Taking Sides: Clashing Views
in US History, V1-The Colonial
Period to Reconstruction, 17e

Larry Madaras
James M. SoRelle

http://create.mheducation.com

ISBN-10: 1259677540   ISBN-13: 9781259677540

Contents

Detailed Table of Contents

Unit 1: Colonial Society

Unit 2: Revolution and the New Nation

Issue: Was the American Revolution a Conservative Movement?
YES: **Robert Eldon Brown**, from "The Nature of the American Revolution, " Boston University Press (1963)
NO: **Alan Taylor**, from "Agrarian Independence: Northern Land Rioters after the Revolution," Northern Illinois University Press (1992)
According to Robert Brown, the British North American colonies were middle-class democracies by the eighteenth century; hence, the American Revolution was fought to preserve a social order that already existed. Alan Taylor, however, emphasizes the class conflict over property that began before the American Revolution and continued for two decades after, in which yeoman farmer's organized local resistance to large proprietors in an effort to realize the revolutionary commitment to liberty by obtaining free or cheap access to land.

Issue: Was the Second Amendment Designed to Protect an Individual's Right to Own Guns?
YES: **Robert E. Shalhope**, from "The Armed Citizen in the Early Republic," *Law and Contemporary Problems* (1986)
NO: **Lawrence Delbert Cress**, from "A Well-Regulated Militia: The Origins and Meaning of the Second Amendment," in Jon Kukla, ed., *The Bill of Rights: A Lively Heritage* (1987)
According to Robert Shalhope, in eighteenth-century America the Second Amendment guaranteed individuals the right to own guns in order to maintain freedom and liberty in a republican society by fulfilling their communal responsibilities within a "well-regulated militia." Lawrence Delbert Cress argues that British common law and the laws of various state legislatures in the United States during the 1780s were designed only to permit armed and "well-regulated militia" to protect citizens from domestic insurrections as well as from tyrannical rule by the national government.

Issue: Was Alexander Hamilton an Economic Genius?
YES: **John Steele Gordon**, from "The Hamiltonian Miracle," Walker and Company (1997)
NO: **Carey Roberts**, from "Alexander Hamilton and the 1790s Economy: A Reappraisal," New York University Press (2006)
John Steele Gordon claims that Alexander Hamilton's brilliant policies for funding and assuming the debts of the Confederation and state governments and for establishing a privately controlled Bank of the United States transformed the new nation's financial circumstances and propelled the United States into a position as a major world economic power. Carey Roberts argues that in the 1790s Hamilton's financial policies undermined popular faith in the Federalist Party and diminished confidence in the federal government.

Issue: Did the Election of 1828 Represent a Democratic Revolt of the People?
YES: **Sean Wilentz**, from *The Rise of American Democracy: Jefferson to Lincoln*, W. W. Norton (2005)
NO: **Daniel Walker Howe**, from *What Hath God Wrought: The Transformation of America, 1815-1848*, Oxford University Press (2007)
Bancroft Prize winner Sean Wilentz argues that in spite of its vulgarities and slanders, the 1828 election campaign "won by Andrew Jackson produced a valediction on the faction-ridden jumble of the Era of Bad Feelings and announced the rough arrival of two distinct national coalitions." Daniel Walker Howe denies that Jackson's victory represented the coming of democracy to the United States and claims that, in the dirtiest campaign in American history, Jackson won on his personal popularity as a military hero and appealed to the agrarian virtues of an earlier age, while John Quincy Adams lost on a program of planned economic development and a diversified economy led by the national government.

Issue: Did Improved Educational Opportunities for Women in the New Nation Significantly Expand Their Participation in Antebellum Society?
YES: **Mary Kelley**, from *Learning to Stand and Speak: Women, Education, and Public Life in America's Republic*, University of North Carolina Press (2006)
NO: **Lucia McMahon**, from "Between Cupid and Minerva" and "Education, Equality, or Difference," Cornell University Press (2012)
Mary Kelley describes how expanding educational opportunities encouraged women to redefine themselves by opening doors to careers beyond the domestic sphere, economic self-support, and public participation in civil society that transformed their understanding of the rights of citizenship in the post-revolutionary and antebellum United States. Lucia McMahon concludes that the unprecedented access to education afforded women in the early national period fostered recognition of women's intellectual capacity, but she argues that most educated women confronted a limited range of opportunities in a society that remained largely committed to a social and political order rooted in notions of sexual difference and male hierarchy.

Unit 3: Antebellum America

Unit 4: Conflict and Resolution

Issue: Are Historians Wrong to Consider the War Between the States a "Total War"?

YES: Mark E. Neely, Jr., from "Was the Civil War a Total War?" *Civil War History* (2004)

NO: James M. McPherson, from "From Limited War to Total War, 1861-1865," in *Gateway Heritage; Magazine of the Missouri Historical Society* (1992)

Professor Mark E. Neely, Jr., argues that the Civil War was not a total war because President Lincoln and the Union military leaders, such as General William T. Sherman, respected the distinction between soldiers and civilians, combatants and noncombatants. In addition, the North did not fully mobilize its resources nor engage in centralized planning and state intervention as was typical of twentieth century wartime economies. Professor James M. McPherson argues that the Civil War was a total war. While conceding the distinction between combatants and noncombatants, he insists that the war accomplished the abolition of slavery and the extinction of national state system—the Confederacy.

Issue: Was Abraham Lincoln America's Greatest President?

YES: Phillip Shaw Paludan, from *The Presidency of Abraham Lincoln*, University Press of Kansas (1994)

NO: Melvin E. Bradford, from *Remembering Who We Are: Observations of a Southern Conservative*, University of Georgia Press (1985)

Phillip Shaw Paludan contends that Abraham Lincoln's greatness exceeds that of all other American Presidents because Lincoln, in the face of unparalleled challenges associated with the Civil War, Succeeded in preserving the Union and freeing the slaves. Melvin E. Bradford characterizes Lincoln as a cynical politician whose abuse of authority as president and commander-in-chief during the Civil War marked a serious departure from the republican goals of the Founding Fathers and established the prototype for the "imperial presidency" of the twentieth century.

Issue: Did Reconstruction Fail as a Result of Racism?

YES: LeeAnna Keith, from *The Colfax Massacre: The Untold Story of Black Power, White Terror, and the Death of Reconstruction*, Oxford University Press (2008)

NO: Heather Cox Richardson, from *The Death of Reconstruction: Race, Labor, and Politics in the Post-Civil War North, 1865-1901*, Harvard University Press (2001)

LeeAnna Keith characterizes the assault on the Grant Parish courthouse in Colfax, Louisiana on Easter Sunday, in 1873 as a product of white racism and unwillingness by local whites to tolerate African American political power during the era of Reconstruction. Heather Cox Richardson argues that the failure of Radical Reconstruction was primarily a consequence of a national commitment to a free labor ideology that opposed an expanding central government that legislated rights to African American that other citizens had acquired through hard work.

Preface

Since 1985, our aim has been to create an effective instrument to enhance classroom learning and to foster critical thinking in the subject area of United States history. Historical facts presented in a vacuum are of little value to the educational process. For students, whose search for historical truth often concentrates on *when* something happened rather than on *why*, and on specific events rather than on the *significance* of those events, Taking Sides is designed to offer an interesting and valuable departure. The understanding arrived at based on the evidence that emerges from the clash of views encourages the reader to view history as an *interpretive* discipline, not one of rote memorization. In this edition, we have continued our efforts to maintain a balance between traditional approaches to political, economic, and diplomatic topics on one hand and the new social history, which depicts a society that benefited from the presence of Native Americans, African Americans, women, and workers of various racial and ethnic backgrounds, on the other. The success of the past 16 editions of *Taking Sides: Clashing Views in United States History* has encouraged us to remain faithful to its original objectives and methods, but previous users of this reader will notice several changes in the format of this new edition.

Book Organization

As in previous editions, issues and their accompanying pairs of essays are arranged in chronological order and can be incorporated easily into any American history survey course. Each issue has an Introduction, which sets the stage for the debate that follows in the pro and con selections and provides historical and methodological background to the problem that the issue examines. For this new edition, each introduction has been expanded to focus more intentionally on *alternative perspectives* that are applicable to the question at hand in order to demonstrate that these issues contain a level of complexity that cannot be addressed fully in a simple Yes/No format. Additionally, each introduction is accompanied by a set of student-focused *Learning Outcomes* which are designed to highlight what knowledge the reader should take away from reading and studying the issue. Also, at the end of each essay we have included a brief biographical sketch of each of the authors whose selections you have just read.

Following the essays, there are several features that are designed to generate further understanding of the issue question and the individual selections. First, there are several questions that relate to the learning outcomes and to the material in the preceding essays that are designed to stimulate *Critical Thinking and Reflection*. Second, *Is There Common Ground?* attempts to encourage students to think more deeply about the issue by highlighting points shared by scholars on the subject at hand and tying the readings to alternative perspectives within the debate. Third, *Additional Resources* offers a brief list of important books and/or journal articles relating to the issue. Also, Internet site addresses (URLs), which should prove useful as starting points for further research, have been provided on the *Internet References* page that accompanies each issue.

Acknowledgments Many individuals have contributed to the successful completion of this edition. We appreciate the evaluations submitted to McGraw-Hill Contemporary Learning Series by those who have used Taking Sides in the classroom. Special thanks to those who responded with specific suggestions for past editions. We are particularly indebted to Maggie Cullen, Cindy SoRelle, the late Barry Crouch, Virginia Kirk, Joseph and Helen Mitchell, Jean Soto, Thomas Kidd, Julie Ann Sweet, and Andrea Turpin, who shared their ideas for changes, pointed us toward potentially useful historical works, and provided significant editorial assistance, as well as to the staffs at the University of Tennessee–Knoxville Library and the Interlibrary Loan Office at Moody Library at Baylor University for aiding in the acquisition of source materials for our consideration of new issue topics. Lynn Wilder performed indispensable typing duties connected with this project. Finally, we are sincerely grateful for the commitment, encouragement, advice, and patience provided in recent years by Jill Meloy, senior product developer for McGraw-Hill Create®/ CLS, and the entire staff of McGraw-Hill Education.

Editors of This Volume

LARRY MADARAS is professor of history emeritus at Howard Community College in Columbia, Maryland. He received a BA from the College of Holy Cross in 1959 and an MA and PhD from New York University in 1961 and 1964, respectively. He has also taught at Spring Hill College, the University of South Alabama, and the University of Maryland at College Park. He has been a Fulbright Fellow and has held two fellowships from the National Endowment for the Humanities. He is the author of dozens of journal articles and book reviews and also has edited another volume in this series, *Taking Sides: Clashing Views in United States History Since 1945*.

JAMES M. SORELLE is professor and undergraduate program director of the Department of History at Baylor University in Waco, Texas. He received a BA and MA from the University of Houston in 1972 and 1974, respectively, and a PhD from Kent State University in 1980. In addition to introductory courses in United States history, he teaches advanced undergraduate classes in African American history, the American civil rights movement, and the 1960s, as well as a graduate seminar on the civil rights movement. His scholarly articles have appeared in *Houston Review, Southwestern Historical Quarterly*, and *Black Dixie: Essays in Afro-Texan History and Culture in Houston* (Texas A & M Press, 1992), edited by Howard Beeth and Cary D. Wintz. He also has contributed entries to *The New Handbook of Texas, The Oxford Companion to Politics of the World, Encyclopedia of African American Culture and History, Encyclopedia of the Confederacy*, and *Encyclopedia of African American History*.

Academic Advisory Board Members

Members of the Academic Advisory Board are instrumental in the final selection of articles for Taking Sides books. Their review of articles for content, level, and appropriateness provides critical direction to the editors and staff. We think that you will find their careful consideration reflected in this volume.

Introduction

The Study of History

In a pluralistic society such as ours, the study of history is bound to be a complex process. How an event is interpreted depends not only on the existing evidence but also on the perspective of the interpreter. Consequently, understanding history presupposes the evaluation of information, a task that often leads to conflicting conclusions. An understanding of history, then, requires the acceptance of the idea of historical relativism. Relativism means that redefinition of our past is always possible and desirable. History shifts, changes, and grows with new and different evidence and interpretations. As is the case with the law and even with medicine, beliefs that were unquestioned 100 or 200 years ago have been discredited or discarded since.

Relativism, then, encourages revisionism. There is a maxim that "the past must remain useful to the present." Historian Carl Becker argued that every generation should examine history for itself, thus ensuring constant scrutiny of our collective experience through new perspectives. History, consequently, does not remain static, in part because historians cannot avoid being influenced by the times in which they live. Almost all historians commit themselves to revising the views of other historians, synthesizing theories into macro-interpretations, or revising the revisionists.

Schools of Thought

Three predominant schools of thought have emerged in American history since the first graduate seminars in history were given at the Johns Hopkins University in Baltimore in the 1870s. The *progressive* school dominated the professional field in the first half of the twentieth century. Influenced by the reform currents of Populism, Progressivism, and the New Deal, these historians explored the social and economic forces that energized America. The progressive scholars tended to view the past in terms of conflicts between groups, and they sympathized with the underdog.

The post–World War II period witnessed the emergence of a new group of historians who viewed the conflict thesis as overly simplistic. Writing against the backdrop of the Cold War, these *neoconservative,* or *consensus,* historians argued that Americans possess a shared set of values and that the areas of agreement within our nation's basic democratic and capitalistic framework are more important than the areas of disagreement.

In the 1960s, however, the civil rights movement, women's liberation, and the student rebellion (with its condemnation of the war in Vietnam) fragmented the consensus of values upon which historians and social scientists of the 1950s had centered their interpretations. This turmoil set the stage for the emergence of another group of scholars. *New Left* historians began to reinterpret the past. They emphasized the significance of conflict in American history, and they resurrected interest in those groups ignored by the consensus school. In addition, New Left historians critiqued the expansionist policies of the United States and emphasized the difficulties confronted by Native Americans, African Americans, women, and urban workers in gaining full citizenship status.

Progressive, consensus, and New Left history is still being written. The most recent generation of scholars, however, focuses upon social history. Their primary concern is to discover what the lives of "ordinary Americans" were really like. These new social historians employ previously overlooked court and church documents, house deeds and tax records, letters and diaries, photographs, and census data to reconstruct the everyday lives of average Americans. Some employ new methodologies, such as quantification (enhanced by advancing computer technology) and oral history, whereas others borrow from the disciplines of political science, economics, sociology, anthropology, and psychology for their historical investigations.

The proliferation of historical approaches, which are reflected in the issues debated in this book, has had mixed results. On the one hand, historians have become so specialized in their respective time periods and methodological styles that it is difficult to synthesize the recent scholarship into a comprehensive text for the general reader. On the other hand, historians know more about the American past than at any other time in history. They dare to ask new questions or ones that previously were considered to be germane only to scholars in other social sciences. Although there is little agreement about the answers to these questions, the methods employed and issues explored make the "new history" a very exciting field to study.

The topics that follow represent a variety of perspectives and approaches. Each of these controversial issues can be studied for its individual importance to our nation's history. Taken as a group, they interact with one another to illustrate larger historical themes. When grouped thematically, the issues reveal continuing motifs in the development of American history.

The New Social History

Some of the most innovative historical research over the last 40 years reflects the interests of the new social historians. The work of several representatives of this group who treat the issues of race, gender, and class appears in this volume.

The intersection of ethnicity, economics, and culture can be investigated through an understanding of the relations between Native Americans and various groups of European colonists in the seventeenth and eighteenth centuries. These relations ran the gamut from cordial and mutually beneficial trade ties to violent atrocities. Particular Native American tribes allied themselves at various times with the English, Dutch, or French; therefore, conflicts among these European nations could impact in significant ways the relations between whites and American Indians. In New England, the Pequot Indians fell victim to settlers' land lust that produced inevitable hostilities culminating in the near extermination of the tribe by 1637.

The field of women's history has been another beneficiary of the new social history. Some scholars have concluded that, given the circumstances of life in the early colonies, women in America were better off than their English counterparts. This view has been countered by the argument that colonial American women occupied a subordinate status in virtually every aspect of their daily lives. This debate continues in the analysis of women's status in the nineteenth century. For example, some historians claim that as educational opportunities expanded women were able to take advantage of new careers in the public sphere. This interpretation is challenged by other historians who conclude that most women in Jacksonian America, despite improvements in education, faced only limited opportunities in a society still rooted in patriarchy.

Study of the Salem witch trials also has produced several quite imaginative scholarly explanations reflecting this social history perspective. While women were the central targets of witchcraft accusations, a wide assortment of socioeconomic tensions can be identified to explain the circumstances in Salem in 1692 that do not necessarily focus on gender. At least one student of this event takes an epidemiological approach and attributes the witchcraft hysteria to physical and neurological behaviors resulting from an undiagnosed epidemic of encephalitis.

Revolution, Religion, and Reform

Historians have identified numerous factors contributing to the American colonists' decision to seek independence through a war with England. They continue to ask whether the War for Independence was essentially a conservative or a radical movement. Did colonists simply want to protect a social order committed to middle-class democracy that a British policy of benign neglect had incubated for some time? Or were there genuine conflicts between small-scale farmers and large landholders with each group seeking its own version of liberty?

Religion has played a significant role in the development of American society. For example, during the first Great Awakening, preachers such as George Whitefield engineered a powerful series of revivals in the 1730s and 1740s that influenced all of the British North American colonies and gave birth to a spirit of evangelicalism that initiated a major alteration of global Christian history. Such a view ignores the contention of one historian who claims that to describe the religious revival activities of the eighteenth century as the "Great Awakening" is to seriously exaggerate their extent, nature, and impact on pre-revolutionary American society and politics. The effort to convert residents of the American colonies to Christianity also extended to enslaved African Americans, and by the 1800s, most slaves had adopted the religion of their masters. Many were instructed in the faith by those masters and attended religious services with them, but religious expression also could be found in remote areas of the rural South where slaves conducted their own religious ceremonies beyond the supervision of their owners.

In the nineteenth century, several reform initiatives were motivated by religious impulses. Most historians recognize that the temperance movement was launched by evangelical ministers in an effort to gain converts who were liberated from "demon rum." This is not the only explanation for the temperance reform movement, however. The attack on strong drink bore important implications for the labor force and can be viewed as a product of a pro-capitalist market economy whose entrepreneurial elite led the way toward abstinence and prohibition campaigns in order to guarantee the availability of a more productive work force.

The major and most controversial reform effort in the pre–Civil War period was the movement to abolish slavery. Evangelical Christianity clearly played a significant role in the attempt to eliminate the "peculiar institution" on the part of abolitionists such as Theodore Dwight Weld, Arthur and Lewis Tappan, and the messianic John Brown. Brown's activities in Kansas and Virginia were so violent that much recent discussion has been given to the question of whether Brown was a domestic terrorist. A number of scholars conclude that Brown's actions conform to the modern definition of terrorist behavior in that he considered the United States incapable of reforming itself by abolishing slavery, believed that only violence would accomplish that goal, and justified his actions by proclaiming adherence to a "higher" power. In contrast, others insist that Brown's commitment to higher moral and political goals conformed to the basic principles of human freedom and political and legal equality that formed the heart of the creed articulated by the founders of the American nation.

War, Leadership, and Resolution

As a nation committed to peace, the United States has faced some of its sternest tests in times of war. Such conflicts inevitably have challenged the leadership abilities of the commanders in chief, the commitment of the nation to involve itself in war, and the ideals of the republic founded on democratic principles. In the first half of the nineteenth century, Americans went to war against England, Mexico, and themselves. The war with Mexico from 1846 to 1848 was fueled by expansionist designs imbedded in the commitment to Manifest Destiny. Many historians of this clash have concluded that President James K. Polk was an imperialist motivated to use the power of the presidency to force Mexico to cede California and the current Southwest to the United States. Those more sympathetic to Polk contend that he pursued an aggressive (but not imperialistic) policy that would force Mexico to recognize U.S. annexation of Texas and to sell New Mexico and California to its northern neighbor without starting a war.

Historians have debated the causes of the Civil War for generations and continue to do so. Most scholars of the conflict accept the centrality of slavery to this tragic event. It seems quite clear that white southerners whose job it was to promote the cause of secession following Abraham Lincoln's election in 1860 appealed to their audiences' commitment to the preservation of slavery and the doctrine of white supremacy. But for those who fought for the United States, slavery may have been less of a motivation. For white northern troops, most of whom harbored prejudicial views of African Americans, whether slave or free, their service was less a humanitarian venture than it was an attempt to preserve the Union.

Students of the military engagements of the Civil War have attempted to characterize the type of war that was fought. The contention of those who insist that the twin goals of restoring the Union and freeing the slaves required the United States to conduct a "total war" against the Confederate troops has been challenged by specialists who dispute the "total war" model because the North did not fully mobilize its resources nor engage in centralized planning and state intervention to defeat the Confederacy.

With the end of slavery, one of the most controversial questions confronting those responsible for reconstructing the nation following the war involved the future of African Americans. Perhaps no other period of American history has been subjected to more myths than has this postwar era. Even though most scholars today recognize that Reconstruction did not achieve its most enlightened economic and social goals, they differ in their explanations about the source of this failure. It is apparent to many that while slavery died with the war, racism did not. Consequently, efforts to bring full citizenship rights to blacks in the South met almost uninterrupted opposition from most white southerners who sought to reinstitute the doctrine of white supremacy. Another line of argument, however, insists that Radical Reconstruction failed primarily as a consequence of a national commitment to a free-labor ideology that opposed an expanding central government that legislated rights to African Americans that other citizens had acquired through hard work.

Politics in America

The American people gave legitimacy to their revolution through the establishment of a republican form of government. The United States has operated under two constitutions from 1781 to the present; the second was written in 1787 and remains in effect over 225 years later. Still, debates continue between broad and strict constructionists over the respective powers lodged by the Constitution in the federal government and the individual states. Other constitutional debates flare up regarding the "original intent of the founders," which tend to focus on the Bill of Rights. Most recently, a hornet's nest of controversy has been stirred up over whether the Second Amendment was meant to secure the right of individuals to possess firearms or whether the authors had in mind only the desire to maintain militia forces to thwart the enemies of the new nation, including a tyrannical central government.

While the United States is a representative government based on democratic ideals, there was some question in the early national period as to how democratic the government under the Constitution truly was. Even if the followers of Charles Beard were wrong, and the Constitution was not a cruel hoax played by an elitist economic minority on "the people" of America, the United States in the early 1800s was a far cry from a fully developed democracy. Many scholars argue that this pattern changed with the rise of Andrew Jackson to political prominence, especially with Jackson's popular election to the presidency in 1828.

No discussion of American politics is complete without examining some of the key individuals who laid the foundation for and preserved the nation in times of crisis. Two of the greatest, according to professional historians, were Alexander Hamilton and Abraham Lincoln. Hamilton served as President George Washington's secretary of the treasury and almost single-handedly placed the government under the new Constitution of the United States on a sound financial foundation. Some scholars may dispute the value of Hamilton's contributions, but his reputation remains intact, especially as he has become the subject of a popular and critically acclaimed Broadway musical.

The majority of historians contend that Lincoln deserves to be recognized as the nation's greatest president for facing the unparalleled challenges associated with the Civil War, preserving the Union, and freeing the slaves. A few neo-Confederates and states' rights defenders, however, characterize Lincoln as a cynical politician whose abuse of authority as president and commander-in-chief during the Civil War marked a serious departure from the republican goals of the Founding Fathers and established the prototype for the "imperial presidency" of the twentieth century.

Comparative History: America in a Global Perspective

How is American history seen within the larger framework of world history? Many Americans, including many scholars, view the United States as a nation unlike any other, including the countries of Western Europe. This idea of American exceptionalism was articulated by Frenchman Alexis de Tocqueville in the 1830s but had its roots in the early colonial era in places like Massachusetts Bay Colony, which was promoted as "a city upon a hill" by John Winthrop. This religious notion became secularized over time, and American politicians continue to invoke the concept of exceptionalism in their campaigns and speeches. At the same time, some scholars debate the validity of this ideal and describe the "end of exceptionalism" in the early twenty-first century or emphasize the many qualities that the United States shares with other countries around the world.

Conclusion

The process of historical study should rely more on thinking than on memorizing data. Once the basics of who, what, when, and where are determined, historical thinking shifts to a higher gear. Analysis, comparison and contrast, evaluation, and explanation take command. These skills not only increase our knowledge of the past but also provide general tools for the comprehension of all the topics about which human beings think.

The diversity of a pluralistic society, however, creates some obstacles to comprehending the past. The spectrum of differing opinions on any particular subject eliminates the possibility of quick and easy answers. In the final analysis, conclusions often are built through a synthesis of several different interpretations, but, even then, they may be partial and tentative.

The study of history in a pluralistic society allows each citizen the opportunity to reach independent conclusions about the past. Since most, if not all, historical issues affect the present and future, understanding the past becomes essential to social progress. Many of today's problems have a direct connection with the past. Additionally, other contemporary issues may lack obvious direct antecedents, but historical investigation can provide illuminating analogies. At first, it may appear confusing to read and to think about opposing historical views, but the survival of our democratic society depends on such critical thinking by acute and discerning minds.

Larry Madaras
Howard Community College

James M. SoRelle
Baylor University

Unit 1

UNIT

Colonial Society

*T*he exploration and settlement of the Western Hemisphere took place in a global context of migration, empire-building, and national rivalries. Europeans who settled in North America encountered various circumstances that reinforced their localist sensibilities by limiting their contacts across colonial lines, but over time they recognized much that they had in common with one another and that set them apart from their native homelands. For many, this experience led them to insist upon the uniqueness of American society.

The ethnic identity of these European colonists affected their relations with Native Americans as well as with each other. These contacts ranged from cordiality to conflict and differed by time and place. The opportunities for success that presented themselves to individual residents often varied by gender, ethnicity, and race.

Religion, too, impacted life in colonial America in both the seventeenth and eighteenth centuries. Some, though not all, colonists migrated specifically for religious purposes, but not all of these migrants shared the same religious precepts. Consequently, religion occasionally produced tensions that affected the society and interpersonal relations in profound ways.

Selected, Edited, and with Issue Framing Material by:
Larry Madaras, *Howard Community College*
and
James M. SoRelle, *Baylor University*

ISSUE

Is America Exceptional?

YES: Seymour Martin Lipset, from "Still the Exceptional Nation?" *The Wilson Quarterly* (2000)

NO: Godfrey Hodgson, from "The Corruption of the Best," Yale University Press (2010)

Learning Outcomes

After reading this issue, you will be able to:

- Define what is meant by the term "American exceptionalism."
- Understand that American exceptionalism possesses both positive and negative characteristics.
- Discuss the characteristics that set the United States apart from the rest of the developed nations in the world.
- Consider the global context of the American historical experience.

ISSUE SUMMARY

YES: Seymour Martin Lipset (1922–2006) claims that the United States remains an "outlier" nation in that it is much less welfare-oriented, the federal government taxes and spends less, Americans are more heavily influenced by Protestant Christianity, and Americans benefit from a higher rate of mobility into elite positions than is the case in other developed nations.

NO: Godfrey Hodgson criticizes what he describes as the "myth of American exceptionalism" that emphasizes the uniqueness of American values while largely ignoring the extent to which the development of the United States has been connected to international, especially European, historical processes and ideologies.

In 1994, Speaker of the House of Representatives Newt Gingrich told members of the Heritage Foundation that it was time to "reassert American exceptionalism." The message was clear: the United States had lost those qualities that distinguished it from other nations around the world. Indeed, Gingrich was merely recognizing what a number of social scientists and historians had been saying for the past 20 years—that the concept of American exceptionalism had diminished as U.S. claims to preeminence in global affairs had dwindled. It seemed that publisher Henry Luce's 1941 prophecy that the twentieth century would be "The American Century" was in jeopardy.

While Alexis de Tocqueville is frequently credited with originating the concept of American exceptionalism in his classic *Democracy in America* (1835), the idea predates the French aristocrat's arrival in the United States

by two centuries. John Winthrop's lay sermon, "A Modell of Christian Charity," delivered to the Puritan passengers aboard the *Arbella* bound for Massachusetts Bay Colony in 1630, was probably the earliest reference to America (or a small portion thereof) having a distinctive, special mission to play on the world stage. Drawing upon the Sermon on the Mount, Winthrop explained the importance of establishing a pure Christian commonwealth in the New World. "For we must be as a city upon a hill," he intoned. "The eyes of all people are upon us." A secularized version of this mission was presented in 1776 with the publication of Thomas Paine's famous Revolutionary-era pamphlet *Common Sense*. Following the creation of the United States, Thomas Jefferson, Noah Webster, and other prominent citizens of the new nation voiced the belief that the country possessed a number of characteristics that set it apart from corrupt and decaying Europe.

While Tocqueville identified the twin components of democracy and equality as the basis for American distinctiveness, it was an American historian, Frederick Jackson Turner, who captured the attention of scholars and students by associating the unique qualities of national character in the United States with the frontier experience. Turner first presented this argument at the annual meeting of the American Historical Association in 1893 in a paper entitled "The Significance of the Frontier in American History." The Turner thesis remained a hot topic of historical discussion for three-quarters of a century as Turnerians and anti-Turnerians debated the details of the impact of the frontier on American life.

An important extension of the Turner thesis is offered in David M. Potter, *People of Plenty: Economic Abundance and the American Character* (University of Chicago Press, 1954), which identifies another factor contributing to the distinctive American character. Michael Kammen, in *People of Paradox: An Inquiry Concerning the Origins of American Civilization* (Alfred A. Knopf, 1972), argues that American distinctiveness is derived from the contradiction produced by a culture created from an interaction of Old and New World patterns. Students interested in pursuing these questions of culture and character should consult Michael McGiffert, ed., *The Character of Americans: A Book of Readings*, rev. ed. (Dorsey Press, 1970).

The issue of exceptionalism is also at the heart of discussions of the nature of American culture carried on by historians interested in the Old World and New World roots of the American people and the society they created beginning in the seventeenth century. Just how new and different was that early American culture? How much did it depart from the cultural heritage of those tens of thousands of immigrants who arrived in England's North American colonies prior to the American Revolution? Opposing historical perspectives can be found in Gary Nash's *Red, White, and Black: The Peoples of Early America*, 3d ed. (Prentice Hall, 1992), which emphasizes the need to appreciate the numerous non-English and non-European elements of American culture, and David Hackett Fischer's *Albion's Seed: Four British Folkways in America* (Oxford University Press, 1989), which suggests that there is a distinctly British tone in American culture and society.

For more than 50 years Seymour Martin Lipset provided a broad-based defense of the concept of American exceptionalism in a number of scholarly works. The most important of these included *Agrarian Socialism* (University of California Press, 1950; rev. and expanded ed., 1971);

The First New Nation: The United States in Historical and Comparative Perspective (Basic Books, 1963); and *American Exceptionalism: A Double-Edged Sword* (W. W. Norton, 1996). Support for Lipset's interpretation can be found in Daniel Boorstin, *The Genius of American Politics* (University of Chicago Press, 1953); Louis Hartz, *The Liberal Tradition in America* (Harcourt, Brace & World, 1955); and the essays collected in Byron Shafer, ed., *Is America Different? A New Look at American Exceptionalism* (Oxford University Press, 1991). Critics of the exceptionalism model are represented in Laurence Veysey, "The Autonomy of American History Reconsidered," *American Quarterly* (Fall 1979); and William C. Spengemann, *A Mirror for Americanists: Reflections on the Idea of American Literature* (University Press of New England, 1989). Michael Kammen's "The Problem of American Exceptionalism: A Reconsideration," *American Quarterly* (March 1993), presents a valuable summary of both sides of the debate.

Is the United States different in fundamental ways from other nations? Has its historical development produced distinctive institutions and citizens? Is it legitimate to focus upon certain characteristics that may appear to separate the United States from other nations at a time when more emphasis is being placed upon global integration? These are some of the questions generated by the following selections.

In the first selection, Seymour Martin Lipset reaffirms the notion of American exceptionalism while claiming that the United States is not as exceptional politically as it once was. Drawing upon the statistical evidence of the social scientist's polling and survey techniques, Lipset argues that the United States is set apart from developed European nations by being less committed to the welfare state, spending and taxing much less than European governments, and maintaining a stronger commitment to religious faith. On the darker side, the U.S. possesses a higher proportion of nonvoters, the highest crime rate and prison population, and a greater maldistribution of income than its European counterparts.

English-born Godfrey Hodgson recognizes certain unique characteristics of colonial British North America and the early United States but claims that much of what was exceptional about early America had faded in the post–Civil War environment of industrialization and urbanization. He criticizes the presentation of U.S. history as a "patriotic commemoration" which largely ignores the extent to which America was shaped by vast international historical processes.

YES

Seymour Martin Lipset

Still the Exceptional Nation?

Was Karl Marx right? More than 100 years ago, he declared in *Capital* that "the country that is the most developed shows to the less developed the image of their future," and his early followers had little doubt that the United States was that most developed harbinger country. "Americans will be the first to usher in a Socialist republic," declared the German Social Democrat August Bebel in 1907—even though the American Socialist Party was faring miserably at the polls while his own party held many seats in the Reichstag. Only after the Russian Revolution in 1917 did the Left and its liberal sympathizers begin to look elsewhere for a vision of the future. Now Europe set the standard and America followed—all too sluggishly, in the minds of many.

How could the world's most advanced capitalist society also be the most impervious to the socialist idea? Even the Great Depression failed to alter its course—America's minuscule Socialist and Communist parties emerged from the 1930s with even less support than they had enjoyed at the beginning of the decade. The American experience cast doubt on the inner logic of historical materialism, the essential Marxist doctrine which holds that the shape of a nation's culture and politics is determined by underlying economic and technological forces. The question engaged the attention of many socialists, as well as Lenin and Trotsky; Stalin attended a special commission of the Communist International on "the American Question."

What was a source of perplexity to some was, of course, a source of pride to others. To scholars, it was a phenomenon in need of explanation. Out of this puzzlement came the rebirth of the idea of "American exceptionalism," a concept first developed by Alexis de Tocqueville in *Democracy in America* (1835–40). The young Frenchman wrote that the United States, the lone successful democracy of his time, differed from all the European nations in lacking a feudal past and in being more socially egalitarian, more meritocratic, more individualistic, more rights-oriented, and more religious. These American tendencies

were reinforced by the country's religious commitment to the "nonconformist," largely congregationally organized Protestant sects, which emphasized the individual's personal relationship with God, a relationship that was not mediated by state-supported, hierarchically organized churches of the kind that prevailed in Europe.

In 19th-century America, the ideology of the American Revolution was transformed into an all-encompassing liberalism stressing liberty, antistatism, and individualism. In Europe, a dominant conservativism was wedded to the state—it was conservatives such as Britain's Benjamin Disraeli, for example, who invented the welfare state—and it naturally gave birth to state-centered opposition, social democracy. Because its liberal ideology stifled the emergence of a state-centered opposition, the United States became an anomaly.

Today, however, the United States once again finds itself the apparent image of the future. Not only is it the world's sole superpower and its economic colossus, but it seems to be pointing the way toward the political future. The American political system, long considered an aberration because its two main parties embrace liberal capitalism, now looks like the model for the developed world.

Nothing symbolizes this change more dramatically than the political pep rally cum summit meeting that brought four social democratic heads of government to Washington in April 1999 under the auspices of America's centrist Democratic Leadership Council. Britain's Tony Blair, Germany's Gerhard Schröder, the Netherlands' Wim Kok, and Italy's Massimo D'Alema did not come to press the cause of democratic socialism on their backward cousins across the Atlantic. They wanted to join with Democrat Bill Clinton in affirming what they called the Third Way. And they have done so more than once, meeting most recently in Florence last November, where they were joined by Brazil's Fernando Henrique Cardoso. These putative social democratic leaders, as *Washington Post* columnist E. J. Dionne notes, "accept capitalism as a given, but promise to do something about its inequalities and

Lipset, Seymour Martin. From *The Wilson Quarterly*, 2000, pp. 31–36, 40–45 (edited). Copyright © 2000 by Martin Seymour Lipset. Reprinted by permission of his wife, Sydnee Lipset.

uncertainties. They talk not of 'socialism' but of 'community,' not of 'collectivism' but of 'solidarity.'" They sound, in other words, very much like America's New Democrats.

All of this suggests that Marx may have been right: the development of an economically and technologically advanced society follows a certain logic, and the United States shows where that logic leads—even if it is not to socialism. But if this is true, will it make sense any longer to speak of American exceptionalism? Will the political cultures of other advanced societies increasingly converge with that of the United States?

The change in the character of Europe's political parties largely reflects the remaking of Europe's economic and class structures along American lines. The European emphasis on *stände*, or fixed, explicitly hierarchical social classes rooted in a feudal and monarchical past, is increasingly a thing of the past. Growing economic productivity is opening access to everything from clothes, cars, and other consumer goods to advanced schooling, powerfully muting the "lifestyle" differences, including accents and dress, that traditionally separated Europe's social classes. The new economic order has been accompanied by demographic shifts, notably a drastic decline in birthrates and an extension of life spans, that have confronted all the developed nations with a common dilemma: raise taxes significantly to pay for more social security, health care, welfare, and other expensive government services, or find ways to cut spending.

The United States has led the economic transformation, shifting sharply away from the old industrial economy built on manual labor, a process that was especially agonizing during the 1970s and '80s. The old economy of General Motors, U.S. Steel, and Standard Oil has given way to the economy of Microsoft, Citigroup—and McDonald's. The proportion of workers employed in manufacturing dropped from 26 percent in 1960 to 16 percent in 1996. In the United Kingdom, manufacturing employment declined from 36 percent of the total to 19 percent, a pattern that prevails from Sweden (with a drop from 32 to 19 percent) to Australia (from 26 to 13.5 percent).

The Old World societies are also following the American lead away from class awareness and organization. Union membership, for example, is declining almost everywhere. Between 1985 and 1995, the proportion of the American labor force carrying a union card fell by 21 percent. Today, only 14 percent of all employed Americans—and only 10 percent of those in the private sector—belong to unions. The proportional losses in France and Britain have been even greater, 37 percent and 28 percent, respectively. In Germany, the decline is a more modest 18 percent.

During the post–World War II era, the distribution of income and occupational skills in Europe has reshaped itself to fit American contours. It has changed from something best illustrated by a pyramidal shape, enlarging toward the bottom, to one better illustrated by a diamond, widest in the middle. The traditional working class, in other words, is shrinking. The middle class is growing, creating solidly bourgeois societies in Europe. Political parties on the left now have little choice but to appeal more to the growing middle strata than to their traditional constituencies, industrial workers and the poor.

Call it what you will—"postindustrial society," "postmaterialism," or the "scientific-technological revolution"—the changing cultures of the emerging societies closely fit the Marxian causal model. The political and cultural "superstructures" are determined, as sociologist Daniel Bell has noted, by the technological structures and the distribution of economic classes.

Many of the trends that Marx anticipated, especially a steady increase in the size of the industrial proletariat, have not occurred. Throughout the industrialized world, job growth is concentrated in the technological and service occupations. College enrollments have swelled, and the degree-bearing population has grown enormously. Alain Touraine, a leading French sociologist and leftist intellectual, writes: "If property was the criterion of membership in the former dominant class, the new dominant class is defined by knowledge and a certain level of education."

With their roots in the university and the scientific and technological worlds, and with a heavy representation in the public sector, the professions, and the industries spawned by computers, the new workers have developed their own distinctive values. Political scientist Ronald Inglehart of the University of Michigan, pointing as well to the influence of a half-century of affluence, argues that these changes have spawned a new set of "postmaterialist" values. An affluent, better-educated citizenry has shifted its political attention away from bread-and-butter economic issues to new concerns: the environment, health, the quality of education, the culture, equality for women and minorities, the extension of democratization and freedom at home and abroad, and last, but far from least, the definition of a more permissive (and highly controversial) morality.

The United States has also been in the forefront of the postmaterialist new politics, quickly exporting the latest concerns of Berkeley, Madison, and other university towns to Paris and Berlin. It gave birth to all the major successful modern movements for egalitarian social change and for improving the quality of life—feminism, environmentalism, civil rights for minorities, and gay rights—just as it did the democratic revolutions of the 19th century. Writing in 1971, as the new politics was beginning to emerge, the French political analyst Jean-François Revel observed in *Without Marx or Jesus* that the "revolutionary stirrings have had their origin in the United States." The Continent's "dissenters . . . are the disciples of the American movements." . . .

The United States clearly is no longer as exceptional politically as it once was. Its political life—dominated by two procapitalist political parties and defined by traditional, moralistic, sectarian religion, classical liberalism (laissez faire), and environmentalist and other post-materialist tendencies—is setting a model for other developed countries. The convergence has even stripped the United States of its past monopoly on populist politics, the traditional outlet of the discontented and dispossessed in a country without a working-class political party. . . .

Yet for all that, the United States remains exceptional in other important ways. It is still an outlier at one end of many international indicators of behavior and values. It is still much less statist and welfare oriented, and its governments (federal and state) tax and spend much less in proportionate terms than European governments. It is the most religious country in Christendom, the only one still strongly influenced by the moralistic and individualistic ethos of Protestant sectarianism. It has higher rates of mobility into elite positions than any other nation. It combines exceptional levels of productivity, income, and wealth with exceptionally low levels of taxation and social spending, and equally exceptional levels of income inequality and poverty.

The United States remains well ahead of other large developed countries in per capita income, retaining the lead it has held since the second half of the 19th century. In 1997, U.S. per capita income (measured in terms of purchasing power parity) was $28,740. Switzerland was the only developed country to come close, at $26,320, while Norway ($23,940), Japan ($23,400), and Denmark ($22,740) followed. At the same time, the United States boasts the lowest rate of unemployment in the developed world, about four percent, while Europe has some 20 million out of work, or more than 10 percent of the labor force. Poverty, currently the condition of 13.7 percent of Americans, is more widespread than in Europe, though rates are dropping. (Among African Americans, the poverty rate dropped to 29 percent in 1995, passing below 30 percent for the first time in the nation's history. Today it stands at 28.4 percent.)

The United States is the only Western country in which government extracts less than 30 percent of the gross domestic product in taxes—it took 28.5 percent in 1996. Spending on social welfare is correspondingly low. One has to go outside the Western world to find societies with a smaller state. The Japanese tax take was a tenth of a percent lower, but among the remaining member states of the Organization for Economic Cooperation and Development (OECD), only Turkey (25.4 percent), South Korea (23.2 percent), and Mexico (16.3 percent) have lower taxation levels.

American exceptionalism is distinctly double-edged. The United States is not as egalitarian in economic terms as the rest of the developed world. It has the highest proportion of nonvoters in national elections, as well the highest rates of violent crime and the biggest prison population (in per capita terms). Thanks to its meritocratic orientation, it is among the leaders in the unequal distribution of income. Gauged by the Gini coefficient, the social scientist's standard measure of income inequality, the U.S. score of 37.5 is almost 10 percent higher than that of the next closest country (Britain) among the Western democracies, and far above Sweden's 22.2. To put it in simpler terms, the richest 20 percent of Americans have incomes about nine times greater than the poorest 20 percent, while in Japan and Germany the affluent enjoy incomes only four and six times greater, respectively.

Yet because individualism and meritocratic ideals are so deeply ingrained in them, Americans are much less troubled by such differences than Europeans. According to a 1990 study, Americans are more likely to believe that there should be "greater incentives for individual effort," rather than that "incomes should be made more equal." Proportionately fewer Americans (56 percent) agree that "income differences are too large," as compared with Europeans (whose positive responses range from 66 to 86 percent). In a survey reported in 1995, people in six countries were asked: "How would you prefer to be paid—on a fixed salary . . . or mostly on an incentive basis which will allow you to earn more if you accomplished a lot, but may result in less earnings if you don't accomplish enough?" A majority of Americans (53 percent) opted for the incentive plan; the survey's British, French, Spanish, and German respondents chose a fixed salary by margins ranging from 65 to 72 percent.

A 1996 survey shows that a policy that reduces income disparities is supported by less than one-third (28 percent) of Americans, while positive responses elsewhere range from 42 percent in Austria to 82 percent in Italy. The British fall in the middle at 63 percent.

Americans are more likely than Europeans to agree that "large income differences are needed for the country's prosperity." Nearly one-third of Americans surveyed in 1987 justify inequality this way, as compared with an average of 23 percent among seven European countries (Great Britain, Austria, West Germany, Italy, Hungary, Switzerland, and the Netherlands). A 1992 review of American public opinion data over 50 years reports: "Surveys since the 1930s have shown that the explicit idea of income redistributing elicits very limited enthusiasm among the American public. . . . Redistributive fervor was not much apparent even in [the] depression era. Most Americans appear content with the distributional effects of private markets."

The historian Richard Hofstadter wrote that the 1930s introduced a "social democratic tinge" into the United States for the first time in its history. The Great Depression brought a strong emphasis on planning, on the welfare state, on the role of the government as a major regulatory actor, and even on redistribution of income. The great crisis challenged the historic American national commitment to the assumptions of classical liberalism and laissez faire, spawning, among other things, New Deal-inspired policies and a growth in trade union strength. These trends, however, have gradually inverted in the reasonably prosperous half-century since the end of World War II. The tinge—which never approached the full flush of Europe—has faded.

Despite the European Left's embrace of the free market, European governments are still, by American standards, very deeply involved in the economy and society. The differences stem in part from historical identities and values, in part from institutions that have been established over the last century. Once in place, government policies are defended by those who benefit from them, even as they continue to shape expectations about what government can do. The major European countries provided important social services long before the United States, which did not enact pension, unemployment, or industrial accident insurance until the 1930s. It is the only developed nation that does not have a government-supported, comprehensive medical system, and it is one of the few that do not provide child support to all families.

Today, Americans are still more opposed than Europeans to government involvement in economic affairs, whether through wage and price controls, publicly funded job creation, or the length of the work week. Nor are they favorably disposed toward government regulation in other realms, such as seat belt laws. Only 23 percent of Americans believe it is government's responsibility "to take care of very poor people who can't take care of themselves," according to a 1998 study by the late public opinion expert Everett Carll Ladd. They are less disposed than Europeans to believe that the state is obligated to supply a job for everyone who wants one, to provide a

decent standard of living for the unemployed, or to guarantee a basic income.

The value differences between the United States and Europe are also reflected in attitudes toward social mobility and personal achievement. Americans are more likely than Europeans to see personal effort, hard work, ambition, education, and ability as more important for getting ahead in life than social background. Confronted with the proposition that "what you achieve depends largely on your family background" in a 1990 survey, only 31 percent of Americans agreed, compared with 53 percent of the British, 51 percent of the Austrians, and 63 percent of the Italians. Asked to choose between hard work and "luck and connections" as the most likely route to a better life, 44 percent of Americans pointed to hard work. Only 24 percent of the most like-minded European group, the British, agreed.

The American commitment to meritocracy is also reflected in the fact that Americans are more disposed than Europeans to favor increased spending on education. (And Americans tend to oppose offering help as a "handout" in the form of outright government grants to students, which Europeans back, preferring instead student loans.) Given that education is seen as the key to upward mobility, it is not surprising that the United States has spent proportionally much more public money on education than Europe, while Europe has devoted much more to welfare. The United States has led the world in providing the kinds of general education needed to get ahead. Since the early 19th century, it has been first in the proportion of citizens graduating from public elementary school, then high school, and more recently in the percentages attending college and receiving postgraduate training.

The other developed countries are now rapidly closing the education gap, however. College entry rates increased by more than 25 percent in 16 OECD countries between 1990 and '96, while the rate in the United States remained about the same. This change and others in education suggest that American-style individualism and ambition have spread to the point where the United States cannot be considered exceptional in these respects.

Does it still make sense to speak of the United States as the exceptional nation? As social democratic parties the world over shift toward the free market, the differences between the United States and other Western democracies may continue to narrow. Yet deeply rooted institutions and values do not easily lose their influence. The Western democracies may now all fit the liberal mold, but liberalism, too, has its divides. Europe still tends toward the economically egalitarian side, with a penchant for active government; Americans prefer a competitive, individualist society with equality of opportunity and effective but weak government.

There is no reason, moreover, to believe that we have seen the end of change—much less the "end of history." For all its rewards, the free market is not a source of great inspiration. Capitalism does not pledge to eliminate poverty, racism, sexism, pollution, or war. It does not even promise great material rewards to all. Neoconservative thinker Irving Kristol echoes a long line of capitalism's defenders when he allows that it offers "the least romantic conception of a public order that the human mind has ever conceived."

It is hard to believe that the West's now-contented young will not some day hunger again for the "exalted notions" that Aristotle described more than 2,000 years ago. Yet when they do, America will still have an ideological vision, the individualist, achievement-oriented American Creed, with which to motivate its young to challenge reality. The evolving social vision of Europe will necessarily hearken back to the very different ideals of the French Revolution and social democracy.

One does not have to peer far into the future to see that the contest between the forces of change and the defenders of the status quo is not over. In the formerly communist countries of Europe, left and liberal advocates of the free market and democracy confront conservative defenders of the power of state bureaucracies. Elsewhere in Europe, Green parties press the cause of environmentalism and other postmaterialist concerns. And nobody can predict what forces may be put into play by future events, from economic crisis to the rise of China. New movements and ideologies will appear and old ones will be revived. Economic hardship may bolster communitarian efforts to relegitimate the state's role in attacking social, sexual, and racial inequalities.

Even looking only at what is already in view, the United States still stands out. For instance, in every one of the 13 richest countries in the European Union, Green parties are represented in the national parliament or the country's delegation to the European Parliament. Greens have recently participated in ruling government coalitions in Belgium, Finland, France, Germany, and Italy. Only the United States lacks even a minimally effective Green party. One of the great puzzles of the 20th century was posed by the title of German sociologist Werner Sombart's 1906 book, *Why Is There No Socialism in the United States?* The puzzle of the next century may be, Why is there no Green party in the United States?

SEYMOUR MARTIN LIPSET (1922–2006) was the Hazel Professor of Public Policy and Sociology in the Institute of Public Policy at George Mason University. A senior fellow of the Hoover Institution at Stanford University and a senior scholar of the Wilstein Institute for Jewish Policy, his publications include *American Exceptionalism: A Double-Edged Sword* (W. W. Norton, 1995) and *Jews and the American Scene*, coauthored with Earl Raab (Harvard University Press, 1995).

Godfrey Hodgson

The Corruption of the Best

I have criticized American exceptionalism, sometimes sharply, on several different grounds. I first argued that the history of the United States ought to be seen as only one part of a broader history, not as the teleological preparation of a present and future perfection; as history, that is, and not as patriotic commemoration.

That history has not exclusively been the product of Puritan religion or the frontier, or any other purely American influences. On the contrary, it has been shaped by vast international historical processes, from the expansion of Europe and the African slave trade, through the Reformation and the Enlightenment, the global competition between the European powers, especially Britain and France, and the industrial revolution. America's development was greatly affected by two world wars, the Depression of the 1930s, and the Cold War. It has continued in the context of the rise of a global economy, first in the early years of the twentieth century and then, after the interruptions of the "short twentieth century," in the past few decades.

Of course there were events and processes that were specific to the United States. They included mass immigration, the frontier, slavery, and the minting of an American political ideology. Their part in shaping the modern nation should never be underestimated. Yet nor should they be exaggerated at the expense of the wider processes that affected the world as a whole. Indeed, the first three of those four cardinal factors in American history also affected the development of many other nations. Historians, in other words, should not cherry-pick what was unique in the American experience and ignore its historical context. And there is an important reason for this. If Americans are brought up in their education, and encouraged by their leaders, to believe that they are a unique and special people, that will affect the way they behave toward the rest of the world, over which they now have so much influence and so much power.

I have suggested that in the early decades after the Revolution, in part as a result of developments in the colonial period, American society truly was more exceptional than it has subsequently become. That exceptionalism consisted in a relatively greater achievement of both freedom and equality, at least for white males, than was to be found elsewhere. The development of freedom and equality in America was always, however, more limited, more constrained, and more under attack than patriotic myth would sometimes have us believe.

After the Civil War, I have maintained, at the very time when the myth of the unique democratic influence of the frontier was coming into existence, America was in many ways becoming less exceptional. That was in part because the United States was beginning to experience the consequences of the industrial revolution, of unregulated capitalism, and of urbanization, in the same way that these forces were already affecting the British Isles and western and central Europe. In some respects, no doubt, the United States had greater resources for resisting or deflecting those dangerous consequences. But by the 1880s, to contrast a Europe enslaved by poverty with a land of opportunity inhabited by "people of plenty" was historically inaccurate. After the abolition of slavery, in fact, American politics were more and more about the "social question": about poverty, inequality, injustice—exactly the matters that were concerning writers, social reformers, and political leaders in Europe. On the one hand, the period brought the development, for the first time on American soil, of what was called in Europe a "proletariat." On the other, in what Mark Twain called the Gilded Age, America bred, on a far larger scale than ever before, a class of plutocrats whose wealth gave them social and political power. So far from being the mother of capitalism, as is sometimes suggested, the United States, though always a capitalist country, came later than several European countries to fully developed industrial capitalism.

America was also becoming less exceptional in reality (though not necessarily less exceptionalist in rhetoric) precisely because—largely unnoticed or at least unappreciated in the United States—Europe, too, was going through an Age of Liberalism. Mid-nineteenth-century Europe was the world of John Stuart Mill and William Ewart Gladstone. Greater freedom, equality, and democracy were aspired to, and—albeit imperfectly—achieved. This was admittedly more painful in Europe, because of the strength of established powers, vested interests, and traditions. But then it was not that easy in America, either. You could say that America was becoming less exceptional because Europeans, or many of them, were adopting American values. But those values had in any case long been European values too for most Europeans.

Many of the historical realities that had once made Europe appear so different from America were disappearing or at least were under attack in late-nineteenth-century and early-twentieth-century Europe. Absolute monarchy had been displaced by constitutional monarchy in Britain, Holland, and Scandinavia. The power of aristocracy was being crippled, not least by the effects of imported American foodstuffs on agricultural rents. Empire was dividing the politics of the imperial powers from 1900 on, the time of the Boer War, and by the second decade of the twentieth century two of the three major political parties in Britain, the Liberals and Labour, were already committed to decolonization in the long term. Americans, and especially American conservatives, have a high opinion of Winston Churchill. British people remember that in the 1930s he was one of the rather few British politicians who strenuously opposed independence for India.

In the twentieth century, America was exceptional not so much for a commitment to democratic ideals but for two other reasons. For one thing, the United States became exceptionally rich, partly because of its natural and human resources, but also because, unlike its European rivals, it was not devastated and impoverished but was enriched by two world wars. At first, and especially in the generation immediately after World War II, that wealth was widely and generously spread. Inequality declined sharply in America during and immediately after World War II. But the "glorious thirty years" after 1945 were a time of rapidly increasing prosperity, far more widely distributed than ever before, in Western Europe and in Japan as well. Workers in automobile plants in Britain and Germany, France and Italy, like auto workers in the United States, were improving their standard of living, buying their own homes, seeing their children go to college, helped by powerful trade unions. More recently, in America and in Europe, economic growth has been disproportionately appropriated by the very rich, both by those who have inherited and by those who have earned their good fortune for themselves. But the differences in the standard of living between America and the rest of the developed world are now differences of degree, not, as they had been before the 1960s, differences of kind.

Once, American incomes were something Europeans could only dream of. Now, in Western Europe at least, it is a question of whether the American average income is reached next year or the year after.

In the 1930s and 1940s the United States also escaped the political disaster of fascism, and indeed played an important, though not (as exceptionalists sometimes imply) the only, role in destroying fascist and Nazi rule. The fact that fascism never seriously threatened the American political system (or, for that matter, the political systems in Britain, the British dominions, or Scandinavia) reflects the strength of the democratic tradition and the political skill of President Roosevelt, as well as the robust common sense of most Americans. Yet even in America some fascist tendencies and quasi-fascist movements appeared.

Untouched by foreign invasion, the American economy boomed in both world wars, at the very time when America's rivals were in their greatest difficulties. The United States "did well" out of the two world wars. After 1945 it was natural for American exceptionalism to be seen in large measure as the consequence of exceptional economic success and military power, not to mention the Faustian power of nuclear weapons and the ability to deliver them almost everywhere at will. So in the 1950s the current version of exceptionalism was a new blend of the moral exceptionalism of Roosevelt's fight for the Four Freedoms and pride in economic recovery, material progress, and military power. A good example is the book by David Potter, *People of Plenty*. "In every aspect of economic welfare," Potter wrote, "the national differentials between the United States and other countries are immense." The United States, he said, had 7 percent of the world's population and 42 percent of the world's income. The equivalent figures today show that the U.S. gross national product is $13.2 trillion out of a world GNP of $48 trillion, or about 27 percent (slightly less than the European Union's share of $14.5 trillion), and the U.S. population, though much larger at about 300 million, is only 4.5 percent of the world's estimated population of 6.6 billion people, a lower proportion than fifty years earlier. The average American in 1949, Potter stated, consumed 3,186 calories, "unquestionably the highest nutritional standard in the world." Half a century later, few would equate calorie consumption with nutritional standards. Moreover, Potter claimed, the high American standard of living was the result much less of natural resources than of the "economic efficiency of all kinds of Americans." The phrase now evokes a gentle smile. Potter's book, like many works of the 1950s, was explicitly devoted to disproving "zany" Marxist or socialist ideas. Many similar books written in the 1950s—for example, works by Max Lerner or Daniel Boorstin—were predicated on similar assumptions of incomparable American material superiority in areas where today the American advantage is comparatively slight and sometimes depends on what precise method of comparison is used.

In recent decades this second, material exceptionalism, now less clear, has helped to breed or to strengthen a third, missionary exceptionalism. This is the belief that it is the destiny, some say the God-given destiny, of the United States to spread the benefits of its democratic system and of its specific version of capitalism to as many other countries as possible. This view is not wholly new. Seeds of it can be seen in early Protestant religion. It played a part in the patriotic rhetoric of the new Republic, in tile confidence of the champions of Manifest Destiny that theirs was an "empire of liberty,"and in the belief system of many American leaders, including especially Woodrow Wilson but also, in different ways, Theodore Roosevelt, Franklin D. Roosevelt, Harry Truman, and John F. Kennedy.

One specific new element in the American belief system, from the last quarter of the twentieth century, was the elevation of American capitalism, alongside American freedom and American democracy, in the pantheon of American exceptionalism. Of course, America has been the home of capitalism from the start, though not its only home. There was a fascinating episode in the earliest years of the Pilgrims' struggle to survive in Plymouth Colony, described in William Bradford's classic account. At first the Pilgrims intended to hold all land and wealth in common. But when the young colony was desperately worried about the shortage of food, the governor, Bradford, "with the advice of the chiefest among them," assigned land as property to each family. This experience, Bradford comments, "may well evince the vanity of that conceit of Plato's and other ancients applauded by some of later times; that the taking away of property and bringing in community [meaning communism or at least common ownership] into a commonwealth would make them happy and flourishing, *as if they were wiser than God.*"

Although ideas of communal ownership of property were to be found in the sixteenth and seventeenth century—for example, among the Anabaptists in sixteenth-century Westphalia, Moravia, and Bohemia and the seventeenth-century Levellers and Diggers in England—capitalism was closely associated with Protestantism, in Holland and Germany as well as in Britain and New England, as has been argued by great modern historians, including Max Weber and R.H. Tawney. If modern capitalism was largely developed in Holland and Britain in the sixteenth and seventeenth centuries, and carried across the Atlantic by Protestant colonists, capitalism itself is as old as civilization. Its fundamental ideas, such as the idea of investing in the hope of future profit, are as old as agriculture, and the part played by markets in setting prices can be traced back at least as far as the earliest towns in the Near East. It is true that at certain times and in certain places—for example, in the ancient river valley civilizations, when economic behavior and prices were regulated by royal authority, and in the European Middle Ages, when usury was prohibited by the church—capitalism was subordinated to temporal or spiritual authority. But capitalism existed long before the United States of America.

Economic historians distinguish a series of successive phases in the development of capitalism, for example, petty capitalism, mercantile capitalism, industrial capitalism, and finance capitalism. None of these can be said to have developed exclusively or even mainly in the United States. It is true, however, that in the twentieth century many European societies reacted to economic crisis by adopting one or another version of socialism. Even in the United States, from 1933 to the 1970s, the federal government embraced a form of social democracy, though control of enterprise was exercised not mainly by state ownership but by state regulation. In Western Europe, as well as in the former British dominions and in Latin America, though various "socialist" devices, including public ownership, were more widespread than in the United States, the economic system was still one variant or another of capitalism, more or less regulated. (Sometimes it was described as a "mixed economy.") It is possible therefore to speak of the United States as having led the way in the propagation of neoliberal ideas in the late twentieth century, but misleading to suggest that capitalism as such is in any way an American invention.

In the past thirty years or so, however, and especially after the presidency of Ronald Reagan, an exceptionalist philosophy has been more confidently enunciated and more openly accepted as the basis for American foreign policy. This missionary spirit has come in two variants. One is the gentler and more consensual version, as preached and practiced by the Clinton administration. Its leaders acknowledged that they were followers of Woodrow Wilson, and that they inherited his desire to bring the benefits of American democracy to the world. But they wanted to do so, as far as possible, only to the extent that others wanted those benefits. They were keen that America should be the leader. But they interpreted that to mean that others were eager to be led. They wanted to act out their beliefs, so far as possible, with the agreement of as many other nations as possible. This, too, had been the instinct, or at least the practice, of the previous Republican administration of George H. W. Bush.

At least as long ago as the debates in the early Cold War years over the National Security Act, and over NSC-68 and the sharp consequent increases in defense budgets, there had been those, the "hawks," who were impatient of restraint. They saw the nation as being virtually at war with communism. They resented the occasional reluctance of allies to endorse American interests or to go along with American initiatives. They called for maximum military readiness and brushed aside those who warned of the dangers of transforming America into a "garrison state" or a "national security state." Surprisingly, perhaps, it was not when the danger of communism was at its height, but when it had to all intents and purposes disappeared in the early 1990s, that the partisans of aggressive, unilateral missionary policies finally triumphed.

I have argued, as many others have now done, that these policies have been disastrous, not only for the damage they have inflicted on the domestic American economy or even for America's reputation in the world, but also for any realistic prospect of achieving their own goals. There can be little doubt that the prospects of spreading American ideals of democracy have weakened, not improved, especially in the Middle East, since the invasion of Iraq in 2003. Survey data from late 2007 suggest that roughly two-thirds to three-quarters of the world's population disapprove of the American invasion and occupation of Iraq. The prospects of American democracy would be seriously damaged by an attack on Iran or even by a nod and a wink to an Israeli attack on Iran. Nor has the prosperity of the United States been enhanced by the new aggressive foreign policy. An America on bad terms with its suppliers of energy, raw materials, cheap manufactured goods, migrants, and credit is not going to be a stronger America, especially if its finite resources have been dissipated in incompetently planned military adventures. Finally, the domestic regime that accompanies conservative foreign policy seems unlikely to strengthen the society in the long term. An America, for example, in which the richest 1 percent were piling up ever greater fortunes, and chief executives of corporations earned many hundreds of times more than their average employee, while half the population could not afford to buy a home or go to the doctor, would not be a stronger America, however spectacular the fortunes accumulated by a few. . . .

From the beginning, one legitimate and positive component of American national pride has been the idea that the United States had unique qualities as a society and a special destiny as a nation. That conviction has been a powerful motivating incentive. It has caused Americans on the whole to set themselves high standards, especially in their public life. If they sometimes supposed that their standards were higher than anyone else's, that may not have been altogether a bad thing. If it set an example for other nations to emulate, so much the better.

At different times in the past, exceptionalism has admittedly taken the objectionable shape of a pompous and intolerant "Americanism," or even "100 percent Americanism." This was the stuff of blowhard Fourth of July oratory in every generation. It took the form of the odious prejudices of nineteenth-century Nativists and of the second Klan of the 1920s, with its bigoted hatred of Catholics and Jews as well as African Americans.

This was the soil in which the Red-baiting and witch-hunting of the 1950s grew. One of my students recently showed me a strip cartoon booklet circulated to schools in 1950 by the service organization Lions International. It recited a propaganda version of "history" in which cavemen, ancient Egyptians, and Spartans were portrayed as slaves. It contrasted the Spartans, directly compared to Russians, with the freedom-loving Athenians, though of course there was slavery in Athens as well as in Sparta. Americans were portrayed as uniquely brave soldiers for freedom, explicitly contrasted with British "socialism." As this cockamamie version of world history went on, to be told to the children, it was made clear that Americans were in danger of being enslaved . . . by taxation.

There is no means of telling how widespread such propaganda about American history was in the early Cold War years. It was certainly not far to seek. Nor perhaps should it be taken too seriously. Some of George Bush's admirers at the 2004 convention carried posters asking how they were to shoot liberals if their guns were taken from them, but everyone knew that that was only a joke in bad taste, not the portent of an American fascism.

The American exceptionalism I am describing is quite different from such coarse prejudice. It has been on the whole a tradition that stresses the superiority of America and Americans, not the inferiority of anyone else. That may be irritating to those of us who are not Americans, but it is generously meant. George W. Bush may not have taken the trouble to find out whether the people of Iraq were pleased to have him impose his conception of democracy on them, but at least it was liberty, not slavery, that he thought he was offering.

The corruption of the best, says the old Latin tag, is the worst. My thesis is not that American exceptionalist thought is intrinsically corrupting or that it was destructive in the past, but that what has been essentially a liberating set of beliefs has been corrupted over the past thirty years or so by hubris and self-interest into what is now a dangerous basis for national policy and for the international system.

Even in the times when its overall thrust was beneficent, the exceptionalist narrative of American history left out half the story. The history of the migration to America, I have suggested, could not be understood in isolation from the conditions and the political and religious beliefs of Europe at the time, certainly not by simply contrasting an American commitment to "liberty" with the presumably servile cultures of every one else. The religious faith of New England was not antithetical to European Christianity; it was one variant of the Protestant faith shared by Ulstermen and Swedes, Afrikaners and Prussians. The impulses that pushed Europeans to migrate to the United States were not wholly different from the motives of those who settled in Canada, or Australia, or the Argentine, or from those of the Russians who broke the black soils of the Ukraine, or even of the settlers from all over Europe who mined the gold and diamonds of South Africa.

Even in the twentieth century, at least the first two-thirds of it, if the American experience was more fortunate than that of other countries, still life in the United States was always influenced and conditioned by what was happening everywhere else. The United States was hardly untouched by the breakdown of the European diplomatic system in 1914 and of the world economic system in 1929, by the invention of the internal combustion engine in Germany in the 1890s or of radio by an Italian working in England, or by the work of nuclear physicists in Cambridge or Berlin in the 1920s. . . .

For more than two centuries Americans have been motivated to set themselves the highest public standards, both in the conduct of their own affairs and in their dealings with the rest of the world, by a national ideology. The essentials of that system of belief concerned such values as liberty, the political sovereignty of the people, equality before the law, and the paramount rule of constitutional law. From the beginning, that national ideology contained both exceptionalist and universalist elements. "The cause of America," said Tom Paine, "is in a great measure the cause of all mankind." The victory of the Union, said Abraham Lincoln, was "the last, best hope of earth." The emancipation of the slaves, he meant, would guarantee the freedom of all Americans. So the United States would be an example to the world. Some Americans in the nineteenth century believed that the "empire of liberty" would inevitably "overspread" at least the whole of North America and perhaps Central America and the Caribbean, and even the whole of the Americas as far as Tierra del Fuego. But public holiday rhetoric aside, there was no idea then that the United States either could or should bring freedom to the entire world. To this day, even the most messianic neo-Wilsonians have allowed their universalist ambitions to be checked by realism. It is one thing to invade Grenada, Lebanon, or at a stretch Iraq. No one is speaking of bringing democracy, by shock and awe, to nations with millions of soldiers and nuclear weapons, such as Russia, India, or China.

It was not until the twentieth century that this combination of exceptionalism with at least a theoretical universalism—a belief, that is, that the United States has a special destiny to bring freedom to the Americas, brought to bear on the idea that the United States could be an example of freedom to the world—began to take on the characteristics of a program. . . .

Underlying the whole story was a fabric of assumptions that were indeed predicated on a new, aggressive interpretation of the exceptionalist creed. The United States, it was said, would act as it saw fit. It neither needed nor wanted international agreement, approval, or cooperation. Those in the world who dissented in any way from the wrath to come were, by administration officials, not to mention their loyal journalists, ignored, or insulted, or derided.

So long as the world was threatened by dictators, first by fascist dictators, then by communists, the world was happy to accept American leadership. It helped that for decades that leadership was exerted in a spirit of generosity and comity. In those days, many around the world who were not Americans found it easy to share the ideals of the traditional American exceptionalist creed, among them freedom, democracy, and popular sovereignty. But in those days, such ideals were not presented in bluntly exceptionalist terms. Now the common ideals of what had come to be known as "the free world" were claimed as the private property of Americans.

To the world, however, freedom cannot mean military occupation. Democracy cannot mean a world's political decisions made behind closed doors in Washington. Popular sovereignty, as an ideal for the world, cannot be reduced to the wishes of the electorate in one country, still less to the instincts of an elite "within the Beltway" that seemed increasingly isolated from the rest of America. Prosperity, for the world, cannot mean the monopoly of the planet's resources by a few hundred corporations and a handful of financial enterprises.

Nothing is more passionately to be hoped for than that the American government will once again hold before it the values that inspired Jefferson and Madison, Lincoln and Roosevelt. Nothing is more heartily to be wished than that the American people should once again see itself, not as a master race whose primacy is owed to the shock and awe inspired by terrifying weaponry, but once again, freely and generously, as first among equals.

Such a change in the face America shows to the world will not come, of course, until Americans have shown once again, as they have so often done in the past, that they will not allow their generous instincts and sound values to be travestied by charlatans and bullies. Until American democracy girds itself to recapture the political system and reasserts its healthiest instincts, the United States is not likely to recapture the admiration and affection the American people earned by their achievements over the first two centuries of their national history. . . .

The point at which the principles of American democracy are reduced to mere boasting and bullying, justified by a cynical "realism," is the point at which the practice of American democracy, at home as well as abroad, is in mortal danger. It is also the point at which the best of the exceptionalism in the American tradition has been corrupted into the worst. We can only hope that mortal danger will be avoided.

The late **GODFREY HODGSON** was an English journalist and former Director of the Reuters Foundation Programme at Oxford University. The author of eleven books, most of them on some aspect of United States history, he served as the Washington bureau chief for *The Observer* and was the foreign editor for the *Independent*.

EXPLORING THE ISSUE

Is America Exceptional?

Critical Thinking and Reflection

1. How does Seymour Martin Lipset define "American exceptionalism"? Why does he believe that the United States is still different from the rest of the world?
2. According to Alexis de Tocqueville, how did the United States of the 1830s differ from all European nations?
3. According to Lipset, how does the United States today still differ from other nations?
4. According to Godfrey Hodgson, what qualities of the United States that are often described as unique are characteristics shared with other nations around the world?
5. According to Hodgson, what factors have contributed to a decline in the notion of American exceptionalism?

Is There Common Ground?

What do people mean when they talk about American exceptionalism? Most scholars approach this term from the perspective that the United States is in certain ways different from other nations. In other words, the United States is an exception to the rule when examining particular national characteristics; in Seymour Martin Lipset's terms, America is an "outlier" when compared to other countries, especially developed European nations to which it is frequently compared. And as Lipset suggests, those identifiable characteristics that set the United States apart from other nations, give it a unique quality, can be either positive or negative traits.

Many Americans, including political leaders ranging from John F. Kennedy to Newt Gingrich to Ronald Reagan to Barack Obama, have employed this term in something of a patriotic fashion and assumed that those features that presumably set the United States apart from other nations are, by definition, good things. They are prone to think of the United States as a model nation, not only set apart from others but also set above. From this vantage point, America is exceptional in the sense that it is superior to other nations, and there is an assumption that other countries should want to emulate the United States.

Critics of the use of this term approach their arguments from a variety of perspectives. Some disapprove because they consider the idea of American exceptionalism to be an expression of arrogance. Others, on the other hand, insist that the problem is that the United States is not different in many of the ways attributed to it. After all, they point out, the United States and its institutions grew out of Western European political and intellectual traditions shared with many other countries today. Generations of Americans, for example, have insisted that American national traditions and character were inherited from England or Germany or even the Celtic areas of Europe. Godfrey Hodgson recognizes that in an earlier time—the colonial era and early national period, in particular—Americans were more justified in claiming a uniqueness. After the Civil War, however, Hodgson believes that the United States became more like other industrializing nations in Europe. Lipset and others, according to Hodgson, miss the point that the United States is a nation among nations whose entire history has operated in a global context, whether individual Americans liked that or not.

Additional Resources

Thomas Bender, *A Nation Among Nations: America's Place in World History* (Hill & Wang, 2006)

Michael Ignatieff, ed., *American Exceptionalism and Human Rights* (Princeton University Press, 2005)

Deborah L. Madsen, *American Exceptionalism* (University Press of Mississippi, 1998)

David Noble, *Death of a Nation: American Culture and the End of Exceptionalism* (Cambridge University Press, 2002)

Sylvia Soderlind and James Taylor Carson, eds., *American Exceptionalisms: From Winthrop to Winfrey* (State University of New York Press, 2012)

Internet References . . .

The Alexis de Tocqueville Tour

www.tocqueville.org

Frederick Jackson Turner

nationalhumanitiescenter.org/pds/gilded/empire
/text1/turner.pdf

Institute for the Study of Civic Values

http://www.sustainable.org/creating-community
/civic-engagement/535-institute-for-the-study-of
-civic-values-iscv-

Selected, Edited, and with Issue Framing Material by:
Larry Madaras, *Howard Community College*
and
James M. SoRelle, *Baylor University*

ISSUE

Was the Pequot War Largely a Product of Native American Aggression?

YES: Steven T. Katz, "The Pequot War Reconsidered," *The New England Quarterly* (1991)

NO: Alfred A. Cave, from "The Pequot War and the Mythology of the Frontier," University of Massachusetts Press (1996)

Learning Outcomes

After reading this issue, you will be able to:

- Understand some of the differences between the traditional and revisionist interpretations of the causes of the Pequot War.
- Summarize several key events leading up to the Pequot War.
- Evaluate the role played by religion in the conflicts between Native Americans and British American colonists.
- Identify the competing perspectives of Native Americans and colonists with regard to the causes of the Pequot War.
- Explain the concept of a "clash of cultures" as it pertains to the interactions of Native Americans and colonists in New England and throughout the British North American colonies.

ISSUE SUMMARY

YES: Steven Katz argues that the Pequot Indians, through a series of raids, ambushes, and murders in the 1630s, sought to realize their geopolitical ambitions by destroying European settlement in New England and that, after efforts to negotiate failed, New England colonists sought to protect themselves from Pequot aggression by waging a defensive war to prevent further assaults on colonial settlements in the region.

NO: Alfred Cave insists that the Pequot War resulted from a clash of cultures in which Puritan leaders, preoccupied with the idea that Native Americans were part of a Satanic conspiracy, were convinced that violence was essential to intimidate indigenous Americans in order to secure colonial settlements, terminate Indian autonomy, and control land and resources in New England.

Relations between Native Americans and Europeans were marred by the difficulties that arose from people of very different cultures encountering each other for the first time. These encounters led to inaccurate perceptions, misunderstandings, and failed expectations. While at first the American Indians deified the explorers, experience soon taught them to do otherwise. European opinion ran the gamut from admiration to contempt; for example, some European poets and painters who expressed admiration for the Noble Savage while other Europeans accepted as a rationalization for genocide the sentiment that "the only good savage is a dead one."

Spanish, French, Dutch, and English treatment of Native Americans differed and was based to a considerable extent on each nation's hopes about the New World and how it could be subordinated to the Old. The Spanish exploited the Indians most directly, taking their gold and silver, transforming their government, religion, and society, and even occasionally enslaving them. The French were less of a menace than the others because there were fewer of them and because many French immigrants were itinerant trappers and priests rather than settlers. The Dutch presence in North America was relatively short-lived. In the long run, the emigration from the British Isles was the most threatening of all. Entire families came from England, and they were determined to establish a permanent home in the wilderness.

The juxtaposition of Native American and English from the Atlantic to the Appalachians resulted sometimes in coexistence, other times in enmity. William Bradford's account of the Pilgrims' arrival at Cape Cod describes the insecurity the new migrants felt as they disembarked on American soil. "[T]hey had now no friends to welcome them nor inns to entertain or refresh their weather beaten bodies; no houses or much less towns to repair to, to seek for succor. . . . Besides, what could they see but a hideous and deserted wilderness, full of wild beasts and wild men. . . . If they looked behind them there was the mighty ocean which they had passed and was now a main bar and gulf to separate them from all the civil parts of the world." Historical hindsight, however, suggests that if anyone should have expressed fears about the unfolding encounter in the Western Hemisphere, it should have been the Native Americans because their numbers declined by as much as 95 percent in the first century following Columbus's arrival. Although some of this decline can be attributed to violent encounters with Europeans, there seems to have been a more hostile (and far less visible) force at work. As historian William McNeill has suggested, the main weapon that overwhelmed indigenous peoples in the Americas was the Europeans' breath which transmitted disease germs for which most American Indians had no immunities.

Upon arrival, English settlers depended on the Indians' generosity in sharing the techniques of wilderness survival. Puritan clergymen tried to save their neighbors' souls, going so far as to translate the Bible into dialects, but they were not as successful at conversion as the French Jesuits and Spanish Franciscans. Attempts at coexistence did not smooth over the tension between the English and the Indians. They did not see eye to eye, for example, about the uses of the environment. Indian agriculture, in the eyes of English settlers, was neither intense nor efficient. Native Americans observed that white settlers consumed larger amounts of food per person and cultivated not only for themselves but also for towns and villages that bought the surplus. Subsistence farming collided with the market economy.

Large-scale violence erupted in Virginia in the 1620s, the 1640s, and the 1670s. In the latter decade, frontiersmen in the Virginia piedmont led by Nathaniel Bacon attacked tribes living in the Appalachian foothills. In New England, from the 1630s through the 1670s, Pequots, Wampanoags, Narragansetts, Mohegans, Podunks, and Nipmunks united to stop the encroachments into their woodlands and hunting grounds. King Philip's War lasted from June 1675 to September 1676, with isolated raids stretching on until 1678. Casualties rose into the hundreds, and Anglo-Indian relations deteriorated.

In the next century Spain, France, and England disputed each other's North American claims, and Native Americans joined sides, usually as the allies of France against England. These great wars of the eighteenth century ended in 1763 with England's victory, but disputes over territorial expansion continued. Colonial officials objected to the Proclamation of 1763 by which King George III's imperial government forbade his subjects from settling west of the Appalachian watershed. The area from those mountains to the Mississippi River, acquired from France at the recently negotiated Peace of Paris, was designated as an Indian reservation. From 1763 to 1783, as Anglo-colonial relations moved from disagreement to combat to independence, the London government consistently sided with the Native Americans.

The full range of experiences of Europeans encountering Native Americans in the New World does not lend itself to easy, unalterable conclusions regarding the nature of those contacts. The consequences of these interactions depended upon when and where they took place and which particular groups were involved, and there was rarely any constant or consistent pattern of behavior. One tribe might experience cordial relations with European colonists at one point in time but not another. A particular tribe would get along well with the French but not the English or Dutch; in another generation, the same tribe might enter into an alliance with its former enemies. A case in point is the history of Indian–white relations in early Virginia. The colonists participating in the Jamestown expedition, for example, were attacked by a group of Indians almost as soon as they set foot on American soil. A few months later, however, Powhatan, the dominant chief in the region, provided essential food supplies to the Jamestown residents who were suffering from disease and hunger. By the latter part of 1608, however, the colonists, under the leadership of John Smith, had begun to take an antagonistic stance toward Powhatan and his people. Smith attempted to extort food supplies from the Indians by threatening to burn their villages and canoes. These hostilities continued long after

Smith's departure from Virginia and did not end until the 1640s, when colonial leaders signed a formal treaty with the Powhatan Confederacy.

Similar experiences occurred in New England where colonists and Native Americans maintained reasonably cordial relations in the early years of settlement. Tensions over land usage, trade, and acts of violence, however, soon produced warfare in southern New England in the 1630s. Following the murder of several Englishmen, Puritan officials demanded that the Pequots, who were held responsible for the deaths despite evidence that members of other tribes in the region were culpable, turn over the guilty parties for prosecution by colonial courts. The Pequot sachem Sassacus refused but did provide restitution in the form of wampum, believing this to be a satisfactory response. Subsequently, in 1637, New England officials sent armed colonists to exact revenge on the Pequots at Fort Mystic, where raids resulted in the deaths of all but a few of the Indian inhabitants, and the village was put to the torch. Plymouth Colony governor William Bradford described the scene in his autobiography: "It was a fearful sight to see them [mainly Pequot women and children] thus frying in the fire and the streams of blood quenching the same, and horrible was the stink and scent thereof; but the victory seemed a sweet sacrifice, and they gave the praise thereof to God, who had wrought so wonderfully for them, thus to enclose their enemies in their hands and give them so speedy a victory over so proud and insulting an enemy."

Responsibility for the outbreak of the Pequot War (1636–1638) has become the topic of considerable debate among scholars of colonial America and specialists in Native American history. While most of the nineteenth-century treatments of this conflict are marred by racist characterizations of Native Americans generally, in the twentieth century, historians have traditionally recognized that New England Puritans certainly were guilty of the slaughter of their Pequot adversaries. At the same time, however, many like Alden Vaughan in *New England Frontier: Puritans and Indians, 1620–1675* (Little, Brown, 1965) have argued that the Pequots represented a threat to New England security and that Puritans acted in self-defense to resist Pequot aggression. Revisionists have been far more critical of the Puritans. Most notable in this regard is Francis Jennings, whose book *The Invasion of America: Indians, Colonialism, and the Cant of Conquest* (University of North Carolina

Press, 1975) refocused the argument on Puritan greed, prejudice, and bigotry. For Jennings, the Pequots were trapped in the middle of an ongoing competition among colonial residents in Massachusetts Bay Colony, Plymouth, and Connecticut over land and control of trade in the region. Neal Salisbury avoids Jennings' polemical style and concludes in *Manitou and Providence: Indians, Europeans, and the Making of New England, 1500–1643* (Oxford University Press, 1982) that the conflict with the Pequots succeeded in bringing the New England Puritan community together to refocus on its divine mission of dispatching the indigenous peoples from their midst. In her book *Settling with the Indians: The Meeting of English and Indian Cultures in America, 1580–1640* (Rowman & Littlefield, 1980), Karen Ordahl Kupperman insists that the Pequot War was prompted by English efforts to exercise undisputed power in New England.

In the following essays, the reader will find two very different interpretations of the causes of the Pequot War. In the first selection, Steven T. Katz challenges revisionists who view the conflict as an act of racist genocide on the part of New England Puritans. According to Katz, Massachusetts Bay Colony leaders attempted unsuccessfully to negotiate with the Pequots in an effort to bring the murderers of John Stone, John Oldham, and other colonists to justice. English colonists, Katz argues, had every reason to fear for their safety and lives as the Pequots attempted to destroy English settlement throughout New England. The Puritans fought a defensive war that included the decision to burn the Pequot village at Fort Mystic and had no intention of carrying out a full-scale war against these Native American adversaries.

Alfred Cave views the Puritans as the aggressors in this conflict as they attempted to make the New England frontier safe for their followers. Cave disputes the argument that the Pequots were a threat to Puritan security except insofar as they attempted to control European trade and maintain a network of allied tribes throughout New England. Characterizing the Pequots (and all Native Americans for that matter) as savages, instruments of Satan, and enemies of Christianity, the Puritans overreacted to rumors promulgated by the Mohegan sachem Uncas that the Pequots were preparing to assault the expanding Puritan settlements. The attack at Fort Mystic resulted and ultimately destroyed Pequot hegemony in the region.

YES ⤹

Steven T. Katz

The Pequot War Reconsidered

It is well known that in the 1970s and 1980s traditional scholarly analyses and judgments of the motives and events surrounding the Pequot War of 1637 came to be revised. In place of the view that the English were simply protecting themselves by preemptively attacking the Pequots, the revisionists argued that the Europeans used earlier, limited threats against them as cause to bring mass destruction on the Pequots. That assault is then taken to be a harbinger, a symbol of a larger, premeditated exterminatory intent that characterized the invasion of the New World. While there is surely room for a more penetrating critical reconstruction of the meaning of America's conquest and settlement than has yet appeared, one must be cautious in allowing legitimate moral outrage at the treatment of the Indians to substitute for a careful sorting of the evidence about the Pequot War. If we examine the facts closely and try to analyze them within their particular historical context, our judgments of the wrongs done the Native Americans will be more nuanced, balanced, and discriminating than radicalizing polemics allow and thus ultimately will better serve our efforts to understand the processes and consequences of colonization.

I

My first cautionary comment regarding the war is that it should not be viewed in strictly racial or ethnic terms of Red vs. White. I do not dispute that the colonists viewed the Indians through racial stereotypes, or that those stereotypes affected their behavior, but the particular circumstances of the Pequot War certainly seem to argue against the charge that It was a universal offensive against "Indianness" per se. The most telling of these circumstances is the presence of rival Indian groups on the side of the colonists. The crucial role of the Narragansetts, first in rejecting Pequot overtures to join a pan-Indian front against the English and then, in October 1636, in allying with the English against the Pequot, is but the earliest and most prominent case of European-Indian

collaboration in the conflict. Following this alliance, the Mohegans, the Massachusetts and River Tribes, and later the Mohawks all sided with the British. Although the reasons for these alliances have been disputed for three centuries, seventeenth-century evidence—for example, the "Remonstrance of New Netherland," John Winthrop's *History of New England*, and John De Forest's *History of the Indians*—is clear that at least intermittent hostility between the Pequots and the Narragansetts and their tributaries preceded the war.

Once we are able to hold our charges of racism in reserve, we can attend to the specifics of the war. Our distance from the events obviously blurs our vision. Many facts about the war have been contested, including the particular causes for the outbreak of hostilities; however, there can be no doubt that both sides had cause to feel aggrieved. From the perspective of most Indians, exceptions notwithstanding, the very presence of the European was an act of aggression. Filling in the outlines of this generalized aggression was an already considerable and well-documented body of particular crimes committed by unscrupulous individuals like John Oldham, whose murder in 1636 set in motion the events that led to the war. Oldham was not, moreover, the only Englishman the Pequots or their tributaries had murdered. In 1634 they had killed two English captains, including the notorious and disreputable John Stone, who had kidnapped and held several Indians for ransom, and in the next two years they had killed at least six more colonists. Alternatively, the English leadership was disturbed that the Pequots had taken no action against the guilty among them and disheartened that the Pequots had abrogated the terms of the treaty they had signed. Fears increased when Jonathan Brewster, a Plymouth trader, passed word that Uncas, sachem of the Mohegans, had reported that

> the Pequents have some mistrust, that the English will shortly come against them (which I take is by indiscreet speeches of some of your people here to the Natives) and therefore out of desperate

madnesse doe threaten shortly to sett upon both Indians [Mohegans] and English, joyntly.

Uncas may well have fabricated the rumor, but the colonists were certainly in a frame of mind to take it seriously. Their numbers were small, and news of the Virginia uprising of 1622, with its 350 casualties, had still not faded from memory. What the Puritans sought was a stratagem that would put an end to unpredictable, deadly annoyances as well as forestall any larger, more significant Indian military action like that suggested by Uncas's report. However one estimates the "good faith" or lack thereof of the Massachusetts leadership, efforts were made to negotiate, but these efforts failed, or at least were perceived to have failed. The colonists then chose as their best course of action a retaliatory raid, intended both to punish and to warn, on the Indians of Block Island, who were specifically charged with Oldham's murder. The Pequots were involved, according to William Hubbard, because the murderers had "fled presently to the Pequods, by whom they were sheltered, and so became also guilty themselves of his blood."

Ninety Englishmen participated in the raid commanded by John Endecott. John Winthrop noted that Endecott was ordered

> to put to death the men of Block Island, but to spare the women and children, and to bring them away, and to take possession of the Island; and from thence to go to the Pequods to demand the murderers of Capt. Stone and other English, and one thousand fathom of wampom for damages, etc., and some of their children as hostages.

None of the mainland Pequot at Pequot Harbor were to be harmed if they capitulated to his demands. In the event, the raid on Block Island turned into an extensive assault, and the Indian settlement there was looted and burned. However, although property was destroyed and several Indians were wounded, "the Naymen killed not a man, save that one Kichomiquim, an Indian Sachem of the Bay, killed a Pequot." The fact that only one Indian was killed seems to confirm John Winthrop's belief that the colonists "went not to make war upon [the Pequots] but to do justice." Not all colonists defined "justice" as Winthrop did, however, for the Endecott raid on the Harbor Indians was condemned by the colonial leaders of Plymouth, Connecticut, and Fort Saybrook.

In response to Endecott's assaults, the Pequots plagued the settlers with a series of raids, ambushes, and annoyances. On 23 April, Wethersfield, Connecticut, was attacked. Nine were killed, including a woman and child,

and two additional young women were captured. A number of other raids claimed the lives of thirty Europeans, or five percent of all the settlers in Connecticut. In addition to these offensive actions, the Pequot set about developing alliances, particularly with the Narragansett, to galvanize support for a war to destroy European settlement in their territory, if not in New England entirely. Many colonists who learned of the plan for a broad effort against them, which was frustrated only at the last minute through the intervention of Roger Williams, rightly felt, given their demographic vulnerability, that their very survival was threatened. Even Francis Jennings, the most severe critic of Puritan behavior, acknowledges that "Had these [Pequot] proposals [for alliance with the Narragansetts] been accepted by the Narragansetts, there would have without a doubt arisen a genuine Indian menace. . . . Whether the colonies could long have maintained themselves under such conditions is open to serious question."

The Pequot War was the organized reaction of the colonists of Connecticut and Massachusetts to these intimidating events. In choosing to make war, they were choosing to put an end to threats to their existence as individuals and as a community. They did not decide to fight out of some a priori lust for Indian blood based on some metaphysical doctrine of Indian inferiority, however much they may have held that view, or some desire for further, even complete, control over Indian territory, much as they coveted such land. They fought, initially, a defensive war. They may well have provoked events, as even Winthrop tacitly acknowledged, by their over-reactive raid on Block Island, but, in the early stages of the conflict, they did not intend to enter into a full-scale war with the Pequot until the Pequot raised the stakes with their response to the events at Block Island and Pequot Harbor. Of course the Indians cannot be blamed for so replying, for they too saw themselves as acting legitimately in self-defense, both narrowly and more generally in defense of traditional Indian rights to their own native lands. In effect, both sides acted to defend what they perceived as rightly theirs. In this context, if either side can be said to have harbored larger geo-political ambitions, it was the Pequot, though defeat would certainly bury those desires.

The major action of the war was an attack by 70 Connecticut and 90 Massachusetts colonists along with 60 Mohegans, plus some scattered Narragansett and Eastern Niantics, against the Pequot Fort at Mystic, which held an Indian population of between 400 and 700, including women and children. The colonists and their Indian allies surprised the Pequots and burned their fort to the ground. During the battle two English soldiers were killed and about 20 were wounded, while almost half the Indians allied with them were killed or wounded; almost all the Pequots were killed.

Richard Drinnon, in his *Facing West: The Metaphysics of Indian Hating and Empire Building* (1980), has argued that the unusual violence of the operation signals the colonists' "genocidal intentions." In evaluating the behavior of the English in this particular instance, however, it should be recognized that the tactics employed were neither so unconventional nor so novel that they can be taken to mark a turning point in Puritan-Indian relations, nor were they so distinctive as to indicate a transformation in Puritan awareness of the otherness of their adversaries. Given the relative strength of the enemy, the inexperience of the colonial forces, and the crucial fact that Sassacus, chief of the Pequot, and his warriors were camped only five miles from Mystic Fort and were sure to arrive soon, as in fact they did, one need not resort to dramatic theories of genocidal intentionality to explain the actions of the English. The simple, irrefutable fact is that had the battle been prolonged, Sassacus would have had time to reach Mystic and deflect the English attack.

II

Although he does not use the term *genocide* per se, it is clear from the rhetorical thrust of his argument and his use of phrases like "deliberate massacre" that Francis Jennings is an insistent advocate of the genocidal thesis. Given the force of his prose, the popularity of his work, and its long-standing influence, it is useful to deconstruct Jennings's argument to evaluate the legitimacy of the heinous charge leveled against the English colonists.

Jennings attributes to Capt. John Mason, the expedition's leader, an overt, *ab initio* desire to massacre the Indians. "Mason proposed," he writes,

> to avoid attacking Pequot warriors, which would have overtaxed his unseasoned, unreliable troops. Battle, as such, was not his purpose. Battle is only one of the ways to destroy an enemy's will to fight. Massacre can accomplish the same end with less risk, and Mason had determined that massacre would be his objective.

Ignoring all other reports of Mason's intentions and actions, Jennings bases his conclusions on Mason's own terse account of the event. Jennings cites Mason's reasons for his strategy, with special reference to his concluding "'and also some other [reasons],'" which he says "'I shall forebear to trouble you with.'" Even Jennings labels this comment cryptic, but he still does not forebear using it as

unambiguous evidence of a hidden, premeditated plan to massacre all the Indians at Fort Mystic.

Jennings also refers to Mason's discussion with his colleagues Lt. Lion Gardiner and Capt. John Underhill as well as with the expedition's Chaplain Stone. He takes Mason's request that the chaplain "'commend our Condition to the Lord, that night, to direct how in what manner we should demean our selves'" to be a covert reference to the existence of a plan to massacre the Indians the next day. But on the eve of such a battle, especially given Puritan sensibilities, such a request is neither surprising nor, given the text before us, indicative of any special intent; to read it as an implicit confession of genocidal desire, Jennings has to overinterpret the brief original source dramatically.

Jennings charges that "all the secondary accounts of the Pequot conquest squeamishly evade confessing the deliberateness of Mason's strategy, and some falsify to conceal it." What Jennings adduces as confirmation of both the premeditated plot to massacre and the later conscious suppression of that fact emerges in the course of a curious argument, which I quote in full.

> Mason's own narrative is the best authority on this point. The Massachusetts Puritans' William Hubbard brazened out his own misquotation by telling his readers to "take it as it was delivered in writing by that valiant, faithful, and prudent Commander Capt. Mason." With this emphatic claim to authority he quoted Mason as saying, "We had resolved a while not to have burned it [the village], but being we could not come at them, I resolved to set it on fire." Despite Hubbard's assurance, these were not Mason's words. His manuscript said bluntly, "we had formerly concluded to destroy them by the Sword and save the Plunder."

Jennings's conclusion does not follow logically from the texts he cites nor from his juxtaposition of them. They neither suggest premeditation to massacre nor falsification of the record; instead, Hubbard's paraphrase of Mason's words accords perfectly with his stated intent to plunder the settlement. Jennings himself recognizes that such economic motives were central to the Block Island raid, as well as other actions by the English. Burning Fort Mystic would, of course, severely limit its economic potential; the sword was a less efficient tool of human destruction but would preserve goods of value to the English. In fact, Mason's vow to "destroy" the Pequots "by the Sword" is a phrase not at all unusual to the language of military conflict and in that context such comments almost always signal not the annihilation of the enemy but the disruption of its capacity to fight. This understanding of Mason's comment is supported by the Puritans' further prosecution of the war.

Jennings continues to press home his point in his increasingly confused and confusing reconstruction of events. I quote:

> The rest of Mason's manuscript revealed what sort of inhabitants had been occupying the Mystic River village and proved conclusively that mere victory over them was not enough to satisfy Mason's purpose. After telling how the attack was launched at dawn of May 26, and how entrance to the village was forced, the account continued thus:

> At length William Heydon espying the Breach in the Wigwam, supposing some English might be there, entred; but in his Entrance fell over a dead Indian; but speedily recovering himself, the Indians some fled, others crept under their Beds: the Captain [Mason] going out of the Wigwam saw many Indians in the Lane or Street; he making towards them, they fled, were pursued to the End of the Lane, where they were met by Edward Pattison, Thomas Barber, with some others; where seven of them were Slain, as they said. The Captain facing about, Marched a slow Pace up the Lane he came down, perceiving himself very much out of Breath; and coming to the other End near the Place where he first entred, saw two Soldiers standing close to the Pallizado with their Swords pointed to the Ground: The Captain told them that We should never kill them after that manner: The Captain also said, WE MUST BURN THEM: and immediately stepping into the Wigwam where he had been before, brought out a Fire Brand, and putting it into the Matts with which they were covered, set the Wigwams on Fire.

From this sparse, unsophisticated description, Jennings concludes that "It is terribly clear . . . that the village, stockaded though it was, had few warriors at home when the attack took place." Mason himself, however, asserts that just the day before the English attack, 150 braves had reinforced the Indian garrison holding the fort, but Jennings cavalierly dismisses this claim in a marvelous display of selective reading. The reasons he musters for denying Mason's express testimony on such a vital matter are offered both in Jennings's text and in a dizzying footnote. The burden of the main argument is that insofar as Mason's account portrays Indians fleeing and creeping under their beds for protection, those so described could only have been "women, children, and feeble old men,"

who had no other recourse but to resort to such cowardly stratagems. Surely 150 warriors—and the Pequots had already well demonstrated "their willingness to fight to the death"—would not have "suddenly and uncharacteristically turned craven." At the end of this convoluted denial of part—and only part, indeed the most straightforward and factual part—of Mason's account is Jennings's assumption that Mason marched on Fort Mystic because he had received advance intelligence from Narragansett allies that "there were no 'reinforcements.'" Destroying the "wretches" would be easily accomplished.

But the original narratives of the battle suggest a very different reading. Mason indicates that he found his first plan unworkable, that only after the attack had begun did he realize how costly it might prove for the English; only then, in self-protection, did he make the decision to burn rather than to plunder the settlement. This analysis of events is confirmed by Underhill's record of the battle, which also has the virtue of emphasizing the bravery of the Indians involved. "Most courageously," he writes, "these Pequots behaved themselves." Only when the battle grew too intense did the British, out of necessity, torch the fort. Even then, Underhill states, "many courageous fellows were unwilling to come out and fought most desperately through the palisadoes . . . and so perished valiantly. Mercy did they deserve for their valor, could we have had opportunity to bestow it." Jennings does not cite Underhill's crucial and disarming testimony; instead, he engages in some more verbal sleight of hand, carefully choosing the texts he wishes to manipulate.

[H]e replays his charge against Mason. Leaving out only the citations, I quote in full:

> . . . Underhill and Hubbard omitted the reinforcements assertion. Winthrop assigned as Pequot casualties "two chief sachems, and one hundred and fifty fighting men, and about one hundred and fifty old men, women, and children." . . . Mason's and Winthrop's "reinforcements" thus became Winthrop's total of warrior casualties. Even if this is true, it means that Mason planned the attack before those warriors arrived, but the likelihood of its truth is remote. No matter how these wriggly texts are viewed, they testify to Mason's deliberate purpose of massacring noncombatants. He had advance information of the Pequot dispositions.

First, it should be recognized that because Underhill and Hubbard do not mention the 150 Indian reinforcements, Jennings uses their silence as confirmation of the dishonesty of Mason's account. But arguments from silence "say" very little, and extreme caution should be exercised in employing them, especially in the face of explicit testimony to the contrary. Jennings next uses Winthrop's narrative, which supports Mason's claim about reinforcements, to diminish that claim by impugning Winthrop's veracity. But such doublethink will not do, for if Winthrop is unreliable, the truth of his account "remote," he cannot serve to discredit Mason; if he is reliable, his depiction of events cannot be taken lightly. Then, out of this morass of conflicting facts and conclusions, Jennings draws the non sequitur that Mason was intent on massacring noncombatant Pequots; in fact, all contemporary accounts simply state that noncombatants were massacred, not that there was any premeditated plan to do so. It appears that Jennings would have us believe that his highly ambiguous, contradictory reconstruction of the facts proposed 340 years after the event and premised on a dubious dialectical analysis of silence, a great deal of hermeneutical confusion, and a series of non sequiturs is to be given precedence over the description of circumstances provided by several contemporary and first-person accounts in our possession. Assuredly, the Connecticut militiamen acted reprehensibly and with unnecessary severity against noncombatants that spring day in 1637, but they did not do so for the reasons, nor in the manner, advanced in Jennings's moving, but untrue, retelling of the tale.

III

Following the destruction of Mystic Fort, the colonists and their Indian allies pursued the surviving Pequots. In the first major encounter of this subsequent stage in the conflict, approximately 200 Indians were captured, of whom 22 or 24 were adult males; these braves were executed. The remaining women and children, almost 80 percent of the total captured, were parceled up about evenly, as was common Indian practice, among the victorious Indian allies and the colonists of Massachusetts Bay. A second and larger engagement took place on 14 July near modern Southport, Connecticut, where Sassacus and the majority of the remaining Pequots, numbering several hundred, were surrounded. In the ensuing battle, women, children, and old men, again a majority of the Pequots present, were allowed to seek sanctuary while about 80 warriors fought to their death. In the final phase of the war, various Indian tribes in the area, vying for English friendship and seeking to settle old tribal debts, hunted down and murdered Pequot braves while dispersing their womenfolk and children. Sassacus was killed, and in early August the Mohawks sent his head to the British in Hartford.

Alden Vaughan describes the aftermath of these events:

> Toward the end of 1637 the few remaining sachems begged for an end to the war, promising vassalage in return for their lives. A peace convention was arranged for the following September. With the Treaty of Hartford, signed on September 21, 1638, the Pequots ceased to exist as an independent polity.

The treaty arrangement as well as the previous pattern of killing all adult males suggests that the anti-Pequot forces, both Indian and European, were determined to eliminate the Pequot threat once and for all. The 180 Pequots captured in the assault on Sassacus were parceled out among the victors: 80 to the Narragansett, 80 to the Mohegans, and 20 to the Eastern Niantics. The survivors were now no longer to be known as Pequots or to reside in their tribal lands, and the Pequot River was renamed the Thames and the Pequot village, New London. These treaty stipulations, which required the extinction of Pequot identity and the assignment of Pequot survivors to other tribes, and some to slavery, suggest an overt, unambiguous form of *cultural* genocide, here employed in the name of military security, However, the dispersement of the remaining communal members—the elderly, the women, and the children, almost certainly a majority of the tribe as a whole—directly contradicts the imputation of any intent to commit *physical* genocide, as some revisionists insist.

A more constrained reading of events would not deny that the Puritans, as their post-war writings reflect, were conscious that they had acted with great, perhaps even excessive, destructive force. Almost certainly composed as responses to English and Indian critics, these after-the-fact appraisals should not, however, be misconstrued as evidence of either genocidal intent prior to the event or even of genocidal behavior during and after the war. Rather, given the Puritan mentality, saturated as it was with concerns to detect God's providential design in temporal matters, these post-hoc accountings, even were we to call them rationalizations, were attempts to satisfy the Puritans' own internal axiological demand that their taking of lives on such a large scale, and in such a bloody way, was justified. Puritans had to know, and they wanted their critics to know, that what they had done was sanctioned by heaven. This concern for ethical legitimation should not be mistaken as evidence that the Puritans, however aware they were *after the event* of the contentious nature of the massacre they had wrought, looked upon this happening as signaling some fundamental re-orientation in their relationship either to their New World surroundings in general or with their New England Indian neighbors in particular. Neither Edward Johnson's approval of the Puritan preachers' exhortation to "execute vengeance upon the heathen," nor William Bradford's description of the burning of the inhabitants at Fort Mystic as a "sweet sacrifice" to the Lord, nor Underhill's appeal to scriptural precedent that in conquering a grossly evil people, such as the Pequot, "women and children must perish with their parents" are proof to the contrary. Indeed, they are exactly the sort of theological pronouncements one would expect within the Puritan conceptual environment, fed as it was by recycled scriptural paradigms.

In general, the English did not relish their victory in an unseemly way. John Mason, for example, "refused to publish his accounts of his exploits, deeming them too immodest and likely to detract from the glory ascribed to God in those events." Captain Underhill, by contrast, did publish his version of the tale, but as Richard Slotkin has written, "Captain Underhill was a man clearly out of step with the Massachusetts way and one proscribed and exiled by the Puritan community." Underhill's "enthusiasms," in fact, were repeatedly met with censure rather than emulation. Mason, by contrast, the modest, self-effacing, God-extolling leader, was considered a worthy model in early American literature.

IV

When the actions of the Puritans are placed in their appropriate context, when they are deconstructed as part and parcel of the historical reality of the seventeenth century, the accusations of genocide leveled against them are recognized to be exaggerations. However excessive the force wielded by the colonists, they had already seen—and would continue to see—their own die at the hands of the Indians. The Virginia Indian uprisings of 1622 have already been mentioned. In April 1644, a second uprising took the lives of approximately 500 whites, and in 1675, 300 more colonists were killed. The bloody events of King Philip's War (1675–76) would certainly have intensified the fears that had long plagued those living at the edge of the frontier. Much Indian violence was, of course, a response to English greed, but for those charged with protecting the members of expanding English communities, the violence had to be stopped at all costs. In the New World—an environment so uncertain, so hostile—the colonists' need to limit threats to their survival was intense. Their responses could be excessive, but their fears were not unfounded.

From our point of view, it is easy to sympathize with the Pequots and to condemn the colonists' actions, but the scope of our condemnation must be measured against the facts. After the Treaty of Hartford was signed, Pequots were not physically harmed. Indeed, in 1640 the Connecticut leadership "declared their dislike of such as would have the Indians rooted out," that is, murdered. Before the Pequots capitulated, many of their tribe had died, but the number killed probably totaled less than half the entire tribe. Sherburne Cook's estimate is even lower: "If the initial population [of Pequots] was 3,000 and 750 were killed, the battle loss was twenty-five percent of the tribe."

While many Pequots were absorbed by other tribes—it is estimated that Uncas's Mohegan tribe, for example, received hundreds—evidence clearly indicates that soon after the conclusion of the war, the Pequot began to regroup as a tribe. By 1650 four special towns were created to accommodate them, each ruled by a Pequot governor, and in 1667 Connecticut established permanent reservations for the tribe, which by 1675 numbered approximately 1,500–2,000 members. That year, no more than two generations after the Pequot War had ended, the Pequots allied with the colonists to fight King Philip's War. As recently as the 1960s, Pequots were still listed as a separate group residing in Connecticut. Such factors suggest that while the British could certainly have been less thorough, less severe, less deadly in prosecuting their campaign against the Pequots, the campaign they actually did carry out, for all its vehemence, was not, either in intent or execution, genocidal.

This revision of the revisionists is not meant to deny the larger truth that the conquest of the New World entailed the greatest demographic tragedy in history. The wrongs done to the Native Americans, the suffering they experienced, the manifest evil involved in the colonial enterprise is in no way to be deflected or minimized. However, this sorry tale of despoliation and depopulation needs to be chronicled aright, with an appropriate sense of the actuality of seventeenth-century colonial existence. False, if morally impassioned, judgments cannot substitute for carefully nuanced and discriminating appraisals. Thus, while it is appropriate to censure the excesses, the unnecessary carnage, of the Pequot War, to interpret these events through the radicalizing polemic of accusations of genocide is to rewrite history to satisfy our own moral outrage.

STEVEN T. KATZ earned his PhD at Cambridge University in 1972. He is the director of the Elie Wiesel Center for Judaic Studies at Boston University, where he holds the Alvin J. and Shirley Slater Chair in Jewish and Holocaust Studies. Katz is the author of *The Holocaust in Historical Context* (Oxford University Press, 1994) among numerous other books on Jewish history.

Alfred A. Cave

 **NO**

The Pequot War and the Mythology of the Frontier

Although the Pequot War was a small-scale conflict of short duration, it cast a long shadow. The images of brutal and untrustworthy savages plotting the extermination of those who would do the work of God in the wilderness, developed to explain and justify the killing of Pequots, became a vital part of the mythology of the American frontier. Celebration of victory over Indians as the triumph of light over darkness, civilization over savagery, for many generations our central historical myth, finds its earliest full expression in the contemporary chronicles and histories of this little war. The myth from its inception was grounded in a distorted conception of Indian character and behavior. The Pequot War was not waged in response to tangible acts of aggression. It cannot be understood as a rational response to a real threat to English security. It was, however, the expression of an assumption central to Puritan Indian policy. Puritan magistrates were persuaded that from time to time violent reprisals against recalcitrant savages would be necessary to make the frontier safe for the people of God. The campaign against the Pequots was driven by the same assumption that had impelled Plymouth to massacre Indians suspected of plotting against them at Wessagusett in 1623. The incineration of Pequots at Fort Mystic served the same symbolic purpose as the impalement of Wituwamet's head on Plymouth's blockhouse. Both were intended to intimidate potential enemies and to remind the Saints that they lived in daily peril of massacre at the hands of Satan's minions.

Two letters written by clergymen to civil authorities in 1637 tell us much about the Puritan mind-set. Both warn of the dangers of hesitation or leniency in dealing with the Pequots. The Reverend Thomas Hooker, responding to the attack on Wethersfield, predicted that any delay in undertaking a punitive war against them would lead other Indians to conclude that Englishmen were cowards. If that happened, Hooker predicted, all of the tribes would "turne enemyse against us." In a similar vein, the Reverend

John Higginson, writing from Fort Saybrook, declared that "the eyes of all the Indians of the country are upon the English. If some serious and very speedie course not be taken to tame the pride and take down the insolency of these now insulting Pequots . . . we are like to have all the Indians in the country about our ears." The assumption, voiced here by Hooker and Higginson, that all Indians are natural enemies of Christians and that the English frontier in Connecticut can therefore be made secure only through the employment of extreme measures against the Pequots, was obviously shared by the English commanders whose cruelty to noncombatants and prisoners of war shocked their Indian allies.

In their reflections on the Pequot War, Puritan apologists argued that English troops were instruments of divine judgment. Early Puritan historians portrayed the war as a key episode in the unfolding of God's plan for New England. Captain John Mason, who believed that the English had been saved from a general Indian uprising only by divine intervention, ended his "Brief History of the Pequot War" with praise of the Almighty: "Let the whole Earth be filled with his Glory! Thus the lord was pleased to smite our Enemies in the hinder Parts, and give us their land for an Inheritance." Mason's colleague, Captain John Underhill, concurred. Through God's providence, "a few feeble instruments, soldiers not accustomed to war," defeated a barbarous and insolent nation," putting to the sword "fifteen hundred souls." Underhill rejoiced that through God's will "their country is fully subdued and fallen into the hands of the English," and he called on his readers to "magnify his honor for his great goodness." A dissenting note was struck by Lieutenant Lion Gardener who, in a work written in 1660, wondered why the Bay Colony leaders made war against the Pequots to avenge the worthless old reprobate Stone, while the Narragansetts, whom he presumed guilty of the murder of the worthy Captain Oldham, went scot-free. But Gardener, no less a Puritan than his colleagues, warned against trusting Indians and complained about lax military preparedness. After describing Indian tortures, he predicted that hundreds of Englishmen would die in agony and dishonor, "if God should deliver us into their hands, as justly he may for our sins."

No other Puritan writer expressed any misgivings about whether the English had attacked the right adversary in 1637. The Massachusetts Bay Colony historian Edward Johnson, writing of the English massacre of Pequots at Fort Mystic, declared that "by this means the Lord strook a trembling terror into all the Indians round about, even to this very day." Through righteous violence, Johnson believed, God had pacified the forces of Satan in the wilderness. That theme dominated Puritan thinking about Indian wars. The commissioners of the United Colonies of New England in 1646 called for the writing of histories that would record how God "hath cast the dread of his people (weak in themselves) upon the Indians." Increase Mather, in his *Brief History of the War with the Indians in New England* (1676), wrote that the defeat of the Pequots in 1637 "must be ascribed to the wonderful Providence of God, who did (as with Jacob of old, and after that with the children of Israel) lay the fear of the English and the dread of them upon all the Indians. The terror of god was upon them round about." Incorporating that notion into his grand history of New England, Cotton Mather later declared that, through God's providence, the Puritans were enabled to achieve not only "the utter subduing" of the Pequots but "the affrighting of all the other Natives" as well, and thereby secured several decades of peace.

As the evidence reviewed in this study demonstrates, Puritan preoccupation with the idea that Indians were part of a satanic conspiracy against God's true church in the wilderness led them to interpret Pequot recalcitrance as evidence of malevolent intent. But it does not follow that we can therefore explain the Pequot War solely and simply as the result of an unfortunate misunderstanding about certain specific occurrences, for the conflict was more fundamentally the outgrowth of a profound incompatibility of cultures. Puritan ideology precluded long-term coexistence with a "savage" people unwilling to acknowledge Christian hegemony. Clarification of Pequot intentions in the short run would not necessarily have changed the long-term outcome. A reading of their commentaries on Indian affairs suggests that our assumptions about the desirability of peaceful coexistence were not necessarily shared by the founders of Puritan New England or by their immediate successors. Although they feared Indian war and prayed that they be spared its horrors, they also suspected that it was both necessary and inevitable. Apologists for the Fort Mystic massacre did not

invent the image of the Indian as a savage killer to excuse the Pequot War, nor did Pequot actions inspire a new view of Indian character. There is ample evidence, as we noted in the first chapter of this study, that from the founding of the first English settlements in North America onward, Englishmen in general and Puritans in particular saw in Native American culture only the "degeneracy" of those who follow the Devil rather than God; they accordingly were predisposed to regard Indians as untrustworthy and treacherous and were thus prone to overreact to rumors of impending Indian attacks.

Their acceptance of customary English anti-Indian prejudice in itself does not fully explain Puritan behavior. We must also examine Puritan ideas about the role of Indians in God's providential plan for New England. Here we encounter concepts quite alien to modern sensibilities, embedded in explanations so far removed from our sense of historical processes that it is tempting to dismiss them as irrelevant. But let us look more closely, for we must try to understand the seventeenth century on its own terms. Fundamental to the Puritan understanding of the dynamics of New England history was the assumption that only through God's special protection of his people could Christians survive in a wilderness realm dominated by Satan and inhabited by satanic savages. God intervened early to soften the hearts of the godless heathens who lurked in New England's forests and wastelands. Ultimately, he controlled their behavior. It therefore followed that troubled Indian relations might well be a frightening sign that God's protection had been, or was about to be, withheld for some reason. Throughout the seventeenth century, rumors of impending Indian attack occasioned deep soul-searching and calls for reformation in Puritan New England.

The Pequot War inspired the earliest expressions of the idea that Indian wars were providentially ordained events intended to test and chastise God's people. John Higginson suggested that the Lord had set "the Indians upon his servants, to make them cleave more closely together, to prevent contentions of brethern." Edward Johnson hinted that God had unleashed the Pequots in order to punish the Puritans for their lack of proper severity in dealing with Anne Hutchinson and the antinomians. Those suggestions foreshadowed the portrayals of the role of divine providence in Indian warfare that would dominate the literature inspired by King Philip's War half a century later. Historians of that conflict spoke of God's need to test his Saints in the fire of battle, punish his people for straying from the true way, and give them also opportunity to serve as the vehicles of God's wrath in exterminating heathen who refused to embrace the Gospel. Those themes were exploited most thoroughly by Puritan divines who, in later years, warned of the fearful consequences of declension. Thus, Increase Mather in a sermon preached in 1676 declared King Philip's War God's "heavy judgment," a punishment of the "sin of man's unfaithfulness. . . . Alas that New England should be brought so low in so short a time (for she is come down wonderfully) and that by such vile enemies by the Heathen, yea by the worst of the Heathen." Cotton Mather, in his 1689 election sermon, declared that the "molestations" the English in New England had suffered at the hands of the Indians had come about because God was angry that his people had "indianized"; in other words, they had allowed themselves to succumb to what Mather regarded as Indian vices: idleness, self-indulgence, and dishonesty. The belief that God used Indians as a rod with which to discipline his people became an enduring and vital aspect of the Puritan sense of the past. In his election sermon of 1730, the Reverend Thomas Prince, reviewing more than a century of New England history, exclaimed, "how often has he made the eastern Indians the rod of his anger and the staff of indignation with us! He has sent them against us and given them the charge to take the spoil and tread us down as the mire of the street. They came with open mouth upon us; they thrust thro' everyone they found abroad; they ensnared and slew our mighty men who went forth for our defense; they spoil'd our fields and pastures; they burnt up our houses; they destroy'd our towns and garrisons; they murdered our wives; they carried our young men and virgins into captivity; they had no pity on the fruit of the womb; their eyes spared not our children, they dashed them in pieces." Prince reminded the citizenry that they had survived only because the Lord, although rightly provoked, finally took pity on his own true people and turned against the savages. "He rebuk'd them and set them one against another . . . as wax melteth before the fire, so they perished at the presence of God." But his favor and protection were not to be taken for granted.

God's wrath, in Puritan formulations of the providential view of New England's history, was not reserved for errant Saints. Historians of King Philip's War assured their readers that, although the war was in part intended to punish the English in New England for straying from the true way, the Lord's anger against the Indians was far greater. For our purposes, perhaps the most revealing statement in the later Indian war literature was a declaration from the Bay Colony's superintendent of Indian affairs that God had ordained the war against King Philip in order to punish the Indians who had refused to embrace Puritan Christianity. This was not an entirely new theme. Although lack of receptivity to the Christian Gospel was not stated explicitly as a reason for killing Pequots by any

of the chroniclers of that early war, the preacher's charge to the Connecticut militia to "execute vengeance against the heathen" rested upon the assumption that the English were indeed called upon by the Almighty to visit his wrath upon a very sinful people. Puritan literary celebrations of the Fort Mystic massacre, which strike us as rather grotesque, are grounded in the belief that the burning of Pequots was a righteous act of divine retribution.

Assessments of the causes and consequences of the Pequot War must take into account Puritan ideas about God's attitude toward the unregenerate. The Pequots were not the last indigenous group in New England to suffer what the Puritans believed to be divinely mandated punishment. The Narragansetts and the Wampanoags, friends of the English in 1636–37, both discovered, before the seventeenth century ended, that the Puritan conception of God's providential plan for New England ultimately left no room for vigorous assertions of Native American autonomy, for such assertions offended the Puritan sense of mission. Puritan toleration of Indian independence was never anything more than an expedient; as the population ratio between Englishmen and Native Americans in New England shifted in favor of the English, the Puritan authorities grew increasingly overbearing in their dealings with their Indian counterparts. Puritan Indian policy from its inception was driven by the conviction that, if the Puritans remained faithful to their covenant with the Almighty, they were destined to replace the Indians as lords of New England. Puritan ideology required that Indian control of land and resources be terminated, on the grounds that "savages" did not exploit natural bounty in the manner that God intended. The pressures created by the burgeoning of the English population in the latter half of the seventeenth century reinforced that ideological imperative. Economic changes, such as the declining importance of the fur trade and the expansion of English agriculture and industry, which reduced the need for Indian commerce, further jeopardized the status of Native American communities in a New England dominated by Euro-Americans. The Indian uprising led by Metacom (King Philip) in 1675 represented a desperate, belated, and ultimately futile effort to protect the last remnants of Indian sovereignty in southern New England.

Although Puritan apologists for the war against the Pequots provided one of the earliest English statements of the belief in Indian war as a divinely sanctioned means of extending the light of civilization and true religion into the wilderness, their version of the frontier drama contained some elements that later generations would find strange and uncongenial. Over the years, the myth of heroic struggle against savagery underwent some important changes in emphasis as secular doctrines of scientific progress and historical evolution, along with a new sense of "manifest destiny," largely but not entirely replaced Puritan notions of divine providence. The idea that Indians might be used by the Almighty to punish the sins of Christians fell from favor. Puritan misgivings about the wilderness as a place of spiritual peril gave way to a more optimistic and uncritical celebration of the frontier as the birthplace of uniquely American virtues. Indian rejection of progress replaced their disinterest in the Gospel or their presumed alliance with Satan as the reason most often advanced to explain their imminent extinction. But in one important particular, the central theme remained the same. On a succession of frontiers, as Winthrop Jordon reminds us, "conquering the Indian symbolized and personified the conquest of American difficulties, the surmounting of the wilderness. To push back the Indian was to prove the worth of one's own mission, to make straight in the desert a highway for civilization."

Once the eastern Indians were no longer a threat, some nineteenth-century writers transformed the Native American into a victim rather than a villain. In their pages, the American "savage" emerged as an innocent and hapless primitive doomed by the imperatives of historical progress, an object of pity for whom the sentimental might shed a tear. Historians, novelists, and dramatists now sometimes castigated Puritans and other pioneers for their mistreatment of such a simple and defenseless people. It goes without saying that such sympathy for the Indian as a "much injured race" is not to be found in seventeenth-century Puritan commentaries on Indian wars. But we must not assume that its appearance in later historical writing necessarily meant abandonment of the idea that the conquest and dispossession of Indians were historical imperatives. Until quite recently, the attitude of paternalistic benevolence cultivated by architects of Indian policy as well as by their critics was generally qualified by a condition: The Indian must now cease to be an Indian, must embrace the values, culture, and religion of his dispossessors, if he is to be deemed worthy of survival. Here we are once again face to face with the premise that drove Puritan Indian policy: denial of the validity and viability of Native American life. Whether the Indian was to be displaced by the workings of divine providence or by the inexorable march of progress, the outcome was much the same. Moreover, it did not matter whether Indians were portrayed as noble or degraded; white Americans over the years generally thought of them as a backward people without history and without a future.

While the frontier struggle for control of land continued, misgivings about mistreatment of Native Americans had only a very limited impact upon events. As Michael Paul Rogin notes, "not the Indians alive . . . but their destruction, symbolized the American experience." Violence against Indians cannot be explained fully as the outgrowth of the white man's acquisitive instincts. There were other motives at work. Rogin argues that Native American societies in their communal aspects "posed a severe threat," as they inspired "forbidden nostalgia for the nurturing, blissful and primitively violent connection to nature that white Americans had to leave behind." Hence, "the only safe Indians were dead, sanitized, or completely dependent upon white benevolence." Indians were "at once symbols of a lost childhood bliss, and, as bad children repositories of murderous negative projections." Those Indians who physically survived plague, war, and dispossession were therefore not only relegated to reservations, where they lived in abject poverty, but subjected to an onslaught on their cultural integrity through measures such as the so-called Religious Crimes Acts, which outlawed the sun dance and other expressions of Native American spirituality.

Intolerance of Indian cultures reflected the persistence of essential elements of the Puritan vision of the struggle between heathen savagery and Christian civilization. Puritan ideology as it pertained to encounters with Indians contained three premises which later provided vital elements in the mythology of the American frontier. One was the image, not original with the Puritans but embellished by them, of the Indian as the Other, primitive, dark, and sinister. Another was the portrayal, first developed in the Pequot War narratives, of the Indian fighter as the agent of God and of progress, redeeming the land through righteous violence. And finally, it is to the apologists for the Pequot War that we owe the justification of the expropriation of Indian resources and the extinction of Indian sovereignty as security measures necessitated by their presumed savagery.

Few historians today confuse these elements of our founding myth with historical fact. The "triumphalist" tone that once characterized the narration of Euro-American victories over presumably savage foes is now muted, or silenced, as scholars struggle to come to terms with the ambiguities as well as the cruelties and injustice now perceived in the encounters of indigenous peoples and European invaders. What place should the Pequots occupy in the new history of intercultural conflict? Despite the ample evidence of arrogance, ignorance, and brutality in the English treatment of Sassacus and his people, it will not do to cast them in the role of passive victims. They were not guilty of the enormities, real or anticipated, with which they are charged in the traditional, pro-Puritan literature. They were not a threat to the survival of the Puritan colonies. But in their efforts to establish and maintain a far-flung tributary network and to control European trade, the Pequots provoked powerful Indian opposition. Their murder of Indian rivals en route to trade at the House of Good Hope in 1632, the exile of the Mohegan sachems shortly thereafter and the occupation of their hunting preserves, along with the subsequent treatment of Mohegans living in Pequot villages after the final defection of Uncas, all give evidence of a ruthless determination to maintain power that suggests that Sassacus would be seriously miscast were we now to describe him simply as an inoffensive noble savage wronged by the white man. He was inept; he lost, but he was hardly a hapless innocent. Neither were the Mohegan, River Indian, and Narragansett sachems who engineered his downfall.

In seeking to use the English as pawns in their power struggles, the sachems made a serious miscalculation. The consequences of alliance with the Puritan colonies were not immediately apparent. The sachems no doubt believed that they could maintain control. The English, as we have seen, were susceptible to manipulation by those who knew how to play on their expectations and anxieties. It was a game that Uncas easily mastered, that Sassacus never learned how to play, and that Miantonomi ultimately lost. But the final outcome was loss of Algonquian autonomy. A revisionist history of the Pequot War written from the Native American point of view—and this present study does not pretend to accomplish that—might well deemphasize decisions made at Boston, Plymouth, Saybrook, and Hartford and focus instead on the miscalculations and blunders in Pequot, Mohegan, and Narragansett councils that paved the way for the early establishment of English hegemony in southern New England. Unfortunately, given the limitations in the source materials, such a reconstruction would be highly conjectural. But we do know enough about Native American politics in southern New England in the early seventeenth century to realize that viewing the conflict from an Algonquian perspective would immediately expose the absurdity of the English belief that they were engaged in some sort of holy war against murderous heathens determined to exterminate Christians. Although the Puritans believed that their actions were driven by their own security needs, and by divine providence, the conflicts that culminated in the Pequot War originally were the outgrowth of the ambitions of rival sachems, not of an anti-English conspiracy. Believing themselves endangered, the Puritan colonies, to the later sorrow of many of their Indian allies, transformed the quarrel with the Pequots into a successful campaign to establish English dominance.

In their justification of the war against the Pequots, Puritan mythmakers invoked old images of treacherous savages and told tales of diabolical plots. It is now clear that their portrayals of the Pequots bear little resemblance to reality. The Puritans transformed their adversary into a symbol of savagery. Rumors of Pequot conspiracy, although flimsy in substance and of dubious origin, reinforced expectations about savage behavior and justified preemptive slaughter and dispossession. Not only did the Pequot War engender its own myths in reinforcement and embellishment of Puritan ideology; it was the fulfillment of a prewar mythology that foretold conflicts in the wilderness between the people of God and the hosts of Satan. The fact that the triumph of Christians in such conflicts would open the way to English control of land and trade, and to the receipt of tribute, provided powerful material incentives to maintain intact ideas about savagery that justified the domination of indigenous peoples. Puritan apologists for their assault on the Pequots made a significant contribution to the development of an ideological rationale for Christian imperialism. The images they framed of their adversary have been remarkably persistent but now should be recognized as the products of wartime propaganda.

The Pequot War in reality was the messy outgrowth of petty squabbles over trade, tribute, and land among Pequots, Mohegans, River Indians, Niantics, Narragansetts, Dutch traders, and English Puritans. The Puritan imagination endowed this little war with a metahistorical significance it hardly deserved. But the inner logic of Puritan belief required creation of a mythical conflict, a cosmic struggle of good and evil in the wilderness, and out of that need the Pequot War epic was born.

ALFRED A. CAVE is Professor Emeritus of History at the University of Toledo. Previously, he held academic positions at the City College of New York, the University of Utah, and the University of Florida. Among his many publications in the fields of Native American and Jacksonian era history, he is the author of *Prophets of the Great Spirit: Native American Revitalization Movements in Eastern North America* (University of Nebraska Press, 2006) and *Lethal Encounters: Englishmen and Indians in Colonial Virginia* (University of Nebraska Press, 2013).

EXPLORING THE ISSUE

Was the Pequot War Largely a Product of Native American Aggression?

Critical Thinking and Reflection

1. Evaluate Steven Katz's perception of historical revisionism with regard to the Pequot War.
2. How does Alfred Cave support his argument that previous interpretations of the Pequot War were a product of Puritan mythmaking?
3. Compare and contrast the conclusions reached by Katz and Cave regarding the causes of the Pequot War.
4. What role did religion play in the outbreak of the Pequot War?
5. Based on your reading of these two essays, to what extent was the Pequot War inevitable?

Is There Common Ground?

The complexities associated with the relations between Native Americans and colonists from Europe are evident from the foregoing essays. Together they suggest the difficulty associated with efforts to generalize about the clash of cultures that occurred on New World shores.

By the end of the colonial period in British North America, the Native American populations in the original 13 colonies had been significantly reduced in terms of numbers and power. Was this reality an inevitable consequence of intercultural hostilities, or are their other viable explanations for Indian decline? Undoubtedly, many European colonists harbored attitudes that allowed them to rationalize aggressive action toward the indigenous peoples they encountered in America. As was the case with their European counterparts, Indians, too, saw themselves and their culture as superior to the new arrivals from across the Atlantic. Both sides viewed the other as uncivilized savages. These general attitudes, however, did not prevent cordial relations and other forms of beneficial alliances from developing. Trade alliances did not end conflict, but they did reinforce recognition of the mutual benefit derived from such connections.

As Gary Nash has observed, American culture derived much of its uniqueness from the interaction of Indian and European, as well as African, traditional folkways. The physical presence of each of these groups played a fundamental role in the emerging political, economic, and social development of early America. The day-to-day lives of the residents of the New World were dramatically affected by the presence of these various human populations and not solely in negative ways.

Additional Resources

James Axtell, *The Invasion Within: The Contest of Cultures in Colonial North America* (Oxford University Press, 1985)

Karen Ordahl Kupperman, *Indians and English: Facing Off in Early America* (Cornell University Press, 2000)

Jill Lepore, *The Name of War: King Philip's War and the Origins of American Identity* (Alfred A. Knopf, 1998)

Daniel R. Mandell, *King Philip's War: Colonial Expansion, Native Resistance, and the End of Indian Hegemony* (Johns Hopkins University Press, 2010)

Gary Nash, *Red, White, and Black: The Peoples of Early America*, 3rd ed. (Prentice-Hall, 1982)

Internet References . . .

Colonial Settlement, 1600s-1763: Virginia's Early Relations with Native Americans

http://www.loc.gov/teachers/classroommaterials
/presentationsandactivities/presentations/timeline
/colonial/indians/

Document Showcase: American Indians in Colonial New York

http://nysa32.nysed.gov/education/showcase
/201111nativeamerican/index.shtml

Native American Archaeology

http://www.portal.state.pa.us/portal/server.pt
/community/native_american_archaeology/3316

Native American Legends: Colonial Era Indian Wars, Battles & Massacres

http://www.legendsofamerica.com
/na-colonialindianwars.html

Virginia's Indians, Past and Present

http://virginiaindians.pwnet.org/

Selected, Edited, and with Issue Framing Material by:
Larry Madaras, *Howard Community College*
and
James M. SoRelle, *Baylor University*

ISSUE

Was the Colonial Period a "Golden Age" for Women in America?

YES: Gloria L. Main, "Gender, Work, and Wages in Colonial New England," *William and Mary Quarterly* (1994)

NO: Cornelia Hughes Dayton, from "Women Before the Bar," University of North Carolina Press (1995)

Learning Outcomes

After reading this issue, you will be able to:

- Discuss the type of work women in colonial New England did for pay compared to men.
- Appreciate how women's opportunities to earn wages for their work changed over time in the colonial period.
- Understand the intersection of legal culture and gender relations in colonial New England.
- Discuss the ways in which women possessed a voice in colonial American courts.
- Realize how women's legal status declined in colonial Connecticut from the seventeenth to the eighteenth century.

ISSUE SUMMARY

YES: Gloria Main notes that New England women were highly valued for their labor and relative scarcity in the early colonial period and that their economic autonomy increased in the years during and following the Seven Years War as more women entered the paid work force and received higher wages for their work.

NO: Cornelia Hughes Dayton offers a nuanced challenge to the "golden age" thesis, concluding that women in seventeenth-century Connecticut enjoyed direct access to the county courts but that new rules and practices in the eighteenth century reinforced patriarchal authority and significantly limited women's access to the courts, which instead came to serve the interests of commercially active men.

For generations students in American history classes have read of the founding of the colonies in British North America, their political and economic development, and the colonists' struggles for independence, without ever being confronted by a female protagonist in this magnificent historical drama. The terms "sons of liberty" and "founding fathers" reflect the end result of a long tradition of gender-specific myopia. In fact, only in the last generation have discussions of the role of women in the development of American society made their appearance in standard textbooks. Consequently, it is useful to explore the status of women in colonial America.

The topic is quite complex. The status of colonial women was determined by cultural attitudes that were exported to the New World from Europe, by the specific conditions confronting successive waves of settlers—male and female—in terms of labor requirements, and by changes produced by colonial maturation over time. It would be impossible to pinpoint a single, static condition in which all colonial women existed.

What was the status of women in the British North American colonies? To what degree did the legal status of women differ from their de facto status? For much of the past century, scholarship has produced the notion that colonial women enjoyed a more privileged status than either their European contemporaries or their nineteenth-century descendants. Support for the "golden age" theory can be found in Elizabeth Anthony Dexter, *Colonial Women of Affairs*, 2nd ed. (Houghton Mifflin, 1931); Mary Ritter Beard, *Woman as Force in History* (Macmillan, 1946); Eleanor Flexner, *Century of Struggle* (Belknap Press, 1959); and Richard B. Morris, *Studies in the History of American Law*, 2nd ed. (Octagon Books, 1964). This interpretation was reinforced in the 1970s in John Demos, *A Little Commonwealth: Family Life in Plymouth Colony* (Oxford University Press, 1970); Roger Thompson, *Women in Stuart England and America: A Comparative Study* (Routledge and Kegan, 1974); and Page Smith, *Daughters of the Promised Land: Women in American History* (Little, Brown, 1977). For example, Demos contends that despite the fact that Plymouth Colony was based on a patriarchal model in which women were expected to subordinate themselves to men, women still shared certain responsibilities with their husbands in some business activities and in matters relating to their children. N. E. H. Hull's *Female Felons: Women and Serious Crime in Colonial Massachusetts* (University of Illinois Press, 1987) concludes that men and women received equal justice in the colonial period.

Women were crucial to the economic success of the colonial experiments and performed numerous functions in various occupations and professions. They not only performed all the household duties but also assisted the menfolk with agricultural duties outside the home when the necessity arose. In colonial America and during the American Revolution, they practiced law, pounded iron as blacksmiths, trapped for furs and tanned leather, made guns, built ships, and edited and printed newspapers. In their path-breaking article "The Planter's Wife: The Experience of White Women in Seventeenth-Century Maryland," *William and Mary Quarterly* (October 1977), Lois Green Carr and Lorena S. Walsh assessed this issue against the backdrop of four factors in colonial Maryland: the predominance of an immigrant population; the early death of male inhabitants; the late marriages of women due to their indentured servitude; and the sexual imbalance in which men greatly outnumbered women. As a result of these conditions, according to Carr and Walsh, Maryland women experienced fewer restraints on their social conduct and enjoyed more power than did their English counterparts. Most who survived became planters' wives, enjoyed considerable freedom in choosing their husbands, and benefited from a substantial right to inherit property.

At the same time, colonial society viewed women as subordinate beings. They were closed off from any formal public power in the colonies even when they performed essential economic functions within the community. Society as a whole viewed them as "weaker vessels," physically, intellectually, and morally. Nor was it a coincidence that most suspected witches were female. Many of those accused of witchcraft in late-seventeenth-century New England were older women who had inherited land that traditionally would have gone to males. Such patterns of inheritance disrupted the normative male-dominated social order. Witchcraft hysteria in colonial America, then, was a by-product of economic pressures and gender exploitation. These views are developed particularly well in Lyle Koehler, *A Search for Power: The "Weaker Sex" in Seventeenth Century New England* (University of Illinois Press, 1980), and Carol F. Karlsen, *The Devil in the Shape of a Woman: Witchcraft in Colonial New England* (Random House, 1987).

As several of the titles cited above suggest, many of the scholarly monographs on the lives of colonial women focus on New England. These include Edmund S. Morgan, *The Puritan Family: Religion and Domestic Relations in Seventeenth-Century New England* (Boston Public Library, 1944) and Laurel Thatcher Ulrich, *Good Wives: Image and Reality in the Lives of Women in Northern New England, 1650–1750* (Knopf, 1980). For another Chesapeake colony, women in colonial Virginia are treated in Darrett B. Rutman and Anita H. Rutman, *A Place in Time: Middlesex County, Virginia, 1650–1750* (W. W. Norton, 1984) and Kathleen M. Brown, *Good Wives, Nasty Wenches, and Anxious Patriarchs: Gender, Race, and Power in Colonial Virginia* (University of North Carolina Press, 1996).

Women in the age of the American Revolution are the focus of Carol Ruth Berkin, *Within the Conjurer's Circle: Women in Colonial America* (General Learning Press, 1974); Linda Grant DePauw and Conover Hunt, *"Remember the Ladies": Women in America, 1750–1815* (Viking Press, 1976); Mary Beth Norton, *Liberty's Daughters: The Revolutionary Experience of American Women, 1750–1800* (Little, Brown 1980); Linda Kerber, *Women of the Republic: Intellect and Ideology in Revolutionary America* (North Carolina, 1980); Charles W. Akers, *Abigail Adams: An American Woman* (Little, Brown, 1980), and Joy Day Buel and Richard Buel, Jr., *The Way of Duty: A Woman and Her Family in Revolutionary America* (W. W. Norton, 1984). For the conclusion that the American Revolution failed to advance women's status, see Joan Hoff Wilson's "The Illusion of Change: Women and the American Revolution" in Alfred F. Young, ed., *The American Revolution: Explorations in the History of American Radicalism* (Northern Illinois University Press, 1976).

The following selections explore the status of women in the colonial period. Gloria Main focuses on women's economic status by comparing types of work, pay scales, and trends in wages in the seventeenth and eighteenth centuries and discovers that the division of labor between men and women was less clearly defined than traditionally assumed. Because they were relatively scarce, she concludes, women were valued for their labor and, as time passed, New England women developed a significant degree of economic autonomy.

Cornelia Hughes Dayton examines women's legal status in colonial Connecticut through a study of county court cases treating the subjects of debt, divorce, illicit consensual sex, rape, and slander in which women were involved. She finds that although the seventeenth-century Puritan sense of justice created opportunities for women to be heard in court in ways that had not been available within English legal tradition, these opportunities had begun to fade by the early eighteenth century, and women's presence in court declined dramatically as legal public space was transformed from an inclusive forum to an institution primarily serving the interests of commercially active men.

YES ⤶

Gloria L. Main

Gender, Work, and Wages in Colonial New England

... **H**istorians of colonial women . . . tend to ignore economic issues when debating trends in women's status and condition. Most believe that white women were more highly regarded in the colonies than at home, because of the higher value of their labor and their relative scarcity, at least in the seventeenth century in regions such as the Chesapeake. Others posit that economic opportunities for women narrowed as colonial society developed beyond primitive conditions in which women shouldered burdens customarily borne by men. Data presented below lend support to the first proposition but dispute the second.

This article examines the types of work women in early New England did compared to men, weighs relative pay scales, and explores trends in the wages of both sexes. Evidence comes from two types of sources: wage ceilings discussed or imposed by governments in 1670 and 1777 and pay rates found in account books, diaries, and probate records. These sources also supply the basis for estimating women's rates of participation in the paid labor force and for tabulating the types of work women performed for pay. All of this material can be conveniently summarized by dividing the colonial period into four phases: initial growth (1620–1674), crisis and recovery (1675–1714), stability (1715–1754), and expansion (1755–1774). The sequence, however, defies simple linear interpretations of progression, either from good conditions to bad, declension, or from bad conditions to good, progress. Both the status of women and the region's economy experienced cycles of good and bad times, but the closing decades of the period saw real improvement for both. Perhaps the most important lesson of this investigation is that even relatively modest economic changes can, by their cumulative actions, significantly alter family relations and living standards. . . .

Settlers in a new land must find ways to acquire the goods they want and cannot make for themselves. For New Englanders, this proved a major challenge. Probably the most notable characteristic of the economy that is evident in probate inventories was the economy's dependence on England for manufactures of all sorts, including textiles. In the first generation after settlement, few women could have engaged in spinning, weaving, or dyeing simply because unprocessed textile fibers were in short supply. "Farmers deem it better for their profit to put away [sell] their cattel and corn for cloathing, then to set upon making of cloth." Flax production was labor intensive, and sheep did not thrive under pioneering conditions: wolves found them easy prey, and the woodland underbrush tore away their wool. By the 1670s these conditions had changed. An aggressive bounty system and the spread of settlements into the interior gradually exterminated the wolves and cleared enough pastureland so that sheep became a more familiar sight on mainland farms. Spinning wheels, mentioned in Plymouth Colony inventories as early as 1644, gradually became common, and most mid-century householders' inventories in Plymouth and neighboring colonies listed wool and flax, and some mention sheep, cotton, and even homemade cloth. Still, textile production must have continued to fall short of potential demand, because few people chose to invest their time in weaving. Of roughly 1,500 inventories dating from before 1675, only thirty, all for men, list looms. Similarly, when Carl Bridenbaugh recorded the occupations of men in the early volumes of Rhode Island land evidences, he identified only one weaver and one cloth worker out of forty-two artisans before 1670.

Nor did many early households possess the tools for such women's tasks as brewing, baking, or dairying. Only a few women appear anywhere in John Pynchon's Connecticut Valley accounts. Of the four women he mentioned in the 1640s, one received pay for chickens and eggs, one for weeding, one for making hay, and the fourth for domestic service. There is no mention of brewing, baking, or butter making, although in 1648 Pynchon paid Henry Burt for making malt, probably from the barley mowed by Richard Excell that year, and Pynchon paid another man for milking his cows in 1666–1667. The first reference to spinning appears in 1663, to knitting in 1668, and to sewing in 1669.

Most of New England's people were farmers. Women who were not tied down by young children probably spent their time outdoors working in gardens or with their men in the fields. Although English women did not customarily do heavy field work, they did garden with hoes, and in the colonies the hoe played a major role wherever families could use existing Indian fields. In early Saybrook Alice Apsley marketed medicinal herbs and onions from her garden. Goody Macksfield supplied a Boston shopkeeper with apples, squashes, beans, cucumbers, carrots, and cabbages, as well as honey, butter, cheese, and eggs. C. Dallett Hemphill examined the work activities of Salem women recorded in testimony before the Essex County court between 1636 and 1683 and found them engaged in men's work or working with men: servant Ann Knight winnowed corn, another woman carried grain to the mill, and others milked cows and branded steers in the company of men; a witness in one case remembered seeing the wife of Joseph Dalaber working alongside her husband planting and covering corn.

. . . [T]he ratio of women's pay to men's pay was at its highest point in this early period when the division of labor between men and women was less clearly defined than in contemporary England or as it later came to be in New England. Women could hoe in already-cleared Indian fields, and meadows and salt marshes supplied their small herds of animals with forage. When these sites filled up and the numbers of livestock expanded, newcomers had to break new ground and create meadows planted with English grasses. Inventories record the gradual advent of a more English farming style using heavy plows drawn by teams of oxen, while tax lists and town genealogies trace the growing supply of sturdy young sons. Similarly, the appearance of spinning wheels, firkins, brewing vats, and dye pots attests to the kinds of activities that came to employ women. The division of labor between the sexes widened and, as it did so, separated them physically.

The use of ox teams, restricted to older men, effectively segregated family members into field and home workers. Men and older boys also did the sowing and harrowing at the beginning of the farm year and the reaping and mowing at harvest. In early spring they planted and pruned orchards and carted and spread dung. In June they washed and sheared sheep. In fall they pressed cider and slaughtered hogs. In the slack seasons men cut and dragged timber, built and maintained fences, cleared underbrush,

ditched bogs, and dug out stones. In most of these activities, handling draft animals was essential and was work for males only. The men used oxen to remove stumps and boulders, drag timber, cart dung, and haul hay and horses to drive cider presses. Only men and older boys paddled canoes, steered scows, piloted "gundalows" (gondolas), or rowed boats.

Women participated in none of these activities except at harvest time, when their help was welcomed. Even then, they did not mow grass or grain, because most did not have the height or upper body strength to handle scythes. Diaries after 1750 show them helping with the reaping, probably binding sheaves and sickling wheat and rye. Young Jabez Fitch of Norwich, Connecticut, reported enthusiastically in his diary on July 24, 1759, "there was a great Reeping[;] we Liv'd very well[;] we had Women anough & Some more." A story related in a town history about one woman's feat is no doubt apocryphal but interesting for its celebration of women's physical achievements in a less genteel age: a Mrs. Brown of Chester, New Hampshire, around the year 1800 or earlier, with others had sowed rye for its seed. At harvest time she prepared breakfast, nursed her child, walked five or six miles to the field, reaped her rye (finishing before any of the men), and walked back home.

Men's diaries also describe both sexes and all ages gathering corn by day and husking together at night, making the work an occasion for a frolic. Both sexes and all ages went berrying and nutting together. Young people often turned such occasions to their own devices, especially when gathering strawberries on long June evenings. The excitement these occasions could create is recorded in the diary of a Harvard undergraduate, who, with other young men, succeeded in transforming a quilting party into a late night gala.

Many farm tasks fell more or less exclusively to the female members of the household. Girls and women tended the fowl and small animals. They milked the cows at dawn and dusk, separated the cream, churned the butter, and made the cheese. They planted and hoed kitchen gardens in plots men had prepared by plowing and harrowing. Women boiled the offal for such by-products as sausage casings, head cheese, calf's foot jelly, and rennet after men killed, cleaned, and butchered animals. Gender-based assignment of many farm chores centered on objective differences in body height and strength rather than on what was deemed culturally appropriate to one sex or the other. Females carried out some of the same tasks as younger boys—they helped hay, hoe, weed, harvest crops, and husk corn.

Yet gender ordered male and female spheres in ways that went beyond obvious physical distinctions. For instance, men and older boys not only cut timber but operated sawmills, erected buildings, dug wells and cellars, laid stone, pointed chimneys, and shaved shingles and staves. Men tanned and curried hides, made saddles or gloves, and bound shoes. Older boys got the bark for tanning, shaved it, ground it, and laid the leather away. . . . [S]killed craftsmen in these trades earned substantially more than farm laborers. Females never participated in these activities. Nor did girls drive cattle or carry grain on horseback to the mill, as boys did. Women did not thresh grain, even though boys of thirteen or fourteen did so. Although men and boys traveled abroad freely in their duties, women's work more often kept them inside or near their own home or those of kinsmen or employers. In and around the home they earned income from tasks that males assiduously avoided: cleaning, cooking, sewing, spinning, washing clothes, nursing, and caring for children.

Thus, people allocated work among themselves based on physical capacity but also on gender. The advent of English-style agriculture, involving large draft animals and deep plowing, helped fix many boundaries between the sexes. The case of John Graves II of East Guilford is illustrative. Five daughters and four sons survived infancy; all of them appear in his accounts at one time or another credited for a day's or a week's work. Of the eighty-nine work occasions he recorded between 1703 and 1726 (the year he died), he identified daughters on twenty-one occasions and sons on sixty-eight. Thus, sons appeared more than three times as often. Graves hired occasional male help in addition to his sons and kept a young servant named Thome for two years when his younger boys were too small to hoe, make fences, or mow hay. Meanwhile, his girls did chores—but never farm work—for his neighbors. They sewed, spun, nursed, and kept house.

An account book of great interest because of the economic activities of women that it records is that of merchant Elisha Williams of Wethersfield, Connecticut, a commercial farm town situated on the Connecticut River just south of Hartford. Williams's ledger begins in 1738, and its pages are filled with references to women credited for onions. A bunch of roped onions weighed about three or four pounds, and Williams bought them for 5d. per bunch in 1738. Women earned a penny per bunch for tying them in the early 1740s. They generally took their pay in the form of store merchandise, mostly luxury imports such as sugar, chocolate, pepper, rum, cotton lace, and silk romall, a silken handkerchief used as a head covering. Other goods paid for by women's onions included medicine, a pair of spectacles, and a copy of Homer's *Iliad*.

So far, the evidence from account books and diaries has helped locate the boundaries demarcating women's work from men's work. Those boundaries, however, were permeable. Men could and did cross into women's domain when the size of the market justified a larger scale of operations than the home could provide. For example, baking and brewing were normally women's work, but men in port towns also made their living by these activities. Men in New England did not lose self-respect if they milked cows, but they did not normally make cheese or churn cream into butter.

If, however, the family began to specialize in dairying for sale, the men might take part. Matthew Patten of New Hampshire mentioned husbands as well as wives buying and selling butter. Thus, when nominally feminine tasks became important to household income, men undertook a share of the responsibility, even if only to keep track of the profits. Male account keepers commonly listed payments due from boarders and lodgers but never credited the work by their wives that made the hospitality possible. On the other hand, some male-dominated occupations were always open to women. Retail trade was perhaps the most common, although before 1740 such opportunities arose in only a few commercial areas. Most women in retailing were widows who had taken over a deceased husband's shop, although one Mary Johnson of Boston, who was not identified as a widow, owned shop goods worth over two hundred pounds, according to the 1669 inventory of her estate. Helen Hobart ran a shop in Hingham in 1682 with her husband's approval. By the late colonial period, such opportunities had spread deeper into the interior. In Worcester County in 1760, for instance, twelve out of 267 licensed dispensers of spirituous liquors (4.5 percent) were women.

Though women had always acted as midwives, nursed the sick, and disbursed homemade remedies, a few also "doctored." The administrator of the estate of David Clark of Wrentham listed payment to Mary Johnson, "Doctoress" for "Physick and Tendance." William Corbin, minister of the Anglican church in Boston, willed his medical books to Jane Allen of Newbury, spinster and daughter of the Honorable Samuel Allen, Esquire. In 1758 the Reverend Ebenezer Parkman went to see the widow Ruhamah Newton, who had broken her leg in a fall. Friends had called a Mrs. Parker to set the leg, and the time it took her to get her apparatus in order and carry out the operation delayed the diarist's return home "till night."

Women taught school, as did men. Generally speaking, women taught young pupils of both sexes to read and spell, and men instructed more advanced classes in writing and arithmetic. Seventeenth-century records occasionally identify "school dames" who took students for fees, but they do not seem to have been common outside the largest settlements.

In the eighteenth century, women usually taught the younger children and girls during the summer, often for only half the wages of the young male college graduates who took the older children the rest of the year. The town of Amesbury, Massachusetts, voted in 1707 that the selectmen "hire four or five school Dames for the town to teach children to read" and allowed five pounds to two men "to keep a school to teach young parsons to write and sifer two months this year." Most towns seem to have found the two-tier system a cheap and efficient way to comply with the provincial school laws. The town meeting of Hingham instructed its selectmen to "hire a schoolmaster as cheap as they can get one, provided they shall hire a single man and not a man that have a family."

There was also a two-tier system in making apparel. Men normally tailored coats and breeches, and women sewed shirts and gowns; however, women in the eighteenth century also engaged in tailoring to a limited extent. In 1708, the estate of Simon Gross, deceased mariner of Hingham, paid for forty weeks of training as a tailor for his daughter Allis. John Ballantine, minister at Westfield, Massachusetts, mentioned two occasions in 1768 when Ruth Weller came for a week to make garments; in 1773 he noted that "Sally Noble, Tailer" was working at his house.

Gender distinctions were very clear in the processing of textiles. Females did not comb worsted or hackle flax, which was men's work, although women, along with boys, pulled flax, carded wool, and picked seeds out of cotton. Girls and women spun, dyed, and knitted yarn, but few engaged in weaving, traditionally a male occupation in England. Women did take up the craft in the eighteenth century, doing simple weaves while men concentrated on more complex patterns.

Few inventoried estates mention looms in the seventeenth century, and only 6 percent in Essex County, Massachusetts, list them around 1700. By 1774, the proportion of inventories with looms in Alice Hanson Jones's New England sample ranged from a low of 17 percent in Essex County to a high of 37.5 percent in Plymouth County. The spread of looms did not mean that the region's textile industry was in the throes of protoindustrialization. Rather, households in less commercial areas were producing more cloth for home use in order to spend their cash and vendible products on new consumer goods like tea and sugar. The newer weavers included women who took up weaving as a nearly full-time activity in the years before marriage or during widowhood. Growing numbers of married women also wove part time to conserve or expand family income.

Weaving may be the only occupation in the colonial period for which there is sufficient documentation to compare men's and women's pay for the same type of work. Women weavers appear in account books as early as 1704 in Norwich, Connecticut, and in 1728, when Mary Stodder purchased a loom from John Marsh of Litchfield. Altogether, eighteen women weavers appear in the diaries, probate records, and account books consulted for this study, of whom just four are identified as "widow." Of those for whom pay rates are available, comparisons with contemporary male weavers show that the sexes earned similar rates per yard for common kinds of cloth. We can conclude that, in this instance, women did earn equal pay for equal work. However, only two women weavers in the sample, Mary Parker and Hannah Smith of Hingham, received credit for weaving more than the common fabrics— "plain," drugget, shirting, linen, tow, and "blanketing." Men produced a much wider variety, including relatively fancy weaves. Judging from these examples, an expanding demand for domestic cloth created opportunities for women to do simple weaving. They could do so without driving down piece rates, which rose by a third between the 1750s and the 1770s; from 4.1d. to 5.4d. and then to 5.5d. in the early 1770s. Although the sources do not reveal great numbers of women working at looms, women's growing presence in the late colonial period signals a trend that accelerated during the Revolution.

The history of weaving and tailoring in New England illustrates the flexibility inherent in the region's gender-based work roles. The further removed the activity was from hard-core masculine tasks associated with oxen, plows, and heavy equipment, the more likely that respectable women did it. The history of work and gender in New England during the colonial years divides readily into four periods of unequal duration. In the earliest period, before the 1670s, the economy simplified compared to England's economy, and the variety of occupations open to either sex contracted sharply. Women spent more time outdoors and working alongside men. The second period came with the proliferation of activities by which men habitually and strictly segregated themselves from women, and women undertook domestic manufacturing tasks with which historians have so often associated them: brewing beer, baking bread, churning butter, making cheese, spinning yarn, and knitting stockings and mittens. Not every housewife practiced all these arts, and specialization encouraged exchange between them.

The third period, beginning about 1715, constituted the farm maintenance stage in older settlements during which demand for unskilled labor declined relative to skilled labor. Increasing population densities created exchange opportunities that encouraged both men and women to specialize and invest more time in nonfarm occupations. This stage might have continued indefinitely, with population growth putting continuous downward pressure on wages, but outside forces intervened, creating the fourth and final phase of New England's colonial development. Beginning in 1739, wars and their aftermaths administered a succession of shocks to the system, creating sudden demands for men and provisions and putting large amounts of money into circulation. The conclusion to the Seven Years' War opened up northern New England and Nova Scotia to British settlement, and the treaty that ended the War for Independence swung open the gates to Iroquoia in New York, as did the Battle of Fallen Timbers (1794) for the Ohio Valley. Much of the labor supply that might have depressed wage rates emigrated instead; in New England, it was not replaced by immigrants.

Despite New England's limited resources and the absence of technological change, demand generated by war and export markets drove the region's economy at a faster rate than its population grew. Evidence for economic expansion appears in both account books and probate inventories. First, stores with new consumer wares appeared. Storekeepers began moving into the rural interior during the 1740s, and their numbers grew dramatically in the ensuing decades. Proportionately, there were nearly as many retailers in Massachusetts in 1771 as there were in the United States in 1929. Many hopeful young businessmen were assisted by merchants in port cities who had advanced their wares on credit to the neophytes.

The lure was the money jingling in farmers' pockets from increasing prices for their products, beginning with the preparations against Louisbourg in 1744–1745. Prices for livestock began to soar faster than inflation, offering strong inducements to farmers to expand their herds. The sterling equivalent of Connecticut inventory values of oxen, for instance, jumped 19 percent in the 1740s, continued to rise in the 1750s, and by the early 1760s reached 80 percent above levels of the 1730s. During the height of the Seven Years' War, Connecticut prices for cows and barreled pork climbed 50 percent, while prices for sheep doubled. After dropping modestly in the late 1760s, prices for oxen and cows rose sharply in the early 1770s, attaining levels not seen since the 1640s. Livestock values in Massachusetts did not keep up with this torrid pace, but the cost of oxen ballooned by more than 70 percent in 1758–1763 and grew again in the early 1770s. Connecticut wheat prices ascended a bit more demurely: 43 percent in the 1750s and 48 percent in 1772–1774. Farmers in newer settlements sent off, besides barreled meat and draft animals, loads of lumber products, such as staves and shingles,

potash, tar, turpentine, and maple syrup. New Englanders also shipped thousands of pounds of well-preserved butter and cheese every year.

For men with resources, the rational reaction to such prices would have been to devote more of their own and their sons' time to farming and less time to crafts such as weaving. To raise and feed more livestock, farmers had to create more pasture and mowing lands, plant more timothy and clover, maintain longer fence lines, and store many more tons of hay in their newly erected barns. Winter chores expanded, cutting the time available for craft activities.

When farmers endeavored to raise more livestock and the grass to feed them, and when farm wives found themselves milking more cows, churning more butter, and making more cheese, men and women were putting pressure on a labor force that in the short run could expand only by crossing the gender division of labor. Every attempt by the colonial governments during the Seven Years' War to recruit soldiers for the summer campaigns further reduced the available pool of young men, and farmers found themselves engaged in a bidding war that raised wages and bounties. According to Fred Anderson, men in military service during these years could earn far more than a fully employed farm laborer. With an eight-month enlistment, plus bounty, minimum income for soldiers in Massachusetts rose from £10.1 sterling in 1755 to £13.9 in 1757, and bounced between a high of £21.75 and a low of £15.75 thereafter. When bounties for *re*enlistment are figured in, estimated maximum incomes reached £32.3 in 1760 and £29.2 in 1762. Anywhere from one-fourth to one-third of men aged sixteen to twenty-nine served with Massachusetts forces at some point during the war.

The rise in wages beginning in the 1740s at first touched only men but in the long term affected everyone by loosening the bonds between parents and their grown children as daughters found work outside the home and sons joined the military or emigrated. The account books show that men abruptly began employing greater numbers of women in the final two decades of the colonial period. Women had already begun moving into tailoring and weaving, but the labor shortages of the Seven Years' War boosted demand for their services, and the migration out of southern New England in the 1760s apparently worked to cushion the postwar depression in farm wages and prices.

Rising wages and expanding employment meant higher incomes for those who did not emigrate. The probate inventories of the late colonial period show that most New England families were prospering. The estimated sterling value per capita of consumer goods in 1774 was

10 percent higher than in the middle colonies, for instance, and an index of amenities in probate inventories from rural New England registered substantial gains in the decades before 1774, catching up and then keeping pace with Chesapeake households that had long been engaged in a commercial economy.

The New England economy took time to recover from the crises of war and destruction in 1675–1694; it grew only slowly for a long period before heating up during the Seven Years' War. That war accelerated economic change, bringing more women into the paid labor force and expanding the penetration of the market into the rural interior. The growing proportion of young women working outside the home in the final decades of the colonial period accompanied a rise in their wages, which no doubt helped attract them. When combined with evidence that increasing numbers of country girls were attending school and learning how to write, the growing ability of women to earn money and conduct business at the local store can be viewed as a positive good, giving them greater control over their own lives. Furthermore, the addition of tea, sugar, and spices to their diets, painted earthenware to their tables, featherbeds to sleep on, and greater privacy, all surely added pleasures to generally hard lives. Although marriage still meant coverture, more women chose to remain single and access to divorce became easier. There is also a demographic indicator that women's lot was improving: life expectancy of married women rose. Mean age at death increased from sixty-two to sixty-six for women marrying between 1760 and 1774 and to sixty-eight for those marrying between 1775 and 1800. On balance, these changes appear beneficial. Women would not gain politically or legally from American Independence, and equality was never even a prospect, but in the decades before 1776 they had won a little liberty, and comfort is no mean thing.

GLORIA L. MAIN is professor of history at the University of Colorado, Boulder. She is also the author of *Tobacco Colony: Life in Early Maryland, 1650–1720* (Princeton University Press, 1983) and *Peoples of a Spacious Land: Families and Cultures in Colonial New England* (Harvard University Press, 2001).

Cornelia Hughes Dayton

Women Before the Bar

More than half a century separated the first and last courtroom appearances of Rebecca Baldwin of Milford, Connecticut. In 1719, when she was seventeen, Rebecca came before the bar in the New Haven courthouse to confess to the crime of fornication; her father, a prosperous wheelwright, paid her fine of forty-three shillings. The man whom Rebecca named as the father of her infant was a newly married local physician, from whom the court extracted a pledge of child support. Despite the embarrassment of bearing a child out of wedlock, Rebecca avoided forfeiting the respectable status of the family she was born into. At age 24, she married her first cousin Phineas Baldwin; they soon became full church members and had three children, all of whom survived to marry well. In her thirties Rebecca inherited two small tracts of land and one hundred pounds from her father and in her sixties a generous testamentary property settlement when her husband died. In 1775 and 1778—well before her death at age 89—Rebecca again crossed the threshold of the courthouse, now as a widow and the sole surviving executor of her husband's estate.

Rebecca Baldwin's adult life was thus bracketed by two quintessential encounters with the law among those experienced by the hundreds of New England women in each county jurisdiction who found their way into court. Although many women never made the trip to the courthouse, the presence of women in court was not unusual. In the early part of the colonial period, spectators on court days would have found it routine that one-third of those waiting to plead or to give testimony were women. Taking shame upon oneself for the illicit act of fornication, as young Rebecca Baldwin did, and suing to collect a debt, as Rebecca did as a widow, were the most common guises in which Connecticut women appeared before the judges of the county courts, the forums to which the bulk of civil and criminal cases were funneled. In addition, scores of women came into county court to sue over slanderous words or inheritance disputes. In Connecticut,

the Superior Court, which rode circuit holding sessions in each county seat, heard a smattering of felony and capital cases inherently involving women—rape, adultery, infanticide—amid a much larger stream of divorce petitions, most of which were brought by deserted wives.

This study takes as its central subjects the many women who entered early Connecticut courtrooms: women suing and being sued over debt and slander, women petitioning for divorce, women prosecuted for sexual transgressions, women advancing rape charges. To ask what the everyday practice of the law courts meant for women is to ask how both women *and* men used available legal procedures to advance their own interests and in what ways they were treated by magistrates and the panoply of community members who, as grand jurors, jurors, and witnesses, made the legal system function. Drawing on colonywide criminal cases and the extensive court records of one jurisdiction, New Haven, in its incarnation as a separate colony until 1665 and afterward as a Connecticut county, this work traces how the gendered patterns of civil, criminal, and divorce litigation changed over 150 years.

Although it follows a design uniquely its own, this investigation builds on three types of scholarly works: analyses of litigation patterns in a single jurisdiction over time, in-depth community studies of towns and their inhabitants, and inquiries into specific aspects of women's relationship to the law. When I began this project, excellent work was emerging on women's legal position as it was defined by colonial statutes, early modern English treatises, and late-eighteenth-century appellate case law, but gender as an important analytical category was missing from new studies on the actual workings of early American courts. Setting out to remedy the deficit, I chose to eschew sampling, a traditional social science technique that can yield a useful portrait of a legal system but that fails to capture all the courtroom encounters that individuals like Rebecca Baldwin might have had over their lifetime. In order to paint an accurate and telling portrait of the early

American courts, treatment of subordinate groups such as women, African-Americans, and Indians, the best strategy, I believe, is a systematic profiling of everything occurring in court in a given jurisdiction.

The extensive, nearly complete records surviving for colonial Connecticut and New Haven make this study possible. For the seventeenth and eighteenth centuries, court records provide an extraordinary window in to behaviors, self-fashionings, and idiomatic uses of language that would otherwise go unrecorded. In a period when few adults left letters or diaries, women and men speak through court records more openly than through almost any other set of documents. Slander writs quote speech fragments verbatim, depositions offer a person's deliberate construction of events, and local magistrates' records transcribe criminals' examinations in a question-and-answer format. Thus we can hear women talking and being talked to, we can see the extent to which they were recognized or ignored in the courtroom, in a more tangible way than is possible for other public settings, such as the tavern, the street, and the meetinghouse.

Besides their usefulness in capturing random, individual voices and in documenting the literal and symbolic work of an important public institution, court records disclose the agency of laypersons. In the seventeenth and eighteenth centuries the legal system could function only with the cooperation of ordinary men and women. New Englanders with legal standing could choose, after all, whether to submit their disputes to the magistrates and courts or resort instead to other forms of mediation, such as the parish or neighborhood arbitration. Indeed, because civil litigation occupied the bulk of the courts' business, local inhabitants by their decisions on whom to sue and how to plead gave shape to the rhythms of court sessions and breathed life into, spelled atrophy for, or prompted modification of legal forms and actions. Similarly, in the realm of criminal justice, without the modern-day apparatus of police, prosecutors, and investigators, the colonial court's effectiveness in keeping the peace depended on the public's willingness to bring complaints and testimony to it.

As members of the lay population, women could contribute to the dynamics of legal business as litigants, witnesses, and criminal defendants. Indeed, they did so with unparalleled frequency in the earliest decades of settlement, when simplified legal rules and a ban on lawyers gave all residents direct access to the legal system. But women stood outside the loose group of brokers who coalesced in the early eighteenth century, a group I call the legal fraternity. Wider than the clusters of judges, justices of the peace, and professional attorneys serving each

county, the legal fraternity should be seen as encompassing the many propertied heads of household who rotated on and off duty as trial jurors and grand jurors. Since the men chosen as jurors were typically in their thirties or forties with average landholdings and dense kinship networks in Connecticut, the system ensured that legal decisions were influenced by men of middling ranks, not just the wealthiest, most prominent figures in the county or those few trained in the law. Thus, after 1700, women's cases were filtered through several layers of men dispensing legal advice and decrees. For New Haven women encountering the law in the eighteenth century, this arrangement represented a different sort of paternalism from that exemplified by the unmediated power of seventeenth-century magistrates. As in affairs of church governance, women operated informally, behind the scenes, to shape legal outcomes, but with the expansion of the legal fraternity through the century their activities became more and more invisible to the public record.

Alongside any brief for the value of early modern court records must come recognition of their recalcitrance. Writs in certain civil actions, notably debt, assault, and trespass, usually fail to record the actual nature of the underlying transaction or conflict. Moreover, no matter how voluminous the depositions surviving in a particular case, as historians we can capture only a small fraction of the information that came before the bench and jury. There were no stenographers in colonial Connecticut courtrooms to transcribe oral testimony, lawyers' arguments, and defendants' exact words. The gestures of the various participants, the gasps and sighs and catcalls of the audience, and in general the dramaturgy of early New England courtrooms—these are almost always lost to us. Much of what the judges said from the bench went unrecorded, including instructions to juries in criminal trials. The practice of issuing judicial opinions to explain rulings and verdicts began, spottily, only in the 1780s. Few eighteenth-century Connecticut judges and lawyers wrote diaries or left papers containing legal briefs and correspondence. Lay men and women, introspective over spiritual matters but not yet inspired to self-revelatory consciousness by Romanticism or modernist impulses, would never have conceived the value of recording in detail what motivated them to attend court, what they observed in the courtroom, or why they might have altered their testimony from one hearing to the next.

Thus our interpretations of what happened in court are inevitably dependent on records full of omissions and silences and on testimonies refracted through faulty memories and calculation. Supplemental information from nonlegal sources can shed light on such issues as who was in court by age or social status and what sorts of disputes failed to come before the bar, but it rarely supplies direct evidence on the attitudes and motivations of courtroom actors. Court records, of course, can be a springboard to investigations of all sorts of topics—from witchcraft beliefs and courtship rituals to credit networks. Yet principally the record books and file papers speak to what issues came before the courts and how laypeople and officials negotiated the terrain marked as law. Thus, the present study keeps a steady focus on the courtroom itself. In its pursuit of the story of New Englanders' use of and reception by the courts over time, it is institutional history. In its close attention to the gender, age, and social standing of litigants, it relies heavily on social history methods. Above all, it is meant to contribute to our understanding of change in early American legal culture and in gender relations and gender ideology.

. . . Five topical categories—debt, divorce, illicit consensual sex, rape, and slander—were chosen because of the sheer quantity of cases or the utility of the legal record for illuminating important aspects of women's relationship to the courts over time. For example, women were party to more than a thousand debt suits in New Haven County alone in the seventeenth and eighteenth centuries, A comparison of women's and men's litigated debt significantly expands our grasp of an understudied aspect of colonial development—the gendered dimensions of commercialization and rural economic growth. In contrast, cases involving rape were few, yet file papers permit us to reconstruct women's and men's conflicting stories and to compare community responses to charges against acquaintances and outsiders, whites and blacks. Considering major aspects of civil, criminal, and divorce law together highlights important currents of legal and social change that can remain obscured when legal actions are studied in isolation.

I make no claim, however, that the study covers every aspect of women's experience before the courts in early New England. Readers will not find extended discussions of several issues. Witchcraft is omitted because the number of cases in New Haven was small and because two fine, in-depth studies of early New England witch-hunting exist that cover Connecticut, including one that makes gender central to its analysis. Furthermore, singular criminal cases in which women played a central role, like a rare 1740s Connecticut abortion prosecution of a doctor and his alleged accomplices, did not fit easily into a study that was geared to examine change in legal actions over time. Finally, legal scholars may argue for the importance of studying women's roles in land and inheritance disputes, but I found it difficult to tease conclusions about

gender out of the records for trespass, ejectment, trover, or inheritance suits, since most involved joint heirs—siblings suing together. To my mind, the differential pattern of men's and women's participation in debt litigation was the most important area of private law to address: debt, after all, was the major engine of change in the colonial legal system.

[T]he courtrooms of the seventeenth-century New Haven and Connecticut colonies had a very different character from those of the late eighteenth century. I argue that the most critical period of change for women's relation to the public space of the courtroom came in the decades surrounding the end of the seventeenth century. By then a collective commitment to upholding a God-fearing society through the courts had been abandoned, and Puritan resistance to the technicalities of English common law practice had faded. From the 1690s to the 1720s rules were implemented that shifted New Haven courtrooms from the utopian reform platform of the Puritan founders to a selective embrace of English formalism. Toward the end of that transition, an enormous expansion in indebtedness reshaped civil litigation. As a result of these transformations in law and society, by the end of the colonial period women's presence in court declined dramatically.

In essence, women's courtroom participation throws into sharp relief the realignment of court and community. The seventeenth-century courts had been occupied by the sorts of community activities to which women were integral: maintaining harmonious neighborly relations, ensuring equitable local trading, and monitoring sexual and moral conduct. After the turn of the century, the courts increasingly became adjuncts and facilitators of vast credit networks that provided farmers and tradesmen with the capital to expand their farms and enterprises. The constituency served by the courts narrowed to propertied men active in the expanding economy; at the same time the volume of court business was growing exponentially. Women's economic and social activities did not change markedly at the beginning of the eighteenth century, but in a schematic sense what was happening in court reveals a new set of divergences in men's and women's spheres taking hold gradually throughout the century. These divergences—in women's and men's relations to commercialization, to the public theater of the courtroom, and to religious attitudes toward sin and human culpability—were silent foreshadowings of the more explicit nineteenth-century ideology that reserved the public realms of commerce, law, and politics to men and gave white women moral dominion over privatized families.

If New Haven's evolving courtroom scenes illumine the restructuring of public and private space, putting law at the center of the story of gender and social change in early New England also enables us to perceive important shifts in a system of power relations that is often viewed as static: patriarchy, or the legal and cultural rules by which men held authority over women in the household and polity. It is my contention that the seventeenth-century Puritan courtroom occupies an anomalous position in the long histories of Anglo-American law and of patriarchy. The New England Puritans struck out on idiosyncratic legal paths, the twisted strands of which included some policies harshly intolerant of unsubmissive women and others remarkably unforgiving of men's ungodly behavior.

On the one hand, the familiar characterization of Puritan justice as repressive of women is borne out in many respects. Puritan legal regimes across New England unquestioningly cast women as witches and condoned a prosecutorial double standard for accused men and women such that twenty-eight women and only seven men were hanged for the crime of witchcraft. In the 1630s and 1640s, New England's leaders used showcase trials against Anne Hutchinson and other female dissenters to silence women as political beings and religious leaders. Finally, the Puritan compulsion to punish a wide range of moral lapses with whippings meant that women were frequently haled before the bar to confess their sins publicly and to submit to the lash.

On the other hand, Puritan jurisprudence, by encouraging lay pleading and by insisting on godly rules, created unusual opportunities for women's voices to be heard in court. The prohibition against lawyers, the simplification of procedural rules, and the magistrates' confidence that God would help them discern the truth behind a dispute or criminal charge meant that women's testimony was invited and encouraged in ways that clashed with English legal traditions. Not only was women's access to courts eased, but the Puritans' emphasis on each individual's obedience to God's strictures led them to insist on punishing men's abuse of authority and sinful behavior. In cases of sexual assault, wife-abuse, and premarital sex, seventeenth-century magistrates gave credence to women's charges and meted out swift, severe sentences to men. Indeed, New Haven Colony came close to establishing a single standard for men and women in the areas of sexual and moral conduct. In sum, policies that were intended to create the most God-fearing society possible operated to reduce the near-absolute power that English men by law wielded over their wives, to undercut men's sense of sexual entitlement to women's bodies, and to relieve women in some situations from their extreme dependency on men. Thus, when Puritanism ceased to be the organizing force in New England society and courtrooms, there were losses for women as well as gains.

Along with new work on the Chesapeake, this study urges that we examine the early and middle decades of the eighteenth century as a period that saw the return to a more traditional type of patriarchy in Britain's New World colonies. Quite different material and ideological conditions explain why some traditional supports of patriarchy were loosened in seventeenth-century colonies as distinct as Virginia and Connecticut and why women in various regions encountered a tightening of patriarchal authority in the eighteenth century. I attempt to account only for women's experience in New Haven as suggestive of the cultural shifts characterizing colonies that began as intensely Puritan settlements. Here, judges, lawmakers, and other men of influence and wealth launched no coordinated, self-conscious campaign to roll back the slight openings and advances women had enjoyed under seventeenth-century legal approaches. Rather, their implicit endorsement of rules and practices that would reinforce male authority was integrally bound up in their promulgation of two pervasive cultural trends: anglicization and embourgeoisement.

Anglicization, the importation of English ways by colonists newly and self-consciously eager to bind themselves to the cultural sophistication of the empire's urban centers, has gained much attention in recent years. In the realm of law, the process can be discerned in early-eighteenth-century New England not only in the licensing of professional attorneys but also in the stricter attention paid to common law procedures and rules of evidence. These shifts internal to the legal system raised barriers to women's easy use of the courts and introduced skeptical attitudes toward the reliability of women's charges of male abuse. Beyond the law, newspapers and almanacs show that by midcentury New England culture also became more English (and more European) in its new toleration of misogynist, antimatrimonial, and bawdy themes. Having been invoked by historians to illuminate such diverse areas as professionalization, political culture, consumer tastes, and national integration, anglicization needs also to be recognized as the bearer of ideas about woman's nature that had been largely suppressed in seventeenth-century New England.

Although there has been much hesitation over applying the language of class to early America before wage dependency was extensive, a social stratum and a set of practices later identified as middle-class were emerging in the eighteenth century. The various processes that one scholar calls the "refinement of America" reflect not just the formation of a distinct American gentry but also the fact that many colonials were taking on genteel habits that the post-Independence, republican context would remake into bourgeois habits. The signs of interest in acquiring the badges of cultivation appeared as early as the 1690s. Expanded trade and sources of credit, denser kinship networks, and ideological shifts released New Englanders from insular preoccupations with family and community survival. Wealthy and ambitious families became caught up in elaborating their material world by adding rooms to their dwelling houses, dividing household space into public and private areas, and acquiring luxury goods. Along with those trends came a new ethic of privacy among the emergent bourgeoisie. The social, religious, and political values of the men who breathed life into the legal system no longer called upon them to insist that their dependents or peers submit moral transgressions—slander, premarital sex, drunkenness—to the regulation of the community embodied in the county court. In the area of regulating premarital sexual relations, for example, Connecticut officials moved toward a narrowly selective approach targeting poor, marginal women and sheltering the middling classes from public scrutiny, humiliation, and penalty. These changes in the types of transgressors and transgressions subject to legal action point to a general reformulation of status and identity, a reformulation that authorized propertied male family heads to distance themselves from . . . some of the key communal values espoused by Puritan founders. What was at work was a simultaneous intensification of class definitions and a "restructuring of morality as a category of private or individual rather than communal life."

Studying gendered patterns of litigation and criminal prosecution over 150 years of New Haven's and Connecticut's shared early history allows us to glimpse not only forces that dramatically changed the face of court business but also divergences in women's and men's lives that led to a redefinition of the public space of the courtroom as a male arena. Crucial to this process were both material conditions, as in women's increasingly attenuated link to their menfolks' economic dealings, and cultural fashions, notably perceptions of appropriate behavior for respectable women. Moreover, that women's voices were largely emptied out of the theater of the courtroom by the era of the new Republic was not a maneuver engineered by elites. Laypersons, through their strategies in civil suits, their pleas in criminal cases, and the wording of their writs and petitions, were critical participants in the renegotiations played out in the courts over how reputation was measured, how culpability for sexual transgressions was calculated, how male power within marriage would be buttressed, and how much women could manage property and have access to credit networks.

Men's and women's actions together, then, over the eighteenth century reshaped the county court from an inclusive forum representative of community to a rationalized institution serving the interests of commercially active men. The refashioning of the court into a public space designed solely to shape and nurture the civic identity of bourgeois men powerfully illustrates that fraternity in its deliberately gendered sense would determine access to the new nation's political and public spheres. The refusal of the statesmen, jurists, and political pamphleteers of the Revolutionary and nation-building era to see women as anything but dependent, apolitical beings emerges clearly in their writings. It is through the narrative trail left in court records predating the Constitution that we can discern that writing women out of the original American political contract had a structural history and experiential base many decades in the making.

CORNELIA HUGHES DAYTON, a specialist in early British North American, legal, and women's history, currently serves as associate professor of history at the University of Connecticut. She earned her PhD at Princeton University in 1986 and taught at the University of California–Irvine from 1988 to 1997.

EXPLORING THE ISSUE

Was the Colonial Period a "Golden Age" for Women in America?

Critical Thinking and Reflection

1. How did the economic status of New England women change over the course of the seventeenth and eighteenth centuries?
2. How did the jobs assigned to New England women differ from those deemed appropriate for men?
3. What are the basic assertions that support the "golden age" thesis as presented by Main?
4. According to Hughes, how did the legal status of New England women change over the course of the seventeenth and eighteenth centuries?
5. What factors contributed to the transformation of the county courts in Connecticut from a gender-inclusive venue to an arena primarily serving the interests of men?

Is There Common Ground?

Both of these essays address the "golden age" thesis that became a significant focus of historical debate in the 1970s and 1980s at a time when the women's liberation movement was at high tide. Both authors ground their research in New England and trace change in women's status from the seventeenth to the eighteenth centuries, although Gloria Main finds improving economic opportunities for women as time passes, while Cornelia Hughes Dayton identifies a clear decline in women's legal status by the early eighteenth century. Both authors also appear to be evaluating the status of white women. What might happen to the conclusions of each had they also factored in the status of nonwhite women in the colonies, or if data from Virginia, Maryland, Pennsylvania, or some other British North American colony had been added to their analyses?

The British North American colonies were clearly a part of a larger, Western European patriarchal structure, so similarities in the status of women undoubtedly existed. Some interesting comparisons could be made between colonial families and modern families. The status of women in the two eras is markedly different, especially in the political realm, but what about average family size and the age of women at first marriage? How were women treated outside of the traditional domestic sphere? This question is central to Hughes's study. To what degree have these spheres changed over time since the colonial period? One obvious difference is the extent to which women have become the focus of historical research.

Mary Beth Norton explores the changes in the status of colonial women more fully in "The Evolution of White Women's Experience in Early America," *American Historical Review*, vol. 89 (June 1984), pp. 593–619. Here she surveys the basic elements of the "golden age' theory and perceptively pronounces the thesis to be "simplistic and unsophisticated" because it concentrates primarily upon the economic function of women in colonial society. Hughes's essay, therefore, represents a corrective to traditional analysis by focusing upon women's roles in the courts.

Additional Resources

Carol Berkin, *First Generations: Women in Colonial America* (Hill & Wang, 1997)

Nancy F. Cott, "Divorce and the Changing Status of Women in Eighteenth-Century Massachusetts," *William and Mary Quarterly*, 3rd series, vol. 33, pp. 586–614 (October 1976)

Mary Beth Norton, *Founding Mothers & Fathers: Gendered Power and the Forming of American Society* (Alfred A. Knopf, 1996)

Elizabeth Reis, *Damned Women: Sinners and Witches in Puritan New England* (Cornell University Press, 1999)

Marylynn Salmon, *Women and the Law of Property in Early America* (University of North Carolina Press, 1986)

Internet References . . .

A Colonial Lady's Clothing: A Glossary of Terms

www.history.org/history/clothing/women/wglossary .cfm

American Women's History: A Research Guide: The Colonial Period

capone.mtsu.edu/kmidlet/history/women/wh-colonial.html

Women of the American Revolution

www.americanrevolution.org/women/women.html

Selected, Edited, and with Issue Framing Material by:
Larry Madaras, *Howard Community College*
and
James M. SoRelle, *Baylor University*

ISSUE

Were Socioeconomic Tensions Responsible for the Witchcraft Hysteria in Salem?

YES: Paul Boyer and Stephen Nissenbaum, from *Salem Possessed: The Social Origins of Witchcraft* (Harvard University Press, 1974)

NO: Laurie Winn Carlson, from *A Fever in Salem: A New Interpretation of the New England Witch Trials* (Ivan R. Dee, 1999)

Learning Outcomes
After reading this issue, you will be able to:
• Understand multicausal explanations of historical events.
• Appreciate the negative impact that social and economic forces had on the sense of community among Salem residents.
• Discuss the possible impact of biological and/or ecological forces in history.

ISSUE SUMMARY

YES: Paul Boyer and Stephen Nissenbaum argue that the Salem witchcraft hysteria of 1692 was prompted by economic and social tensions that occurred against the backdrop of an emergent commercial capitalism, conflicts between ministers and their congregations, and the loss of family lands, which divided the residents in Salem Town and Salem Village.

NO: Laurie Winn Carlson believes that the witchcraft hysteria in Salem was the product of people's responses to physical and neurological behaviors resulting from an unrecognized epidemic of encephalitis.

Although an interest in the occult, including witchcraft and devil worship, exists in modern society, for most of us the images of witches are confined to our television and movie screens or perhaps to the theatrical stage where a Shakespearean tragedy is being performed. We can watch the annual presentation of The Wizard of Oz and reruns of Bewitched or hear the cries of "Bubble, bubble, toil and trouble" in a scene from Macbeth, with as little concern for the safety of our souls as we exhibit when black-garbed, broomstick-toting children appear on our doorsteps at Halloween. But such was not always the case.

Prehistoric paintings on the walls of caves throughout Europe, from Spain to Russia, reveal that witchcraft was of immediate and serious concern to many of our ancestors. The most intense eruptions in the long history of witchcraft, however, appeared during the sixteenth and seventeenth centuries. In the British North American colonies, there were over 100 witchcraft trials in seventeenth-century New England alone, and 40 percent of those accused were executed. For most Americans the events

that began in the kitchen of the Reverend Samuel Parris in Salem, Massachusetts, in 1692 are the most notorious.

A group of young girls, with the assistance of Parris's West Indian slave, Tituba, were attempting to see into the future by "reading" messages in the white of a raw egg they had suspended in a glass. The tragic results of this seemingly innocent diversion scandalized the Salem community and reverberated all the way to Boston. One of the participants insisted she saw the specter of a coffin in the egg white, and soon after, the girls began to display the hysterical symptoms of the possessed. Following intense interrogation by adults, Tituba, Sarah Good, and Sarah Osborne were accused of practicing magic and were arrested. Subsequently, Tituba confessed her guilt and acknowledged the existence of other witches but refused to name them. Accusations spread as paranoia enveloped the community. Between May and September 1692 hundreds of people were arrested. Nineteen were convicted and hanged (not burned at the stake, as is often assumed), and another, a man who refused to admit either guilt or innocence was pressed to death under heavy weights.

Finally, Sir William Phips, the new royal governor of the colony, halted court proceedings against the accused (which included his wife), and in May 1693, he ordered the release of those who were still in jail. After 1692, a few witches were tried in the British North American colonies: in Virginia (1706), North Carolina (1712), and Rhode Island (1728). The last execution for witchcraft in England occurred in 1712 and in Scotland in 1727. On the Continent, royal edicts put an end to such persecutions before the close of the seventeenth century.

The Salem witch trials represent one of the most thoroughly studied episodes in American history. Throughout history, witchcraft accusations have tended to follow certain patterns, most of which were duplicated in Salem. Usually, they occurred during periods of political turmoil, economic dislocation, or social stress. In Salem, a political impasse between English authorities and the Massachusetts Bay Colony, economic tensions between commercial and agricultural interests, and disagreements between Salem Town and Salem Village all formed the backdrop to the legal drama of 1692. In addition, the events in Salem fit the traditional pattern that those accused were almost always women. In *A Search for Power: The "Weaker Sex" in Seventeenth-Century New England* (University of Illinois, 1980), Lyle Koehler points out that not only were three-fourths of the persons accused of witchcraft in Salem females but also, of the 56 men accused, half were related to accused women. In addition, most of the accused women in some way openly flouted the ideal role established for women in Puritan society. According to Koehler, the accusers were seeking to overcome their own feelings of personal powerlessness by speaking out in the patriarchal world in which they lived. Moreover, these women relished the sense of power they received from court officials' attention to their allegations designed to conquer the supernatural forces around them. Carol F. Karlsen, in *The Devil in the Shape of a Woman: Witchcraft in Colonial New England* (W. W. Norton, 1987), reveals that negative views of women as the embodiment of evil were deeply embedded in the Puritan (and European) world view. But through most of the seventeenth century, according to Karlsen, New Englanders avoided explicit connections between women and witchcraft. Nevertheless, the attitudes that depicted witches as women remained self-evident truths and sprang to the surface in 1692.

Several scholars have concluded that the enthusiasm for learning more about the Salem witches and their accusers far outweighs the importance of the event; yet essays and books continue to roll off the presses, including a spate of works in the 1990s to commemorate the 300th anniversary of the events in Salem. Those interested in pursuing this topic further should examine Marion Starkey's *The Devil in Massachusetts: A Modern Enquiry into the Salem Witch Trials* (Knopf, 1949), which blames the episode on the lies told by the accusers. An intriguing alternative is Chadwick Hansen's *Witchcraft at Salem* (George Braziller, 1969), which insists that several Salem residents did practice black magic, thereby heightening the fears of their neighbors. Mary Beth Norton has postulated that borderland threats from Native Americans and the French were conflated by Salem and Essex County residents with alleged assaults by witches to explain problems confronting seventeenth-century residents of Massachusetts Bay Colony. John Putnam Demos's *Entertaining Satan: Witchcraft and the Culture of Early New England* (Oxford University Press, 1982) applies theories and insights from the fields of psychology, sociology, and anthropology to explore the influence of witchcraft throughout New England. Also of value is Demos's earlier essay, "Underlying Themes in the Witchcraft of Seventeenth-Century New England," *American Historical Review* (June 1970).

The following selections offer two varying interpretations that seek to explain the events in Salem over 300 years ago. Paul Boyer and Stephen Nissenbaum, in *Salem Possessed: The Social Origins of Witchcraft* (Harvard University Press, 1974), detail the socioeconomic conflicts (over such issues as the rise of commercial capitalism, the loss of family lands by third-generation sons, and disputes between local ministers and their congregations) that existed between the residents of Salem Town and Salem Village in the late seventeenth century. By mapping out the residences of those who were accused of witchcraft and those who leveled the charges, Boyer and Nissenbaum conclude that the accusers and the accused generally were not acquainted with one another and that the witchcraft hysteria was based on politics and economics.

Laurie Winn Carlson, on the other hand, insists that previous explanations for the events in Salem fail to take into account the physical and neurological symptoms exhibited by many of the residents of the town. Those symptoms, she argues, correspond very closely to behaviors described during the pandemic of encephalitis lethargica that struck the United States in the early twentieth century and provide a reasonable explanation for many of the unanswered questions about the events in Salem.

Paul Boyer and Stephen Nissenbaum

Salem Possessed: The Social Origins of Witchcraft

1692: Some New Perspectives

Salem witchcraft. For most Americans the episode ranks in familiarity somewhere between Plymouth Rock and Custer's Last Stand. This very familiarity, though, has made it something of a problem for historians. As a dramatic package, the events of 1692 are just too neat, highlighted but also insulated from serious research by the very floodlights which illuminate them. "Rebecca Nurse," "Ann Putnam," "Samuel Parris"—they all endlessly glide onto the stage, play their appointed scenes, and disappear again into the void. It is no coincidence that the Salem witch trials are best known today through the work of a playwright, not a historian. It was, after all, a series of historians from George Bancroft to Marion Starkey who first treated the event as a dramatic set piece, unconnected with the major issues of American colonial history. When Arthur Miller published *The Crucible* in the early 1950's, he simply outdid the historians at their own game.

After nearly three centuries of retelling in history books, poems, stories, and plays, the whole affair has taken on a foreordained quality. It is hard to conceive that the events of 1692 could have gone in any other direction or led to any other outcome. It is like imagining the *Mayflower* sinking in midpassage, or General Custer at the Little Big Horn surrendering to Sitting Bull without a fight.

And yet speculation as to where events might have led in 1692 is one way of recapturing the import of where they did lead. And if one reconstructs those events bit by bit, as they happened, without too quickly categorizing them, it is striking how long they resist settling into the neat and familiar pattern one expects. A full month, maybe more, elapsed between the time the girls began to exhibit strange behavior and the point at which the first accusations of witchcraft were made; and in the haze of those first uncertain weeks, it is possible to discern the shadows of what might have been.

Bewitchment and Conversion

Imagine, for instance, how easily the finger of witchcraft could have been pointed back at the afflicted girls themselves. It was they, after all, who first began to toy with the supernatural. At least one neighboring minister, the Reverend John Hale of Beverly, eventually became convinced that a large measure of blame rested with these girls who, in their "vain curiosity to know their future condition," had "tampered with the devil's tools." And Hale's judgment in the matter was shared by his far more influential colleague Cotton Mather, who pinpointed as the cause of the outbreak the "conjurations" of thoughtless youths, including, of course, the suffering girls themselves.

Why then, during 1692, were the girls so consistently treated as innocent victims? Why were they not, at the very least, chastised for behavior which itself verged on witchcraft? Clearly, the decisive factor was the interpretation which adults—adults who had the power to make their interpretation stick—chose to place on events whose intrinsic meaning was, to begin with, dangerously ambiguous.

The adults, indeed, determined not only the direction the witchcraft accusations would take; it was they, it seems, who first concluded that witchcraft was even in the picture at all. "[W]hen these calamities first began," reported Samuel Parris in March 1692, "... the affliction was several weeks before such hellish operations as witchcraft was suspected." Only in response to urgent questioning—"Who is it that afflicts you?"—did the girls at last begin to point their fingers at others in the Village.

It is not at all clear that the girls' affliction was initially unpleasant or, indeed, that they experienced it as an "affliction" at all. Unquestionably it could be harrowing enough once witchcraft became the accepted diagnosis, but the little evidence available from late February, before the agreed-upon explanation had been arrived at, makes the girls' behavior seem more exhilarated than tormented, more liberating than oppressive. One of the early published accounts of the outbreak, that of Robert Calef in 1700, described the girls' initial manifestations as "getting into holes, and creeping under chairs and stools . . . , [with] sundry odd postures and antic gestures, [and] uttering foolish, ridiculous speeches which neither they themselves nor any others could make sense of." . . .

Some Patterns of Accusation

Pace. By the time the storm subsided in October, several hundred persons had been accused of witchcraft, about 150 of them formally charged and imprisoned, and nineteen executed. But when it first broke out in February, there had been no indication that it would reach such proportions, or that it would be any more serious than the numerous isolated witchcraft outbreaks that had periodically plagued New England since at least 1647—outbreaks that had resulted in a total of only fifteen or so executions. The initial accusations at the end of February had named three witches, and most people outside Salem Village, if they heard of the matter at all, probably assumed that it would end there. But the symptoms of the afflicted girls did not subside, and toward the end of March the girls accused three more persons of tormenting them. Still, by early April (a month and a half after the accusations began) only six people had come under public suspicion of witchcraft.

It was at this time, however, that the pace of accusations picked up sharply, and the whole situation began to assume unusual and menacing proportions. Twenty-two witches were accused in April, thirty-nine more in May. After a dip in June, probably reflecting the impact of the first actual execution on June 10, the arrests picked up again and increased steadily from July through September. Indeed, toward the end of the summer, accusations were being made so freely and widely that accurate records of the official proceedings were no longer kept.

Status. But it was not only in the matter of numbers that the episode changed dramatically as it ran its course; there was a qualitative change as well. The first three women to be accused could be seen as "deviants" or "outcasts" in their community—the kinds of people who anthropologists have suggested are particularly susceptible to such accusations. Tituba, as we have seen, was a West Indian slave; Sarah Good was a pauper who went around the Village begging aggressively for food and lodging; "Gammer" Osborne, while somewhat better off, was a bedridden old woman.

In March, however, a new pattern began to emerge. Two of the three witches accused in that month—the third was little Dorcas Good—were church members (a sign of real respectability in the seventeenth century) and the wives of prosperous freeholders. This pattern continued and even intensified for the duration of the outbreak: the twenty-two persons accused in April included the wealthiest shipowner in Salem (Phillip English) and a minister of the gospel who was a Harvard graduate with a considerable estate in England (George Burroughs). By mid-May warrants had been issued against two of the seven selectmen of Salem Town; and by the end of the summer some of the most prominent people in Massachusetts and their close kin had been accused if not officially charged. These included:

Several men with "great estates in Boston";

a wealthy Boston merchant, Hezekiah Usher, and the widow of an even wealthier one, Jacob Sheafe;

a future representative to the General Court;

the wife of the Reverend John Hale of Beverly (a man who had himself supported the trials);

Captain John Alden, one of the best-known men in New England (and son of the now legendary John and Priscilla of Plymouth Colony);

the two sons of a distinguished old former governor, Simon Bradstreet, who were themselves active in provincial government;

Nathaniel Saltonstall, a member of the Governor's Council and for a time one of the judges of the witchcraft court;

and Lady Phips herself, wife of the governor.

Indeed, according to one account, a specter of Cotton Mather and another of his mother-in-law were spied late in the summer. As the attorney who prepared the cases against the accused wrote at the end of May, "The afflicted spare no person of what quality so ever."

True, none of these persons of quality was ever brought to trial, much less executed. Some escaped from jail or house arrest, others were simply never arraigned. Nevertheless, the overall direction of the accusations remains clear: up the social ladder, fitfully but perceptibly, to its very top. Whatever else they may have been, the Salem witch trials cannot be written off as a communal effort to purge the poor, the deviant, or the outcast.

Geography. Just as the accusations thrust steadily upward through the social strata of provincial society, so, too, they pressed outward across geographic boundaries. Beginning within Salem Village itself, the accusations moved steadily into an increasingly wide orbit. The first twelve witches were either residents of the Village or persons who lived just beyond its borders. But of all the indictments which followed this initial dozen, only fifteen were directed against people in the immediate vicinity of Salem Village. The other victims came from virtually every town in Essex County, including the five which surrounded the Village. (In the town of Andover alone, there were more arrests than in Salem Village itself.)

While almost all these arrests were made on the basis of testimony given by the ten or so afflicted girls of Salem Village (although in some cases they merely confirmed the validity of others' accusations), it is clear that the girls themselves did not actually know most of the people they named. The experience of Rebecca Jacobs—arrested only to go unrecognized by her accusers—was far from unique. Captain Alden, for example, later reported that at his arraignment in Salem Village, the afflicted girls who had named him were unable to pick him out until a man standing behind one of them whispered into her ear. After finally identifying Alden, the girl was asked by one of the examiners if she had ever seen the man before; when she answered no, her interrogator asked her "how she knew it was Alden? She said, the man told her so."

Accusers and accused, then, were in many if not most cases personally unacquainted. Whatever was troubling the girls and those who encouraged them, it was something deeper than the kind of chronic, petty squabbles between near neighbors which seem to have been at the root of earlier and far less severe witchcraft episodes in New England.

But if the outbreak's geographic pattern tends to belie certain traditional explanations, it raises other, more intriguing, interpretive possibilities. More than a hundred years ago, Charles W. Upham, a public figure in Salem whose lifelong avocation was the study of the witch trials, published a map which located with some precision the home of nearly every Salem Village resident at the beginning of 1692. Using Upham's careful map as a basis, it is possible to pinpoint the place of residence of every Villager who testified for or against any of the accused witches and also of those accused who themselves lived within the Village bounds. A pattern emerges from this exercise—a pattern which further reinforces the conclusion that neighborhood quarrels, in the narrow sense of the phrase, played a minor role indeed in generating witchcraft accusations:

There were fourteen accused witches who lived within the bounds of Salem Village. Twelve of these fourteen lived in the eastern section of the Village.

There were thirty-two adult Villagers who testified against these accused witches. Only two of these lived in that eastern section. The other thirty lived on the western side. In other words, the alleged witches and those who accused them resided on opposite sides of the Village.

There were twenty-nine Villagers who publicly showed their skepticism about the trials or came to the defense of one or more of the accused witches. Twenty-four of these lived in the eastern part of the Village—the same side on which the witches lived—and only five of them in the west. Those who defended the witches were generally their neighbors, often their immediate neighbors. Those who accused them were not. . . .

Witchcraft and Social Identity

What we have been attempting . . . is to convey something of the deeper historical resonances of our story while still respecting its uniqueness. We see no real conflict between these two purposes. To be sure, no other community was precisely like Salem Village, and no other men were exactly like embittered Samuel Parris, cool and ambitious Israel Porter, or Thomas Putnam, Jr., grimly watching the steady diminution of his worldly estate.

This irreducible particularity, these intensely personal aspirations and private fears, fairly leap from the documents these Salem Villagers, and others, left behind them. And had we been able to learn to know them better—heard the timbre of their voices, watched the play of emotion across their faces, observed even a few of those countless moments in their lives which went unrecorded— we might have been able to apprehend with even greater force the pungent flavor of their individuality.

But the more we have come to know these men for something like what they really were, the more we have also come to realize how profoundly they were shaped by the times in which they lived. For if they were unlike any other men, so was their world unlike any other world before or since; and they shared that world with other people living in other places. Parris and Putnam and the rest were, after all, not only Salem Villagers: they were also men of the seventeenth century; they were New Englanders; and, finally, they were Puritans.

If the large concepts with which historians conventionally deal are to have any meaning, it is only as they can be made manifest in individual cases like these. The problems which confronted Salem Village in fact encompassed some of the central issues of New England society in the late seventeenth century: the resistance of back-country farmers to the pressures of commercial capitalism and the social style that accompanied it; the breaking away of outlying areas from parent towns; difficulties between ministers and their congregations; the crowding of third-generation sons from family lands; the shifting locus of authority within individual communities and society as a whole; the very quality of life in an unsettled age. But for men like Samuel Parris and Thomas Putnam, Jr., these issues were not abstractions. They emerged as upsetting personal encounters with people like Israel Porter and Daniel Andrew, and as unfavorable decisions handed down in places like Boston and Salem Town.

It was in 1692 that these men for the first time attempted (just as we are attempting in this book) to piece together the shards of their experience, to shape their malaise into some broader theoretical pattern, and to comprehend the full dimensions of those forces which they vaguely sensed were shaping their private destinies. Oddly enough, it has been through our sense of "collaborating" with Parris and the Putnams in their effort to delineate the larger contours of their world, and our sympathy, at least on the level of metaphor, with certain of their perceptions, that we have come to feel a curious bond with the "witch hunters" of 1692.

But one advantage we as outsiders have had over the people of Salem Village is that we can afford to recognize the degree to which the menace they were fighting off had taken root within each of them almost as deeply as it had in Salem Town or along the Ipswich Road. It is at this level, indeed, that we have most clearly come to recognize the implications of their travail for our understanding of what might be called the Puritan temper during that final, often intense, and occasionally lurid efflorescence which signaled the end of its century-long history. For Samuel Parris and Thomas Putnam, Jr., were part of a vast company, on both sides of the Atlantic, who were trying to expunge the lure of a new order from their own souls by doing battle with it in the real world. While this company of Puritans were not the purveyors of the spirit of capitalism that historians once made them out to be, neither were they simple peasants clinging blindly to the imagined security of a receding medieval culture. What seems above all to characterize them, and even to help define their identity as "Puritans," is the precarious way in which they managed to inhabit both these worlds at once.

The inner tensions that shaped the Puritan temper were inherent in it from the very start, but rarely did they emerge with such raw force as in 1692, in little Salem Village. For here was a community in which these tensions were exacerbated by a tangle of external circumstances: a community so situated geographically that its inhabitants experienced two different economic systems, two different ways of life, at unavoidably close range; and so structured politically that it was next to impossible to locate, either within the Village or outside it, a dependable and unambiguous center of authority which might hold in check the effects of these accidents of geography.

The spark which finally set off this volatile mix came with the unlikely convergence of a set of chance factors in the early 1690's: the arrival of a new minister who brought with him a slave acquainted with West Indian voodoo lore; the heightened interest throughout New England in fortune telling and the occult, taken up in Salem Village by an intense group of adolescent girls related by blood and faction to the master of that slave; the coming-of-age of Joseph Putnam, who bore the name of one of Salem Village's two controlling families while owing his allegience to the other; the political and legal developments in Boston and London which hamstrung provincial authorities for several crucial months early in 1692.

But beyond these proximate causes lie . . . deeper and more inexorable ones. . . . For in the witchcraft outburst in Salem Village, perhaps the most exceptional event in American colonial history, certainly the most bizarre, one finds laid bare the central concerns of the era. And so once again, for a final time, we must return to the Village in the sorest year of its affliction.

Witchcraft and Factionalism

Predictably enough, the witchcraft accusations of 1692 moved in channels which were determined by years of factional strife in Salem Village. The charges against Daniel Andrew and Phillip English, for example, followed closely upon their election as Salem Town selectmen—in a vote which underscored the collapse of the Putnam effort to stage a comeback in Town politics. And Francis Nurse, the husband of accused witch Rebecca Nurse, was a member of the anti-Parris Village Committee which took office in October 1691.

Other accusations, less openly political, suggest a tentative probing around the fringes of the anti-Parris leadership. For example, George Jacobs, Jr.—accused with several members of his family—was a brother-in-law of Daniel Andrew, whose lands he helped farm. Jacobs was close to the Porter group in other ways as well. In 1695, for example, he was on hand as the will of the dying Mary Veren Putnam was drawn up, and his name appears with Israel Porter's as a witness to that controversial document.

In May 1692 Daniel Andrew and George Jacobs, Jr., were named in the same arrest warrant, and they evidently went into hiding together.

Another of Daniel Andrew's tenants was Peter Cloyce whose wife, Sarah (a sister of Rebecca Nurse) was among the accused in 1692. And Michael DeRich, whose wife Mary was also charged that year, seems at one time to have been a retainer or servant in the household of the elder John Porter, and his ties to the family may well have continued into the next generation. (Mary DeRich, in turn, was a close relative—perhaps even a sister—of Elizabeth Proctor, convicted of witchcraft along with her husband John.)

Indeed, as the accused are examined from the perspective of Village factionalism, they begin to arrange themselves into a series of interconnected networks. These networks were not formally organized or rigidly structured, but they were nonetheless real enough. The kinds of associations which underlay them were varied: kinship and marriage ties were crucial, but marriage, in all likelihood, was simply the final step, the institutionalization of less tangible bonds built up gradually over a period of time. The traces of such bonds lie buried in a wide variety of sources, including real-estate transactions, court testimony, genealogies, and lists of witnesses and executors in wills and estate settlements. Ultimately, the evidence for these relationships fades off into shadowy associations which are frustratingly difficult to document with precision—although they were certainly well known at the time.

One such network . . . links Israel Porter with a startling number of "witch" families, most notably the Proctors and the Nurses. Other anti-Parris networks (and, for that matter, pro-Parris networks) could be reconstructed. Though this chart is hardly complete or definitive—it could certainly be elaborated with additional research, or even extended outward to encompass additional witches—it does show the various kinds of connections which could hold such a network together. Perhaps the nature of these ties provides a key to one of the ways in which political "factions" were established, cemented, and enlarged in Salem Village (and in other communities as well) during the last part of the seventeenth century. If so, the pattern of witchcraft accusations may itself be a more revealing guide than even the maps or tax lists to the origin of political divisions in the Village.

Given all this, it is not surprising to discover a high correlation between Salem Village factionalism and the way the Village divided in 1692 over the witchcraft outbreak. There are forty-seven Villagers whose position can be determined both in 1692 (by their testimonies or other involvement in the witchcraft, trials) and in 1695 (by their signatures on one or the other of the two key petitions). Of the twenty-seven of those who supported the trials by testifying against one or more of the accused witches, twenty-one later signed the pro-Parris petition, and only six the anti-Parris document. Of the twenty who registered their opposition to the trials, either by defending an accused person or by casting doubt on the testimony of the afflicted girls, only one supported Parris in 1695, while nineteen opposed him. In short, supporters of the trials generally belonged to the pro-Parris faction, and opponents of the trials were overwhelmingly anti-Parris.

Almost every indicator by which the two Village factions may be distinguished, in fact, also neatly separates the supporters and opponents of the witchcraft trials. Compare, for example, . . . the residences of accusers and defenders in 1692 with . . . Parris's supporters and opponents. The connection is clear: that part of Salem Village which was an anti-Parris stronghold in 1695 (the part nearest Salem Town) had also been a center of resistance to the witchcraft trials, while the more distant western part of the Village, where pro-Parris sentiment was dominant, contained an extremely high concentration of accusers in 1692.

Similarly with wealth: just as the average member of the anti-Parris faction paid about 40 percent more in Village taxes than his counterpart in the pro-Parris faction, so the average 1695–96 tax of the Villagers who publicly opposed the trials was 67 percent higher than that of those who pushed the trials forward—18.3 shillings as opposed to 11 shillings. . . .

As early as 1689, in his *Memorable Providences Relating to Witchcrafts and Possessions*, Cotton Mather had urged his readers to "shun a frame of discontent" if they wished to avoid becoming witches: "When persons through discontent at their *poverty*, or at their *misery*, shall be always murmuring and repining at the providence of God, the Devils do then invite them to an agreement . . . , [and d]ownright *witchcraft* is the upshot of it."

From the perspective of those who led the attack in 1692, such an analysis might have seemed to explain not only disruptive malcontents at the lower end of the scale—people like Job Tookey and Sarah Good—but also prospering and upwardly mobile people like John Proctor, John Willard, and Rebecca Nurse. There were, after all, various ways to betray "discontent" with one's natural station: one could turn embittered and spiteful, to be sure; but on the other hand, like the young Proctor and Nurse, one might combine aggressive behavior with good fortune and improve one's status. From a seventeenth century viewpoint, swift economic rise was just as tangible an expression of "discontent" as was muttering or complaining.

Everybody knew that by 1692 John Proctor was wealthier than any of his accusers, yet they also knew that he remained "Goodman" Proctor while Thomas Putnam, by virtue of his father's station, bore the more honorific

designation "Mr. Putnam." As Abigail Williams cried out during a spectral visitation in mid-April, running down a list of newly accused witches: "Oh yonder is Goodman Proctor and his wife and Goody Nurse and Goody Cory and Goody Cloyse!" (Abigail's own uncle may not have been receiving his salary at the time, but he was nevertheless "Mr. Parris.") And at the witchcraft examination of Mary Clarke of Haverhill, young Ann Putnam commented sarcastically that even though the accused woman was now addressed as "Mistress Mary Clarke," Ann well knew "that people used to call her Goody Clarke."

All of these people were on the move, socially and economically. Yet to many New Englanders of the seventeenth century, the stability of the social order rested on the willingness of everyone to accept his given station in life. Refusal to do so was more than a personal weakness; it represented a tangible threat to the social fabric itself. When Cotton Mather preached a sermon in 1689 in response to a Boston witchcraft case of that year, he chose a Biblical text which made this very point: *"Rebellion is as the sin of witchcraft."* The rebellion Mather had in mind here was surely not the political sort—not in the very year that he had supported the successful overthrow of Governor Andros!—but the even more menacing variety implicit in both the spiteful turbulence of those who were sliding down the social ladder and the pushy restlessness of those who were climbing up. The feeling that Mather articulated in this 1689 sermon was one shared by many people in Salem Village three years later: the social order was being profoundly shaken by a superhuman force which had lured all too many into active complicity with it. We have chosen to construe this force as emergent mercantile capitalism. Mather, and Salem Village, called it witchcraft. . . .

PAUL BOYER (1935–2012) was the Merle Curti Professor of History at the University of Wisconsin-Madison. A cultural and intellectual historian, he also authored *Urban Masses and Moral Order in America, 1820–1920* (Harvard University Press, 1978), *By the Dawn's Early Light: American Thought and Culture at the Dawn of the Atomic Age* (2nd ed., University of North Carolina Press, 1994), and *Purity in Print: Book Censorship in America from the Gilded Age to the Computer Age* (2nd ed., University of Wisconsin Press, 2002).

STEPHEN NISSENBAUM is a professor of history emeritus at the University of Massachusetts, Amherst. He is the author of *Sex, Diet, and Debility in Jacksonian America: Sylvester Graham and Health Reform* (Praeger, 1980) and *The Battle for Christmas* (Alfred A. Knopf, 1996).

Laurie Winn Carlson  **NO**

A Fever in Salem: A New Interpretation of the New England Witch Trials

During the latter part of the seventeenth century, residents of a northeastern Massachusetts colony experienced a succession of witchcraft accusations resulting in hearings, trials, imprisonments, and executions. Between 1689 and 1700 the citizens complained of symptoms that included fits (convulsions), spectral visions (hallucinations), mental "distraction" (psychosis), "pinching, pin pricking and bites" on their skin (clonus), lethargy, and even death. They "barked like dogs," were unable to walk, and had their arms and legs "nearly twisted out of joint."

In late winter and early spring of 1692, residents of Salem Village, Massachusetts, a thinly settled town of six hundred, began to suffer from a strange physical and mental malady. Fits, hallucinations, temporary paralysis, and "distracted" rampages were suddenly occurring sporadically in the community. The livestock, too, seemed to suffer from the unexplainable illness. The randomness of the victims and the unusual symptoms that were seldom exactly the same, led the residents to suspect an otherworldly menace. With the limited scientific and medical knowledge of the time, physicians who were consulted could only offer witchcraft as an explanation.

These New Englanders were Puritans, people who had come to North America to establish a utopian vision of community based upon religious ideals. But, as the historian Daniel Boorstin points out, their religious beliefs were countered by their reliance on English common law. The Puritans did not create a society out of their religious dogma, but maintained the rule of law brought from their homeland. They were pragmatic, attempting to adapt practices brought from England rather than reinventing their own as it suited them. When problems arose that were within the realm of the legal system, the community acted appropriately, seeking redress for wrongs within the courts.

Thus when purported witchcraft appeared, church leaders, physicians, and a panicked citizenry turned the problem over to the civil authorities. Witchcraft was a capital crime in all the colonies, and whoever was to blame for it had to be ferreted out and made to stop. Because no one could halt the outbreak of illness, for ten months the community wrestled with sickness, sin, and the criminal act of witchcraft. By September 1692, nineteen convicted

witches had been hanged and more than a hundred people sat in prison awaiting sentencing when the trials at last faded. The next year all were released and the court closed. The craze ended as abruptly as it began.

Or did it? There had been similar sporadic physical complaints blamed on witchcraft going back several decades in New England, to the 1640s when the first executions for the crime of witchcraft were ordered in the colonies. Evidence indicates that people (and domestic animals) had suffered similar physical symptoms and ailments in Europe in still earlier years. After the witch trials ended in Salem, there continued to be complaints of the "Salem symptoms" in Connecticut and New Hampshire, as well as in Boston, into the early eighteenth century. But there were no more hangings. The epidemic and witchcraft had parted ways.

By examining the primary records left by those who suffered from the unexplainable and supposedly diabolical ailments in 1692, we get a clear picture of exactly what they were experiencing. *The Salem Witchcraft Papers,* a three-volume set compiled from the original documents and preserved as typescripts by the Works Progress Administration in the 1930s, has been edited for today's reader by Paul Boyer and Stephen Nissenbaum. It is invaluable for reading the complete and detailed problems people were dealing with. Like sitting in the physician's office with them, we read where the pain started, how it disappeared or progressed, how long they endured it.

A similar epidemic with nearly exact symptoms swept the world from 1916 to 1930. This world-wide pandemic, sleeping sickness, or encephalitis lethargica, eventually claimed more than five million victims. Its cause has never been fully identified. There is no cure. Victims of the twentieth-century epidemic continue under hospitalization to the present day. An excellent source for better understanding encephalitis lethargica is Oliver Sacks's book *Awakenings,* which is now in its sixth edition and has become a cult classic. A movie of the same title, based on the book, presents a very credible look at the physical behaviors patients exhibited during the epidemic. While encephalitis lethargica, in the epidemic form in which it appeared in the early twentieth century, is not active today, outbreaks of insect-borne encephalitis do appear infrequently throughout the country; recent outbreaks of mosquito-borne encephalitis have nearly brought Walt Disney World in Florida to a halt, have caused entire towns to abandon evening football games, and have made horse owners anxious throughout the San Joaquin Valley in California.

Using the legal documents from the Salem witch trials of 1692, as well as contemporary accounts of earlier incidents in the surrounding area, we can identify the "afflictions" that the colonists experienced and that led to the accusations of witchcraft. By comparing the symptoms reported by seventeenth-century colonists with those of patients affected by the encephalitis lethargica epidemic of the early twentieth century, a pattern of symptoms emerges. This pattern supports the hypothesis that the witch-hunts of New England were a response to unexplained physical and neurological behaviors resulting from an epidemic of encephalitis. This was some form of the same encephalitis epidemic that became pandemic in the 1920s. In fact, it is difficult to find anything in the record at Salem that *doesn't* support the idea that the symptoms were caused by that very disease. . . .

What Happened at Salem?

. . . Historical explanations of witchcraft dwell on what Thomas Szasz calls the "scapegoat theory of witchcraft," which explores who was accused and why in the context of larger societal issues. Inevitably they fail to examine the accusers or the "afflicted," who themselves were often tried for witchcraft.

Sociologists have pointed to community-based socioeconomic problems as the causative agent in the events at Salem. They propose that there were really two Salems: Salem Town (a prosperous sector on the well-developed east side of town) and Salem Village (a less-developed, very swampy and rocky area on the west side). Likening Salem Village to a troubled backwater, the accusations and afflictions emanated from the west side, where the residents directed their animosity toward their wealthier, more powerful eastern counterparts by accusing individuals on the east side of witchcraft. Examining the struggles, failures, broken dreams, and lost hopes of the Salem Village residents, sociologists began to view the village as "an inner city on a hill." Social conflict, in this case between prosperous merchants and struggling subsistence farmers, was examined. In the case of the Salem witch hunts, the theory may better explain who was accused and convicted of witchcraft than why individuals were afflicted. Division along class and religious lines has been well documented in determining criminal accusations.

Other investigators have blamed the situation on village factionalism, claiming that Salem Village was rife with suspicious, disgruntled, jealous settlers whose frustrations had festered for years before exploding in the court record with witchcraft accusations and trials. But that does not explain why twenty-two *other* towns in New England were

eventually connected to the proceedings in some way; villagers throughout Maine, New Hampshire, Connecticut, Massachusetts, and Rhode Island were brought into the trial records. Victims, accused witches, and witnesses came from other locales as far away as the Maine frontier. Other locations, such as Connecticut, conducted witch trials that preceded or coincided with those at Salem. Choosing to view the problems as power struggles or personality differences within a small village strikes one as too parochial. Many of the possessed claimants barely knew the people they named as their tormenters, in fact several had never even met the persons they accused of fostering their problems—hardly enough tension to support the idea that the entire uproar was based on long-standing animosities. Socioeconomic divisions did engender problems in the region, and while they ultimately may be used to explain who was accused and why, they do not explain the many physical symptoms or who experienced them.

Carol Karlsen has viewed what happened at Salem in her book *The Devil in the Shape of a Woman*, which relates the events to women's oppressed status within Puritan society. She considers New Englanders' "possession" to have been a cultural performance—a ritual—performed by girls, interpreted by ministers, and observed by an audience as a dramatic event. Karlsen claims the possessed individuals exhibited learned behavior patterns and that words and actions varied only slightly among them. The affected women experienced an inner conflict which was explained by ministers as a struggle between good and evil: God versus Satan. The outcome revolved around whether or not the young women would later lead virtuous lives or fall into sin. Karlsen suggests that a woman's possession was the result of her indecision or ambivalence about choosing the sort of woman she wanted to be. She views the possession as a "collective phenomenon" among women in Connecticut between 1662 and 1663, and in Massachusetts from 1692 to 1693. It was a "ritual expression of Puritan belief and New England's gender arrangements," and a challenge to society. It was ultimately a simple power struggle between women and their oppressors.

As to the physical symptoms: the fits, trances, and paralyzed limbs, among others, Karlsen attributes them to the afflicted girls' actual fear of witches as well as the idea that once they fell into an afflicted state they were free to express unacceptable feelings without reprisal. The swollen throats, extended tongues, and eyes frozen in peripheral stares were manifestations of the inner rage they felt toward society; they were so upset they literally *couldn't* speak. Their paralysis was based on anger over having to work; their inability to walk meant they could not perform their expected labor—in other words, a passive-aggressive response to a situation that incensed them. Karlsen views witchcraft possession in New England as a rebellion against gender and class powers: a psychopathology rooted in female anger.

Misogyny may well explain who was accused of witchcraft, but it lacks an explanation for the wide-ranging symptoms, the ages of the afflicted, and the patterns of symptoms that occurred across time and distance in seventeenth-century New England. Scholars who take this route, however, conveniently ignore the fact that men too were accused, tried, and hanged for witchcraft, both in the colonies and in Europe. In fact, Robin Briggs states that though "every serious historical account recognizes that large numbers of men were accused and executed on similar charges, this fact has never really penetrated to become part of the general knowledge on the subject." His research shows that a misogynistic view of witch-hunts lacks complete credibility.

Many researchers have proposed that mass hysteria affected the young women of Salem. The term *hysteria*, essentially a female complaint, has recently been dropped from use by the psychiatric profession in favor of "conversion symptom," which describes the manner in which neurotic patients suffer emotional stress brought on by an unconscious source. This stress or tension can undergo "conversion" and reveal itself in a variety of physical ailments. Conversion, a very pliable disorder, can be explained by almost any societal pressure in any particular culture. It is a psychological catchall for unexplained neurological or emotional problems. But its victims are always the same, according to analysts: unstable females.

Jean-Martin Charcot, a French physician, worked extensively with epileptic and hysteric female patients at the Salpêtrière Hospital in Paris between 1862 and 1870. He laid the groundwork for hysteria theory, calling it hystero-epilepsy. He accused his patients of being deceitful, clever actresses who delighted in fooling the male physician. Charcot's medical students claimed to be able to transfer diseases from hysterics with the use of magnets, something they called the "metal cure." Eventually his professional standing as a neurologist diminished and faded, and he turned to faith healing. Sigmund Freud, one of his students, began his work under Charcot's direction.

A more modern version of the hysteria complex is called Mass Psychogenic Illness, or MPI, which is defined as the contagious spread of behavior within a group of individuals where one person serves as the catalyst or "starter" and the others imitate the behavior. Used to describe situations where mass illness breaks out in the school or workplace, it is usually connected to a toxic agent—real or imagined—in a less than satisfactory institutional or factory setting. MPI is the sufferer's response to overwhelming life and work stress. It relies on the individual's identification with the index case (the first one to get sick, in effect the "leader") and willingness to succumb to the same illness. A classical outbreak of MPI involves a group of segregated young females in a noisy, crowded, high-intensity setting. It is most common in Southeast Asian factories crowded with young female workers; adults are not usually affected. Symptoms appear, spread, and subside rapidly (usually over one day). Physical manifestations usually include fainting, malaise, convulsions with hyperventilation, and excitement. Transmission is by sight or sound brought about by a triggering factor which affects members of the group, who share some degree of unconscious fantasies. A phenomenon more related to the industrial world of the nineteenth and twentieth centuries than to pastoral village life in colonial New England, MPI does not address the question of why men and young children, who would not have identified emotionally and psychologically with a group of young girls, suffered. The New England colonists scarcely fit the pattern for this illness theory that demands large groups of people of similar age, sex, and personality assembled in one confined location.

Salem's witches cannot, of course, escape Freudian critique. Beyond the hysteria hypothesis, John Demos, in *Entertaining Satan,* looked at the evidence from the perspective of modern psychoanalysis. He pointed out that witchcraft explained and excused people's mistakes or incompetence—a failure or mistake blamed on witches allowed a cathartic cleansing of personal responsibility. Witches served a purpose; deviant people served as models to the rest of society to exemplify socially unacceptable behavior. But Demos's explanation that witch-hunts were an integral part of social experience, something that bound the community together—sort of a public works project—does not address the physical symptoms of the sufferers.

For the most part, examinations of the afflicted individuals at Salem have focused on the young women, essentially placing the blame on them instead of exploring an organic cause for their behaviors. Freudian explanations for the goings-on have attributed the activities of the possessed girls to a quest for attention. Their physical manifestations of illness have been explained as being conversion symptoms due to intrapsychic conflict. Their physical expression of psychological conflict is a compromise between unacceptable impulses and the mind's attempt to ignore them. Demos uses the example of Elizabeth Knapp, whose fits became increasingly severe while strangers gathered to view her behavior. Instead of considering that she was beset by an uncontrollable series of convulsions which were likely worsened by the excited witnesses who refused to leave her alone, he attributes her worsening condition to her exhibitionist tendencies, motivated by strong dependency needs. Elizabeth's writhing on the floor in a fetal position is seen as an oral dependency left over from childhood, causing her regression to infancy.

But "inner conflict" simply does not explain the events at Salem. Neither does the idea that the young afflicted girls were motivated by an erotic attraction to church ministers who were called in to determine whether Satan was involved. The girls' repressed adolescent sexual wishes (one girl was only eleven years old) and their seeking a replacement for absent father figures scarcely explains the toll the disease was taking on victims of both sexes and all ages. No Freudian stone has been left unturned by scholars; even the "genetic reconstruction" of Elizabeth Knapp's past points out that her childhood was filled with unmet needs, her mother's frustration because of an inability to bear additional children, and her father's reputation as a suspected adulterer. "Narcissistic depletion," "psychological transference," "a tendency to fragment which was temporarily neutralized"—the psycho-lingo just about stumbles over itself in attempts to explain the afflicted girls at Salem. But unanswered questions remain: Why the sharp pains in extremities? The hallucinations? The hyperactivity? The periods of calm between sessions of convulsions? Why did other residents swear in court that they had seen marks appear on the arms of the afflicted?

The opinion that the victims were creating their own fits as challenges to authority and quests for fame has shaped most interpretations of what happened in 1692. But would the colonists have strived for public notice and attention? If the afflicted individuals were behaving unusually to garner public notice, why? Did women and men of that era really crave public attention, or would it have put them in awkward, critical, and socially unacceptable situations? How socially redeeming would writhing on the ground "like a hog" and emitting strange noises, "barking like a dog," or "bleating like a calf" be for a destitute young servant girl who hoped to marry above her station? It is difficult to accept that these spectacles, which horrified viewers as well as the participants themselves, were actually a positive experience for the young women. That sort of suspicious activity usually met with social stigma, shunning, or, at the least, brutal whipping from father or master.

Puberty, a time of inner turmoil, is thought to have contributed to the victims acting out through fits, convulsions, and erratic behavior. The victims' inability to eat is explained away as a disorder related to the youthful struggle for individuality: anorexia nervosa. What about the young men who reported symptoms? Freudian interpretation attributes their behavior to rebellion against controlling fathers. How have psycho-social interpretations explained the reason witch trials ended after 1692 in Salem? As communities grew into larger urban units, people no longer knew their neighbors, grudges receded in importance as a factor in social control, and witches were no longer valuable to society. John Demos observes that witchcraft never appeared in cities, and that it lasted longest in villages far removed from urban influence. That linkage between witchcraft outbreaks and agricultural villages is important when establishing a connection with outbreaks of encephalitis lethargica, which appeared largely in small towns and rural areas in the early twentieth century. Rather than accepting the idea that witchcraft receded because it was no longer useful in a community context, one must examine why epidemics occurred in waves and how particular diseases affected isolated population groups.

The situation in seventeenth-century New England fails psycho-social explanation because too many questions remain unanswered. Not only can we not make a strong case that infantilism, sexual repression, and a struggle for individuality caused the turmoil in Salem, but a psycho-social explanation does not answer why the symptoms, which were so *obviously physical,* appeared with such force and then, in the autumn of 1692, largely disappeared from Salem.

Because the complexity of psychological and social factors connected with interpreting witchcraft is so absorbing, the existence of a physical pathology behind the events at Salem has long been overlooked. Linnda Caporeal, a graduate student in psychology, proposed that ergot, a fungus that appears on rye crops, caused the hallucinogenic poisoning in Salem. Her article appeared in 1976 in *Science* while Americans were trying to understand the LSD drug phenomenon. Hers is one of the few attempts made to link the puzzling occurrences at Salem with biological evidence.

Ergot was identified by a French scientist in 1676, in an explanation of the relation between ergotized rye and bread poisoning. It is a fungus that contains several potent pharmacologic agents, the ergot alkaloids. One of these alkaloids is lysergic acid amide, which has ten percent of the activity of LSD (lysergic acid diethylamide). This sort of substance causes convulsions or gangrenous deterioration of the extremities. Caporeal proposed that an ergot infestation in the Salem area might explain the convulsions attributed to witchcraft. If grain crops had been infected with ergot fungus during the 1692 rainy season and later stored away, the fungus might have grown in the storage area and spread to the entire crop. When it was distributed randomly among friends and villagers, they would have become affected by the poisoned grain.

Caporeal's innovative thinking was challenged by psychologists Nicholas Spanos and Jack Gottlieb, who were quick to point out that her theory did not explain why, if food poisoning were to blame, families who ate from the same source of grain were not affected. And infants were afflicted who may not have been eating bread grains. Historically, epidemics of ergotism have appeared in areas where there was a severe vitamin A deficiency in the diet. Salem residents had plenty of milk and seafood available; they certainly did not suffer from vitamin A deficiency. Ergotism also involves extensive vomiting and diarrhea, symptoms not found in the Salem cases. A hearty appetite, almost ravenous, follows ergotism; in New England the afflicted wasted away from either an inability to eat or a lack of interest in it. The sudden onset of the Salem symptoms in late winter and early spring would be hard to trace to months of eating contaminated grain. Ergot was never seriously considered as the cause of problems at Salem, even by the colonists themselves who knew what ergotism was (it had been identified sixteen years earlier) and were trying desperately to discover the source of their problems.

An explanation that satisfies many of the unanswered questions about the events at Salem is that the symptoms reported by the afflicted New Englanders and their families in the seventeenth century were the result of an unrecognized epidemic of encephalitis. Comparisons may be made between the afflictions reported at Salem (as well as the rest of seventeenth-century New England) and the encephalitis lethargica pandemic of the early twentieth century. This partial list, created from the literature, reveals how similar the two epidemics were, in spite of the variation in medical terms of the day:

1692 SALEM	1916–1930s ENCEPHALITIS EPIDEMIC
fits	convulsions
spectral visions	hallucinations
mental "distraction"	psychoses
pinching, pricking	myoclonus of small muscle bundles on skin surface
"bites"	erythmata on skin surface, capillary hemorrhaging
eyes twisted	oculogyric crises: gaze fixed upward, downward, or to the side
inability to walk	paresis: partial paralysis
neck twisted	torticollis: spasm of neck muscles forces head to one side, spasms affect trunk and neck
repeating nonsense words	palilalia: repetition of one's own words

In both times, most of the afflicted were young women or children; the children were hit hardest, several dying in their cradles from violent fits. The afflictions appeared in late winter and early spring and receded with the heat of summer. . . . Von Economo noted that most encephalitis lethargica epidemics had historically shown the greatest number of acute cases occurring in the first quarter of the year, from midwinter to the beginning of spring. The "pricking and pinching" repeated so often in the court records at Salem can be explained by the way patients' skin surfaces exhibited twitches—quick, short, fluttering sequences of contractions of muscle bundles. Cold temperatures cause them to increase in number and spread over the body. Twitches were seldom absent in cases of hyperkinetic encephalitis lethargica during the 1920s epidemic. The skin surface also exhibited a peculiar disturbance in which red areas appeared due to dilation and congestion of the capillaries. Red marks that bleed through the skin's surface would explain the many references in court documents to suspected bites made by witches.

Examining the colonists' complaints in the trial papers uncovers many other symptom similarities: inability to walk, terrifying hallucinations, sore throat, or choking—the list goes on and on. . . .

Ultimately the witch-hunts—or at least the complaints of afflictions—ended in Salem in the autumn of 1692, and there were no more complaints the following year. An arboviral encephalitis epidemic would have receded in the fall, when the air and water grew too cold for mosquitoes' survival. By the time spring arrived, the situation had altered, and the epidemic appeared to fade. Encephalitis epidemics, like many other contagious epidemics, often recede for years—sometimes decades—between recrudescence periods. Either the agents mutate and disappear to return years later, or they run out of susceptible hosts—the only ones left are those who have an immunity to the infection.

Ticks too might have been to blame. Just as in the spread of tick-borne encephalitis throughout the northern region of Russia, ticks played a part in spreading the disease across the virgin forests of temperate North America. Peasants who worked in the forest as woodcutters were affected in Russia during the epidemic of the 1950s; in Salem, in the seventeenth century, residents also worked as woodcutters and loggers. The Putnam family, in particular, were engaged in logging and woodcutting (and in fact were involved in arguments over whether they were taking logs from property they did not own). If the Putnams brought ticks bearing disease into their homes on their bodies or clothing, other members might have been affected. Reverend Parris's household could have been infected from the large amount of firewood he negotiated to supply his family, as part of his salary. Because they were his strongest supporters, the Putnams would likely have been the ones to cut and deliver the wood to his doorstep. Firewood, in the form of large logs used in colonial fireplaces, might have harbored wood ticks that had gone into winter hibernation but came out of the bark when logs were stored beside the hearth in a warm New England house. Infestations of ticks and body lice were common in colonial homes where laundry could not be done during the winter (nowhere to dry the wet clothing) and baths were rarely taken.

Another disease that results in encephalitis is endemic to the New England area even today. Lyme disease is a contemporary problem in New England, and there is little reason to think that it would have been absent from the area in colonial times. It is an infectious disease caused by bacteria spread by deer ticks. Both people and animals can be infected with Lyme disease. It is a serious but not fatal disease today. Found throughout the United States, it is most common along the East Coast, the Great Lakes, and the Pacific Northwest. In Massachusetts, deer ticks are most often found along the coast and are common in the Connecticut River Valley. The disease most likely spreads between late May and early autumn, when ticks are active. So tiny that the larvae are no bigger than a pencil point, the ticks live for two years, during which they can infect wild and domestic animals as well as people.

Symptoms of Lyme disease include a rash where the tick was attached—which may appear anywhere between three days and a month after the innocuous bite. Sometimes the rash looks like a small red doughnut. Other signs include itching, hives, swollen eyelids, and flulike symptoms such as fever, headache, stiff neck, sore muscles, fatigue, sore throat, and swollen glands. The symptoms go away after a few weeks, but without medical treatment nearly half the infected people will experience the rash again in other places on their bodies. In the later stages, three major areas—the joints, the nervous system, and the heart—may be affected even months after the tick bite. People with Lyme disease can develop late-stage symptoms even if they have never had the rash. About 10 to 20 percent of the people who do not get treatment develop nervous system problems: severe headache, stiff neck, facial paralysis, or cranial nerve palsies, and weakness and/or pain in their hands, arms, feet, or legs. Symptoms may last for weeks, often shifting from mild to severe and back again.

These symptoms are found in the present form of Lyme disease; the disease could likely have mutated over the centuries, because hallucinations and paranoia, along with lethargy, are not found in today's tick-borne version of Lyme disease. Questions and problems arise when connecting Lyme disease to the situations in 1692 or 1920, but it is another factor to consider. Could ticks have been common in Salem? The colonists did not bathe regularly, and they lived close by their domestic animals. Ticks could have wintered inside the home, carried in on firewood. They would have found ample hiding places in the seams of the heavy woolen clothing commonly worn by the colonists.

What about 1920? A common nuisance of that era was the "bedbug," chinch bug, or *Cimex lectularius*. Jar lids filled with arsenic were placed under bedsteads to keep the critters from climbing into bed and feeding on people's blood. Head lice have been common throughout the ages; today's rampant epidemics in schools are nothing to ignore, though scientists reassure us that neither bedbugs nor head lice carry any type of disease. Perhaps they did at one time. Many avenues must be explored, much research must be done. Perhaps we will never know what caused encephalitis lethargica. . . .

Laurie Winn Carlson is an assistant professor of history at Western Oregon University. She is the author of several scholarly historical studies, including *Cattle: An Informal Social History* (Ivan R. Dee, 2002); *Seduced by the West: Jefferson's America and the Lure of Land Beyond the Mississippi* (Ivan R. Dee, 2003); and *William J. Spillman and the Birth of Agricultural Economics* (University of Missouri Press, 2005).

EXPLORING THE ISSUE

Were Socioeconomic Tensions Responsible for the Witchcraft Hysteria in Salem?

Critical Thinking and Reflection

1. Compare and contrast the characteristics of witchcraft accusers and accused in Salem.
2. What were the basic differences between the residents who lived in Salem Town and those who resided in Salem Village?
3. What do Boyer and Nissenbaum's conclusions suggest about the consequences of material growth and progress in colonial America?
4. What specific evidence does Laurie Winn Carlson give to support her interpretation of the events in Salem in 1692? How persuasive is her argument?

Is There Common Ground?

The Salem witch hysteria and subsequent trials and executions were an unfortunate, but not unique, event and must be understood within the larger context of attitudes toward the supernatural. While Salem seems always to attract the attention of the curious among students and the general public, scholars are well aware that similar episodes erupted in Western Europe and other parts of the American colonies. Because the vast majority of those accused of practicing witchcraft were women, it is no surprise that some historians would focus on the nature of gender relations in the colonies to gain a better understanding of why these accusations occurred and why they were believed by so many.

At the same time, the accusations can be viewed from a much broader perspective of political, economic, and social transformations that were occurring in the late seventeenth century and which generated enormous tensions and anxieties among the people experiencing that changing world. A comparative framework could be established that examines peoples' reactions to the profound changes produced by rapid industrialization and the shift from rural to urban values that took place in the late nineteenth century or the fears demonstrated by many Americans in the post–World War II era as they attempted to come to grips with the atomic age and the rising power of the Soviet Union.

Dramatic changes often spawn concerns about the impact of such changes on individuals within society. The Carlson essay, however, takes the discussion of Salem in an entirely different direction and reinforces the importance of our willingness to recognize the impact of biological forces in history. This recognition relates well to historical arguments made by William McNeill, Jared Sparks, and Alfred Crosby, among others, regarding the influence of germs in shaping human history.

Create Central

www.mhhe.com/createcentral

Additional Resources

Paul Boyer and Stephen Nissenbaum, eds., *Salem-Village Witchcraft: A Documentary Record of Local Conflict in Colonial New England* (Northeastern University Press, 1993)

Elaine G. Breslaw, *Tituba, Reluctant Witch of Salem: Devilish Indians and Puritan Fantasies* (New York University Press, 1995)

Larry Gragg, *The Salem Witch Crisis* (Praeger, 1992)

Frances Hill, ed., *The Salem Witch Trials Reader* (Da Capo Press, 2000)

Bernard Rosenthal, *Salem Story: Reading the Witch Trials of 1692* (Cambridge University Press, 1993)

Internet References . . .

Famous American Trials: Salem Witchcraft Trials, 1692

law.umkc.edu/faculty/projects/ftrials/salem/salem.htm

National Geographic Salem Witch Hunt

www.nationalgeographic.com/features/97/salem/

Salem Witch Trials

school.discoveryeducation.com/schooladventures/salemwitchtrials

Salem Witch Trials Documentary Archive

salem.lib.virginia.edu/home.html

The Salem Witch Trials of 1692

www.salemwitchmuseum.com/education/

Selected, Edited, and with Issue Framing Material by:
Larry Madaras, *Howard Community College*
and
James M. SoRelle, *Baylor University*

ISSUE

Was There a Great Awakening in Mid-Eighteenth-Century America?

YES: **Thomas S. Kidd,** from *The Great Awakening: The Roots of Evangelical Christianity in Colonial America,* Yale University Press (2007)

NO: **Jon Butler,** from "The Plural Origins of American Revivalism," Harvard University Press (1990)

Learning Outcomes

After reading this issue, you will be able to:

- Discuss the role played by religion in the British North American colonies.
- Identify George Whitefield and explain his contributions to the Great Awakening.
- Understand the origins, goals, leaders, and consequences of the First Great Awakening.
- Evaluate the relationship between evangelical Protestantism and democracy in early America.
- Identify multiple factors that contributed to colonial American religious life in the eighteenth century.

ISSUE SUMMARY

YES: Thomas Kidd insists that preachers such as George Whitefield engineered a powerful series of revivals in the mid-eighteenth century that influenced all of the British North American colonies and gave birth to a spirit of evangelicalism that initiated a major alteration of global Christian history.

NO: Jon Butler claims that to describe the religious revival activities of the eighteenth century as the "Great Awakening" is to seriously exaggerate their extent, nature, and impact on prerevolutionary American society and politics.

Although generations of American schoolchildren have been taught that the British colonies in North America were founded by persons fleeing religious persecution in England, the truth is that many of those early settlers were motivated by other factors, some of which had little to do with theological preferences. To be sure, the Pilgrims and Puritans of New England sought to escape the proscriptions established by the Church of England. Many New Englanders, however, did not adhere to the precepts of Calvinism and therefore were viewed as outsiders. The Quakers who populated Pennsylvania were mostly fugitives from New England, where they had been victims of religious persecution. But to apply religious motivations to the earliest settlers of Virginia, South Carolina, or Georgia is to engage in a serious misreading of the historical record. Even in New England the religious mission of Massachusetts Bay Colony Governor John Winthrop's "city upon a hill" began to erode as the colonial settlements matured and stabilized.

Although religion was a central element in the lives of the seventeenth- and eighteenth-century Europeans who migrated to the New World, proliferation of religious sects and denominations, emphasis upon material gain in all parts of the colonies, and the predominance of reason over emotion that is associated with the Deists of the Enlightenment period all contributed to a gradual but obvious movement of the colonists away from the church and clerical authority. William Bradford of Plymouth Colony, for example, expressed grave concern that many Plymouth residents were following a path of perfidy, and Pennsylvania founder William Penn was certain that the "holy experiment" of the Quakers had failed. Colonial clergy, fearful that a fall from grace was in progress, issued calls for a revival of religious fervor. The spirit of revivalism that spread through the colonies in the 1730s and 1740s, therefore, was an answer to these clerical prayers.

The episode known as the First Great Awakening coincided with the Pietistic movement in Europe and England and was carried forward by dynamic preachers such as Gilbert Tennant, Theodore Frelinghuysen, and George Whitefield. They promoted a religion of the heart, not of the head, in order to produce a spiritual rebirth. These revivals, most historians agree, reinvigorated American Protestantism. Many new congregations were organized as a result of irremediable schisms between "Old Lights" and "New Lights." Skepticism about the desirability of an educated clergy sparked a strong strain of anti-intellectualism. Also, the emphasis on conversion was a message to which virtually everyone could respond, regardless of age, sex, race, or social status.

For some historians, the implications of the Great Awakening extended beyond the religious sphere into the realm of politics and were incorporated into the American Revolution. William G. McLoughlin's essay "'Enthusiasm for Liberty': The Great Awakening as the Key to the Revolution," in Jack P. Greene and William G. McLoughlin, eds., *Preachers & Politicians: Two Essays on the Origins of the American Revolution* (American Antiquarian Society, 1977), claims that the Great Awakening paved the way for the American Revolution by promoting religious revitalization, inter-colonial unity, and democracy. In his book *Religion in America: Past and Present* (Prentice-Hall, 1961), Clifton E. Olmstead argues for a broader application of religious causes to the origins of the American Revolution. First, and consistent with McLoughlin and others, Olmstead contends that the Great Awakening did foster a sense of community among American colonists, thus providing the unity required for an organized assault on English control. Moreover, the Awakening further weakened existing ties between colonies and Mother Country by drawing adherents of the Church of England into the evangelical denominations that expanded as a result of revivalist Protestantism. Second, tensions were generated by the demand that an Anglican bishop be established in the colonies. Many evangelicals found in this plan

evidence that the British government wanted further control over the colonies. Third, the Quebec Act, enacted by Parliament in 1774, not only angered American colonists by nullifying their claims to western lands, but also heightened religious prejudice in the colonies by granting tolerance to Roman Catholics. Fourth, ministers played a significant role in encouraging their parishioners to support the independence movement. Olmstead claims that Congregationalist, Presbyterian, Dutch Reformed, and Baptist ministers overwhelmingly defended this revolutionary movement in the colonies. Finally, many of the revolutionaries, imbued with the American sense of mission, believed that God was ordaining their revolutionary activities.

Further support for these views can be found in Alan Heimert, *Religion and the American Mind from the Great Awakening to the Revolution* (Cambridge University Press, 1966); Cedric B. Cowing, *The Great Awakening and the American Revolution: Colonial Thought in the Eighteenth Century* (University of Chicago, 1971); Richard Hofstadter, *America at 1750: A Social Portrait* (Knopf, 1973); Rhys Isaac, *The Transformation of Virginia, 1740–1790* (University of North Carolina Press, 1982); Ruth H. Bloch, *Visionary Republic* (Cambridge University Press, 1985); Patricia U. Bonomi, *Under the Cope of Heaven: Religion, Society, and Politics in Colonial America* (Oxford University Press, 1986); Harry S. Stout, *The New England Soul: Preaching and Religious Culture in Colonial New England* (Oxford University Press, 1986); and Mark A. Noll, *Christians in the American Revolution* (Regent College Publishing, 2006).

In the following selections, Thomas S. Kidd writes from the traditional assumption that a powerful revivalist force known as the "Great Awakening" occurred in the American colonies in the mid-eighteenth century. Recognizing that these revivals began before 1740 and continued well into the Revolutionary era, Kidd focuses on the activities of George Whitefield in the early 1740s. In his essay, Kidd challenges Jon Butler's contention that the influence of the Great Awakening was limited to New England and produced little change in colonial American religion. In contrast, Kidd argues that the Great Awakening produced a powerful impact in the colonies and sparked a rise in evangelical fervor that would have significant implications for global Christianity.

Jon Butler's revisionist essay questions the importance and even the existence of a cohesive, colony-wide period of revivalism that deserves to be called a "Great Awakening." Scholars' obsession with the Great Awakening, according to Butler, is in fact an "interpretive fiction" that obscures several other aspects of eighteenth-century American religious development that proved far more consequential. For example, Butler focuses more attention on state church traditions prior to 1740 and religious pluralism and doctrinal diversity after as the essential traits of colonial American religious life and concludes that, despite the revivals led by itinerants such as George Whitefield, most colonists exhibited an indifference to religion that was not significantly reversed until the nineteenth century.

YES ⬅

Thomas S. Kidd

The Great Awakening: The Roots of Evangelical Christianity in Colonial America

... Until 1982, historians took the Great Awakening as a given, but then historian Jon Butler argued that it was only an "interpretative fiction" invented by nineteenth-century Christian historians. Although Butler's argument was overextended, it helpfully provoked a revaluation of what we actually mean by "the Great Awakening." He contended that the event really amounted to just "a short-lived Calvinist revival in New England during the early 1740s." No doubt the eighteenth-century awakenings were centered in New England, but over time they came to influence parts of all the colonies, and more important, they helped birth an enormously important religious movement, evangelicalism, which shows no sign of disappearing today.

Butler also asserted that the "revivals had modest effects on colonial religion" and that they were "never radical." But if the revivals helped create evangelicalism, then not only did the awakenings make a profound change in colonial religion, but they began a major alteration of global Christian history. Moreover, ... the revivals featured all manner of radical spiritual manifestations, unnerving antirevivalists and moderate evangelicals alike. Butler's critique does show, however, that it is not enough to evaluate evangelicalism as a homogenous whole. It had radical implications, but those implications were hotly contested by moderates, and its social potential often came to naught for women, African Americans, and Native Americans. Some evangelicals also began a great assault on the churchly establishments of colonial America, and the revolutionary move for disestablishment on the federal and state levels can largely be attributed to evangelical and deist cooperation in favor of the separation of church and state.

Butler finally claimed that, contrary to the suggestions of previous scholars, "the link between the revivals and the American Revolution is virtually nonexistent." ...

I am in substantial agreement with Butler on this point. Moreover, evangelicals' responses to the Revolution covered the whole range of opinions from enthusiastic Patriotism to staunch Loyalism. But we should also note that evangelical rhetoric and ideology helped to inspire and justify the Patriot cause for both evangelical and nonevangelical leaders. Evangelicalism did not start the Revolution, but the Patriot side certainly benefited from the support of many evangelicals.

... I contend that there was, indeed, a powerful, unprecedented series of revivals from about 1740 to 1743 that touched many of the colonies and that contemporaries remembered for decades as a special visitation of the Holy Spirit. Calling this event "the" Great Awakening does present historical problems. Chief among them is that the standard framework of the "First" and "Second" Great Awakenings may obscure the fact that the evangelical movement continued to develop after 1743 and before 1800. There were important, widespread revivals that happened before the First, and between the First and Second, Great Awakenings. ... I examine, instead, what we might call the *long* First Great Awakening and the contest to define its boundaries. Although many revivals, including the major season from 1740 to 1743, happened during this period, revivals alone did not delineate the early evangelical movement. Instead, persistent desires for revival, widespread individual conversions, and the outpouring of the Holy Spirit distinguished the new evangelicals. The long First Great Awakening started before Jonathan Edwards's 1734–35 Northampton revival and lasted roughly through the end of the American Revolution, when disestablishment, theological change, and a new round of growth started the (even more imprecise) "Second" Great Awakening. The controversial emergence of the religion of the new birth demarcated the long First Great Awakening and the first generation of American evangelical Christianity.

Kidd, Thomas S. From *The Great Awakening: The Roots of Evangelical Christianity in Colonial America* (Yale University Press, 2007), pp. xviii–xix, 83–90, 91, 92–93 (excerpts). Copyright © 2007 by Yale University. Reprinted by permission of Yale University Press.

. . . New Englanders began to hear about George Whitefield in 1739, and many hoped that he would soon visit them. Benjamin Colman of Boston's Brattle Street Church wrote to Whitefield in December 1739 after having received a letter from him. Whitefield estimated that he might come to New England by summer 1740. Colman was deeply impressed by what he had learned about Whitefield. He had read Whitefield's *Journals,* as well as some of his sermons. Colman wrote that he had never encountered anything comparable to Whitefield's ministry, although he had witnessed "uncommon Operations of the holy Spirit . . . ; as in our Country of Hampshire of late; the Narrative of which by Mr. Edwards, I suppose you may have seen." If Whitefield would come to New England, he would find the churches' Calvinist doctrine to his liking, "how short soever we may come of your Fervours." Colman told him that the churches had been praying for him publicly, and that when he arrived he could use the commodious Brattle Street Church for meetings. In a letter to Gilbert Tennent, Whitefield wrote that he found Colman's published sermons "acute and pointed, but I think not searching enough by many degrees." If anything, Colman was too polite for Whitefield. Nevertheless, Whitefield wrote back to Colman and promised that when he came to New England "I shall endeavour to recommend an universal charity amongst all the true members of CHRIST's mystical body." Because of this universal spirit, he suggested that he might stay in the fields to preach, and out of the meetinghouses. He appreciated Colman's latitudinarianism, and they both hoped that the old division of Anglican versus dissenter would become irrelevant in light of the ministry of the new birth.

Jonathan Edwards also received word of Whitefield's revivals, and in November 1739 Whitefield wrote to him, desiring to visit Northampton to see for himself the fruit of the 1734–35 awakening. Edwards wrote back in February 1740, encouraging Whitefield to travel to Northampton but warning him not to expect much. Edwards was heartened by God's raising up Whitefield in the Church of England "to revive the mysterious, spiritual, despised, and exploded doctrines of the gospel." This might be a sign of the coming Kingdom of God, Edwards thought.

The Boston and Philadelphia newspapers began picking up stories about Whitefield's prodigious meetings in England in spring 1739, and Whitefield's fame began to spread into the hinterlands by early 1740. For instance, pastor Nicholas Gilman of Exeter, New Hampshire, on a visit to Boston, began reading Whitefield's *Journals* in mid-January 1740 and commented with admiration on Whitefield's "most Indefatigable labours to Advance the Kingdom of Christ." He borrowed more of Whitefield's sermons from Colman. In June, Gilman noted that "Mr. Whitefield [was] Now much the Subject of Conversations."

In July, Whitefield wrote to Colman to announce that he was coming soon, perhaps within a month, and to ask Colman to spread the word in friendly churches. This advance publicity worked wonderfully, and when Whitefield arrived in Newport. Rhode Island, on September 14, 1740, New England was abuzz with talk of his coming. In Newport, Whitefield was welcomed by Nathaniel Clap, a venerable Congregational minister, and the wandering Jonathan Barber of Oysterponds, Long Island. Whitefield had earlier written the disconsolate Barber, telling him that he did not presume to judge whatever dealings God had with him. As for his visionary experiences, "I rather rejoice in them, having myself been blessed with many experiences of the like nature." He told Barber to expect persecution when God dealt with him in extraordinary ways. These encouraging words led Barber to come to Newport to receive Whitefield. Upon meeting, they agreed that Barber would become part of Whitefield's entourage.

After some successes in preaching, particularly at Clap's meetinghouse, Whitefield traveled north to Boston, where he arrived on September 18. Boston was the largest town in the colonies but still only a small provincial capital with about 17,000 people. In 1740, it was in decline, and it would slowly lose population up through the American Revolution. War with Spain, and later with France, left many widows in Boston, and the city faced high taxes and inflation. The poor in Boston were many, and they responded exuberantly to Whitefield, as they would to the radical piety of James Davenport and others.

As usual, Whitefield met with Anglican authorities in Boston, most notably the Commissary Timothy Cutler, the former Congregationalist rector of Yale turned Anglican "apostate." Cutler was the most formidable proponent of Anglicanism in the colonies, and he and Whitefield did not see eye to eye about Whitefield's relationship with non-Anglicans. Cutler argued that dissenters had no legitimate ordination because they did not follow in the line of apostolic succession. Whitefield thought their ordinations were legitimate, primarily because they preached the new birth: "I saw regenerate souls among the Baptists, among the Presbyterians, among the Independents, and among the Church folks—all children of God, and yet all born again in a different way of worship," he told Cutler. Whitefield was able to leave Cutler on friendly terms, but he would receive a much warmer welcome among the Congregationalists, especially from Benjamin Colman. After visiting Cutler he preached at the Brattle Street Church to about four thousand.

Whitefield spoke from supporters' Boston pulpits as well as on Boston Common. On September 20, he preached at Joseph Sewall's Old South Church to about six thousand, and in the afternoon he addressed a crowd at the common that he estimated at eight thousand, although the papers guessed five thousand. The next day he attended Sunday morning services at the Brattle Street Church and spoke at Thomas Foxcroft's Old Brick Church in the afternoon. The crowd pressing to see him was so large that he went out to the common again and preached to an enormous assembly he totaled at fifteen thousand, close to the whole population of Boston (the newspapers guessed eight thousand). On Monday morning he sermonized at John Webb's New North Church to about six thousand. Then, in the afternoon, tragedy struck the tour. At Samuel Checklcy's New South Church, the sound of a breaking board in the gallery triggered a stampede among the overflow crowd. A number of people were severely trampled, and some jumped from the balcony. Five people died. Whitefield decided to go on with the message he planned to deliver, only moving out to the common. No doubt this suggested insensitivity in Whitefield's character, but the crowd wanted him to go on, and one could hardly imagine a better moment for people to contemplate their mortality.

Whitefield visited Harvard and was not impressed with the size of the school or its spirit. He noted that "bad books," such as those by John Tillotson and Samuel Clarke, defenders of natural religion, were popular there, not the Puritan classics. Whitefield would later regret his harsh assessment of Harvard and Yale and would become a great supporter of the colleges. Whitefield also toured neighboring towns, including Roxbury and Charlestown, in his circuit. On September 27, Whitefield preached to one of his greatest crowds yet, fifteen thousand, on the common. Many were deeply affected, and Whitefield himself wrote that he felt like shouting, "This is no other than the House of God and the Gate of Heaven." Boston Common had become a portal to divine glory.

Whitefield began taking collections for the Bethesda Orphanage, and the number of pounds given was truly remarkable: perhaps £3,000 in local currency. Boston outpaced collections even in London. On September 28 alone, he collected more than £1,000 in services at the Old South and Brattle Street churches. After speaking at Brattle Street in the afternoon, Whitefield held two private meetings that showed the breadth of his appeal. The first was with the governor, Jonathan Belcher, who was an evangelical supporter of Whitefield. The second was with "a great number of negroes," who requested a private session with him. He preached to them on the conversion of the Ethiopian in Acts 8.

Whitefield visited towns up the coast from Boston from September 29 to October 6, finding some successes but also a great deal of passivity. Maine and New Hampshire had a substantial revival tradition, having seen large numbers of conversions and admissions to full communion in the 1727–28 earthquake awakening, and to a lesser extent in 1735–36 as a devastating "throat distemper" (diphtheria) raged there. He preached as far north as York, Maine, at the church of the well-respected Samuel Moody. His northern tour gave Nicholas Gilman of Exeter, who had been reading Whitefield's *Journals* and sermons for almost a year, a chance to meet him. Gilman was perhaps not as adulatory in his initial response to Whitefield as one might expect, noting that "there are Various Conjectures about Mr. Whitefield," but expressing hope that he truly was "a Man of an Excellent Spirit." Whitefield's appearance precipitated a conversion crisis for Gilman, as well, and set him on the path to becoming one of the most radical of New England's evangelicals. Whitefield won some notable converts in Maine, especially John Rogers. The pastor at Kittery, Rogers had been in the ministry for thirty years when he heard Whitefield, but he had never experienced conversion. Whitefield's ministry convinced him of his need for the new birth, and afterwards he became one of Whitefield's foremost proponents in Maine. Rogers's son Daniel, a tutor at Harvard, would soon join Whitefield's entourage and seek his own assurance of salvation. The revivals in Maine and New Hampshire would not begin in force until late 1741, however.

Returning to Boston, Whitefield continued seeing large audiences, but he also gravitated toward Tennent's confrontational style as he spoke against unconverted ministers. "I am persuaded," he wrote in his journal, "[that] the generality of preachers talk of an unknown and unfelt Christ." He felt energized by confronting the unsaved clergy: "Unspeakable freedom God gave me while treating on this head." Although some of the ministers may have grown uneasy at such talk, Whitefield drew ever-larger crowds, until he finally announced a farewell sermon on October 12, which drew a crowd estimated at twenty thousand. If reasonably accurate, this was the largest crowd ever assembled in America up to that time.

From Boston, Whitefield traveled west through New England. Delivering on his promise, Whitefield went slightly out of his way to visit Northampton. It was a poignant occasion for Edwards, who had waited five long years for revival fire to reignite in Northampton. Edwards shed tears during Whitefield's preaching. Whitefield, too, was deeply affected by his visit and impressed with Edwards's wife and children, who seemed to him models of piety and propriety. Whitefield's preaching in Northampton reached a crescendo on the Sabbath, as "Mr. Edwards wept during the whole time of exercise" in the morning. "Mr. Whitefield's sermons were suitable to the circumstances of the town," Edwards wrote later to Thomas Prince, "containing just reproofs of our back-slidings." He reported to Whitefield that the revival bore lasting fruit, including the conversion of some of the Edwardses' children. Immediately after Whitefield's departure, however, Edwards did begin a sermon series on the parable of the sower (Matthew 13), including warnings that short-lived episodes of heated preaching and crying did not make for saving religion. He subtly warned that Whitefield's brand of revivalism was ripe for religious hypocrisy. Edwards would continue to support Whitefield, but he insisted that Northampton would experience revival on his terms.

Accompanied by Edwards, Whitefield made his way south to East Windsor, the home of Edwards's parents. Along the way Whitefield kept preaching on unconverted ministers, and at one point Edwards cautioned Whitefield about not judging other ministers too harshly or trying to ascertain whether they were converted. Edwards supported Whitefield overall, but he certainly had doubts about the emotionalism and rash judgments that seemed to characterize the itinerant's ministry. In East Windsor, Whitefield preached to Timothy Edwards's congregation and then visited the elderly pastor and his wife Esther Stoddard Edwards, sharing supper and staying the night in their home.

Out of Whitefield's journey through Connecticut came two remarkable testimonies of conversion. The first was from the East Windsor saddler Samuel Belcher. Though Belcher grew up in the family of Joseph Belcher, pastor at Dedham, Massachusetts, he became "Cold and Dull" in matters of salvation, and though he experienced some concerns for his soul before 1740, they had not lasted. Whitefield's arrival signaled the beginning of a six-month-long conversion crisis. When "mr Whitefield p[re]ached here, . . . I was Greatly effected with his preaching both here and att Hartford," Belcher wrote. Belcher grew cold again, but then in April he met a man in Lebanon, Connecticut, who told of the revival there, which deeply impressed him. Then pastors Eleazar Wheelock of Lebanon and Benjamin Pomeroy of Hebron preached at East Windsor, and Belcher fell under deeper convictions than ever before. He felt the terrors of sin and the threat of damnation, "but God was pleased to enable me to Cry mightily unto him in the bitterness of my Soul for mercy in and through Jesus Christ." While he was praying, "I felt my Load Go of and my mouth was Stopt and I Could not utter one word for Some time and I felt as if my heart was Changed." When Belcher could speak again, he began praising God and he knew

he had been saved. For Belcher, Whitefield's exhortations began the conversion process, but Wheelock's and Pomeroy's preaching, and his own prayers, finished the ordeal.

Whitefield's appearance also represented a beginning point for the conversion of Nathan Cole, a farmer and carpenter from Kensington, Connecticut. Cole grew up as what he called an "Arminian," likely meaning that he casually assumed that good works would save him. He began to hear reports about Whitefield's tour, and he "longed to see and hear him, and wished he would come this way." News arrived in October that Whitefield had left Boston for Northampton. Then on October 23, a messenger arrived and told him that Whitefield was coming to nearby Middletown later that morning. Cole ran in from the field to tell his wife that they were leaving immediately, fearing they would not have time to get there. As they neared the road to Middletown, he wrote that

> I saw before me a Cloud or fogg rising; I first thought it came from the great River, but as I came nearer the Road, I heard a noise something like a low rumbling thunder and presently found it was the noise of Horses feet coming down the Road and this Cloud was a Cloud of dust. . . . I could see men and horses Sliping along in the Cloud like shadows . . . every horse seemed to go with all his might to carry his rider to hear news from heaven for the saving of Souls, it made me tremble to see the Sight, how the world was in a Struggle.

When they arrived at the Middletown meeting house, Cole guessed that perhaps three or four thousand had assembled there, the countryside having emptied of its residents. Then Whitefield came to the scaffold:

> He Looked almost angelical; a young, Slim, slender, youth before some thousands of people with a bold undaunted Countenance . . . he looked as if he was Cloathed with authority from the Great God. . . . And my hearing him preach, gave me a heart wound; By Gods blessing: my old Foundation was broken up, and I saw that my righteousness would not save me; then I was convinced of the doctrine of Election: and went right to quarrelling with God about it; because that all I could do would not save me; and he had decreed from Eternity who should be saved and who not.

Cole's "quarrelling" with God lasted almost two years. Like Jonathan Edwards, he wrestled with the doctrine of predestination, thinking it abhorrent, while at the same time wondering if he himself was damned. "Hell fire was most always in my mind; and I have hundreds of times put my fingers into my pipe when I have been smoking to feel how fire felt." In the midst of his fears of hell's torments, however, God gave him a vision:

> God appeared unto me and made me Skringe: before whose face the heavens and the earth fled away; and I was Shrinked into nothing; I knew not whether I was in the body or out, I seemed to hang in open Air before God, and he seemed to Speak to me in an angry and Sovereign way what won't you trust your Soul with God; My heart answered O yes, yes, yes. . . . Now while my Soul was viewing God, my fleshly part was working imaginations and saw many things which I will omitt to tell at this time. . . . When God appeared to me every thing vanished and was gone in the twinkling of an Eye, as quick as A flash of lightning; But when God disappeared or in some measure withdrew, every thing was in its place again and I was on my Bed. My heart was broken; my burden was fallen of[f] my mind; I was set free, my distress was gone.

Cole's long conversion culminated, as it did for many early evangelicals, with a vision of God.

In New Haven, Whitefield visited with Rector Thomas Clap, who would later become one of his most bitter opponents. For now, Whitefield received a universally polite, if not entirely zealous, reception at Yale, despite his speaking to the students about "the dreadful ill consequences of an unconverted ministry." Whitefield then continued toward New York, and when he reached the border, he evaluated New England as impressive because of its godly heritage, but he feared that "Many, nay most that preach . . . do not experimentally know Christ." He loved the excitement his visit generated, though, and he thought New England was pliable enough for true revival. Pastor William Gaylord of Wilton, Connecticut, brother-in-law of James Davenport, wrote that many thought Whitefield "has a Touch of Enthusiasm" but that overheatedness could be forgiven more easily than lukewarmness. He believed Whitefield's most profound effect might have been "stirring up" the ministers themselves, though he did have reservations about Whitefield's comments on unconverted ministers. Much of the power of Whitefield's tours lay in his ability to excite the local ministers to more fervent gospel preaching.

As Whitefield's band crossed into New York, the Harvard tutor Daniel Rogers came to the spiritual awakening he had sought during weeks of travel. After a meeting at King's Bridge (now a part of the Bronx), Rogers wrote,

"It pleased God of his free Sovreign Grace to come into my poor Soul with Power and so to fill me with Peace: yea with Such Joy in the Holy Ghost as I never Experienced before—I cd not forbear Smiling nay Laughing for Joy and Gladness of Heart." Rogers shared the news with an elated Whitefield, but soon after Satan was tormenting Rogers with "Abominable Horrible Shocking Tho'ts." Assurance was not always easily gained by the new evangelicals. . . .

Whitefield continued to preach with considerable success in New York City, then moved on to Staten Island where he rendezvoused with Gilbert Tennent and John Cross. Tennent told him of his recent itineration through south Jersey, Delaware, and northern Maryland, while Cross reported that he had recently "seen great and wonderful things in his congregations." They arrived at Cross's Basking Ridge congregation on November 5, where James Davenport had been preaching in the morning. At an affecting afternoon service, Daniel Rogers recalled that a nine- or ten-year-old boy began speaking loudly, at which time Whitefield called on the crowd "to hear this Lad preaching to them." This led to a "General motion" during which many cried out, some fainted, and some fell into fits. A young man near Rogers was so moved that he had to lean on Rogers during much of the sermon until he finally fell to his knees.

The large crowd then retired to Cross's barn for the evening lecture. Tennent preached first, followed by Whitefield. Whitefield estimated that he had spoken for six minutes when one man began to shout, "He is come, He is come!" (Rogers recalled the man as crying "I have found him!") Many others began crying out "for the like favour," and Whitefield stopped to pray over them, which only heightened their fervent emotions. Rogers struggled to adequately describe the meeting, but noted that many were "weeping, Sighing, Groaning, Sobbing, screaching, crying out." The ministers finally retired, but Rogers and Davenport returned at one o'clock in the morning to resume preaching. Many in the congregation stayed up all night in the barn, praying and worshipping. "Tis a night to be remembered," Rogers wrote.

The next morning many penitents approached the departing Whitefield, including a "poor negro woman," a slave, who asked to join his entourage. Her master actually agreed to this idea (it is unlikely that he had permanent emancipation in mind), but Whitefield told her to go home and "serve her present master." Whitefield and most white evangelicals were unprepared to let the social implications of his gospel run a course to abolitionism. . . .

. . . Whitefield's tour moved on to New Brunswick, where Whitefield began telling Gilbert Tennent and Daniel

Rogers to go to New England to follow up on the work there. Tennent initially refused, but after encouragement from Whitefield and an apparent vote by the entourage, Tennent agreed. Whitefield headed south with Davenport while Rogers and Tennent began planning their new tours. In Philadelphia, Whitefield began preaching in the so-called New Building, a structure erected by supporters specifically for his visits. The one-hundred-by-seventy-foot building became Whitefield's usual pulpit in Philadelphia, and though the fervor of his earlier visit had abated, wondrous visitations continued. At one meeting, many reported experiencing the sensation of being pierced by "pointed arrows" as he preached, and a young woman fell down senseless during the meeting and had to be carried home. On another occasion Whitefield reported that he spontaneously spoke against "reasoning unbelievers," and he later found out that "a number of them were present" at his sermon. He attributed his well-timed admonition to the leading of the Holy Ghost.

Through November, Whitefield continued his tour of southern New Jersey, Pennsylvania, Delaware, and Maryland, making stops at friendly congregations in Whiteclay Creek, Fagg's Manor, Nottingham, and Bohemia Manor. Whitefield, as was often the case, fell terribly ill at Fagg's Manor, writing that "straining caused me to vomit much." But he continued preaching and praying, and "soon every person in the room seemed to be under great impressions, sighing and weeping." On December 1, Whitefield departed for South Carolina and Georgia, noting with satisfaction that he had preached perhaps one hundred seventy-five times since he arrived in Rhode Island two-and-a-half months earlier. The presence of God that attended his meetings convinced him that the British American provinces would remain his "chief scene for action." The fall 1740 tour had been a gigantic success for Whitefield. His method of theatrical field preaching rejuvenated New England's substantial revival tradition and captivated tens of thousands of listeners. His incautious remarks about unconverted ministers, however, and his friendship with such figures as Tennent, Davenport, and Cross laid the groundwork for great controversies concerning the awakenings in the years ahead.

THOMAS S. KIDD is professor of history at Baylor University where he also serves as co-director of the Program on Historical Studies of Religion for the Institute for Studies in Religion. His other books include *The Protestant Interest: New England after Puritanism* (Yale University Press, 2004); *The Great Awakening: The Roots of Evangelical Christianity in Colonial America* (Yale University Press, 2007); *God of Liberty: A Religious History of the American Revolution* (Basic Books, 2010); and *Patrick Henry: First Among Patriots* (Basic Books, 2011).

Jon Butler

 **NO**

The Plural Origins of American Revivalism

. . . **H**istorians usually focus on the "Great Awakening" of the 1740s as the principal religious occurrence of pre-revolutionary American society. Since its first elucidation in Joseph Tracy's *The Great Awakening*, which was published in 1841 to provide historical support for America's nineteenth-century revivals, its interpretative significance has multiplied a thousandfold. In the 1970s and 1980s, various historians have seen in it nothing less than the first unifying event of the colonial experience, the origins of the American evangelical tradition, and a major source of revolutionary antiauthoritarian and republican rhetoric.

This emphasis on the "Great Awakening" may say more about subsequent times than about its own. The term was not contemporary, nor was it known to the historians of the revolutionary and early national periods. Nowhere in George Bancroft's magisterial history of the United States can a single reference to this "event" be found. Although Tracy coined the term, he limited his history to New England and wrote only fleetingly about revivals elsewhere in the 1740s. Internal descriptive and analytical inconsistencies belie the event's importance and even its existence; it is difficult to date, for example, because revivals linked to it started in New England long before 1730 yet did not appear with force in Virginia until the 1760s. Its supporters questioned only certain kinds of authority, not authority itself, and they usually strengthened rather than weakened denominational and clerical institutions. It missed most colonies, and even in New England its long-term effects have been greatly exaggerated. On reflection, it might better be thought of as an interpretive fiction and as an American equivalent of the Roman Empire's Donation of Constantine, the medieval forgery that the papacy used to justify its subsequent claims to political authority. More important, an obsessive concern with it distorts important historical subtleties and obscures other crucial realities of eighteenth-century American religious development.

For better or worse, the state church tradition, rather than Dissenting evangelicalism or voluntaryism, gave Christianity its primary shape in eighteenth-century colonial American society, at least through 1740. The state church tradition took its power from three major characteristics: coercion, territoriality, and public ceremonialism. Different varieties in different colonies used these means in very different ways. But they produced a remarkably similar product, especially when viewed from the perspective of the laity whose religious needs and desires they sought to direct.

The principal task of congregations enjoying the benefits of legal establishment was to construct an effective parish life. This was true of all the colonial state church systems, whether in ·the Anglican middle and southern colonies or the Congregationalist commonwealths of Massachusetts and Connecticut. The territorial parish designated the physical boundaries within which clergymen exercised their ministry. The parish minister assumed responsibility for propagating and maintaining Christian practice and belief among the entire population, not just among a few knowledgeable and loyal believers. Indeed, the state church minister rightly assumed that evangelism—spreading the Christian gospel—was the major obligation of his ministry. Even where the state church minister might reach for saints, he ministered to everyone.

For the Church of England, a central premise guided ministerial work: successful Christian adherence intersected and informed community life. Such a premise underlay Bishop Gilbert Burnet's *Discourse of the Pastoral Care,* a 1692 tract that was typical of reforming Anglican sentiment about the role of the clergy. Burnet criticized lazy "Mass-Priests," who, like their Catholic counterparts, merely manipulated symbols before a gullible and uninformed populace. "Parish-Priests" were Burnet's ideal, and they fused Christian teaching to a vital parish social life. Parish priests would "be well instructed in their Religion, lead regular Lives," and would gain their living from the parish in which they ministered, thus avoiding the notorious evil of "multiple benefices," through which clergymen increased their income from parishes in which they never or seldom served. "Parish priests . . . almost perpetually employ[ed] themselves in the several parts of their Cures." They led Sabbath services, performed marriages, conducted funerals, preached, catechized, visited the sick, and heard confession throughout the length and breadth of their jurisdictions. . . .

A striking pluralism of Christian expression soon supplemented the state churches of eighteenth-century America. This pluralism provided an astonishing variety of European religious traditions in a maturing, increasingly complex society. Although eighteenth-century American religious pluralism most likely did not exceed that found throughout Europe as a whole, by 1760 it probably had no equal in any single European society. As important as Its existence was its effect. It soon underwrote a wide variety of ways to support religious renewal in prerevolutionary society and laid down complex patterns of revival that would persist into the nineteenth and even twentieth centuries.

Institutional proliferation became a major sign of eighteenth-century colonial religious pluralism. The diversity of individual opinion long characteristic of English settlement from Boston to Virginia in the seventeenth century took on institutional expression after 1680. This was most obvious, of course, in the rise of the great Dissenting denominational institutions organized in and around Philadelphia between 1685 and 1710 and extending into other colonies in later decades of the eighteenth century. Baptists, Presbyterians, and Quakers all had appeared in New England by the 1670s but gained significance through their persistence across the next half century. In the case of the Quakers, this occurred despite the execution of three Public Friends from England in 1658 and jailings of Quaker leaders in Salem. Less well known groups, descended from the region's complex Puritan history, further complicated the New England mosaic. "Rogerenes," former Seventh Day Baptists who followed John Rogers of Newport, Rhode Island, combined Baptist and Quaker principles with a belief in miraculous healing and attracted adherents in both Rhode Island and Connecticut, usually from among well-to-do rather than poor settlers. Seventh Day Baptists themselves sustained small but persistent congregations in Rhode Island and Connecticut. Finally, of course, Anglicans enjoyed the fruit of SPG proselytization, especially in Connecticut. As elsewhere, Anglican appeal was broad, not narrow. Often they attracted poorer settlers squeezed out of dominant parish and town churches. At the same time, by mid-century,

Anglicans enjoyed their own favor among new elites in new and changing towns and began to hold public office in numbers out of proportion to their numbers in society.

The middle and southern colonies offered even broader examples of Christian pluralism. As in New England, some of this pluralism descended from English Baptist, Presbyterian, and Quaker sources. Increasing ethnic pluralism soon engendered further religious variety. French Protestants (Huguenots) and Sephardic Jews who arrived in the 1680s and 1690s were joined in the next half century by settlers from Scotland, northern Ireland, a wide variety of German states and principalities, and Switzerland.

The new ethnic mix brought with it an even richer variety of religious groups. This was first noticeable among Scots. The first Scottish immigrants settled largely in West New Jersey and were Quakers, but they were quickly followed by Scottish Anglicans and, of course, by Presbyterians. German-speaking immigrants settling in Pennsylvania provided even greater variety. The first group, arriving in 1683 from the Rhine town of Krefeld, reflected both the vibrancy and the complexity of late seventeenth- and early eighteenth-century German pluralism. Most of the Krefeld immigrants had only recently become Mennonites, followers of the sixteenth-century reformer Menno Simons, and though they expressed an interest in Quaker principles in indicating their desire to emigrate to Pennsylvania, they had not yet joined the Quaker movement. In fact, most never did. In Germantown, just outside Philadelphia, they were joined by visionary Lutherans and more than a few avowed sectarians, some led by the mysterious Johannes Kelpius.

Between 1695 and 1740 Christian pluralism exploded in the middle colonies. The Keithian schism among the Quakers stimulated a flurry of sectarian groups. Keithian Quakers became Keithian Baptists who, in turn, became Calvinist or Particular Baptists only to watch others become Anglicans and even Presbyterians. Kelpius's Wissahickon settlement disintegrated before 1710, after which a few followers traveled west. Near Lancaster, with newly immigrating German Seventh Day Baptists, they formed a new settlement at Ephrata (meaning "fruitful"), renowned for its seeming prefigurement of nineteenth-century American communitarianism. It was characterized by antiworldly sectarianism, division into male and female segments, and a special musical regimen that prompted Thomas Mann to model one of his principal figures in *The Magic Mountain* after Ephrata's mid-eighteenth-century leader, Conrad Beisel. "Dunkers," the derisive name applied to the adherents of the Church of the Brethren, were antipaedobaptists who believed in complete immersion during adult baptism. Followers of the reformer Kaspar Schwenkfeld arrived in Pennsylvania in 1734, and in 1741 Count Nicholas Zinzendorf arrived in Philadelphia, bringing a major group of Moravian settlers to the colony.

Although the southern colonies could not compete with the spiritual jangle heard in Pennsylvania, its landscape was by no means silent. As in Pennsylvania, some of its pluralism came through Continental sources. Followers of Jean de Labadie, a former Jesuit, formed a communitarian settlement in Maryland in 1683, and in 1728 Schwenkfeldian refugees who had fled Silesia settled in Georgia, where they were followed in the 1730s by Moravian immigrants. Older Quaker meetings persisted but did not expand. More important was Dissenter activity. The Presbyterians experienced considerable growth in the 1750s as the result of Scottish and Scots-Irish immigration. Especially in Virginia, Baptists expanded after 1750, though usually at Anglican expense. They challenged Anglican hegemony in the colony, both figuratively and literally, and lured Anglicans into foolish contests over preaching and taxes that the Baptists could not lose.

International cosmopolitanism accompanied this growing eighteenth-century American religious pluralism. Cotton Mather maintained an extensive European correspondence, particularly with Pietists. Charleston's French Protestant minister, Paul L'Escot, corresponded with two theologians in Neuchâtel and Geneva, Jean Frederick Ostervald and Jean Alphonse Turrettini, sending Turrettini rattlesnake skins. Henry Melchior Muhlenberg kept up an enormous correspondence with Lutheran leaders in Halle and elsewhere in Germany from the 1740s until his death in 1787. Quakers in Pennsylvania, New England, and the southern colonies used the "transatlantic connection" with traveling or Public Friends to keep the movement spiritually cohesive before 1750 and to promote religious change and reformation after 1750. English Seventh Day Baptists in New Jersey, Pennsylvania, and Rhode Island kept in close touch both through correspondence and through frequent emigration from one colony to the other. Even a settlement like Ephrata, physically far removed from the challenge of a city like Philadelphia, maintained a remarkably cosmopolitan theology, fusing together diverse elements of German pietism, anabaptism, and social experimentation in its communitarian setting.

This burgeoning pluralism and its broad public acceptance was perhaps best displayed in New York City in August 1763, when the governor proclaimed a day of thanksgiving to celebrate the British victory over France in the French and Indian War. The city's two Anglican clergymen were joined in their sermons by their Dutch, French, Presbyterian, Baptist, and Moravian counterparts. Even the "hazan," or prayer chanter, at Congregation Shearith Israel, Joseph Jesuron Pinto, delivered a thanksgiving sermon, taking for his text Zechariah 2:10: "Sing and rejoice, O daughter of Zion: for lo, I come, and I will dwell in the midst of thee, saith the Lord."

The increase in religious pluralism provides an important clue to understanding the attempts at religious renewal in eighteenth-century America. It was the breadth and diversity of these efforts—not their cohesion or their limitation to the 1740s—that solidified their significance. Even in New England, Perry Miller described efforts at renewal and revival as episodically persistent. They appeared as early as the 1670s, and reappeared in major forms in the 1680s, the 1730s, and the 1760s, with a major peak between 1740 and 1745. Middle colony religious renewal began tumultuously with the rise of "singing Quakers" on Long Island in the 1680s and continued with efforts to create a piety of suffering among French Huguenots in the 1690s, with Dutch revivals in the 1720s in New Jersey, and with Presbyterian and German revivals (the latter largely failures) in the 1740s in Pennsylvania. In the southern colonies efforts at religious renewal appeared for short periods in both South Carolina and Virginia in the 1740s, stimulated by the preaching of the Anglican itinerant, George Whitefield, but met with more sustained growth there and in North Carolina after 1760, when Presbyterian and Baptist activity increased.

Although religious revival missed many colonies, it usually attracted notoriety and charges of political radicalism when it occurred. Alexander Garden of Charleston and Charles Chauncy of Boston both charged that the religious "enthusiasm" of the 1740s was modeled on the behavior of London's infamous "French Prophets" of the 1710s, who raised followers from the dead, prophesied Christ's imminent return to earth, and used female preachers. The charges of radicalism actually pointed up the relative modesty of what was taking place. Some prerevolutionary colonial revivals allowed and even encouraged emotional outbursts as a sign of true conversion. Jonathan Edwards apparently permitted such episodes in the early revivals he encouraged, and James Davenport brought them to a climax when he and his New London, Connecticut, followers burned books written by their opponents. Yet heightened emotionalism characterized only some revivals. The revivals in the New Jersey Dutch churches led by Bernardus Freeman and Theodore Frelinghuysen emphasized personal discipline rather than emotion as evidence of conversion, and Baptist revivals in both New England and Virginia defined success more in terms of the listeners' sober reception of the new doctrine that was propounded than in displays of emotional excess.

Doctrinal diversity also characterized eighteenth-century religious renewal. Calvinism clearly dominated New England revival. But it had been preceded in the 1710s by a major interest in German Pietist doctrines, circulated through the writings of a Halle reformer, August Herman Francke, with whom Cotton Mather had begun an intensive correspondence in 1709. In the 1750s revivalism incorporated Wesleyan Arminianism, brought to America through the example of John Wesley's English Methodists. In the middle colonies, not surprisingly, Calvinism was important in the Scottish Presbyterian revivals. But quite different doctrines spurred religious renewal among other communions. Frelinghuysen's and Freeman's disciplinary revival among Dutch Reformed colonists was encouraged by a Dutch renewal tradition with strong seventeenth-century origins. Among Germans, efforts at religious renewal took root in reformed Lutheranism, in a distinct German Calvinist tradition quite unlike that found in New England, and in a Pietism of great breadth and eclecticism. As espoused by immigrants like Christopher Sauer, this Pietism could easily involve Lutheran sacramentalism, Hermetic Rosicrucianism, and universalist Freemasonry. And the spectacular growth of the Baptists in Virginia and North Carolina used Arminian doctrine as its fuel.

Colonial revivals nearly always reflected regional and local conditions. In New England they flourished amid tensions stemming from religious, social, and economic maturation, which had brought increased disparities of wealth, social stratification, and sometimes incomprehensible social diversity. Middle colony revivalism was more narrowly circumscribed and often took root in efforts to articulate ethnic dimensions in religious observance, both Scottish and German. In Virginia, Baptist revivalism prospered alongside the inability and even the refusal of established Anglican churches to comprehend broadening religious needs in the colony, particularly among poorer, less literate settlers.

The peculiar, seemingly contradictory, mix of provincialism, regionalism, and internationalism became especially obvious in the labor of revival and religious renewal. George Whitefield's colonial appeal fed on his English and Scottish success and on the news of that success spread by colonial newspapers and theological sympathizers. Private letters from ministers to each other, read at public occasions on both sides of the Atlantic, created a "concert of prayer" that made the revivals of the 1740s and 1750s seem even more momentous than they were. And the exchange was more than one-way. Thomas Prince's weekly newspaper, *The Christian History*, published in both Boston and Edinburgh in the 1740s, brought as much news of

America to Europe as of Europe to America. George Whitefield, moreover, publicly acknowledged very early colonial models for his mid-century reform work. When he visited Northampton, Massachusetts, in 1740, he expressed more interest in Jonathan Edwards's grandfather than in Edwards himself: "After a little refreshment, we crossed the ferry to Northampton, where no less than three hundred souls were saved about five years ago. Their pastor's name is Edwards, successor and grandson to the great [Solomon] Stoddard, whose memory will be always precious to my soul, and whose books entitled 'A Guide to Christ,' and 'Safety of Appearing in Christ's Righteousness,' I would recommend to all."

In general, revivalism embraced conservative rather than radical or egalitarian approaches to the question of authority. It is true that revivals frequently produced schisms that threatened the old order. In New England, revivals in the 1740s produced more than two hundred schismatic congregations that split away from old churches, and several "New Light" Congregationalist and "Separate" Baptist denominational organizations. In the middle colonies Presbyterian revivalists withdrew from the Synod of Philadelphia to form the Synod of New York. Yet these schisms usually occurred because proponents demanded more, not less, authority from their churches. This became particularly obvious during the Presbyterian schism of the 1740s. Usually interpreted as an attack on authority—as "antiauthoritarian" and as perhaps a preface to the American Revolution—it was actually proauthoritarian. Its instigators, Gilbert Tennent and the ministers of the evangelicals' so-called Log College, had long objected to disciplinary laxness in the old Synod of Philadelphia. When the synod refused to raise its disciplinary standards, the Log College ministers walked out, not into the heady air of antiauthoritarian freedom but to New York. There they created new presbyteries and finally another synod—the Synod of New York—to exercise effective coercive authority over "true" Presbyterian ministers, ministerial candidates, and congregations.

Colonial revivals also raised, rather than lowered, the status of the ordained ministry and did little to increase lay authority within either local congregations or their denominational institutions. Revivalism prompted many ministers to change their style of preaching. Many turned to extemporaneous preaching more frequently than they had before, accelerating a tradition that can be dated back to at least the 1680s. Isaac Backus, the New England Baptist leader, noted that revivalists used sermons to "insinuate themselves into the affections" of the people and even induced opponents to incorporate more "emotion" and "sentiment" in their sermons. At the same time some sermons were clearly more "extemporaneous" than others. Some itinerant ministers, especially Whitefield, memorized sermons and interchanged sections to suit particular moments and audiences. Since they preached without notes their listeners believed these sermons to be products of immediate inspiration.

Revivalists upheld important distinctions between ministers and laypeople. Ministers had rights, the laity had duties. Jonathan Edwards acknowledged, in *Some Thoughs concerning the Present Revival of Religion in New England*, that "some exhorting is a Christian duty" for a few of the converted. But Edwards was quick to protect clerical privilege. "The Common people in exhorting one another ought not to clothe themselves with the like authority, with that which is proper for ministers." Gilbert Tennent spoke even more adamantly. His infamous 1740 sermon, *The Danger of an Unconverted Ministry,* was taken by many as a siren of antiauthoritarianism, and historians have frequently treated it as a prelude to the rhetoric of the Revolution. Tennent attacked "unedifying" ministers who could not lay claim to a conversion experience. They were "Pharisee-shepherds" and "Pharisee-teachers." He argued that listeners and even parishioners had a duty to turn to the sermons of other clergymen if misfits persisted in their office. But Tennent never attacked the ministry itself or suggested that anyone with a conversion experience should begin preaching to others. Only ministers properly ordained by legitimate denominational bodies preached, and only preaching brought men and women to Christ. As early as 1742 Tennent thundered against lay preachers. They were "of dreadful consequence to the Church's peace and soundness in principle . . . [F]or Ignorant Young Converts to take upon them authoritatively to Instruct and Exhort publickly tends to introduce the greatest Errors and the greatest anarchy and confusion."

Revival ministers often took more paternalistic attitudes toward their listeners than did their less enthusiastic colleagues. Regenerate ministers saw themselves as true shepherds, who brought their sheep like listeners to religious conviction they would likely never experience except under proper, inspired guidance. In the 1740 Presbyterian revival at New Londonderry, Pennsylvania, James Blair's "soul exercises" transformed the congregation. His instructions on relating their experiences with God set limits and forms for their spiritual exercises. He constantly exhorted his listeners to "moderate and bound their passions." He warned them against excesses through which they might misconstrue God and, in turn, have their doings misconstrued by others. Finally, he withheld judgment concerning his listeners' state of grace, a proper Calvinist practice that also broadened and extended rather than constrained his authority.

Itineraney likewise solidified ministerial authority. Although some itinerants lacked formal education, none of those who were active in the American colonies are known to have been illiterate. The century's most famous itinerant, George Whitefield, took an Oxford degree in 1736, and its most infamous, James Davenport, stood at the top of his Yale class in 1732. Itinerants opposed settled ministers only selectively. They bypassed local churches when the minister opposed their work and preached in them when the minister was favorable. Nearly all itinerants wore the protective badge of clerical ordination. When he was charged in Virginia with being an unlicensed minister, the evangelical Presbyterian, Samuel Davies, defended his orthodoxy by pointing to his ordination by the Presbytery of New Castle. Only Davenport ventured into the colonial countryside lacking ordination, with just his high-flown spirituality and his Yale degree to protect him. But only Davenport was judged by a court to have been crazy. . . .

The reinvigoration of the state church parishes in New England and in the southern colonies, the expansion of European religious diversity, and the rise of a pluralistic evangelical revivalism kept prerevolutionary rates of church adherence from sinking further in many places, if not everywhere, and improved them in some. At mid-century New England exhibited the greatest range in church adherence rates. Highs in rural membership rates varied from two-thirds of the adults to less than a fifth of the eligible adults, and in Boston Samuel Mather admitted in 1780 that "not one sixth" attended public worship. In New York some rural congregations contained between 40 and 60 percent of eligible adults, but others contained far less, and New York City's church adherence rate probably did not approach 15 percent.

Anglican records suggest some gains early in the century followed by some losses after 1750. The well-known 1724 survey of Anglican congregations ordered by the bishop of London exhibited large and suspicious gaps between attendance as reported by parish ministers and the record of actual communicants. Clergy frequently claimed congregations of between a hundred and two hundred at most Sabbath services but recorded only twenty to forty communicants. Statistics drawn from long series of yearly reports by SPG ministers in the middle colonies suggest both considerable variation in the ratio, depending on location, and in some places, a widening gap between the two figures as the century wore on. At Radnor, Pennsylvania, Anglican ministers reported about 20 percent of the area's eligible nonsectarian, English-speaking residents as communicants; adding Quakers and Welsh Baptists probably brought the church adherence, attendance, or affiliation rate up to as much as 40 percent of the area's adults in this period. In contrast, at Apoquimminy in Delaware, where Anglicans were the largest single Christian group, communicants accounted for no more than 10 to 15 percent of the area's nonsectarian English-speaking residents between 1743 and 1752. At Newcastle, Delaware, the communication rate among potential Anglicans actually declined between 1744 and 1776, from between 15 and 20 percent of the eligible communicants in the 1740s and early 1750s to between 8 and 12 percent between 1760 and 1776, with no known increase in other Christian congregations to account for the difference.

The result was a mixed record for both state churches and Dissenting evangelicals in eighteenth-century America. On the one hand, the renewal of state church activity in both the northern and the southern colonies, the rise of the Dissenting denominations and their vigorous efforts to promote ministerial labor and discipline, the increase of religious groups from the Continent, and the proliferation of a wide and sometimes surprising range of efforts at renewal all probably saved the public expression of Christianity from the kind of collapse that already seemed imminent in many colonies, led by Maryland and the Carolinas, in the 1680s. Without these new expressions of Christian activity and form, moreover, this weakened Christianity would also have been narrowly English and would have alternated between only middle-of-the road Anglicanism and increasingly middle-of-the-road Dissenting groups. Instead the colonies were filled with astonishing varieties of Christian expression, which only increased as ethnic and national heterogeneity accelerated.

On the other hand, the statistics regarding church adherence, meager and frustrating as they are, provide little evidence to reject Hector St. John de Crèvecoeur's judgment that in later eighteenth-century America, "religious indifference is imperceptibly disseminated from one end of the continent to the other." Crèvecoeur put a happy face on this situation. He bypassed the suppression of African national religious systems in the colonies, and found persecution and "religious pride" all but absent from America. He eagerly traced American religious indifference to sectarian pluralism and wilderness spaciousness and ignored the European heritage of erratic lay adherence to institutional Christianity, "Zeal in Europe is confined; [but] here it evaporates in the great distance it has to travel; there it is a grain of powder inclosed; here it burns away in the open air and consumes without effect." Still, however poorly Crèvecoeur understood the causes of American religious indifference, his vivid, enduring metaphors rightly fixed its existence.

What would happen to these conflicting patterns in the Revolution? Though a wide range of eighteenth-century changes salvaged Christianity from some of its seventeenth-century difficulties, they scarcely guaranteed the future. And, worse, the causes, experience, and course of the Revolution all too quickly began to expose the insecurity of Christianity's place in American society.

Jon Butler is the Howard R. Lamar Professor of American History and Dean of the Graduate School of Arts and Sciences at Yale University. He is the author of *The Huguenots in America: A Refugee People in New World Society* (Harvard University Press, 1983); *Awash in a Sea of Faith: Christianizing the American People* (Harvard University Press, 1990); and co-author of *Religion in American Life: A Short History* (Oxford University Press, 2002). He co-edited *Religion in American History: A Reader* (Oxford University Press, 1997) and is currently writing a book on religion in modern New York City.

EXPLORING THE ISSUE

Was There a Great Awakening in Mid-Eighteenth-Century America?

Critical Thinking and Reflection

1. What do historians mean by the term "Great Awakening"? Is there consensus among scholars regarding the significance of the Great Awakening in early America? Explain.
2. According to Thomas Kidd, what were the origins, goals, and consequences of the First Great Awakening?
3. Who was George Whitefield, and what role did he play in mid-eighteenth-century religious revivals?
4. What arguments does Jon Butler make in challenging the validity of an historical event known as the "Great Awakening"?
5. Compare and contrast the conclusions reached by Kidd and Butler concerning the Great Awakening.
6. Contrast the positions taken by Kidd and Butler concerning the influence of the Great Awakening on the American Revolution.

Is There Common Ground?

Few scholars are likely to be persuaded by Butler's insistence upon abandoning the label "Great Awakening" when referring to the colonial revivals of the mid-eighteenth century, but some do find merit in certain aspects of his interpretation. In particular, Butler's critique of efforts to link the Awakening with the American Revolution is part of a longstanding historical debate related to the intersection of religious and political liberty. Was there, in fact, a "Great Awakening"? If so, how extensive was its influence? Is it possible to argue that these religious revivals had little or no influence in some colonies or among some religious denominations, or was it truly the first shared national experience of the British North American colonies? What does the discussion of the Great Awakening suggest about the more general understanding of religious influences in the American colonies?

Additional Resources

Thomas S. Kidd, ed., *The Great Awakening: A Brief History with Documents* (Bedford/St. Martin's, 2008)

Frank Lambert, *Inventing the "Great Awakening"* (Princeton University Press, 1999)

David S. Lovejoy, *Religious Enthusiasm and the Great Awakening* (Prentice-Hall, 1969)

George M. Marsden, *Jonathan Edwards: A Life* (Yale University Press, 2003)

William G. McLoughlin, *Revivals, Awakenings, and Reform: An Essay on Religion and Social Change in America, 1607–1977* (University of Chicago Press, 1978)

Internet References . . .

Unit 2

UNIT

Revolution and the New Nation

*T*he American Revolution led to independence from England and to the establishment of a new nation. As the United States matured, its people and leaders struggled to implement fully the ideals that had sparked the Revolution. What had been abstractions before the formation of the new government had to be applied and refined in day-to-day practice. A constitutional structure with protections against a potentially oppressive central government was developed to stabilize the new nation.

The emergence of political factionalism produced a two-party structure populated by Federalists and Democratic-Republicans in the 1790s and Whigs and Democrats by the 1830s. The expansion of democracy and educational institutions, applauded by many of the nation's leaders, promised new opportunities for "the common man" but had an ambiguous impact in the lives of women, African Americans, and Native Americans.

Selected, Edited, and with Issue Framing Material by:
Larry Madaras, *Howard Community College*
and
James M. SoRelle, *Baylor University*

ISSUE

Was the American Revolution a Conservative Movement?

YES: Robert Eldon Brown, from "The Nature of the American Revolution," Boston University Press (1963)

NO: Alan Taylor, from "Agrarian Independence: Northern Land Rioters after the Revolution," Northern Illinois University Press (1993)

Learning Outcomes

After reading this issue, you will be able to:

- Give two or three definitions of revolution.
- Distinguish between a revolution and a rebellion.
- Critically evaluate whether the American Revolution was a "middle-class" non-revolution, a rebellion, a conservative revolution, or a radical revolution.
- Critically evaluate whether the American Revolution was a struggle for home rule or a struggle for who should rule at home.

ISSUE SUMMARY

YES: According to Robert Brown, the British North American colonies were middle-class democracies by the eighteenth century; hence, the American Revolution was fought to preserve a social order that already existed.

NO: Alan Taylor, however, emphasizes the class conflict over property that began before the American Revolution and continued for two decades after, in which yeoman farmers organized local resistance to large proprietors in an effort to realize the revolutionary commitment to liberty by obtaining free or cheap access to land.

Early historians of the American Revolution were concerned with the political and constitutional issues of the American Revolution. Contemporary writer David Ramsey believed that "taxation without representation" was the main reason for the conflict between colonists and Mother Country. George Bancroft, a historian during the Jackson era, advanced a similar argument, but he vilified King George III and believed the colonists won because God was on their side.

Bancroft's view remained unchallenged until the beginning of the twentieth century, when a group of *imperialist* historians analyzed the Revolution from the perspective of the British Empire. These historians tended to be sympathetic to the economic and political difficulties that Great Britain faced in running an empire in the late eighteenth century. Both the Whig and the imperialist historians assumed that the Revolution was an external event whose primary cause was the political differences between the colonists and their British rulers. In 1909, however, historian Carl Becker paved the way for a different interpretation of the Revolution when he concluded in his study of colonial New York that an *internal* revolution had taken place. The American Revolution, said Becker, created a struggle not only for home rule but also one for who should rule at home. This *progressive*, or *conflict*, interpretation dominated most of the writings on the American Revolution from 1910 through 1945. During this time progressive historians searched for the social and economic conflicts among groups struggling for political power.

Since 1945 most professional historians have rejected what they considered to be an oversimplified conflict interpretation of the Revolution. These post–World War II historians have been called *neo-Whig, neo-conservative,* and *consensus* historians because, like earlier nineteenth-century historians, they consider the taxation issue between England and the colonists to be the major reason for the American Revolution. In his book *Out of Our Past: The Forces That Shaped Modern America* (Harper Collins, 1959, 1970, 1984) Carl Degler summarizes the arguments of the neo-Whig or consensus school of historians. The colonists were rational loyal citizens of the British Empire who accepted the trade regulations of the mercantilist system because of the benefits provided, such as guaranteed markets and the protection of the British navy against pirates. Trouble began when the British acquired Canada from France after the Great War for Empire in 1763. No longer was France a threat to the colonists, but the British needed revenue because they were saddled with a debt of 130 million pounds sterling plus interest. It seemed only fair that the colonists should pay their fair share of taxes. When the British enacted the Sugar, Stamp, and Townshend Acts, the colonists responded with the consistent argument that they were taxed without being represented in Parliament.

The disagreements over virtual and actual representation in Parliament and who had the power to tax centered around two very different assumptions about the nature of the British Empire. "Whereas Englishmen saw America as a part of an empire in which all elements were subordinate to Britain," says Degler, "the Americans, drawing upon their actual history, saw only a loose confederation of peoples in which there were Britons and Americans, neither one of whom could presume to dictate to the other."

In 1991, Professor Gordon S. Wood wrote *The Radicalism of the American Revolution* (Knopf), a book which did not fit neatly into the progressive or conservative school of interpretation; unlike the French and later Russian Revolutions, which produced class conflicts and the violent overthrow of the ruling class, the American Revolution kept its leadership class intact while declaring its departure from the British empire. But in Wood's view the Declaration of Independence was a revolutionary document with worldwide implications when it rejected the theory of the divine right of kings and stated that men had the natural right to choose their own rulers. There also occurred a social transformation between 1760 and the early years of the nineteenth century. Though not everyone was economically equal, the new Americans considered everyone their social equals. The economy also was transformed into a competitive capitalist economy where all white males had the opportunity to participate regardless of their previous status as an indentured servant or a tenant farmer.

Wood's interpretation did not go unchallenged. A group of neo-progressive historians believed that he was describing primarily a middle-class, male-dominated political and economic ruling class from the northeastern states. Wood ignored the impact of the Revolution upon the "lower sorts" of society. Supposedly all whites—be they sailors, artisans, hired laborers, or poor farmers—all subscribed to the ideology of the political leaders as the nation was transformed from a monarchical to republican and democratic society. In addition, Wood has little to say about the impact of the Revolution on women, Indians, or slaves, even though, ironically, the author of the Declaration of Independence was one of the nation's leading slave holders, as was the nation's first President, George Washington.

In recent years the neo-progressive interpretation and the struggle for who should rule at home has dominated the historiography of the American Revolution. Numerous books and articles have recorded the impact of the American Revolution on these groups. The late Alfred F. Young, Ray Raphael, and Gary Nash are the leading writers of the conflict interpretation. See Raphael, *A People's History of the American Revolution: Founding Myths* (Newcress, 2001); Gary Nash, *The Unknown American Revolution: The Unruly Birth of Democracy and the Struggle to Create America* (Viking Press, 2005); three collections of articles of the many radical scholars edited by Alfred F. Young in the series *Explorations in the History of American Radicalism,* 3 vols. (Northern Illinois University Press, 1868–93); and most recently *Revolutionary Founders: Rebels, Radicals and Reformers in the Making of the Nation* (Knopf, 2011).

Was the American Revolution a true revolution? The answer may depend on how the term *revolution* is defined. *Strict constructionists,* for example, perceive revolution as producing significant and deep societal change, while loose constructionists define the term as "any resort to violence within a political order to change its constitution, rulers, or policies." Historians agree that American Revolutionaries fulfilled the second definition because they successfully fought a war that resulted in the overthrow of their British rulers and established a government run by themselves; however, historians disagree over the amount of social and economic change that took place in British North America.

In the first selection, Robert Brown attacks the viewpoints of progressive historians, such as Carl Becker and Charles Beard, who believed that the American Revolution was as much an internal as an external struggle fought between the upper and lower classes for control over the government. In their view, the common man does not attain real political power until the election of 1828. Brown believes on the basis of his research on colonial Massachusetts and Virginia that America had become a "middle-class" society before the American Revolution. In his view, the break with England was a rebellion fought over the tightening political and economic controls which England imposed on the colonists. As Brown put it in *Reinterpretation of the Formation of the American Constitution* (Boston University Press, 1963), "In conclusion, then, our concepts of the colonial society which produced the American Revolution and Constitution are in the process of undergoing some rather drastic revisions. Some of us no longer believe that colonial America was an aristocratic, class-ridden America, with limited opportunities for the common man and sharp class conflict between upper and lower classes. Instead, we are coming to an interpretation of colonial society as predominantly middle-class, with much economic opportunity, a broad franchise, representation that favored the agricultural areas, educational facilities for the common man, and much religious freedom. Colonial America, so some of us think, was much more liberal than we previously believed." Brown makes a decent case that the colonists were better off than their contemporaries in Europe. America was more middle-class because the gap between rich and poor was not as wide as in Europe. Furthermore, voting was more widespread in the colonies than in England because property requirements were more easily fulfilled in the colonies than in the Mother Country.

Critics of Brown have argued that applying twentieth-century concepts of "middle-class" and "democracy" to the eighteenth century is inappropriate. Quantitative historian John Cary has criticized Brown's statistics on property ownership and voting. Even Brown himself admits "most of the elected representatives came from the upper bands of the income spectrum even when the voters usually had a choice of candidates with very modest property holdings." Furthermore, Merrill Jensen points out that the American Revolution altered the political system in the newly formed states with more checks and balances and a more broad-based group of elected officials. Critiques of Professor Brown include: "Statistical Method and the Brown Thesis on Colonial Democracy: John Cary, With a Rebuttal by Robert E. Brown," *William and Mary Quarterly*, vol. 20, no. 2 (April 1963), pp. 251–76; Merrill Jensen, "Democracy and

the American Revolution," *Huntington Library Quarterly*, vol. 20 (August 1957): 321–41; and J. R. Pole, "Historians and the Problem of the Early American Democracy," *American Historical Review*, vol. 68 (April 1962), 626–46.

In the second essay, Alan Taylor is representative of the neo-progressive or New Left historians. Twice a Pulitzer Prize winner, Taylor points out the conflicts on the western frontier that began during the French and Indian War and continued for two decades after the Treaty of Paris of 1783 was signed ending the Revolutionary War. Taylor points out that there was continuing struggle over who owned the western lands that were ceded to the Americans by the British. The clash, said Taylor, was between the yeoman farmers—small producers who were sometimes tenants and sometimes squatters—versus the gentlemen who were "mercantile Capitalists intent on extracting a surplus either as rent, land payments, or legal and judicial fees." Often violence resulted. Taylor gives three examples of the class conflict between the yeoman farmers and the gentlemen who were representatives of speculative land grant companies. In 1788 the "Wild Yankees" from Connecticut broke down the doors of a Pennsylvania judge, Thomas Pickering, in Wilkes-Barre, Pennsylvania, over conflicting claims among individuals of the Susquehanna Company. In New York's Columbia County in 1791 a shootout occurred between seventeen "anti-renters" and the sheriff's party over payments to their landlord, Philip Schuyler, a Federalist United States senator and a Revolutionary War general. In the summer of 1800, the "Liberty-Men" of backcountry Massachusetts disguised themselves as Indians and attacked the surveyors of General Henry Knox, George Washington's artillery commander during the Revolutionary War, a wealthy speculator who claimed large chunks of what today is the middle of Maine. Taylor views these conflicts as a struggle of agrarians versus proprietors. Both sides believed that the frontier was the cutting edge of the America's future. They agreed that private property was "the foundation for family independence and social order—although the *agrarians* stressed the first and *proprietors* the second." Finally, Taylor argues that the Revolution did not end for two decades after the signing of the Peace Treaty of 1783. The agrarians received more favorable settlements after the presidential election of 1800 put the Jeffersonians in power in the national government and eventually eclipsed the Federalist Party on the local level with the ascendency of the agrarian leaders in the state legislatures and as county officers.

YES ←

Robert Eldon Brown

The Nature of the American Revolution

... The late Carl Becker, professor of history at Cornell University, was one of the earliest of the historians to interpret the American Revolution in terms of class conflict. Writing more than half a century ago, Becker said:

"The American Revolution was the result of two general movements: the contest for home rule and independence, and the democratization of American politics and society. Of these movements, the latter was fundamental; it began before the contest for home rule, and was not completed until after the achievement of home rule." Later in the same work Becker characterized the two movements of the Revolution in this way: "The first was the question of home rule; the second was the question, if we may so put it, of who should rule at home."

Becker's injection of the class struggle into the American Revolution caught on quickly with other historians whose immediate background was the liberal Progressive Movement in this country—a movement to improve the lot of the common man. To these historians, colonial society was undemocratic and class-ridden: there were rich and poor, enfranchised and disfranchised, privileged and under-privileged. Thus the Revolution became in large part a movement to improve the lot of the common man, just as was the Progressive Era.

From that day to this, Becker's statement of home rule and who should rule at home has found its way into countless books dealing with the American Revolution. We have come to call this the "dual revolution"—the war for independence against Britain and the internal class struggle within the colonies over which class should dominate. And as with Becker, the internal conflict between classes of Americans has assumed greater significance than has the war with Britain.

But just as our interpretation of colonial society has undergone sharp scrutiny and drastic revision in recent years, so also has our view of the Revolution as a "dual revolution." It would follow naturally that if colonial society was middle-class, democratic, and offered much opportunity for the common man, the ingredients for a class revolution would be largely absent. There had to be some other explanation.

With the new interpretation, we are coming to look upon the American Revolution as one that was fought on the part of Americans to preserve an already-democratic social order rather than to achieve democracy. This aim to *preserve* rather than to *change* made our revolution somewhat unique in world history. Most revolutions occur because men become dissatisfied with the *status quo* and desire to change it. The American Revolution occurred because Americans were reasonably satisfied with the *status quo* and did not want the British to change it. Democracy was involved, but it was a democracy that had already been achieved, not something to be gained from a class conflict between upper and lower classes.

Briefly, the evidence points to the following interpretation. British imperial policies, designed to benefit the Mother Country, had long been ineffective because they could not be enforced, and one of the main reasons for the failure of enforcement was the action of democratic assemblies in the colonies. Fearing colonial growth and the unpleasant prospect of future colonial independence, the British attempted to reform their colonial system after 1760. Since these reforms involved the curtailment of American democracy, Americans objected to British reforms. When objections failed, Revolution resulted, and while American democracy gained a great deal by the elimination of Great Britain, it was not a gain that resulted from internal class war between upper and lower classes. . . .

What I should like to emphasize . . . is that the successful enforcement of British measures after 1760 would probably have been fatal to democracy in the colonies, as, of course, it was intended to be. Colonists especially realized the value of controlling the purse for they understood perfectly the old adage that he who pays the piper calls the tune. An event in Massachusetts well demonstrates colonial attitude when the Governor and Council in effect attempted to levy taxes without the approval of the House. In its remonstrance, the House accused the Governor and Council of taking from the representatives "their most darling privilege, the right of originating all taxes." The remonstrance then went on to say that "it would be of as little consequence to the people, whether they were subject to George or Louis, the king of Great Britain or the French king, if both were as arbitrary as both would be, if both could levy taxes without parliament." Feeling as they did, it was little wonder that they looked upon taxes controlled by Parliament as a grave threat to their liberty and property.

John Adams was another who recognized that successful enforcement of British colonial policies posed a grave threat to colonial democracy. He called the Stamp Act "that enormous engine, fabricated by the British Parliament for battering down all the rights and liberties of America." Then Adams made this significant statement:

> If there is any man, who from wild ideas of power and authority, *from a contempt of that equality in knowledge, wealth, and power, which has prevailed in this country*, or from any other cause, can upon principle desire the execution of the Stamp Act, those principles are a total forfeiture of the confidence of the people. If there is anyone who cannot see the tendency of that act to reduce the body of the people to ignorance, poverty, dependence, his want of eyesight is a disqualification for public employment. Let the towns and the representatives, therefore, renounce every stamp man and every trimmer next May. [Italics mine.]

Next May, of course, was election time, and at the elections, the voters took care of the stamp men and trimmers.

Let me emphasize Adams' statement, "from a contempt of that equality in knowledge, wealth, and power, which has prevailed in this country," for to me this signifies democracy in education, economic opportunity, and politics.

In fact, Adams listed five characteristics of New England which he said had preserved American liberties from the exorbitant powers of governors and other threats. These five items were the purity of blood in New England, religious institutions, public-supported education which he considered the best in the world, political institutions which gave every man an opportunity to display his talents and made knowledge of public business common, and the law for the distribution of intestate estates which caused frequent divisions of landed property and prevented monopolies of land. Certain it is that in Adams' thinking, democracy played a large role in thwarting the impact of imperialism.

Thomas Hutchinson also confirmed the view that the trouble was an external threat from Britain, not an internal one involving class conflict. Hutchinson said that it was necessary to quiet the minds of the people so they would "be better prepared to receive such regulations as are absolutely necessary in order to restore & support authority," and he stated that future rule in America would be the same as that used in Ireland. Then he added:

> *Had our confusions, in this province, proceeded from any interior cause* we have good men enough in the country towns to have united in restoring peace and order and would have put an end to the influence [of] the plebeian party in the town of Boston over the rest of the province. In the town of Boston a plebeian party always has and I fear always will have the command and for some months past they have governed the province. *But as our misfortunes come from a cause without us*, many of those persons who in the other case would have been friends to government are now too apt to approve of measures inconsistent with government & unite with those whom they would otherwise abhor under a notion of opposing by a common interest a power which they had no voice in creating, & which they say has a distinct and separate interest from us. [Italics mine.]

In other words, if the trouble had been internal it could have been taken care of, but since it came from an outside cause, it united men who might overwise not see eye to eye.

Hutchinson also confirmed the view that it was British efforts to restrict democracy, not efforts by the lower classes to gain more democracy, that was causing the trouble. In 1769 he wrote:

> I really wish that there may not have been the least degree of severity beyond what is absolutely necessary for maintaining I think I may say to you *the dependence* which a colony ought to have upon the parent state but if no measures shall be taken to secure this dependence or nothing more than some declaratory acts or resolves it is all over with us. The friends of government will be utterly disheartened and the friends of anarchy will be afraid of nothing be it ever so extravagant. . . . I never think of the measures necessary for the peace and good order of the colonies without pain. There must be an abridgment of what is called liberty. . . . I doubt whether it is possible to project a system

of government in which a colony 3000 miles distant from the parent state shall enjoy all the liberties of the parent state.

Although we once believed that colonial merchants led the opposition to British acts for economic reasons and then backed out when the lower classes threatened to take over for their own benefit, now we think that the merchants came into the opposition late and then only reluctantly. After an incident involving a merchants' meeting in March, 1768, Governor Francis Bernard wrote:

This may be said to be the first movement of the merchants against the acts of Parliament: all the proceedings before were carried on at town meetings and were rather upon refinements of policy than concern for trade. However the merchants are at length dragged into the cause; their intercourse and connection with the politicians and fear of opposing the stream of the people have at length brought it about against the sense of an undoubted majority both of numbers property and weight.

Throughout the period before the Revolution the cry was not to change conditions to bring about more democracy but to go back to the good old days prior to 1760 and before British efforts to enforce mercantilism and imperialism. Thomas Pownall insisted that all would be well if Britain would just return "to that *old safe ground of administration.*" Pownall then explained that Britain had passed laws, independent of the colonists, to raise a revenue for the support of civil government in the colonies. This deviated from the old way, destroyed the checks on government which the colonists had, and should never have been done. The Boston town meeting warned that the only solution was for Parliament to repeal every act raising a revenue without colonial consent, to recall customs commissioners and troops, and to restore conditions as they had formerly been. The Reverend Samuel Cooper pointed out that all the "body of the people" desired was to go back to the "old establishment upon which they have grown and flourished." Examples of this nature are legion in the sources.

To the extent that democracy was involved in the conflict in a positive way, it was the democracy that would ensue from the elimination of British restrictions, not an internal democracy resulting from a victory of the lower classes over the upper classes. As Governor Francis Bernard put it:

If the opposition was directed only against persons and measures a reconciliation might and

soon would take place and all might be well again. But men and measures are only nominal defendants: The authority of the King [,] the supremacy of Parliament [,] the superiority of government are the real objects of the attacks and a general levelling of all the powers of government and reducing it into the hands of the whole people is what is aimed at and will at least in some degree succeed, without some external assistance.

Naturally the extent to which American democracy would be increased by removal of the British was tremendous, but in our interpretation of the Revolution, there is a great difference whether this increase came from eliminating the British or eliminating a local colonial aristocracy.

A final piece of evidence in the background of the Revolution must suffice to show that it was an external conflict with British imperialism, not an internal class conflict. Writing in 1818, John Adams said:

The American Revolution was not a common event. Its effects and consequences have already been awful over a great part of the globe. And when and where are they to cease?

But what do we mean by the American Revolution? Do we mean the American war? The Revolution was effected before the war commenced. The Revolution was in the minds and hearts of the people; a change in their religious sentiments of their duties and obligations. While the king, and all in authority under him, were believed to govern in justice and mercy, according to the laws and constitution derived to them from the God of nature and transmitted to them by their ancestors, they thought themselves bound to pray for the king and queen and all the royal family, and all in authority under them, as ministers ordained by God for their good; but when they saw those powers renouncing all the principles of authority, and bent upon the destruction of all the securities of their lives, liberties, and properties, they thought it their duty to pray for the continental congress and all the thirteen state congresses, & c.

Then Adams continued:

There might be, and there were others who thought less about religion and conscience, but had certain habitual sentiments of allegiance and loyalty derived from their education; but believing allegiance and protection to be reciprocal, when protection was withdrawn, they thought allegiance was dissolved.

Another alteration was common to all. The people of America had been educated in an habitual affection for England, as their mother country; and while they thought her a kind and tender parent, (erroneously enough, however, for she never was such a mother,) no affection could be more sincere. But when they found her a cruel beldam, willing like Lady Macbeth, to 'dash their brains out', it is no wonder if their filial affections ceased, and were changed into indignation and horror.

This radical change in the principles, opinions, sentiments, and affections of the people, was the real American Revolution.

It was in this context that John Adams made the statement quoted earlier that the above principles and feelings, as well as those of the British toward the Americans, should be traced back for two hundred years, and that the perpetual discordance between British and American principles and feelings "came to a crisis, and produced an explosion." . . .

A final argument that the American Revolution was designed to preserve a society, not to change it, comes when we survey the social results of that upheaval. The results of any revolution, as we see them today in Russia, China, and Cuba, should tell us a great deal about the nature of the conflict. And so it is with the American Revolution.

At one time we believed that our Revolution had resulted in significant social change. Formerly, we talked about the lowering of voting qualifications to enlarge the franchise, the establishment of a more equitable system of representation, the ending of such aristocratic items as entail, primogeniture, the established church, and the breakup of large Loyalist estates. In short, we believed that the Revolution to democratize American society had achieved its goals, and that the common man had benefitted tremendously.

Now we are not so sure that all this took place—in fact, when we read some of the exponents of the old interpretation, we discover that they, themselves, were not very sure of their ground. On the one hand they say that there was a social revolution, but then on the other hand they admit that in reality not very much happened internally as a result of the Revolution. Far from being a radical movement, they say that Americans leaned heavily upon colonial experience, that the men who wrote the early state constitutions did not trust the people, that property qualifications remained, and that indirect elections and higher qualifications for office-holders than

for voters meant that the legislature still represented the upper classes.

The truth of the matter is that the American Revolution is remarkable for the paucity of internal change that resulted. As Samuel Adams put it: "We have however gone from step to step, till at length we are arrived at perfection, as you have heard, in a Declaration of Independence. Was there ever a revolution brought about, especially as important as this without great internal tumults & violent convulsions!" Adams, incidentally, ended his sentence with an exclamation mark, not a question mark.

Writing in 1778, John Adams explained why there was so little internal change as a result of the Revolution—the broad extent of both economic and political democracy. "The agrarian in America," he said, "is divided among the common people in every state, in such a manner, that nineteen twentieths of the property would be in the hands of the commons, let them appoint whom they could for chief magistrate and senators." In addition to economic democracy, Adams also believed that there had been political democracy before 1776. "The truth is," he continued, "that the people have ever governed in America; all the force of royal governors and councils, even backed by fleets and armies, has never been able to get the advantage of them, who have stood by their houses of representatives in every instance, and have always carried their points."

A society in which the common people held ninety-five per cent of the property and controlled the government would hardly provide fertile ground for a lower-class revolution. Under these circumstances, one would be surprised to find much internal upheaval.

Naturally there were some changes. American legislatures quickly rectified what they considered inequities in areas where British restrictions had been effective. In various colonies, such as Massachusetts, the British had succeeded in having districts set up without representation and this situation was quickly altered. Ten years after the war broke out, Virginia lowered the voting qualifications from 100 acres of wild land to fifty acres, but the House of Burgesses had attempted to do this previously only to be blocked by the British. It is true that entail and primogeniture were abolished in the Old Dominion, but this was done by representatives who were upper-class, not lower-class, and might well have happened earlier had there been no British restraints. The Church of England also came to an end in Virginia, but again this was something that had been developing for a long time, and even so, the final separation did not come until 1786.

We should not minimize the gains to colonial democracy which accrued through the elimination of Great Britain. These were substantial, but we should not attribute them to internal class conflict and a victory of the lower over the upper classes.

In conclusion, then, we no longer look upon the American Revolution as we have during the past fifty years. Instead of an emphasis on an internal class upheaval to democratize an aristocratic American social order, we are coming to believe that the Revolution was designed primarily to preserve an already democratic middle-class society. Democracy and imperialism were incompatible bedfellows. When the British attempted to reform their imperial system, democracy and imperialism clashed head-on. One or the other had to go. Fortunately, from the standpoint of our Constitution . . . it was British imperialism which departed.

ROBERT BROWN was a professor of history at Michigan State University. He earned his PhD in history from the University of Wisconsin and is the author of *Charles Beard and the Constitution* (Princeton University Press, 1956).

Alan Taylor

 **NO**

Agrarian Independence: Northern Land Rioters after the Revolution

Shortly before midnight 26 June 1788, armed men broke down the bedroom door of Col. Timothy Pickering's house in Wilkes-Barre, Pennsylvania. This was a daring affront, for Pickering was his frontier county's judge, court clerk; register of probate, recorder of deeds, a proprietor of 10,000 acres, and an agent for several other Pennsylvania land speculators. Pickering's alarmed wife lit a candle to reveal that their bedroom was filled with fifteen men armed with muskets and hatchets and disguised as Indians: faces blackened and handkerchiefs tied round their heads. The "Indians" seized the colonel, tied his hands and led him outdoors, through the sleeping village, and up the Susquehanna into the sparsely settled hinterland, where they held Pickering for nearly a month. Known as "Wild Yankees," Pickering's captors were new settlers from New England who had staked homestead claims with the connivance of "the Susquehanna Company," Connecticut land speculators who hoped to wrest the upper Susquehanna country from Pennsylvania and that state's competing proprietors. By freely granting portions of their vast claim to actual settlers the Susquehanna Company's leaders gambled that they could seize and hold the entire northern third of Pennsylvania, and reap great profits from future sales to later settlers. So, they recruited in Pickering's words, "men destitute of property, who could be tempted by the gratuitous offer of lands; on the single condition that they should enter upon them *armed*, 'to man their rights,' in the cant phrase of those people." The violent contest between competing speculators of competing states created an opportunity for landless men willing to fight for free homesteads.

. . .

On 27 October 1791 Cornelius Hogeboom, sheriff of New York's Columbia County, and two assistants rode into Hillsdale, a hill-country town beside the Massachusetts border. They meant to arrest several "Anti-Renters," tenant farmers who had suspended payments to their landlord Philip Schuyler, a Federalist United States senator and a revolutionary war general. Convinced that their farms should be freeholds the Anti-Renters hated tenancy as "tending to degrade your Petitioners from the Rank the God of Nature destined all Mankind to move in, to be SLAVES and VASSALS." The area's settlers had resisted their landlords intermittently since the 1750s. When the sheriff's party reached Jonathan Arnold's farm, seventeen armed men, disguised as Indians, burst from the barn and fired their muskets and pistols in the air. One Anti-Renter rode up to the sheriff and fired, killing him instantly.

. . .

On the morning of 18 July 1800 in Lincoln Plantation (now Thorndike), Maine, seven surveyors stumbled into an ambush laid by armed men "blacked and disguised like Indians." Bullets ripped into the surprised surveyors' ranks. They retreated to the coast, bearing their three wounded. The surveyors worked for Gen. Henry Knox, George Washington's artillery commander during the Revolutionary War and the new nation's first secretary of war. He was also one of the "Great Proprietors," wealthy land speculators who claimed legal title to most of mid-Maine, the frontier region between the Androscoggin River, on the west, and the Penobscot River, to the east (until 1820 Maine belonged to Massachusetts). Determined to build his fortune by retailing homesteads to settlers, General Knox sent the surveyors into the backcountry to subdivide his claim into townships and lots. But the backcountry settlers were squatters who wanted neither to pay for their new homesteads nor have neighbors who would. In June 1801 Knox sent another survey party into the backcountry, but they, too, fell into an ambush that sent them reeling back to the coast with one badly wounded man. Knox's land agents reported. "Our defeat occasioned exultation among the greater part of the people in the suspected regions. . . .

To discover the backcountry settlers' motives, the general sent two emissaries into the hostile region in August 1801. They found self-styled "Liberty-Men," defending their notion of the American Revolution against betrayal by the Great Proprietors. The two men reported:

> Instead of reasoning they resort to harangue. All old & young, husbands & wives, mothers & sons have gotten the same story by rote & two or three demagogues in & about Sheepscott Pond Settlement deliver it with a great deal of impassioned & boisterous eloquence. "We fought for land & liberty & it is hard if we can't enjoy either. We once defended this land at the point of the bayonet & if drove to the necessity are now equally united, ready & zealous to defend it again in the same way. It is as good to die by the sword as by the famine & we shall prefer the [former]. Who can have a better right to the land than we who have fought for it, subdued it & made it valuable which if we had not done no proprietor would ever have enquired after it. God gave the earth to the children. We own no other proprietor. Wild land ought to be as free as common air. These lands once belonged to King George. He lost them by the American Revolution & they became the property of the people who defended & won them. The General Court did wrong & what they had no right to do when they granted them in such large quantities to certain companies & individuals & the bad acts of government are not binding on the subject. . . ."

The harangue summarized three propositions at the heart of the agrarianism prevalent in the American backcountry, among the Wild Yankees of Pennsylvania, the Anti-Renters of New York, and the Liberty-Men of Maine: that laboring men had a God-given right to claim and improve wilderness land, that the American Revolution had been a collective enterprise to secure the natural right, and that communities must resist laws that traduced the Revolution's meaning. This was not what General Knox wanted to read.

What can we make of these incidents of Indian-disguised agrarians resisting the land claims of Federalist grandees? In this essay I will argue that, instead of concluding with the 1783 Treaty of Paris that ended the war with Great Britain, the American Revolution persisted in an attenuated, internal form in parts of the backcountry during the subsequent three decades. During this last phase of the Revolution gentlemen and yeomen who had cooperated against British rule fell out over the nature of property, whether power should be diffused locally or consolidated centrally, and whether extralegal crowds retained any legitimacy in the new republic.

Two competing visions of America's future came into conflict in the Pickering, Schuyler, and Knox incidents. Both visions identified the frontier as the cutting edge of America's future, the point where the process of white expansion westward recurrently created new property, new communities. Both sides shared a devout commitment to private property as the foundation for family independence and social order—although the *agrarians* stressed the first and *proprietors* the second. But the two groups clashed over how property was legitimately created and properly defended, and so over whose property was at stake and who was the aggressor. As holders of large speculative land grants, the Federalist proprietors insisted that property in wilderness land *began* when the domain's sovereign (whether English king or Federal government, colonial or state legislature, or Indian sachem) issued documentary "title" to a specified tract, but the agrarians countered that their improving labor *created* legitimate, private property in the previously common forest. So Henry Knox's land agents were only half right when they charged that "banditti" had formed "a settlement of men in opposition to the rights of property and the utter subversion of all laws relative thereto." For, far from seeking to eliminate "the rights of property," the agrarians meant to defend their own.

As gentlemen of property and standing, Timothy Pickering, Philip Schuyler, and Henry Knox fought a war for national independence, a war intended to place America's government in their own hands and to safeguard their extensive property from arbitrary parliamentary taxation. They expected the new order to safeguard prerevolutionary legal contracts, especially large land grants. Unwilling to entrust ordinary folks with the political decisions affecting great property, Federalist gentlemen sought to consolidate political power as much as possible: in counties rather than towns, in states rather than counties, in a new federal government rather than the states. They hoped that centralization would permit the discerning gentlemen of the commercial centers to govern independently of popular pressure between elections (when they expected the electorate to choose between gentlemen). Otherwise, they feared that the Revolution would spin out of control and humbler men intoxicated with ill-understood liberty would plunder their betters. Consequently, gentlemen regarded extralegal resistance to constituted authority as presaging a collapse into anarchy. Urging the Pennsylvania legislature to send militia to suppress the Wild Yankees, Thomas Fitzsimons insisted, "if the frontiers are suffered to insult your government, the contagion spreads more and more wide, by the accession of all the disselute and idle, until it may reach the centre, and all be anarchy, confusion and total ruin." Safeguarding the gentry's limited Revolution required parrying the "popular license" of backcountry agrarians.

But those agrarians perceived Pickering, Schuyler, and Knox as de facto Tories, greedy betrayers of the American Revolution's proper meaning. The Wild Yankees, Anti-Renters, and Liberty-Men believed in a different American Revolution, one meant to liberate small producers from the moneyed parasites who did not live by their own labor but, instead, preyed on the many who did. They dreaded any prolonged economic dependence as tenant or wageworker as the path to "slavery." So, they sought an American Revolution that maximized their access to, and secured their possession of, freehold land upon which they could realize their labor as their own private property. This meant minimizing the levies of the "great men": taxes, rents, land payments, and legal fees. Convinced that the republic could not endure (except as an exploitative sham) unless property was widely and equitably distributed among adult white males, agrarians regarded free access to frontier land as essential to liberty's survival. Otherwise, they feared, America would ultimately replicate Europe's oppressive regimes where arrogant aristocrats lorded over impoverished peasants.

Agrarians distrusted any translocal establishment, religious or political, as the natural preserve of parasitical great men ever bent on expanding their power and property at the expense of the many. To protect their farms for transmission to their children, agrarians insisted on the right of local communities forcefully to nullify new exactions. In 1771 a land agent explained to New York landlord James Duane why the Yankee settlers on his manor resisted tenancy: "Their whole fear was drawing their Posterity into Bondage. Silly People!" Dispersed over a rough landscape, possessing only limited means, and hindered by their farms' chronic demands on their labor, the agrarians pursued a strategy that was, of necessity, limited and defensive. They organized their own militia companies to prevent the service of legal writs, disrupt surveys, intimidate local opponents, and forcibly liberate imprisoned compatriots. They meant to obstruct particular laws until their rulers could amend them; that done, the yeomen meant to return to their farms, leaving governance to the gentlemen until the next moment that they transgressed their proper bounds.

Extent and Bounds

The Pickering, Schuyler, and Knox episodes belonged to an extensive pattern of backcountry resistance. From the mid-eighteenth century to the mid-nineteenth century, frontier settlement and political interest building frequently clashed, as yeomen seeking free farms confronted gentlemen who exploited their connections to secure large land grants. Yeomen were small producers living by family labor, while the gentlemen were mercantile capitalists intent on extracting a surplus, either as rent, land payments, or legal and judicial fees. Moreover, yeomen and gentlemen moved in distinct circles and possessed starkly different self-conceptions; yeomen sought economic independence while pursuing an evangelical faith that insisted upon man's utter dependence on God; conversely, the gentry were well-educated, well-connected, and outwardly self-confident paternalists determined to guide the common folk and usually contemptuous of evangelical "superstition." Conflict between the two groups was simultaneously and inseparably material and cultural.

In at least eleven areas, settlers fought proprietors to obtain free or cheap access to wilderness land. In New Jersey during the 1740s and 1750s yeomen resisted land laws that favored their proprietors. During the 1750s and early 1760s some settlers in South Carolina's Rocky Mount district violently obstructed surveyors working for nonresident speculators. At the same time settlers in North Carolina's Granville District rioted against unscrupulous land speculators. Beginning in the 1750s and recurring intermittently until about 1860, tenants in east-central New York rebelled against their landlords. Between 1760 and 1815 mid-Maine's "Liberty-Men" resisted their Great Proprietors. From 1762 to 1808, "Wild Yankees" in northeastern Pennsylvania challenged the state's proprietors. Beginning in 1764 and persisting through the revolutionary war, western Vermont's "Green Mountain Boys" rebelled against their New York landlords. In the 1770s settlers around Pittsburgh with cheap Virginia land titles violently resisted Pennsylvania's jurisdiction and land speculators. During the 1780s Ohio squatters evaded federal land laws and federal troops. From 1795 through 1810 squatters in northwestern Pennsylvania waged gang warfare against land speculators' hired hands. Finally, during 1835–36 settlers in western New York's Holland Purchase rioted against the land company that held their burdensome mortgages.

The costs and mode of administering justice represented a second focal point of conflict over the surplus produced by common farmers. Heavy taxes, burdensome debts, excessive judicial fees—or the legal establishment's failure to protect farmers from marauding outlaws and Indians—threatened to impoverish freeholders, raising the dreaded specter of tenancy. In ten "rebellions" rural folk organized to protect their "liberty" (equated with secure and egalitarian possession of freehold property) against apparent extortions or indifference by outside "great men." In 1763 and 1764 central Pennsylvania's "Paxton Boys" massacred government-protected Indians and started (but did not complete) a march on Philadelphia. Beginning in 1764, North Carolina's "Regulators" challenged their rulers until crushed at the Battle of Alamance in 1771. During the late 1760s South Carolina's "Regulators" defied their colony by establishing vigilante justice in the backcountry. During the same decade New Jersey's "Liberty Boys" rioted against their county courts. Similarly, from 1770 through 1775 rioters in eastern Vermont frequently closed their courts. From 1774 until ratification of a new state constitution in 1780, western Massachusetts's "Berkshire Constitutionalists" kept their courts from sitting. In 1782 "Ely's Rebellion" rallied yeomen in parts of western Massachusetts and northern Connecticut against their judges. Four and five years later the New England Regulation (or "Shays's Rebellion" as dubbed by its foes) shut down the courts and hindered tax collection in Massachusetts's hinterland and in parts of Vermont, New Hampshire, and Connecticut. In much of the West, and especially western Pennsylvania, "Whiskey Rebels" defied federal excise taxes during the 1790s. And in 1799, farmers in central Pennsylvania mounted "Fries's Rebellion" against a new federal land tax.

Although widespread, backcountry resistance was localized and episodic rather than universal and perpetual. A dangerous gamble that could cost losers their farms and perhaps their lives, resistance was not embarked upon lightly. Consequently, settlers usually confined their resentments to grumbling, chronically laggard land payments, and plundering the standing timber on unsold lots. To proceed further to armed resistance settlers needed a strong community solidarity, a mutual confidence that all would stand together against the formidable legal pressure that the "great men" could bring to bear, a shared conviction that they deserved to prevail and would certainly succeed. Agrarians insisted that all must cooperate to sustain the aggregate, collective value of the property created by their particular, individual labor applied to the wilderness, and that individuals should not, heeding fears and pursuing self-interest, seek a separate peace with their proprietor. . . .

To sustain the critical solidarity, confidence, and conviction, settlers needed the allegiance of their settlements' *leading men*: political and economic mediators between their communities and the wider world. Men like Nathaniel Allen and Timothy Beach comprised the pivotal, intermediate group in the conflict between gentlemen and the yeomanry. In every protracted resistance the yeomen enjoyed leadership from the substantial farmers and prosperous millers in their midst. A luckless deputy who ventured into Maine's backcountry knew he was in for a long day when the confident locals could boast "that they had all the town to join them, that they had *the first men* in town & were determined that no property should be attached . . .

& [they] would defend it at the expense of their lives. Their language was very abusive & threatening." The deputy returned home with his unserved writs.

Consequently, the agrarian conflicts pivoted around the contest for the allegiance of each settlement's leading men, a contest between community and class notions of duty. The leading men possessed more property and, often, wider ambitions than their yeomen neighbors, but lacked the social graces, family connections, and literary education necessary for acceptance among the new nation's genteel establishment. Such men lay at the conflicts' balance point: a risky, high-stakes position rife with cloudy choices, hidden dangers, and promising opportunities. On the one hand, the leading man felt the pull of his community's expectation that he must protect the people's liberty and property from the encroaching, cosmopolitan "great men." On the other hand, the Federalist gentry wooed or cajoled backcountry leading men to prove their worthiness as fellow gentlemen by converting their neighbors to the "good principles" of orderly submission to the law.

Leading men needed to tread a fine line—for fear of arson, fencetoppling, and livestock mutilation at home or of legal retribution by external authorities. The leading man who misplayed his balancing act could lose his property to a proprietor's lawsuit or to a neighbors' hot coal, placed at night beneath his barn. Conversely, an especially ambitious leading man could reap extensive speculative possession claims by exploiting his neighbors' resistance, as did Vermont's Ethan Allen, despite his masterful denunciations of New York's absentee landlords. As a leading man in Wyalusing, a Wild Yankee settlement, John Ingham had to proceed carefully to retain both his community preeminence and his external standing as a state legislator. In 1806 Pennsylvania's proprietors sent a surveyor to run lines through the settlement. The settlers turned to Ingham for advice. He knew he could channel but not obstruct his neighbors' resistance. "I told them to make any kind of opposition they pleased, only to kill and hurt nobody, nor let anybody appear in arms. When this surveyor came a great many of the inhabitants collected, some in the woods shooting [in the air], others around the surveyor threatening him. I was afraid some worse mischief would happen, so I ordered some one to break the [surveyor's] compass or I would. Upon this one of the company broke the compass and the surveyor went away." . . .

Expansion

Backcountry resistance increased in the wake of the American revolutionary war with the dramatic expansion of the bounds of the contested, marginal, and (relatively) autonomous districts where yeomen and leading men drew together against external gentlemen. Accelerating migration inland away from the Atlantic seaboard multiplied the settled backcountry. During the period 1760–1800 frontier migration redistributed most of the population increase in the United States to new counties virtually unpopulated by whites in 1760. In 1790, counties virtually unpopulated thirty years before claimed one-third of the nation's population; ten years later that share exceeded two-fifths. During the 1790s the post-1760 frontier region's population grew five times faster than the longer-settled seaboard. Except for the first colonists in the early seventeenth century, never before nor since has such a high proportion of America's white population lived in newly settled communities.

This frontier migration occurred at the same moment that the Revolution discredited received authority and legitimated confronting rulers who imperiled "natural rights." As in the English Revolution of the 1640s depicted by Christopher Hill, the American Revolution encouraged a creative, cultural ferment among ordinary men and women seeking to bypass a learned clergy to attain direct contact with divinity. The Revolution's dramatic unpredictability encouraged millennial anticipation. The thoughts of common folk were alive with new possibilities. On 30 December 1781 Jonathan Sayward of York, Maine . . . concluded that the people were "remarkably unsettled in religious as well as political principles." Seven years later, William Frost, a conservative merchant from York, worried, "There is nothing but tumult & noise & free thinkers, prognosticators, & the Deavil knows what stiring about now a days, but I hope the time is near at hand when every lowsey fellow shall not be a law maker." Settlers carried this ferment with them into the many new backcountry settlements formed immediately after the Revolution.

In every agrarian resistance or rebellion antiauthoritarian evangelical preachers encouraged, clarified, spread, and invested with divine meaning their settler neighbors' agrarian notions. Baptist preacher James Finn was one of the Wild Yankees' leaders, moderating a 20 July 1786 meeting that declared, "an equal distribution of property, and not engrossing large domains, is the basis of free and equal government, founded on republican principles. . . . the labours bestowed in subduing a rugged wilderness were our own, and can never be wrested from us without infringing the eternal rules of right." Rev. Jacob Johnson, a New Light Congregationalist who preached among the Wild Yankees, told Timothy Pickering that the Susquehanna "lands belonged to the Con[necticu]t people, by the laws of God & nature; but

that the laws of Penn[sylvani]a would take them from them: that laws contrary to the laws of God & Nature were not to be obeyed." Ethan Allen's idiosyncratic deism was either irrelevant to, or at odds with, his enormous personal popularity in Vermont; indeed, ultraevangelical "Antinomians" (who sought to bypass a learned clergy in pursuit of direct spiritual encounters) played important roles in mobilizing Vermont's resistance. A New York supporter reported:

> Another kind of People who have Contributed much to the Continuing the People In their state of outlawry is a religious order that have lately sprang up. One Reuben Jones is the Father of this Sect and one Alijah Lovejoy is a Fellow Labourer and preacher of the Same—this pious order profess the Greatest Reverence for the Holy Word of God and declare it is the Law of a perfect Lawgiver, and contains in it all Laws necessary for the Well Ruling ordering and Governing all Kingdoms and Counties on the Earth that it is Blasphemy against the g_d given [law] for anybody or bodies of men to make any Laws or ordonances and Sinful to obey such Laws and ordonances when made . . . that in the Holy book of God there is not so much as Magna Charta, Habeas Corpus Act, Writs of Habeas Corpus, Supervisors, Sheriffs, Constables, Grand-jurors or pettit Jurys, . . . and that therefore these words names etc ought to be Treated with a Holy Contempt as becometh Saints, these two Reformers have had Considerable success not having been on their Mission more than a year.

Mid-Maine's agrarian leaders all wrote or spoke in a religious vein, and all claimed religious authority. Prominent in both the North Carolina Regulation and western Pennsylvania's Whiskey Rebellion, Herman Husband was a mystical visionary, itinerant preacher, and prolific religious pamphleteer, who espoused "Antinomian" principles identical to those found in Maine and Vermont, and who also invoked those principles to justify resisting political elites. Husband was also a rare Pennsylvania assemblyman to support the Susquehanna Yankees' homestead claims.

Federalist gentlemen worried that migration to the frontier compounded the destabilizing potential of evangelical religion and recent revolution by removing thousands from older districts where social and political authority combined in the same traditionally recognized and respected families. While touring mid-Maine, Timothy Dwight, arch-Federalist and president of Yale College, observed, "In most new settlements a considerable proportion of the adventurers will, almost of course consist of roving, disorderly, vicious men. In the regular, established society in which they were born, they were awed and restrained. On the new grounds to which they resort, they are set loose, and usually break out into open licentiousness of principle and conduct." In this view, the timing of that migration could not have been worse, for it occurred at the very moment when common folk, newly agitated by the Revolution's exertions and the evangelicals' preaching, most needed elite counsel to calm their expectations and to recognize the proper limits on their "liberty."

Timothy Pickering agreed that frontier "anarchy" ramified "the natural instability of the common people." He, like the other Federalist grandees, saw a civilizing mission as well as potential profits in his frontier lands. He observed of the Susquehanna's settlers, "their [agri]culture is ordinary and often of the most slovenly kind but the hovels they dwell in are beyond description. They are generally built with logs, but in the very worst manner. In a great part of them there is no chimney, but a hole is left in the roof, thro' which the smoke escapes. The children [are] often very ragged & the whole family very dirty. Indeed, I did not imagine such general apparent wretchedness could be found in the United States." Blaming the settlers' poverty on their supposed indolence, Pickering concluded: "I shall have it in my inclination, as it will be not a little in my power, to introduce such means of education as will prevent their degenerating to a savage state; to which they have been verging."

In September 1787 a Connecticut newspaper warned, "a dangerous combination of villains, composed of runaway debtors, criminals, adherents of Shays, &c is now actually forming on the river Susquehanna." The newspaper concluded, "we see *banditties* rising up against law and good order in all quarters of our country." But, although correct in seeing Anti-Renters, Shaysites, Wild Yankees, and Liberty-Men as of a piece, gentlemen grossly overestimated the degree of collusion between them; indeed, the agrarians' defiant localism precluded interregional cooperation, contributing to the eventual frustration of their visions.

Contraction

Agrarian resistance peaked during the two decades following the American Revolution. But, the social collapse into disunion, civil war, and anarchy that many observers forecast in the 1790s on the basis of agrarian discontent, sectional rivalry, political partisanship, and urban

rioting was averted in the succeeding decade by the Jeffersonians' sweeping political triumph. America's more astute, more pragmatic, and more ambitious gentlemen saw Federalist intransigence toward popular discontent as both a national danger and a political opportunity. Confident in their ability to conduct republican governance in a manner that channeled and mollified popular grievances, these more flexible gentlemen rallied around Thomas Jefferson to shatter the Federalists' political predominance. . . .

Jeffersonianism sapped resistance by winning over the leading men. The Jeffersonians' message and approach offered the leading men a path out of the protracted conflicts in a manner that preserved their prosperity and local influence. Wary and weary of their humbler neighbors' armed capacity to attack anyone who violated their notions of community solidarity, most backcountry leading men appreciated the Jeffersonians' promise that, once cleansed of Federalist privilege, republican institutions could peacefully and equitably mediate social conflicts. The Jeffersonians' triumph offered leading men compelling arguments for persuading their neighbors that further resistance was counterproductive, that their new friends in office offered all the relief that was possible. Moreover, the Jeffersonians' liberal social vision made sense to the backcountry's leading men. They had garnered property by hard work and market shrewdness, but could not obtain a full measure of respect and acceptance among the Federalist gentry. Consequently, leading men readily identified with the Jeffersonians' promise to secure a perfectly equitable economy, polity, and society, by allowing the free market and voluntary association—rather than political privilege and social elitism—to allocate wealth, power, and status. In sum, the Jeffersonians' liberal vision offered the leading men an escape from their uncomfortable middle position in the land conflicts, an escape in a manner that promised to complete their drive to respectability in the eyes of the wider world. Over time, the social mobility of a strategic few shrank the contested, marginal, autonomous districts that had temporarily expanded after the Revolution.

Conclusion

During the two decades after the Revolution, the settlers in certain locales found the social space from authority necessary to organize efforts to defend their new freeholds: the property that enabled them to live free from another man's dominion. In the process, the settlers defended their version of the American Revolution. The settlers' resistance helped topple the Federalist regime and inaugurate a more liberal social order guided by Jeffersonian politicians. By defending their values and their lands, these settlers contributed to the preservation, for another generation, of the republic of small producers living in agrarian independence from the domination of would-be landlords.

ALAN TAYLOR is the Thomas Jefferson Memorial Professor of History at the University of Virginia and has won two Pulitzer Prizes for his books, including his latest, *The Internal Enemy: Slavery and War in Virginia, 1772–1832* (Norton, 2013).

EXPLORING THE ISSUE

Was the American Revolution a Conservative Movement?

Critical Thinking and Reflection

1. Provide two definitions of revolution, and distinguish between a revolution and a rebellion.
2. Critically analyze Professor Brown's argument that the United States was a "middle-class" democracy even before the break with England came in 1776. In his view, was the War for Independence a rebellion or a revolution?
3. Brown argues that the American Revolution was more a war to preserve a democratic society than a class war to achieve democracy. Critically analyze.
4. Brown believes that the British mercantilist system that regulated trade and prohibited certain sectors of manufacturing was a reason for the Revolution. Were these economic or political factors? Can you separate the two? Critically analyze.
5. Gordon Wood argues that the American Revolution was different from the French Revolution yet it was still a radical revolution. Critically analyze.
6. a. If Great Britain had taken Guadalupe instead of Canada from France in the Treaty of Paris of 1763, would there have been a Revolutionary War?
   b. If Great Britain had repealed all taxes after 1763 including the tea tax, would there have been an American Revolution?
   c. Is it still possible today that the United States would still be a part of the British Empire with dominion status similar to Canada?
7. Alan Taylor argues that the American Revolution continued for two decades after the Treaty of Paris of 1783 was signed. Critically discuss.
8. Compare Professor Brown's peaceful "middle-class" revolution with Taylor's violent upheavals in Pennsylvania, New York, and western Massachusetts.
9. Critically examine Taylor's thesis that the struggle for power in the two decades after the Revolutionary War ended was between the agrarians and the proprietors.
10. Critically examine how the Federalists and Jeffersonians disagreed over the meaning of "property rights."

Is There Common Ground?

A good starting point on this issue is to discuss the definition of revolution. Do you prefer the strict constructionist or loose constructionist definition? Can a conflict in which only a political change of leadership takes place be called a revolution? Or must each change be accompanied by a radical transformation of social and economic institutions? Was the American Revolution radical, conservative, or not a revolution at all? How do students define such terms as radical and conservative? How do historians define these same terms? For help with the definitions, see the essays in Richard M. Fulton, ed., *The Revolution That Wasn't: A Contemporary Assessment of 1776* (Kennikat Press, 1981).

Is it possible to reconcile Brown's "middle-class" rebellion with Carl Degler's notion of conservative revolution

and Gordon Wood's radical revolution in politics and manners with Taylor's continuing violent revolution 20 years after the war ended? Weren't all these conflicts played out within a political system of government that did not break down until the Civil War of 1861–65?

Additional Resources

Robert E. Brown, *Middle-Class Democracy and the Revolution in Massachusetts, 1691–1780* (Cornell University Press, 1955)

Richard M. Fulton, ed., *The Revolution That Wasn't: A Contemporary Assessment of 1776* (Kennikat Press, 1981)

Edmund Morgan, *The Birth of the Republic, 1763–1789* (University of Chicago Press, 1956)

Alan Taylor, *Liberty, Men and Great Proprietors: The Revolutionary Settlement of the Maine Frontier, 1760–1820* (University of North Carolina Press, 1990)

Alfred E. Young, "American Historians Confront the Transforming Hand of Revolution," in Ronald Hoffman and Peter Albert, eds., *The Transforming*

Hand of Revolution: Reconsidering the American Revolution as a Social Movement (University of Virginia Press, 1996)

Alfred F. Young, ed., *Liberty Tree, Ordinary People, and the American Revolution* (New York University Press, 2006)

Internet References . . .

The American Revolution

revolution.h-net.msu.edu/

The American Revolution: A Documentary History

http://avalon.law.yale.edu/subject_menus
/amerrev.asp

The American Revolution: Lighting Freedom's Flame

www.nps.gov/revwar/

The American Revolution—Teaching American History

teachingamericanhistory.org/static/neh
/interactives/americanrevolution/

Selected, Edited, and with Issue Framing Material by:
Larry Madaras, *Howard Community College*
and
James M. SoRelle, *Baylor University*

ISSUE

Was the Second Amendment Designed to Protect an Individual's Right to Own Guns?

YES: Robert E. Shalhope, from "The Armed Citizen in the Early Republic," *Law and Contemporary Problems* (vol. 49, Winter 1986, pp. 125–126, 132–141 (edited)

NO: Lawrence Delbert Cress, from "A Well-Regulated Militia: The Origins and Meaning of the Second Amendment," in Jon Kukla, ed., *The Bill of Rights: A Lively Heritage* (Library of Virginia, 1987)

Learning Outcomes

After reading this issue, you will be able to:

- Understand the legal precedents set by British common law behind the second amendment.
- Understand the arguments used by the state assemblies in the 1780s to define the role of gun ownership in the state militia in preserving liberty and order in the new republic.
- Understand the theoretical and real roles played by the state militia in fighting in the Revolutionary War and in keeping order within the states.
- Define the major argument between scholars who emphasize that the Constitution guarantees an individual the right to own a gun as opposed to those who believe the individual could own a gun only as a part of a state militia group.

ISSUE SUMMARY

YES: According to Robert Shalhope, in eighteenth-century America the Second Amendment guaranteed individuals the right to own guns in order to maintain freedom and liberty in a republican society by fulfilling their communal responsibilities within a "well-regulated militia."

NO: Lawrence Delbert Cress argues that British common law and the laws of the various state legislatures in the United States during the 1780s were designed only to permit armed and "well-regulated militia" to protect citizens from domestic insurrections as well as from tyrannical rule by the national government.

"**A** well-regulated militia, being necessary to the security of a free state, the right of the people to keep and bear arms, shall not be infringed." The modern controversy over the meaning of the Second Amendment centers around two different interpretations. Opponents of gun control believe that the section which states "the right of the people to keep and bear arms" means that individuals have a right to own guns without interference from the national government. But supporters of gun control believe that the Second Amendment permits gun ownership only if you are a member of "a well-regulated militia."

"The answer to the question, 'Whose right to bear did the Second Amendment protect?', turns out to be more complicated than scholars once thought," says Saul Cornell, the leading historian on Second Amendment rights. "Indeed, the most recent historical scholarship

now accepts that there was a considerable range of opinion in America at the time the Bill of Rights was adopted."

In the eighteenth century, the colonies kept order through the formation of militia organizations. When a crisis occurred, the part-time citizen-soldiers would gather their arms and protect the colony from external and internal threats. Philosophically, the militia drew upon the heritage of the English political philosophers who argued that it was the virtuous yeoman farmers who formed militia units to protect themselves against a tyrannical king.

During the Revolutionary War, a number of militia were called into service. With a few exceptions, the militia were militarily ineffective. George Washington and other military leaders were highly critical of the state units and formed a national army which was responsible for the major military victories at Saratoga and Yorktown. Also during the Revolution, the colonists set up 13 separate state governments under the umbrella of a central government. The Articles of Confederation, the first national government, was severely limited in its powers. It lacked the power to tax or to regulate interstate commerce and trade agreements with foreign countries without the consent of the states. There was to be no standing army. Order would be maintained by state militia. The experiment failed, and by 1786, the national government, dependent on revenues from the individual states, was in dire economic straits. Calls for delegates were made to all the states to meet at Annapolis in early 1787 to address the crisis. When not enough delegates showed up, a second meeting was scheduled for the summer of 1787 in Philadelphia.

Meanwhile, a group of farmers in western Massachusetts, led by a former Revolutionary War officer Daniel Shays, took up arms and closed the courts to prevent their farms from being seized by creditors during the Depression. The rebellion was put down by the state militia after Shays's followers failed to take over the arsenal at Springfield, Massachusetts. Although it was a local event, a number of delegates to the Philadelphia convention, including George Washington, became concerned that the Confederation government was totally ineffective. The delegates went beyond their original charge to revise the Articles and decided to create an entirely new government.

The "Founding Fathers" created a much stronger central government with three separate branches—a president, two separate legislative assemblies—the Senate and the House of Representatives, and a coterie of federal courts under the Supreme Court. There were separate powers given to each branch with a system of built-in checks and balances. Political scientists like to note that while the system prevents tyrannical rule, it often makes it slow, cumbersome, and inefficient in carrying out the government's functions. Of the 55 members who showed upon Philadelphia, 13 left when they realized a new central government was being formed, and only 39 signed the final document. Rather than sending it to the state legislatures for approval where it would possibly have been rejected, the delegates asked the states to establish separate ratifying conventions. When none of the 13 states approved it, the new constitution would go into effect.

There was a tremendous debate among the general public about the merits and weaknesses of the new constitution. The politicians were divided between Federalists, who were really nationalists who supported the new constitution, and the Antifederalists, or localists, who were opposed to the new constitution in its existing form. Their major concern was that the Constitution lacked a bill of rights, which the state constitutions contained.

The Federalists won several early victories, but it was essential for the large states of Massachusetts and Virginia to ratify if the new government was to have any legitimacy. A turning point occurred when Massachusetts, the sixth state to ratify, recommended that a list of amendments be taken up by the First Congress after the Constitution was adopted. Virginia became the tenth state to

ratify but recommended amendments modeled after its own declaration of rights.

Having lost their fight in the state conventions, the Antifederalists concentrated on stacking the House of Representatives with their own followers in the first session and pushed for a Bill of Rights. Seventeen amendments were sent to the Senate, which pared the list down to 12. The first two, dealing with legislative apportionment and salaries, were rejected. The final list contained 10 amendments known as the Bill of Rights, which the states ratified as a mechanism to prevent the central government's abuse of citizenship rights.

In recent years, the Second Amendment has generated a shrill debate that scholars have attempted to address. Historian Michael A. Bellesiles in "The Origins of Gun Culture in the United States, 1760–1865," *Journal of American History* (vol. 83, September 1966, pp. 425–455), embraced quantitative methodology and studied probate and militia records to establish the extent of gun ownership. According to Bellesiles, "We find that gun ownership was exceptional in the eighteenth and early nineteenth centuries, even on the frontier, and that guns became a common commodity only with industrialization, with ownership concentrated in urban areas. The gun culture grew with the gun industry." Unfortunately, shortly after the publication of his book *Arming America* (Knopf, 2000), the author was accused of misinterpreting or fabricating some of his statistics. When he was questioned about his research, Bellesiles did a poor job of defending himself.

Lawyers have also taken up the debate. Sanford Levinson published a seminal article "The Embarrassing Second Amendment," *Yale Law Journal* (vol. 99, December 1989) in which he argued that the Second Amendment guaranteed the individual's right of gun ownership. Legal scholar Glen Harlan Reynolds dubbed this the "Standard Model" maintaining that this was the agreed-upon interpretation of the meaning of the Second Amendment. This interpretation corresponded with the views of modern-day gun rights advocates, as well as judges such as Supreme Court Associate Justice Antonin Scalia, who argue that as "Originalists" they can determine the true meaning of the Constitution and apply it to modern-day issues.

Most historians disagree with the Standard Model and Originalist interpretation. They see conflict rather than consensus in the way the Constitution was viewed in the 1780s and 1790s. The fight between Federalists and Antifederalists over how to interpret the Constitution was often vitriolic and bitter. Even today it is clear that there is little consensus in the U.S. Supreme Court about the Second Amendment.

The readings in this essay reflect the two schools of historical thought regarding the Second Amendment. Professor Lawrence Delbert Cress argues that gun ownership was a part of a collective right of the people to participate in "a well-regulated militia"; therefore owning a gun was a communal responsibility. Professor Robert Shalhope believes that the right "to keep and bear arms" was an individual right. This debate has deeper philosophical roots. Cress believes that eighteenth-century Americans were wedded to the "Republican" ideal of the virtuous citizens who were interested in preserving the communal values of America's ideals. Shalhope argues that Americans believed in "classical liberal" ideas which allowed citizens to pursue their own private interests with limited interference from the government.

Robert E. Shalhope

The Armed Citizen in the Early Republic

I. Introduction

Over the past quarter century concerns about the private possession and use of firearms in the United States have greatly intensified. Indeed, citizens with alternative views of "what America is and ought to be" seem to be waging a great American gun war. This "war," whose operations range from polite public forums to tragic confrontations between individual citizens and the police, finds both sides arrayed behind differing interpretations of the second amendment. Citizens anxious to protect the individual's right to possess firearms stress the "right to bear arms" portion of the amendment. Those concerned with collective rights and communal responsibilities, in contrast, emphasize the "well regulated Militia" phrase in their attempt to gain restrictive gun legislation. Each group rests its case upon an appeal to history. In fact, both sides frequently draw upon the same historical data to support opposing views. Unfortunately, in their efforts to promote disparate views, these polemicists have obscured the historical context within which the second amendment originated.

To grasp the meaning of the amendment, as well as the beliefs of its authors, it is necessary to understand the intellectual environment of late eighteenth-century America. Attitudes toward an armed citizenry in that time had roots in classical philosophy, but drew most fully upon a tradition of "republicanism" received from Niccolo Machiavelli through such intermediaries as James Harrington and James Burgh. The belief system which emerged from the thought of these men joined the twin themes of personal right and communal responsibility. In this belief system the collective right to arms was not antithetic to that of the individual, but rather inclusive of it, indeed, deduced from it. This integration of the individual and the community has escaped modern antagonists, but it is essential to understanding the second amendment and the role of the armed citizen in the early republic.

This article analyzes the influence of republican ideas in the political culture of early America. By focusing on arms, the individual, and society from an eighteenth-century perspective rather than a twentieth-century one, it attempts to recapture the relationship between the individual and the community characteristic of the early republic. Such an approach should provide useful insights into the beliefs of the founders, the intent of the second amendment, and the legacy of the nineteenth century to the modern gun controversy.

II. The Relationship Between Arms and Society in Republican Theory

. . . Joel Barlow clearly articulated the vital relationship of armed citizens to American republican thought. For him, America's strength rested in "making every citizen a soldier, and every soldier a citizen; not only *permitting* every man to arm, but *obliging* him to arm." In Europe this idea "would have gained little credit; or at least it would have been regarded as a mark of an uncivilized people, extremely dangerous to a well ordered society." Quite the reverse characterized America where, "it is *because the people are civilized, that they are with safety armed.*" Such was the value of freedom and equality that Americans' "conscious dignity, as citizens enjoying equal rights," precludes any desire "to invade the rights of others."

> [T]he danger where there is any from armed citizens, is only to the *government,* not to the *society* and as long as they have nothing to revenge in the government (which they cannot have while it is in their own hands) there are many advantages in their being accustomed to the use of arms, and no possible disadvantage.

To the morally uplifting regime of free institutions Barlow contrasted despotisms characterized by professional soldiers

> who know no other God but their king; who lose all ideas of themselves, in contemplating their officers; and who forget the duties of a man, to practise those of a soldier—this is but half the operation: an essential part of the military system is to disarm the people, to hold all the functions of war, as well the arm that executes, as the will declares it, equally above their reach.

Then, by integrating Adam Smith's contention that individuals who lost their martial spirit suffered "that sort of mental mutilation, deformity and wretchedness which cowardice necessarily involves in it" with his own beliefs, Barlow articulated the vital nature of armed citizens in American republican thought: A government that disarmed its people "palsies the hand and brutalizes the mind: an habitual disuse of physical forces totally destroys the moral; and men lose at once the power of protecting themselves, and of discerning the cause of their

Shalhope, Robert E. From *Law and Contemporary Problems*, Winter 1986, pp. 125–126, 132–141 (edited). Copyright © 1986 by Duke Law. Reprinted by permission.

oppression." Only the individual capable of defending himself with arms if necessary possessed the moral character to be a good republican citizen. In democracies "the people will be universally armed: they will assume those weapons for security, which the art of war has invented for destruction." A republican society might retain its vigor and virtue only so long as its individual citizens possessed arms and the capability of using them in the defense of themselves, their property, and their society.

This theme permeated the political observations of the eighteenth century. During the struggle over the ratification of the Constitution, Federalists and anti-Federalists alike had linked the preservation of liberty to an armed populace. Richard Henry Lee considered it "essential that the whole body of the people always possess arms, and be taught alike, especially when young, how to use them." In his defense of the Constitution, Noah Webster echoed Madison's theme: "The supreme power in America cannot enforce unjust law by the sword; because the whole body of the people are armed, and constitute a force superior to any band of regular troops that can be, on any pretence, raised in the United States." Thomas Jefferson, while not a participant in the ratification process, revealed a depth of feeling transcending politics with regard to the relationship among liberty, arms, and the character of the individual republican citizen. Writing to his nephew, Peter Carr, Jefferson advised that "health must not be sacrificed to learning." A few hours each day should be set aside for physical exertion. "As to the species of exercise, I advise the gun. While this gives a moderate exercise to the body, it gives boldness, enterprize [sic], and independence [sic] to the mind." In contrast, he believed that "[g]ames played with the ball and others of that nature, are too violent for the body and stamp no character on the mind. Let your gun therefore be the constant companion of your walks." Here is perhaps the clearest indication that Americans perceived a vital link between the gun and the character of the individual citizen.

III. The Bill of Rights

When James Madison and his colleagues drafted the Bill of Rights, they did so at a time when Americans felt strongly about protecting individual rights from a potentially dangerous central government. Regarding the place of arms within their society, the drafters firmly believed in two distinct principles: (1) Individuals had the right to possess arms to defend themselves and their property; and (2) states retained the right to maintain militias composed of these individually-armed citizens. Further, the drafters felt that professional armies should exist only in wartime and that, in any event, the military should always be subordinate to civilian control.

These principles had been clearly articulated in the several state bills of rights as well as in the amendments to the Constitution proposed by the various state ratifying conventions. The Pennsylvania Bill of Rights, for example, stated:

That the people have a right to bear arms for the defense of themselves and the state; and as standing armies in the time of peace are dangerous to liberty, they ought not to be kept up; And that the military should be kept under strict subordination to, and governed by, the civil power.

In their ratifying convention, New Hampshire men ignored the militia issue, but did claim that "no standing Army shall be Kept up in time of Peace unless with the consent of three fourths of the Members of each branch of Congress, nor shall Soldiers in Time of Peace be quartered upon private Houses without the consent of the Owners." Then, they offered a separate admonition: "Congress shall never disarm any Citizen unless such as are or have been in Actual Rebellion."

The Virginia convention exclaimed:

That the people have a right to keep and bear arms; that a well regulated Militia composed of the body of the people trained to arms is the proper, natural and safe defence of a free State. That standing armies in time of peace are dangerous to liberty, and therefore ought to be avoided, as far as the circumstances and protection of the Community will admit; and that in all cases the military should be under strict subordination to and governed by the Civil power.

New Yorkers, who suggested over fifty amendments to the Federal Constitution, observed: "That the People have a right to keep and bear Arms; that a well regulated Militia, including the body of the People *capable of bearing Arms,* is the proper, natural and safe defence of a free state." Pennsylvania's minority report, a widely publicized anti-Federalist tract, was the most specific:

That the people have a right to bear arms for the defence of themselves and their own State, or the United States, or for the purpose of killing game; and no law shall be passed for disarming the people or any of them, unless for crimes committed, or real danger of public injury from individuals; and as standing armies in the time of peace are dangerous to liberty, they ought not to be kept up; and that the military shall be kept under strict subordination to and be governed by the civil power.

The Massachusetts Declaration of Rights claimed that the people had a "right of enjoying and defending their lives and liberties" (Article I) and "to keep and to bear arms for the common defense" (Article XVII). This wording caused a number of towns to demand more precise language in order to spell out the individual's right to possess arms in his own defense. The citizens of Northampton, for instance, resolved:

We also judge that the people's right to keep and bear arms, declared in the seventeenth article of the same declaration is not expressed with that ample and manly openness and latitude which the importance of the right merits; and therefore propose that it should run in this or some such like manner, to wit. The people have a right to keep and bear arms as well for their own as the common defence. Which mode of expression we are of opinion would harmonize much better with the first article than the form of expression used in the said seventeenth article.

For their part, inhabitants of Williamsburgh stated:

Upon reading the 17th Article in the Bill of Rights. Voted that these words their Own be inserted which makes it read thus: that the people have a right to keep and to bear Arms for their Own and the Common defence.

Voted Nemine Contradic.———

Our reasons gentlemen for making this Addition Are these. 1st that we esteem it an essential priviledge to keep Arms in Our houses for Our Own Defence and while we Continue honest and Lawful Subjects of Government we Ought Never to be deprived of them.

Influential Americans clearly differentiated individual possession of arms from service in the militia. Samuel Adams offered an amendment at his state's convention that read: "And that the said Constitution be never construed to authorize Congress to infringe the just liberty of the press or the rights of conscience; or to prevent the people of the United States who are peaceable citizens from keeping their own arms." Thomas Jefferson did not even mention the militia in his initial draft of a proposed constitution for the State of Virginia. He did, however, oppose standing armies except in time of actual war. Then, in a separate phrase, he wrote: "No freeman shall ever be debarred the use of arms." In succeeding drafts he amended this statement to read: "No freeman shall be debarred the use of arms within his own lands or tenements." Clearly, Jefferson believed that the possession of arms could be entirely unrelated to service in the militia.

James Madison believed in balancing individual rights with communal responsibilities. Having buttressed the corporate nature of society with the Constitution, Madison and others set out to protect the individual from the potentially overweening power of the community. When he offered the amendments comprising the Bill of Rights, Madison suggested they be inserted directly into the body of the Constitution in article I, section 9, between clauses 3 and 4. He did not separate the right to bear arms from other rights designed to protect the individual; nor did he suggest placing it in section 8, clauses 15 and 16, which dealt specifically with arming and organizing the militia. When preparing notes for an address supporting the amendments, Madison reminded himself: "They relate 1st to private rights"; and when he consulted with Edmund Pendleton, Madison emphasized that "amendments may be employed to quiet the fears of many by supplying those further guards for private rights."

Others assumed the same stance. Madison's confidant, Joseph Jones, believed the proposed articles were "calculated to secure the personal rights of the people so far as declarations on paper can effect the purpose." Tench Coxe, writing as "Pennsylvanian," discussed individual guarantees and then, in reference to the second amendment, maintained that "the people are confirmed by the next article in their right to keep and bear their private arms." "Philodemos" exclaimed; "Every freeman has *a right to the use of the press,* so he has to *the use of his arms.*" Clearly, Madison and his colleagues intended the right to bear arms, like that of free speech or the press, to be a guarantee for every individual citizen whether or not he served as part of the militia.

When Madison and his select committee drafted the Bill of Rights, they did their best to combine briefly the essential elements of the various state bills of rights as well as the many suggestions made by state ratifying conventions. The effort resulted in a good deal of cutting, revising, and synthesizing. This drafting approach was certainly used with the second amendment, as the committee incorporated two distinct, yet related, rights into a single amendment.

The brief discussion of the amendment in Congress makes clear that the committee had no intention of subordinating one right to the other. Elbridge Gerry attacked the phrase dealing with conscientious objectors, those "scrupulous of bearing arms," that appeared in the original amendment. Revealing a libertarian distrust of government, Gerry maintained that the declaration of rights in the proposed amendment "is intended to secured the people against the mal-administration of the Government," and indicated that the federal government might employ the conscientious objector phrase "to destroy the constitution itself. They can declare who are those religiously scrupulous, and prevent them from bearing arms." This would return America to a European-style society in which governments systematically disarmed their citizens. Thomas Scott of Pennsylvania also strenuously objected to this phrase for fear it might "lead to the violation of another article in the constitution, which secures to the people the right of keeping arms."

While congressmen firmly believed in the right of individual citizens to possess arms, no consensus existed regarding whether or not these people should be required to bear arms in the militia. One representative declared: "As far as the whole body of the people are necessary to the general defence, they ought to be armed; but the law ought not to require more than is necessary; for that would be a just cause of complaint." But another representative observed that "the people of America would never consent to be deprived of the privilege of carrying arms. Though it may prove burdensome to some individuals to be obliged to arm themselves, yet it would not be so considered when the advantages were justly estimated." Other congressmen even went so far as to argue that the states should supply firearms to those Americans without them. Regardless of their voicers' feelings about the militia, such statements clearly revealed an urge to get arms into the hands of all American males between the ages of eighteen and forty-five, and not to restrict such possession to those in militia service.

While late eighteenth-century Americans distinguished between the individual's right to *possess* arms and the need for a militia in which to *bear* them, more often than not they considered these rights inseparable. Observations by Madison, George Washington, Dwight, and Joseph Story provide excellent insight into why it was so natural to combine these two rights into a single amendment.

Madison observed that in the case of oppressed Europeans "it is not certain that with this aid alone [possession of arms], they would not be able to shake off their yokes." Something beyond individual possession of weapons was necessary:

> But were the people to possess the additional advantages of local governments chosen by themselves, who could collect the national will, and direct the national force; and of officers appointed out of the militia, it may be affirmed with the greatest assurance, that the throne of every tyranny in Europe would be speedily overturned, in spite of the legions which surround it.

Similarly, Washington declared: "To be prepared for war, is one of the most effectual means of preserving peace. A free people ought not only to be armed, but disciplined; to which end, a uniform and well-digested plan is requisite."

Several decades later, Dwight exalted the right of the individual to possess arms as the hallmark of a democratic society. But he observed: "The difficulty here has been to persuade the citizens to keep arms, not to prevent them from being employed for violent purposes." A similar lament characterized the observations of Story, whose *Commentaries* captured the vital essence of the relationship between armed citizens and the militia. Regarding the second amendment, Story wrote:

> The right of the citizens to keep and bear arms has justly been considered, as the palladium of the liberties of a republic; since it offers a strong moral check against the usurpation and arbitrary power of rulers; and will generally, even if these are successful in the first instance, enable the people to resist and triumph over them. And yet, though this truth would seem so clear, and the importance of a well regulated militia would seem so undeniable, it cannot be disguised, that among the American people there is a growing indifference to any system of militia discipline, and a strong disposition, from a sense of its burdens, to

be rid of all regulations. How it is practicable to keep the people duly armed without some organization, it is difficult to see. There is certainly no small danger, that indifference may lead to disgust, and disgust to contempt; and thus gradually undermine all the protection intended by this clause of our national bill of rights.

Such observations divulge a fascinating relationship between the armed citizen and the militia. Clearly, these men believed that the perpetuation of a republican spirit and character within their society depended upon the freeman's possession of arms as well as his ability and willingness to defend both himself and his society. This constituted the bedrock, the "palladium," of republican liberty. The militia remained equally important to them, however, because militia laws insured that American citizens would remain armed and, consequently, retain their vigorous republican character. Beyond that, the militia provided the vehicle whereby the collective force of individually-armed citizens might become most effectively manifest. By consolidating the power of individual Americans, the militia forced those in power to respect the liberties of the people and minimized the need for professional armies, the greatest danger a republican society could face. This belief lay behind Jefferson's oft-quoted statement: "[W]hat country can preserve it's [sic] liberties if their rulers are not warned from time to time that their people preserve the spirit of resistance. Let them take arms." Thus, the armed citizen and the militia existed as distinct, yet dynamically interrelated elements within American thought; it was perfectly reasonable to provide for both within the same amendment to the Constitution.

IV. Post-Revolution America and the Importance of the Individual

With the passage of time, the importance of the militia faded in American thought while the image of the privately-armed citizen assumed increased importance. This shift in thought, resulting from changes in perceptions of republicanism during and after the Revolution, has exerted an enormous influence over time and plays a major role in the current discussion of the private ownership of guns.

Many Americans entered the Revolution with the millenial expectation of creating a new republican society comprised of virtuous citizens free of Old World corruption. During the course of the war, however, American behavior manifested disturbing and disappointing signs of European vices. Public officials and contractors indulged in graft; farmers and merchants displayed greed; many Americans traded with the enemy; and the government had to rely on conscription of men and confiscation of property in order to prosecute the war. Most important, the militia—the backbone of a republican society—proved ineffective; only the presence of a regular army saved the cause. Despite these facts, following Yorktown, Americans chose to believe that their victory was a confirmation of their moral strengths. In 1783 it was public virtue, not its failure, that was crucial. To preserve their millenial vision of the future, Americans could not recognize the reality of the many questionable expedients employed to win the war. Concerned about their failures and anxious about their bequest to posterity, the revolutionary generation redefined its experiences and made them as virtuous and as heroic as they ought to have been. Thus, victory—gained by the fallible, partial, and selfish efforts of most Americans—allowed an entire generation to ignore this unpleasant reality and to claim that it had remained true to the standard of 1775. They offered that standard and the image of a unified, virtuous republican citizenry to future generations.

The impulse to glorify the revolutionary effort led to exaggerated claims of success and helps to explain the significance accorded the militia by Americans in the 1780s. The popular interpretation of victory in the Revolution ignored the role played by the regular army and reinstated the people's militia as the vital pillar of American virtue and essential to the preservation of the nation's unique republican character. Thus, at the time the Founders drafted the Bill of Rights, reaffirmation of the militia principle seemed important along with the guarantee of arms to the individual. In the face of nineteenth-century developments, however, the symbolic importance of the militia would fade, while that of the armed individual gained increased stature.

Americans of the revolutionary generation had made a profession of virtue and committed their republic to the escape from corruption, but Enlightenment thought taught them that natural laws of social and economic development gripped all societies in an evolutionary process that carried them inevitably from brutal savagery to the decadent civilization of commerce and corruption. In response, following Harrington's reasoning that commerce could not corrupt so long as it did not overwhelm agrarian interests, Americans believed that in order to accommodate both virtue and commerce a republic must be as energetic in its search for land as it was in its search for commerce. A vast supply of land, occupied by an armed and self-directing yeomanry, might establish an endless reservoir of virtue. This belief is what gave point to Jefferson's observation that "our governments will remain virtuous for many centuries; as long as they are chiefly agricultural; and this will be as long as these shall be vacant lands in any part of America." If American virtue was threatened by the increase in commercial activity following the Constitution of 1787, it could revitalize itself on the frontier through the efforts of the armed husbandman. America might yet escape the evils of history by remaining forever in a "middle state" in which the people were constantly reinvigorated through their contact with nature. The "aggressive *virtu* of agrarian warriors" could thrive forever on the frontier. Thus, Americans became caught up in a flight from history into nature.

A violently activist democratic ideology, based on nature's abundance and vitality, emerged in the nineteenth century. Americans would not have to create their history in closed space, which could only foster decadence and decay. They could perpetually return to youthful vigor on the frontier. There they could begin again and regenerate themselves and their society through heroic combat with the wilderness and its creatures. The frontiersman gained self-realization through the prideful display of individual prowess and by a manly independence of social or other restraints. The myth of the frontiersman became one of self-renewal or self-creation through acts of violence. Believing in the possibility of regeneration, hunters, Indian fighters, and farmers gradually destroyed the natural conditions that supported their economic and social freedom as well as their democracy of social mobility. Yet the mythology and the value system it spawned survived long after the objective conditions that had justified it disappeared. By this process, the armed individual, free to act on his environment as he saw fit, free to control his own destiny, became an integral part of the nineteenth century's legacy to modern America, It is this inheritance that undergirds the emotional commitment of so many Americans today to the private ownership of guns. This is the legacy with which gun control advocates must contend.

V. Conclusion

When lawyers contest the "correct" interpretation of the past, history is often the loser. Angry polarization and distortion, rather than clarification and understanding, can be the result. This is certainly the case with the current argument between those emphasizing the right-to-bear-arms part of the second amendment and those stressing its well-regulated militia phrase. Such contentiousness obscures the Founders' efforts to create a nation that would foster communal responsibilities while at the same time guaranteeing the individual rights of its citizens. It may very well be true that *neither* the militia nor the armed citizen is appropriate for modern society. In any event today's needs, however urgently they are felt, must not be allowed to obscure our understanding of the origins of the second amendment and, in the process, our understanding of revolutionary America. The second amendment included *both* of its provisions because the Founders intended both of them to be taken seriously. They intended to balance as best they could individual rights with communal responsibilities.

Robert E. Shalhope is the George Lynn Cross Research Professor of History at the University of Oklahoma. A specialist on American political culture in the eighteenth and nineteenth centuries, he is the author of *Bennington and the Green Mountain Boys: The Emergence of Liberalism in Vermont, 1763–1850* (Johns Hopkins University Press, 1996).

Lawrence Delbert Cress

NO

A Well-Regulated Militia: The Origins and Meaning of the Second Amendment

Unlike provisions of the Bill of Rights that guaranteed such individual rights as freedom of speech, due process, and religious choice, the Second Amendment to the United States Constitution was not written to assure private citizens the prerogative of carrying weapons. To the leaders of the American Revolution it meant something very different. The Second Amendment was intended to guarantee that the sovereign citizenry of the republic (armed, propertied, and able to vote) would always remain a vital force in America's constitutional order. Despite the militia's poor showing during the revolutionary war, Americans remained convinced that republican government would fail without a "well-regulated militia."

The lessons of history, they believed, were clear. Only a citizenry organized into local militia companies could deter ambitious tyrants or foreign invaders. Republics, whether ancient or modern, thrived only when their citizens were willing and able to leave the plow for the field of battle. When a professional army usurped the citizenry's role in national defense, especially as a consequence of political intrigue or moral decadence, republics withered and liberty fell victim to tyranny and oppression.

A well-regulated militia not only protected citizens against the intrigues of ambitious rulers, it also protected the body politic against civil disorder. Daniel Shays's Rebellion, an armed insurrection in western Massachusetts in 1786, had sent tremors through the nation. And, history suggested that republican governments were especially vulnerable to domestic turmoil. To the generation that wrote it, the Second Amendment was at once a declaration of a fundamental principle of good government and a means to protect the stability of republican institutions. It did not guarantee individuals, such as Daniel Shays and his followers, the right to stockpile armaments.

The Second Amendment had roots deep in Anglo-American political and constitutional theory. Since the mid-seventeenth century, English political theorists had linked the militia to the maintenance of a balanced, stable, and free constitution. James Harrington, whose *Commonwealth of Oceana* (London, 1656) was widely read by Americans of the revolutionary generation, recommended the militia both for national defense and to deter the misuse of political power. Political writers at the time of the Glorious Revolution of 1689 emphasized the

militia's importance for constitutional stability. Algernon Sidney warned that tyranny arose whenever the militia was allowed to decay. John Trenchard, later popular in the colonies as the author with Thomas Gordon of *Cato's Letters,* began his career as a pamphleteer by chiding Parliament for providing William III with a standing army after the Treaty of Ryswick in 1697. Standing armies, he wrote, were the agents of political intrigue and corruption. Only a militia could be counted upon to protect both the territory and the liberties of free people.

Between 1763 and 1776, Americans felt the truth of Trenchard's indictment. The occupation of Boston by British soldiers in 1768 and again in 1774, to say nothing of the Boston Massacre of 1770, confirmed the belief that hired soldiers were agents of political oppression. Although America did resort to professional soldiers in the revolutionary war, the country emerged from the Revolution no less persuaded by Trenchard's condemnation of standing armies. When they framed the Bill of Rights with an eye to preserving the republican gains of the Revolution, both the danger of standing armies and the militia's positive role as the armed manifestation of the sovereign people were important considerations.

The statutory antecedents of the Second Amendment reached far into the Anglo-American past. Magna Carta, a feudal compact accepted by King John at Runnymede in 1215 in exchange for renewed pledges of loyalty from his rebellious nobles, outlined the prerogatives of the nobility and the limits of royal authority. As an agreement between the king and the politically articulate community of the realm, Magna Carta served as an important touchstone for the development of Anglo-American law. Chapter 29 guaranteed every knight the right to serve in the castle-guard or to send someone of his own choosing to perform that duty and prohibited the king from forcing noblemen to pay taxes in lieu of personal service. The nobles in effect prevented King John from creating an army supported by their taxes but independent of their control. Magna Carta was the first step toward insuring the citizenry (then narrowly defined as the nobility) a role in the realm's defense.

Parliament grappled with similar matters during the Glorious Revolution. In the 1680s James II increased the number of Roman Catholic military officers and excluded Protestant officers in violation of the 1673 Test Act, and he imported Irish Catholics to fill the army's expanding ranks. Thus, as the English Bill of Rights phrased it, he "did endeavor to subvert and extirpate the Protestant religion, and the laws and liberties of this kingdom" by "raising and keeping a standing army . . . without consent of parliament" and by "causing several good subjects, being Protestants, to be disarmed, at the same time when papists were both armed and employed." To correct this, the Bill of Rights of 1689 prohibited the English monarchy from raising an army during peacetime without Parliament's consent and guaranteed that "subjects which are Protestants, may have arms for their defence suitable to their conditions, and as allowed by law." The English Bill of Rights did not create an unlimited right to bear arms, however, for Protestants were to "have arms for their defence" only as was "suitable to their conditions and as allowed by law." Arms were denied to men who did not own lands worth at least £100, unless they were the sons or heirs of an esquire, knight, or nobleman. Parliament also reserved the future option of restricting "by law" access to arms. These provisions were intended to ensure a stable government free from the threat of disruptions by Catholic Jacobites and the intrigues of future monarchs.

A century later, the framers of the American states' declarations of rights also sought to lay the foundations for constitutional stability. When Thomas Jefferson indicted George III in the Declaration of Independence for keeping "among us in time of peace, standing armies without the consent of our legislatures," he underscored the American concern about the relationship between liberty and citizen soldiers, but the militia tradition had more than just rhetorical significance. Patriot leaders in the colonies during the winter and spring of 1774–1775 adopted resolutions declaring "that a well-regulated Militia, composed of the gentlemen, freeholders, and other freemen, is the natural strength and only stable security of free Government." With independence at hand, the states' declarations of rights identified the militia as an institution necessary for the preservation of liberty.

Virginia's Declaration of Rights—adopted on 12 June 1776, nearly a month before the American colonies officially announced their independence—set the pattern. Article 13, drafted by George Mason and approved by a committee that included James Madison, declared "that a well regulated Militia, composed of the Body of the People, trained to Arms, is the proper, natural, and safe Defence of a free State." Two months later, Pennsylvania adopted in article 13 of its own declaration of rights the proposition that "the people have a right to bear arms for the defence of themselves and the state." The language was slightly different, but the meaning was the same. Only the trained, armed, and organized citizen militia could be depended upon to preserve republican liberties for "themselves" and to ensure the constitutional stability of the "state." Both Virginians and Pennsylvanians warned that standing armies were "dangerous to liberty" and stipulated that the military be kept "under strict subordination" to the civil

government. Without a strong, popularly based militia, liberty would succumb to the dictates of tyrants.

Delaware, Maryland, and North Carolina adopted similar declarations during the first year of independence, the first two states by borrowing language from Virginia's article 13, and North Carolina following Pennsylvania's lead by declaring that "the people have a right to bear arms, for the defence of the state." Vermont, though not formally a state until 1792, quoted Pennsylvania's article 13 in its 1777 declaration of rights. In the same year, New York incorporated an equally clear statement in the body of its constitution. Announcing it to be "the duty of every man who enjoys the protection of society to be prepared and willing to defend it," New Yorkers proclaimed that the "militia . . . at all times . . . shall be armed and disciplined."

In Massachusetts, John Adams drafted the bill of rights that was ratified with the 1780 constitution. "The people," he wrote, "have a right to keep and bear arms for the common defence." New Hampshire's 1783 bill of rights made the same point, declaring "A well regulated militia is the proper, natural, and sure defence of a state." Both documents condemned standing armies and subordinated the military to civil authority, while affirming the citizen militia's collective role as the protector of personal liberty and constitutional stability against ambitious tyrants and uncontrolled mobs.

Several states put limits on citizens' militia obligation. Pennsylvania, Delaware, and Vermont provided that no "man who is conscientiously scrupulous of bearing arms" could be "compeled" to serve in the militia, but they required that conscientious objectors meet their obligations with "equivalents," payments equal to the cost of their militia service. These clauses permitting conscientious objection to military service demonstrate yet again that for eighteenth-century Americans "to bear arms" meant militia service. State after state guaranteed a role in the common defense collectively to the "people" or the "militia." On the other hand, when describing individual rights such as freedom of conscience they used the terms "man" or "person." New Hampshire's bill of rights—the last written during the Confederation period and, as such, a compendium of previous thinking on the matter—is a case in point. It declared the importance of "a well regulated militia" to the defense of the state and exempted from service any "person . . . conscientiously scrupulous about the lawfulness of bearing arms." The individual right of conscience was asserted against the collective responsibility for the common defense. These same concerns surfaced in the debate about the Constitution.

During the last days of the Philadelphia convention, Virginia delegate George Mason, having failed to secure a separate bill of rights, sought an explicit statement of the militia's place in republican government. He wanted a clause explaining that the congressional power to arm, organize, and discipline the militia was intended to secure "the Liberties of the People . . . against the Dangers of regular Troops or standing Armies in time of Peace." When the Convention failed to agree, Mason refused to sign the Constitution. As he explained in his widely read "Objections to the Constitution of Government formed by the Convention," the document contained "no Declaration of Rights" and specifically lacked a "declaration of any kind . . . against the danger of standing armies." To correct this omission, Mason backed an amendment, drafted on the eve of Virginia's ratification convention, declaring that the "People have a Right to keep & bear Arms" because "a well regulated Militia [is] the proper natural and safe Defence of a free State." Mason's proposal also rehearsed the dangers of standing armies and the need for the "strict Subordination" of military to civil authority. A separate amendment would have provided that a person "religiously scrupulous of bearing Arms" be allowed "to employ another to bear Arms in his Stead." Never did Mason challenge the Constitution's failure to guarantee individual access to weapons.

During the debates over the Constitution, many critics worried that the proposed government threatened the militia's important role in the republic. Maryland Antifederalist Luther Martin challenged the proposed government's military prerogatives: "Instead of guarding against a standing army, . . . which has so often and so successfully been used for the subversion of freedom," Martin argued, the Constitution gave "it an express and constitutional sanction." Congress's authority over the state militias, he warned, could be used "even to disarm" them. Worse, the militia might be needlessly mobilized and sent marching to the far reaches of the Union so that the people would be glad to see a standing army raised in its stead. "When a government wishes to deprive its citizens of freedom," Martin noted, "it generally makes use of a standing army [while leaving] the militia in a situation as contemptible as possible, lest they might oppose its arbitrary designs." Pennsylvania's Antifederalists demanded that the states be given a veto over any call for militia service outside a state's borders.

Concern arose too over the Constitution's failure to protect conscientious objectors. Antifederalist candidates for the New York convention charged that the Constitution left "men conscientiously scrupulous of bearing arms . . . liable to perform military duty." Reflecting the sentiments of the state declarations of rights, the Antifederalists were determined to preserve the militia as a bulwark of republican government but also anxious to protect the individual's free exercise of conscience.

The notion that individual citizens should be guaranteed access to weapons surfaced several times during the debate over the Constitution. A minority report from the Pennsylvania ratifying convention borrowed language from the state's own declaration of rights to declare not only the people's right "to bear arms for the defence of themselves and their own State or the United States" but also the right to bear arms "for the purpose of killing game," while adding the proviso that "no law

shall be passed for disarming the people or any of them." Samuel Adams, of Massachusetts, argued that the Constitution should never be construed "to authorize Congress to . . . prevent the people of the United States, who are peaceable citizens from keeping their own arms" but then renounced that position after reflecting on Shays's Rebellion in western Massachusetts. Finally, among a series of amendments recommended for consideration by the First Congress, New Hampshire proposed that "Congress shall never disarm any citizen unless such as are or have been in Actual Rebellion."

The principles of these resolutions were close to the classical republican understanding of the armed citizenry. In each case, bearing arms was linked to the citizenry's collective responsibility for defense, familiar warnings about the danger of standing armies, and affirmations, of the need to subordinate military to civil authority. Neither Pennsylvania's critics nor New Hampshire's cautious supporters of the Constitution had moved far, if at all, beyond the eighteenth-century notion that bearing arms meant militia service, and no other state followed their lead. Pennsylvania's Antifederalists provided for the disarming of criminals and conceded that further action would be appropriate if society faced "real danger of public injury from individuals." The order and safety of society always took precedence over the individual's claim to possess weapons, and constitutional stability remained the preeminent consideration. The only other hint that Americans may have viewed bearing arms as an individual right occurs in one of Thomas Jefferson's early draft proposals for Virginia's new state constitution. Jefferson's draft had a clause guaranteeing every freeman the use of arms "within his own lands or tenements," but this provision was not incorporated in the Constitution of 1776. Virginia's statesmen were satisfied that George Mason's thirteenth article of the Declaration of Rights protected the "Militia, composed of the body of the people, trained to arms" and accurately stated the armed citizenry's proper role in a republic.

The amendments proposed in the state ratifying conventions reflected the concerns about national military power and the republican principles embodied in the states' declarations of rights. New York and North Carolina wanted to limit congressional power to raise a peacetime army by requiring "the consent of two thirds" of the House and Senate. Maryland suggested limiting a soldier's enlistment to four years to prevent Congress from creating a permanent military force. More than half of the states advocated strong state militias to counter the tyrannical potential of the Constitution. Fearing that the militia would be purposely neglected, some states proposed guarantees that the states could organize, arm, and discipline their citizens if Congress failed to fulfill its responsibilities. Against the more common fear that Congress's right to call out the militia would prove detrimental to republican liberties, New Yorkers recommended that a state's militia not be allowed to serve outside its borders longer than six weeks "without the consent of the legislature thereof." Others worried that the subjection of the militia to martial law might lead to abuses. The Maryland and North Carolina conventions asked Congress to amend the Constitution so that the militia could be placed under martial law only "in time of war, invasion, or rebellion." Finally, several state conventions stated firmly that no person "religiously scrupulous of bearing arms" should be compelled to serve in the military.

Virginia's proposed amendments, which directly influenced Madison's draft of the Bill of Rights, bring into focus the concerns that ultimately produced the Second Amendment. Indeed, the changes proposed by the commonwealth's ratifying convention neatly defined the issues raised during later congressional debates. Declaring that "the people have a right to keep and bear arms," Virginians asked for constitutional recognition of the principle that "a well regulated Militia, composed of the Body of the People trained to Arms, is the proper, natural, and safe Defence of a free State." This proposition addressed the fear that the new government might disarm the citizenry while raising an oppressive standing army. To reinforce the point, the convention urged a constitutional declaration that standing armies "are dangerous to liberty, and therefore ought to be avoided, as far as the circumstances and protection of the community will admit." The Constitution was also found wanting for failing to pronounce the military "in all cases" subordinate to "civil power." The Virginia convention prepared a separate amendment "That any person religiously scrupulous of bearing arms ought to be exempted, upon payment of an equivalent to employ another to bear arms in his stead." No one expressed concern about an individual citizen's access to weapons.

Madison had Virginia's recommendations in mind when, on 8 June 1789, he proposed to Congress that the Constitution be amended to provide that "The right of the people to keep and bear arms shall not be infringed; a well armed and well regulated militia being the best security of a free country: but no person religiously scrupulous of bearing arms shall be compelled to render military service in person." Six weeks later, a committee composed of Madison and ten representatives (one from each of the other states that had ratified the Constitution), began preparing a formal state of amendments, using as a guide both Madison's recommendations and those proposed by the states. The committee revised Madison's original recommendation and stated more explicitly the armed citizenry's importance to the constitutional order.

Such doubts as were raised remind us of the militia's importance in the political theory of the day. The failure to link freedom of conscience with the obligation to find a substitute or pay an "equivalent" troubled many members of the House. Requiring one part of the population to provide for the defense of the other was simply "unjust," argued James Jackson, of Georgia. Others believed that matters of "religious persuasion" had no place in an amendment designed to guarantee a fundamental principle of republican government. "It is extremely injudicious," warned one congressman, "to intermix matters of doubt with fundamentals." Such concerns brought the House of Representatives within two votes of striking the conscientious objection clause from the proposed amendment.

Congressman Ædanus Burke, of South Carolina, proposed a clause declaring that a "standing army . . . in time of peace is dangerous to public liberty, and such shall not be raised . . . without the consent of two-thirds of the members present of both Houses" and an explicit statement of the subordination of military to civil authority. Burke's motion was defeated because some congressmen thought a simple majority vote was sufficient and other congressmen complained that the debate had already been closed. Nevertheless, Burke's amendment again demonstrates what Congress meant by the Second Amendment. The aim was to confirm a fundamental principle of republican government, that a well-regulated militia was "the best security of a free State."

Little is known about the Senate debate on the Second Amendment; it seems to have been similar to that in the House. The Senate joined the House in rejecting the proposal to restrict Congress's power to raise armies during peacetime but denied approval to the controversial conscientious objection clause. The Senate's changes were accepted by a joint conference committee of both houses, and on 24 and 25 September 1789, the House and Senate respectively voted their approval.

We also know little about debate on the Second Amendment in the states. No state legislature rejected it. As a statement of republican principles already commonplace in state declarations of rights, it probably evoked little discussion. If any doubts were raised, they might have focused on the amendment's failure explicitly to describe the dangers of a standing army.

When Virginia ratified the Second Amendment on 15 December 1791 the statement that "A well regulated militia, being necessary to the security of a free State, the right of the people to keep and bear arms, shall not be infringed," became a part of the United States Constitution. The militia had played an important role in stemming the tide of oppression that necessitated independence from Great Britain, and it alone offered a republican remedy to domestic disorders such as Shays's Rebellion. The Second Amendment gave constitutional sanction to the idea that the militia was the institutional expression of the citizenry's collective obligation to bear arms against the internal and external enemies of the state—"a well regulated militia" to defend the liberties of the people against a demagogue's armed mob or a tyrant's standing army.

LAWRENCE DELBERT CRESS was the former dean of the College of Liberal Arts at Willamette University where he served as professor of history. He is the author of *Citizens in Arms: The Army and Militia in American Society to the War of 1812* (University of North Carolina Press, 1982, 2010).

EXPLORING THE ISSUE

Was the Second Amendment Designed to Protect an Individual's Right to Own Guns?

Critical Thinking and Reflection

1. In your own words, define the philosophy of Republicanism and Liberalism. (If necessary check a standard American history reference book as your lecture notes.)
2. According to Professor Shalhope, what role did the right to bear arms play in Republican thought?
3. (a) What role did the militia play in the Revolutionary era? Distinguish between the theoretical and actual roles.
   (b) What does the militia's role in Shays's Rebellion reveal about the way Americans understood its purpose?
   (c) Why did eighteenth-century Americans fear standing armies?
4. Both Cress and (especially) Shalhope surveyed a wide array of sources; these included philosophical writings, the private correspondence of the Founders, the proceedings of state ratifying conventions, and the debates within the First Congress over the Bill of Rights.
   (a) What does each source tell us about the meaning of the Second Amendment?
   (b) Whose point of view is represented in each of these bodies of evidence?
5. Cress relies heavily on the arguments of the Antifederalists in the state assemblies and ratifying conventions.
   (a) Who were the Antifederalists?
   (b) What role did they play in the evolution of the Second Amendment?
   (c) How should we weigh Antifederalist ideas when seeking to understand the meaning of the Second Amendment?

Is There Common Ground?

Both Professors Shalhope and Cress stretch their arguments back to the political philosophers in English history. Cress goes back to the Magna Carta of 1215 which gave the people (meaning the noblemen) the right to bear arms against the potential tyranny of the King. By the eighteenth century, many of these English libertarians had grieved over the "loss of virility and virtue" in their society and abdicated their military responsibilities to professionals.

Both Shalhope and Cress also agree that it was America that remained an agrarian society where armed men would consider it their civic duty to join their state militia as armed citizens and protect themselves from the tyranny of our national government or any other external threat. Both use similar sources such as the debates at the Constitutional Convention of 1787 and the states' ratifying conventions to bolster their arguments, but they reach different conclusions. Cress believes that the Second Amendment meant that an individual could possess arms only if he were a member of the militia, while Shalhope maintains that all virtuous citizens had the right to bear arms. In his view, the argument centered on whether or not citizens were required to be members of the militia.

Cress does not extend his argument for limiting arms to members of the militia past the 1780s. Shalhope, however, argues that with the passage of time, the symbolic

importance of the militia faded while "a violently activist democratic ideology" produced a mythological frontiersman ready to rid the environment of wild animals and Indians. "This is the legacy," says Shalhope, "which gun control advocates must contend."

Create Central

www.mhhe.com/createcentral

Additional Resources

Saul Cornell, *A Well-Regulated Militia: The Founding Fathers and the Origins of Gun Control in America* (Oxford University Press, 2006)

Lawrence D. Cress, "An Armed Community: The Origins and Meaning of the Right to Bear Arms," *Journal of American History* (vol. 71, June 1984)

Glenn H. Reynolds, "A Critical Guide to the Second Amendment," *Tennessee Law Review* (Spring 1995)

Robert Shalhope, "The Ideological Origins of the Second Amendment," *Journal of American History* (vol. 69, December 1982)

Mark V. Tushnet, *Out of Range: Why the Constitution Can't End the Battle Over Guns* (Oxford University Press, 2007)

Internet References . . .

Michael Bellesiles, "Disarming the Critics"

www.oah.org/pub/nl/2001nov/bellesiles.html

National Rifle Association News and Information

www.NRANEWS.com/

U.S. Department of Justice's Bureau of Justice Statistics

www.ojp.usdoj_gov/bjs/homicide/tables/weaponstab

Selected, Edited, and with Issue Framing Material by:
Larry Madaras, *Howard Community College*
and
James M. SoRelle, *Baylor University*

ISSUE

Was Alexander Hamilton an Economic Genius?

YES: John Steele Gordon, from "The Hamiltonian Miracle," Walker and Company (1997)

NO: Carey Roberts, from "Alexander Hamilton and the 1790s Economy: A Reappraisal," New York University Press (2006)

Learning Outcomes

After reading this issue, you will be able to:

- Analyze the major components of Hamilton's economic program.
- Compare and contrast the arguments supporting or opposing Hamilton's economic program.
- Distinguish between loose and strict construction of the Constitution and apply it to interpreting Hamilton's economic program.
- Understand the legacy of Hamilton's economic program in today's political policy debates.

ISSUE SUMMARY

YES: John Steele Gordon claims that Alexander Hamilton's brilliant policies for funding and assuming the debts of the Confederation and state governments and for establishing a privately controlled Bank of the United States transformed the new nation's financial circumstances and propelled the United States into a position as a major world economic power.

NO: Carey Roberts argues that in the 1790s Hamilton's financial policies undermined popular faith in the Federalist Party and diminished confidence in the federal government.

$\mathbf{A}$lexander Hamilton remains the most enigmatic, elusive, and highly criticized of the group we call "the founding fathers." When contrasted with Thomas Jefferson, Hamilton comes off second best as arrogant, crude, and manipulative, an embezzler who was worst of all a "crypto-monarchist." Yet nationally syndicated conservative columnist George Will astutely observes: "There is an elegant memorial in Washington to Jefferson, but none to Hamilton. However, if you seek Hamilton's monument, look around. You are living in it. We honor Jefferson but live in Hamilton's country."

Hamilton grew up in very humble circumstances. Born out of wedlock in the West Indies in 1755, Hamilton was abandoned by his father at age 9, orphaned by the death of his mother at age 13, and left penniless. He and his older brother were assigned by the courts to live with a cousin who committed suicide less than a year after he had taken in the boys. In spite of such a volatile childhood that limited his formal schooling, Hamilton was a voracious reader who taught himself French and became skilled in mathematics and economics. As a 16-year-old, he was employed as a clerk in the firm of Beckman and Cruger, where he performed important accounting and administrative duties. Hugh Knox, a Presbyterian minister, recognized Hamilton's talents and changed the young man's life forever when he collected funds to send him to the mainland for an education.

Talented and very ambitious, Hamilton arrived in the British North American colonies in 1773 as revolutionary fervor was boiling. After studying at an academy in New Jersey, Hamilton enrolled at Kings College (now Columbia University), where he remained until March 14, 1776, when he was appointed captain of a New York artillery company. General George Washington appointed Columbia's most distinguished student his aide-de-camp and promoted him to the rank of lieutenant colonel in the Continental Army. Hamilton served with Washington at key battles including the near disaster at Valley Forge.

Hamilton's military experiences with the financially starved Continental Army, along with his service as a delegate from New York in the Confederation Congress, turned him into a staunch nationalist. He attended the Annapolis Convention of 1786 to discuss the problems of interstate commerce under the Articles of Confederation, but so few delegates showed up, he introduced a resolution for a meeting at Philadelphia the following year.

At the Constitutional Convention of 1787, Hamilton's proposal to model the new government after the British system, with lifetime appointments of the president, Supreme Court, and Senate, met with strong hostility. His two fellow New York delegates were even opposed to the structure of government supported by the majority of the delegates. But Hamilton wrote a majority of the articles, along with James Madison and John Jay, in the New York City newspaper that were instrumental in securing the ratification of the Constitution. These articles, collectively known as *The Federalist Papers,* were later published in book format and have become the bible in interpreting the Constitution.

The highpoint of Hamilton's career was his appointment as President George Washington's secretary of the treasury, where his proposals for funding the new government, assuming the debts of the states, and establishing a private Bank of the United States, created a political furor that is still being debated by historians today. Supporters of Hamilton's proposals argue that the national government needed these programs to give the country order and stability. Opponents of such programs as the establishment of a Bank of the United States believed that the bank had too much power in directing the economy of the country. In the 1830s, President Andrew Jackson achieved a political victory when he withdrew federal deposits from the Bank of the United States and refused to re-charter "the Monster." In doing so, says historian Alan Brinkley, "the country lost an important financial institution and was left with a fragmented and chronically unstable banking system that would plague the economy for many years." The establishment of the Federal Reserve System in 1913 was a testament to the legacy of Alexander Hamilton.

After his resignation from Washington's cabinet in 1795, Hamilton's advice was still sought by Washington, and he penned the president's famous farewell address. Though out of office, he dominated the cabinet of his opponent, President John Adams, but lost influence after his Federalist Party was thrown out of office. In the election of 1800, he supported Jefferson over Aaron Burr when a tie resulted in the electoral-college vote. When Hamilton labeled Burr "a dangerous man who ought not to be trusted with the reins of government" and cost him the gubernatorial election in New York in 1804, Burr challenged Hamilton to a duel. Hamilton accepted and was mortally wounded on July 11, 1804. He died a day later, bidding farewell to his wife and children.

The bibliography on Alexander Hamilton is enormous. Hamilton was compulsive in publishing his essays on politics and economics. Harold C. Syrett et al., have published 27 volumes of *The Papers of Alexander Hamilton* (Columbia University Press, 1961–1987). Among the many shorter versions of Hamilton's essays and letters are: Michael Lind, ed., *Hamilton's Republic: Readings in the American Democratic Nationalist Tradition* (Free Press, 1997); Richard B. Morris, ed., *Alexander Hamilton and the Founding of the Nation* (The Dial Press, 1957); and Jo Anne Freeman, *Alexander Hamilton: Writings* (Library of America, 2001). Quotations in Donald R. Hickey and Connie D. Clark, *Citizen Hamilton: The Wit and Wisdom of an American Founder* (Rowman and Littlefield, 2006) attempt to make Hamilton relevant today. For the best journal articles published between 1925 and 1966, see Jacob E. Cooke's *Alexander Hamilton: A Profile* (Hill and Wang, 1967). The most recent interpretations can be found in Douglas Ambrose and Robert W. T. Martin, eds., *The Many Faces of Alexander Hamilton: The Life and Legacy of America's Most Elusive Founder* (New York University Press, 2006). The most recent and comprehensive biography is Ron Chernow's prize-winning *Alexander Hamilton* (Penguin Press, 2004) with new information on his youth. Other important biographies include Forrest McDonald, *Alexander Hamilton: A Biography* (W. W. Norton, 1979), which contains an excellent discussion on his career as secretary of the treasury; John C. Miller, *Alexander Hamilton: Portrait in Paradox* (Harper and Brothers, 1959); and Richard Brookhiser, *Alexander Hamilton: American* (Free Press, 1999).

Was Hamilton an economic genius or was he overrated in terms of his influence of the future American economy? In the first essay, historian John Steele Gordon believes that Hamilton's policies for funding and assuming the debts of the Confederation and state governments, and for establishing a privately controlled Bank of the

United States laid the foundation for the rich and powerful national economy the country enjoys today. But Professor Carey Roberts disagrees. He argues that in the context of the 1790s, Hamilton's financial policies were politically unpopular and helped undermine popular faith in the Federalist Party. Such policies also diminished confidence in the federal government because of the increasing tax burden necessary to fund the full debt and enabled some people to increase their own wealth through political influence.

YES ↵

John Steele Gordon

The Hamiltonian Miracle

. . . **B**ecause the financial situation had been the most powerful impetus to the establishment of the new government, the most important of the new executive departments was certain to be the Treasury. It soon had forty employees to the State Department's mere five. And its tasks were as clear as they were monumental. The department would have to devise a system of taxation to fund the new government. A monetary system would have to be developed to further the country's commerce and industry. The national debt needed to be refunded and rationalized. The Customs Service had to be organized. The public credit had to be established so that the government could borrow as necessary.

All this was to be brilliantly accomplished in the first two years of the new government. It was, almost entirely, the work of the first secretary of the treasury, Alexander Hamilton. Among the Founding Fathers, Hamilton, because of his financial genius and despite never holding elective office, would have an impact on the future of the United States that only Washington, Madison, and Jefferson equaled.

But Hamilton was not like the other Founding Fathers. He was the only one of the major figures of the early Republic who was not born in what is now the United States. Instead he was born on the minor British West Indian island of Nevis and came to manhood on what was then the Danish island of St. Croix, now part of the U.S. Virgin Islands. . . .

With the rapidly deteriorating relations between Great Britain and its American colonies, Hamilton threw in his lot with his new country. His immense talents and his capacity for work soon secured him an important role in the Revolution—as Washington's aide-de-camp—and its aftermath. When Washington became president under the new Constitution, on April 30th, 1789, he asked Robert Morris, known as "the financier of the Revolution" because of his success at finding money and supplies for the Continental army, to become secretary of the treasury. But Morris, intent on making money, turned him down.

He recommended Hamilton instead. Morris and Hamilton had been in correspondence for several years about the country's fiscal crisis and how to solve it, and Hamilton, still in his early twenties, had greatly impressed the elder man. As early as 1781, as the Revolution still continued, Hamilton had written Morris regarding the establishment of a proper national debt on the British model. "A national debt, if it is not excessive, will be to us a national blessing," he wrote. "It will be a powerful cement to our union. It will also create a necessity for keeping up taxation to a degree which, without being oppressive, will be a spur to industry."

Washington was happy to appoint his old comrade in arms, and Hamilton, now in his early thirties, gladly gave up a lucrative law practice in New York to accept.

Hamilton's background would always set him apart and give him an outlook on life and politics the other Founding Fathers did not share. It also made him uniquely qualified to establish the financial basis of the new United States. Far more than Jefferson, Washington, Adams, and Madison, Hamilton was a nationalist. Perhaps because he had grown up viewing the colonies on the continent only from afar, his loyalty to the United States as a whole was unalloyed by any loyalty to a particular state, not even New York where he spent his adult life.

Also, Hamilton was by far the most urban and the most commercial-minded of the men who made the country. He had grown up, almost literally, in a counting house and lived most of his life in what had already long been the most cosmopolitan and commercial-minded city in the country. In 1784 he had founded a bank that continues to this day, the Bank of New York, and would found a newspaper that also lives, the *New York Post*. Washington, Jefferson, Madison, and even Adams were far more tied to the land than was Hamilton. Jefferson, especially, longed to see the United States as a country filled with self-sufficient yeoman farmers who shunned urban life. Hamilton, at home in the city and deeply learned in both the theory and practice of finance, saw far more clearly than Jefferson how the winds of economic change were blowing in the late eighteenth century. . . .

Very nearly Congress's first act was to set about devising a federal tax system. On July 4, 1789, it passed the first Tariff Act, largely written by Hamilton, and henceforth import duties would usually provide the bulk of the federal government's revenues until the First World War (although the proceeds from the sale of public land in the West, not a tax at all, increasingly contributed to the government's revenues as the frontier pushed westward).

But, at first, tariffs were not enough. To gain more revenue, Congress passed excise taxes on carriages, distilled spirits, sugar, salt, and other items. Excise taxes are internal taxes on specific goods or on the privilege of doing business, and the tax on carriages was clearly a tax on the rich (only the rich, after all, could afford carriages) but a very modest one. Virginia quickly sued, claiming that the tax on carriages was a direct tax and thus had to be apportioned among the states according to population (in other words, according to the number of people, not carriages). Hamilton, at the request of the attorney general, argued the case for the federal government before the Supreme Court. The Court agreed with Hamilton that the carriage tax was an excise. This, as it happens, was the first time the Court addressed the constitutionality of an act of Congress.

The tax on liquor might seem to be the first of the "sin taxes," but the idea of alcohol as "demon rum" was, in fact, largely a nineteenth-century concept. Instead, liquor, sugar, and salt were taxed simply because they were three of the relatively few commodities then manufactured on an industrial scale and thus amenable to efficient tax collection.

The federal government quickly ran into a serious problem with the so-called whiskey tax. In most areas of the country, liquor distillers were too few in number to effectively protest the new tax, and, in any event, they could easily pass it along to their customers in higher prices. But the small farmers in western areas were blocked from eastern markets by the Appalachian Mountains. They had to convert their grain to whiskey before it was in a valuable enough form to bear the cost of transportation across the mountains. A 25 percent excise tax was a heavy economic burden for them, and they flared into rebellion in 1794, the first direct challenge to the authority of the new federal government. The rebellion was quickly and easily suppressed, and the two rebels who were convicted of treason were pardoned by President Washington. But the point was made that the new federal government could, and would, enforce its writ.

A revenue stream in place, Hamilton quickly turned to refunding the debt incurred in the Revolution and by the old national government. Indeed there was not much choice for the new Constitution commanded that the federal government assume the debts of the Confederation. The argument was over who should benefit from this refunding. Much of the debt, in the form of bonds, requisition IOUs, and continentals had fallen into the hands of wealthy merchants in the major cities, who had acquired it at far below par (its nominal face value), some for as little as 10 percent of that face value.

On January 14th, 1790, Hamilton submitted his first "Report on the Public Credit," which called for redeeming the old national debt on generous terms and issuing new bonds to pay for it, backed by the revenue from the tariff. The plan immediately became public knowledge in New York City—then the nation's temporary capital—but news of it spread only slowly, via horseback and sailing vessel, to the rest of the country. New York speculators moved at once to take advantage of the situation. They bought as many of the old bonds as they could, raising the price from 20–25 percent of par to about 40–45 percent.

There was an immediate outcry that these speculators should not be allowed to profit at the expense of those who had patriotically taken the old government's paper at par and then sold it for much less in despair or from necessity. James Jackson, a member of the House of Representatives from the sparsely settled frontier state of Georgia, was horrified by the avaricious city folk. "Since this report has been read in this house," he said in Congress, "a spirit of havoc, speculation, and ruin, has arisen, and been cherished by people who had access to the information the report contained, . . . Three vessels, sir, have sailed within a fortnight from this port [New York], freighted for speculation; they are intended to purchase up the State and other securities in the hands of the uninformed, though honest citizens of North Carolina, South Carolina, and Georgia. My soul rises indignant at the avaricious and immoral turpitude which so vile a conduct displays."

Elias Boudinot of New Jersey, wealthy and heavily involved in speculation himself, demurred. "I should be sorry," he said in reply, "if, on this occasion, the House should decide that speculations in the funds are violations of either the moral or political law. A government hardly exists in which such speculation is disallowed; . . . [I agree] that the spirit of speculation had now risen to an alarming height; but the only way to prevent its future effect, is to give the public funds a degree of stability as soon as possible." This, undoubtedly, was Hamilton's view as well.

James Madison, in the House of Representatives for Virginia, led the attempt to undercut the speculators. He proposed that the current holders of the old bonds be paid only the present market value and that the original bond-holders be paid the difference between market value and face value. There were two weighty objections to this plan.

The first was one of simple practicality. Identifying the original holders of much of this paper would have been a bureaucratic nightmare, in many cases entirely impossible. Fraud would have been rampant. The second objection was one of justice. If an original bond holder had sold his bonds to another, "are we to disown the act of the party himself?" asked Elias Boudinot. "Are we to say, we will not be bound by your transfer, we will not treat with your representative, but insist on resettlement with you alone?"

Further, to have accepted Madison's scheme would have greatly impaired any future free market in U.S. government securities and thus greatly restricted the ability of the new government to borrow in the future. The reason was simple. If the government of the moment could decide, on its own, to whom it owed past debts, any government in the future would have a precedent to do the same. Politics would control the situation, and politics is always uncertain. There is nothing that markets hate more than uncertainty, and they weigh the value of stocks and bonds accordingly.

Hamilton, deeply versed in the ways of getting and spending, was well aware of this truth. Madison, a land-owner and intellectual, was not. Hamilton, in his report, had been adamant. "It renders property in the funds less valuable, consequently induces lenders to demand a higher premium for what they lend, and produces every other inconvenience of a bad state of public credit."

Hamilton was anxious to establish the ability of the U.S. government to borrow when necessary. But he was also anxious to establish a well-funded and secure national debt for other reasons, for he was fully aware of the British experience with its national debt. Perhaps the greatest problem of the American economy at this time was a lack of liquid capital, which is to say, capital available for investment. Hamilton wanted to use the national debt to create a larger and more flexible money supply. Banks holding government bonds, he argued, could issue bank notes backed by them. He knew also that government bonds could serve as collateral for bank loans, multiplying the available capital, and that they would attract still more capital from Europe.

But there were still many people who failed to grasp the power of a national debt, properly funded and serviced, to bring prosperity to a national economy. John Adams,

hardly stupid, was one. "Every dollar of a bank bill that is issued beyond the quantity of gold and silver in the vaults," he wrote, "represents nothing, and is therefore a cheat upon somebody."

Hamilton's reasoning eventually prevailed over Madison's, although not without a great deal of rhetoric. Hamilton's father-in-law, Philip Schuyler, by this time a senator from New York, owned more than $60,000 worth of government securities, a small fortune by the standards of the day. It was said that listening to the opposition speakers in the Senate made his hair stand "on end as if the Indians had fired at him." Rhetoric or no, the House passed Hamilton's funding proposals 36–13.

The second major part of Hamilton's program was for the new federal government to assume the debts that the individual states had incurred during the Revolutionary War. Hamilton thought these debts amounted to $25 million, although no one really knew for sure. It eventually turned out that only about $18 million in state bonds remained in circulation.

Again, opinion was sharply divided. Those states, such as Virginia, that had redeemed most of their bonds were adamantly opposed to assumption. Needless to say, those states, like the New England ones, that had not were all in favor of it. Financial speculators, hoping for a rise to par of bonds they had bought at deep discount, also favored the federal government assuming the state debts. But land speculators were opposed. Many states allowed public lands to be purchased with state bonds at face value, even when the bonds were selling in the open market for much less. Any rise in the price of bonds would increase the cost of land.

Madison and others argued that it was simply unfair for Virginians, who had nearly liquidated their state's bonded indebtedness, to pay all over again for the debts incurred by other states that had not. "Where, I again demand," thundered James Jackson of Georgia, "is the justice of compelling a State which has taxed her citizens for the sinking of her debt, to pay another proportion, not of her own, but the debts of other States, which have made no exertions whatever?"

Fisher Ames, a congressman from Massachusetts, argued that since the new Constitution gave all revenues from tariffs—the best and surest source of funds with which to pay the interest on the bonds—to the federal government, the federal government should now assume the debt. "Let the debts follow the funds," he demanded.

In the middle of April 1790, the House voted down Hamilton's proposal 31–29. Four more times it was voted down, each time by so narrow a margin that Hamilton had hopes of making a deal. He had to do something, for he had tied the funding of the old national debt and the assumption of the state debt into one bill. Many thought that the state debt issue was "a millstone about the neck of the whole system which must finally sink it."

Hamilton might have abandoned his effort to fund the state debts, but he had still one more reason for extinguishing as much state paper as possible and replacing it with federal bonds. The debts, of course, were largely held by the prosperous men of business, commerce, and agriculture—the oligarchs, in other words. These men's loyalties lay mainly with their respective states and the cozy local societies in which they had grown up. Although they had largely supported the creation of the new Union, Hamilton had every reason to suppose that their support would quickly fade away if their self-interest dictated it.

Hamilton, therefore, was anxious to make it in the self–interest of these men to continue their support of the Union. If they had a large share of their assets held in federal bonds, they would have powerful incentives for wishing the Union well. . . .

Hamilton was right that the bonds would find acceptance in the marketplace, and the entire issue sold out in only a few weeks. The new government, with a monopoly on customs duties and possessing the power to tax elsewhere, was simply a much better credit risk than the old government and the states had been. When it became clear that the U.S. government would be able to pay the interest due on these bonds, they quickly became sought after in Europe, just as Hamilton had hoped, especially after the outbreak of the war in which the other European powers tried to reverse the tide of the French Revolution.

The third major portion of Hamilton's program was the creation of a central bank, modeled after the Bank of England. Hamilton saw it as an instrument of fiscal efficiency, economic regulation, and money creation. Jefferson saw it as another giveaway to the rich and as a potential instrument of tyranny. Furthermore, Jefferson and Madison thought it was patently unconstitutional for the federal government to establish a bank, for the Constitution nowhere gives the federal government the explicit power to charter a bank or, for that matter, any other corporation.

There are three main purposes to a central bank. It acts as a depository for government funds and a means of transferring them from one part of the country to another (no small consideration in the primitive conditions of Hamilton's day). It is a source of loans to the government and to other banks, and it regulates the money supply.

The last was a great problem in the new Republic. Specie—gold and silver—was in critically short supply. Colonial coinage had been a hodgepodge of Spanish, Portuguese, and British coins, often cut into pieces in order to make small change.

The lack of specie forced merchants to be creative. In the southern colonies warehouse receipts for tobacco often circulated as money. Hamilton knew that foreign bonds could serve the same purpose. In his "Report on the Public Credit" he wrote: "It is a well-known fact that in countries in which the national debt is properly funded, and an object of established confidence, it answers most of the purposes of money. Transfers of stock, or public debt, are there equivalent to payments in specie; or, in other words, stock, in the principal transactions of business, passes current as specie. The same thing would, in all probability, happen here, under the like circumstances."

But the bonds, of course, were of very large denomination. There were a few state banks (three in 1790) to issue paper money, but these notes did not circulate on a national basis. Many business deals had to be accompanied by barter simply because there was no money to facilitate them.

Hamilton did not like the idea of the government itself issuing paper money because he felt that governments could not be trusted to exert self-discipline. Certainly the Continental Congress had shown none when it came to printing paper money, although at least it had the pretty good excuse of utter necessity. Hamilton thought that an independent central bank could supply not only a medium of exchange but the discipline needed to keep the money sound. If it issued notes that were redeemable in gold and silver on demand and accepted by the federal government in payment of taxes, those notes would circulate at par and relieve the desperate shortage of cash. Further, because the central bank could refuse the notes of state banks that got out of line—which would mean that no one else would take them either—it could supply discipline to those banks as well.

Hamilton proposed a capitalization of $10 million, a very large sum when it is considered that the three state banks in existence had a combined capital of only $2 million. The government was to subscribe 20 percent of this, but Hamilton intended the bank to be a private concern. "To attach full confidence to an institution of this nature," Hamilton wrote in his "Report on a National Bank" delivered to Congress on December 14th, 1790, "it appears to be an essential ingredient in its structure, that it shall be under a *private* not a *public* direction—under the guidance of *individual interest*, not of *public policy*; which would be supposed to be, and, in certain emergencies, under a feeble or too sanguine administration, would really be, liable to being too much influenced by *public necessity*." In other words, Hamilton did not believe that politicians could be trusted with the power to print money, whereas a privately held bank could, because its owners would go broke if they printed excessive amounts. The history of many countries, including, in his own time, France under the First Republic, would prove him right.

To make sure that the private owners of the bank did not pursue private interests at public expense, Hamilton wanted the bank's charter to require that its notes be redeemable in specie, that 20 percent of the seats on the board of directors be held by government appointees, and that the secretary of the treasury would have the right to inspect the books at any time.

There was little political discussion of the bank outside of Congress, which passed Hamilton's bill, the two houses splitting cleanly along sectional lines. Only one congressman from states north of Maryland voted against it, and only three from states south of Maryland voted for it.

Hamilton thought the bank was a fait accompli, but he had not reckoned on Thomas Jefferson and James Madison. Jefferson, the lover of rural virtues, had a deep, almost visceral hatred of banks, which he thought the epitome of all that was urban. "I have ever been the enemy of banks," he wrote years later to John Adams. "My zeal against those institutions was so warm and open at the establishment of the Bank of the U.S. that I was derided as a Maniac by the tribe of bank-mongers, who were seeking to filch from the public their swindling, and barren gains."

Jefferson and Madison, along with their fellow Virginian Edmund Randolph, the attorney general, wrote opinions for President Washington that the bank bill was unconstitutional. Their arguments revolved around the so-called necessary and proper clause, giving Congress the power to pass laws "necessary and proper for carrying into Execution the foregoing Powers."

The Constitution nowhere specifically authorizes the federal government to establish a central bank, they argued, and therefore one could be created only if it were indispensable for carrying out the government's enumerated duties. A central bank was not *absolutely* necessary and therefore was absolutely unconstitutional. This line of reasoning is known as *strict construction*—although the phrase itself was not actually coined until 1838—and has been a powerful force in the American political firmament ever since.

President Washington recognized the utility of a central bank, but Jefferson's and Randolph's argument had much force for him. Further, he may have worried that if the bank were established in Philadelphia, the capital might never make its way to his beloved Potomac. He told Hamilton that he could not sign the bill unless Hamilton was able to overcome Jefferson's constitutional argument.

To counter Jefferson's doctrine of strict construction, Hamilton devised a counter doctrine of *implied powers*. He said that if the federal government was to deal successfully with its enumerated duties, it must be supreme in deciding how best to perform those duties. "Little less than a prohibitory clause," he wrote to Washington, "can destroy the strong presumptions which result from the general aspect of the government. Nothing but demonstration should exclude the idea that the power exists." Moreover, he asserted that Congress had the right to decide what means were necessary and proper. "The national government like every other," he wrote, "must judge in the first instance of the proper exercise of its powers."

Hamilton's complete response to Jefferson and Randolph runs nearly 15,000 words and was written under an inflexible deadline, for the Constitution required President Washington to sign or veto the bill within ten days of its passage. Hamilton thought about his response for nearly a week but seems to have written it entirely in a single night. To read it today is to see plain the extraordinary powers of thought he possessed. Even John Marshall was awed by them. "To talents of the highest order," the great chief justice wrote, "he united a patient industry, not always the companion of genius, which fitted him in a peculiar manner for the difficulties to be encountered by the man who should be placed at the head of the American finances."

Washington, his doubts quieted, signed the bill in 1791, and the bank soon came into existence. Its stock subscription was a resounding success, for investors expected it to be very profitable, which it was. It also functioned as Hamilton intended and did much to further the early development of the American economy. . . .

Hamilton's financial program quickly, indeed utterly, transformed the country's financial circumstances. In the 1780s the United States had been a financial basket case. By 1794 it had the highest credit rating in Europe, and some of its bonds were selling at 10 percent over par. Talleyrand, who later became the French foreign minister, explained why. The United States bonds, he said, were "safe and free from reverses. They have been funded in such a sound manner and the prosperity of this country is growing so rapidly that there can be no doubt of their solvency." By 1801 Europeans held $33 million in U.S. securities, and European capital was helping mightily to build the American economy.

Less than two years after Hamilton's funding bill became law, trading in state and federal bonds had become so brisk in New York that brokers who specialized in them got together and formed an organization to facilitate trading. This organization would evolve into the New York Stock Exchange, and within a little more than 100 years it would be the largest such exchange in the world, eclipsing London's.

But Hamilton's program and its enactment had one great and entirely unanticipated consequence. It produced the first big political fight of the new federal union. It revealed deep and heretofore unsuspected cleavages in the American body politic. "When the smoke of the contest had cleared away," wrote Albert S. Bolles in his majestic *Financial History of the United States*, published a century ago, "two political parties might be seen, whose opposition, though varying much in conviction, power, and earnestness, has never ceased." It still hasn't, and the American political nation can be divided to this day largely into Jeffersonians and Hamiltonians, those who look more closely at the trees of individual liberty and justice and those for whom the forests of a sound economy and an effective government are most important.

Jefferson never ceased to rail against Hamilton's program. His "Remarks Upon the Bank of the United States," published a few years after the bank was chartered, is a savage attack upon Hamilton. Jefferson, for instance, considered only the inevitable inequities that had resulted from Hamilton's funding scheme. "Immense sums were . . . filched from the poor and ignorant," he wrote, "and fortunes accumulated by those who had themselves been poor enough before."

Hamilton, understandably, preferred to look at the results and felt abused. "It is a curious phenomenon in political history," he wrote in reply, "that a measure which has elevated the credit of the country from a state of absolute prostration to a state of exalted preeminence, should bring upon the authors of it obloquy and reproach. It is certainly what, in the ordinary course of human affairs, they could not have anticipated."

But by then, 1797, the political pendulum was swinging toward the Jeffersonians, and they would run the country for years to come. In the fullness of time, however, as the very few who were actually harmed by Hamilton's program faded from the scene and the very many who benefited, generation after generation, remained, it came to enjoy the praise it deserves. Of Hamilton's work Daniel Webster, with typical grandiloquence, would one day say "the whole country perceived with delight, and the world saw with admiration. He smote the rock of the national resources, and abundant streams gushed forth. He touched the dead corpse of the public credit, and it sprung to its feet. The fabled birth of Minerva from the brain of Jove was hardly more sudden or more perfect than the financial system of the United States as it burst forth from the conception of Alexander Hamilton."

JOHN STEELE GORDON is a specialist in business and financial history whose articles have appeared in numerous prominent magazines and newspapers for the past 20 years. He is a contributing editor to *American Heritage* and since 1989 has written the "Business of America" column. His other books include *Hamilton's Blessing: The Extraordinary Life and Times of Our National Debt* (Walker, 1977), *The Great Game: The Emergence of Wall Street as a World Power: 1653–2000* (1999), and *A Thread Across the Ocean: The Heroic Story of the Transatlantic Cable* (Walker, 2002).

Carey Roberts

 **NO**

Alexander Hamilton and the 1790s Economy: A Reappraisal

Historians and political scientists commonly credit Alexander Hamilton's economic plans for revitalizing the American economy and providing the impetus for extended economic progress. Such arguments usually take for granted many of the criticisms levied against the policies of the states and Confederation during the 1780s. They further assume that the weakness of the American economy stemmed from the decentralized nature of its financial institutions, lack of specie, and burdensome problems of the Revolutionary debt.

There is little doubt that economic problems prevailed under the Articles of Confederation; however, it remains unclear how much Hamilton's policies corrected those problems. Hamilton's program of assumption and funding resulted in an overall increase in the nation's monetary base. The Bank of the United States (BUS) furthered the monetary expansion by following a pattern of fractional-reserve lending up until 1795. As a result, inflation continued to affect the economy during the early 1790s. Burdensome taxes were levied to pay off government debts at face value rather than at prevailing market values. And significant opposition formed against Federalist officials due to the perceived joining of monied interests to the federal government.

Without understanding the short-term consequences, our praise for the long-term results seems strained at best. If what is called "Hamiltonian" finance resulted in short-term problems, or even disasters, long-term success would be less likely. If long-term success could actually be attributed to Jeffersonian policies carried forward by Jacksonian Democrats, the place of Hamiltonian finance in our history would change drastically. Furthermore, even if it is determined that the American economy surged after 1791, attributing the rise to beneficial market conditions totally independent from federal politics could jeopardize Hamilton's place as a financial genius. Such is not the scope of this essay, nor is it a challenge to the dominant interpretation of Hamilton's character and financial vision. However, puzzling discrepancies present themselves when one compares the effects of the Federalist financial plan and its short-term consequences in the 1790s. Limitation of space prevents a full treatment of the period, but it is hoped that the following might serve as a prolegomena for further study.

Economic Problems of the 1790s

The first decade under the new constitution was not a period of strong economic growth, nor was it free from periods of economic distress. Data are sketchy at best, and debate still rages as to whether the economy of antebellum America was rapidly expanding or mediocre. Likewise, we may never have a complete grasp on the economic condition for the period between 1789 and 1800, a problem further complicated by the loss of records, especially those of the BUS, during the War of 1812.

While the fine details of economic growth remain elusive, much can still be said about economic conditions both before and after Hamilton and Congress implemented Hamilton's plan for the national economy. A speculative crash occurred in New York City in 1792 and spread sporadically across the eastern seaboard. Steep inflation rates existed between 1791 and 1796. And while infrastructure investments bustled throughout the East and the developing West, their creation coincided with a rapid increase in bankruptcy and insolvency. Even at this early date, the cyclical activity of the American economy appeared in short booms and busts.

Several explanations could be offered for the development of an early boom-bust cycle. One might suggest business cycles are a natural element of capitalism, and as the economy modernized, cyclical fluctuations would be expected. Sheer greed on the part of speculators could have produced more services than consumers demanded, thus causing overproduction. The financial infrastructure may have remained too immature to adequately finance the needs of investors despite Hamilton's attempt to strengthen it. State governments may have improperly managed their economic situation either by refusing to cooperate with other states or by failing to sufficiently support newly chartered companies. Investors and promoters may have been unsuccessful in getting farmers and minor merchants to see how they could benefit from a vigorous—and united—national economy.

Another explanation for a business cycle emerging early in the 1790s suggests that far from stabilizing the economy, Hamilton and the Federalist Congress destabilized financial markets causing entrepreneurs to misread the market and make incorrect business decisions.

Many important entrepreneurs in the early republic also held most of the domestic debt. As the country's public credit rose, debt holders profited from debt redemption. The Bank of the United States added to the potential for increased investment by pursuing a policy of easy money until 1796. By receiving higher profits and easier credit than market conditions allowed, entrepreneurs took much greater risks with their subsequent investments. They also mistook the dramatic deflation of the late 1780s and the inflation of the early 1790s as evidence of a strengthening economy. Prices surged after ratification of the Constitution due to perceived political actions of Congress, not due to Americans being in a position to demand more goods and services. The resulting malinvestments in transportation improvements, banking, and manufacturing far exceeded market demand and resulted in the Panic of 1792 and would add to the distress in 1796. To complicate matters further, the Treasury, following Hamilton's "Report on the Mint," fixed the exchange rate of specie so that gold slightly overvalued silver. The decision instigated a classic example of Gresham's Law, where "bad" money chases out "good" money, and in this case, the country's gold supply was steadily depleted in favor of silver

Debt Funding, Conversion, and the Bank of the United States

There is no need to regurgitate the intricacies of the financial program proposed by Alexander Hamilton while Secretary of Treasury. Yet misunderstanding Hamilton's goals and the monetary effects of his plans creates a distorted view of Hamilton's role. Hamilton was neither a defender of an aristocracy of wealth nor was he the architect of America's economic "take-off."

Alexander Hamilton laid clear plans as to what he wished to do with the Revolutionary debt. Though not a dedicated bullionist, like most economic nationalists of his day Hamilton believed the country's economic problems grew from a lack of sufficient specie in circulation. The underlying goal required augmenting existing specie by coverting federal and state government securities into a capital pool for financiers and entrepreneurs. Financiers, traders, merchants, manufacturers, and all other businessmen would benefit by having access to cheap credit while consumers would have sufficient currency with which to purchase products. Hamilton never questioned the federal government's role in providing specie, albeit to him, that role was supervisory rather than regulatory.

Hamilton publicly reasoned that the country's credit problems weakened the federal government's ability to get more specie. Low public credit also prevented private citizens from getting loans at reasonable interest rates. The economy needed a jump-start, but not by a direct infusion of specie. Entrepreneurs, who knew how to use capital to spur on economic growth, needed the specie before average citizens. Getting specie to entrepreneurs first (or at all) proved problematic given the immature state of the country's commercial credit system. Hamilton's solution involved bringing in enough specie and then using the federal government to provide a financial network to dispense capital where it was best used. The Revolutionary War debt offered the means of accomplishing both.

Influenced by the predominant view that the economy suffered from a shortage of specie, Hamilton assumed a new credit network needed something other than a finite amount of specie. To be feasible, it must grow with the needs of the people. A rigid specie standard and a credit market where all banknotes equaled specie reserves would be too tight. The best strategy must include a combination of specie, redeemable bank notes, and government securities, where all forms of money and money substitutes traded as currency. Hamilton envisioned nothing less than a sophisticated credit market that could aid investors and supply the country with much needed currency, or as he called it, "the active capital of a country."

Hamilton believed banks could issue more credit than they held in specie reserves as long as all notes were fully redeemable in specie on demand. Like many advocates of commercial banking, Hamilton understood that a bank's depositors rarely demanded all their specie at once. At any given time, banks easily lent out more credit than they held on deposit. He did not understand, however, that the subsequent alteration in the overall purchasing power of money distorted rather than stabilized prices.

Three distinct but interrelated events came together between 1788 and 1791: funding the federal debt through the federal government, not the states; converting the old debt into new debt; and using the Bank of the United States to facilitate the acceptance of securities and bank notes as currency. Only Hamilton advocated all three from a position of high political office. Some congressmen supported him on this. But like many of the great compromises in American history, a majority probably did not exist in support of all three segments combined, only on each segment individually.

As the Philadelphia convention met and produced a new constitution, the market value of debt securities rose based on the expectation of payment. Never did the securities become worthless, but never did they actually reach par with their face value before conversion in 1790. Speculators stood to make impressive gains from buying the debt cheap in the early 1780s and selling high, as many did, in the late 1780s. Furthermore, those who kept their securities through the conversion process stood to gain even more. As late as 1789, confused debt holders did not know what to expect from Congress with regard to the debt. Their only anchor during the hectic first session of Congress was that most congressmen favored paying the debt in some manner.

Congressmen differed on whom to pay and how much. Many opponents of funding, James Madison and Thomas Jefferson excepted, knew the problem was not forsaking the initial common people and soldiers who held the debt. Rather, they saw the issue as a battle between market value on the one hand and a sizable expansion of credit, high taxation, and enlargement of the federal debt's market value, on the other. There were few if any true "repudiationists" in Congress at the time it debated funding.

Thanks to James Madison, the discrimination, or market value forces, lost. Madison, knowingly or not, sidetracked to opponents of face value funding on to questions of morality and social obligation as opposed to financial questions and taxation. By the end of the debate, discrimination meant giving original holders a portion of *face* value, illustrating how Hamilton's most vocal opponents moved toward the center. To make the opposition's position on discrimination less tenable, the difference between market value and face value shrank as the debate dragged on.

Indeed, talk of funding during the ratification process had already increased the market value of the debt and caused a wave of deflation to sweep the economy. Between 1787 and 1789 prices fell between 4 and 7 percent across the country. In Philadelphia alone, extending the dates from 1784 to 1790 shows a 20 percent deflation rate overall. By itself, deflation probably caused some market distortions, and regardless of which policy Congress

followed, whether Hamilton's or an alternative, some malinvestments likely would have occurred.

Congress finally agreed to take specie from a new European loan and apply it to the national debt and the assumed value of state debts. Congress offered to exchange old securities for stock, substituting two-thirds of the principal for 6 percent stock and one-third for 6 percent deferred stock. It also paid all remaining interests and indents at 3 percent and old continental currency at 100:1. The process of conversion both raised the market value of the debt by fully backing it with specie and turned it into usable currency. But conversion also reduced the new currency's purchasing power by infusing the economy with new specie and new notes whose value must have been slightly higher than the highest market value of old notes in the summer of 1790.

One would think conversion continued the process of deflation, but such was not the case since new notes were issued based on the face value of old notes. Because conversion exchanged notes rather than allowed the old ones to continue in circulation and because the federal government injected more notes than the total market value of the old notes, the overall supply of money increased. The resulting inflation appeared immediately as prices increased nationwide. Between 1791 and 1796, prices in Charleston increased 57 percent, Cincinnati grew by 38 percent, and Philadelphia prices rose an astonishing 98 percent. Additional foreign loans (of specie) and creating the Bank of the United States compounded the situation by further increasing the supply of specie *and* redeemable notes. Had Congress followed a policy of paying the old debt at market value, even market value over a period of months, Congress might have continued the deflation. Corresponding taxation may have softened the monetary expansion, but it was unlikely to significantly counteract its effects given the variety of products taxed and the variation of the tax burden.

It is important not to focus merely on general monetary phenomena, but to suggest monetary changes that affected individual entrepreneurs. One must be careful to keep in mind that holders of the debt purchased the bulk of it at prices far below what they were worth after 1790. Prices paid for the debt and the profits debt holders made did not reflect market demand for the debt so much as it reflected Congress's demand for its own debt. In other words, the American economy did not cause the price of securities to increase, Congress's decisions did. The subsequent rise in prices cannot be attributed to a rise in consumer spending, but to a drop in the purchasing power of government securities and BUS notes.

Far ahead of his time, Hamilton took possible inflation into account. In fact, he expected it and anticipated its effect on government securities in terms of bringing down the rate of interest. When Hamilton's proposal went to Congress, some congressmen wished to pay interest on the new stock at present rates of interest, or around 8 percent. But having more money and money substitutes available for banks to lend, the price of money dropped. Betting on interest rates to fall, Hamilton hoped to get debt holders to agree to 6 percent stock that would sell at a premium if interest rates dropped below 6 percent.

Beyond conversion and assumption, other aspects of Hamilton's plan exercised significant influence over prices. Hamilton hoped the Bank of the United States would create a commercial credit network, pool capital for investors, and strengthen the country's merchant base. But like funding and conversion, the Bank exercised an inflationary effect. It certainly increased available commercial credit to individual entrepreneurs as well as to new commercial banks chartered by various states. The bank and its branches fully redeemed its notes upon demand, but the banknotes were not fully backed by specie reserves, and notes circulated in a high proportion to specie in the vaults especially before 1796.

During the first years of the Bank's operation, it followed a course of fairly rapid credit expansion. The BUS played a substantial role in the Panic of 1792, and it may have accounted for some of the economic distress of the period up to 1796. Taking into account the Bank's proportion of notes to specie between 1792 and 1794, the Bank held about a 2:1 ratio. By January 1795, the ratio increased to 5:1 only to drop down slightly by the end of the year. The excess of fiduciary currency, or the notes issued in excess of specie reserves, likely contributed to the rise in prices from 1792 forward. New commercial banks, which pyramided their assets on top of BUS notes and stock, compounded the situation. Wisely, BUS officials changed course by late 1796, boosted their specie holdings, and the notes to specie ratio evened out to near equity by 1799–1800. Not coincidentally, 1796 marked a turning point where the Bank began loaning more capital to private investors than it did to the federal government.

Even assuming the BUS followed a conservative path, those banks whose capital came from BUS notes pursued a different course until competition from BUS branches intensified. Hamilton's consternation with state banks rested on their willingness to expand credit through fiduciary offerings at a much faster rate than the BUS. While some Federalists supported the coexistence of state banks with the Bank and its branches, Hamilton worried the inflationary tendency of the combined circulation of BUS notes and notes of state banks would wreck the fledgling commercial credit system. State banks, Hamilton thought, could not be trusted to control their credit emissions. Should the notes of state banks begin to depreciate, BUS notes might slip as well, thus jeopardizing the whole system. Hamilton must also have known other banks could curtail credit, making loans more expensive, thereby raising interest rates and detrimentally affecting the BUS.

Hamilton mistakenly saw credit as a means of stimulating investment and failed to recognize that demand for credit does not correlate to demand for the investments created with it. If credit expansion prompted investors to place that credit in things for which the economy was not strong enough to endure, then consumer demand would not be strong enough to make investments pan out. At least publicly, Hamilton insisted the opposite would occur. Investors, he claimed, would place their money in ventures sure to make a profit instead of "permanent" improvements like canals and manufacturing. Such was not the case.

A counterargument to the one given here might suggest that inflation is desirable and that deflation is to be avoided. Critics might also insist that the purpose of Hamiltonian finance, as he stated, was to raise the credit rating of the United States government and American businessmen seeking capital or credit from abroad, or to set better terms on foreign contracts. From this perspective, Hamilton was successful, thus contributing to the increase of foreign trade and the export-led expansion of the economy. If not this, then he helped lay the groundwork for institutions that used securities for a finance-led expansion of the economy.

Another way of examining Hamilton's contributions may be in order. Though many debt holders did quite well, many notable exceptions occurred that cannot be attributed to poor luck or lack of entrepreneurial wisdom. Instead, it seems that the inflationary tendencies of Hamiltonian finance produced faulty economic "signals" that misled entrepreneurs into thinking the economy was better than it actually was. Rather than analyzing what influence debt holders exerted over the formation of the new government and Hamilton's plan, a focus on how federal policies influenced their business practices reveals much about the effects of funding, conversion, and the First Bank. Such an approach would follow the one briefly outlined below concerning William Duer.

The Panic of the Early 1790s

The example of the much-maligned William Duer illustrates how economic repercussions from funding and assumption were far from positive. Duer was English by birth and, like Hamilton, spent time in the West Indies, though Duer did so only long enough to manage his father's plantation. Also like Hamilton, Duer settled in New York and married into a wealthy family. The wives of both men were even cousins. Duer briefly served in the Continental Congress but made a fortune fulfilling contracts with the Continental Army. Following the war, he speculated in real estate holdings and served on the Confederation's Treasury Board. He then became Assistant Secretary of Treasury under Hamilton in 1789 and assisted Hamilton in the creation of the Society of Useful Manufactures. Duer often used inside information to exploit the government securities market, but his misapplication—or corrupt application—of this information can account for most of his financial mistakes.

Duer lost with deflation leading up to debt conversion and with the subsequent inflation. Scholars rightly distance Hamilton from Duer with regard to their personal relationship. And Hamilton had no control over Duer's speculations. However, lack of personal involvement does not mean that repercussions from Hamilton's financial plan failed to influence Duer's decisions.

No doubt Duer's life followed that of a frontier gambler more than it did a New York aristocrat. Yet the most incredible of his speculative endeavors depended on specific actions of the federal government, either under the Articles of Confederation or under the Constitution. Two examples merit mentioning: his role in the Scioto land company and his direct influence over the Panic of 1792.

Following the Revolution, Americans started pushing the bounds of the western territory. Given the perceived shortage of specie, prospective land customers petitioned Congress in the late 1780s to accept debt certificates in the place of hard currency. Two companies led the way: the Ohio Company of Association and the Scioto Company. Duer participated in the creation of both since they were part of the same deal, though he directly influenced the Scioto Company. Land developers wished to use the companies to purchase land cheaply and sell it to needy settlers. When Congress agreed to accept specie and debt certificates as payment, Duer and his clients stood to make a substantial profit if the market value of the debt certificates remained low. In other words, they based their assessment of the situation on current prices in 1787 and did not expect the rapid rise in market value. In the end, the Scioto Company went broke due to mismanagement and the substantial increase of land costs as government debt values increased.

The Scioto example should not be used to discount Hamiltonian finance, which began operation after the Scioto Company became insolvent. It does, however, indicate

how entrepreneurs based their decisions on the value of government securities and how changes in their value harmed some investors. Regardless of what Congress did, debt certificates would have fluctuated in value to some extent. In hindsight, Scioto investors should have known better. But how could they? There was no certainty in 1787 that Congress would even pay the national debt, and less certainty existed over whether Congress would pay the debt at face value.

Integral to Duer's association with the Scioto Company was his use of it to manage his personal speculation in government securities. In fact, the same forces that injured the land company encouraged Duer to try his hand at another form of speculation. While assistant to Hamilton, Duer counted on uncertainty about a new congressional policy: full funding of state debts. He busily purchased as much outstanding debt as possible before Congress reached a final decision in August 1790.

Afterwards, as interest rates dropped, new government debt traded at a premium. Additional stock and securities came onto the market as the Bank of the United States commenced business and supported the creation of new commercial banks. BUS shares, bank stocks, and new securities traded openly in major American cities, but no city contained as much speculative buying as New York. At the center of all this stood William Duer.

Duer participated in the selling of most forms of stocks and securities, and he worked both sides of the market. Able to control vast sums of capital, Duer bought and traded the same stock, virtually cornering the market and creating his own profits. Like other speculators in government securities, Duer commenced planning a number of important new companies ranging from banks and factories to bridges and canals. Thinking the market rise in securities knew no limit, Duer plunged everything he had into the market. He began buying on margin by taking out loans from all possible sources, including the fledgling Society for the Erection of Useful Manufacturers and wealthy New Yorkers. The activity of speculators, drawing on the extensive new credit system created by the Federalists under Alexander Hamilton, peaked in March 1792. When directors of the Bank of New York realized credit had been extended too much, their decision to stop all loans commenced a credit contraction spelling the end to William Duer's operation. By the end of March, the panic that began in New York became nationwide.

Ultimately, the federal government and Hamilton bore the greatest economic cost of the Panic of 1792. By late 1792 Hamilton and members of Congress realized projected revenue would not meet the government's demands for expenses and interest payments on the debt. The situation forced Hamilton to take out another foreign loan. The combination of economic distress and the apparent inability of the funding system and BUS to "fund" the debt without more loans elicited stern attacks from Hamilton's opponents in Congress. William B. Giles of Virginia, with the assistance of William Findley of Pennsylvania and Nathaniel Macon of North Carolina, pushed through a series of resolutions questioning Hamilton's leadership of the Treasury and accusing him of misallocation of funds.

The economy momentarily improved, but inflation rates continued to climb until 1796. At that point, the economy slipped back into a panic, albeit less severe than the one in 1792.

The question must be asked: Was William Duer representative of American entrepreneurs during the 1780s and 1790s? Certainly not, especially when considering that all American entrepreneurs did not speculate in government securities and lose all their investments in the Panic of 1792. However, Duer illustrates how expansive credit systems, like that proposed by Hamilton, cannot be sustained indefinitely and how credit booms mislead entrepreneurs and thus lay the groundwork for credit bursts. More importantly, if an insider like William Duer could not make good decisions based on the information at his disposal, how could average entrepreneurs?

Duer shows how politically generated conditions encourage speculative behavior. He based his decisions in part on the signals he received from the securities market—prices boosted by funding and assumption. And if Winifred Rothenberg is correct, debt holders were not the only people basing their decisions on market prices. Though Rothenberg's coverage covers mainly New England, it is safe to say that by the 1780s and 1790s an increasing number of Americans relied exclusively on market prices for economic decisions, prices made possible by moving away from bartering. A different policy, one that allowed for the gradual redemption of securities at market value, may have alleviated some of the extreme cases of speculation and price distortions.

Other speculators who benefited from funding and assumption followed a pattern similar to Duer's. Men like Robert Morris, Thomas Willing, James Greenleaf, Nathaniel Massie, and John Nicholson took profits made from government securities and invested them in projects the market could not sustain.

Land prices rose faster than any other investment in the inflationary climate of the early 1790s, leading numerous speculators to place investments on western expansion (or even on undeveloped land in the East). The Ohio Company, the North American Land Company, the Connecticut Land Company, and the Yazoo land claims,

to name a few, began after investors wildly exaggerated the gains to be made in land development. One of the best examples fueled by inflating land prices, Washington, D.C., included several prominent debt holders like Uriah Forrest and Robert Morris, who plunged into an uncertain market and were financially ruined.

Investors thought higher land prices resulted from higher demand for property. When land prices began dropping, developers went to great lengths to get returns on their investments. William Blout, Nicholas Romayne, and John Chisholm went so far as inviting Great Britain to get Spanish holdings in North America.

The credit boom of the early 1790s also coincided with the expansion of internal improvement companies and commercial banks, whose capital was often pyramided on BUS funds, state subsidies, or mutual credit extensions. To help prospective settlers move west, or to link local eastern markets together, transportation companies quickly emerged with the assistance of state legislatures. The number of banks grew from one in 1790 to twenty in 1795. Thirty-two new navigation companies, including canals and waterways, were charted between 1790 and 1795. States granted twelve new charters in 1796, alone. Charters for bridges increased from one per year in 1791 to as many as fourteen per year in 1795, totaling forty-four between 1791 and 1796. And by 1796, there were sixteen new turnpike charters. Naturally, not all of these new companies relied on bank credit, nor did former debt holders promote them all by themselves. Some companies evolved from lucrative family holdings or from capital raised from investors. But even if some did not rely directly on credit expansion, their customers and investors often did.

New internal improvement companies faced obstacles similar to those encountered by land companies. Most investors wished to build improvements in order to expand their markets. They assumed that Federalist financial measures reinvigorated the economy and continued growth would offset the expense of linking markets together. In doing so, rural markets could be tapped to further commercial potential. Those relying exclusively on prices and available commercial credit, however, ignored the economy's weakness as well as latent hostility to their projects from farmers.

State laws required companies to have charters, which carried certain advantages such as monopoly status, state grants, and the ability to exercise eminent domain. However, charters also carried numerous restrictions that ultimately hindered profitability. And since companies often undermined the property rights of common people, rural farmers condemned the new companies for their special, political privileges. Like the land schemes, most internal improvement projects faced substantial losses. Promoters repeatedly returned to state legislatures for additional support only to be turned away by politicians weary of mounting demands and disillusioned with development schemes. In the end, national fiscal measures encouraged investment, whereas state and local policies were ignored only to the detriment of uncanny or misled investors.

Great wealth was made, as such prominent examples of John J. Astor and Stephen Girard show. But the 1790s were far from the boom time many speculators imagined. In fact, business failures, missed opportunities, and collapsed fortunes may have been the norm. Even wealth made in the decade later diminished as competition intensified and the monetary shocks wore off.

Detractors of this argument may be prepared to accept both the benefits and costs of this boom-bust cycle. The market would never have produced the transportation improvements so quickly. And in the long run, society still enjoys the fruits of the products such as better roads, canals, and a commercial banking network. All modernization efforts proceed along a bumpy path, but society ultimately benefits by laying the foundation for future stages of economic growth.

However, one must take into account that insolvent companies cannot maintain their investments. Bridges fell into disrepair, roads washed away, and canals remained unfinished. Above all, long-run benefits must take into account not only the material costs of malinvestments, but the social and political costs as well. The Federalist financial system did not solidify broad support for the federal government and Federalist Party. In fact, Hamilton's financial program failed to secure the continued support of the "monied" interests to which his opponents claimed he catered. No elite group of financiers found continued fortune at the hands of the Federalists.

Political Ramifications of Hamiltonian Finance and Federalist Policy

The political success of the Federalist Party depended upon the success of Alexander Hamilton and his financial policies. From the beginning, supporters of the Federalists counted on the new government to meet their financial interests. Three major political results proceeded from Federalist financial arrangements.

First, the economic malaise of the early 1790s undermined popular faith in the Federalist Party. As Albert Gallatin insisted in 1796, "Far from strengthening government," aspects of Hamiltonian finance "created more discontent and more uneasiness than any other measure." It is inconceivable to assume political and cultural differences alone could have instigated the first party system. It is true that issues like Jay's Treaty, for example, aggravated party feelings, as did the economic conditions of the late 1790s, for which Hamilton was not directly responsible. It is also true that the self-appointed leaders of the opposition, Madison and Jefferson, worked with Hamilton to pass key aspects of the Federalist program, including the BUS and assumption. Nevertheless, partisan attacks against Hamilton and the Federalists carried great weight as inflation intensified during the mid-1790s.

Second, confidence in the federal government shrank in light of the increasing tax burden to fund the full debt. Direct taxes, particularly that on liquor, provoked heated debate in Congress, which ultimately spilled over into the Whiskey Rebellion. However, direct taxes continued after Hamilton's departure from Philadelphia. Whether Fries's Rebellion or the Virginian assault on the carriage tax, animosities toward Federalist finance served as a conduit for even greater animosity toward the federal government.

Third, in a few cases, Hamiltonian finance enabled some people to aggrandize their wealth through political influence. John Beckley, James Monroe, and John Taylor attacked the Federalists early on for creating a privileged elite. They pointed to the large number of debt holders in Congress who passed the major elements of Hamilton's program as evidence of corruption. Examples of privilege enabled the Jeffersonians to adopt portions of the anti-wealth rhetorical tradition of eighteenth-century England and extend it well into the nineteenth century.

The link between Hamiltonian finance and the business problems of the 1790s is not tenuous. Many investors profited handsomely from debt conversion and found additional resources available from new commercial banks. They had to put their new money somewhere, and, though risky, land companies and internal improvements seemed to offer the best returns. Here was the problem. Because of the new credit and steep profits from conversion, investors could afford to take advantage of pioneering companies, whereas those with limited funds were more careful with their investments. Not everyone lost, but overall, new investments in the 1790s offered disappointing results and intensified political conflict. By the late 1790s, when the Federalist leadership under John Adams began questioning financial incentives for business, or when Federalists in Congress could not pass bankruptcy protection for suffering ventures, those entrepreneurs most dependent on state aid migrated to the Republican Party.

Alexander Hamilton cannot be blamed for all of this. But the bulk of his defense of the Constitution implied that it protects and promotes the various interests of the country. Far from classical republicanism, Hamilton recognized that a government cannot deny the existence of different interest groups, nor can it seek to destroy those interests most people consider legitimate. Hoping to promote as many economic interests as possible, Hamilton constructed a financial plan from which as many people as possible got something. Entrepreneurs gained easy credit, debt holders received payment, assumption restored stability for debtor states, moral nationalists got taxes on whiskey, and politicians at least paid lip service to manufacturers and then promised farmers that grain exports would lift them to prosperity.

Entrepreneurs received mixed signals as new government securities and credit spread through the economy. The increased value of debt certificates, the lowering of interest rates, the ready availability of capital, and the expansion of banking reflected an artificial boom. The federal government was in no position to sustain the boom, and even if it were, the economy could not elevate consumer demand high enough to return investors' profits on their infrastructure improvements. At precisely the same time that Americans embraced a mature market system based on prices rather than barter, monetary shocks implemented by Alexander Hamilton and the Federalists rendered available prices insufficient to support entrepreneurial decisions.

CAREY ROBERTS is assistant professor of history at Arkansas Tech University. He has presented papers and written articles on eighteenth- and nineteenth-century American history.

EXPLORING THE ISSUE

Was Alexander Hamilton an Economic Genius?

Critical Thinking and Reflection

1. Discuss and critically analyze the major components of Hamilton's economic program as secretary of the treasury. These include:
   a. Tariff and tonnage acts;
   b. The assumption and funding program of old debts;
   c. Assumption of state debts;
   d. The establishment and role of the Bank of the United States.
2. Critically analyze those economic programs which both Federalists and Republican-Democrats agreed upon. Where did they disagree? What arguments did both sides employ? Explain the differences between strict and loose construction of the constitution. Use the constitutional arguments employed by Hamilton and Jefferson to support or oppose the creation of the Bank of the United States.
3. Historian John Steele Gordon favors Hamilton's views on the 1790s economy. Carey Roberts is much more sympathetic to the arguments of Hamilton's critics—Jefferson and Madison. Compare and contrast their opposing interpretations and give your own opinion on which side you support.
4. Carey Roberts believes that Hamilton''s economic policies were partially responsible for the decline of the Federalist Party after 1800 and that the new investments offered disappointing results for many of the entrepreneurs. Critically analyze his arguments.

Is There Common Ground?

Authors Gordon and Roberts are analyzing Hamilton's economic policies as secretary of the treasury from totally different perspectives. Gordon is sympathetic to the aims of Hamilton. As a staunch nationalist, Hamilton tried to establish the new nation on a firm credit basis. His funding and debt programs where the nation goes in debt to itself were designed to establish credit worthiness of the new nation in the eyes of its European trading partners. The assumption of state debts and the establishment of a Bank of the United States were also designed to increase the power of the national government over the states and to curb reckless spending. Controls were loosened during the Jefferson and post-Jackson years when there was no strong national bank in operation, but the establishment of the Federal Reserve System in 1913 was a testament to the legacy of Hamilton.

Carey Roberts is one of the few writers about Hamilton today who is critical of his economic policies. Roberts places Hamilton in the context of the political and economic environment of the 1790s. He argues that Hamilton was concerned about the country's "lack of sufficient specie in circulation." In order to jump start the economy, Hamilton reasoned that the specie needed to be funded to entrepreneurs and not the average citizen. The Bank of the United States was supposed to act as a check on bad investments, but in Roberts' view the Bank often encouraged reckless speculation on projects of dubious merit. His program often favored certain business interests and did little for the agricultural sector where the vast majority was employed. The resultant hostility towards Hamilton, brought on by both his arrogant attitude and unpopular fiscal program, was partially responsible for the defeat of the Federalist Party in the congressional and presidential elections of 1800.

There is some merit in both Gordon's and Roberts' assessments of Hamilton. Roberts examines in detail some of the land deals and speculations in government securities of the reckless William Duer, a former assistant secretary of the treasury under Hamilton. Gordon downplays the negative effects of Duer and others on the economy and argues that Hamilton had gotten rid of Duer, who eventually died in debtors' prison, and moved quickly "to stabilize the market and ensure that panic did not bring down basically sound institutions." Finally, Roberts underplays the importance of Hamilton's policies in improving foreign trade, though Gordon does admit that Hamilton and the nation had the good fortune to have a major European war break out in 1793 after Louis XVI, the King of France, lost his head.

Additional Resources

Joyce Appleby, *Inheriting the Revolution: The First Generation of Americans* (The Belknap Press of Harvard University Press, 2000)

Ronald Chernow, *Alexander Hamilton* (The Penguin Press, 2004)

John Ferling, *Jefferson and Hamilton: the Rivalry That Forged a Nation* (Bloomsbury Press, 2013)

Thomas Fleming, *Duel: Alexander Hamilton, Aaron Burr, and the Future of America* (Basic Books, 2000)

Stephen F. Knott, *Alexander Hamilton and the Persistence of Myth* (University Press of Kansas, 2002)

Thomas S. McCaw, *The Founders and Finance: How Hamilton, Gallatin and Other Immigrants Forged a New Economy* (The Belknap Press of Harvard University Press, 2012)

Internet References . . .

Alexander Hamilton: The Man Who Made Modern America

www.alexanderhamiltonexhibition.or

Birth of a Nation & Antebellum America

www.academicinfo.net/usindnew.html

The Papers of Alexander Hamilton

http://founders.archives.gov/about/Hamilton

The Thomas Jefferson Papers

https://www.loc.gov/collections/thomas-jefferson
-papers/about-this-collection/

Selected, Edited, and with Issue Framing Material by:
Larry Madaras, *Howard Community College*
and
James M. SoRelle, *Baylor University*

ISSUE

Did the Election of 1828 Represent a Democratic Revolt of the People?

YES: Sean Wilentz, from *The Rise of American Democracy: Jefferson to Lincoln* (W. W. Norton, 2005)

NO: Daniel Walker Howe, from *What Hath God Wrought: The Transformation of America, 1815–1848* (Oxford University Press, 2007)

Learning Outcomes

After reading this issue, you will be able to:

- Describe the changes that had taken place in politics by the 1820s.
- List the major issues of the campaign of 1828, if there were any.
- Describe the tactics used by both political organizations.
- Describe the different visions and policies for the country of both the Jacksonians and National Republicans of John Quincy Adams and Henry Clay.

ISSUE SUMMARY

YES: Bancroft Prize winner Sean Wilentz argues that in spite of its vulgarities and slanders, the 1828 election campaign "won by Andrew Jackson produced a valediction on the faction-ridden jumble of the Era of Bad Feelings and announced the rough arrival of two distinct national coalitions."

NO: Daniel Walker Howe denies that Jackson's victory represented the coming of democracy to the United States and claims that, in the dirtiest campaign in American history, Jackson won on his personal popularity as a military hero and appealed to the agrarian virtues of an earlier age, while John Quincy Adams lost on a program of planned economic development and a diversified economy led by the national government.

According to conventional wisdom, Andrew Jackson's election to the presidency in 1828 began the era of the common man in which the mass of voters, no longer restrained from voting by property requirements, rose up and threw the elite leaders out of our nation's capital. While recent historians are not quite sure of what constituted Jacksonian democracy or who supported it, and they question whether there ever existed such an era of egalitarianism, American history textbooks still include the obligatory chapter on the age of Jackson.

There are several reasons the old-fashioned view of this period still prevails. In spite of the new scholarly interest in social history, it is still easier to generalize about political events. Consequently, most texts continue to devote the major portion of their pages to detailed examinations of the successes and failures of various presidential administrations. Whether Jackson was more significant than other presidents is difficult to assess because "Old Hickory's" forceful personality, compounded with his use

of strong executive authority, engendered constant controversy in his eight years in office.

Another reason the traditional concept of Jacksonian democracy has not been abandoned is because critics of the progressive interpretation have not been able to come up with an acceptable alternative view. Culminating with Arthur Schlesinger, Jr.'s Pulitzer Prize-winning and beautifully written *The Age of Jackson* (Little, Brown, 1945), the progressive historians viewed Jackson's election in 1828 as the triumph of the common man in politics. Oversimplified as this interpretation may be, there is little doubt that a major change was taking place in our political system during these years. The death of both Thomas Jefferson and John Adams on July 4, 1826, the fiftieth anniversary of our Declaration of Independence from England, signified the end of the revolutionary generation's control over American politics. The first six presidents had been leaders or descendants of leaders in the revolutionary movement. At the Constitutional Convention in 1787, most of the time was spent discussing the powers of the presidency.

Because of the recent experience with the British king, the Founding Fathers were fearful of strong executive authority. Therefore, the presidency was entrusted only to those individuals whose loyalty remained unquestioned. Jackson was the first president of the United States who did not come from either Virginia or Massachusetts. Though Jackson was only a teenager at the time of the American Revolution, his career was similar to those of the early Founding Fathers. Like Washington and Jefferson, Jackson became a living legend before he was 50 years old. His exploits as an Indian fighter and the military hero of the Battle of New Orleans in the War of 1812 were more important than his Western background in making him presidential material.

Starting in the 1960s, a number of historians have studied the effects of presidential elections on the development and maintenance of our two-party system. Borrowing concepts and analytical techniques from political scientists and sociologists, the "new political" historians have demonstrated the effectiveness of political parties in selecting candidates, running campaigns, developing legislation, and legitimizing conflicts within our democratic system. By 1815, the first-party system of competition between the Federalists and the Democratic-Republicans had broken down, in part because the Federalists had refused to become a legitimate opposition party. A second-party system developed during the Jacksonian era between Old Hickory's Democratic Party and his Whig opponents. It lasted until the 1850s when the slavery issue led to the formation of a new system of party competition between Republicans and Democrats.

In a key article on the 1828 presidential election written for the *American Historical Review* (October 1960), Richard P. McCormick removed Jackson from the center of the political era usually associated with Jacksonian democracy. A veteran analyst of nineteenth-century politics, McCormick viewed the 1828 election through the lens of quantitative history. He used statistics to break down a number of generalizations about the significance of Jackson's election, discounting the removal of property qualifications for voting, the influence of the Western states, and the charisma of Jackson as the major reasons why twice as many voters turned out in the 1828 presidential race than they had four years earlier. McCormick argued that in spite of such statistics, a higher percentage of voters had turned out for earlier gubernatorial and legislative elections in most states than for the 1828 presidential election. In McCormick's view, the key election was 1840, not 1828. Why? Because by this time, the two parties—Whigs and Democrats—were equally balanced in all sections of the country, and voters typically turn out in larger numbers when they perceive a closely contested presidential race.

McCormick's article raises a number of questions. Is he comparing apples and oranges in contrasting local and national elections? Using McCormick's data, is it possible for other historians to reach different conclusions? How does one explain a 50 percent increase in voter turnout between 1824 and 1828? Both authors of the following essays disagree with Professor McCormick and believe that the 1828 election was transformative to the development of the second American party system.

Professor Sean Wilentz, in a selection from his Pulitzer Prize-winning *The Rise of American Democracy* (W. W. Norton, 2005), restores Jackson to the center of the era. He disagrees with McCormick and other historians such as Lee Benson whose *Concept of Jacksonian Democracy: New York as a Test Case* (Princeton Paperback, 1970) stressed ethno-cultural factors in determining voting patterns and removed Jackson from the center of the era. Wilentz argues that the second-party system started with the presidential election of 1828 when Jackson's personality enabled state coalitions in New York, Ohio, and Kentucky, among others, to organize a national presidential campaign in support of Jackson. According to Wilentz, McCormick may be correct in arguing that some state and local elections prior to 1828 had a larger proportional turnout of voters, but local elections and issues were far more important to a nation barely unified in its transportation and economic systems. Jackson's election and presidency, he believes, shifted the locus of power to Washington, DC.

Wilentz's 1,000-page book is especially strong on the development and mobilization of political organizations in the years from Jefferson through Lincoln. His description of the campaign with its sloganeering, mobilization of voters, and mudslinging (Jackson's wife was called a "harlot" and Adams a "pimp"), set the tone for the way presidential elections would be run in the future. Contemporaries realized the shift when on inauguration day, March 4, 1829, 20,000 people from all parts of the country converged on Washington, broke into the White House reception, and cheered wildly for Jackson. Wrote one sour contemporary: "It was like the inundation of the northern barbarians into Rome, save that the tumultuous tide came in from all parts of the compass."

Daniel Walker Howe's *What Hath God Wrought* is a major synthesis of the transformation of the United States in the years from 1815 to 1848. While Wilentz's book is primarily a political narrative of the years from Jefferson to Lincoln, Howe weaves the politics within a social cultural framework. As one reviewer aptly put it, "the significant transformations in Howe's story are the burgeoning technologies and networks of infrastructure and communication that conducted messages of religious revival, social reform, and party politics, as well as goods and people, ever more rapidly across an expanding country."

There are many similarities in the narrative of both authors regarding the election of 1828. Both emphasize the development of rival political organizations that developed from the breakdown of the caucus system and bargains made between Henry Clay's and John Quincy Adams's forces that deprived Jackson of the presidency in the 1824 election. Both writers describe the importance of the state organizations and the rise of the newspapers as voices of propaganda. Both describe the smearing of the two candidates—Jackson for marrying a woman who was still officially married to her previous husband and Adams for procuring an American woman as a prostitute for the Czar of Russia. But Howe is clearly sympathetic to the Whig point of view. After all he dedicates this book "to the memory of John Quincy Adams." The author sees Adams's vision of the United States as a country with a diversified economy with new forms of transportation and communications emerging. Jackson, on the other hand, looked back toward an agrarian past, according to Howe, much as the Jeffersonians had idealized a nation of free white farmers.

YES

Sean Wilentz

The Rise of American Democracy: Jefferson to Lincoln

"Under *Whip & Spur*": Politics, Propaganda, and the 1828 Campaign

Although he looked like a distinguished old warrior, with flashing blue eyes and a shock of whitening steely gray hair, Andrew Jackson was by now a physical wreck. Years of ingesting calomel and watered gin to combat his chronic dysentery had left him almost toothless. (In 1828, he obtained an ill-fitting set of dentures, but he often refused to wear them.) An irritation of his lungs, caused by a bullet he had caught in one of his early duels, had developed into bronchiectasis, a rare condition causing violent coughing spells that would bring up what he called "great quantities of slime." The bullet itself remained lodged in his chest, and another was lodged in his left arm, where it accelerated the onset of osteomyelitis. Rheumatism afflicted his joints, and his head often ached, the effect of a lifetime of chewing and smoking tobacco. He had survived near-total collapse of his health in 1822 and 1825, but for the rest of his life, he enjoyed few days completely free of agony. His outbursts of irascible fury, which sometimes shocked even his old friends and allies, owed partly to his suffering and to his efforts to suppress it. But after the debacle of 1825, they also owed to his determination to vindicate not just his own honor but that of the American people. For Jackson and his admirers, the two had become identical.

Willfulness did not mean rashness. In preparing to wreak his vengeance on Adams (whom he respected) and Clay (whom he despised), Jackson took care not to violate the accepted etiquette of presidential campaigning and appeal directly for the job. He was available to serve his country once more, but to look or sound less elevated than that would have been dishonorable (as well as onerous, given the state of his health). Jackson made only one major public appearance over the months before the election, at a public festivity in New Orleans on January 8, commemorating his great victory thirteen years earlier—an invitation, issued by the Louisiana legislature, that he could not refuse without seeming churlish. Yet while he stuck close to the Hermitage, Jackson threw himself into the fray as no other previous presidential candidate before him had, making himself available for visiting delegations of congressmen, giving interviews to interested parties, and writing letters for newspaper publication. When

personal attacks on his character began, he became even more active, his sense of honor on the line. Some of his chief supporters, including Van Buren, asked that "we be let alone" and that Jackson "be *still*," but Jackson would command this campaign just as surely as he had any of his military exploits.

His positions on several key issues were moderate and flexible, replicating much of what he had said in 1824, in generalities that would not upset the national coalition his agents were assembling. On the tariff, the primary political issue in 1828, Jackson remained blandly middle-of-the-road, repeated his support for a "judicious" tariff, and allowed men of different views to imagine that his sympathies lay with them. On internal improvements, Jackson modified his stance somewhat to support a distribution of surplus federal monies to the states for any road and canal projects they wished to undertake, but generally he restated his cautious support for projects that were genuinely national in scope. On the Indian question, he remained persuaded that, for the good of white settlers and natives alike, orderly removal was the only sound solution, but he refrained from saying anything that might be interpreted as an endorsement of the more extreme state-rights removal position.

Instead of a long list of positions and proposals, Jackson's campaign revolved around calls for "reform," a theme broad enough to unite a disparate coalition without merely resorting to platitudes. At one level, "reform" meant undoing what Jackson considered the theft of the presidency in 1825, and ending the political climate that had permitted it. Sometimes, Jackson and his supporters proposed specific changes. Jackson himself said he would exclude from his cabinet any man who sought the presidency—one obvious way to help prevent any future "corrupt bargain." He also called for a constitutional amendment to bar any member of Congress from eligibility for any other federal office (except in the judiciary) for two years beyond his departure from office. Other Jacksonians spoke of the candidate's support for the principle of rotation in office, for limiting presidents to a single term, and for banning the executive from appointing congressmen to civil posts—all means to disrupt insider exclusivity and what Jackson called the "intrigue and management" that had corrupted the government. Otherwise, the Jackson campaign simply reminded the voters of what had happened in 1825—and went further, to charge that "Lucifer" Clay had, during the House negotiations, offered to throw his support to Jackson if Jackson promised he would name him secretary of state.

At another level, "reform" meant returning American government to Jeffersonian first principles and halting the neo-Federalist revival supposedly being sponsored under the cover of the American System. President Adams, Jackson and his men charged, had made the mistake of following his father's footsteps, balancing a "hypocritical veneration for the great principles of republicanism" with artful manipulation of political power. All of "the asperity which marked the struggle of 98 & 1800," Jackson wrote, had returned. Having "gone into power contrary to the voice of the nation," the administration had claimed a mandate it did not possess, and then tried to expand its authority even further. Illegitimate from the start, the new Adams regime raised what Jackson called the fundamental question at stake in the election: "[S]hall the government or the people rule?"

While Jackson and his closest advisors refined this message and called the shots from Nashville, his supporters built a sophisticated campaign apparatus unlike any previously organized in a presidential election, a combination so effective that it obviated the need for either a congressional caucus nomination or a national convention. At the top, Jackson's most capable Tennessee operatives, including John Overton, William Lewis, and John Eaton, concentrated their efforts in a central committee headquarters established in Nashville, where decisions about strategy and tactics could be taken efficiently, in rapid response to continuing events and with Jackson's approval. (A similar, smaller Jackson committee headquarters was established in Washington, to work closely with the pro-Jackson caucus in Congress that met regularly under Van Buren's aegis.) The central committee in turn dispatched its messages to (and received intelligence from) Jackson campaign committees established in each state. Finally, the Jacksonians responded to the reforms in presidential voting around the country—reforms that, by 1828, had included, in all but two states, giving the power to choose presidential electors directly to the voters—by coordinating activities at the local level. The state pro-Jackson committees linked up with local Jackson committees, sometimes called Hickory Clubs, that stirred up enthusiasm with rallies and parades and made sure that their supporters arrived at the polls.

Even more extraordinary than the campaign committees was the dense network of pro-Jackson newspapers that seemed to arise out of nowhere beginning in the spring of 1827. Early in the campaign, Jackson's congressional supporters had caucused and pledged to establish "a chain of newspaper posts, from the New England States to Louisiana, and branching off through Lexington to the Western States." In North Carolina alone, nine new Jacksonian papers had appeared by the middle of 1827, while in Ohio, eighteen new papers supplemented the five already in existence in 1824. In each state, the Jackson forces arranged for one newspaper to serve as the official organ of their respective state committees, refining the broadcast of an authoritative message while promoting a cadre of prominent loyal editors, including Ritchie at the *Enquirer,* Amos Kendall at the *Argus of Western America,* Edwin Croswell at the *Albany Argus,* Isaac Hill at the New Hampshire *Patriot,* and, above all, in Washington, Calhoun's friend Duff Green at the anti-administration *United States Telegraph.*

Funding (as well as copy) for the campaign sheets came directly from Jackson's congressional supporters and their friends, who pioneered numerous fundraising gimmicks, including five-dollar-a-plate public banquets and other ticketed festivities. More substantial sums, including money raised from local bankers and businessmen in the New York–Philadelphia region, were collected and disbursed by Martin Van Buren, who served as the campaign's de facto national treasurer. Some of these monies went to the newspaper editors; others were spent on printing campaign books and pamphlets and producing paraphernalia such as campaign badges. Much of this material made its way to supporters at government cost, thanks to Jacksonian congressmen's liberal partisan use of their personal postal franking privileges.

Jackson's friends made special efforts to solidify their connections to various popular democratic movements, urban and rural, while also winning over more established and politically influential men. The alliances ranged from complete mergers to testy but effective ententes. Kentucky was a special prize for the Jacksonians, having cast its congressional vote for Adams in 1825 at Henry Clay's insistence. The 1828 tariff's high protective rates for hemp growers and manufacturers helped Van Buren offset Clay's advantage among the Kentucky elite, recently aligned with the Old Court Party—but the Jacksonians mainly pinned their hopes on Amos Kendall, Francis Blair, and the revitalized New Court Party machine. In protection-mad Pennsylvania, where the tariff proved extremely popular among the state's ironmongers, the Jacksonians appealed to all of the elements of the old Jeffersonian coalition—including manufacturers, western farmers, and rural Germans—with a propaganda effort headed by the papermaking magnate Congressman Samuel Ingham. In Philadelphia, the presence of numerous New School candidates for state and local office on the Jacksonian ticket alienated the new Working Men's Party, but Jackson's friends reached out to the labor insurgents in various ways, including a direct fifteen-hundred-dollar contribution to rescue Stephen Simpson's financially strapped paper, the *Columbian Observer.* Ultimately, the Workies devised their own Jackson ticket, picking and choosing among the official nominees, offering joint nominations to those they deemed reliable, but running their own candidates for the other slots.

New York, which Jackson had lost in 1824, was a different and, as ever, more difficult story. Under the revised state constitution, voters now chose the state's presidential electors. Unlike in most other states, however, New York's electoral votes would be apportioned on a district-by-district basis, meaning that even if Van Buren's agents carried the overall popular vote, Adams was bound to win a portion of the state's Electoral College total. DeWitt Clinton's death resolved much of the early bickering within the New York pro-Jackson camp, leaving Van Buren in control, but it also raised the possibility that some pro-Clinton Jackson men, who had supported the Tennessean chiefly to promote Clinton, might now drift over to Adams. And then there was the perplexing Anti-Masonic uprising in western New York, an outburst of democratic outrage that could never be won over to Grand Master Mason Andrew Jackson. Even with all of the southern states plus Pennsylvania likely to support Jackson, it would not be enough to elect him president. New York's result would be crucial.

The outlook for Jackson improved when political operatives determined that the Anti-Masonic movement remained, for the moment, localized, and that its chief advocates, Thurlow Weed and William Henry Seward, were having difficulty merging it with the Adams campaign. The outlook improved even more when Jackson's operatives confirmed that Henry Clay was not only a Mason but, as one delighted Manhattan pol put it, "a Mason of rank." Van Buren, meanwhile, decided to make the most of his New York strongholds, above all New York City, where the old Tammany Society, after a history of recurrent factionalism, turned into one of the most united and reliable pro-Jackson organizations in the state. As early as January, Tammany began hosting giant public events touting Jackson, and after the death of DeWitt Clinton—who was hated by the Tammany braves—the way was cleared for an all-out effort to spike the city's vote. Hickory Clubs appeared in every ward, sponsoring hickory tree-planting ceremonies and barroom gatherings to toast the general's success. A clutch of partisan editors in the already well-established New York press churned out reams of pro-Jackson material. "The more he is known," one pro-Jackson paper boasted of its man, "the less and less the charges against him seem to be true."

Against this juggernaut, Adams's supporters—their candidate an awkward public figure who spurned involvement in campaign organization—were badly overmatched. But they tried their best and performed credibly as organizers. Henry Clay, ignoring advice that he resign and let Adams bear the full brunt of defeat, took charge of creating a national campaign and of stumping at dinners and celebrations around the country to make the administration's case. Daniel Webster pitched in as well, overseeing the canvassing of potential financial backers (fully exploiting his ample personal connections to New England capitalists), collecting substantial sums, and keeping track of accounts. Although they could not equal the Jacksonians,

the Adamsites created a substantial pro-administration press, headed in Washington by Joseph Gales and William Seaton's *National Intelligencer* and Peter Force's *National Journal*. The Adamsites printed forests' worth of pamphlets, leaflets, and handbills, organized their own state central committees, and sponsored countless dinners and commemorations. In at least one state, New Jersey, the Adamsites probably outorganized their opponents. And everywhere outside of Georgia, where Jackson ran unopposed, there was a genuine contest under way, with both parties, as one Marylander wrote, "fairly in the field, under *whip & spur.*"

Adamsite strategic and tactical errors at the state and local level repeatedly undermined whatever enthusiasm the administration's loyalists generated. High-minded stubbornness, linked to an aversion to what looked to some National Republicans like Van Buren–style wheeling and dealing, killed Adams's chances of carrying the middle Atlantic states. In upstate New York, the National Republicans insulted the Anti-Masons by rejecting their nominee for governor, a close friend of Thurlow Weed's, and then bidding the insurgents to show their good faith by adopting the pro-administration slate, ruining any chance of an alliance. In New York City, a protectionist movement, geared to halting the dumping of foreign manufactures on the New York market, arose in the spring; and, by autumn, it had gained a sizable following that cut across class and party lines. But the Adamsites, seemingly unable to believe that their protectionism might appeal to urban workers, held back from the movement. The protectionists ran their own ticket, and the opportunity was wasted. Similar shortsightedness prevailed in Philadelphia, where the Adamsites refused to make common cause with the surviving Federalist establishment, encouraging Jacksonian hopes of taking the city.

The Adamsites did excel in one area, the dark art of political slander. In 1827, a Cincinnati editor and friend of Clay's named Charles Hammond took a fact-finding tour into Kentucky and Tennessee, and unearthed some old stories about alleged legal irregularities in Jackson's marriage (supposedly he was a bigamist), along with charges that Jackson's wife, Rachel, was an adulteress and his mother a common prostitute. The charges were not simply mean-spirited: they evoked broader cultural presumptions that stigmatized Jackson as a boorish, lawless, frontier lowlife, challenging the Christian gentleman, John Quincy Adams. Clay immediately recommended his mudslinger friend to Webster, calling Hammond's paper "upon the whole, the most efficient and discreet gazette that espouses our cause," and suggested that the editor get direct financial support. Hammond, meanwhile, became a fountain of wild and inflammatory charges—that Jackson's mother had been brought to America by British soldiers, that she married a mulatto who was Jackson's father—all of which found their way into what may have been the lowest production of the 1828 campaign, a new journal entitled *Truth's Advocate and Monthly Anti-Jackson Expositor*.

Jackson, enraged to the point of tears, held Clay responsible and sent John Eaton to confront the Kentuckian. Clay vehemently denied the charges, though his private correspondence with Hammond contains hints he was lying. Jackson continued to blame everything on Clay.

Character assassination in presidential politics was hardly invented in 1828—recall, for example, the lurid attacks on Thomas Jefferson and "Dusky Sally" Hemings—and Clay could easily and rightly complain of the Jackson campaign's unceasing attacks about the corrupt bargain as the basest sort of slander. But the Hammond affair, beginning more than a year before the 1828 electioneering commenced in earnest, marked the arrival of a new kind of calculated, mass cultural politics, pitting a fervent sexual moralism against a more forgiving, secularist, laissez-faire ethic. Hammond's attacks also ensured that a great deal of the campaign would be fought out in the sewer. The Jacksonians spread sensational falsehoods that President Adams was a secret aristocratic voluptuary who, while minister to Russia, had procured an innocent American woman for the tsar. Clay came in for merciless attacks as an embezzler, gambler, and brothel habitué. The Adamsites responded with a vicious handbill, covered with coffins, charging Jackson with the murder of six innocent American militamen during the Creek War, and labeling him "a wild man under whose charge the Government would collapse." The competition turned largely into a propaganda battle of personalities and politically charged cultural styles instead of political issues. A campaign slogan from four years earlier, coined in support of a possible Adams–Jackson ticket, assumed completely new meaning and summed up the differences, contrasting the nominees as "Adams who can write/Jackson who can fight."

And yet, for all of the vulgarities and slander, the campaign of 1828 was not an unprincipled and demagogic theatrical. Neither was it a covert sectional battle between a pro-slavery southerner and an antislavery New Englander; nor was it a head-on clash between pro-development Adamsite capitalists and antidevelopment Jacksonian farmers and workers, although strong views about slavery and economic development certainly came into play. The campaign pronounced a valediction on the faction-ridden jumble of the Era of Bad Feelings and announced the rough arrival of two distinct national coalitions, divided chiefly over the so-called corrupt bargain and the larger political implications of the American System. It was, above all, a contest over contrasting conceptions of politics, both with ties to the ideals of Thomas Jefferson.

For all of his setbacks and suffering, John Quincy Adams had never abandoned his moral vision of energetic government and national uplift. Protective tariffs, federal road and canal projects, and the other mundane features of the American System were always, to him, a means to that larger end. A fugitive from Federalism, Adams embodied one part of the Jeffersonian legacy, devoted to intellectual excellence, rationality, and government by the most talented and virtuous—those whom Jefferson himself, in

a letter to Adams's father, had praised as "the natural aristoi." The younger Adams took the legacy a large step further, seeing the federal government as the best instrument for expanding the national store of intelligence, prosperity, beauty, and light.

Objections to the political ramifications of that vision united the opposition—objections rooted in another part of the Jeffersonian legacy, a fear of centralized government linked to a trust in the virtue and political wisdom of ordinary American voters. Jackson and his polyglot coalition contended that human betterment meant nothing without the backing of the people themselves. Lacking that fundamental legitimacy, Adams, Clay, and their entire administration had, the Jacksonians contended, been engaged from the start in a gigantic act of fraud—one that, to succeed, required shifting as much power as possible to Washington, where the corrupt few might more easily oppress the virtuous many, through unjust tariffs, costly federal commercial projects, and other legislative maneuvers. Were the Adamsites not removed as quickly as possible, there was no telling how far they might go in robbing the people's liberties, under the guise of national improvement, the American System, or some other shibboleth. Hence, the opposition's slogan: "Jackson and Reform."

Jackson himself laid out the stakes in a letter to an old friend, on the omens in what he called the Adamsites' exercise of "patronage" (by which he simply meant "power"):

> The present is a contest between the virtue of the people, & the influence of patronage[. S]hould patronage prevail, over virtue, then indeed "the safe precedent," will be established, that the President, appoints his successor in the person of the sec. of state—Then the people may prepare themselves to become "hewers of wood & drawers of water," to those in power, who with the Treasury at command, will wield by its corrupting influence a majority to support it—The present is an important struggle, for the perpetuity of our republican government, & I hope the virtue of the people may prevail, & all may be well.

Or as one of his New York supporters put it (presuming to speak on behalf of "the sound planters, farmers & mechanics of the country"), the Jacksonians beheld the coming election as "a great contest between the aristocracy and democracy of America."

The balloting began in September and, because of widely varying state polling laws, continued until November. Early returns from New England unsurprisingly gave Adams the lead, although not quite the clean sweep he had expected. (In Maine, a hardy band of ex-Crawford Radicals in and around Portland managed to win one of the state's electoral votes for Jackson.) The trend shifted heavily in mid-October, when Pennsylvania (overwhelmingly, including a strong plurality in Philadelphia) and

Ohio (narrowly) broke for Jackson. It remains a matter of speculation how much this news affected the vote in other states, where the polls had not yet opened, but the Jacksonians took no chances, especially in New York, where the three days of voting did not commence until November 3. Holding back until the moment was ripe, the New York Jackson committee suddenly spread the word in late October that Jackson's election was virtually assured, in order to demoralize the opposition. In the end, Jackson carried the state's popular vote, although only by about 5,000 ballots out of 275,000 cast.

The state-by-state reporting of the vote, with news of one Jackson victory after another rolling in, heightened the impression that a virtual revolution was underway. The final tallies showed a more complicated reality. As expected, Adams captured New England, and Jackson swept the South below Maryland. But apart from Jackson's lopsided victory in Pennsylvania, the returns from the key battleground states were remarkably even. If a mere 9,000 votes in New York, Ohio, and Kentucky had shifted from one column to the other, and if New York, with an Adams majority, had followed the winner-takes-all rule of most other states, Adams would have won a convincing 149 to 111 victory in the Electoral College. In other races for federal office the Adamsites actually improved their position. Above all, in the U.S. Senate, what had been a strong six-vote opposition majority in the Twentieth Congress would be reduced to a Jacksonian majority of two when the new Congress assembled in December 1829. Despite all their blunders, and despite Adams's unpopularity, the friends of the administration had not lost future political viability.

These wrinkles in the returns were lost amid Jackson's overwhelming victory nationwide. Jackson won 68 percent of the electoral vote and a stunning 56 percent of the popular vote—the latter figure representing a margin of victory that would not be surpassed for the rest of the nineteenth century. The totals came from a vastly larger number of voters than ever before in a presidential election, thanks to the adoption of popular voting for electors in four states and the bitterness of the one-on-one contest in the middle Atlantic states. More than a million white men voted for president in 1828, roughly four times the total of 1824. Jackson alone won three times as many votes as the total cast for all candidates four years earlier. The magnitude of it all left Adamsites, including the normally sanguine Henry Clay, miserable, and Jacksonians jubilant.

Perhaps the only Jacksonian not thoroughly overjoyed was Jackson himself. Well before the voting was over, he had understood what the outcome would be, and the news confirming his election caused no particular stir at the Hermitage. After all the months of campaigning behind the scenes, and now faced with actually assuming the presidency, the victor reported that "my mind is depressed." Sadness turned to panic and then grief in mid-December, when Rachel Jackson, preparing for the move to Washington, suddenly collapsed and, after five days of violent heart seizures, died. Her husband, who sat up with her throughout her ordeal, would never really recover from the shock. His great biographer James Parton wrote that it henceforth "subdued his spirit and corrected his speech," except on rare occasions when, in a calculated effort to intimidate his foes or inspire his allies, he would break into his customary fits of table pounding and swearing. Yet Rachel's death also steeled Jackson for the political battles to come. Her health had been precarious for several years before she died. Jackson was absolutely certain that the slanders of the 1828 campaign had finally broken her. And for that cruel and unforgivable blow, he would forever blame, above all others, his nemesis, Henry Clay.

Jackson and Reform

Jackson's victory marked the culmination of more than thirty years of American democratic development. By 1828, the principle of universal white adult male suffrage had all but triumphed—and accompanying that victory, much of the old politics of deference still left over from the Revolutionary era had collapsed. The country and city democracies of the 1790s had attained a legitimacy only barely imaginable a generation earlier. Once-impregnable political establishments—the Connecticut Standing Order, the Philadelphia Federalist regime, the planter and financier political elites of Georgia and Tennessee and Kentucky—had either fallen or been shaken to their foundations. Even where democratic reformers achieved the least—above all in the seaboard South, and there, above all, in South Carolina—local rulers granted cosmetic changes that permitted them to claim that they fairly represented the citizenry's will. . . .

SEAN WILENTZ is the George Henry Davis Professor of History at Princeton University. His book *Chants Democratic: New York City and the Rise of the American Working Class, 1788–1850* (Oxford University Press, 1984) won the prestigious Frederick Jackson Turner Award and the Albert J. Beveridge Award. His most recent books include *The Age of Reagan, 1974–2008* (Harper, 2008) and *Bob Dylan in America* (Doubleday, 2010).

Daniel Walker Howe    **NO**

What Hath God Wrought: The Transformation of America, 1815–1848

The Improvers

The campaign for the presidential election of 1828 lasted the whole four years of John Quincy Adams's administration. Eventually defenders of the national administration started calling themselves "National" Republicans, while the supporters of the man who claimed the popular mandate called themselves "Democratic" Republicans, later simply "Democrats." The terms came into use only very slowly. For Adams and his followers, to recognize the emergence of partisanship was to confess failure. Jackson and his followers saw themselves as the legitimate Jeffersonian Republican party and referred to their opponents as a corrupt clique of "federalists." Accustomed as we are to a two-party system, we seize upon labels that contemporaries hesitated to employ. By the time the new party names gained acceptance, the election was over.

What came to be called the National Republicanism of Adams and Clay represented a continuation of the new Republican nationalism that had arisen out of the experience of the War of 1812. The Democratic Republicans of Jackson, Van Buren, and the recently transformed Calhoun recruited the proslavery Radicals of William H. Crawford and embraced the state-rights tradition of Old Republicanism. Despite the role played by Van Buren in putting together the opposition coalition, Jackson always controlled his own campaign, operating it from his headquarters in Nashville, Tennessee. The few remaining Federalists generally joined the Adams party in New England, the Jackson party in the South, and divided between them in the middle states.

Each side embraced its own version of modernity. The administration's supporters endorsed economic modernization and appealed for votes on the basis of their improvement program. The Jacksonians emphasized their candidate rather than a program but developed a very modem political organization with attendant publicity and rallies. The one step they did not take was to hold a national party convention, but they did sponsor many state conventions. The Adams supporters followed suit; in the face of Jackson's political machine, their aspiration to classical nonpartisanship could not practically be maintained. Taking advantage of improvements in communications, both sides relied heavily on partisan newspapers

to get across their message, though Jackson's followers kept theirs under tighter control. Handbills and campaign biographies also made use of the new opportunities for printed propaganda. Mindful of ethnic divisions, both sides published some campaign literature in German. The techniques of electioneering reflected the increased public participation in the election of the president. By 1828, all but two states (Delaware and South Carolina) chose their presidential electors by popular vote. Most states opted for electing them at large, since that maximized the state's influence, although it would have been more democratic (that is, reflected public opinion more accurately) to choose the electors by congressional district.

As in 1824, Jackson campaigned against Washington insiders. He himself described the contest as a "struggle between the virtue of the people and executive patronage"—an ironic expression indeed, in view of his party's exploitation of the spoils of office once in power, but there is no reason to suppose it not sincerely felt. Rather than debate policy, Jacksonians harped on the "corrupt bargain" that had robbed the people of their preferred candidate. The charge played well in provincial America, where Yankees like Adams were often unpopular peddlers and storekeepers, notorious for cheating farm wives with wooden nutmegs and driving many a small "corrupt bargain." (Through much of the American hinterland, Yankees were the functional equivalent of Jews in rural Europe.) Contrasted with such a figure of metropolitan guile appeared the Old Hero Jackson, a leader of stern virtue, a frontiersman who had made his own legend. To celebrate his victory at New Orleans, Jackson's campaign marketed the song "The Hunters of Kentucky"—in defiance of the historical record, which showed that Jackson had reproached the Kentucky militia for their conduct in the battle. Where Adams exhorted his countrymen to a program of deliberate "improvement," the Jacksonians celebrated their unrefined "natural" leader. Old Hickory was portrayed as a straightforward man of action, a hero the common man could trust.

The Adams press responded that Jackson's personal attributes actually disqualified, rather than qualified, him for the presidency. He possessed a notoriously fiery temper and had repeatedly displayed vindictive anger. Adams partisans reminded the public that Jackson had been involved in several brawls and duels, killing a man in one of them. The "coffin handbill" distributed by Philadelphia newspaperman John Binns called sympathetic attention to the six militiamen executed by Jackson's orders in February 1815. (In retaliation, pro-Jackson mobs persecuted Binns and his wife.)

The Adams–Clay supporters also indicted Jackson's character on the basis of his sex life. Back in 1790, young Jackson had set up housekeeping with Rachel Robards, a woman married to another man. Though divorce was difficult and rare, Rachel's husband, Lewis Robards, successfully divorced her on grounds of desertion and adultery. In 1794, after learning of the divorce, Andrew and Rachel underwent a marriage ceremony; prior to that time they had been "living in sin," as respectable nineteenth-century opinion understood it. (On the eighteenth-century frontier, people did not inquire closely into such matters; Andrew and Rachel had simply been accepted as Mr. and Mrs. Jackson.) This juicy story was resurrected by an Adams newspaper, the *Cincinnati Gazette*, on March 23, 1827. Jackson's Nashville campaign office responded with an elaborately contrived narrative claiming that Andrew and Rachel had participated in an earlier marriage ceremony in 1791 under the mistaken belief that Lewis Robards had obtained a divorce then, so their adultery had been inadvertent and merely technical. No evidence has ever been found of this alleged wedding, and Jackson's scrupulous biographer Robert Remini must be right in concluding that no 1791 ceremony took place, and that in any case Andrew and Rachel were living together as husband and wife as early as 1790.

Raising the subject of adultery related to the larger issue of Jackson's character, the charge that he was so willful, impetuous, and impatient of restraint that he could not be trusted with supreme responsibility. In the vocabulary of the time, it was said that Jackson's "passions" ruled him. The general almost played into his critics' hands during the campaign. When Samuel Southard (Adams's secretary of the navy) suggested at a dinner party that Secretary of War Monroe might have been entitled to some of the credit for the New Orleans victory, Old Hickory wrote a furious message to him preparing the way for a duel. Jackson's friend Sam Houston managed to get the letter rephrased.

The Jackson campaign did not confine its falsehoods to defenses of the candidate's honor but invented others to attack his rival. The scrupulous, somber Adams might not seem to offer much of a target for salacious arrows, but Jacksonians did not let this inhibit their imagination. Jackson's New Hampshire supporter Isaac Hill retailed the libel that while U.S minister to Russia, Adams had procured an American girl for the sexual gratification of the tsar. Less preposterous, and therefore perhaps more dangerous, was the accusation that Adams had put a billiard table in the White House, at public expense. In truth, Adams did enjoy the game and had bought such a table, but paid for it out of his own pocket. Adams's religion was not exempt

from attack: The Presbyterian Ezra Stiles Ely denounced the president's Unitarian theological views as heresy and called on all sound Christians to vote for Jackson. Taken together, the accusations against Adams were designed to show him as aristocratic, intellectual, and un-American.

The hope that Adams and Clay had entertained that the election might constitute a referendum on the American System evaporated. Instead, the presidential campaign of 1828 was probably the dirtiest in American history. It seems only fair to observe that while the hostile stories circulated about Adams were largely false, those about Jackson were largely true. An exception was the charge appearing in an Adams paper that Jackson's mother had been a prostitute. However, shifting the focus of the campaign from program to personalities generally benefited the Jacksonians. They were only too willing to see the choice posed as a popular ditty had it: "Between J. Q. Adams, who can write/And Andy Jackson, who can fight." Depressed by the turn the campaign was taking, Adams stopped recording events in his diary in August and did not resume until after the election.

The bitterness with which the campaign was waged manifested the intensity of the feelings it aroused. For beyond the mudslinging, important national issues were at stake. Adams stood for a vision of coherent economic progress, of improvement both personal and national, directed by deliberate planning. Instead of pursuing improvement, Jacksonians accepted America the way it was, including its institution of slavery. They looked upon government planners as meddlesome, although they were more than willing to seek government favors on an ad hoc basis, as when a particular internal improvement or tariff rate gratified a particular local interest. They did not publicize a comprehensive program as the national administration did. But they too had a vision of the future, and theirs centered not on economic diversification but on opening new lands to white settlement, especially if those lands could be exploited with black labor. Jackson the frontier warrior personified this vision, and it had potential appeal not only to the slaveholders of the South but also among the common white men of both sections.

Martin Van Buren set out the strategic logic behind the Jackson campaign in a letter he wrote to Thomas Ritchie on January 13, 1827. Editor of the *Richmond Enquirer*, Ritchie was a key opinion-maker in the southern Radical circles that had supported Crawford in 1824. Van Buren wanted Ritchie to swing his influence behind Jackson in 1828. But this time the Little Magician had more than just a temporary, tactical purpose in mind; he aspired to forge a fundamental realignment in American politics. Van Buren despised the nonpartisan, meritocratic ideal of James Monroe and John Quincy Adams; he wanted to re-create the party system that had divided Republicans from Federalists. Van Buren wrote to persuade Ritchie of the merits of a political alliance "between the planters of the South and the plain Republicans of the North." This alliance around Jackson should claim the mantle of the

Jeffersonian Republican party and stigmatize its opponents as Federalists. Political parties are inevitable, Van Buren argued, so it behooved the Jackson supporters not only to embrace partisanship openly but also to define the parties in as advantageous a way as possible. If a second party system were not created, Van Buren believed, the result would be a politics based on sectionalism. In the absence of strong party distinctions, "prejudices between free and slave holding states will inevitably take their place," he warned Ritchie. The Missouri debate illustrated the danger, he pointed out. The senator from New York did not scruple to appeal to the southern Radical's desire to preserve slavery from northern interference. "Party attachment in former times furnished a complete antidote for sectional prejudices by producing counteracting feelings." Van Buren held out the creation of the Jacksonian Democratic Party as a promised means of containing antislavery. Ritchie was persuaded.

As Van Buren's letter foretold, the campaign saw the commencement of a novel acceptance of parties in American political life. And not surprisingly, given the commitment of Van Buren and most other Jacksonians to protecting slavery, the campaign also shaped up as highly sectional. For the only time in American history, the two sides presented the electorate with opposing sectional tickets. To run with him against the two southerners, Jackson and Calhoun, President Adams picked his Treasury secretary, Richard Rush of Pennsylvania, creating an all-northern team. In the South, Jackson's popularity was enhanced by the feeling that only he could be relied upon to maintain white supremacy and expand the white empire, to evict the Indian tribes, to support and extend slavery.

In the North, the race was tight. Appeals to defend slavery would not work for Old Hickory, and the Adams–Clay economic development program enjoyed widespread support. Moreover, the populistic, egalitarian Antimasons were opposing Jackson. Without Van Buren's brilliant strategy, his party organization, and his tariff abominations, it is hard to see how the all-southern ticket could have won, even given Jackson's legend. Van Buren gave the effort his all, even sacrificing his Senate seat to run for governor of New York in 1828, so as to hold back the tide of Antimasonry in the state.

The election returns, as they gradually came in, gave Jackson the victory, 178 to 83 in the electoral college. His 56 percent of the popular vote set a record that was not surpassed until the twentieth century. His followers also won control of both houses of Congress, by a particularly impressive 138 to 74 in the House of Representatives. Jackson racked up awesome majorities across the South and West—except, ironically, in Louisiana, scene of his greatest battle. There his high-handed conduct was remembered, he was unpopular with the French Creoles, and the sugarcane planters needed a tariff. The Jacksonians, who believed in partisan politics wholeheartedly, not surprisingly had waged it more effectively than the Adamsites,

some of whom engaged in it only grudgingly. Everywhere outside New England and New Jersey, Jackson benefited from more effective organization. In Georgia, where Indian Removal was the big issue, Adams got no popular votes at all. Calhoun's record on Indian Removal did not satisfy Georgians either, so seven of the Georgia electors cast their vice-presidential votes for the South Carolina Radical William Smith, Calhoun's longtime rival.

As in 1824, Adams carried his core constituency: New England, the Antimasonic and evangelical areas of New York state, the shores of the Great Lakes. He also won New Jersey, Delaware, and some of the congressional districts of Maryland. Under his leadership, New England had emerged from Federalist particularism and embraced Republican nationalism. The attack on his theology did not hurt Adams among Christians of the Universal Yankee Nation (as the New England zone of settlement was called). In the South, Adams showed pockets of strength in the towns and commercial areas like the Kentucky Bluegrass. But his running mate Rush failed to deliver Pennsylvania, and Clay failed to deliver any electoral votes in the Ohio Valley. The Tariff of Abominations had effectively counteracted the political appeal of the American System in those areas.

The popular vote tripled in size from 1824, partly because of states changing their method of choosing electors, but mostly because of heightened public interest and organized get-out-the-vote efforts. A two-way race captured the public imagination more clearly than a five-way race had done. Participation of eligible voters, 57.5 percent overall, was generally highest in states where the race was close, like New York and Ohio, and where good local transportation made it not too inconvenient to get to the polling place. Where state offices were more hotly contested than the presidency, turnout was higher in those races. Legal enfranchisement of new voters did not represent a significant factor in increasing the size of the turnout, although some states were in the process of removing the remaining property and religious tests for voting. The great majority of adult white males had long enjoyed the legal right to vote.

Did Jackson's victory constitute the coming of democracy to America? Certainly the Jackson political machine tried to persuade voters to see it that way. But continuities with an earlier time are evident: Jackson's campaign slogans celebrated antique agrarian virtue and promised to restore Old Republicanism. His personal popularity rested to a large extent on military prowess, which of course is the oldest political appeal of all, and by no means democratic. If Jackson was the candidate of the "common man," as he was so often described, it was specifically the common *white* man, and one not bothered by slavery or the abuses of Freemasonry. The Jacksonians cultivated an antielitist image. How far this corresponded with the reality of their support has not been easy for historians to document. Most voters in antebellum America, on both sides of the political divide, were farmers. The few industrial wage-earners who were male often voted for the American System, not Andrew Jackson, in the belief that a tariff protected their jobs. Adams did well among people living along commercial routes. Jackson did well in economically undeveloped regions, among non-English white ethnic groups, and among first-time voters (young men, immigrants, or the previously apathetic). But Jackson's leading newspaper editor, the ardently proslavery Missourian Duff Green, knew how to exploit the communications revolution: He distributed his *United States Telegraph* through the mails using the franking privilege of Jackson congressmen. Jackson's successful campaign owed as much to improvements in communications as to the democratization of the electorate.

The vote displayed striking sectional characteristics. Jackson managed a bare majority in the free states (50.3%) while racking up 72.6 percent in the slave states. The South provided most of his electoral votes. Thanks to the peculiarities of the Electoral College (with the notorious three-fifths clause inflating the power of the slaveholding states), the 400,000 popular votes Jackson got in the North brought him only 73 electoral votes, while the 200,000 southerners who voted for him produced 105. There is no justification for claiming that the states Jackson carried were more democratic than the ones Adams carried; indeed, in some tangible ways state governments in the North, where Adams ran better, were the more democratic. To be sure, Jackson and his supporters had successfully encouraged and exploited broadening political participation. They had laid the groundwork for a new two-party system. But much of what they had done could as fairly be called demagogy as democracy. In the words of an antebellum newspaperman, the Adams campaign had "dealt with man *as he should be*," while the Jackson campaign had "appealed to him *as he is*."

The election of 1828 proved a pivotal one; it marked the end of one kind of politics and the beginning of another. During the so-called Era of Good Feelings, presidential politics had been unstructured by party rivalry and had been driven less by issues than personal ambitions. In 1828, the incumbent, Adams, had boldly based his campaign on a national economic program. The challenger, Jackson, had run on a combination of personal popularity, organization, and the evocation of symbolism. The Jackson campaign, while claiming to be anti-politics, had in practice created a new and far more potent political machinery. Having won, Jackson did not feel content to bask in the glory of his record as a military hero vindicated by the electorate. He became an activist president. His administration would witness novel assertions of presidential power, rancorous debate over issues, and the rebirth of political parties. After 1828, the classical ideal of nonpartisan leadership, which Adams and Monroe had shared with Washington and countless political philosophers, was dead—killed in battle with Old Hickory as surely as General Pakenham.

There was another aspect of the outcome, less often noticed by historians but no less important. The National Republican improvement program of planned economic development would have encouraged a diversified economy in place of reliance on the export of slave-grown agricultural staples. Its strong central government would have held long-term potential for helping the peaceful resolution of the slavery problem, perhaps in connection with some kind of colonization program, while weaning portions of the South, especially in the border states, away from plantation agriculture toward mixed farming, industry, and commerce. Whatever such promise Adams's program held had been frustrated, to a large extent by defenders of slavery who recognized in it a vision of America's future incompatible with their own. Still, the Adams–Clay vision of government-sponsored national economic development, though temporarily checked, lived on. The second American party system, originating in the election of 1828, was strongly issue-oriented. It would be characterized by fierce debates over both economic policy and the enforcement of white supremacy.

Daniel Walker Howe is professor of history emeritus at UCLA. He is the author of *The Political Culture of the American Whigs* (University of Chicago Press, 1980) and *Making the American Self: Jonathan Edwards to Abraham Lincoln* (Harvard University Press, 1997).

EXPLORING THE ISSUE

Did the Election of 1828 Represent a Democratic Revolt of the People?

Critical Thinking and Reflection

1. Describe the changes that had taken place in politics by the 1820s.
    (a) List three of the major issues in the campaign of 1828, if there were any.
    (b) Describe the organization that Jackson built to run his campaign.
    (c) Describe the tactics used by the Jackson organization.
2. (a) What do political scientists mean by the term "political systems of competition"?
    (b) Discuss why Professors Wilentz and Howe believe that the election of 1828 led to the development of the two-party system of competition.
3. Compare and contrast and critically evaluate, according to both Professors Wilentz and Howe, the presidential campaigns in 1828 run by Jackson and Adams. In your answer, consider:
    (a) Organizations in various states;
    (b) Funding;
    (c) Issues;
    (d) Methods;
    (e) Campaign literature;
    (f) Political mudslinging;
    (g) Reasons why Jackson won and Adams lost.
4. Jackson won 68 percent of the electoral college and 56 percent of the popular vote in 1828. Yet a shift of 9,000 votes in New York, Ohio, and Kentucky would have swung the election to Adams. Explain how this could have happened under our system of voting.
5. Compare the similarities and differences in tactics, advertisements, organization, and issues in the 1828 presidential election with the 2008 and 2012 presidential elections.

Is There Common Ground?

At first glance it appears that both authors are discussing the presidential election of 1828 from two competing perspectives. Sean Wilentz has synthesized the new political history frameworks with an old-fashioned pro-Jackson narrative interpretation. Daniel Walker Howe has also synthesized the new political history within a broader socioeconomic cultural context and is more sympathetic to the Whig nationalistic interpretation of history.

Yet both authors agree that the 1828 election was the first modern presidential election as far as having the Electoral College choose our president instead of the old-fashioned caucus system. A two-party system of competition developed with similar organizations set up with full-time professional politicians and partisan newspaper editors whose main job was to get out the vote on Election Day.

Since both authors consider the 1828 election to be the first modern presidential election, they raise a number of questions about our method of selecting a president. What were the issues in the campaign? Were they coherently and logically expressed by the two major candidates so that the voter could make an intelligent choice? If not, why? Why was organization such a key factor in this election? In fact, why is organization the most important element in any election? List any distortion of facts which

occurred in this election. Do you feel voters are more intelligent today than in the early nineteenth century? Compare the presidential campaigning system which developed during the 1828 election with the system which functioned in our most recent presidential race? Should we make major changes in this selection and election processes for choosing our president?

Create Central

www.mhhe.com/createcentral

Additional Resources

Ronald P. Formisano, *The Transformation of Political Culture: Massachusetts Parties, 1790–1840* (Oxford University Press, 1983)

Richard P. McCormick, *The Second American Party System: Party Formation in the Jacksonian Era* (University of North Carolina Press, 1966)

Robert V. Remini, *The Election of Andrew Jackson* (J. P. Lippincott, 1963)

John W. Ward, *Andrew Jackson: Symbol for an Age* (Oxford University Press, 1955, 1983)

Harry L. Watson, *Liberty and Power: The Politics of Jacksonian America* (Noonday Press, 1990)

Internet References . . .

Andrew Jackson

www.history.com/topics/andrew-jackson

The Age of Jackson

www.gilderlehrman.org/history-by-era/national
-expansion-and-reform-1815-1860/age-jackson

The Hermitage: The Jackson Family

www.thehermitage.com/jackson-family
/andrew-jackson

The Papers of Andrew Jackson

thepapersofandrewjackson.utk.edu/

Selected, Edited, and with Issue Framing Material by:
Larry Madaras, *Howard Community College*
and
James M. SoRelle, *Baylor University*

ISSUE

Did Improved Educational Opportunities for Women in the New Nation Significantly Expand Their Participation in Antebellum Society?

YES: **Mary Kelley,** from *Learning to Stand and Speak: Women, Education, and Public Life in America's Republic,* University of North Carolina Press (2006)

NO: **Lucia McMahon,** from "Between Cupid and Minerva" and "Education, Equality, or Difference," Cornell University Press (2012)

Learning Outcomes

After reading this issue, you will be able to:

- Understand the impact of antebellum female academies and seminaries.
- Assess the role of education in opening new opportunities for women in the antebellum period.
- Differentiate women's access to the domestic and public spheres of American society.
- Consider whether or not women's status in the antebellum period improved or declined in comparison with the colonial era.
- Discuss and evaluate the concept of "mere equality" as it applies to antebellum American women.

ISSUE SUMMARY

YES: Mary Kelley describes how expanding educational opportunities encouraged women to redefine themselves by opening doors to careers beyond the domestic sphere, economic self-support, and public participation in civil society that transformed their understanding of the rights of citizenship in the post-revolutionary and antebellum United States.

NO: Lucia McMahon concludes that the unprecedented access to education afforded women in the early national period fostered recognition of women's intellectual capacity, but she argues that most educated women confronted a limited range of opportunities in a society that remained largely committed to a social and political order rooted in notions of sexual difference and male hierarchy.

Until the late 1960s, the serious student of American women's history could store all the important scholarly studies of women on one shelf of a bookcase. These works typically fell into two categories: broad surveys based upon the limited sources available, such as Eleanor Flexner's *Century of Struggle: The Woman's Rights Movement in the United States* (Harvard University Press, 1959) and Andrew Sinclair's *The Better Half: The Emancipation of the American Woman* (Harper & Row, 1965); and "great women" biographies, studies of pioneering women in the fields of abolitionism, education, and the suffrage movement. As important as these works were, most early historians of American women wrote within a traditional framework of political history, despite the fact that women were essentially excluded from the public sphere until the Nineteenth Amendment went into effect in 1920.

The decade of the 1960s, however, laid the groundwork for a significant transformation in the volume and approach to women's history. In 1961, John F. Kennedy established the Presidential Commission on the Status of Women, with former First Lady Eleanor Roosevelt as its chair. Following the commission's report in 1963, Kennedy issued an executive order ending sex discrimination in federal civil service employment and signed into law the Equal Pay Act guaranteeing women equal pay for equal work. Also in 1963, journalist Betty Friedan published *The Feminine Mystique*, a stinging indictment of sex inequality in the United States in which she characterized the traditional domestic sphere for women as "a comfortable concentration camp" that infantilized its female inhabitants. These efforts coalesced with the youth rebellion of the decade, with its condemnation of puritanical attitudes toward sex and demand for the extension of freedom and democracy to all sectors of the society, to generate momentum for the women's liberation movement of the late 1960s and 1970s. Against this backdrop, it is not surprising that young historians, including many women whose numbers were surging in graduate programs across the nation, began to focus on women's status as a legitimate and timely avenue of scholarly inquiry.

In order to write a real history of women, new sources and approaches would have to be employed. The traditional political-military-diplomatic framework would have to be abandoned. A new generation of historians—men and women influenced by the fourth wave of immigration, the civil rights movement, and the women's liberation movement—would begin to write about the lives of ordinary people. Their histories would be written from the bottom up instead of the top down, employing the source materials and methodologies of the new social history. In one path-breaking work, a study of religious literature and gift books, such as Sarah Josepha Hale's *Godey's Lady's Book*, historian Barbara Welter defined the characteristics of what American society believed to be "true womanhood" in the antebellum period. Her seminal essay "The Cult of True Womanhood, 1820–1860," *American Quarterly* (Summer 1966), identified the attributes by which a woman judged herself and was judged by her husband, neighbors, and the larger American community. According to Welter, there were four cardinal virtues—"piety, purity, submissiveness and domesticity. Put them all together and they spelled mother, daughter, sister, wife, woman. Without them, no matter whether there was fame, achievement, or wealth, all was ashes. With them, she was promised happiness and power."

One of the pioneer scholars of women's history was Gerda Lerner. An Austrian refugee who settled in New York City in 1939, Lerner earned her bachelor's degree at the New School for Social Research before pursuing a doctoral degree in history at Columbia University. She convinced her mentors at Columbia that a study of the Grimké sisters, two white southern abolitionists, would make a viable dissertation topic, and she turned this manuscript into *The Grimke Sisters from South Carolina: Rebels Against Slavery* (Houghton Mifflin, 1967) after a number of major publishers rejected the project. In 1962, Lerner taught the first course in women's history at the New School. Recognizing that women "are and always have been at least half of humankind and most of the time have been a majority," Lerner argued that women have their own history, which should not be marginalized by male scholars. With other historians of women, she led the search for nontraditional sources—demographic records, census figures, parish and birth records, property tax rolls, organizational files of churches, schools, police departments, and hospitals, diaries, family letters, and autobiographies—that are more attuned to a woman's point of view. Lerner suggested that scholars of women's history should (1) search for women whose experiences deserve to be well known; (2) identify women associated with topics and issues deemed important to the American mainstream; (3) test familiar narratives and revise generalizations when they appear to be wrong; and (4) understand gender as a social construct, and rewrite and develop new frameworks and concepts to understand women's history.

Drawing upon Welter's conceptual framework of the "cult of true womanhood," Lerner published a classic essay that explores the economic status of American women in the age of Jacksonian democracy. "The Lady and the Mill Girl: Changes in the Status of Women in the Age of Jackson," *American Studies Journal* (Spring 1961), argued that the experiences of middle-class and working-class women in the 1830s were different from those of men since women were unable to vote and were driven out of the medical, legal, and business professions, all of which provided occupations of upward mobility for men. Lerner's article concluded that industrialization had retarded women's attempts at economic advancement outside the home. While Jacksonian democracy provided political and economic opportunities for men, she pointed out, the "lady" and the "mill girl" were equally disenfranchised and isolated from vital centers of economic opportunity.

A more optimistic analysis of antebellum women's economic status can be found in the work of Thomas Dublin. In *Women at Work: The Transformation of Work and*

Community in Lowell, Massachusetts, 1826–1860 (Columbia University Press, 1979), Dublin argues that women employed in the Lowell textile mills developed a collective consciousness through which they enforced moral standards in the boarding houses and organized strikes when owners cut their wages, as in 1834 and 1836. Similarly, Nancy Cott, in *The Bonds of Womanhood: "Women's Sphere" in New England, 1780–1835* (Yale University Press, 1977), believes that when the modern factory system developed in the 1830s, economic opportunities opened up outside the home in industry, journalism, and within a limited sphere in business, law, and medicine. Drawing upon letters and diaries of literate New England women, Cott documents the shifting role of women inside and outside the family.

The following issue treats the impact of education on the status of women in the first half of the 1800s. As common school education expanded throughout the United States, middle-class families began to view more advanced training for their daughters as almost a prerequisite. New England, with the nation's highest literacy rate, took the lead by establishing female academies and seminaries. The founders of these institutions did not always agree on the purpose for this advanced curriculum. Emma Willard, for example, believed that further educational training not only would increase women's moral influence in society but also improve their performance in the domestic sphere by making them better mothers and housekeepers. Mary Lyon, who founded Mount Holyoke Seminary in Massachusetts in 1837 as an endowed institution of higher learning, also included a program of study in keeping with the "cult of true womanhood," but she also sought to prepare her students for a wider range of social roles. While women still were restricted in the types of professional or commercial jobs they were allowed to hold, the expansion of the common school movement opened up significant numbers of jobs for women as teachers, especially as male teachers abandoned the field of primary and secondary education to take jobs in newly emerging commercial occupations that paid significantly higher salaries. To what extent, then, did improved educational opportunities for women in the antebellum period improve their status in the public sphere?

Mary Kelley argues that the changes in educational opportunities for women were largely positive in advancing the movement of women into the nation's public life. Educated women gained leadership skills for activities outside their households by experiencing a course of study that often matched that of male colleges. By the 1850s, she concludes, women were viewed as the intellectual equals of men and had transformed the face of American civil society by contributing to the national discourse on religious doctrine, politics, and sexual and racial discrimination.

Lucia McMahon agrees that educational opportunities were available for women in the antebellum years but claims that in most instances the purpose of that education was to enable women to better serve men, not to provide women with personal autonomy. Most proponents of women's education, she asserts, insisted that women were both equal to and different from men. Moreover, they believed that maintaining social and political order demanded male hierarchy and the recognition of the differences between the sexes. As a result, American women did not achieve substantial equality or emancipation through legal channels and were victims of a continuing ambivalence regarding the proper role of educated women in American society.

YES ⤶

Mary Kelley

Learning to Stand and Speak: Women, Education, and Public Life in America's Republic

In an essay that appeared in the *School Gazette*, which students published at Hartford Female Seminary in the 1820s, one student took stock of the aspirations generated in becoming a learned woman and of the risks in claiming that mantle in post-Revolutionary and antebellum America. The author, who chose to remain anonymous, asked her classmates to consider an "Enigma." She introduces herself as "both the feminine and neuter gender." There are those who disdain her as a deviant, as "a good for nothing weed growing out of doors." Uneasy in her presence, they "would be glad to be rid of me." But she is not so easily dismissed and instead is always present in the hours devoted to schooling in the seminary's Study Hall. In those hours and in that setting, she reckons, "my company is welcome to all." Students reading their classmate's "Enigma" might have looked around the Study Hall to try to identify the author. Was she the current editor? Or was she instead one of the other contributors to the *Gazette*? Then they might have turned to an equally important project—deciphering the code and solving the riddle. Did the author's subject symbolize the promise of an advanced education for women? Did that education challenge conventional gender relations? Still playful and still elusive, the anonymous author might have answered both of these questions in the affirmative, telling her classmates that this was the "Enigma."

The student who calculated the potential benefits and costs was an actor in one of the most profound changes in gender relations in the course of the nation's history—the movement of women into public life. In asking how and why post-Revolutionary and antebellum women shaped their lives anew, *Learning to Stand and Speak* measures the significance of this transformation in individual and social identities. As the subtitle, *Women, Education, and Public Life*, suggests, it looks to the role schooling at female academies and seminaries played in mediating this process. In recasting women's subjectivity and the felt reality of their collective experience, that education was decisive. Employing the benefits of their schooling, women redefined themselves and their relationship to civil society. As educators, as writers, as editors, and as reformers, they entered the "public sphere," or the social space situated between the institutions of the family and the nation-state. The large majority of the women who claimed these careers and who led the movement of women into the world beyond their households were schooled at these institutions.

Consider Harriet Beecher Stowe. Stowe's parents, Lyman and Roxana Foote Beecher, had relatively little economic capital. The minister of the Congregational church at Litchfield, Connecticut, Lyman relied upon his parishioners for a modest salary, which included a yearly supply of firewood. But what Lyman and Roxana did command had a telling salience. The descendants of families who had migrated to New England in the seventeenth century, both had a large network of social connections. The skillful deployment of this form of capital accomplished its purpose for the Yale-trained minister, who was called from an isolated parsonage in East Hampton, Long Island, to Litchfield's prestigious Congregational church in 1810. Now at the center of a powerful network, Lyman and Roxana claimed the privileges of families long accustomed to leadership in their communities. Lyman substituted social capital for the economic resources typically needed to educate his daughter, Harriet, who was born the year after the family had moved to Connecticut. In return for pastoral services at Litchfield Female Academy, he was able to barter the costs of her education at one of the nation's most prominent academies. Harriet's schooling did not end at Litchfield. Having attended Sarah

Pierce's Academy for the four years between 1819 and 1824, Harriet was then sent to Hartford Female Seminary, which her sister, Catharine, had founded in 1821.

Educated at institutions that took the lead in providing a course of study that matched that of male colleges, Stowe was schooled in the competencies post-Revolutionary and antebellum Americans identified as the basis for cultural capital. Pierce and her nephew John Brace provided an education that certified Stowe's command of the canon of Western literature Alexis de Tocqueville identified as necessary for "remain[ing] civilized or to becom[ing] so." Familiarity with this canon was central to Stowe's education, both formal and informal. Well before she was sent to Litchfield Female Academy, Stowe had received from her family a cultural inheritance that predisposed her to books and ideas. She took to the printed page from the moment she was able to make meaning of the words and read widely in history, fiction, and poetry. As the child of a minister enthralled with his Calvinist predecessors, Cotton Mather's *Magnalia Christi Americana* was an obvious choice. Harriet leavened Mather's millennial visions with the novels of Scott and the poetry of Byron. The education did not stop there. Roxana and her sister, the beloved Harriet Foote, with whom the younger Harriet spent a year after her mother's death, disciplined her in the manners and bearing displayed by members of post-Revolutionary America's elite and aspiring middling classes. Six decades later, Stowe would inscribe this training on the pages of *My Wife and I* and its sequel, *We and Our Neighbors*, two novels that doubled as conduct manuals for the middling classes.

Was Stowe representative? No more nor less than other women schooled at a female academy or seminary. Some had more economic capital at their disposal. Others had less opportunity than Stowe to acquire cultural capital before they began their education at one of these schools. Still others came from families well supplied with both social and economic capital. However, if one compares them with other women of their generation, these differences matter relatively little. Two factors set these women apart, first, their parents' access to resources needed for the accumulation of capital in one or more of its forms and, second, their decision to commit that capital to the education of daughters.

Although there were a host of variables that shaped the decisions individual families made, certain patterns can be discerned. The convergence of a market revolution fueled by innovations in transportation and communication, capital accumulation, and increasing shortages in available land transformed the lives of all Americans. Nowhere was the impact more profound than in rural America, where 80 percent of the nation's population

resided between the American Revolution and the Civil War. Once able to provide sons with farms and daughters with dowries, parents found it increasingly difficult to sustain these traditions. Those who looked to education as an alternative endowment made the same commitment as Lyman and Roxana Beecher, contributing their economic, social, and cultural capital to the education of children. Some sons and daughters took their schooling at local academies that instructed men and women together. Others, whose families invested more of their capital in education, attended male colleges or female academies and seminaries. Some who attended these schools returned to their local communities. Many more populated the two migrations that marked these decades, one from East to West and the other from countryside to town or city.

Perhaps the most important article in the baggage these generations took with them, an advanced education opened the door to economic self-support. Men entered traditional professions as lawyers, doctors, and ministers or market-oriented careers as merchants, bankers, retailers, and manufacturers. Women, with these possibilities closed to them, took advantage of newly emerging opportunities to be writers and editors. An unprecedented number also embarked on careers as teachers. Many women pursued these opportunities simultaneously. Stowe's sister, Catharine Beecher, is emblematic in this regard. Not only did she establish three female seminaries, but she also published influential volumes on moral philosophy, physical health, and domestic economy. Compared with other women who attended a female academy or seminary, Stowe ranked as perhaps the most influential in the making of public opinion. But this difference matters not at all if compared with the influence wielded by these women as a whole. Thousands of women who had access to sufficient resources and who were educated at one of these schools followed the same trajectory as Stowe, entering civil society and taking its practice and discourse in an unprecedented direction.

Civil Society

. . . To the degree that this project is a study of social roles and institutions, it challenges the familiar model that divides the nineteenth century into private and public, feminine and masculine, household and marketplace. Teachers and students at female academies and seminaries simultaneously deployed and dismantled these binaries as they linked them to the reciprocal rights and obligations of citizenship inscribed in the nation's Constitution.

Women boldly entered civil society beginning in the 1790s and in increasingly large numbers in later decades. Sarah Josepha Hale, editor of the *Lady's Book* (later, *Godey's Lady's Book*), spoke to the importance of the institutional and discursive spaces in which they exercised influence. In the aptly titled "Conversazione," which she published in January 1837, Hale called the public broadly conceived "civil society." In its most inclusive form, antebellum Americans defined civil society as a national public in which citizens were secured in basic freedoms before the law. Embodied in the Constitution's Bill of Rights, these freedoms included speech, press, and assembly. Hale and her contemporaries also invested civil society with a more specific meaning, marking it as a public inhabited by private persons. In addition, they set the boundaries of this public, excluding the operations of the market economy from its domain. If the post-Revolutionary compromise denied women access to participation in the public sphere of organized politics, it left civil society fully open as a public sphere in which first white and then black women were able to flourish as never before. Instead of restricting them to the household, the Republic's establishment facilitated the entry of women into this rapidly expanding social space.

Post-Revolutionary and antebellum European Americans constituted civil society at a series of sites, each of which emerged in a specific historical context. Free African Americans in the North and to a lesser extent in the South acted in parallel settings, challenging discriminatory premises and practices of European Americans. Despite differences in temporal identity and emphasis, European and African American sites were all linked in a common understanding of civil society as composed of private citizens meeting together. These discursive and institutional spaces emerged in the middle of the eighteenth century as institutions of sociability where the propertied gathered for conversation; they were transformed in the post-Revolutionary decades into entities more explicitly engaged in the making of public opinion; and they came to the fore yet again in the 1830s in the voluntary associations Tocqueville identified as the key medium for articulation of the citizenry's concern with cultural uplift and moral reform. From the post-Revolutionary academies to the antebellum seminaries, students prepared themselves for engagement in civil society. Most notably, they fashioned a subjectivity in which rights and obligations of citizenship were fundamental to their sense of self.

Elite white women took their places at tea tables and salons, institutions of sociability that along with male clubs, taverns, and coffeehouses were dedicated to making public opinion. The sociability the eighteenth-century elite practiced not only separated European Americans from multiple others but also marked them as privileged relative to their counterparts in the lower ranks. Post-Revolutionary and antebellum European Americans established a host of institutions, ranging from organizations dedicated to benevolence to movements for social reform—including white women's rights and black people's emancipation—to institutions variously called literary societies, reading circles, and mutual improvement associations. Described by Tocqueville as "intellectual and moral" in their orientation, these voluntary associations were a powerful resource in the making of public opinion. Like their eighteenth-century predecessors, antebellum European Americans who engaged in organized benevolence demarcated the elite and the emerging "middling classes" from the multiple others whom they defined as "uncivilized" objects of reform. European Americans and African Americans enlisted in movements calling for the rights of white women and the end of slavery took the opposite tack. In contrast to those who insisted upon conformity to the prevailing order, they protested sexual and racial discrimination.

In addition to editing *Godey's Lady's Book*, Hale published *Woman's Record; or, Sketches of All Distinguished Women, from "the Beginning" till A.D.* 1850, a compilation of sixteen hundred individual biographies. In a volume that spanned the centuries from the birth of Christ to 1850, she devoted more than a third of the pages to women still living. Herself one of the nation's powerful makers of public opinion, Hale introduced readers to post-Revolutionary and antebellum America's most visible contributors to civil society. Although *Woman's Record* purported to sketch all women who had distinguished themselves in voluntary associations, it celebrated elite and middle-class Protestants with whom Hale shared social status and religious inclinations. African American and white working-class women were excluded, although these women were also prominent in associational life. The approaches taken by all these women illustrate the importance of class and race in defining an individual's engagement in organized benevolence, social reform, and associations devoted to reading and writing. In contrast to their elite and middle-class counterparts, white working-class women concentrated their energies on mutual aid societies. Free African American women in the North were likely to link mutual aid not only with benevolence but also with self-improvement and social reform. Free women of color in Savannah, Georgia, began to organize church-based benevolent societies in the 1830s. In the same decade, free African American women in the North organized literary societies. Doubling as acts of resistance, the collective acts of interpretation they produced in these societies took as their subjects slavery and racial prejudice, both of which were excoriated in essays, stories, and poems that members published in antislavery newspapers.

Hale also introduced readers of *Woman's Record* to founders of female academies and seminaries, whom she celebrated as exemplars. Columns and articles in *Godey's Lady's Book*, which Hale edited for four decades, praised their counterparts, the teachers in the nation's common schools. In the decades before the Civil War, the proportion of women in the classroom was higher in urban than in rural America. By 1860, women constituted between 65 and 80 percent of the teachers in the towns and cities of every region. In rural America, where 80 percent of the population lived, the proportions of women teaching varied considerably. In New England, fully 84 percent of the region's rural teachers were female. The proportions were lower in the Middle Atlantic and in the South, 59 percent and 36 percent, respectively. In Michigan and Minnesota, 86 percent of the teachers were women. In the other seven states of the Middle West, the proportion was a significantly lower 58 percent. Regional differences aside, the trend was unmistakably clear: America's classrooms were rapidly becoming a woman's domain. The women who embarked on careers as teachers were largely responsible for the rapid increase in literacy between the American Revolution and the Civil War. The students whom they taught entered a world of print that enlarged the horizon of a reader's imagination and encouraged a reflective consciousness, both of which were crucial to participation in civil society. Conversely, readers shaped that world, not only by advancing the circulation of print but also by claiming careers as writers and editors.

Woman's Record included these writers and editors whom Hale presented as an increasingly influential presence in the literary marketplace. In terms of their social and cultural importance, she was right. Between the American Revolution and the Civil War, women in the North and the South emerged as leaders in the nation's lively trade in texts. The number of genres in which they wrote expanded rapidly, as did the role they took in shaping a distinctively American literature. In the novels, histories, poems, and biographies they published and in the magazines they edited, these women contributed to national discourses on religious doctrine and denominationalism, on politics and political parties, on women and domesticity, and on the nation and its potential as the world's redeemer. By the 1840s and the 1850s, the most successful of these writers and editors could expect to make a livelihood with their pen.

Remaining Civilized or Becoming So

Like Hale's "Conversazione," which appeared three years before the publication of *Democracy in America* in 1840, Tocqueville's foundational text in American exceptionalism focused on voluntary associations that were designed to cultivate an individual's intellectual and moral potential. Indeed, these organizations stood at the center of the civil society Tocqueville described in the second volume of his treatise. In contrast to associations devoted to commerce and politics, Tocqueville told readers, voluntary associations had received relatively little consideration. And yet for him, as for Hale, they were as critical, indeed "perhaps more so," to the success of the political democracy constituted by antebellum white males. Grounded in networks of social interaction, these associations were, according to Tocqueville, the key to "remain[ing] civilized or to becom[ing] so."

In ascribing this double purpose to voluntary societies, Tocqueville went to the crux of antebellum associational life. Like those who had led the institutions of sociability that preceded them, members of voluntary organizations aligned themselves with social and cultural values they insisted were required for "remain[ing]" a "civilized" people. In women's literary societies, reading circles, and mutual improvement associations, members engaged the culturally privileged knowledge European Americans had defined as the possession of "civilized" peoples. British American women established the precedent. Gathering in reading circles a decade before the American Revolution and dedicating themselves to reading and writing, they pursued history, biography, poetry, and fiction. Through conversation and presentation of essays, they disciplined their minds and sharpened their analytical faculties. Not least, they applied the knowledge they had garnered to social and political issues. In all, they laid the basis for women's claim to the public voice and intellectual authority necessary for the making of public opinion. Students at female academies and seminaries engaged in the same critical thought and cultural production in literary societies, which were designed to intersect with and serve as a supplement to classroom instruction. These institutions were a crucial resource as students crafted subjectivities inflected by the advanced education they were learning to command. Women whose schooling had been completed extended their education in the hundreds of organizations dedicated to reading and writing they founded in villages, towns, and cities in the nation. In these settings, as in literary societies at female academies and seminaries, women addressed the larger meanings of the knowledge they were pursuing, practiced the art of persuasive self-presentation, and instructed themselves in the values and vocabularies of civil society.

Women in organized benevolence embarked on the project that Tocqueville had considered as critical as remaining "civilized"—schooling others in becoming "civilized," which they identified as the basis for citizenship. Those whom they marked as the other, or the yet-to-be elevated intellectually and morally, were expected to yield their principles to the values of reformers who claimed the right to define what it meant to be "civilized." That peoples as diverse as immigrant Catholics and native Americans resisted what we now label "cultural imperialism" should surprise no one. Others, if they suspected the motives of those who sought to impose their values, nonetheless welcomed the aid provided by evangelical Protestants, who rallied their communities on behalf of support for the indigent, education for the less privileged, aid for the widowed, and homes for the orphaned. Social reformers in the North, some evangelical, some not, took on the much more controversial issues of white women's rights and black people's emancipation.

The assemblage of associations that so impressed Hale and Tocqueville has long fascinated scholars investigating the foundations of political democracy in the nineteenth and twentieth centuries. Leading neo-Tocquevillean Robert Putnam has argued that voluntary associations are a liberal society's linchpin in "making democracy work." Envisioned as socializing agents in the nation's communities, these associations reflect and reinforce a public-spiritedness akin to the republican virtue celebrated by the post-Revolutionary elite. In creating and consolidating shared values, these organizations also serve as a counterweight to the divisiveness of antebellum America's conventional politics. However, nineteenth-century voluntary associations also played an opposite role in relation to consensus, bringing individuals together to interrogate the dominant social and political order. Whether they defended or called into question dominant values, the thousands of women who participated in voluntary associations forged lives at the intersection of newly available educational opportunities and engagement with civil society in local, regional, and national communities.

If the neo-Tocquevillean model sees voluntary associations as providing support for the masculine state, the model presented here has as its center a civil society in which women and men engaged in individual action and critical thought. In its female voluntary associations, civil society was constructed as the feminine other of the masculine state. Of course, feminist scholars, and I include myself here, have been taught to beware of binary oppositions. I am introducing this opposition, however, not as an exclusive or limiting binary, but as one among others. The household has been proposed as the binary opposite of the state, for example, and its counterpart domesticity as the feminine other to the masculine state. Introducing the concept of civil society as an additional complement to the state opens more possibilities. It also helps us to see that exclusion from one sphere of action does not necessarily imply confinement to another. The presence of women in the public sphere of civil society dismantles the false binary that identifies women exclusively with the household, even as it calls into question the symbiotic relationship between this institutional and discursive space and the masculine state. Not all women constituted this site any more than all men constituted the state. That certain women came to play leading roles in this public sphere and to shape the course it took in post-Revolutionary and antebellum America highlights the significance of education as the key both to women's entering civil society and to the influence they exercised as makers of public opinion. . . .

In the letter in which Lucy Stone recalled that she and Antoinette Brown Blackwell had "learned to stand and speak" as members of literary societies, she herself was speaking from the perspective of more than five decades of activism on behalf of women's rights. Stone, one of the movement's most influential leaders and a graduate of Mount Holyoke Seminary, understood the transformative potential of these societies and the schools that housed them. In cultivating reasoning and rhetorical faculties, modeling persuasive self-presentation, and disciplining the mind, literary societies reinforced the formal instruction provided in the classrooms of female academies and seminaries. We can be certain that Antoinette Brown Blackwell agreed with her friend. In an exchange of letters some forty years earlier, she told Stone about the impact of one such society. In the winter of 1847, the fifty members, including Brown, had organized themselves in typical fashion. In a weekly rotation, six submitted compositions for all to read and then led the debate at the meeting. *"All take a deep* interest in the exercises," Brown declared. Brown herself had "never before improved so rapidly in my life in the use of the tongue." The experience led her to repeat the claim that champion of female education Judith Sargent Murray had made a half-century earlier. With no little confidence, Brown predicted, "There is soon to be a new era in womans history." In 1798, when Murray told the *Gleaner's* readers that women who were attending the newly emerging female academies would inaugurate "a new era in female history," she looked forward to an exponential increase in women's influence in civil society. By the 1850s, women had transformed the face of civil society, and Brown was ready to extend that influence to suffrage.

The subjectivities of thousands of women were shaped by their experience as students at a female academy or seminary. Educated at institutions created exclusively for women, they attended schools with a clearly articulated mission, a faculty that offered inspiring role models, and a curriculum that introduced them to female exemplars. In educational practices ranging from classroom instruction to literary societies to reading protocols to emulation of intellectually accomplished women, students were schooled in a curriculum that matched the course of study at male colleges. Embracing the convictions of principals and teachers who held that an improved mind was a woman's greatest treasure, they committed themselves to earning the mantle of learned women.

. . . Contributors to this discourse made advanced education integral to the role they projected for women in civil society. From the Judith Sargent Murrays to the Antoinette Brown Blackwells, post-Revolutionary and antebellum women asked themselves what it meant to be a learned woman. Initially, there were those who saw little reason for a female education that went beyond reading, writing, and ciphering. Ranking women as inferior to men in matters of the mind, they doubted that a woman could be truly learned. With the establishment of female academies in the 1780s, the issue of women's intellectual potential was debated for the next three decades. In catalogs, circulars, and plans of study that highlighted schooling in reason as a primary objective, educators asserted that women were fully able to engage in critical thinking and cultural production. They also called on the women who were attending these schools to "vindicate the equality of female intellect," as Sarah Pierce charged her students in 1818. Beginning in the 1820s, the introduction of a curriculum as rigorous as that in male colleges and the performance of students at hundreds of female academies and seminaries settled the question. There were exceptions, of course. But, in most circles, women were now regarded as the intellectual equals of men.

A second and related issue generated a debate that has yet to be fully resolved. More than two centuries ago, newly independent Americans asked themselves: What should a woman do with her learning? In linking the right to an advanced education to the fulfillment of gendered social and political obligations, post-Revolutionary Americans forged an enduring compromise. Instead of claiming that women had the right to pursue knowledge for individual ends, those who were constituting gendered republicanism debated the boundaries of the domain within which women ought to meet obligations to the larger social good. Those who subscribed to the more conservative model insisted that they deploy their influence only as wives and mothers. Others pressed those boundaries. Although they acknowledged that responsibilities to one's family remained primary, they asked that women take the lead in instructing their nation in republican virtue. Even as women claimed the moral authority sanctioning their roles in the household and in the larger society and as the impact of their presence and power became increasingly visible in the latter domain, most chose not to challenge a social and political system that still rendered them subordinate to men. Instead, they proclaimed their loyalty to deference, one of the fundamental principles in systems of gender relations in which women are not accorded the same standing as men. "Woman," as Catharine Beecher declared in *Suggestions respecting Improvements in Education, Presented to the Trustees of the Hartford Female Seminary* in 1829, was "bound to 'honor and obey' those on whom she depends for protection and support." Claims to deference such as Beecher's masked women's newly acquired agency with the rhetoric of subordination. Behind this rhetoric existed a larger social reality in which thousands of women were steadily enlarging upon the power they wielded in civil society. By the middle of the 1850s, Beecher, who was founding her third and final seminary, could proclaim confidently that women had the mandate to "civilize the world." Mandate or not, women who had focused initially on their local communities were now claiming responsibility for schooling native American, South Asian, and Eastern European peoples in the tenets of republican virtue and its corollary, American exceptionalism.

The women who attended a female academy or seminary were white, and whatever their status in terms of property or income they had access to one or more forms of economic, social, and cultural capital. As its title indicates, *Notable American Women* recovers women who are "notable" in terms of social, intellectual, political, and cultural leadership. The three volumes of entries show that the large majority of the leaders of post-Revolutionary and antebellum America's organized benevolence and social reform attended a female academy or seminary. The same can be said for the educational reformers, who not only attended women's schools but also became founders and teachers. The correlation between being educated at a female academy or seminary and becoming a member of the nation's community of letters is equally strong for the writers and editors who came to maturity between 1790 and 1860. The combined privileges of skin color, social standing, and advanced education provided these women with an unparalleled opportunity to set the terms of women's engagement with public life. In elaborating an increasingly expansive gendered republicanism and in calling women to the role they projected, they did exactly that.

. . . These schools institutionalized women's access to higher education. They established the foundations of a collegiate course of study. They provided models for negotiating between the aspirations generated by higher education and the feminine conventions women were expected to practice. And they extended to generations of women the rights and obligations of citizenship.

Let me return to the riddle with which we began. For the thousands of women whose subjectivities had been shaped at female academies and seminaries, the "Enigma" the student presented to her classmates was a deeply felt reality. With little or no hesitation, these women embraced an education wrapped in the values and vocabularies of gendered republicanism. In puzzling through the challenge to the prevailing system of gender relations entailed in that education, they tacked back and forth between personal aspiration and social constraint. The paths they fashioned and the strategies they invented were multiple and complex. Decade by decade, they revised and elaborated the choices they had made. Acting on local, regional, and national stages, they became influential makers of public opinion. In all this they enacted a transformation in women's relationship to public life that has proved an enduring legacy.

Mary Kelley is the Ruth Bordin Collegiate Professor of History, American Culture, and Women's Studies at the University of Michigan. She received her PhD from the University of Iowa in 1974 and has previously held academic appointments at the City University of New York, the University of North Carolina at Charlotte, and Dartmouth College. She is also the author of *Woman's Being, Woman's Place: Female Identity and Vocation in American History* (G. K. Hall, 1979) and (with Jeanne Boydston and Anne Margolis) *The Limits of Sisterhood: The Beecher Sisters on Women's Rights and Woman's Sphere* (University of North Carolina Press, 1988), and has edited *The Power of Her Sympathy: The Autobiography and Journal of Catherine Maria Sedgewick* (Northeastern University Press, 1993).

Lucia McMahon    **NO**

Between Cupid and Minerva

In an 1802 essay provocatively titled, "Plan for the Emancipation of the Female Sex," an anonymous author suggested that women "would willingly relinquish that authority which they have so long enjoyed by courtesy, in order to appear formally on the theatre of the world merely as the equals of man." To achieve mere equality, women could "petition the legislature to sanction their emancipation by law." To gain equality, women needed only to ask for it—equality was, in essence, already theirs for the taking because no "gallant man" would allow his wife or mother to "sue in vain." This author recognized the law as one road to female emancipation, but he also underscored the early national connection between education and equality. As part of his "Plan for Emancipation," he proposed that the nation "found a college for the instruction of females in the arts and sciences." The faculty at this college would be women devoted entirely to their careers. "For the better preservation of female rights," he insisted, "the professors should all be enjoined celibacy." In addition to teaching, these "fair sages" would publish works on "the nobler subjects of civil polity or philosophy." Yet female students would be trained not to emulate their professors' public careers but to assume traditional domestic roles: "Young women entrusted to the tuition of female philosophers in this university, may when they become mothers, instruct their children; . . . and thus a gradual increase of wisdom, and consequently, of happiness, will be diffused throughout the community."

By 1802, when this essay was published, scores of female academies were being established throughout the young nation, yet the idea of a college for women was still outside serious consideration. Indeed, it is difficult to discern if the essay's author was principally serious or sarcastic. If the "Plan for Emancipation" was meant as a parody, its stance on women's education did not contain enough true derision. The author presented the female college and its students in largely positive terms and failed, unlike most critics, to disparage educated women as pedants or bluestockings. As another author noted, "Few men would (I imagine) wish their wives and daughters to prefer Horace and Virgil to the care of their families." Whatever the intentions of this 1802 "Plan for Emancipation," the fluid, nebulous nature of early national ideas about women's education and gender roles made it difficult to distinguish where possibility ended and parody began.

In 1819, less than two decades after the publication of the "Plan for Emancipation," Emma Willard, educator, echoed many of its suggestions and strategies in her "Plan for Improving Female Education." Willard petitioned the New York legislature not for female emancipation as such but, rather, for official improvements in and government support of women's education. Willard insisted that schools for women needed the same "respectability, permanency, and uniformity of operation" that characterized male institutions. As Willard argued, "It is the duty of a government, to do all in its power to promote the present and future prosperity of the nation, over which it is placed. This prosperity will depend on the character of its citizens." Women were citizens, and their proper education was vital to the success of the nation. Yet, according to her nineteenth-century biographer, Willard struggled "to find a suitable name for her ideal institution," and reportedly asserted, "It would never do to call it a 'college,' for the proposal to send young ladies to college would strike everyone as an absurdity." She instead decided upon the term "female seminary," hopeful that such naming "will not create a jealousy that we mean to intrude upon the province of the men." Willard was careful to insist that she had no desire to offer "a masculine education," stressing that education needed to reflect men and women's "difference of characters and duties."

Whether presented as parody or possibility, early national articulations of women's education were marked by this persistent tension between intellectual equality and sexual difference. In essence, proponents of women's education insisted that women were at once equal to and different from men. This paradox found expression in Willard's rejection of "masculine education" for women, as well as in the assertion in the 1802 "Plan for Emancipation" that education would put women in positions *merely* as the equals of man. Yet it is also striking that both plans proposed legal and educational measures as paths to women's equality. Women in post-Revolutionary America did not achieve substantial measures of equality or emancipation through legal channels. Early national women could not vote or hold office; and once married, women were subject to the doctrine of coverture, which made it challenging for them to hold property or acquire independent wealth. Within the educational landscape, however, progress was well underway. The period from approximately 1785 to 1825 represented a watershed moment in women's institutional access to education. Although colleges remained closed to them, women enjoyed unprecedented access to a variety of new educational opportunities.

As the institutional landscape changed, so did representations of educated women within the literary public sphere. Through a variety of forms—including engravings, poetry, essays, anecdotes, character sketches, and novels—prescriptive writers explored the place of educated women in early national America. Although many supported advancements in women's education, early national Americans were troubled by the idea that women's intellectual equality might disrupt the social, economic, and political frameworks that were sustained by the notion of sexual difference. Understanding how prescriptive writings articulated the tensions between education, equality, and difference is a crucial first step that will inform subsequent explorations of how individual women understood and experienced the boundaries of mere equality within their own lives.

"The Female Mind Shall Equal Prove"

Prior to the American Revolution, as one 1810 essayist recalled, women were "systemically shut out of Minerva's Temple." The young nation sought to expand women's access to education: "Thanks to the liberal and aspiring spirit of the age and country, the genius and education of women are not shamefully neglected." Educators established scores of new academies and seminaries for both women and men, insisting that education was an essential component of nation building. "It must therefore be a pleasure to all who wish for the prosperity and glory of this rising nation," the *Pennsylvania Gazette* reported in 1786, "to observe the zealous and liberal exertions of its citizens, in promoting the cause of literature, and

providing for the instruction of youth in every useful and ornamental science." The need for well-educated men reflected political and social ideals about well-informed citizens who would take the lead in matters concerning the political, economic, and literary spheres of the nation. Yet many early national Americans asserted that the proper education of women was equally important. As advocates insisted, women's education involved nothing less than "the most effectual means of establishing, promoting, and securing, on the most solid foundation, the domestic and social happiness of the present and future ages." Education was both a symptom and cause of the commitment of the young nation to liberty, freedom, and independence.

Such enlightened faith in the powers of education was accompanied by an optimistic, and potentially radical, belief in the equality of women's and men's intellectual capacities. Educators asserted that women "were beings endowed with reason," who possessed intellectual capacity and "an equality of mind" with men. As one author contended, women "possess a strength of reason equal to ours . . . and can attain the knowledge of every thing they are required to do, with at least, an equal facility." Another essay on female education began with a poem that captured the era's optimistic faith in women's intellectual potential: "When'er the female mind shall equal prove . . . No longer shall it vauntingly be said /*Her's is inferior to the mind of man.*" This widespread belief in women's intellectual equality had promising potential, suggesting that women could perhaps live merely as the equals of man. As John Burton, author of *Lectures on Female Education and Manners*, argued, "it cannot be denied, that your sex have given equal proofs with the men, of genius, judgment, taste, and imagination." Burton tantalizingly intimated that women were, in theory, as capable of receiving the same education as men, perhaps for the same ends: "It is not necessary, neither it is expedient for the purpose of civil society, that girls should be educated in the same manner as boys: but were a similar plan to be adopted, the women, without doubt, would be as well informed in the system of human knowledge, as the men." As Burton suggested, women's station in society was a matter of custom and access to education, not due to any lack of intellectual ability. Yet, because it was deemed neither "necessary" nor "expedient" for women to be granted full access to political and economic equality, writers such as Burton repeatedly tempered their celebratory remarks about women's intellectual capacities by evoking prescribed gender roles: "The respective employments of the male and female sex being different, a different mode of education is consequently required. For whatever equality there may be in the natural powers of their minds, which I shall not consider at present, yet the female sex, from their situation in life, and from the duties corresponding with it, must evidently be instructed in a manner suitable to their destination, and to the tasks which they will have to perform."

Despite their enlightened faith in women's intellectual equality, early national Americans continued to believe that men and women were dissimilar beings with contrasting manners, morals, and dispositions—and duties. Although the female mind was capable of intellectual equality, the female body apparently was not fitted for political equality: "'Tis Nature herself that prescribes for them a sedentary life, and devotes them to domestic occupations;' tis Nature herself that secludes from public offices, the functions of which could not be combined with the duties of a mother and a nurse." The enthusiasm for women's educational accomplishments stopped well short of extending the rights of suffrage and direct political power to women. This tension produced the notion of mere equality that dominated early national discussions of women's education.

The belief that women were indeed mere equals of men, at least intellectually and socially, while at the same time profoundly different in body and station, generated conflicting models of womanhood. To negotiate this thorny realm of equality and difference, early national Americans explored complementary gender roles that celebrated certain elements of equality (intellectual and social) while simultaneously insisting that "natural" distinctions (gender and race) defined the parameters of full political citizenship. Stressing the mutuality of relations between the sexes, writers urged women to find contentment in a model of gender identity that remained inherently hierarchical. "Do not these facts justify the order of society, and render some difference in rank between the sexes, necessary to the happiness of both?" This complementary model of gender relations attempted to square the overriding insistence on prescribed gender roles with a positive characterization of women's intellectual capacities. In the process, the prescriptive literature obscured questions of power and authority inherent in this model of social organization. Although granting women intellectual capacity equal to that of men, prescriptive writers ultimately focused on maintaining a social and political order rooted in sexual difference and male hierarchy.

Discussions of women's education thus revealed a persistent contradiction between women's intellectual capacity (which many agreed was equal to that of men), and the decidedly different uses intended for education

in their everyday lives. In essence, once having agreed that women could learn, proponents of women's education could not agree about what women should learn because their universal faith in the capacity of women's intellectual abilities came into conflict with their adherence to conventional gender roles. As one author insisted, "A *good* education is that which renders the ladies correct in their manners, respectable in their families, and agreeable in society. That education is always *wrong*, which raises a woman above the duties of her station." Instead of selfishly acquiring knowledge for their own sakes, women were asked to educate themselves for the benefit of early republican society. "How much better it would be then, were females educated, in order to make useful and ornamental members of society." As John Burton stressed, "the accomplishments, therefore, which you should acquire, are those that will contribute to render you serviceable in domestic, and agreeable in social life." The main purpose of women's education, then, was not to provide women with the means to develop personal autonomy and ambition but, rather, to enable them to serve men and society. . . . [A]ccess to education dramatically affected how individual women made sense of themselves and the world around them. But such changes in women's identity formation were of little interest to most prescriptive writers. Instead, educated women's roles were defined almost exclusively in relationship to men; they were to exercise moral influence, to provide pleasing conversation, and to serve as attractive companions. Prescriptive writers expressed little regard for the individual aspirations of educated women; rather, they worried about how women's pursuit of education would affect men.

Thus, while recognizing that the acquisition of education could enable women to live as mere equals to men, writers repeatedly warned that too much intellectual "sameness" between men and women would jeopardize domestic and social harmony by creating rivalry and competition. Prescriptive writings asserted that there was "a line of character between the sexes, which neither can pass without becoming contemptible." Women overly interested in the "masculine attainments" associated with certain forms of education and knowledge were accused of selfishness, pedantry, and affectation, traits considered "repugnant to female delicacy, so derogatory to the natural characteristic of her sex." As another author, identified as "Alphonzo," insisted, "A strong attachment to books in a lady, often deters a man from approaching her with the offer of his heart. This is ascribed to the pride of our sex." Implicitly, men did not want women who were smarter than they were, women who would disagree with them, or women who would seek opportunities in the spheres of government and business:

> When a woman quits her own department, she offends her husband, not merely because she obtrudes herself upon *his* business, but because she departs from that sphere which is assigned *her* in the order of society—because she neglects *her* duties and leaves *her own* department vacant. . . . The same principle which excludes a man from an attention to domestic business, excludes a woman from law, mathematics, and astronomy. Each sex feels a degree of pride in being best qualified for a particular station, and a degree of resentment when the other encroaches upon their privilege. This is acting conformably to the constitution of society.

In promoting a separate spheres model, writers insisted that women could not occupy themselves with "masculine" concerns without necessarily neglecting their domesticity and desirability. Accordingly, the prescriptive literature urged women to make themselves "lovely" to men, and as Alphonzo insisted, "to be *lovely* you must be content to be *women*; to be mild, social and sentimental— to be acquainted with all that belongs to your department— and leave the masculine virtues, and the profound researches of study to the province of the other sex." Prescriptive writings stressed the need for educated women to retain their feminine attractiveness and desirability to men, fearful of what might occur if educated women were no longer "content to be *women*"—in other words, if they sought to live *merely* as the equals of man.

"Knowledge, Combined with Beauty"

Part celebratory, part cautionary, prescriptive representations were important tools by which social commentators attempted to teach particular lessons about the proper content, forms, and effects of women's education. The frontispiece of the 1791 volume of the *Massachusetts Magazine* presented an inspirational model of womanhood meant to guide educated women. Surrounded by mythological and material embodiments of education, this representative woman exhibited an aura of intellectual seriousness *and* attractive femininity. The editors offered an "Explanation of the Frontispiece":

> The Fair Daughters of Massachusetts, are collectively represented by the symbolic figure of an elegant and accomplished young Lady, seated in her study, contemplating the various pages of the Magazine. Their general acquaintance with the necessary branches of reading and writing, and the more ornamental ones, of History and Geography, is happily depicted, by those instruments of Science, which adorn the Hall of Meditation. *Minerva*, the Goddess of Wisdom, assisted by *Cupid*, crowns her with a chaplet of Laurel: *Hymen*'s burning Torch is displayed aloft— a delicate intimation, that knowledge, combined with beauty, enkindles the purest flames of love.

In this representation, love and learning were coupled seamlessly in that both Cupid and Minerva crowned the achievements of this symbolic figure. "Knowledge, combined with beauty," enabled women to spread happiness and harmony throughout the young nation. As Daniel Bryan, educator, insisted, "the influence of enlightened Beauty" was "inconceivable." An attractive and intelligent woman, as a student at a female academy remarked, represented the ideal form of womanhood: "I do not know any thing which so nearly approaches the *acme* of human excellence, as a young female of an enlightened understanding, a well-informed mind, and a pure and virtuous heart, united in a fair-proportioned and beautiful form."

An "enlightened beauty" presented no apparent contradiction between love and learning, yet prescriptive thinkers frequently expressed concern about the potentially negative effects of women's education. In an 1809 essay titled, "On Female Education," James Milnor, a trustee of the Philadelphia Academy, aptly described the merits, as well as the possible dangers, inherent in women's pursuit of education. Milnor noted, "that as a polite and well-informed woman is the most welcome companion of the intelligent of our sex, a female pedant is in all respects the reverse." By failing to acquire "useful" knowledge, a pedant was given to affectation and the "ostentatious display of the decorations of her mind." But Milnor also recognized that in the effort to avoid pedantry, educators "may err on the contrary extreme." Young women also had to fear the consequences of a poor education, produced most often by reading novels. "Instead of the evil of pedantry, these are calculated to seduce the unsetted minds of young persons into the adoption of erroneous and immoral principles." Such women entertained "frivolity" and "false views of life" that often led to "disastrous course of conduct."

In his essay, Milnor identified two extremes on a spectrum of ideas about educated women. Education and knowledge were presented as important antidotes to frivolity and coquetry (symptoms of undereducation), but the danger of overeducation (specifically, pedantry) was ever-present. In effect, educated women were asked to perform a delicate balancing act. They constantly risked falling into one or the other of these perceived extremes—extremes that can be thought of as representing either too much love or too much learning. A poorly educated woman was in danger of becoming too coquettish, too sexualized, and too susceptible to seduction. On the other end of the spectrum was the woman with too much education, or more precisely, one who had gained knowledge considered inappropriate for women. Both the undereducated coquette and the overeducated pedant let their level of education interfere with their attractiveness to men—thus threatening compatibility between the sexes. The figures of the pedant and the coquette served as foils against which model republican wives and mothers were measured.

On one end of the spectrum was the pedant. Both supporters and critics of women's education agreed that the pedant was a dangerous figure—a woman who selfishly pursued knowledge to the detriment of her domestic and social duties. "Female pedantry is the object of my ridicule," one author remarked with obvious disdain. When a woman "applied herself to her study" too much, her actions resulted not in "that deference and respect which she had vainly expected" but, rather, "desertion and contemption." Instead of properly preparing herself for participation in early national society, the pedant exhibited behavior that was antisocial, selfish, and vain. It was best, as *The American Lady's Preceptor* recommended, for women to avoid "all abstract learning, all difficult researches, which may blunt the finer edges of their wit, and change the delicacy in which they excel into pedantic coarseness." Even the strongest proponents of women's education were careful to warn about the dangers of overeducating women. As Susanna Rowson, author of several books and founder of a female academy, underscored, "many are the prejudices entertained, and the witticisms thrown out against what are called learned women." Rowson summarized this mindset in her *Present for Young Ladies:* "The mind of a female is certainly as capable of acquiring knowledge, as that of the other sex; but if an enlightened mind must consequently be a conceited one it were better to remain in ignorance, since pedantry and presumption in a woman is more disgusting than an entire want of literary information, the one often awakens compassion, the other invariably excites contempt."

Pedantry was rooted in conceit and vanity. As John Burton warned, young women needed to avoid becoming "vain enough to imagine, that your boasted merit is held in the same estimation by others." Such affectation, he

asserted, implied that women were "so full of their own importance" as to exhibit an "egotism" that was "intolerable." Samuel Whiting, author of *Elegant Lessons*, agreed, remarking, "affectation of learning and authorship, in a woman with very little merit, draws upon itself the contempt and hatred of both sexes." . . .

"The Arts of Coquetry"

If a woman was too engrossed with education, she risked being labeled a pedant. Yet, if a woman's attention to education was too superficial, she could be criticized for that as well. Samuel Whiting, author, warned about the dangers awaiting any "utterly uncultivated" young woman: "What is there to correct her passions, or to govern her practice? What is there to direct her in the choice of companions and diversions; to guard her against the follies of her own sex, and the arts of ours?" As critics warned, the path to coquetry was most often laid "by a false Education, the folly of parents, or the flattery of a corrupted world." Unlike the pedant, who was preoccupied with learning, the coquette neglected her education, afraid that any overexertion might interfere with her beauty and charm. As one author quipped, "useful studies must by no means be attended to, as possibly it might damp Miss's vivacity."

Neglecting useful studies, coquettes instead were more likely to spend countless hours engaged in reading novels. Indeed, novel reading was perhaps the surest path to coquetry. Prone to coquettish behavior, novel readers were ill prepared for the realities of courtship and marriage, preferring instead to inhabit a dreamlike world of their own imagination. Such was the case for "Melissa," a young woman whose "invincible attachment to novels" turned her into a coquette. Melissa felt herself "well qualified for a heroine, as any, who shine in the page of romance. . . . Indeed she had charms, and her mind was well stored with modern female erudition; (for she had perused numberless novels)." Melissa replaced real education with romantic fancies, and through her voracious novel reading, "the arts of coquetry were. . . . carefully studied." Given to affectation and flirting, Melissa rejected many sound marriage proposals, "knowing that once sacrificed at the altar of Hymen, she could no longer enjoy the felicity of coquetry." Instead, Melissa spent her entire life an unmarried woman, and when her charms no longer worked, "she professed herself a *man hater*."

Whereas the pedant was cast as an unattractive, masculine figure, the coquette represented disorder in the form of excessive female sexuality. The "ultimate aim" of the coquette was to gain "power" over male admirers and the surrounding social scene. Ultimately, however, this power was chimerical: "However flattering it may be to the vanity of the female sex, to make conquests, or to have many admirers, yet it betrays a kind of coquetry by no means admirable." Although coquettes reveled in their ability to attract men, they represented a disruptive form of desirability—one that ultimately led to rejection and embarrassment for men. Expecting to meet heroic men who resembled characters from novels, coquettes hesitated to accept "several offers that would otherwise have appeared highly advantageous and proper." By rejecting marriage proposals from respectable men, coquettes eventually found themselves alone and unwanted. As critics repeatedly warned, any worthy man would come to recognize the insincere flirtations of a coquette and would refuse to consider her as an ideal mate. "How faint and spiritless are the charms of a coquet [sic], with the real loveliness of . . . innocence, piety, good-humour, and truth." By disrupting marital models, coquettes were as problematic as pedants. . . .

"On an Equal Footing"

Through myriad warnings and cautionary tales, the literary public sphere revealed a continued sense of ambivalence about educated women's roles in society. Rather than clarifying the relationship among education, equality, and difference, such prescriptive models may have created confusion for any woman who was relying on them to guide her behavior. As one proponent of women's education rhetorically asked, "How can a pretty woman fail to be ignorant, when the first lesson she is taught, is that beauty supersedes and dispenses with every other quality; . . . [and] that to be intelligent is to be pedantic?" Women recognized that the charge of pedantry could be used to discredit their intellectual pursuits. Yet, by stressing the need for women to remain desirable and attractive to men, prescriptive writers could be guilty of encouraging coquettish practices. "Shall we blame her for being a coquette," this author continued, "when the indiscriminate flattery of every man teaches her that the homage of one is as good as that of another?"

The censure of both coquettish and pedantic behavior reflected two extremes on a spectrum of fears about the implications of women's education. . . . Both the pedant and coquette challenged gender roles by insisting on living merely as the equals of man on their own misguide terms.

. . . [I]t was not educated women themselves but rather early national society as a whole that was unready for woman to explore the possibilities of mere

equality. . . . Early national woman eagerly embraced opportunities to acquire education and put it to good use. As a student at a female academy in New York insisted, "Since we have the same natural abilities as themselves, why should we not have the same opportunity of polishing and displaying them by the principles of an independent and virtuous education." This young woman rejoiced that enlightened Americans "wish to see the fair sex on an equal footing with themselves, enjoying all the blessings of freedom."

Inspired by this equal footing, educated women began to imagine what it would be like to live merely as the equals of man—at least in their personal and social relationships. . . . Female academies inspired women to develop identities that celebrated their intellectual ambitions. Enthusiastic about their studies, young women were determined to defend their ardent interest in education against prescriptive warnings about both coquettish and pedantic behavior.

When they left the safe, nurturing space of the female academy, educated women searched for new ways to enact identities founded in the promise of mere equality. . . . In all stages of their lives, women self-consciously crafted personal and social relationships in which their intellectual achivements were valued, appreciated, and celebrated. Through relationships with like-minded individuals, educated women searched for mere equality, inextricably linking their intellectual, emotional, and social aspirations. In particular, women believed that egalitarian relationships between men and women *were* possible, and to their credit, they found men willing and eager to enact relationships that emphasized shared intellectual and emotional interests.

Despite prescriptive fears about masculine, pedantic women, early national men did not seem troubled by the intellectual women in their lives, nor did early national women reject their domestic roles after acquiring education. In fact, we could argue that most educated women faced the inverse of the disruptive scenarios envisioned by prescriptive writers: Could they sustain the promise of mere equality when faced with the increasing demands of family life and domesticity? That is, could individual women enact identities and relationships rooted in expressions of mere equality *within* their assigned gender roles? The first generation of educated women did not, as a whole, make larger claims for political equality—they asked primarily for the right to be educated. Accepting the constraints of prescribed gender roles with respect to the law and politics, women who acquired education channeled those energies primarily toward their individual identities and relationships. "Ask those gentlemen of this assembly whose wives have been the best educated whether they find them to be less attentive to domestic concerns," Anna Harrington suggested to the audience of a Ladies' Exhibition held at an academy in Lincoln, Massachusetts. "May not more women be trusted with knowledge, as well as these. Or is there any fear that women shall gain too much influence; and become mistresses of the world in spite of man?" The fear that intellectual equality would lead women to seek "too much influence" was not borne out by the everyday lives of educated women. "When we shall quit our domestic employments, put on offensive armor, and become fond of the art of war," Anna asserted, "then such an event may be feared." While accepting (for the time being) the limited range of such efforts, educated women began to explore—and without "offensive armor"—what the promises of mere equality might entail in their individual lives. . . .

Education, Equality, or Difference

Pray you excuse me, if I have gone too far
In telling you what we've learnt: and what we are
We'll strive to show, if you will deign to hear us;
If worthy, let your approbation cheer us.

Miss A. M. Burton read this poem at commencement exercises held at Susanna Rowson's Female Academy in October 1803. The poem was published in the *Boston Weekly Magazine*, making Burton's acquisition of education at once a lived experience and a literary representation. The interplay between the personal and prescriptive was also reflected in the poem itself, which asserted women's steadfast determination to acquire and demonstrate knowledge ("we'll strive to show"), along with persistent concerns about male reception ("if you will deign to hear us"). Such worries about male criticism were not unfounded, but the story is more complicated than that. As early national women acquired education, many advocates expressed confidence that women would easily achieve a state of near, or mere, equality with men. "By giving *mind* to the fair sex," as one author asserted, "we shall make them equal to any thing that is attainable by rational beings." Another essayist proudly noted that human qualifications, "when properly cultivated and exerted, put men and women nearly on an equal footing with each other, and share the advantages and disadvantages of life impartially between them."

Left unresolved were more precise discussions of what it meant for women to live merely as the equals of man—how near an equal footing was possible, given the legal, political, and economic realities of early American life? Many women succeeded, as one essayist noted, in achieving "moments of transient equality," demonstrating intellectual "ability equal to ours." But those moments remained transient. After promoting women's intellectual capacities and celebrating their importance to civic society, prescriptive writers failed to advocate for women's legal, political, and professional equality with men. Unable to concede the possibility of women's full participation in political and economic spheres, social and political thinkers instead relied on the murky notion of mere equality in an effort to contain the potentially liberating aspects of their own rhetoric. Educated women learned to settle for social and cultural expressions of "approbation" rather than more expansive opportunities to fully utilize their intellectual capacities.

Despite these tensions, early national Americans clearly recognized that women's acquisition of education represented a critical step in their path to equality. Yet more than fifty years later, the subject of women's intellectual equality remained open to debate. In an 1840 essay published in *Godey's Lady Book*, author Mary Hale echoed sentiments expressed half a century earlier, insisting, "with proper cultivation, with the enjoyment of equal advantages, the intellectual attainments of women may equal those of men." Over the course of fifty years, educated women had proven their intellectual capacities in ever-increasing number and in an ever-expanding variety of subjects. "Has the short space of a half century given woman new powers," Hale wondered, "or is the spirit of our institutions more favourable to an enlarged cultivation of those she already possessed?" According to Hale, the answer was obvious: expanded access to educational opportunities had clearly led to women's increased attainment of knowledge and understanding.

Women had repeatedly demonstrated that they possessed intellectual capacity equal to that of men; why, then, did Hale still have to defend this assertion? Moreover, why had expanded access to education not led to even more expansive opportunities for women? In 1840, when Hale's article was published, only a handful of colleges admitted women. The clergy, law, and legislature all remained closed to women. Women continued to occupy "a less *public* station" than men, not from lack of intellectual capacity but from lack of access and opportunity. Despite her ardent support of women's educational capacities, Hale largely accepted these constraints as the will of Providence. Yet her essay also pointed to a more secular explanation—the continued criticism leveled against "a literary lady." Any woman who appeared too interested in education risked being tainted with the stain of "pedantry, self-sufficiency and insipidity." Nineteenth-century Americans remained deeply suspicious of women's intellectual accomplishments.

Reading Hale's essay, we may wonder whether little had actually changed in the course of fifty years. Fears of educated women continued to proliferate in the literary public sphere, perhaps in part because women's access to education continued to expand exponentially. By 1840, scores of academies, seminaries, and collegiate institutes existed, offering a variety of advanced educational opportunities for women. Schools such as the Troy Female Seminary (founded by Emma Willard in 1821), the Hartford Female Seminary (founded by Catherine Beecher in 1823), and Mount Holyoke (founded by Mary Lyon in 1837) offered women the equivalent of a college education—although without explicitly referring to it as such. In 1837, Oberlin College admitted its first female students, paving the way for women's admission to other colleges in the decades to follow. Well-educated women filled the ranks of teachers, authors, missionaries, and reformers. In essence, educated women attended institutions and engaged in the types of activities proposed in the 1802 "Plan for the Emancipation of the Female Sex"—yet without resolving the thorny issue of mere equality.

As women's access to education expanded, nineteenth-century Americans remained at once celebratory and cautious about educated women's influence in society. Articles proudly boasted that the United States "can vie with any nation on earth in a good proportion of intelligent and pious females." To those skeptics who doubted the need for women's education, one author suggested that such critics undoubtedly held "very limited views" of the importance of education or that they had conflated education with affectation: "Perhaps their idea of an 'educated lady' is associated in their mind with nothing better than some starched nun, or round-mouthed pedant." Despite impressive institutional advancements and individual achievements in women's education, prescriptive writers still relied on the figure of the pedant to discredit women's intellectual ambitions. Improperly educated women could still be dismissed as "trifflers and silly women," as one female essayist noted, "but if any of us have resolution enough to soar beyond those narrow limits, . . . we are called critics, wits, female pedants, &c." For over half a century, women steadfastly acquired education, but the potential uses of their intellectual capacities remained constrained by custom, law, and prejudice. Accordingly, the prescriptive literature continued to define women's education through a series of contradictions—between

capacity and utilization, between learning and desirability, between coquetry and pedantry.

In their everyday lives, educated women attempted to sort through competing sets of discourses, resisting negative representations while favoring models that validated their intellectual interests. Skeptical of both the pedant and the coquette, women refashioned narrow representations of womanhood into more expansive models. Women experimented with personal interpretations of print, reshaping discourses to suit their individual needs and aspirations. At every stage of their lives, women explored the boundaries of mere equality. In particular, educated women sought relationships with like-minded individuals willing to accept them as their intellectual and social equals. Women such as Eunice Callender, Sarah Ripley Stearns, Elizabeth and Margaret Shippen, Linda Raymond Ward, Jane Bowne Haines, and Jane Bayard Kirkpatrick all enjoyed platonic or romantic relationships with men who valued their intellectual attainments. Shared intellectual interests became a key means by which men and women crafted fulfilling relationships that celebrated areas of affinity and mutuality, in contrast to prescriptive ideas that insisted on models of gender difference and hierarchy. These women's efforts remind us that prescriptive literature can tell us only part of the history of an era, and they illustrate the continued interplay between prescriptive literature and lived experience that informed women's emotional and intellectual lives.

It is important to underscore, and tempting to celebrate, how early national women achieved some measures of mere equality in their everyday lives and relationships, even as we recognize that their efforts failed to challenge structural systems of inequality and inequity. That early national women did not advocate more fully for political rights may be seen as a lost opportunity, yet the paradoxical nature of mere equality offered them few avenues to pursue such broad goals. The narrow expressions of mere equality that educated women achieved reflected not just their own individual limitations but also larger cultural and prescriptive constraints. Despite their enlightened faith in women's intellectual capacity, early national Americans struggled to sustain the malleable and elusive concept of mere equality. Ultimately, when faced with the fundamental question of whether women could be simultaneously equal to and different from men, nineteenth-century Americans could not square the search for mere equality with their overriding belief in sexual difference. In their own lives, women accepted these constraints even as they bristled against them. "I think if we had the advantages of the other sex, we should be equally as reasonable and orderly a set of beings as they are." Elizabeth Lindsay mused to her friend Apphia Rouzee in 1806. Yet, like most of her contemporaries, Elizabeth stopped short of articulating a more radical call for equality: "but enough on the superiority of the sexes, for after all, I believe it is the best way to content ourselves with the station of life in which we have been placed." To best serve society, Elizabeth reflected, educated women needed to learn a final lesson—to "bend all our ambition on becoming as useful as we can." It can be argued that the women of this study bent their ambition, living quiet lives that until recently warranted little historical inquiry. They were well educated and determined to enact useful lives as learned women, but they had few avenues to directly challenge patriarchal systems of inequity.

The more well-known stories in women's history often revolve around those women who were able to express their desires for equality in more ambitious ways. These women, it should be noted, typically enjoyed access to educational opportunities pioneered by the early national generation. In 1848, Elizabeth Cady Stanton—a graduate of Emma Willard's Troy Seminary—presented her *Declaration of Sentiments* at the Seneca Falls convention. Recognizing the link between knowledge and power, Stanton argued that women's educational status contributed to their subordinated place in American society: "He has denied her the facilities for obtaining a thorough education, all colleges being closed against her." Women's rights activists understood that the franchise was only one path to equality; thus, they sought not only the right to vote but further access to education, reforms to divorce and property rights legislation, and expanded economic opportunities, including "an equal participation with men in the various trades, professions and commerce." Women's rights activists called for something greater than mere equality—they sought a comprehensive vision of gender equality largely unconstrained by narrow representations of difference. Perhaps it was, in part, the limits of mere equality that inspired these activists to develop a more expansive women's rights agenda.

We know that most nineteenth-century Americans sharply resisted women's efforts to claim a more fundamental equality with men, as they evoked reformulated arguments about separate spheres and sexual difference in their efforts to maintain patriarchal systems of power. As the idea of mere equality evolved into struggles for wide-ranging forms of equality, the reactions against women became more vigorous. Indeed, the doctrine of separate spheres found its fullest expression in the prescriptive literature *after* women began to assert larger

claims for political and economic equality. Writers articulated a narrowly defined private sphere of domesticity at the very time that numerous women were carving out public roles for themselves and making demands for equal access to educational and economic opportunities. Thus, the notion of separate spheres that has dominated the historiography for decades can be better understood as a *reaction* to early national women's experiments with mere equality rather than as an accurate depiction of women's lives during this time period. The sharp emphasis of the antebellum era on difference came to dominate after women had attempted to live merely—and then more fully—as the equals of man.

Perhaps most worthy of future study are the thorny questions of how and why so many women learned to adopt the rhetoric of difference and, indeed, often did so as a conscious, deliberate strategy to justify their public roles. "On the whole, (even if fame be the object of pursuit)," Hannah More, author, argued, "is it not better to succeed as women, than to fail as men?" A leading advocate of women's education, More promoted a model of female excellence sustained not by mere equality but by sharp delineations of difference. She asked women to consider whether it was better "to shine, by walking honorably in the road which nature, custom, and education seem to have marked out, rather than to counteract them all, by moving awkwardly in a path diametrically opposite?" Like other prescriptive writers, More urged women to find cultural authority by seeking "to be excellent women, rather than indifferent men." Such arguments proved persuasive, and as the nineteenth century progressed, many women rejected the complex challenges of mere equality for such clear articulations of difference.

Why did women retreat from the idea of becoming merely the equals of man and embrace a social order rooted in sexual difference? What did the rhetoric of difference offer women that mere equality failed to provide or sustain? As scholars have shown, the prescriptive rhetoric promoting women's "sphere of influence" enabled women to enact a number of expanded roles for themselves as reformers, missionaries, educators, and authors. "There is an influence spread abroad in society," wrote M. H. S. Brown, a member of the Young Ladies' Association of the New Hampton Female Seminary, in 1840. "It is felt, though it may be unacknowledged, in the halls of legislation, as well as in the drawing room, and exerts itself powerfully upon the most gifted as upon the most unintellectual of men. . . . This influence is woman's." Yet such influence came at a price—it was sustained by the explicit notion that women were acting in these influential roles as *women*, not as the mere equals of men.

The abandonment of mere equality was perhaps inevitable, in that it represented a paradoxical expression of gender identity that simultaneously reified sexual difference even as it promoted intellectual equality. Faced with this contradiction, . . . educated women often experienced a sense of ambivalence that complicated their understandings of the connections among education, equality, and difference. Although their efforts met with only limited success, the stories of how individual women attempted to live merely as the equals of man raise fundamental questions about the place of difference in a nation dedicated to the proposition that all men are created equal. Such questions have resonance today, as we consider the ways in which women continue to achieve certain measures of equality that have not required men to cede significant power or privilege. At stake, then and now, has been nothing less than (mere) equality.

Lucia McMahon is an associate professor and assistant chair in the Department of History at William Paterson University. A specialist in U.S. early national and women's and gender history, she earned her PhD from Rutgers University in 2004.

EXPLORING THE ISSUE

Did Improved Educational Opportunities for Women in the New Nation Significantly Expand Their Participation in Antebellum Society?

Critical Thinking and Reflection

1. What impact did female education have on women's status in antebellum American public life?
2. In what specific ways were American women able to use their education to participate in civil society?
3. To what extent did education produce equality between men and women in antebellum America?
4. How did notions of sexual difference impact women's opportunities in the antebellum United States?
5. Compare and contrast Kelley's and McMahon's assessments of the influence of education on antebellum women's lives.

Is There Common Ground?

Despite the different conclusions reached in their studies, Kelley and McMahon agree that educational opportunities for women clearly increased in the United States in the first half of the nineteenth century. The expansion of the common school system and the establishment of institutions of higher learning for women were important consequences of the extension of democracy in America. Even if limitations to that democratic structure denied women full access to the public sphere, this educational training laid the groundwork for women to use their training and talents to carve out meaningful roles for themselves, especially in the area of social reform. As they worked to improve the circumstances of others through their involvement in the abolitionist, temperance, and peace movements, many of these women would conclude that it was time to advance their own status by demanding a voice in the political sphere. The Women's Rights Convention at Seneca Falls, New York, in 1848 highlighted the growing awareness of women to their second-class citizenship and initiated a long campaign that would culminate in the passage of the Nineteenth Amendment at the close of the Progressive era and, ultimately, in the women's liberation movement in the late 1960s and 1970s.

What impact have these changes had on the "cult of true womanhood"? Have the divisions been completely erased between the domestic and public spheres? Traditional notions are very powerful. Despite more egalitarian ideals of contemporary society, women continue to carry out most of the responsibilities associated with child rearing and housekeeping, even as they represent a larger and larger percentage of students attending colleges and universities. Economic aspirations and necessity have produced "Super Moms," who are expected to juggle employment outside the home with responsibilities in the domestic arena. Do we need new frameworks to discuss the reality of women's experiences in the past as well as in contemporary society? For help in reconceptualizing, see Joan W. Scott, "Gender: A Useful Category of Historical Analysis?" *American Historical Review* (December 1986).

Additional Resources

Barbara J. Berg, *The Remembered Gate: Origins of American Feminism: The Woman and the City, 1800–1860* (Oxford University Press, 1978)

Carl Kaestle, *Pillars of the Republic: Common Schools and American Society* (Hill and Wang, 1983)

Margaret A. Nash, *Woman's Education in the United States, 1780–1840* (Palgrave Macmillan, 2005)

Barbara Miller Solomon, *In the Company of Educated Women: A History of Women and Higher Education in America* (Yale University Press, 1985)

Kim Tolley, *Heading South to Teach: The World of Susan Nye Hutchinson, 1815–1845* (University of North Carolina Press, 2015)

Internet References . . .

The Antebellum Women's Movement

https://www.learner.org/courses/amerhistory/pdf
/AntebellumWomen_LOne.pdf

Education Reform in Antebellum America

www.gilderlehrman.org/history-by-era/first-age
-reform/essays/education-reform-antebellum-america

Harriet Robinson: Lowell Mill Girls

www.fordham.edu/halsall/mod/robinson-lowell.asp

Lowell Mill Girls

http://faculty.uml.edu/sgallagher/Mill_girls.htm

Women's Reform Movement

http://teachinghistory.org/history-content/beyond
-the-textbook/24124

Unit 3

UNIT

Antebellum America

*P*ressures and trends that began building in the early years of the American nation continued to gather momentum until conflict was almost inevitable. The institution of slavery persisted in fifteen states, and population growth and territorial expansion brought the country into conflict with other nations under the banner of "Manifest Destiny."

The twin beliefs in democracy and progress produced an era of reform to address a variety of challenges that confronted a rapidly changing society. A dedicated group of activists, motivated by both intellectual and religious principle, determined that the ideals of human rights and democratic participation that guided the founding of the nation had been applied only to selected segments of the population and set out to eliminate social evils where they found them.

Selected, Edited, and with Issue Framing Material by:
Larry Madaras, *Howard Community College*
and
James M. SoRelle, *Baylor University*

ISSUE

Was Antebellum Temperance Reform Motivated Primarily by Religious Moralism?

YES: W. J. Rorabaugh, from *The Alcoholic Republic: An American Tradition* (Oxford University Press, 1979)

NO: John J. Rumbarger, from "The Social and Ideological Origins of Drink Reform, 1800–1836," in *Profits, Power, and Prohibition: Alcohol Reform and the Industrializing of America, 1800–1930* (State University of New York Press, 1989)

Learning Outcomes

After reading this issue, you will be able to:

- Understand the forces that produced an "age of reform" in the first half of the nineteenth century.
- Discuss the connection between religion and social reform in the first half of the nineteenth century.
- Evaluate the economic arguments that promoted attacks on American drinking habits.
- Analyze ways in which temperance reform represented a mechanism of social control over undesirable individual behavior.
- Differentiate between the goals of "temperance," "abstinence," and "prohibition."

ISSUE SUMMARY

YES: W. J. Rorabaugh points out that in the first half of the nineteenth century, evangelical Christian ministers portrayed liquor as the tool of the Devil and developed temperance societies as socializing institutions to ease social tensions and anxieties that contributed to alcohol consumption.

NO: John J. Rumbarger concludes that nineteenth-century temperance reform was the product of a pro-capitalist market economy whose entrepreneurial elite led the way toward abstinence and prohibition campaigns in order to guarantee the availability of a more productive work force.

In the era following the War of 1812, several dramatic changes occurred in the United States. Andrew Jackson's military triumph over the British at the Battle of New Orleans generated a wave of nationalistic sentiment in the country, even though the victory had come two weeks *after* the Treaty of Ghent officially ended the conflict with England. The republic experienced important territorial expansion with the addition of new states in each of the half-dozen years following the end of the war. A "transportation revolution" produced a turnpike, canal, and railroad network that brought Americans closer together and enhanced the opportunities for economic growth. In politics, the demise of the nation's first two-party system, following the decline of the Federalists, was succeeded by the rise to prominence of the Democratic and later, the Whig Parties.

Although some historians have characterized this period as the "era of good feelings," it is important to remember that many Americans were aware that the nation was not without its problems. Drawing upon intellectual precepts associated with the Enlightenment, some citizens believed in the necessity of and potential for perfecting American society. Ralph Waldo Emerson captured the sense of mission felt by many nineteenth-century men and women when he wrote: "What is man for but to be a Re-former, a Re-maker of what man has made; a renouncer of lies; a restorer of truth and good, imitating that great Nature which embosoms us all, and which sleeps no moment on an old past, but every hour repairs herself, yielding to us every morning a new day, and with every pulsation a new life?" These ideas were reinforced by the encouragement for moral and spiritual perfection produced by the revival movement known as the Second Great Awakening. Significantly, revivalists such as Charles G. Finney combined a desire to promote salvation through faith and spiritual conversion with an active interest in social change.

This "age of reform" was a multifaceted and often interrelated movement. Reformers, most of whom were from the middle and upper classes, hoped to improve the condition of inmates in the country's prisons and asylums or to encourage temperance or even total abstinence from drinking. Some reformers emphasized the necessity of maintaining peace in the world, while others hoped to improve the educational system for the masses. Still others directed their energies into movements emphasizing clothing reform for women or dietary reform. Finally, large numbers of Americans sought to stimulate human progress through campaigns to improve the status of women and to eliminate slavery.

Thousands of Americans belonged to one or more of these antebellum reform societies, but some controversy exists as to the motivations of these reformers. Were they driven by humanitarian impulses that surfaced in the reinvigorated American republic after 1815? Or was it merely self-interest that encouraged middle- and upper-class Americans to attempt to order society in such a way as to preserve their positions of power? Who were these reformers, and what were their strategies and goals for improving the society in which Americans lived?

Much of the scholarly writing pertaining to the "age of reform" represents a response to the path-breaking compendium published by Alice Felt Tyler over 65 years ago. Her study, *Freedom's Ferment: Phases of American Social History from the Colonial Period to the Outbreak of the Civil War* (University of Minnesota Press, 1944), offered the thesis that antebellum reformers were motivated largely by humanitarian ideals and hoped to perfect American society. These impulses, Tyler claimed, stemmed from America's democratic spirit and the evangelical sentiment produced by the Second Great Awakening. In the following decade, other scholars began to suggest other explanations for why nineteenth-century American reformers responded as they did. For example, David Donald, in his influential essay "Toward a Reconsideration of Abolitionists," in *Lincoln Reconsidered: Essays on the Civil War Era* (Alfred A. Knopf, 1956) concluded that abolitionists were responding to a society in which power had shifted into the hands of slave owners and industrialists, thereby depriving them of leadership positions. Their crusade against slavery, then, was part of a "status revolt" designed to create for these reformers a new leadership niche and a sense of personal fulfillment.

Another significant interpretation of the antebellum reformers comes from the "social-control" school of thought. Drawing upon the works of Michel Foucault, Erving Goffman, Howard Becker, Thomas Szasz, and others, these scholars characterize American reformers as being more interested in serving their own interests than in providing assistance to mankind. As a result, middle- and upper-class reformers responding to momentous changes within their society (the same types of changes described by Donald) imposed their standards of morality and order on the lower classes and, thus, denied the latter group freedom to act as a diverse set of individuals.

Ronald G. Walters, in *American Reformers, 1815–1860* (Hill and Wang, 1978), concludes that although many nineteenth-century reformers expressed sentiments that were self-serving and bigoted, their motivations were not based entirely upon a desire to control the lower classes. Rather, reformers were convinced that improvements could and should be made to help people.

The following essays address these varying interpretations from the perspective of those involved in the efforts to moderate or abolish the consumption of alcohol in the United States in the first half of the nineteenth century.

In the YES selection, W. J. Rorabaugh insists that religious practices and temperance both were responses to the same set of underlying social tensions and anxieties. He describes a temperance movement that was launched around 1810 by evangelical Calvinist ministers who advocated religious faith as a cure for the consumption of "demon rum." Camp meeting revivals, says Rorabaugh, focused on religious conversion in general while also targeting the conversion of alcoholics, and temperance societies served as important "moral machines" and socializing agents for the nation.

In the NO selection, John J. Rumbarger argues that American temperance reform was grounded in a market economy in which employers sought to impose limits on the traditional drinking habits of their employees as a means of improving the productive capacity of their work force. Temperance reform, according to Rumbarger, became a political effort to create a social order congenial to entrepreneurial capitalism.

YES    W. J. Rorabaugh

The Alcoholic Republic: An American Tradition

Demon Rum

During the 1820s per capita consumption of spirituous liquor climbed, then quite suddenly leveled off, and in the early 1830s began to plummet toward an unprecedented low. This decline marked a significant change in American culture, as a zestful, hearty drinking people became the world's most zealous abstainers. Just why this dramatic change took place is not entirely clear, due at least in part to the fact that historians who have studied the temperance movement have not analyzed it adequately. . . .

The antiliquor campaign was launched about 1810 by a number of reform-minded ministers, who were evangelical Calvinists associated with the newly founded Andover Seminary. Indeed, it appears that the movement began at one of a series of Monday night gatherings where Justin Edwards, Moses Stuart, Leonard Woods, and Ebenezer Porter met in the latter's study to discuss social questions. Early fruits of this Andover meeting were a number of militant antiliquor articles in Jeremiah Evarts' *Panoplist*, a Boston religious periodical with strong Andover ties. These articles were followed in 1814 by a seminal temperance pamphlet issued by Andover's New England Tract Society. This pamphlet was widely used by ministers to prepare sermons opposing the use of alcohol. The founders of the movement soon discovered that their cause had broad appeal, and when the Massachusetts Society for the Suppression of Intemperance was organized in 1812, its leaders included not only the Andover crowd but such prominent figures as Abiel Abbot, Jedidiah Morse, and Samuel Worcester. Within the next two decades these clergymen and others who subsequently joined them spread their message across the country.

Militant moral reformers succeeded in attracting public attention. A populace that had not responded to Benjamin Rush's rational warnings that spirits brought disease and death was captivated by emotional, moral exhortations warning that the drinker would be damned. The success of this emotional appeal shows clearly that Americans were more receptive to a moral argument against liquor than to a scientific argument. To persuade people to quit drinking, temperance leaders used two techniques. On the one hand, they advocated religious faith as a way for people to ease the anxieties that led to drink; on the other hand, they made drinking itself the source of anxieties by portraying liquor as the agent of the devil. Those Americans who were persuaded that Satan assumed "the

shape of a bottle of spirits" found that liquor did more to increase anxieties than to lessen them. Such people preferred abstinence to alcohol.

The leaders of the temperance crusade created a significant socializing institution, the temperance society. These "moral machines" were established in many villages and towns following a visit from an agent of a state or national temperance organization. An agent commonly wrote ahead to the ministers of a town to seek support for the cause. He then visited the town, gave a public address in one of the churches, and urged the clergymen and leading citizens to form a temperance society. The agent furnished a model constitution for such an organization, blessed the project; and proceeded to the next town. If successful, he left behind a concern about drinking and a group of prominent local people who would organize a society, adopt a constitution, write a pledge against drinking intoxicants, and undertake to get members of the community to sign it. Copies of the pledge were circulated among friends and neighbors, and new signers were initiated at monthly meetings where members congratulated themselves on the strength and vigor of their organization. When a temperance society had gathered sufficient popular support, it might plan to celebrate a holiday, such as the 4th of July, with a dry parade, picnic, or public speech designed to counter traditional wet festivities. These celebrations did not always succeed. Sometimes rival wet and dry programs sparked controversy, and at least one temperance group fought a pitched battle with its opponents. What is more surprising is how often temperance societies came to dominate the life of a town. Perhaps the best indication of their strength and influence is the fact that in some localities drinkers felt sufficiently threatened to form antitemperance societies. . . .

While the campaign against alcohol was of benefit to expansionary industrialism, it also met the needs of a growing religious movement. In the last quarter of the eighteenth century the influence of religion on American life had declined, the victim of Revolutionary chaos, a loss of English subsidies to the Episcopal church, popular distrust of authority, and the prevailing ideology of Reason. After 1800 the situation changed, and Americans, particularly those on the frontier, began to take a new interest in religion. The preachers soon saw that the Lord intended them to lead a great revival, to cleanse the nation of sin and to prepare for judgment, which might well be at hand. Some, especially the Methodist preachers, organized camp meeting revivals, where hordes of people pitched their tents, gathered for days on end, listened to numerous exhortations from a host of ministers, and were converted by the dozens amid frenzy and emotion. At one such meeting in Tennessee, "hundreds, of all ages and colors, were stretched on the ground in the agonies of conviction. . . ."

Camp meetings became one of the focal points of frontier life, attracting not only those who sought salvation but also curiosity seekers, scoundrels, and scoffers. Troublemakers often crept along the edges of the camp, threatening to steal provisions, shouting obscenities, and drinking. These intoxicated scoffers presented the leaders of a revival with a dilemma. If they posted sentinels to protect the camp and bar entry, the rowdies would taunt them from the darkness of the forest. Moreover, such a policy precluded what could be the highlight of the meeting, the dramatic and inspiring conversion of a drunkard. On the other hand, if half-drunk rowdies were admitted, they might heckle or even try to force whiskey down the throat of an abstaining minister. In either case a preacher must be ever vigilant, like the incomparable Peter Cartwright. Once that pious Methodist swung a club to knock a mischief-maker off his horse; another time he stole the rowdies' whiskey. On a third occasion he drove off troublemakers by hurling chunks of a camp fire at them. As he threw the burning wood, he shouted that fire and brimstone would descend upon the wicked. Sometimes, however, the antagonists had their joke. The Reverend Joseph Thomas was horrified when several intoxicated men, having joined the celebration of the Lord's Supper, produced a loaf of bread and a bottle of spirits.

These conditions led frontier revivalists to preach sermons contrasting the defiant, unrepentant drinker with the pietistic, humble churchgoer. The consumer of alcohol was portrayed as a man of depravity and wickedness, and this idea was supported both by the presence of rowdies at camp meetings and by the emergence of a religious doctrine that demanded abstinence. Although most denominations had long condemned public drunkenness as sinful, it was revivalistic Methodists who most vigorously opposed alcohol. After 1790 the Methodist Church adopted rules that imposed strict limitations on the use of distilled spirits. In 1816 the quadrennial general conference barred ministers from distilling or selling liquor; in 1828 it praised the temperance movement; and in 1832 it urged total abstinence from all intoxicants. A similar rise in opposition occurred among Presbyterians. In 1812 their official body ordered ministers to preach against intoxication; in 1827 it pledged the church to support the temperance movement, in 1829 expressed regret that church members continued to distill, retail, or consume distilled spirits, and in 1835 recommended teetotalism.

This increased hostility to drink showed the impact of the camp meetings and revivals upon all sects. Even conservative Congregationalists and Presbyterians were, in the words of one evangelical, moving "from the labyrinth of Calvinism . . . into the rich pastures of gospel liberty." Ministers of these denominations were relieved, after a long period of religious quiescence, to find people thirsting for salvation. Although theological conservatives tried to bend the enthusiasm for revivals to their own interest, they were less successful than the Methodists, whose feverish, anti-intellectual, nondoctrinal spirit was most in harmony with the national mood. To compete in winning converts, conservative ministers were compelled to adopt an evangelical style that the public demanded and to subordinate doctrine to the task of winning hearts.

Ministers of many denominations followed the lead of the Methodists, who preached that a man was saved when he opened his heart unto the Lord. This simple doctrine appealed to millions of Americans, but it also endangered religious authority, for the concept of personal salvation meant that it was impossible for an outsider, even a preacher, to know whether a man had actually received saving grace. A man might either claim salvation falsely or believe it mistakenly. The possibility of deceit or delusion so haunted evangelical clergymen that most came to believe that salvation was only likely when inner feelings were matched by outer deeds. When a man claimed grace, the preacher looked for a visible proof of conversion, an indication of true faith and allegiance, a token of the renunciation of sin and acceptance of the Lord.

One visible outward sign of inner light was abstinence from alcoholic beverages. A man reborn of God had no need to drink spirits, since his radiant love for the Lord would fully satisfy him. Conversely, concluded one minister, "we may set it down as a probable sign of a false conversion, if he allows himself to *taste a single drop.*" In the same vein it was held that a drinking man could not give himself to God; his drinking confirmed his hardness of heart; he was damned of God, because he would not save himself. Warned one clergyman, "Few intemperate men ever repent." This view led evangelicals to see alcohol as the devil's agent, the insidious means by which men were lured into Satan's works, such as gaming, theft, and debauchery and, worse still, trapped and cut off from their own eternal salvation. Said one preacher, "From the United States, then, what an army of drunkards reel into Hell each year!"

Not all Americans adopted the view that abstinence signified holiness and that drinking was damnable. Among the most prominent opponents of the temperance cause were the primitive Baptists, sometimes called Hard Shells or Forty Gallon Baptists. They were antinomians who believed that faith alone insured salvation and that the demand for proof of faith, such as requiring abstinence, was blasphemous. Indeed, some held that abstinence was sinful, because "God gave the spirit in the fruit of grain, and the ability to extract and decoct it, and then he gave them the inclination to drink." Furthermore, they believed that temperance organizations, like home missions, Sunday schools, and moral tract societies, threatened the purity of religion by involving the church in social problems that were best left to secular authority. Doctrine, however, may not have been the most important reason for this sect's opposition to temperance, for it was claimed that their illiterate preachers were "engaged largely in making and selling whisky." In any event, many primitive Baptist congregations expelled a member either for public intoxication or for joining a temperance society. This bifurcated policy led one exasperated man to bring a flask before his church board and ask, "How much of this 'ere critter does a man have to drink to stay in full fellership in this church?"

Most Americans, however, did accept abstinence as a sign of grace. During the late 1820s religious fervor peaked in a wave of revivals that swept across the country, that brought large numbers of new members into old congregations, and that led to the establishment of many new churches. This period of rising interest in religion coincided with the first popular success of the campaign against alcohol. The two were inexorably linked. In many localities revivals were held, church rosters bulged, and then six months or a year later temperance societies were organized. If this pattern had been universal, we could conclude that antiliquor sentiment was an outgrowth of religious enthusiasm, that the signing of a pledge was nothing more than proof of conversion, a symbolic act with no significance of its own. In some places, however the establishment of temperance societies preceded the revivals, a pattern that suggests a different interpretation of the relationship between abstinence and holiness. It appears that some Americans rejected liquor for secular reasons and only afterward turned to religion. The prevalence of both patterns indicates that temperance and revivalism were not causally connected. I would argue, rather, that they were interwoven because both were responses to the same underlying social tensions and anxieties.

We have already seen how the stresses of rapid change had made Americans anxious, how the failure to implement Revolutionary ideals of equality and liberty had heightened that anxiety, and how the decay of traditional institutions had left citizens of the young republic with few orderly outlets for their emotions, few acceptable means of satisfying their emotional needs. Under such circumstances many Americans had turned to strong drink, but they found alcohol emotionally unsatisfying. Then came the revivals and the temperance movement, which offered Americans new ways to resolve tensions, reduce fears, and organize their emotional impulses. The camp meeting, the evangelical church, and the temperance society were institutions that provided new mechanisms for coping with frustrations and for controlling, structuring, rationalizing, and channeling emotions. "It is *religion*," declared one tract, "... which alone contains in it the seeds of social order and stability, and which alone can make us happy and preserve us so." Both evangelical religion and the temperance cause encouraged people to subordinate emotions to rational, institutional processes. In my view the inexorable link between holiness and abstinence was that both

called for emotions to be expressed and controlled, and at times repressed, within an orderly, institutional framework. . . .

Misdirection of energies is common among moral crusaders, since principled and well-intentioned leaders are often self-deluded and unable to perceive their goals objectively. Temperance advocates did not comprehend their own arrogance in attempting to impose their views upon segments of the populace that were hostile, nor did they understand that effective moral codes must develop out of a social consensus, that they cannot be dictated by an elite group that seeks reform. The cry for abstinence was an attempt to cement the broken fragments of American society, but the leaders of the temperance movement could never gain the kind of unanimous consent that would have been necessary for the success of the cause. In another, broader sense the failure of the reformers to persuade all Americans to forego alcoholic beverages voluntarily was inevitable because of a peculiarity of evangelical religion. Since abstinence was the creed of those converted to godliness, universal salvation would have insured its triumph. Such unanimity, however, would have undermined revivalistic religion, whose vitality demanded a steady flow of repentant sinners. The damned drunkard was essential to the cause. On the other hand, if abstinence were not universal, this failure to achieve complete success would show that evangelical religion was not able to improve public morals greatly and would doom the idea of temperance as a consensual social value.

Antiliquor crusaders never understood these contradictions. Instead, they emerged from each bitter clash with their enemies determined to escalate the war against alcohol in order to achieve final success. And, of course, in one sense they were right; only escalation of their efforts could keep attention focused on their goal of a dry America and obscure the contradictions inherent in their position. During the 1830s, when new pledges began to fall off, reformers turned to attacking beer and wine and proving that the wine used in the biblical accounts of the Christian sacrament was the unfermented pure wine of the grape—i.e., grape juice. Not everyone was convinced. The failure of exhortation to procure universal teetotalism led to a campaign for legal prohibition, which brought about local option licensing in the 1840s, state prohibition in the 1850s, and, ultimately, in 1919, the national constitutional prohibition of all intoxicating liquor. Each effort failed to achieve the universal abstinence that reformers sought. Again and again it was demonstrated that those who believed in abstinence could not succeed in imposing their own view of morality upon that portion of the population that did not share their vision. In 1838, when Massachusetts outlawed the retail sale of distilled spirits, Yankee ingenuity triumphed. An enterprising liquor dealer painted stripes on his pig and advertized that for 6¢ a person could see this decorated beast. The viewer also got a free glass of whiskey. Such ploys spurred a hurried repeal of the nation's first prohibition law.

The moral of the striped pig was that a belief in temperance was only one component of the American ethos. This moral was lost on antiliquor zealots, who attempted to transcend the contradictions within American society with a combination of religious fervor, postponed gratification, and promises of heavenly rewards. While the faithful found these ideas appealing, others chose to forego religious commitment for the pursuit of economic gain. They were led to a kind of pragmatism that stressed industrialization, materialism, and progress. As worldly success became the counterweight to reform, the chance for Americans to develop a consensual, holistic ethos that would serve them during the period of industrialization was lost. Some, such as abolitionist John Brown, would lapse into self-deluding fanaticism; others, such as Wall Street stock manipulator Daniel Drew, into self-destructive cynicism. Most Americans would be content with a contradictory mixture of morality and materialism that would be mindlessly played out in the years ahead. The heroes of the next generation would be entrepreneurs like Cornelius Vanderbilt, who had so few scruples that he could ignore his avaricious and rapacious pursuit of millions and without embarrassment deliver public lectures on virtue. Somehow, despite his utter baseness, Vanderbilt was more admirable than a hypocritical Henry Ward Beecher, who preached against sin while facing charges of adultery. In the years after the Civil War the hope for financial gain overshadowed the search for righteousness, although neither quest could express all the contrary desires of Americans. The times favored men such as Vanderbilt, who ignored principles, followed instincts, and subordinated both his head and his heart to his gut.

In my view the kind of society that Americans built in the nineteenth century resulted both from the way that ideology and institutions interacted with changing contemporary conditions and from the way in which society itself evolved as a consequence of those interactions. Just as historical circumstances and economic developments had led to the opportunity for increased drinking in the 1820s, the binge itself created another opportunity; the impulses toward materialism and evangelicalism dictated the shape and contour of the response to that opportunity. The campaign for abstinence and the transformation of alcohol from the Good Creature into the Demon Rum were a logical outgrowth of prevailing attitudes, values, and institutions. As drinking declined, as society was reshaped, as the framework for modern capitalism developed, and as the churches organized their moral campaign, the chance for a holistic ethos disappeared.

America was left as a culture dominated by an ambivalence that could be transcended only through an anti-intellectual faith. The potential for powerful intellects to influence American life had diminished; a unified moral code was no longer possible. By 1840 the pattern that would dominate the country for a century was set. Entrepreneurial capitalism, the corporate structure, the cult of private enterprise, and the glorification of profit were to dominate the rational, hard, masculine, and efficient side of the culture; evangelical religion, the voluntary reform society, the cult of Christian charity, and the glorification of God were to dominate the emotional, soft, feminine, and inspirational side. Institutions representing the two sides were to work in tandem to build the country. Important among those institutions were temperance societies. They were, in many ways, the crucial link between the two contrasting sides of American culture. A majority of the participants in the early temperance movement were women, but, in contrast to a later era, the leaders were men, mostly evangelical clergymen. These ministers were to be the bridge between the two sides of American culture, the men who connected the masculine and feminine, hard and soft, rational and emotional aspects. Or as one American said in the 1830s, clergymen were "a sort of people between men and women." This remark has a second, deeper meaning. Being neither men nor women, the clergy were clearly impotent, and, ultimately, incapable of sustaining a coherent, holistic, living culture.

W. J. Rorabaugh is professor of history at the University of Washington. His current published research focuses on the 1960s and includes *Berkeley at War: The 1960s* (Oxford University Press, 1989), *Kennedy and the Promise of the 1960s* (Cambridge University Press, 2002), and *The Real Making of the President: Kennedy, Nixon, and the 1960 Election* (University Press of Kansas, 2009).

John J. Rumbarger

 **NO**

The Social and Ideological Origins of Drink Reform, 1800–1836

The roots of the temperance movement can be found in those social forces working to develop the expansionist tendencies of the American economy. Neither an abstract Puritan heritage nor paternalist conservatism can explain satisfactorily the dynamics that produced the movement to extirpate liquor drinking from America's culture. The earliest temperance societies, like that organized in Litchfield, Connecticut, in 1787, resulted from the efforts of wealthy farmers to curtail drinking among their laborers during harvest time. . . .

Nevertheless, these early societies defined the movement's strategic objective: the increase of productivity by the elimination of daily work breaks for alcoholic refreshment and its unpredictable consequences. These societies also illustrated a mutual desire on the part of property holders to obtain a uniform standard of labor, regardless of considerations that worked to set them in opposition to each other. These employers assumed that it was their prerogative to determine the social conditions that would lower the costs of production. In a market economy such considerations constituted sufficient reason to eliminate customary drinking, and the more so when labor scarcity deprived employers of a traditional instrument of capital accumulation, low wages.

Early concern about popular drinking was forcefully articulated by Benjamin Rush, whose writing on the subject became an ideological touchstone for the temperance movement. . . . His objective could best be obtained by employing "the force of severe manners" to curtail the social habits of drinking. . . .

Typical of the fruits of Rush's pioneering efforts was the temperance society formed by property owners in the Moreau-Northumberland region of Saratoga County, New York. At the beginning of the nineteenth century these agriculturally rich townships supported a diversified local economy of farming, lumbering, milling, and some rudimentary manufacturing. The political and social life of the area was dominated by a squirearchy, but, as elsewhere, it was difficult for them to engage in business enterprise without supplying workers with their customary alcoholic beverages. What distinguished Moreau-Northumberland's temperance pioneers was professional training among those who galvanized the squirearchy into action against liquor drinking.

Billy Clark had studied medicine; Esek Cowan had read law; Lebbius Armstrong was trained for the ministry. All three invested their surplus professional income in land and agricultural production. Clark, for example, owned several farms and had a large investment in a local paper mill. Cowan was a prosperous farm owner with a reputation for innovative husbandry. More important, however, for the purposes of temperance reform, was the common world view—quite like Rush's—the three shared. In one degree or another Moreau's temperance reformers believed society could improve with individual discipline and practical innovation, and that the criterion of improvement was business profits. William Hay, who subsequently headed the society, recalled that Clark was "convinced of the necessity of self-culture, and consequently acquired what are pertinently termed *business habits*." Hay admiringly described Clark as "pecuniarily successful as a physician and a businessman," and also wrote approvingly of Esek Cowan's various employments as a jurist, farmer, and classical scholar. For this kind of man "recreation was only change of employment," and employment was directed towards profit. . . .

These ideological conceptions nurtured temperance reform. But the reformers' stance towards other social classes was flexible: traditional rank or position was not an obstacle for association with like-minded men, provided the requisite social virtues of practical knowledge and disciplined effort could be demonstrated. Despite this apparent democratic appeal, the political ideology of a temperance "middle" class did not look to a reordering of society. Forged as it was in the crucible of business enterprise, it sought ultimately to redirect the energies and activities of capital and labor, but not to alter their social relationship. In the social context of Jeffersonian America, however, temperance ideology was radical in both theory and practice since it claimed to seek another reallocation of wealth and property according to utilitarian norms even as it sought an increase in social productivity. The assumption of the permanency of social stratification, to be dominated by a rationally selected elite, was but poorly masked by notions of individual worth taken to be demonstrated by the social virtues of innovation and discovery wedded to a discipline, including temperance, congenial to business. Because of this critical defect, temperance reformation, insofar as it envisioned a distinct "middle" class, was necessarily procapitalist.

Rumbarger, John J. Reprinted by permission from *Profits, Power, and Prohibition: Alcohol Reform and the Industrializing of America, 1800–1930* (State University of New York Press, 1989), pp. 3, 4, 5–10, 11–15, 19–20 (excerpts, notes omitted). Copyright © 1989 by State University of New York. Reprinted by permission of State University of New York Press, Albany NY. All rights reserved.

The idea of a middle class proved especially valuable to the socialization process required by young America, which in the period 1820–50 could not compel people to alter their customary behavior sufficiently to modify the social order's value system. Indeed, the idea that personal characteristics and behavior were a form of capital may be seen as the *sine qua non* of American economic development in these years. Thus, all manner of ideologies, both secular and religious, that encouraged the development of internal modes of self-discipline as forms of "moral capital" were encouraged by the early advocates of liquor reform.

During the decades of the 1820s and 1830s temperance reform wherever it appeared became a political effort to create a social order universally congenial to entrepreneurial capitalism. It was during these years that the perceptions of men like Benjamin Rush and Billy Clark took root in business activity outside of agriculture, and attracted attention from such established institutions as the Protestant churches. But while local societies of employers who mutually agreed "that hereafter we will carry on our business without the use of distilled spirits as an article of refreshment, either for ourselves or those whom we may employ" remained on the reform scene, they proved insufficient to the task of extending temperance sentiment. To meet this need and to deal with the realities facing various enterprises, their politicization was required.

In Jeffersonian and Jacksonian America, maritime commerce ranked with agriculture in its importance to the economy. Here, too, liquor was customarily provided for laborers. . . .

In shipbuilding, workers enjoyed ceremonial provisions of strong drink in addition to their daily rations. At the completion of each major stage of construction they joined with shipowners and masters to toast their work's progress. Thus when the keel was put down, the ribs erected, the decking laid, and the masts raised and stepped there would be general celebrations fueled by large amounts of whiskey.

The earliest efforts at reform in these employment areas followed the boycott tactics that were being developed by agricultural temperance societies. In Medford, Massachusetts, for example, a local shipbuilder, Thacher Magoun, refused to permit rum or distilled spirits to be used in his shipyard. Magoun's 1817 no-rum edict was immediately interpreted by his laborers as "practically an increase in the working time, the employer thus saving the cost of time as well as the cost of the rum." Other Medford shipbuilders followed Magoun's lead, even to the point of raising wages. These boycotts could only be partially effective, however, because of the apprentice system and the grog shop, which furnished money and the means to smuggle the contraband refreshment into the yards.

By 1819, temperance advocates outside of agricultural societies had developed an analysis of the liquor problem that would eventually permit them to go beyond the limits of the boycott, and thus politicize the temperance movement. Thomas Hertell's *An Expose of the Causes of Intemperate Drinking and the Means by which It May Be Obviated* considered the entire social order to be the obstacle to temperance reform. Hertell implied that reform could only succeed if society in general were reformed with respect to drinking.

Hertell, who served for more than a dozen years on the bench of New York City's maritime court, asserted that his antiliquor convictions proceeded from the fact that "intemperate drinking is inimical to agricultural and mechanical, as well as moral improvement." He maintained that neither distillers nor the grog shop lay at the root of the problem; both were symptoms and consequences. The real cause of society's intemperate drinking was to be found in the "intemperate use of ardent liquor [which] originates in the fashions, habits, customs, and examples of what are called the upper or wealthy classes of the community." Because of the universal employment of such drinks by society's elites in both public and private, Hertell concluded that "inebriating drinks" had gained sanction as the "median universally adopted by society for manifesting friendship and good will, one to another."

Hertell believed that society's lower orders habitually emulated the upper, and so he argued that self-reformation by the wealthy must come before a general reform. Moreover, Hertell insisted that without a general temperance reform, nascent manufacturing enterprizes could not hope to succeed for "there is scarcely to be found among the laboring class, any who do not drink, and drink too much." Drinking customs were depriving manufacturers of quality manpower. "What single measure," he asked rhetorically, "would do more to further [manufacturing and agricultural development] than the destruction of the custom of giving ardent spirits to working people of every description."

Hertell's analysis of the liquor problem pulled together several strands in the developing temperance movement, and extended the focus of the reformers' concerns beyond agriculture and commerce to manufacturing. The reform impulse had derived from the pragmatic observation that customary drinking diminished productivity. Initially, reformers focused on the ordinary drinks—"ardent spirits"—of the working class as the principal source of abuse, and they continued to rely on the boycott as the means of curtailing and eliminating drinking.

On the other hand, Hertell insisted on the need of society's elites (including the churches) to exercise rigid self-restraint. Only when this class acted to end its sanction of drinking would "useful industry . . . become fashionable," and would "the already over-run and overrated learned professions" be abandoned for the "honorable calling" of the mechanical trades. Hertell looked to the formation of an antiliquor class consciousness that would act not only to protect its traditional base in agriculture and commerce, but also extend its concerns to American manufacturing. Of primary significance, however, is the fact that this attention to the responsibility of America's elite for the general well-being of society gave the temperance reform its peculiarly moralistic character, its ambivalence about the use of the state, and its connection with the Protestant churches.

During the years leading to the politicization of the temperance movement, American society underwent severe stress. Between 1800 and 1820, war and depression, accompanied by the introduction of the factory system, released latent hostilities that frequently expressed themselves in inchoate public drunkenness and disrespect towards religious and secular authority—or so it seemed to men like Lyman Beecher, the Congregationalist clergyman-reformer. Yet Beecher's consideration of social policy did not produce any effort to define the liquor problem in ways fundamentally different from those discussed. Indeed, during these years the established churches wedded themselves firmly to the emerging temperance movement in ways that sought to reinforce the movement's fundamental purposes. In 1812, for example, Beecher brought an ad hoc report before the General Association of Congregational and Presbyterian clergy wherein he asserted that intemperance was the mutual problem of the "Civil and Religious order," and recommended that employers cease providing liquor to their employees. Beecher also warned his colleagues that their efforts must remain within the boundaries of the "sanction of public sentiment," and thus echoed Benjamin Rush's plea for a regime of severe manners.

Ultimately the concerns of activist clergymen like Beecher were identical to those of men like Thomas Hertell and Mathew Carey, the Philadelphia publisher who helped establish the Philadelphia Society for the Promotion of National Industry. In 1820 Carey brought out Beecher's sermon, "The Means of National Prosperity," which encouraged the expansion of manufacturing, presupposing an abstemious social order, and outlined a role for the nation's churches in fostering this development. . . .

The larger vision of temperance reform articulated by Thomas Hertell and Lyman Beecher took firm root within the establishments of the Northeast during and immediately following the Napoleonic wars. Mercantile capital, the center of much early temperance concern, fueled the expansion of the nation's young manufacturing enterprises and brought to them the problems of absentee owners seeking to insure their investments in an unsure world. Made aware during these years of their own role in perpetuating the "drinking usages" of society, American capitalists organized to secure a dry working class. By 1834, Walter Channing, a pioneering member of the Massachusetts Society for the Suppression of Intemperance, recalled with some exaggerated pride that it was only when "men of great consideration . . . solemnly impressed with the ruinous progress of intemperance . . . came out as one man to make an open declaration of their convictions" that temperance reform began to progress.

The American Temperance Society (ATS), founded in January 1826 by Marcus Morton, a colleague of Channing,

became the vehicle for the unified expression of class interest and coordinated action that Channing was to praise. Morton, who was "ahead of his time" in matters pertaining to labor reform, organized an umbrella society because of the deepening conviction that existing temperance societies were weak and ineffective. "Their object was," the ATS complained, "to regulate the use of ardent spirits, not to abolish it."

ATS envisioned a decentralized temperance apparatus, hierarchically organized from the local through the national level so that the smallest antiliquor organizations could "regulate their own movements and efforts according to their own views of necessity and expediency, and . . . their own wants and ability." The work of the ATS itself was to provide each and all with a common analysis of the liquor problem that corresponded to the class-conscious need for property owners to abstain totally from the use of distilled liquor, and to aid in the formation of state and local societies that adhered to this view of the problem. To oversee this work, Morton's group decided that a full-time paid secretary would be necessary and solicited contributions from "men of known and expansive benevolence, who are blessed with property," and who shared the view "that a system of general and powerful cooperation may be formed, and that a change may in a short time be effected, which will save an incalculable amount of property, and vast multitudes of valuable lives."

The man chosen to carry out the ATS reform was Justin Edwards of Andover Theological Seminary. In part Edwards's own previous skepticism about the efficacy of total abstinence from the use of distilled liquor became a major asset to the new organization. Prior to joining ATS as its secretary, Edwards had "thought [total abstinence] was going much too far . . . that the temperate use of ardent spirit was, for men who labor, in hot weather, necessary." What persuaded Edwards that the pledge of total abstinence by property owners was indeed efficacious was not theological conviction but an experiment conducted at one of the farms of a member of Morton's group in 1825. The result, Edwards testified, was that laborers "performed more labor with greater ease."

Equally and perhaps more important, in the eyes of ATS, total abstinence from hard liquor produced an apparent change in the attitude of laborers. According to Edwards the regime of enforced abstinence made the men "more respectful and uniform in their deportment . . . more contented with their living; more desirous of being present at morning and evening family devotion . . . more attentive at public worship on the Sabbath." Clearly this class-based reform effort saw a vital link between the docility of workers and their productivity on the one hand, and depriving them of liquor on the other.

The ATS, through the work of Edwards and secretaries of state societies affiliated with it, made repeated attempts to use the churches to advance the goal of abolition. Recognizing that distilleries were, for the most part, owned and operated by members of their own social class,

ATS and its affiliates viewed the churches as the most appropriate vehicles available to them for the persuasion and coercion of their own. These efforts had profound and disruptive effects upon the churches and the movement itself, but what should not be lost sight of in the dogmatic hairsplitting over the extent to which abstinence was to be demanded is the intent of the reformers. "Ardent spirits" was the ordinary alcoholic beverage of workers. It had been the indifferent success of societies like the Massachusetts Society for the Suppression of Intemperance in seeking "to discontinue the too free use of ardent spirit" that had led to demands for total abolition. The ATS pledge committed affiliated societies to exclude all who "traffic" in ardent spirits and to "discountenance the use of them throughout the Community." It was thus that the churches became putative instruments of the reformers.

In their endeavor to persuade the churches to condemn both moderate drinking and the liquor traffic, ATS concentrated its efforts on the governing bodies of the various Protestant denominations. Such attempts met with indifferent success. The General Conference of the Methodist Episcopal Church, for example, condemned "the pestilential example of temperate drinking," but only inquired rhetorically if churches which tolerated manufacturers and sellers of whisky could be innocent of wrongdoing. The conference did not condemn the latter or move to excommunicate offending individuals. Thus, ATS had to rely upon the vague hopes of "some leading men" of the conference that by 1836 the church would be rid of the traffickers in drink.

The ATS also sought to bring pressure on the churches to expel liquor dealers through the efforts of such men as Wilbur Fisk, president of Wesleyan University, who castigated total abstinence church members for not insisting upon such expulsions and charged the churches with similar complicity. The ATS executive committee joined in this criticism: "From all parts of the country . . . the greatest difficulties in the way of Temperance Reformation . . . are those members of the church, who still sell ardent spirit."

Such pressures divided the established churches even though they produced condemnations of varying strength from national and state ecclesiastical organizations. The larger ones usually confined their expressions of opinion to vague generalities and left it to specific congregations to act. The Protestant clergy was also encouraged to advance the utilitarian purposes of the reformers. Thus, a Connecticut clergyman maintained that the cause would be well served "if farmers and mechanics would agree not to drink spirits themselves, and not provide them for their workmen."

By 1834 it was clear that the established churches had not made any deep inroads against either moderate drinking or the liquor traffic. In addition, their involvement in reform entailed a necessary hindrance to it since wine was of central importance to the Christian ritual as well as the ordinary drink of the wealthy. When, in the mid-1830s, ATS pushed for total abstinence from all alcoholic beverages and demanded state action against the liquor traffic, the difficulties posed by the churches appeared to outweigh their assets. As one clerical reformer acknowledged to the 1834 New York State Temperance Convention: "I have therefore been pained to see so many inclined to connect their religion with temperance. . . . And I know many individuals, who keep themselves aloof from the temperance society on this account, who would undoubtedly join the ranks, if the cause of temperance could be kept separate from everything else."

While the American Temperance Society concentrated its efforts on arousing the consciousness of property holders through the churches, state societies continued to recruit such people to the cause of temperance by stressing the utilitarian benefits of reform. In July 1833, the *Temperance Recorder*, the official organ of the New York State Temperance Society, reported that the consolidation of the Erie Canal's several towing firms into the Albany and Buffalo Towing Company had enabled the teamsters' employers to gain "control and government" over them, with the result that their intemperate drinking habits had been effectively checked. The same issue praised the society's forwarding of a circular letter to American consuls in Europe, warning émigrés that those who drank would find it difficult to obtain employment, and urging them to affiliate with a temperance society as an aid to finding work. The New York Society, which was dominated by mercantile and landed capitalists like Edward C. Delavan of Albany and Stephen Van Rensselaer of Saratoga, urged "the proprietors of our large, as well as our small manufacturing establishments . . . to take their subject into immediate consideration," since it was clear that intemperance was more dangerous to business prosperity than even foreign competition. The New Yorkers advised that temperance societies be organized within the factories themselves, and that proprietors and owners become the officers: "Unless proprietors or agents take the lead, nothing need be expected; but by their taking the course recommended . . . all under their control will be brought speedily into this 'ark of safety.'"

But the efforts of the New York Society and ATS to use the churches to arouse a class-conscious temperance sentiment in favor of overseas economic expansion ran afoul of the churches' difficulties and weakened the desired condemnation and divided the reformers. Many reformers recognized that the association of temperance with specific political and economic issues detracted from its class appeal. If the temperance movement were to gain the class support that its adherents believed was crucial, temperance morality would have to be divorced from specific secular and religious issues, and its moral appeal would have to come from an agency not associated with the churches.

In May 1833 ATS directors convened a national convention in Philadelphia to consider these questions and to chart the future course of reform. The four hundred delegates from twenty-four states represented the country's mercantile, manufacturing, and landed capital. Indicative of the range and scope of this class of men are Gerrit Smith and Stephen Van Rensselaer. Together with John Jacob Astor, Smith's father had acquired over one million acres of land in upstate New York, some 700,000 acres of which he passed on to his son in 1819. Van Rensselaer's holdings were equally vast. Both men were outstanding proponents of internal improvements and expanded trade with the West. Smith violently opposed a governmental role in expanding these markets, but Van Rensselaer was a strong advocate of such aid.

Other representatives of mercantile wealth included Edward C. Delavan, Roberts Vaux and his son, Richard, of Philadelphia, Samuel Ward of New York whose family's wealth had been invested in the banking firm of Prime, Ward, and King, Samuel Mifflin of Philadelphia, and John Tappan of Boston. Typical of emerging manufacturing representatives were Amasa Walker of Boston, Jonas Chickering, whose piano manufacturing concern of Stewart and Chickering developed the single casting iron frame for making grand pianos, and Matthew Newkirk, whose cotton goods business provided the funds for his railroad investments. Many of them, Delavan, Newkirk, and Smith, for example, had multiple investments in land, transportation, and manufacturing.

Also attending the first national temperance convention were luminaries from the first ranks of law, politics, religion, and science, many bearing some of the oldest family names in America. Reuben Hyde Walworth, chancellor of New York State, was named the convention's president. Joseph H. Lumpkin (whose brother Wilson was a Georgia planter and governor of the state), who would himself become a member of Georgia's Supreme Court, was named convention vice president. Timothy Pitkin, the author of the first major statistical account of American commerce, was a delegate from Connecticut. John McLean, who was to become president of the College of New Jersey, was a delegate. So also was Samuel L. Southard, Democractic senator from New Jersey. Amos Twitchell, a pioneer heart surgeon, represented New Hampshire. Jonas K. Converse of Burlington, Vermont, was a delegate, as were Philadelphia philanthropists John Sargent and Joseph B. Ingersoll; businessmen-publicists such as Mathew Carey, William Goodell, Thomas Bradford, Jr., and Sylvester Graham were typical delegates.

Other men of similar stature, like chemist Benjamin Silliman of Yale, or perhaps less well known, such as George Chambers, largest landowner in Franklin County, Pennsylvania and a reformer in education and agriculture, filled out the complement of delegates to the Philadelphia meeting. Their differences in economic interest, political affiliation, and religious persuasion were transcended by a fundamental class problem: the liquor question. . . .

In the end, this effort to rely solely upon the resources of property would fail because, as Gerrit Smith had already pointed out, America was a society where the demand for labor could not be met. Would-be employers would find the pledge inadequate and the law insufficient. But from the vantage point of 1834, the antiliquor movement had achieved astounding success. It had aroused the consciousness of virtually the entire propertied class, regardless of particular economic or political interest, to the importance of extirpating the use of distilled alcohol as a precondition of capitalist development. It had created a secular temperance morality that avoided the rigidities of various theologies while, at the same time, it had been able to enlist the churches in raising the consciousness of the "employing class." And it had developed its archetypal propaganda institution, the American Temperance Society, which was controlled by entrepreneurs of all sorts, and state and local temperance societies, which were to organize local property interests for the cause. Finally, the reform was being urged in the direction of a political attack on the liquor traffic itself.

When the United States Temperance Union and its affiliates met at Saratoga Springs in 1836, there appeared to remain but two mutually compatible tasks for the reform: first, spread the new gospel that "it has been proved a thousand times, that more labor can be accomplished in a month, or a year, under the influence of simple nourishing food and unstimulating drink than through the aid of alcohol"; second, organize and launch a political assault on the liquor traffic itself. To further these ends, the USTU named Reverend John Marsh and Edward C. Delavan to its principal offices. Both were fitting choices for the work. Marsh was related by marriage to the Tappan mercantile family of Boston and New York; his cousin Samuel would head the New York and Erie railroad. Delavan, on the other hand, was an active entrepreneur whose fortune had been made, ironically, as an importer of wine, and who came to the temperance reform after Nathaniel Prime, Lynde Catlin, and he had lost three hundred thousand dollars invested in the manufacture of steam engines and other heavy iron work because, they claimed, of "the unfortunate drinking habits [of the workers], which for best of motives, we ourselves encouraged."

John J. Rumbarger (1938–1996) taught American political history at Rutgers University. A former editor of *Prologue*, he later served as chief historian of the Federal Emergency Management Agency.

EXPLORING THE ISSUE

Was Antebellum Temperance Reform Motivated Primarily by Religious Moralism?

Critical Thinking and Reflection

1. What role did religion play in the efforts to reform the drinking habits of Americans in the first half of the nineteenth century? Were there some denominations that were more active in this reform than others? If so, why?
2. How were camp meeting revivals particularly useful in converting alcoholics?
3. Were there other reform initiatives of this time period in which religious moralism was a prominent component? If so, what were some of these reforms?
4. Why were industrial entrepreneurs so interested in the personal behavior of their workers? How successful were they in reforming the drinking habits of these employees?
5. To what extent can one argue that ministers and entrepreneurs both operated from a "social control" perspective in their efforts to institute temperance reform?

Is There Common Ground?

Mark Edward Lender and James Kirby Martin, in *Drinking in America: A History* (The Free Press, 1982), examine the characteristics of temperance reformers in the first half of the nineteenth century. These reformers, they argue, drew upon the perfectionist message presented during the Second Great Awakening in an effort to create a more virtuous nation. They describe a moral elite consisting of ministers and laypeople who served as "stewards of society" by leading a mass reformation in the drinking culture of the United States that shifted over time from a focus on moral suasion to bring about more moderate consumption of "ardent spirits" to political movements for total abstinence.

Both Rorabaugh and Rumbarger offer explanations for the motivations of temperance reformers that could fall into the "social control" model. Clearly, the consumption levels of alcohol in the American republic were significant enough for many Americans to conclude that the nation faced a drinking problem. To what degree did the efforts to limit this consumption fly in the face of personal freedoms that were being touted in the "age of Jackson"? Also, is it reasonable to assume that some of the demand for temperance or prohibition stemmed from a rising tide of Irish and German immigration to the United States in the 1830s and 1840s and the drinking habits these immigrants brought with them as part of their cultural baggage? Neither author pays much attention to the fact that women comprised a significant portion of the membership of temperance societies both before and after the Civil War. Some scholars

have attributed this pattern to the fact that women volunteered for a wide variety of humanitarian organizations, but one could also hypothesize that they were particularly concerned about alcohol consumption because of the potential deleterious impact it had on family structure and relationships.

Create Central

www.mhhe.com/createcentral

Additional Resources

Ellen C. Du Bois, *Feminism and Suffrage: The Emergence of an Independent Woman's Movement in America, 1848–1869* (Cornell University Press, 1978)

Barbara L. Epstein, *The Politics of Domesticity: Women, Evangelism, and Temperance in Nineteenth-Century America* (Wesleyan University Press, 1981)

Clifford S. Griffin, *Their Brothers' Keepers: Moral Stewardship in the United States, 1800–1865* (Rutgers University Press, 1960)

Joseph R. Gusfield, *Symbolic Crusade: Status Politics and the American Temperance Movement* (University of Illinois Press, 1966)

Carolyn J. Lawes, *Women and Reform in a New England Community, 1815–1860* (University Press of Kentucky, 2000)

Internet References . . .

American Reform Movements

www.gilderlehrman.org/history-now/2012-01
/reform-movements

**Religion and Reform in Nineteenth-
Century America**

nationalhumanitiescenter.org/ows/seminarsflvs
/religionreform.html

**Temperance Reform in the Early
Nineteenth Century**

www.teachushistory.org/Temperance/

**The Second Great Awakening and the Age
of Reform**

www.teachushistory.org/second-great-awakening
-age-reform

Selected, Edited, and with Issue Framing Material by:
Larry Madaras, *Howard Community College*
and
James M. SoRelle, *Baylor University*

ISSUE

Did African American Slaves Exercise Religious Autonomy?

YES: Albert J. Raboteau, from "Slave Autonomy and Religion," *Journal of Religious Thought* (1982)

NO: John B. Boles, from *Masters & Slaves in the House of the Lord: Race and Religion in the American South, 1740–1870*, University Press of Kentucky (1988)

Learning Outcomes

After reading this issue, you will be able to:

- Explain how slave owners could employ religion to control their slaves.
- Understand ways in which slaves used religious activities to gain personal autonomy.
- Discuss the importance of African American preachers in the antebellum period.
- Evaluate the biracial religious culture of the antebellum South.
- Assess the extent to which Christianity pacified slaves or caused them to resist their enslavement.

ISSUE SUMMARY

YES: Albert J. Raboteau claims that the religious activities of enslaved African American were characterized by institutional and personal independence, which undermined the ability of slave owners to exercise effective control over their chattel property.

NO: John B. Boles recognizes that slaves often worshiped apart from their masters, but he asserts that the primary religious experience of southern slaves occurred within a biracial setting in churches dominated by whites.

Since the mid-1950s, few issues in American history have generated more interest among scholars than the institution of slavery. Books and articles analyzing the treatment of slaves, comparative slave systems, the profitability of slavery, slave rebelliousness (or lack thereof), urban slavery, the slave family, and slave religion have abounded. This proliferation of scholarship, stimulated in part by the civil rights movement, contrasts sharply with slavery historiography between the two world wars, which was monopolized by a single book—Ulrich B. Phillips's apologetic and blatantly racist *American Negro Slavery* (D. Appleton, 1918). Phillips, a native Georgian who taught for most of his career at Yale, based his sweeping view of the southern slave system upon plantation records left by some of the wealthiest slave owners. He concluded that

American slavery was a benign institution controlled by paternalistic masters. These owners, Phillips insisted, rarely treated their bondservants cruelly but, instead, paternalistically provided food, clothing, housing, and other necessities of life to their slaves, who he characterized as childlike, acquiescent human property.

Although African American historians such as George Washington Williams, W. E. B. Du Bois, Carter G. Woodson, and John Hope Franklin produced scholarly works emphasizing the brutal impact of slavery, their views received almost no consideration from the wider academic community. Consequently, recognition of a "revisionist" interpretation of slavery was delayed until the post–World War II era when, in the wake of the *Brown* desegregation case, Kenneth Stampp, a white northern historian, published *The Peculiar Institution: Slavery in the*

Ante-Bellum South (Alfred A. Knopf, 1956). Stampp also focused primarily upon antebellum plantation records, but his conclusions were literally a point-by-point rebuttal of the Phillips thesis. The institution of slavery, he said, was a harsh, oppressive system in which slave owners controlled their servants through fear of the lash. Further, in contrast to the image of the passive, happy-go-lucky "Sambo" described by Phillips, Stampp argued that slaves were "a troublesome property" who resisted their enslavement in subtle as well as overt ways.

Three years later, Stanley Elkins synthesized these seemingly contradictory interpretations in his controversial study *Slavery: A Problem in American Institutional and Intellectual Life* (University of Chicago Press, 1959). Elkins clearly accepted Stampp's emphasis on the harshness of the slave system by hypothesizing that slavery was a "closed" system in which masters dominated their slaves in the same way that Nazi concentration camp guards in World War II had controlled the lives of their prisoners. Such an environment, he insisted, generated severe psychological dysfunctions which produced the personality traits of Phillips's "Sambo" character type.

As the debate over the nature of slavery moved into the 1960s and 1970s, several scholars, seeking to provide a history of the institution "from the bottom up," began to focus upon the slaves themselves as a contributing force in the slave system. Interviews with ex-slaves had been conducted in the 1920s and 1930s under the auspices of Southern University in Louisiana, Fisk University in Tennessee, and the Federal Writers Project of the Works Progress Administration. Drawing upon these interviews and previously ignored slave autobiographies, sociologist George Rawick's *From Sundown to Sunup: The Making of the Black Community* (Greenwood, 1972) and historians John Blassingame's *The Slave Community: Plantation Life in the Antebellum South* (Oxford University Press 1972) and Eugene D. Genovese's *Roll, Jordan, Roll: The World the Slaves Made* (Pantheon, 1974), among others, portrayed a multifaceted community life over which slaves held a significant degree of influence. This community, operating beyond the view of the "Big House," was, in Genovese's phrase, "the world the slaves made."

Religion was an integral part of that community life among slaves by the antebellum period and has received attention in virtually every scholarly treatment of the institution of slavery. In the colonial period, however, whites made little more than sporadic attempts to proselytize among newly arrived Africans who brought with them their traditional religious belief systems. More attention began to be directed toward the religious lives of enslaved peoples during the evangelical Protestant revivals from the mid-eighteenth century to the early decades of the 1800s, as masters offered religious instruction to their chattel property, various Christian denominations directed missionary activities toward slaves, and as African American bondservants began to adapt the white man's religion to their own spiritual needs. Genovese's *Roll, Jordan, Roll* (cited above) places religious practice at the heart of the slave community. Slaves, says Genovese, were able to create a syncretized African-Christianity that served them in multiple ways: as an instrument of accommodation or resistance, emotional fervor, and spiritual comfort and relief from their daily labors and troubles. They took from their master's religion what was useful to them, particularly the themes of faith, love, and deliverance, and gave less thought to doctrine or denominational structure. Lawrence W. Levine, in *Black Culture and Black Consciousness: Afro-American Folk Thought from Slavery to Freedom* (Oxford University Press, 1977), studies slave songs, spirituals, and folk tales to conclude that slaves practiced their religion in a world that they shared with one another apart from their masters. Albert Raboteau's *Slave Religion: The "Invisible Institution" in the Antebellum South* (Oxford University Press, 1978) insists that this separate religious life enabled slaves to develop a strong sense of community and to develop leaders within that community. Sterling Stuckey offers a slightly different conclusion in *Slave Culture: Nationalist Theory and the Foundations of Black America* (Oxford University Press, 1987) by pointing out that many slaves lacked access to regular religious services or embraced Sunday as a day off and, hence, were scarcely touched by Christianity. In contrast to the interpretations presented in the preceding works, Orville Burton's *In My Father's House Are Many Mansions: Family and Community in Edgefield, South Carolina* (University of North Carolina Press, 1985) suggests that Christianity functioned as a means of social control over slaves to maintain docility and obedience.

Some of these contrasting interpretive currents are reflected in the following essays on the nature of slave religion. In the first selection, Albert Raboteau describes the ways in which the acceptance of Christianity produced numerous opportunities for slaves to assume control over their own religious activities. Slave preachers assumed positions of leadership in the black community that could not be limited by whites, and slaves realized greater autonomy in black-controlled churches or in secret religious gatherings. This religious autonomy, according to Raboteau, permitted slaves to resist some of the dehumanizing elements of the slave system.

John Boles admits that slaves in the antebellum South worshiped in a variety of ways (in independent black churches, plantation chapels, or informal, secret gatherings), but he concludes that the typical site for slave religious activities was the church of their masters. Although potentially restrictive, such a setting vitalized the slave community by offering bondservants from different plantations an opportunity to mingle freely with one another.

Moreover, says Boles, nowhere else in southern society were blacks treated so nearly as equals to whites than in these biracial churches, where they were admitted to membership, addressed by whites as "brother" or "sister" (the same terms used for fellow white members), and allowed to participate with limited equality in church discipline.

YES ↩

Albert J. Raboteau

Slave Autonomy and Religion

One of the perennial questions in the historical study of American slavery is the question of the relationship between Christianity and the response of slaves to enslavement. Did the Christian religion serve as a tool in the hands of slaveholders to make slaves docile or did it serve in the hands of slaves as a weapon of resistance and even outright rebellion against the system of slavery? Let us acknowledge from the outset that the role of religion in human motivation and action is very complex; let us recognize also that Christianity played an ambiguous role in the stances which slaves took toward slavery, sometimes supporting resistance, sometimes accommodation. That much admitted, much more remains to be said. Specifically, we need to trace the convoluted ways in which the egalitarian impulse within Christianity overflowed the boundaries of the master-slave hierarchy, creating unexpected channels of slave autonomy on institutional as well as personal levels. To briefly sketch out some of the directions which religious autonomy took among slaves in the antebellum South is the purpose of this essay.

Institutional Autonomy

From the beginning of the Atlantic slave trade in the fifteenth century. European Christians claimed that the conversion of slaves to Christianity justified the enslavement of Africans. For more than four centuries Christian apologists for slavery would repeat this religious rationalization for one of history's greatest atrocities. Despite the justification of slavery as a method of spreading the gospel, the conversion of slaves was not a top priority for colonial planters. One of the principal reasons for the refusal of British colonists to allow their slaves religious instruction was the fear that baptism would require the manumission of their slaves, since it was illegal to hold a fellow Christian in bondage. This dilemma was solved quickly by colonial legislation stating that baptism did not alter slave status. However, the most serious obstacle to religious instruction of the slaves could not be legislated away. It was the slaveholder's deep-seated uneasiness at the prospect of a slave laying claim to Christian fellowship with his master. The concept of equaility, though only spiritual, between master and slave threatened the stability of the system of slave control. Christianity, complained the masters, would ruin slaves by allowing them to think themselves equal to white Christians. Far worse was the fear, supported by the behavior of some Christian slaves, that religion would make them rebellious. In order to allay this fear, would-be missionaries to the slaves had to prove that Christianity would make better slaves. By arguing that Christian slaves would become obedient to their masters out of duty to God and by stressing the distinction between spiritual equality and worldly equality, the proponents of slave conversion in effect built a religious foundation to support slavery. Wary slaveholders were assured by missionaries that "scripture, far from making an Alteration in civil Rights, expressly directs, *that every Man abide in the Condition wherein he is called, with great indifference of Mind* concerning outward circumstances."

In spite of missionary efforts to convince them that Christianity was no threat to the slave system, slaveowners from the colonial period on down to the Civil War remained suspicious of slave religion as a two-edged sword. Clerical assurances aside, the masters' concern was valid. Religious Instruction for slaves had more than spiritual implications. No event would reveal these implications as clearly as the series of religious revivals called the Great Awakenings which preceded and followed the Revolution. The impact of revival fervor would demonstrate how difficult it was to control the egalitarian impulse of Christianity within safe channels.

The first Great Awakening of the 1740s swept the colonies with the tumultuous preaching and emotional conversions of revivalistic, evangelical Protestantism. Accounts by Whitefield, Tennent, Edwards, and other revivalists made special mention of the fact that blacks were flocking to hear the message of salvation in hitherto unseen numbers. Not only were free blacks and slaves attending revivals in significant numbers, they were taking active part in the services as exhorters and preachers. The same pattern of black activism was repeated in the rural camp meetings of the second Great Awakening of the early nineteenth century.

The increase in slave conversions which accompanied the awakenings was due to several factors. The evangelical religion spread by the revivalists initiated a religious renaissance in the South where the majority of slaves lived. The revival became a means of church extension, especially for Methodists and Baptists. The mobility of the Methodist circuit rider and the local independence of the Baptist preacher were suited to the needs of the rural South. Among the Southerners swelling the ranks of these denominations, were black as well as white converts.

Moreover, the ethos of the revival meeting, with its strong emphasis upon emotional preaching and congregational response, not only permitted ecstatic religious behavior but encouraged it. Religious exercises, as they were termed, including fainting, jerking, barking, and laughing a "holy laugh," were a common, if spectacular, feature of revivals. In this heated atmosphere slaves found sanction for an outward expression of religious emotion consonant with their tradition of danced religion from Africa. While converting to belief in a "new" God, slaves were able to worship in ways hauntingly similar to those of old.

Extremely important for the development of black participation in revival religion was the intense concentration upon individual inward conversion which fostered an inclusiveness that could become egalitarianism. Evangelicals did not hesitate to preach to racially mixed congregations and had no doubt about the capacity of slaves to share the experience of conversion to Christ. Stressing plain doctrine and emotional preaching, emphasizing the conversion experience instead of religious instruction, made Christianity accessible to illiterate slave and slaveholder alike. The criterion for preachers was not seminary training but evidence of a converted heart and gifted tongue. Therefore, when an awakened slave showed talent for preaching, he preached, and not only to black congregations. The tendency of evangelical Protestantism to level the souls of all men before God reached its logical conclusion when blacks preached to and converted whites.

By the last quarter of the eighteenth century a cadre of black preachers had begun to emerge. Some of these pioneer black ministers were licensed, some not; some were slaves, others free. During the 1780s a black man named Lewis preached to crowds as large as four hundred in Westmoreland County, Virginia. Harry Hosier traveled with Methodist leaders, Asbury, Coke, Garretson, and Whatcoat and was reportedly such an eloquent preacher

that he served as a "drawing card" to attract larger crowds of potential converts, white and black. In 1792 the mixed congregation of the Portsmouth, Virginia Baptist Church selected a slave, Josiah Bishop, as pastor, after purchasing his freedom and also his family's. Another black preacher, William Lemon, pastored a white Baptist church in Gloucester County, Virginia, for a time at the turn of the century.

In 1798, Joseph Willis, a freeman, duly licensed as a Baptist preacher, began his ministry in southwest Mississippi and Louisiana. He formed Louisiana's first Baptist church at Bayou Chicot in 1812 and served as its pastor. After developing several other churches in the area, he became the first moderator of the Louisiana Baptist Association in 1818. Uncle Jack, an African-born slave, joined the Baptist church and in 1792 began to preach in Nottoway County, Virginia. White church members purchased his freedom and he continued to preach for over forty years. Henry Evans, a free black licensed as a local preacher by the Methodists, was the first to bring Methodist preaching to Fayetteville, North Carolina. Initially preaching to black people only, he attracted the attention of several prominent whites and eventually the white membership of his congregation increased until the blacks were crowded out of their seats. Evans was eventually replaced by a white minister, but continued to serve as an assistant in the church he had founded until his death.

That black preachers should exhort, convert, and even pastor white Christians in the slave South was certainly antithetical to the premise of slave control. Though such occasions were rare, they were the ineluctable result of the impulse unleashed by revivalistic religion. Of greater importance for the development of autonomy in the religious life of slave was the fact that black preachers, despite threats of punishment, continued to preach to slaves and in some few cases even founded churches. An early historian of the Baptists applauded the anonymous but effective ministry of these black preachers:

> Among the African Baptists in the Southern states there are a multitude of preachers and exhorters whose names do not appear on the minutes of the associations. They preach principally on the plantations to those of their own color, and their preaching though broken and Illiterate, is in many cases highly useful.

Several "African" Baptist churches sprang up before 1800. Some of these black congregations were independent to the extent that they called their own pastors and officers, joined local associations with white Baptist churches, and sent their own delegates to associational meetings. Though the separate black church was primarily an urban phenomenon, it drew upon surrounding rural areas for its membership, which consisted of both free blacks and slaves, Sometimes these black churches were founded amidst persecution. Such was the case with the African Baptist Church of Williamsburg, Virginia, whose history was chronicled in 1810:

> This church is composed almost, if not altogether of people of colour. Moses, a black man, first preached among them, and was often taken up and whipped, for holding meetings. Afterwards Gowan Pamphlet . . . became popular among the blacks, and began to baptize, as well as to preach. It seems, the association had advised that no person of colour should be allowed to preach, on the pain of excommunication; against this regulation, many of the blacks were rebellious, and continued still to hold meetings. Some were excluded and among this number was Gowan. . . . Continuing still to preach and many professing faith under his ministry, not being in connexion with any church himself, he formed a kind of church out of some who had been baptized, who, sitting with him, received such as offered themselves; Gowan baptized them, and was moreover appointed their pastor; some of them knowing how to write, a churchbook was kept; they increased to a large number; so that in the year 1791, the Dover association, stat[ed] their number to be about five hundred. The association received them, so far, as to appoint persons to visit them and set things in order. These making a favourable report, they were received, and have associated ever since.

Several features of this narrative deserve emphasis as significant examples of black religious autonomy. Ignoring the threat of excommunication, not to mention physical punishment, blacks rebelled against white religious control and insisted on holding their own meetings, led by their own ministers. They gathered their own church, apparently according to the norms of Baptist polity, accepted their own members, kept their own minutes, and finally succeeded in joining the local association, all the while growing to a membership of five hundred by 1791!

In Savannah, Georgia, a slave named Andrew Bryan established an African Baptist Church, against white objection and persecution. In 1790, Bryan's church included two hundred and twenty-five full communicants and approximately three hundred and fifty converts, many of whom did not have their masters' permission to be baptized. In 1803, a Second African Church of Savannah was organized from the first, and a few years later a third came

into being. Both of the new churches were led by black pastors. After Bryan's death, his nephew, Andrew Marshall, became pastor of the First African Church and by 1830 his congregation had increased in size to two thousand, four hundred and seventeen members.

The labors of these early black preachers and their successors were crucial in the formation of slave religion. In order to adequately understand the development of Christianity among the slaves, we must realize that slaves learned Christianity not only from whites but from other slaves as well. Slave preachers, exhorters, and church-appointed watchmen instructed their fellow slaves, nurtured their religious development, and brought them to conversion in some cases without the active involvement of white missionaries or masters at all. The early independence of black preachers and churches was curtailed as the antebellum period wore on, particularly in periods of reaction to slave conspiracies, when all gatherings of blacks for whatever purpose were viewed with alarm. For slaves to participate in the organization, leadership, and governance of church structures was perceived as dangerous. Surely it was inconsistent, argued the guardians of the system, to allow blacks such authority. As the prominent South Carolinian planter, Charles Cotesworth Pinkney, declared before the Charleston Agricultural Society in 1829, the exercise of religious prerogatives left slaves too free from white control. "We look upon the habit of Negro preaching as a widespreading evil; not because a black man cannot be a good one, but . . . because they acquire an influence independent of the owner, and not subject to his control. . . . when they have possessed this power, they have been known to make an improper use of it." No doubt, Pinkney and his audience had in mind the African Methodist Church of Charleston which had served as a seedbed of rebellion for the Denmark Vesey conspiracy of 1822. (Following discovery of the plot, whites razed the church to the ground.)

Regardless of periodic harassment by civil and ecclesiastical authorities, black preachers continued to preach and separate black churches continued to be organized. Just as Pinkney and others warned, in preaching and in church life some blacks found channels for self-expression and self-governance. To be sure, the exercise of such autonomy was frequently modified by white supervision, but it was nonetheless real. In various sections of the antebellum South, black churches kept gathering members, over the years swelling in size to hundreds and in a few instances thousands of members. Certainly, the vast majority of slaves attended churches under white control. However, even in racially mixed churches some black Christians found opportunities to exercise their spiritual gifts and a measure of control over their religious life. This was so especially in Baptist churches because Baptist polity required that each congregation govern itself. In some churches committees of black members were constituted to oversee their own conduct. These committees listened to black applicants related their religious experience and heard the replies of members charged with moral laxity. Meeting once a month, committees of "brethren in black" conducted business, reported their recommendations to the general meeting and gave to black church members experience in church governance. This experience laid a foundation upon which freedmen would rapidly build their own independent churches after emancipation.

Hampered though it was, the exercise of religious autonomy among slaves was a fact of antebellum life. It was due to the nature of the revival fervor of the Great Awakenings of the eighteenth and early nineteenth centuries which first brought the slaves to conversion in large numbers and also created a situation in which it became possible for black freemen and slaves to preach and even pastor. (By way of contrast, these avenues to spiritual authority would not open for blacks in either the Church of England or the Roman Catholic Church for a long time to come.) To the extent possible, then, black Christians proved not at all reluctant about deciding their own religious affairs and managing their own religious institutions. For the vast majority of slaves, however, institutional religious autonomy was not possible. This did not stop them from seeking religious independence from whites in more secretive ways.

Personal Autonomy

Like their colonial predecessors, antebellum missionaries to the slaves had to face objections from whites that religion for slaves was dangerous. Beginning in the 1820s, a movement led by prominent clerics and laymen attempted to mold southern opinion in support of missions to the slaves. Plantation missionaries created an ideal image of the Christian plantation, built upon the mutual observance of duties by masters and by slaves. One leader of the plantation mission stated the movement's basic premise when he predicted that "religious instruction of the Negroes will *promote our own morality and religion.*" For, when "one class rises, so will the other; the two are so associated they are apt to rise or fall together. Therefore, servants do well by your masters and masters do well by your servants." In this premise lay a serious fallacy: for while the interests of master and slave occasionally coincided, they could never cohere. No matter how devoted master was to the ideal of a Christian plantation, no matter how pious he might be,

the slave knew that the master's religion did not countenance the slaves' freedom in this world.

Precisely because the interests of master and slave extended only so far and no further, there was a dimension of the slaves religious life that was secret. The disparity between the master's ideal of religion on the plantation and that of the slaves led the slaves to gather secretly in the quarters or in brush arbors (aptly named hush harbors) where they could pray, preach, and sing, free from white control. Risking severe punishment, slaves disobeyed their masters and stole off under cover of secrecy to worship as they saw fit. Here it was that Christianity was fitted to their own peculiar experience.

It was the slaveholding gospel preached to them by master's preacher which drove many slaves to seek true Christian preaching at their own meetings. "Church was what they called it," recalled former slave Charlie Van Dyke, "but all that preacher talked about was for us slaves to obey our masters and not to lie and steal." To attend secret meetings was in itself an act of resistance against the will of the master and was punished as such. In the face of the absolute authority of the Divine Master, the authority of the human master shrank. Slaves persisted in their hush harbor meetings because there they found consolation and communal support, tangible relief from the exhaustion and brutality of work stretching from "day clean" to after dark, day in and day out. "Us niggers," remarked Richard Carruthers, describing a scene still vivid in his memory many years later, "used to have a prayin' ground down in the hollow and sometimes we come out of the field . . . scorchin' and burnin' up with nothin' to eat, and we wants to ask the good Lawd to have mercy. . . . We takes a pine torch . . . and goes down in the hollow to pray. Some gits so joyous they starts to holler loud and we has to stop up they mouth. I see niggers git so full of the Lawd and so happy they draps unconscious."

In the hush harbor slaves sought not only substantive preaching and spiritual consolation they also talked about and prayed for an end to their physical bondage. "I've heard them pray for freedom," declared one former slave. "I thought it was foolishness then, but the old time folks always felt they was to be free. It must have been something 'vealed unto 'em." Though some might be skeptical, those slaves who were confident that freedom would come, since God had revealed it, were able to cast their lives in a different light. Hope for a brighter future irradiated the darkness of the present. Their desire for freedom in this world was reaffirmed in the songs, prayers, and sermons of the hush harbor. This was just what the master—those who didn't believe in prayer, as well as those who did—tried to prevent. The external hush harbor symbolized an internal resistance, a private place at the core of the slaves' religious life which they claimed as their own and which, in the midst of bondage, could not be controlled.

For evangelical Christians, black or white, full admission into membership in the church required that the candidate give credible testimony about the inner workings of the Spirit upon his or her heart. The conversion experience, as described by ex-slaves, was typically a visionary one, inaugurated by feelings of sadness and inner turmoil. Frequently the individual "convicted of sin" envisioned Hell and realized that he was destined for damnation. Suddenly, the sinner was rescued from this danger and led to a vision of Heaven by an emissary from God. Ushered into God's presence, the person learned that he was not damned but saved. Awakening, the convert realized that he was now one of the elect and overwhelmed with the joyful feeling of being "made new" shouted out his happiness. For years afterwards, this "peak" experience remained a fixed point of identity and value in the convert's life. He knew that he was saved, and he knew it not just theoretically but experientially. Confident of their election and their value in the eyes of God, slaves who underwent conversion, gained in this radical experience a deeply rooted identity which formed the basis for a sense of purpose and an affirmation of self-worth—valuable psychic barriers to the demeaning and dehumanizing attacks of slavery.

Conversion, as an experience common to white and black Christians, occasionally led to moments of genuine emotional contact, in which the etiquette of racial relationships was forgotten. A dramatic instance of one such occasion was recounted by a former slave named Morte:

> One day while in the field plowing I heard a voice . . . I looked but saw no one . . . Every thing got dark, and I was unable to stand any longer . . . With this I began to cry, Mercy! Mercy! Mercy! As I prayed an angel came and touched me, and I looked new . . . and there came a soft voice saying, "My little one, I have loved you with an everlasting love. You are this day made alive and freed from hell. You are a chosen vessel unto the Lord." . . . I must have been in this trance more than an hour. I went on to the barn and found my master waiting for me. . . . I began to tell him of my experiences . . . My master sat watching and listening to me, and then he began to cry. He turned from me and said in a broken voice, "Morte I believe you are a preacher. From now on you can preach to the people here on my place . . . But tomorrow morning. Sunday. I want you to preach

> to my family and my neighbors." . . . The next morning at the time appointed I stood up on two planks in front of the porch of the big house and, without a Bible or anything. I began to preach to my master and the people. My thoughts came so fast that I could hardly speak fast enough. My soul caught on fire, and soon I had them all in tears . . . I told them that they must be born again and that their souls must be freed from the shackles of hell.

The spectacle of a slave reducing his master to tears by preaching to him of his enslavement to sin certainly suggests that religion could bend human relationships into interesting shapes despite the iron rule of slavery. Morte's power over his master was spiritual and (as far as we know) it was temporary. It was also effective.

While commonality of religious belief might lead to moments of religious reciprocity between blacks and whites, by far the more common relationship, from the slaves' side, was one of alienation from the hypocrisy of slaveholding Christians. As Frederick Douglass put it, "Slaves knew enough of the orthodox theology of the time to consign all bad slaveholders to hell." On the same point, Charles Ball commented that in his experience slaves thought that heaven would not be heaven unless slaves could be avenged on their enemies. "A fortunate and kind master or mistress, may now and then be admitted into heaven, but this rather as a matter of favour, to the intercession of some slave, than as a matter of strict justice to the whites, who will, by no means, be of an equal rank with those who shall be raised from the depths of misery in this world." Ball concluded that "The idea of a revolution in the conditions of the whites and blacks, is the cornerstone of the religion of the latter. . . ."

Slaves had no difficulty distinguishing the gospel of Christianity from the religion of their masters. Ex-slave Douglas Dorsey reported that after the minister on his plantation admonished the slaves to honor their masters whom they could see as they would God whom they could not see, the driver's wife who could read and write a little would say that the minister's sermon "was all lies." Charles Colcock Jones, plantation missionary, found that his slave congregation did not hesitate to reject the doctrine preached in a sermon he gave in 1833:

> I was preaching to a large congregation on the *Epistle of Philemon:* and when I insisted upon fidelity and obedience as Christian virtues in servants and upon the authority of Paul, condemned the practice of *running away*, one half of my audience deliberately rose up and walked off with themselves, and those that remained looked any

thing but satisfied, either with the preacher or his doctrine. After dismission, there was no small stir among them: some solemnly declared "that there was no such an Epistle in the Bible:" others, "that I preached to please the masters:" others, "that it was not the Gospel:" others, "that they did not care if they ever heard me preach again!" . . . There were some too, who had strong objections against me as a preacher because I was a *master* and said, "his people have to work as well as we."

The slaves' rejection of white man's religion was clearly revealed in their attitudes toward morality. While white preachers repeated the command, "Do not steal," slaves simply denied that this precept applied to them since they themselves were stolen property. Josephine Howard put the argument this way: "Dey allus done tell us it am wrong to lie and steal, but why did de white folks steal my mammy and her mammy . . . Dat de sinfulles' stealin' dey is." Rachel Fairley demanded, "How could they help but steal when they didn't have nothin'? You didn't eat if you didn't steal." Henry Bibb declared that under slavery "I had a just right to what I look, because it was the labor of my hands." Other slaves concluded that it was not morally possible for one piece of property to steal another since both belonged to the same owner: it was merely a case of taking something out of one tub and putting it in another. This view of stealing referred only to master's goods, however, for a slave to steal from another slave was seriously wrong. As the saying went, "a slave that will steal from a slave is called *mean as master*." Or as one ex-slave remarked, "This is the lowest comparison slaves know how to use: just as mean as white folks." . . .

Not all slaves, however, were able to distinguish master's religion from authentic Christianity, and were led to reject this religion totally. In 1839, Daniel Alexander Payne explained how this could happen:

> The slaves are sensible of the oppression exercised by their masters: and they see these masters on the Lord's day worshipping in his holy Sanctuary. They hear their masters professing Christianity; they see their masters preaching the gospel; they hear these masters praying in their families and they know that oppression and slavery are inconsistent with the Christian religion; therefore they scoff at religion itself—mock their masters, and distrust both the goodness and justice of God.

Frederick Douglass too remembered being shaken by "doubts arising . . . from the sham religion which everywhere prevailed" under slavery, doubts which "awakened in my mind a distrust of all religion and the conviction that prayers were unavailing and delusive." Unable to account for the evil of slavery in a world ruled by a just God, some slaves abandoned belief. "I pretended to profess religion one time," recalled one former slave, "I don't hardly know what to think about religion. They say God killed the just and unjust; I don't understand that part of it. It looks hard to think that if you ain't done nothing in the world you be punished just like the wicked. Plenty folks went crazy trying to get that straightened out." There is no way of estimating how many slaves felt these doubts, but they indicate how keenly aware slaves were of the disparity between the gospel of Christ and what they termed "white man's religion."

At the opposite extreme from the agnostic slave was the slave who developed a life of exemplary Christian virtue which placed him in a position of moral superiority over his master. William Grimes, for example, was possessed of a sense of righteousness which led him to take a surprising attitude toward his master when punished for something he had not done:

> It grieved me very much to be blamed when I was innocent. I knew I had been faithful to him, perfectly so. At this time I was quite serious, and used constantly to pray to my God. I would not lie nor steal. . . . When I considered him accusing me of stealing, when I was so innocent, and had endeavored to make him satisfied by every means in my power, that I was so, but he still persisted in disbelieving me, I then said to myself if this thing is done in a green tree what must be done in a dry? I forgave my master in my own heart for all this, and prayed to God to forgive him and turn his heart.

Grimes is of course alluding to the sacrifice of Christ and identifying himself with the innocent suffering servant who spoke the words concerning green and dry wood on his way to death on Calvary. From this vantage point Grimes is able forgive his master. Note however the element of threat implied in the question, "if this thing is done in a green tree (to the innocent) what must be done in a dry (to the guilty)?" Those who are guilty of persecuting the innocent, like Grimes's master, will be judged and punished. (The full context of the biblical allusion includes a terrifying prediction of the destruction of Jerusalem.) What did it mean to Grimes's self-image to be able to have moral leverage by which he might elevate his own dignity. A similar impulse lay behind the comment of Mary Younger, a fugitive slave in Canada, "if those slaveholders were to come here, I would treat them well, just to shame them by showing that I had humanity." To assert one's humanity in the face of slavery's power to dehumanize, perhaps explained Grimes's careful adherence to righteousness, a righteousness which might at first glance seem merely servile.

Conclusion

In the slave society of the antebellum South, as in most societies, the Christian religion both supported and undermined the status quo. On the one hand, Nat Turner claimed that God's will moved him to slaughter whites, on the other, "good" slaves protected their masters out of a sense of duty. Slave religion, however was more complex than these alternatives suggest. Institutionally, the egalitarian impulse of evangelical Protestantism, leveling all men before God and lifting some up to declare his word with power and authority, gave slaves and free blacks the opportunity to exercise leadership. Usually this leadership was not revolutionary and from the perspective of political strategy it was overwhelmingly conservative. Yet political action is not the only measure of resistance to oppression. Despite political impotence, the black preacher was still a figure of power as an unmistakable symbol of the talent and ability of black men, a fact which contradicted the doctrine of inherent black inferiority. As white slaveholders occasionally recognized, black preachers were anomalous, if not dangerous, persons under the system of slave control precisely because their authority could not be effectively limited by whites.

Nor were slave owners able to control the spirit of religious independence once it had been imbibed by their slaves. Continually this spirit sought to break out of the strictures confining slave life. When possible, it sought expression in separate institutions controlled by blacks. When that proved impossible, it found expression in secret religious gatherings "out from under the eye of the master." In both cases, the internal autonomy of the slave's own

moral will proved impossible to destroy. Throughout the history of Christianity, earthly rulers (civil and religious) have been troubled by the claim that individuals owed obedience to a higher authority than their own. Antebellum slaveholders and missionaries faced the same problem. When slaves disobeyed their masters in order to obey God, a long tradition of Christian heroism validated their assertion of human freedom

The emotional ecstasy of slave religion has been criticized as compensatory and otherworldly, a distraction from the evils of this world. And so it was. But it was much more. Individually, slaves found not only solace in their religion but, particularly in the conversion experience, a source of personal identity and value. Collectively, slaves found in the archetypical symbol of biblical Israel their identity as a community, a new chosen people bound for Divine deliverance from bondage. From this communal identity mutual support, meaning, and hope derived. In the ecstasy of religious performance individual and communal identity and values were dramatically reaffirmed time and time again. In the handclapping, footstomping, headshaking fervor of the plantation praise house, the slaves, in prayer, sermon, and song, fit Christianity to their own peculiar experience and in the process resisted, even transcended the dehumanizing bonds of slavery.

ALBERT J. RABOTEAU earned his PhD in religious studies at Yale University and has taught at Princeton University since 1982, where he currently serves as the Henry W. Putnam Professor of Religion. He is the author of numerous works on the topic of African American religion, including *A Fire in the Bones: Reflections on African-American Religious History* (Beacon Press, 1995) and *Canaan Land: A Religious History of African Americans* (Oxford University Press, 1999).

John B. Boles

Masters & Slaves in the House of the Lord: Race and Religion in the American South, 1740–1870

Race and religion have probably always been controversial topics in the South, as elsewhere, particularly when their intersection has called into question widely accepted folkways about the place of blacks in southern society. Different interpreters have suggested that the South has been haunted by God and preoccupied with race, so perhaps we should not expect a scholarly consensus on how the two intertwined in the decades from the Great Awakening to Reconstruction. The last generation of our own times has witnessed a remarkable burst of scholarship on blacks and race relations in the region and similar if not quite as prolific discovery of southern religious history. . . .

Most laypersons today seem completely unaware that a century and a half ago many churches in the Old South had significant numbers of black members: black and white co-worshipers heard the same sermons, were baptized and took communion together, and upon death were buried in the same cemeteries. Such practices seem inconceivable today, when the old cliché that Sunday morning at 11:00 A.M. is the most segregated hour in America still rings true. When I was a boy in the rural South thirty years ago, we all supported the Lottie Moon Christmas offering to send missionaries to convert the "heathen" in Africa and elsewhere, but the church deacons and the congregation would have been scandalized had one of the black converts traveled from Africa expecting to worship with us. Yet a century earlier biracial attendance at Baptist churches like ours was the norm in the rural South.

Blacks worshiped in a variety of ways, and some did not participate in any Christian worship, for, especially in the colonial period, a smattering of blacks practiced Islam and others clung tenaciously to traditional African religions. All non-Christian religious activity was discouraged by most slaveowners, who were as ethnocentric as they were concerned about the potential for unrest and rebellion they sensed in their slaves' participation in what to whites were strange and exotic rites. In addition, many slaveowners in the seventeenth and eighteenth centuries were hesitant to attempt to convert their bondspeople to Christianity—if they themselves were Christians—out of fear that conversion might loosen the ties of their bondage. The English knew of slavery long before they had any New World settlements and had considered it a backward institution that might be promoted by Catholic Spain but not by the England of Elizabeth. Even so, the English believed that certain persons might be held in bondage—convicted felons, war prisoners, in some cases heathens, that is, nonbelievers in Christianity. It took several generations before Englishmen in the North American mainland colonies came to accept the practicality of African slavery, then argue the necessity of it, and finally surpass their Spanish rivals in its applications. To the extent that they needed any noneconomic justification, they assumed that the Africans not being Christians made it morally acceptable to enslave them. But if Africans' "heathenism" justified making them slaves, would not their conversion at the very least call into question the rightness of keeping them in bondage? On at least several occasions in the seventeenth century blacks had won their freedom in court by proving they had been baptized. Hence any moral uneasiness that might have existed among less-than-devout slaveowners for nor sharing the gospel with their slaves was entirely overcome by their uneasiness about the stability of their work force should they do so. To clarify this ambiguity obliging laws were passed in the late seventeenth century specifying that a person's "civil state" would not be affected by his conversion to Christianity. . . .

Yet despite the difficulties inherent in converting the slave—the whites' hesitancy to have their slaves hear Christian doctrines and no doubt a hesitancy on the part of some slaves to give up traditional beliefs, even if those beliefs had been attenuated by a long presence in the New World—in the middle decades of the eighteenth century increasing numbers of bondspeople became members of Christian churches. A dramatic shift was occurring in the history of black Americans, most of whom before 1750 had been outside the Christian church, for within a century the majority of slaves were worshiping in one fashion or another as Christians. After emancipation, freedpersons continued to find in their churches solace from the cares of the world and joy and a purpose for living in a society that continued to oppress black people. Everyone acknowledges the significance of the church in the black community after freedom; less understood is black worship during the antebellum era and earlier. Yet the half-century following 1740 was the critical period during which some whites broke down their fears and inhibitions about sharing their religion with the slaves in their midst, and some blacks—only a few at first—came to find in Christianity a system of ideas and symbols that was genuinely attractive. . . .

Several aspects of African traditional religion bore close enough parallels to Christianity that bondspeople who were initially disinterested in the white man's religion could—once they glimpsed another side to it—see sufficient common ground between the whites' Christianity and their own folk religions to merit closer examination. That willingness, that openness, on the part of blacks to the claims of Christianity was all the entée white Christian evangelicals needed. Most West African religions assumed a tripartite hierarchy of deities—nature gods, ancestral gods, and an omnipotent creator god who was more remote though more powerful than the others. This conception was roughly transferable to the Christian idea of the trinity. West Africans understood that spirit possession was a sure sign of contact with the divine, an experience not totally dissimilar from the emotional fervor of evangelistic services. Before the mid-eighteenth century slaves had not come into contact with white evangelicals, who were also largely of the lower social order, who worshiped with emotional abandon, and who spoke movingly of being possessed by the Holy Spirit and knowing Jesus as their personal savior. But such evangelical Christians came increasingly to minister to slaves, and they would bridge the chasm between the races and introduce large and growing numbers of slaves to evangelical Christianity.

During the second quarter of the eighteenth century, Evangelicalism and Pietism swept across England and Europe, and the quickening of heartfelt religion soon leapfrogged to the New World in the person of George

Whitefield. The resulting Great Awakening occurred primarily north of Maryland, but Whitefield's preaching and the example of his life gained disciples in South Carolina and Georgia. None of Whitefield's followers were more devout than members of the prominent Bryan family in Georgia, and . . . the two Bryan brothers sincerely believed Jesus' call for repentance was addressed to all persons, black and white, bond and free. Consequently, they undertook to promote Christianity among their own and neighboring slaves, but they did so in such a way as to support the institution of slavery. From today's perspective, their paternalistic efforts toward the blacks under their control seem a truncated version of Christianity, but they did present the faith to the slaves in a way that was acceptable to the larger society. A subtle shift in rationales had occurred that would have a far-reaching influence on whites and blacks. At first it had been deemed appropriate to enslave Africans because they were considered heathens; by the mid-eighteenth century some Anglican clergy had begun to argue that it was appropriate to enslave Africans because they might thereby be converted to Christianity. In that sense this development foreshadowed an important tradition of elite white evangelism to blacks, and through such efforts then and in the future thousands of slaves came to know Christianity and, in various ways, to appropriate its message for their own ends.

Another development of the mid-eighteenth century was to be even more important for the growth of Christianity among the slaves than the limited Anglican awakening in the aftermath of Whitefield. In the quarter of a century following 1745 three evangelical Protestant groups planted their seeds in the colonial South—first the Presbyterians, then the Separate Baptists (later the term Separate was dropped as this species came almost completely to swallow all competing versions of believers in adult baptism), and finally the Methodists (first only a subset of the Church of England but after 1784 an independent denomination). These three churches grew at different rates and had different constituencies. The Presbyterians never experienced the extensive growth among rural southerners that the other two did but found increasing support from among those on the upper rungs of society, supplanting the erstwhile Anglican (the postrevolutionary Episcopal) church in influence among the elite. Presbyterian church members, disproportionately wealthy, of course owned disproportionate numbers of slaves, and continuing the elite paternalism pioneered by the Anglican Bryans in colonial Georgia, they tended to minister to blacks by providing them special ministers and separate accommodations. A form of religious noblesse oblige motivated some of them to devise ways to bring the gospel message to their blacks, especially after abolitionists charged that southern whites neglected the spiritual well-being of their slaves. Moreover, the developing argument that slavery was a progressive institution designed by God to effect the Christianization of Africans gave slaveholders a moral obligation to consider the religious needs of their bondspeople. This sentiment, especially strong among Presbyterians and Episcopalians, produced the significant "mission to the slaves" movement of the late antebellum period. . . .

Although the Presbyterian church was to remain relatively small but influential beyond its numbers, the Baptists and Methodists experienced remarkable growth, especially after the Great Revival at the beginning of the nineteenth century. It would be inappropriate in this brief overview to rehearse the reasons for the success these two evangelical denominations had in the rural South; to an extraordinary degree they became the folk churches of the region. Certainly in their youthful decades, the 1750s through 1790s, when their appeal was even more emphatically to those whites who lived at the margins of society—poor, isolated, largely nonslaveholding—the Baptists and Methodists maintained a fairly consistent antislavery stance. Especially south of Maryland, both denominations recognized the political explosiveness of such beliefs if preached incautiously. They tended to criticize slavery in the abstract, delineate its evils both to the slaves and even more to the whites, emphasize that slaves were persons with souls precious in the sight of God, and suggest that slavery be ended "insofar as practicable"—or words to that effect. This is not to argue that they were insincere or hypocritical. Rather, they understood the realities of the economic and social-control imperatives of the institution and occasionally stated explicitly that if they boldly attacked slavery, they would not be allowed to preach to the blacks, thereby—by their lights—causing the unfortunate bondspeople not to hear the gospel. It is easy from today's perspective, and probably incorrect, to see as self-serving such remarks as Methodist Francis Asbury's summation of his position in 1809: "Would not an *amelioration* in the condition and treatment of slaves have produced more practical good to the poor Africans, than any attempt at their *emancipation*? The state of society, unhappily, does not admit of this: besides, the blacks are deprived of the means of instruction; who will take the pains to lead them into the way of salvation, and watch over them that they may not stray, but the Methodists? . . . What is the personal liberty of the African which he may abuse, to the salvation of his soul; how may it be compared?"

The point is not the limited emancipationist impulse in the evangelical denominations and how it was thwarted over time by political and racial pressures. More appropriate here is the way the lower-class structure of the early Baptist and Methodist churches, most of whose members did not own slaves and felt estranged from the wealthier whites who did, enabled them to see blacks as potential fellow believers in a way that white worshipers in more elite churches seldom could. From the moment of their organization, typical Baptist or Methodist churches included black members, who often signed (or put their "X") on the founding documents of incorporation. Black membership in these two popular denominations was substantial from the last quarter of the eighteenth century through the Civil War. Without claiming too much or failing to recognize the multitude of ways slaves were not accorded genuine equality in these biracial churches it is still fair to say that nowhere else in southern society were they treated so nearly as equals.

Because church membership statistics for the antebellum period are incomplete, and because churches varied in their definitions of membership, a quantitatively precise portrait of the extent to which blacks and whites worshiped together is impossible to obtain. Historian John Blassingame has written that "an overwhelming majority of the slaves throughout the antebellum period attended church with their masters. Then, after the regular services ended, the ministers held special services for the slaves." Such special services were more typical of Episcopal and Presbyterian churches; Methodist and Baptist preachers would usually, sometimes toward the end of the service, call for something like "a special word for our black brothers and sisters" and then turn to them in the back pews or in the balcony and address them with a didactic sermon that often stressed obedience to their earthly masters. Sarah Fitzpatrick, a ninety-year-old former slave interviewed in 1938, recalled that "us 'Niggers' had our meetin' in de white fo'ks Baptist Church in de town o' Tuskegee. Dere's a place up in de loft dere now dat dey built fer de 'Nigger' slaves to 'tend church wid de white fo'ks. White preacher he preach to de white fo'ks an' when he git thu' wid dem he preach some to de 'Niggers.' Tell 'em to mind dere Marster an' b'have deyself an' dey'll go to Hebben when dey die."

Slaves saw through these words and felt contempt for the self-serving attention they received. More important to them was the remainder of the service that they heard and participated in with the rest of the congregation. Here the slaves heard a more complete version of the gospel, and despite whatever social-control uses some ministers tried to put religion to in a portion of the Sunday service, most slaves found grounds for hope and a degree of spiritual liberation through their participation in these biracial churches. As Blassingame concluded, "Generally the ministers tried to expose the slaves to the major tenets of Christianity. . . . [And] only 15 percent of the Georgia slaves who had heard antebellum whites preach recalled admonitions to obedience."

Slaves worshiped apart from whites on some occasions, often with the knowledge of their owners and often without the white supervision the law called for. Some black churches were adjuncts to white churches, and completely independent and autonomous black churches existed in southern cities. Blacks worshiped privately and often secretly in their cabins and in the fields. Sometimes, and especially when their owner was irreligious, slaves had to slip away to hidden "brush arbors" deep in the woods to preach, shout, sing, and worship. But such practices should not lead us to forget that the normative worship experience of blacks in the antebellum South was in a biracial church. "Including black Sunday School scholars and catechumens," Blassingame writes, "there were probably 1,000,000 slaves under the regular tutelage of Southern churches in 1860." When David T. Bailey examined some 40 autobiographies of blacks and 637 interviews of slaves on the subject of religion, he discovered that 32 percent of the autobiographers who mentioned religion reported that they had gone to white churches, 14 percent said their master led the services for them, and another 14 percent attended worship services at special plantation chapels, whereas 36 percent mentioned that they had attended black prayer meetings. Of the former slaves interviewed, 43.5 percent mentioned attending white churches, 6.5 percent reported master-led services, 6.5 percent described plantation chapels, and only 24 percent discussed attendance at black prayer meetings.

Such substantial black participation in churches normally considered white indicates that white evangelicals, even in the late antebellum period, when they had moved up the social scale, joined the establishment, and come to support the institution of slavery, still felt a Christian responsibility to include slaves in the outreach of the church. Their idea of mission assumed that slaves were persons with souls precious in God's sight. In fact, many white evangelicals came to believe that part of their responsibility to God involved Christianizing the slave work force. It was to that end, they reasoned, that God had sanctioned slavery. . . . [A]bolitionist charges that the southern church ignored the slaves infuriated southern clergymen and caused them to redouble their efforts to bring slaves into the church. During the Civil War clergy feared that God was chastising the region for not sufficiently supporting the mission effort to the blacks, and religiously inspired attempts to amend slavery by correcting the worst abuses,

teaching bondspeople to read (so the Scriptures would be accessible to them), and providing missionaries for them . . . almost reformed slavery out of existence in Confederate Georgia.

Devout white clergy often took seriously their responsibilities toward the blacks in their midst, and their paternalistic and racist assumptions should not blind us to their convictions that slaves too were God's children and that white slaveowners stood under God's judgment for the way they treated their bondspeople. It is difficult to understand today how devout whites could define blacks legally as chattel and yet show real concern for the state of their souls. Could genuine Christians so compartmentalize their charity? Apparently so, given their assumptions that blacks were a race of permanent children. A misguided sense of Christian responsibility led well-meaning, decent whites to justify slavery as the white man's duty to Africans, for it was, they argued, through the order and discipline bondage provided that slaves learned—sampled?—Christianity and Western civilization. Almost like whistling in the dark to drive away one's fears, white churchmen sometimes were particularly anxious to Christianize their slaves as though only thus could the institution be justified and their guilt be lessened.

Blacks too must have derived a substantial reward from their participation in the institutional churches or they would not have been involved with them to such an extent for so long. The manuscript records of hundreds of local Baptist churches across the South allow us to see a seldom-studied aspect of white-black interaction that helps explain the attraction biracial churches held for slaves. First, . . . blacks were accorded a semblance of equality when they joined antebellum Baptist churches. White members often addressed them as brother or sister, just as they did fellow white members. This equality in the terms of address may seem insignificant today, but in an age when only whites were accorded the titles of Mr. and Mrs., and it was taboo for a white to so address a black, any form of address that smacked of equality was notable. Behind it lay the familial idea, accepted by whites in principle if not always in practice, that in the sight of God all were equal and were members of His spiritual family. Incoming or outgoing members of Baptist churches were accepted or dismissed with "letters" attesting to their good standing, and slaves asking to join Baptist churches were expected to "bring their letter" just as prospective white members were. Churches seem to have routinely supplied such letters to their members of both races who moved to other locations. New members, black and white, were usually given the "right hand of fellowship" after their letters were accepted or after they came to the altar following the minister's sermon-ending call for conversion to "confess their sins and accept Christ's mercy." Individual churches often varied in this practice, as in much else in the South, where strict uniformity in anything was the exception.

Blacks usually sat in a separate section of the church, perhaps a balcony or a lean-to. There is evidence, however, that slaves sat scattered throughout Anglican churches in colonial Virginia and that sometimes they sat with or next to the pew of their master. Today, such segregated seating would seem to contradict the idea of spiritual equality, but the contradiction probably did not seem so stark to slaves, who were excluded from most other white-dominated functions. The white women often sat apart from the white men, too; in that age segregation by gender was almost as common as that by race, and the familiarity of such separation might well have lessened the negative connotation although it accentuated each subgroup's sense of separate identity. That is, the sense of both a separate women's culture and a separate black culture might have been inadvertently strengthened by the prevalent mode of segregated seating under a common roof. In fact, for some blacks who were isolated on farms and small plantations with no or only a few fellow slaves, the gathering together on Sunday at the church house with slaves from other farms may have been the primary occasion for experiencing a sense of black community. For such slaves the forced segregation in seating may have seemed both natural and desirable because they hungered for close interaction with persons of their own kind. That interaction may have been a stronger attraction than the worship itself. No doubt many bondspeople found their marriage partners through such social involvement at church—certainly much white courtship began there. Perhaps, then, for slaves dispersed on farms outside the plantation district, the slave community was largely created and vitalized in the one arena in which slaves belonging to different owners could freely mingle—the biracial church service.

As with church membership practices, there was an important but limited degree of equality in slaves' participation in antebellum church discipline. . . . [C]ertainly no one would want to argue that whites completely forgot or transcended the racial mores of a slave society in the confines of the church building, but it is significant that slaves were allowed to give testimony—sometimes even conflicting with white testimony—and that on occasion their witness overruled the charges of whites. This occurred in a society that did not allow blacks to testify against whites in civil courts. Moreover, blacks were not disciplined out of proportion to their numbers; on the whole, they were charged with infractions similar to those of whites; and they were held to the same moral expectations as whites

with regard to profanity, drunkenness, lying, adultery, failure to attend church, and fighting. There surely were charges against blacks that had no parallel for whites—for example, blacks alone were charged with running away. But nowhere else in southern society were slaves and whites brought together in an arena where both were held responsible to a code of behavior sanctioned by a source outside the society—the Bible. The Scriptures were interpreted in culturally sanctioned ways, but whites as well as blacks were occasionally found wanting.

Blacks discovered in the church and in church discipline a unique sphere wherein to nurture (and be recognized by whites to have) moral responsibility and what Timothy L. Smith has called "moral earnestness." Through the church slaves found a meaning for their lives that could give a touch of moral grandeur to the tragic dimension of their bondage. Images of the children of Israel and the suffering servant provided ways to accept their life predicament without feelings of self-worthlessness. The church offered a spark of joy in the midst of pain, a promise of life-affirming forgiveness to soften the hopelessness of unremitting bondage, an ultimate reward in heaven for unrewarded service in this world. Participation in the biracial churches was one of the ways slaves found the moral and psychological strength to survive their bondage.

It is important to remember that social interaction does not necessarily imply social equality, in a variety of contexts outside the churches slaves and masters mingled closely without narrowing the gap between freedom and bondage. In many ways such interaction could even magnify the sense of enslavement. Yet it would be a mistake so to emphasize the belittling possibilities of white-black interaction that we fail to see the alternative possibilities inherent in the biracial churches. Slaves apparently had their image of being creatures of God strengthened by the sermons they heard—even when that was not the intention of the ministers—and the discipline they accepted. Their evident pleasure in occasionally hearing black preachers speak to biracial congregations no doubt augmented their sense of racial pride. Taking communion together with whites, serving as deacons or Sunday school teachers, being baptized or confirmed in the same ceremonies, even contributing their mite to the temporal upkeep of the church, could surely have been seen as symbolic ways of emphasizing their self-respect and equality before God. Slaves certainly were not dependent on white-controlled institutions to nurture their sense of self-worth, but neither were they adverse to seizing opportunities wherever they found them and using them for that purpose. In a society that offered few opportunities for blacks to practice organizational and leadership skills or hear themselves addressed and see themselves evaluated morally on an equal basis with whites, small matters could have large meanings. Blacks did not discover in the biracial churches an equality of treatment that spiritually transported them out of bondage, but they found in them a theology of hope and a recognition of self-worth that fared them well in their struggle to endure slavery.

As Robert L. Hall documents in his analysis of religion in antebellum Florida, blacks worshiped in a variety of ways in the antebellum South besides in biracial Protestant churches. In most southern cities and large towns there were completely independent black churches, with black ministers, black deacons or elders, and a panoply of self-help associations connected to and supported by the church. Usually such churches, like the St. James African Episcopal Church in Baltimore, were under the control of free blacks, although many if not most of the members were slaves. Although the surrounding white-dominated churches tended to ignore societal ills, emphasize conversion, and minister primarily to individuals, the black churches tended to minister to all the social and religious needs of their parishioners. There was a communal and social thrust in the independent black churches that was notably absent from the mainstream white churches of the South. (That difference even today sets many black churches apart from white.) Often the black churches had very large memberships, and sometimes their meeting places had the largest seating capacity in the city.

Blacks also worshiped in black churches that were adjunct to white churches. Such situations typically arose after the biracial church built a new sanctuary and, with the black members perhaps outnumbering the white, the blacks were allowed ("allowed" seems more accurate than "forced") to conduct separate services in the old structure. The motivation of the whites here is not clear; they often indicated that the blacks preferred their own services, but to what extent whites desired segregated white churches for essentially racist reasons is impossible to determine. In most cases when blacks were split off into separate "African" churches, as they were known, a committee of whites was assigned to oversee their services. The supervision seems to have been honored more in the breach, however. In a variety of other ways black church members were often given some autonomy in regulating portions of their worship life, again apparently more because the blacks desired such separation than because whites required it. These small islands of black autonomy within the biracial church were perhaps the beginning of the complete racial separation that would come after the Civil War.

Not all the organized churches in the South were Protestant, although Protestantism was far more dominant in the South than elsewhere in the nation. There were pockets of Catholic strength in Maryland, Kentucky, and Missouri, and in south Louisiana Catholicism was preponderant. Most southern cities had at least one Catholic church, usually attended primarily by immigrant workers. Louisiana and Maryland had rural Catholic churches as well, with numbers of black Catholic parishioners. Catholic masters sometimes required that their slaves worship as Catholics, though their bondspeople may have preferred the neighboring Baptist or Methodist churches either as a subtle form of rebellion against their masters or because of the appeal of the demonstrative emotionalism of the evangelical churches. In various ways the Catholic church ministered to bondspeople; separate black orders and sisterhoods were established and the sacraments extended. Because it was a minority church in a rabidly Protestant region and was concerned not to attract notoriety, the Catholic church never questioned the morality of slavery. An occasional Catholic institution or order might own slaves, as did the Jesuits in Maryland, though this property in humans was divested for reasons of ethics and economics. . . .

In addition to the various kinds of formal churches—biracial, adjunct, and independent black churches and plantation chapels—to which slaves had access, black worshipers also gathered in more informal, often secret settings. The evidence for this is to be found in black memoirs and slave narratives, although even these sources suggest that most blacks worshiped in one or another of the formal churches. There are many reasons why slaves would choose to worship in a manner less subject to white supervision or control. Some masters sought to prevent slaves from worshiping at all, which forced slaves to develop an underground religion and to meet secretly either in their cabins at night or in the brush arbors. Slaves who were allowed (or required) to attend a biracial church (or any formal service carefully monitored by whites) in which the minister placed too much emphasis on the "slaves-obey-your-master" homily and thereby neglected to preach the gospel in its fullness often sought an alternative worship experience. There must have been other times when slaves felt inhibited in the presence of whites and simply desired a time and a place to preach, sing, and shout without having to suffer the condescending glances of less emotionally involved white churchgoers. Although slaves worshiping apart and secretively may have developed a distinctly black Christianity significantly different from that which they heard in the more formal institutions, there is no unambiguous evidence that they did so. More probably the services in the brush arbors were simply a longer, more emotionally demonstrative version of those in the biracial churches, with more congregational participation. No precise record exists of the theology implicit in such brush arbor meetings or of special emphases that might have developed, but the similarity in worship practice and ecclesiology of the autonomous black churches that emerged after the Civil War to the earlier biracial churches argues against the evolution of any fundamentally different system in the brush arbors.

A momentous change in the nature of church practice in the South took place at the beginning of Reconstruction. Blacks in significant numbers—eventually all of them—began to move out of the biracial churches and join a variety of independent black denominations. As Katharine Dvorak notes in her insightful essay, the blacks left on their own volition; they were not forced out. At first many white churchmen tried to persuade them to stay, but within several decades the degenerating racial climate of the region led these same churchmen on occasion to applaud the new segregated patterns of worship, so different from the common practice before the Civil War.

Of course, that freedpersons wanted to leave the biracial churches is a commentary on the less-than-complete equality they had enjoyed in them. Blacks had a strong sense of racial identity, reinforced by their having been slaves and, within the confines of the churches, by their segregated seating. The complete sermons they had heard for years, not just the self-serving words the white ministers directed specifically at them, had engendered in blacks a sense of their moral worth and equality in the sight of God. The biracial churches simultaneously nurtured this sense of moral equality and thwarted it by their conformity to the demands of the slave society. Black participation in the biracial churches—as preachers, deacons, stewards, and Sunday school teachers—had given them practical leadership and administrative experience, as had their islands of autonomy within the demographically biracial churches. Theologically and experientially blacks were ready to seize the moment offered by emancipation to withdraw from their old allegiances and create autonomous denominations. No better evidence of the freedom slaves had not enjoyed in the biracial churches exists than the rapidity with which blacks sought to establish separate denominations after the Civil War. And no better evidence exists of the extent to which slaves in the biracial churches accepted evangelical Christianity as their preferred expression of religious faith and molded their lives to its demands than the denominations they created after emancipation.

The worship services and institutional arrangements in the new black churches bore a very close resemblance to the biracial churches from which the blacks withdrew. In fact, black Baptist and Methodist services were closer to the early nineteenth-century post–Great Revival services of the evangelical churches than those of the postbellum all-white churches. Blacks had assimilated the theology and order of service in the biracial churches. Rejecting the modernizing tendencies of the white churches toward less emotion, shorter sermons, an emphasis on choir singing rather than congregational singing, and seminary-trained ministers, they more truly carried on the pioneer evangelical traditions. It should not have been surprising to anyone that when born-again Baptist presidential candidate Jimmy Carter wanted to appeal to blacks in 1976, he spoke to them in their churches. Despite the differences—black services are longer, the music is more expressive, emotions are more freely expressed, there is greater congregational participation—the kinship between the white and black Baptist churches of today is readily apparent, and it points back to a time more than a century ago when the religious culture of the South was fundamentally biracial.

JOHN B. BOLES earned his PhD from the University of Virginia and currently teaches at Rice University, where he is the William P. Hobby Professor of History. A specialist in the American South and southern religion, Boles served for thirty years as the editor of the prestigious *Journal of Southern History*. He also is the author of numerous books, including *The Great Revival, 1787–1805: The Origins of the Southern Evangelical Mind* (University Press of Kentucky, 1972), *Black Southerners, 1619–1869* (University Press of Kentucky, 1983), and *The Irony of Southern Religion* (Peter Lang, 1994).

EXPLORING THE ISSUE

Did African American Slaves Exercise Religious Autonomy?

Critical Thinking and Reflection

1. According to Raboteau, how did American slaves develop both institutional and personal autonomy in the antebellum South?
2. What impact did Christianity have on the racial status quo in the antebellum South?
3. How could religion be used as a form of resistance to the institution of slavery?
4. What factors contributed to the growth of Christianity among enslaved persons?
5. Discuss in detail the influence of the biracial church on the lives of slaves in the antebellum South.

Is There Common Ground?

Both Albert Raboteau and John Boles recognize that the religious practices of African American slaves in the antebellum South included both formal participation in biracial church congregations and more informal efforts by the slaves to carve out some degree of autonomy free from the supervision of their masters. Both are equally aware that the message of Christianity was subject to different interpretations or understandings depending on whether masters or slaves were in charge of delivering that message. Antebellum white southerners for the most part crafted the Gospel to legitimize slavery and developed a multi-pronged justification to satisfy themselves that slavery and Christianity were not at odds with one another. African American preachers and exhorters, however, were far more inclined to focus upon the liberationist nature of the Exodus and the egalitarian character of the New Testament. The real point of debate, therefore, is which of these religious experiences was most prominent in the lives of American slaves.

One of the most intriguing issues for students of American slavery is the relationship between religion and resistance. Specifically, did slaves find in Christianity a palliative that conditioned them to seek salvation only in God's heavenly kingdom or did it steel their resolve to seek deliverance from their bondage in the earthly realm? Actually, there was a certain dualism evident in the slaves' religious life. Some obviously were pacified by a fatalistic attitude that slavery was their permanent status, yet hopeful that salvation would be achieved in the heavenly afterlife. Slave owners, of course, attempted to ensure their bondservants' loyalty and passivity. For their own part, slaves much preferred to hear Bible readings related to Moses's deliverance of the Israelites from Egypt, and it should be remembered that Gabriel Prosser, Denmark Vesey, and Nat Turner all employed religious symbolism and apocalyptic language to foster their revolutionary conspiracies in the antebellum South.

Additional Resources

Carol V. R. George, *Segregated Sabbaths: Richard Allen and the Rise of Independent Black Churches, 1760–1840* (Oxford University Press, 1973)

Vincent Harding, "Religion and Resistance Among Antebellum Negroes, 1800–1860," in August Meier and Elliott Rudwick, eds., *The Making of Black America*, 2 vols. (Atheneum, 1969); vol. 1, pp. 179–197

Charles Joyner, *Down by the Riverside: A South Carolina Slave Community* (University of Illinois Press, 1984)

Orlando Patterson, *Slavery and Social Death: A Comparative Study* (Harvard University Press, 1982)

Mechal Sobel, *Trabelin' On: The Slave Journey to an Afro-Baptist Faith* (Princeton University Press, 1979)

Internet References . . .

African American Christianity

http://nationalhumanitiescenter.org/tserve/nineteen
/nkeyinfo/aareligion.htm

Facts About the Slave Trade and Slavery

https://www.gilderlehrman.org/history-by-era
/slavery-and-anti-slavery/resources/facts
-about-slave-trade-and-slavery

Slavery and the Making of America

www.pbs.org/wnet/slavery/timeline/

Slavery in America

www.uen.org/themepark/liberty/slavery.shtml

Selected, Edited, and with Issue Framing Material by:
Larry Madaras, *Howard Community College*
and
James M. SoRelle, *Baylor University*

ISSUE

Was the Mexican War an Exercise in American Imperialism?

YES: Ramón Eduardo Ruiz, from "Manifest Destiny and the Mexican War," Dorsey Press (1988)

NO: Norman A. Graebner, from "The Mexican War: A Study in Causation," *Pacific Historical Review* (1980)

Learning Outcomes

After reading this issue, you will be able to:

- Critically evaluate the causes of the Mexican War from the United States' and Mexican points of view.
- Critically analyze the concepts of "manifest destiny" and "imperialism."
- Critically analyze the strengths and weaknesses of the "American Empire."
- Critically analyze the successes and failures of the Mexican War from the viewpoints of both the United States and Mexico.
- Critically analyze the long-range effects of the Mexican War on both the United States and Mexico.

ISSUE SUMMARY

YES: Ramón Eduardo Ruiz argues that for the purpose of conquering Mexico's northern territories, the United States waged an aggressive war against its neighbor to the south from which Mexico never recovered.

NO: Professor of diplomatic history Norman A. Graebner argues that President James Polk pursued an aggressive policy that he believed would force Mexico to sell New Mexico and California to the United States and to recognize the annexation of Texas without starting a war.

The origins of the Mexican War began with the controversy over Texas, a Spanish possession for three centuries. In 1821, Texas became the northern-most province of the newly established country of Mexico. Sparsely populated with a mixture of Hispanics and Indians, the Mexican government encouraged immigration from the United States. By 1835, the Anglo population had swelled to 30,000 plus over 2,000 slaves, while the Mexican population was only 5,000. Fearful of losing control over Texas, the Mexican government prohibited further immigration from the United States in 1830, but it was too late. The Mexican government was divided and had changed hands several times. The centers of power were thousands of miles from Texas. In 1829, the Mexican government abolished slavery, an edict that was difficult to enforce. Finally, General Santa Anna attempted to abolish the federation and impose military rule over the entire country. Whether it was due to Mexican intransigence or the Anglos' assertiveness, the settlers rebelled in September 1835. The war was short-lived. Santa Anna was captured at the battled of San Jacinto in April 1836, and Texas was granted her independence.

For nine years, Texas remained an independent republic. Politicians were afraid that if Texas were annexed it would be carved into four or five states, thereby upsetting the balance of power between the evenly divided free states and slave states that had been created in 1819 by the Missouri Compromise. But the pro-slavery president John Tyler pushed through Congress a resolution annexing Texas in the final three days of his presidency in 1845.

The Mexican government was incensed and broke diplomatic relations with the United States. President James K. Polk sent John Slidell as the American emissary to Mexico to negotiate monetary claims of American citizens in Mexico, to purchase California, and to settle the southwestern boundary of Texas at the Rio Grande River and not farther north at the Nueces River, which Mexico recognized as the boundary. Upon Slidell's arrival, news leaked out about his proposals. The Mexican government rejected Slidell's offer. In March 1846, President Polk stationed General Zachary Taylor in the disputed territory along the Rio Grande with an army of 4,000 troops. On May 9, Slidell returned to Washington and informed Polk that he was rebuffed. Polk met with his cabinet to consider war. By chance that same evening, Polk received a dispatch from General Taylor informing him that on April 25 the Mexican army had crossed the Rio Grande and killed or wounded 16 of his men. On May 11, Polk submitted his war message claiming "American blood was shed on American soil." Congress voted overwhelmingly for war, 174 to 14 in the House and 40 to 2 in the Senate, despite the vocal minority of Whig protestors and intellectuals who opposed the war.

As David M. Pletcher points out in his balanced but critical book *The Diplomacy of Annexation: Texas, Oregon and the Mexican War* (University of Missouri Press, 1973), the long-range effects of the Mexican War on American foreign policy were immense. Between 1845 and 1848, the United States acquired more than 500,00 square miles of territory and increased its size by over a third of its present area. This included the annexation of Texas and the subsequent states of the southwest that stretched to the Pacific Coast, incorporating California and the Oregon Territory up to the 49th parallel. European efforts to gain a foothold in North America virtually ceased. By the 1850s, the British gradually abandoned their political aspirations in Central America, "content to compete for economic gains with the potent but unmilitary weapon of their factory system and their merchant marine." Meanwhile, the United States flexed its muscles at the end of the Civil War and used the Monroe Doctrine for the first time to force the French puppet ruler out of Mexico.

Walter Nugent's *Habits of Empire* (Knopf, 2008) is now the major synthesis of the political and military roots of American expansionism. Nugent bluntly argues that the United States was imperialistic from its very beginnings. American expansionism has gone through three phases: the first was the *continental* expansion across North America (exclusive of Canada) from 1783 to 1853, which resulted in the displacement of the Native Americans. Empire II was *overseas* expansion from 1867 to 1917, which resulted in the acquisition and rule over non-white populations in the Pacific and Central American regions. Since the end of World War II in 1945, the United States established the third *virtual-global* empire, which resulted in regime changes during the cold-war years against Russia and China as well as during the current war on terrorism.

Nugent spent most of his career writing about western American history. In this book he combines the expansion of the American people across the continent with the imperialist thrust of establishing an empire. The motivations are multi-causal—"spontaneous jingoism, national security demands, and visions of overseas markets for imperial goods." If there is one key factor, it is demographics. This is especially true for Empire I when the United States increased its population from one million in 1787 to thirty million on the eve of the Civil War. "During that period," said Stephen A. Douglas in deriding Lincoln's "House Divided" speech in a debate in 1858, "we have extended our territory from the Mississippi to the Pacific Ocean; we have acquired the Floridas and Texas, and other territory sufficient to double our geographical extent."

Nugent is also very critical of the United States' policy toward Mexico. He views Polk as a narrow-minded bigot whose one big idea was to acquire California and as much of the southwest as was possible either through negotiation or force. When the Mexican government, riddled with unstable governments, corrupt politicians, and incompetent generals, refused to negotiate, Polk maneuvered the Mexican government to attack American soldiers stationed in the disputed area between the Rio Grande and Nueces Rivers. This was not the only time, says Nugent, the chief executive maneuvered Congress into a fait accompli with regard to declaring war. "Madison came near to doing so in 1812. George H. W. Bush's troop buildup before the first Gulf War and George W. Bush's before Iraq were not novelties. There may be limits on presidential power, but there are no obvious ones on a president as commander-in-chief in sending troops and ships where he wants to." The two best historiographical essays on this topic are Jerald A. Combs, "Norman Graebner and the Realist View of American Diplomatic History," *Diplomatic History* (Summer 1987), and Dennis E. Berge, "Manifest Destiny and the Historians," in Michael P. Malone, ed., *Historians and the American West* (University of Nebraska Press, 1983).

The following selections reflect two opposing views on the nature of the United States' war with Mexico. In the first selection, Ramón Eduardo Ruiz argues that the United States waged a racist and aggressive war against

Mexico for the purpose of conquering what became the American Southwest. In his view, Manifest Destiny was strictly an ideological rationale to provide noble motives for what were really acts of aggression against a neighboring country. Norman A. Graebner, the author of the second essay, was a very popular teacher with students at the University of Virginia and is considered one of the most prominent members of the "realist" school of diplomatic historians. His writings were influenced by the cold-war realists, political scientists, diplomats, and journalists of the 1950s who believed that American foreign policy oscillated between heedless isolationism and crusading wars without developing coherent policies that suited the national interests of the United States. According to Graebner, President James Polk assumed that Mexico was weak and that acquiring certain Mexican territories would satisfy "the long-range interests" of the United States. But when Mexico refused Polk's attempts to purchase New Mexico and California, he was left with three options: withdraw his demands, modify and soften his proposals, or aggressively pursue his original goals. According to Graebner, the president chose the third option.

YES ⬅

Ramón Eduardo Ruiz

Manifest Destiny
and the Mexican War

All nations have a sense of destiny. Spaniards braved the perils of unknown seas and the dangers of savage tribes to explore and conquer a New World for Catholicism. Napoleon's armies overran Europe on behalf of equality, liberty, and fraternity. Communism dictates the future of China and the Soviet Union. Arab expansionists speak of Islam. In the United States, Manifest Destiny in the 19th century was the equivalent of these ideologies or beliefs. Next-door neighbor Mexico felt the brunt of its impact first and suffered most from it.

What was Manifest Destiny? The term was coined in December 1845 by John L. O'Sullivan, then editor and cofounder of the *New York Morning News*. Superpatriot, expansionist, war hawk, and propagandist, O'Sullivan lived his doctrine of Manifest Destiny, for that slogan embodied what he believed. O'Sullivan spoke of America's special mission, frequently warned Europe to keep hands off the Western Hemisphere, later joined a filibustering expedition to Cuba, and had an honored place among the followers of President James K. Polk, Manifest Destiny's spokesman in the Mexican War.

Manifest Destiny voiced the expansionist sentiment that had gripped Americans almost from the day their forefathers had landed on the shores of the New World in the 17th century. Englishmen and their American offspring had looked westward since Jamestown and Plymouth, confident that time and fate would open to them the vast West that stretched out before them. Manifest Destiny, then, was first territorial expansion—American pretensions to lands held by Spain, France, and later Mexico; some even spoke of a United States with boundaries from pole to pole. But Manifest Destiny was greater than mere land hunger; much more was involved. Pervasive was a spirit of nationalism, the belief that what Americans upheld was right and good, that Providence had designated them the chosen people. In a political framework, Manifest Destiny stood for democracy as Americans conceived it; to spread

democracy and freedom was the goal. Included also were ideals of regeneration, the conquest of virgin lands for the sake of their development, and concepts of Anglo-Saxon superiority. All these slogans and beliefs played a role in the Mexican question that culminated in hostilities in 1846.

Apostles of these slogans pointed out that Mexicans claimed lands from the Pacific to Texas but tilled only a fraction of them, and then inefficiently. "No nation has the right to hold soil, virgin and rich, yet unproducing," stressed one U.S. representative. "No race but our own can either cultivate or rule the western hemisphere," acknowledged the *United States Magazine and Democratic Review*. The Indian, almost always a poor farmer in North America, was the initial victim of this concept of soil use; expansionists later included nearly everyone in the New World, and in particular Mexicans. For, Caleb Cushing asked: "Is not the occupation of any portion of the earth by those competent to hold and till it, a providential law of national life?"

Oregon and Texas, and the Democratic Party platform of 1844, kindled the flames of territorial expansion in the roaring forties. Millions of Americans came to believe that God had willed them all of North America. Expansion symbolized the fulfillment of "America's providential mission or destiny"—a mission conceived in terms of the spread of democracy, which its exponents identified with freedom. Historian Albert K. Weinberg has written: "It was because of the association of expansion and freedom in a means-end relationship, that expansion now came to seem most manifestly a destiny."

Americans did not identify freedom with expansion until the forties. Then, fears of European designs on Texas, California, and Oregon, perhaps, prompted an identity of the two. Not only were strategic and economic interests at stake, but also democracy itself. The need to extend the area of freedom, therefore, rose partly from the necessity of keeping absolutistic European monarchs from limiting the area open to American democracy in the New World.

Other factors also impelled Americans to think expansion essential to their national life. Failure to expand imperiled the nation, for, as historian William E. Dodd stated, Westerners especially believed "that the Union gained in stability as the number of states multiplied." Meanwhile, Southerners declared the annexation of Texas essential to their prosperity and to the survival of slavery, and for a congressional balance of power between North and South. Others insisted that expansion helped the individual states to preserve their liberties, for their numerical strength curtailed the authority of the central government, the enemy of local autonomy and especially autonomy of the South. Moreover, for Southerners extension of the area of freedom meant, by implication, expansion of the limits of slavery. Few planters found the two ideas incompatible. Religious doctrines and natural principles, in their opinion, had ruled the Negro ineligible for political equality. That expansion favored the liberties of the individual, both North and South agreed.

In the forties, the pioneer spirit received recognition as a fundamental tenet of American life. Individualism and expansion, the mark of the pioneer, were joined together in the spirit of Manifest Destiny. Expansion guaranteed not just the political liberty of the person, but the opportunity to improve himself economically as well, an article of faith for the democracy of the age. Further, when antiexpansionists declared that the territorial limits of the United States in 1846 assured all Americans ample room for growth in the future, the expansionists-turned-ecologists replied that some 300 million Americans in 1946 would need more land, a prediction that overstated the case of the population-minded experts. And few Americans saw the extension of freedom in terms other than liberty for themselves—white, Anglo-Saxon, and Protestant. All these concepts, principles, and beliefs, then, entered into the expansionist creed of Manifest Destiny.

None of these was a part of the Mexican heritage, the legacy of three centuries of Spanish rule and countless years of pre-Columbian civilization. Mexico and the United States could not have been more dissimilar in 1846. A comparison of colonial backgrounds helps to bring into focus the reasons the two countries were destined to meet on the field of battle. One was weak and the other strong; Mexico had abolished slavery and the United States had not; Americans had their Manifest Destiny, but few Mexicans believed in themselves.

Daughter of a Spain whose colonial policy embraced the Indian, Mexico was a mestizo republic, a half-breed nation. Except for a small group of aristocrats, most Mexicans were descendants of both Spaniards and Indians. For Mexico had a colonial master eager and willing to assimilate pre-Columbian man. Since the days of the conqueror Hernán Cortés, Spaniards had mated with Indians, producing a Mexican both European and American in culture and race. Offspring of the Indian as well as the Spaniard, Mexican leaders, and even the society of the time, had come to accept the Indian, if not always as an equal, at least as a member of the republic. To have rejected him would have been tantamount to the Mexican's self-denial of himself. Doctrines of racial supremacy were, if not impossible, highly unlikely, for few Mexicans could claim racial purity. To be Mexican implied a mongrel status that ruled out European views of race.

Spain bequeathed Mexico not merely a racial attitude but laws, religious beliefs, and practices that banned most forms of segregation and discrimination. For example, reservations for Indians were never a part of the Spanish heritage. Early in the 16th century, the Spaniards had formulated the celebrated Laws of the Indies—legislation that clearly spelled out the place of the Indian in colonial society. Nothing was left to chance, since the Spanish master included every aspect of life—labor, the family, religion, and even the personal relations between Spaniard and Indian. The ultimate aim was full citizenship for the Indian and his descendants. In the meantime, the Church ruled that the Indian possessed a soul; given Christian teachings, he was the equal of his European conqueror. "All of the people of the world are men," the Dominican Bartolomé de las Casas had announced in his justly famous 1550 debate with the scholar Sepúlveda.

Clearly, church and state and the individual Spaniard who arrived in America had more than charity in mind. Dreams of national and personal glory and wealth dominated their outlook. Yet, despite the worldly goals of most secular and clerical conquerors, they built a colonial empire on the principle that men of all colors were equal on earth. Of course, Spain required the labor of the Indian and therefore had to protect him from the avarice of many a conquistador. Spaniards, the English were wont to say, were notorious for their disdain of manual labor of any type. But Spain went beyond merely offering the Indian protection in order to insure his labor. It incorporated him into Hispanic-American society. The modern Mexican is proof that the Indian survived: all Mexicans are Indian to some extent. That the Indian suffered economic exploitation and frequently even social isolation is undoubtedly true, but such was the lot of the poor in the Indies—Indian, half-breed, and even Spaniard.

Spain's empire, as well as the Mexican republic that followed, embraced not just the land but the people who had tilled it for centuries before the European's arrival. From northern California to Central America, the boundaries of colonial New Spain, and later Mexico, the Spaniard had embraced the Indian or allowed him to live out his life. It was this half-breed population that in 1846 confronted and fell victim to the doctrine of Manifest Destiny.

America's historical past could not have been more dissimilar. The English master had no room for the Indian in his scheme of things. Nearly all Englishmen—Puritans, Quakers, or Anglicans—visualized the conquest and settlement of the New World in terms of the exclusive possession of the soil. All new lands conquered were for the immediate benefit of the new arrivals. From the days of the founding of Jamestown and Plymouth, the English had pushed the Indian westward, relentlessly driving him from his homeland. In this activity, the clergy clasped hands with lay authorities; neither offered the red man a haven. Except for a few hardy souls, invariably condemned by their peers, Englishmen of church and state gave little thought to the Indian. Heaven, hell, and the teachings of Christ were the exclusive domain of the conquerors.

Society in the 13 colonies, and in the Union that followed, reflected English and European customs and ways of life. It was a transplanted society. Where the Indian survived, he found himself isolated from the currents of time. Unlike the Spaniards, whose ties with Africa and darker skinned peoples through .seven centuries of Moorish domination had left an indelible imprint on them, most Englishmen had experienced only sporadic contact with people of dissimilar races and customs. Having lived a sheltered and essentially isolated existence, the English developed a fear and distrust of those whose ways were foreign to them. The Americans who walked in their footsteps retained this attitude.

Many American historians will reject this interpretation. They will probably allege that American willingness to accept millions of destitute immigrants in the 19th century obviously contradicts the view that the Anglo-Saxon conqueror and settler distrusted what was strange in others. Some truth is present here, but the weight of the evidence lies on the other side. What must be kept firmly in mind is that immigration to the English colonies and later to the United States—in particular, the tidal wave of humanity that engulfed the United States in the post–Civil War era—was European in origin. Whether Italians, Jews, or Greeks from the Mediterranean, Swedes, Scots, or Germans from the North, what they had in common far outweighed conflicting traits and cultural and physical

differences. All were European, offspring of one body of traditions and beliefs. Whether Catholics, Protestants, or Jews, they professed adherence to Western religious practices and beliefs. The so-called melting pot was scarcely a melting pot at all; the ingredients were European in origin. All spices that would have given the stew an entirely different flavor were carefully kept out—namely, the Negro and the Indian.

It was logical that Manifest Destiny, that American belief in a Providence of special design, should have racial overtones. Having meticulously kept out the infidel, Americans could rightly claim a racial doctrine of purity and supremacy in the world of 1846. Had not the nation of Polk's era developed free of those races not a part of the European heritage? Had the nation not progressed rapidly? Most assuredly, the answer was yes. When American development was compared to that of the former Spanish-American colonies, the reply was even more emphatically in the affirmative. After all, the Latin republics to the south had little to boast about. All were backward, illiterate, and badly governed states. Americans had just cause for satisfaction with what they had accomplished.

Unfortunately for Latin America, and especially Mexico, American pride had dire implications for the future. Convinced of the innate racial supremacy which the slogan of Manifest Destiny proclaimed throughout the world, many Americans came to believe that the New World was theirs to develop. Only their industry, their ingenuity, and their intelligence could cope fully with the continental challenge. Why should half-breed Mexico—backward, politically a waste-land, and hopelessly split by nature and man's failures—hold Texas, New Mexico, and California? In Mexico's possession, all these lands would lie virgin, offering a home to a few thousand savage Indians, and here and there a Mexican pueblo of people scarcely different from their heathen neighbors. Manifest Destiny simply proclaimed what most Americans had firmly believed—the right of Anglo-Saxons and others of similar racial origin to develop what Providence had promised them. Weak Mexico, prey of its own cupidity and mistakes, was the victim of this belief.

Manifest Destiny, writes Mexican historian Carlos Bosch García, also contradicts an old American view that means are as important as ends. He stresses that the key to the history of the United States, as the doctrine of Manifest Destiny illustrates, lies in the willingness of Americans to accept as good the ultimate result of whatever they have undertaken to do. That the red man was driven from his homeland is accepted as inevitable and thus justifiable. American scholars might condemn the maltreatment of the Indian, but few question the final verdict.

Equally ambivalent, says Bosch García, is the American interpretation of the Mexican War. Though some American scholars of the post–Civil War period severely censured the South for what they called its responsibility for the Mexican War, their views reflected a criticism of the slavocracy rather than a heartfelt conviction that Mexico had been wronged. Obviously, there were exceptions. Hubert H. Bancroft, a California scholar and book collector, emphatically denounced Polk and his cohorts in his voluminous *History of Mexico* (1883–88). Among the politicians of the era, Abraham Lincoln won notoriety—and probably lost his seat in the House of Representatives—for his condemnation of Polk's declaration of war against Mexico. There were others, mostly members of the Whig Party, which officially opposed the war; but the majority, to repeat, was more involved with the problem of the South than with the question of war guilt.

Most Americans, in fact, have discovered ways and means to justify Manifest Destiny's war on Mexico. That country's chronic political instability, its unwillingness to meet international obligations, its false pride in its military establishment—all those, say scholars, led Mexican leaders to plunge their people into a hopeless war. Had Mexico been willing to sell California, one historian declares, no conflict would have occurred. To paraphrase Samuel F. Bemis, distinguished Yale University diplomatic scholar, no American today would undo the results of Polk's war. Put differently, to fall back on Bosch García, American writers have justified the means because of the ends. Manifest Destiny has not only been explained but has been vindicated on the grounds of what has been accomplished in California and New Mexico since 1848. Or, to cite Hermann Eduard von Holst, a late 19th century German scholar whose writings on American history won him a professorship at the University of Chicago, the conflict between Mexico and the United States was bound to arise. A virile and ambitious people whose cause advanced that of world civilization could not avoid battle with a decadent, puerile people. Moral judgments that applied to individuals might find Americans guilty of aggression, but the standards by which nations survive and prosper upheld the cause of the United States. Might makes right? Walt Whitman, then editor of the *Brooklyn Daily Eagle*, put down his answer succinctly:

> We love to indulge in thoughts of the future extent and power of this Republic—because with its increase is the increase in human happiness and liberty. . . . What has miserable Mexico—with her superstition, her burlesque upon freedom, her actual tyranny by the few over the many—what has she to do with

the great mission of peopling the New World with a noble race? Be it ours, to achieve that mission! Be it ours to roll down all of the up-start leaven of the old despotism, that comes our way.

The conflict with Mexico was an offensive war without moral pretensions, according to Texas scholar Otis A. Singletary. It was no lofty crusade, no noble battle to right the wrongs of the past or to free a subjugated people, but a war of conquest waged by one neighbor against another. President Polk and his allies had to pay conscience money to justify a "greedy land-grab from a neighbor too weak to defend herself." American indifference to the Mexican War, Professor Singletary concludes, "lies rooted in the guilt that we as a nation have come to feel about it."

American racial attitudes, the product of a unique colonial background in the New World, may also have dictated the scope of territorial conquest in 1848 and, ironically, saved Mexico from total annexation. Until the clash with Mexico, the American experience had been limited to the conquest, occupation, and annexation of empty or sparsely settled territories, or of those already colonized by citizens of the United States, as were Oregon and Texas. American pioneers had been reincorporated into the Union with the annexation of Oregon and Texas, and even with the purchase of Louisiana in 1803, for the alien population proved small and of little importance. White planters, farmers, and pioneers mastered the small Mexican population in Texas and easily disposed of the Indians and half-breeds in the Louisiana territory.

Expansionists and their foes had long considered both Indian and Negro unfit for regeneration; both were looked on as inferior and doomed races. On this point, most Americans were in agreement. While not entirely in keeping with this view, American opinions of Latin Americans, and of Mexicans in particular, were hardly flattering. Purchase and annexation of Louisiana and Florida, and of Texas and Oregon, had been debated and postponed partly out of fear of what many believed would be the detrimental effect on American democracy resulting from the amalgamation of the half-breed and mongrel peoples of these lands. Driven by a sense of national aggrandizement, the expansionists preferred to conquer lands free of alien populations. Manifest Destiny had no place for the assimilation of strange and exotic peoples. Freedom for Americans—this was the cry, regardless of what befell the conquered natives. The location of sparsely held territory had dictated the course of empire.

James K. Polk's hunger for California reflected national opinion on races as well as desire for land. Both that territory and New Mexico, nearly to the same extent, were almost barren of native populations. Of sparsely settled California, in 1845 the *Hartford Times* eloquently declared that Americans could "redeem from unhallowed hands a land, above all others of heaven, and hold it for the use of a people who know how to obey heaven's behests." Thus it was that the tide of conquest—the fruits of the conference table at Guadalupe Hidalgo—stopped on the border of Mexico's inhabited lands, where the villages of a people alien in race and culture confronted the invaders. American concepts of race, the belief in the regeneration of virgin lands—these logically ordered annexation of both California and New Mexico, but left Mexico's settled territory alone.

Many Americans, it is true, gave much thought to the conquest and regeneration of all Mexico, but the peace of 1848 came before a sufficiently large number of them had abandoned traditional thoughts on race and color to embrace the new gospel. Apparently, most Americans were not yet willing to accept dark-skinned people as the burden of the white man.

Manifest Destiny, that mid-19th-century slogan, is now merely a historical question for most Americans. Despite the spectacular plums garnered from the conference table, the war is forgotten by political orators, seldom discussed in classrooms, and only infrequently recalled by historians and scholars.

But Mexicans, whether scholars or not, have not forgotten the war; their country suffered most from Manifest Destiny's claims to California. The war of 1846–48 represents one of the supreme tragedies of their history. Mexicans are intimately involved with it, unlike their late adversaries who have forgotten it. Fundamental reasons explain this paradox. The victorious United States went to a post-Civil War success story unequaled in the annals of Western civilization. Mexico emerged from the peace of Guadalupe Hidalgo bereft of half of its territory, a beaten, discouraged, and divided country. Mexico never completely recovered from the debacle.

Mexicans had known tragedy and defeat before, but their conquest by Generals Zachary Taylor and Winfield Scott represented not only a territorial loss of immense proportions, but also a cataclysmic blow to their morale as a nation and as a people. From the Mexican point of view, their pride in what they believed they had mastered best—the science of warfare—was exposed as a myth. Mexicans could not even fight successfully, and they had little else to recall with pride, for their political development had enshrined bitter civil strife and callous betrayal of principle. Plagued by hordes of scheming politicians, hungry military men, and a backward and reactionary clergy, they had watched their economy stagnate. Guadalupe Hidalgo clearly outlined the scope of their defeat. There was no success story to write about, only tragedy. Mexicans of all classes are still engrossed in what might have been *if* General Antonio López de Santa Anna had repelled the invaders from the North.

Polk's war message to Congress and Lincoln's famous reply in the House cover some dimensions of the historical problem. Up for discussion are Polk's role in the affair, the responsibility of the United States and Mexico, and the question of war guilt—a question raised by the victorious Americans and their allies at Nuremberg after World War II. For if Polk felt "the blood of this war, like the blood of Abel, is crying to Heaven against him," as Lincoln charged, then not just the war but also Manifest Destiny stand condemned.

RAMÓN EDUARDO RUIZ (1921–2010) was professor emeritus of Latin American history at the University of California–San Diego. He is the author of fifteen books including *Triumphs and Tragedy: A History of the Mexican People* (W. W. Norton, 1972, 1993), *The Great Rebellion: Mexico, 1905–1924* (W. W. Norton, 1982), and *On the Rim of Mexico: Encounters of the Rich and Poor* (Basic Books, 1998).

Norman A. Graebner

 **NO**

The Mexican War: A Study in Causation

On May 11, 1846, President James K. Polk presented his war message to Congress. After reviewing the skirmish between General Zachary Taylor's dragoons and a body of Mexican soldiers along the Rio Grande, the president asserted that Mexico "has passed the boundary of the United States, has invaded our territory and shed American blood upon the American soil. . . . War exists, and, notwithstanding all our efforts to avoid it, exists by act of Mexico." No country could have had a superior case for war. Democrats in large numbers (for it was largely a partisan matter) responded with the patriotic fervor which Polk expected of them. "Our government has permitted itself to be insulted long enough," wrote one Georgian. "The blood of her citizens has been spilt on her own soil. It appeals to us for vengeance." Still, some members of Congress, recalling more accurately than the president the circumstances of the conflict, soon rendered the Mexican War the most reviled in American history—at least until the Vietnam War of the 1960s. One outraged Whig termed the war "illegal, unrighteous, and damnable," and Whigs questioned both Polk's honesty and his sense of geography. Congressman Joshua R. Giddings of Ohio accused the president of "planting the standard of the United States on foreign soil, and using the military forces of the United States to violate every principle of international law and moral justice." To vote for the war, admitted Senator John C. Calhoun, was "to plunge a dagger into his own heart, and more so." Indeed, some critics in Congress openly wished the Mexicans well.

For over a century such profound differences in perception have pervaded American writings on the Mexican War. Even in the past decade, historians have reached conclusions on the question of war guilt as disparate as those which separated Polk from his wartime conservative and abolitionist critics. . . .

In some measure the diversity of judgment on the Mexican War, as on other wars, is understandable. By basing their analyses on official rationalizations, historians often ignore the more universal causes of war which transcend individual conflicts and which can establish the bases for greater consensus. Neither the officials in Washington nor those in Mexico City ever acknowledged any alternatives to the actions which they took. But governments generally have more choices in any controversy than they are prepared to admit. Circumstances determine their extent. The more powerful a nation, the more remote its dangers, the greater its options between action and inaction. Often for the weak, unfortunately, the alternative is capitulation or war. . . . Polk and his advisers developed their Mexican policies on the dual assumption that Mexico was weak and that the acquisition of certain Mexican territories would satisfy admirably the long-range interests of the United States. Within that context, Polk's policies were direct, timely, and successful. But the president had choices. Mexico, whatever its internal condition, was no direct threat to the United States. Polk, had he so desired, could have avoided war; indeed, he could have ignored Mexico in 1845 with absolute impunity.

In explaining the Mexican War historians have dwelled on the causes of friction in American-Mexican relations. In part these lay in the disparate qualities of the two populations, in part in the vast discrepancies between the two countries in energy, efficiency, power, and national wealth. Through two decades of independence Mexico had experienced a continuous rise and fall of governments; by the 1840s survival had become the primary concern of every regime. Conscious of their weakness, the successive governments in Mexico City resented the superior power and effectiveness of the United States and feared American notions of destiny that anticipated the annexation of Mexico's northern provinces. Having failed to prevent the formation of the Texas Republic, Mexico reacted to Andrew Jackson's recognition of Texan independence in March 1837 with deep indignation. Thereafter

Graebner, Norman A. From *Pacific Historical Review*, vol. 49, no. 3, August 1980, pp. 405–426. Copyright © 1980 by University of California Press, Journals Division. Reprinted by permission.

the Mexican raids into Texas, such as the one on San Antonio in 1842, aggravated the bitterness of Texans toward Mexico, for such forays had no purpose beyond terrorizing the frontier settlements.

Such mutual animosities, extensive as they were, do not account for the Mexican War. Governments as divided and chaotic as the Mexican regimes of the 1840s usually have difficulty in maintaining positive and profitable relations with their neighbors; their behavior often produces annoyance, but seldom armed conflict. Belligerence toward other countries had flowed through U.S. history like a torrent without, in itself, setting off a war. Nations do not fight over cultural differences or verbal recriminations; they fight over perceived threats to their interests created by the ambitions or demands of others.

What increased the animosity between Mexico City and Washington was a series of specific issues over which the two countries perennially quarreled—claims, boundaries, and the future of Texas. Nations have made claims a pretext for intervention, but never a pretext for war. Every nineteenth-century effort to collect debts through force assumed the absence of effective resistance, for no debt was worth the price of war. To collect its debt from Mexico in 1838, for example, France blockaded Mexico's gulf ports and bombarded Vera Cruz. The U.S. claims against Mexico created special problems which discounted their seriousness as a rationale for war. True, the Mexican government failed to protect the possessions and the safety of Americans in Mexico from robbery, theft, and other illegal actions, but U.S. citizens were under no obligation to do business in Mexico and should have understood the risk of transporting goods and money in that country. Minister Waddy Thompson wrote from Mexico City in 1842 that it would be "with somewhat of bad grace that we should war upon a country because it could not pay its debts when so many of our own states are in the same situation." Even as the United States after 1842 attempted futilely to collect the $2 million awarded its citizens by a claims commission, it was far more deeply in debt to Britain over speculative losses. Minister Wilson Shannon reported in the summer of 1844 that the claims issue defied settlement in Mexico City and recommended that Washington take the needed action to compel Mexico to pay. If Polk would take up the challenge and sacrifice American human and material resources in a war against Mexico, he would do so for reasons other than the enforcement of claims. The president knew well that Mexico could not pay, yet as late as May 9, 1846, he was ready to ask Congress for a declaration of war on the question of unpaid claims alone.

Congress's joint resolution for Texas annexation in February 1845 raised the specter of war among editors and politicians alike. As early as 1843 the Mexican government had warned the American minister in Mexico City that annexation would render war inevitable; Mexican officials in Washington repeated that warning. To Mexico, therefore, the move to annex Texas was an unbearable affront. Within one month after Polk's inauguration on March 4, General Juan Almonte, the Mexican minister in Washington, boarded a packet in New York and sailed for Vera Cruz to sever his country's diplomatic relations with the United States. Even before the Texas Convention could meet on July 4 to vote annexation, rumors of a possible Mexican invasion of Texas prompted Polk to advance Taylor's forces from Fort Jesup in Louisiana down the Texas coast. Polk instructed Taylor to extend his protection to the Rio Grande but to avoid any areas to the north of that river occupied by Mexican troops. Simultaneously the president reinforced the American squadron in the Gulf of Mexico. "The threatened invasion of Texas by a large Mexican army," Polk informed Andrew J. Donelson, the American charge in Texas, on June 15, "is well calculated to excite great interest here and increases our solicitude concerning the final action by the Congress and the Convention of Texas." Polk assured Donelson that he intended to defend Texas to the limit of his constitutional power. Donelson resisted the pressure of those Texans who wanted Taylor to advance to the Rio Grande; instead, he placed the general at Corpus Christi on the Nueces River. Taylor agreed that the line from the mouth of the Nueces to San Antonio covered the Texas settlements and afforded a favorable base from which to defend the frontier.

Those who took the rumors of Mexican aggressiveness seriously lauded the president's action. With Texas virtually a part of the United States, argued the *Washington Union*, "We owe it to ourselves, to the proud and elevated character which America maintains among the nations of the earth, to guard our own territory from the invasion of the ruthless Mexicans." The *New York Morning News* observed that Polk's policy would, on the whole, "command a general concurrence of the public opinion of his country." Some Democratic leaders, fearful of a Mexican attack, urged the president to strengthen Taylor's forces and order them to take the offensive should Mexican soldiers cross the Rio Grande. Others believed the reports from Mexico exaggerated, for there was no apparent relationship between the country's expressions of belligerence and its capacity to act. Secretary of War William L. Marcy admitted that his information was no better than that of other commentators. "I have at no time," he wrote in July, "felt that war with Mexico was probable—and do not now believe it is, yet it is in the range of possible occurrences. I have officially acted on the hypothesis that our peace may be temporarily disturbed without however believing it will be." Still convinced that the administration had no grounds for alarm, Marcy wrote on August 12: "The presence of a considerable force in Texas will do no hurt and possibly may be of great use." In September William S. Parrott, Polk's special agent in Mexico, assured the president that there would be neither a Mexican declaration of war nor an invasion of Texas.

Polk insisted that the administration's show of force in Texas would prevent rather than provoke war. "I do not anticipate that Mexico will be mad enough to declare war," he wrote in July, but "I think she would have done so but for the appearance of a strong naval force in the Gulf and our army moving in the direction of her frontier on land." Polk restated this judgment on July 28 in a letter to General Robert Armstrong, the U.S. consul at Liverpool: "I think there need be but little apprehension of war with Mexico. If however she shall be mad enough to make war we are prepared to meet her." The president assured Senator William H. Haywood of North Carolina that the American forces in Texas would never aggress against Mexico; however, they would prevent any Mexican forces from crossing the Rio Grande. In conversation with Senator William S. Archer of Virginia on September 1, the president added confidently that "the appearance of our land and naval forces on the borders of Mexico & in the Gulf would probably deter and prevent Mexico from either declaring war or invading Texas." Polk's continuing conviction that Mexico would not attack suggests that his deployment of U.S. land and naval forces along Mexico's periphery was designed less to protect Texas than to support an aggressive diplomacy which might extract a satisfactory treaty from Mexico without war. For Anson Jones, the last president of the Texas Republic, Polk's deployments had precisely that purpose:

> Texas never actually needed the protection of the United States after I came into office. . . . There was no necessity for it after the 'preliminary Treaty,' as we were at peace with Mexico, and knew perfectly well that that Government, though she might bluster a little, had not the slightest idea of invading Texas either by land or water; and that nothing would provoke her to (active) hostilities, but the presence of troops in the immediate neighborhood of the Rio Grande, threatening her towns and settlements on the southwest side of that river. . . . But Donelson appeared so intent upon 'encumbering us with help,' that finally, to get rid of his annoyance, he was told he might give us as much protection as he pleased. . . . The protection asked for was only *prospective* and contingent; the *protection* he had in view was *immediate and aggressive.*

For Polk the exertion of military and diplomatic pressure on a disorganized Mexico was not a prelude to war. Whig critics of annexation had predicted war; this alone compelled the administration to avoid a conflict over Texas. In his memoirs Jones recalled that in 1845 Commodore Robert F. Stockton, with either the approval or the connivance of Polk, attempted to convince him that he should place Texas "in an attitude of active hostility toward Mexico, so that, when Texas was finally brought into the Union, *she might bring war with her.*" If Stockton engaged in such an intrigue, he apparently did so on his own initiative, for no evidence exists to implicate the administration. Polk not only preferred to achieve his purposes by means other than war but also assumed that his military measures in Texas, limited as they were, would convince the Mexican government that it could not escape the necessity of coming to terms with the United States. Washington's policy toward Mexico during 1845 achieved the broad national purpose of Texas annexation. Beyond that it brought U.S. power to bear on Mexico in a manner calculated to further the processes of negotiation. Whether the burgeoning tension would lead to a negotiated boundary settlement or to war hinged on two factors: the nature of Polk's demands and Mexico's response to them. The president announced his objectives to Mexico's troubled officialdom through his instructions to John Slidell, his special emissary who departed for Mexico in November 1845 with the assurance that the government there was prepared to reestablish formal diplomatic relations with the United States and negotiate a territorial settlement. . . .

❧

Actually, Slidell's presence in Mexico inaugurated a diplomatic crisis not unlike those which precede most wars. Fundamentally the Polk administration, in dispatching Slidell, gave the Mexicans the same two choices that the dominant power in any confrontation gives to the weaker: the acceptance of a body of concrete diplomatic demands or eventual war. Slidell's instructions described U.S. territorial objectives with considerable clarity. If Mexico knew little of Polk's growing acquisitiveness toward California during the autumn of 1845, Slidell proclaimed the president's intentions with his proposals to purchase varying portions of California for as much as $25 million. Other countries such as England and Spain had consigned important areas of the New World through peaceful negotiations, but the United States, except in its Mexican relations, had never asked any country to part with a portion of its own territory. Yet Polk could not understand why Mexico should reveal any special reluctance to part with Texas, the Rio Grande, New Mexico, or California. What made the terms of Slidell's instructions appear fair to him was Mexico's military and financial helplessness. Polk's defenders noted that California was not a sine qua non of any settlement and that the president offered to settle the immediate controversy over the acquisition of the Rio Grande boundary alone in exchange for the cancellation of claims. Unfortunately, amid the passions of December 1845, such distinctions were lost. Furthermore, a settlement of the Texas boundary would not have resolved the California question at all.

Throughout the crisis months of 1845 and 1846, spokesmen of the Polk administration repeatedly warned the Mexican government that its choices were limited. In June 1845, Polk's mouthpiece, the *Washington Union,* had observed characteristically that, if Mexico resisted Washington's demands, "a corps of properly organized volunteers . . . would invade, overrun, and occupy Mexico. They would enable us not only to take California, but to keep it." American officials, in their contempt for Mexico, spoke privately of the need to chastize that country for its annoyances and insults. Parrott wrote to Secretary of State James Buchanan in October that he wished "to see this people well flogged by Uncle Sam's boys, ere we enter upon negotiations. . . . I know [the Mexicans] better, perhaps, than any other American citizen and I am fully persuaded, they can never love or respect us, as we should be loved and respected by them, until we shall have given them a positive proof of our superiority." Mexico's pretensions would continue, wrote Slidell in late December, "until the Mexican people shall be convinced by hostile demonstrations, that our differences must be settled promptly, either by negotiation or the sword." In January 1846 the *Union* publicly threatened Mexico with war if it rejected the just demands of the United States: "The result of such a course on her part may compel us to resort to more decisive measures . . . to obtain the settlement of our legitimate claims." As Slidell prepared to leave Mexico in March 1846, he again reminded the administration: "Depend upon it, we can never get along well with them, until we have given them a good drubbing." In Washington on May 8, Slidell advised the president "to take the redress of the wrongs and injuries which we had so long borne from Mexico into our own hands, and to act with promptness and energy."

Mexico responded to Polk's challenge with an outward display of belligerence and an inward dread of war. Mexicans feared above all that the United States intended to overrun their country and seize much of their territory. Polk and his advisers assumed that Mexico, to avoid an American invasion, would give up its provinces peacefully.

Obviously Mexico faced growing diplomatic and military pressures to negotiate away its territories; it faced no moral obligation to do so. Herrera and Paredes had the sovereign right to protect their regimes by avoiding any formal recognition of Slidell and by rejecting any of the boundary proposals embodied in his instructions, provided that in the process they did not endanger any legitimate interests of the American people. At least to some Mexicans, Slidell's terms demanded nothing less than Mexico's capitulation. By what standard was $2 million a proper payment for the Rio Grande boundary, or $25 million a fair price for California? No government would have accepted such terms. Having rejected negotiation in the face of superior force, Mexico would meet the challenge with a final gesture of defiance. In either case it was destined to lose, but historically nations have preferred to fight than to give away territory under diplomatic pressure alone. Gene M. Brack, in his long study of Mexico's deep-seated fear and resentment of the United States, explained Mexico's ultimate behavior in such terms:

> President Polk knew that Mexico could offer but feeble resistance militarily, and he knew that Mexico needed money. No proper American would exchange territory and the national honor for cash, but President Polk mistakenly believed that the application of military pressure would convince Mexicans to do so. They did not respond logically, but patriotically. Left with the choice of war or territorial concessions, the former course, however dim the prospects of success, could be the only one.

Mexico, in its resistance, gave Polk the three choices which every nation gives another in an uncompromisable confrontation: to withdraw his demands and permit the issues to drift, unresolved; to reduce his goals in the interest of an immediate settlement; or to escalate the pressures in the hope of securing an eventual settlement on his own terms. Normally when the internal conditions of a country undermine its relations with others, a diplomatic corps simply removes itself from the hostile environment and awaits a better day. Mexico, despite its animosity, did not endanger the security interests of the United States; it had not invaded Texas and did not contemplate doing so. Mexico had refused to pay the claims, but those claims were not equal to the price of a one-week war. Whether Mexico negotiated a boundary for Texas in 1846 mattered little; the United States had lived with unsettled boundaries for decades without considering war. Settlers, in time, would have forced a decision, but in 1846 the region between the Nueces and the Rio Grande was a vast, generally unoccupied wilderness. Thus there was nothing, other than Polk's ambitions, to prevent the United States from withdrawing its diplomats from Mexico City and permitting its relations to drift. But Polk, whatever the language of his instructions, did not send Slidell to Mexico to normalize relations with that government. He expected Slidell to negotiate an immediate boundary settlement favorable to the United States, and nothing less.

Recognizing no need to reduce his demands on Mexico, Polk, without hesitation, took the third course which Mexico offered. Congress bound the president to the annexation of Texas; thereafter the Polk administration was free to formulate its own policies toward Mexico. With the Slidell mission Polk embarked upon a program of gradual coercion to achieve a settlement, preferably without war. That program led logically from his dispatching an army to Texas and his denunciation of Mexico in his annual message of December 1845 to his new instructions of January 1846, which ordered General Taylor to the Rio Grande. Colonel Atocha, spokesman for the deposed Mexican leader, Antonio López de Santa Anna, encouraged Polk to pursue his policy of escalation. The president recorded Atocha's advice:

> He said our army should be marched at once from Corpus Christi to the Del Norte, and a strong naval force assembled at Vera Cruz, that Mr. Slidell, the U.S. Minister, should withdraw from Jalappa, and go on board one of our ships of War at Vera Cruz, and in that position should demand the payment of [the] amount due our citizens; that it was well known the Mexican Government was unable to pay in money, and that when they saw a strong force ready to strike on their coasts and border, they would, he had no doubt, feel their danger and agree to the boundary suggested. He said that Paredes, Almonte, & Gen'l Santa Anna were all willing for such an arrangement, but that they dare not make it until it was made apparent to the Archbishop of Mexico & the people generally that it was necessary to save their country from a war with the U. States.

Thereafter Polk never questioned the efficacy of coercion. He asserted at a cabinet meeting on February 17 that "it would be necessary to take strong measures towards Mexico before our difficulties with that Government could be settled." Similarly on April 18 Polk told Calhoun that "our relations with Mexico had reached a point where we could not stand still but must treat all nations whether weak or strong alike, and that I saw no alternative but strong measures towards Mexico." A week later the president again brought the Mexican question before the cabinet. "I expressed my opinion," he noted in his diary, "that we must take redress for the injuries done us into our own hands, that we had attempted to conciliate Mexico in vain, and had forborne until forbearance was no longer either a virtue or patriotic." Convinced that Paredes needed money, Polk suggested to leading senators that Congress appropriate $1 million both to encourage Paredes to negotiate and to sustain him in power until the United States could ratify the treaty. The president failed to secure Calhoun's required support.

Polk's persistence led him and the country to war. Like all escalations in the exertion of force, his decision responded less to unwanted and unanticipated resistance than to the requirements of the clearly perceived and inflexible purposes which guided the administration. What perpetuated the president's escalation to the point of war was his determination to pursue goals to the end whose achievement lay outside the possibilities of successful negotiations. Senator Thomas Hart Benton of Missouri saw this situation when he wrote: "It is impossible to conceive of an administration less warlike, or more intriguing, than that of Mr. Polk. They were *men of peace, with objects to be accomplished by means of war;* so that war was a necessity and an indispensability to their purpose."

Polk understood fully the state of Mexican opinion. In placing General Taylor on the Rio Grande he revealed again his contempt for Mexico. Under no national obligation to expose the country's armed forces, he would not have advanced Taylor in the face of a superior military force. Mexico had been undiplomatic; its denunciations of the United States were insulting and provocative. But if Mexico's behavior antagonized Polk, it did not antagonize the Whigs, the abolitionists, or even much of the Democratic party. Such groups did not regard Mexico as a threat; they warned the administration repeatedly that Taylor's presence on the Rio Grande would provoke war. But in the balance against peace was the pressure of American expansionism. Much of the Democratic and expansionist press, having accepted without restraint both the purposes of the Polk administration and its charges of Mexican perfidy, urged the president on to more vigorous action. . . .

Confronted with the prospect of further decline which they could neither accept nor prevent, [the Mexicans] lashed out with the intention of protecting their self-esteem and compelling the United States, if it was determined to have the Rio Grande, New Mexico, and California, to pay for its prizes with something other than money. On April 23, Paredes issued a proclamation declaring a defensive war against the United States. Predictably, one day later the Mexicans fired on a detachment of U.S. dragoons. Taylor's report of the attack reached Polk on Saturday evening, May 9. On Sunday the president drafted his war message and delivered it to Congress on the following day. Had Polk avoided the crisis, he might have gained the time required to permit the emigrants of 1845 and 1846 to settle the California issue without war.

What clouds the issue of the Mexican War's justification was the acquisition of New Mexico and California, for contemporaries and historians could not logically condemn the war and laud the Polk administration for its territorial achievements. Perhaps it is true that time would have permitted American pioneers to transform California into another Texas. But even then California's acquisition by the United States would have emanated from the use of force, for the elimination of Mexican sovereignty, whether through revolution or war, demanded the successful use of power. If the power employed in revolution would have been less obtrusive than that exerted in war, its role would have been no less essential. There simply was no way that the United States could acquire California peacefully. If the distraught Mexico of 1845 would not sell the distant province, no regime thereafter would have done so. Without forceful destruction of Mexico's sovereign power, California would have entered the twentieth century as an increasingly important region of another country.

Thus the Mexican War poses the dilemma of all international relations. Nations whose geographic and political status fails to coincide with their ambition and power can balance the two sets of factors in only one manner: through the employment of force. They succeed or fail according to circumstances; and for the United States, the conditions for achieving its empire in the Southwest and its desired frontage on the Pacific were so ideal that later generations could refer to the process as the mere fulfillment of destiny. "The Mexican Republic," lamented a Mexican writer in 1848, ". . . had among other misfortunes of less account, the great one of being in the vicinity of a strong and energetic people." What the Mexican War revealed in equal measure is the simple fact that only those countries which have achieved their destiny, whatever that may be, can afford to extol the virtues of peaceful change.

NORMAN A. GRAEBNER (1915–2010) was the Randolph P. Compton Professor Emeritus of History at the University of Virginia. A renowned classroom teacher, he also wrote and edited numerous books, articles, and texts on American history, including *Foundations of American Foreign Policy: A Realist Appraisal from Franklin to McKinley* (Scholarly Resources, 1985) and *Empire on the Pacific: A Study in American Continental Expansion*, 2nd ed. (Regina Books, 1983).

EXPLORING THE ISSUE

Was the Mexican War an Exercise in American Imperialism?

Critical Thinking and Reflection

1. Define imperialism by looking up the definition in a dictionary.
   a. Discuss whether or not the dictionary definition is too narrow.
   b. Does a nation need to control a country territorially to be imperialistic?
   c. Discuss whether or not the United States pursued an imperialistic policy toward Mexico in the 1840s.
2. Define Manifest Destiny.
   a. Where did the term originate?
   b. Did Manifest Destiny express the true feelings of the American people? Of American politicians? Or was it an exaggeration?
   c. Was Manifest Destiny merely a cover for American expansionist policies in Mexico?
   d. Was Manifest Destiny racist? Explain.
3. What evidence does Ramón Eduardo Ruiz provide to support his contention that the U.S.-Mexico War was motivated by racism and imperialism?
4. What is a "realist diplomatic historian"?
   a. Examine the influences of the cold war and influences of political scientists on Graebner's thinking.
   b. Analyze the following statement made by Graebner: "Nations do not fight over cultural differences or verbal recriminations; they fight over perceived threats to their interests created by the ambitions or demands of others."
5. Discuss the following three options which Polk could have taken after the Mexican government refused to back down in Texas or to sell New Mexico and California to the United States: (1) withdraw the demands; (2) scale down the demands; and (3) keep up the pressure until demands were met.
6. What other courses of action could President Polk have followed to achieve his objectives and to avoid a war?
7. Could California, like Texas, have become part of the United States through an internal revolution? Explain.
8. Has Mexico been hurt economically for the past 150 years because she lost control of Texas, New Mexico, and California?
9. Compare the cases of President Polk in 1846 with the two Presidents Bush in the ways in which they waged the Iraq Wars in 1991 and 2003.

Is There Common Ground?

Graebner disagrees with Walter Nugent over who started the Mexican War. He argues that Polk truly believed that President Paredes would back down and negotiate. Nugent, along with other writers such as Richard Kluger, in *Seizing Destiny: How America Grew from Sea to Shining Sea* (Knopf, 2007) maintains that Polk really wanted the war, especially after the Oregon boundary dispute with England was settled at the 49th parallel. Other historians support Graebner by putting the events into a broader focus. Walter A. McDougall, in *Promised Land, Crusader State: The American Encounter with the World since 1776*, states that aside from "sheer ambition" or "the fact that

Americans inhabited an undeveloped continent devoid of serious rivals . . . expansion derived from the primordial exceptional American commitment to liberty." The four barriers to expansion, continued McDougall, included Indian tribes, British lords, Mexican juntas, and "U.S. federal authorities themselves telling farmers, trappers, ranchers, merchants and missionaries: No, you can't settle here, or do business there. Go back where you came from!" (p. 78). Finally, Robert Kagan, in *Dangerous Nation* (Knopf, 2006), emphasizes how the acquisition of California and the territories of New Mexico and Arizona could upset the balance of power between the equal number of free and slave states that had been created.

There are many issues that an instructor could discuss with students concerning the early foreign policy of the United States. First is the notion of American "exceptionalism." The policies of American isolationism, neutrality, and the Monroe Doctrine were premised on the rejection of the traditional European notion of balance-of-power politics. Manifest Destiny was a concept that extolled the spread of the unique American ideals of freedom, democracy, and capitalism across the North American continent (not including Canada). Europe, by contrast, was wedded to old-fashioned kingdoms that restrained economic development via mercantilist controls. American foreign policy was based on ideals; European diplomacy was based on cynical realism in which nations played games with one another to maintain a balance of power.

The issue of American "exceptionalism" raises several questions. Was Benjamin Franklin playing power politics when he violated the alliance with France and negotiated a separate peace treaty with England to gain American independence? Are there other examples in the pre–Civil War period in which American presidents negotiated realistic agreements with foreign countries? In his book *Unmanifest Destiny: Mayhem and Illusion in American Foreign Policy—From the Monroe Doctrine to Reagan's War in El Salvador* (Dial Press, 1984), journalist T. D. Allman asserts that American foreign policy has run amok, spreading its unmanifested destiny to Vietnam in the 1960s and early 1970s and to El Salvador and Nicaragua in the late 1980s. Was the American invasion of Grenada a violation of the Monroe Doctrine? Is American foreign policy imperialistic? Was Manifest Destiny merely a cover for American imperialism? Was Manifest Destiny also racist, as some Mexican historians contend? For a view that perceives empire as a way of life in the United States, consult the first chapter of Professor William Appleman Williams's classic *Tragedy of Diplomacy*, 2nd ed. (Delta, 1972). For the perspective of the Mexican side, see the collections on the Mexican War by Archie McDonald, ed., *The Mexican War: Crisis for American Democracy* (D. D. Heath, 1969) and Ramón Eduardo Ruiz, ed., *The Mexican War: Was It Manifest Destiny?* (Holt, Rinehart and Winston, 1969).

Additional Resources

Rodolfo Acuña, *Occupied America: A History of Chicanos*, 3rd ed. (Harper & Row, 1988)

Ernesto Chavez, *The U.S. War with Mexico: A Brief History with Documents* (Bedford/St. Martin's, 2008)

John S. D. Eisenhower, *So Far from God: The U. S. War with Mexico, 1846–1848* (Random House, 1989)

Amy S. Greenberg, *A Wicked War: Polk, Clay, Lincoln and the 1846 U.S. Invasion of Mexico* (Alfred A. Knopf, 2012)

Robert W. Merry, *A Country of Vast Designs: James K. Polk, the Mexican War and the Conquest of America* (Simon & Schuster, 2009)

Internet References . . .

A Continent Divided: The U.S.-Mexico War

library.uta.edu/usmexicowar/

A Guide to the Mexican War

www.loc.gov/rr/program/bib/mexicanwar/

Descendants of Mexican War Veterans

www.dmwv.org/

Mexican War Service Records

www.fold3.com/category_274/

Military Resources: Mexican War, 1846–1848

www.archives.gov/research/alic/reference/military /mexican-war.html

Selected, Edited, and with Issue Framing Material by:
Larry Madaras, *Howard Community College*
and
James M. SoRelle, *Baylor University*

ISSUE

Was John Brown an Irrational Terrorist?

YES: James N. Gilbert, from "A Behavioral Analysis of John Brown: Martyr or Terrorist?" in *Terrible Swift Sword: The Legacy of John Brown* (Ohio University Press, 2005)

NO: Scott John Hammond, from "John Brown as Founder: America's Violent Confrontation with Its First Principles," in *Terrible Swift Sword: The Legacy of John Brown* (Ohio University Press, 2005)

Learning Outcomes
After reading this issue, you will be able to:
• Define "terrorism" and place this concept in a broad historical context that does not simply include the present.
• Determine whether John Brown's actions amount to terrorist tactics.
• Compare the abolitionists' goals for freedom for African American slaves with the political freedom sought by the founders of the American republic.
• Assess the legitimacy of employing violence to end the institution of slavery.

ISSUE SUMMARY

YES: James N. Gilbert says that John Brown's actions conform to a modern definition of terrorist behavior in that Brown considered the United States incapable of reforming itself by abolishing slavery, believed that only violence would accomplish that goal, and justified his actions by proclaiming adherence to a "higher" power.

NO: Scott John Hammond insists that John Brown's commitment to higher moral and political goals conformed to the basic principles of human freedom and political and legal equality that formed the heart of the creed articulated by the founders of the American nation.

Opposition to slavery in the area that became the United States dates back to the seventeenth and eighteenth centuries, when Puritan leaders, such as Samuel Sewall, and Quakers, such as John Woolman and Anthony Benezet, published a number of pamphlets condemning the existence of the slave system. This religious link to antislavery sentiment is also evident in the writings of John Wesley as well as in the decision of the Society of Friends in 1688 to prohibit their members from owning bond servants. Slavery was said to be contrary to Christian principles. These attacks, however, did little to diminish the institution. Complaints that the English government had instituted a series of measures that "enslaved" the colonies in British North America raised thorny questions about the presence of *real* slavery in those colonies. How could American colonists demand their freedom from King George III, who was cast in the role of oppressive master, while denying freedom and liberty to African American slaves? Such a contradiction inspired a gradual emancipation movement in the North, which often was accompanied by compensation for the former slave owners.

In addition, antislavery societies sprang up throughout the nation to continue the crusade against bondage. Interestingly, the majority of these organizations were located in the South. Prior to the 1830s, the most prominent antislavery organization was the American Colonization Society, which offered a twofold program: (1) gradual, compensated emancipation of slaves and (2) exportation of the newly freed to colonies outside the boundaries of the United States, mostly to Africa.

In the 1830s, antislavery activity underwent an important transformation. A new strain of antislavery sentiment expressed itself in the abolitionist movement. Drawing momentum both from the revivalism of the Second Great Awakening and the example set by England (which prohibited slavery in its imperial holdings in 1833), abolitionists called for the immediate end to slavery without compensation to masters for the loss of their property. Abolitionists viewed slavery not so much as a practical problem to be resolved, but rather as a moral offense incapable of resolution through traditional channels of political compromise. In January 1831, William Lloyd Garrison, who for many came to symbolize the abolitionist crusade, published the first issue of *The Liberator*, a newspaper dedicated to the immediate end to slavery. In his first editorial, Garrison expressed the self-righteous indignation of many in the abolitionist movement when he warned slaveholders and their supporters to "urge me not to use moderation in a cause like the present. I am in earnest—I will not equivocate—I will not excuse—I will not retreat a single inch—AND I WILL BE HEARD. . . ."

Unfortunately for Garrison, relatively few Americans were inclined to respond positively to his call. His newspaper generated little interest outside Boston, New York, Philadelphia, and other major urban centers of the North. This situation, however, changed within a matter of months. In August 1831, a slave preacher named Nat Turner led a rebellion of slaves in Southampton County, Virginia, that resulted in the death of 58 whites. Although the revolt was quickly suppressed and Turner and his supporters were executed, the incident spread fear throughout the South. Governor John B. Floyd of Virginia turned an accusatory finger toward the abolitionists when he concluded that the Turner uprising was "undoubtedly designed and matured by unrestrained fanatics in some of the neighboring states."

One of the weaknesses of most studies of abolitionism is that they generally are written from a monochromatic perspective. In other words, historians typically discuss whites within the abolitionist crusade and give little, if any, attention to the roles African Americans played in the movement. Whites are portrayed as the active agents of reform, while blacks are the passive recipients of humanitarian efforts to eliminate the scourge of slavery. Students should be aware that African Americans, slave and free, also rebelled against the institution of slavery both directly and indirectly, although very few rallied to the call of John Brown.

Benjamin Quarles in *Black Abolitionists* (Oxford University Press, 1969) describes a wide range of roles played by blacks in the abolitionist movement. The African American challenge to the slave system is also evident in the network known as the "underground railroad." Larry Gara, in *The Liberty Line: The Legend of the Underground Railroad*

(University of Kentucky Press, 1961), concludes that the real heroes of the underground railroad were not white abolitionists but the slaves themselves who depended primarily upon their own resources or assistance they received from other African Americans, slave and free.

Other studies treating the role of black abolitionists in the antislavery movement include James M. McPherson, *The Struggle For Equality: Abolitionists and the Negro in the Civil War and Reconstruction* (Princeton University Press, 1964); Jane H. and William H. Pease, *They Who Would Be Free: Blacks' Search for Freedom, 1830–1861* (Atheneum, 1974); R. J. M. Blackett, *Building an Antislavery Wall: Black Americans in the Atlantic Abolitionist Movement, 1830–1860* (Louisiana State University Press, 1983) and *Beating Against the Barriers: The Lives of Six Nineteenth-Century Afro-Americans* (Louisiana State University Press, 1986); Ronald K. Burke, *Samuel Ringgold Ward: Christian Abolitionist* (Garland, 1995), Nell Irvin Painter, *Sojourner Truth: A Life, A Symbol* (W. W. Norton, 1997); and Catherine Clinton, *Harriet Tubman: The Road to Freedom* (2004). Frederick Douglass's contributions are evaluated in Benjamin Quarles, *Frederick Douglass* (Atheneum, 1968; originally published 1948), Nathan Irvin Huggins, *Slave and Citizen: The Life of Frederick Douglass* (Little, Brown, 1980), Waldo E. Martin, Jr., *The Mind of Frederick Douglass* (University of North Carolina Press, 1984), and William S. McFeely, *Frederick Douglass* (W. W. Norton, 1991).

The following essays focus on a white abolitionist who perhaps best fits the characterization of an "unrestrained fanatic" but who became a martyr in the antislavery pantheon when he was executed following his unsuccessful raid on the federal arsenal in Harpers Ferry, Virginia in 1859. James N. Gilbert argues that Brown's attack was comparable to recent acts of terrorism in the United States and that, despite the continuing tendency to portray his actions as those of a martyred hero, Brown clearly fits the modern definition of a domestic terrorist.

In the second selection, Scott John Hammond characterizes Brown in a more positive light. While recognizing flaws in Brown's personality and actions, Hammond nevertheless concludes that John Brown acted on the highest of principles to thwart evil by articulating an undiluted commitment to the basic principles of America's founding—individual liberty and political and legal equality.

YES

James N. Gilbert

A Behavioral Analysis of John Brown: Martyr or Terrorist?

The scholarly examination of the topic of terrorism has developed into a significant area of legal and criminological research. Academic and governmental studies pertaining to terrorist crimes and those who perpetrate them are now voluminous and continue to be actively pursued. Emerging as what appeared to be a new form of criminal deviance, the definition and cause of the "disease of the 70s" has challenged criminologists. While most contemporary documented incidents continue to occur outside the United States, the fear of domestic terrorism, as recent events have illustrated, remains a legitimate concern. The public and researchers alike have in the past commonly assumed that this country would continue to be spared from acts that conform to our contemporary definition of terrorist activity. Terrorism was associated with a foreign environment and viewed as exceptional in the history of American criminal violence.

But after February 26, 1993, when the New York World Trade Center was the target of a massive terrorist bombing, the attention of Americans became riveted upon the unique form of criminality that we have collectively termed terrorism. And of course this criminal act was followed by the far more deadly bombing in Oklahoma City and the attacks on the World Trade Center and the Pentagon on September 11, 2001. Although much of the media and public has treated these terrorist acts as precedent-setting domestic attacks, the history of terrorism in the United States actually dates to the founding of the nation. Of the many such violent episodes in our earlier history, John Brown's attack on Harpers Ferry in October 1859 is comparable to these more recent acts in terms of national terror and consequent social and political upheaval.

In late 1859 John Brown and twenty-one followers attempted to rally and arm large numbers of slaves by attacking and briefly holding the United States arsenal at Harpers Ferry, Virginia (presently West Virginia). Captured by federal military forces and local militia, Brown was hastily tried and executed. While the life and deeds of John Brown are immensely important for their impact on abolitionism and the American Civil War, this powerful historical figure is rarely defined as a terrorist. Instead, a vast collection of literature generally portrays Brown as either saint or madman. On one hand, there is the sympathetic traditional portrait of John Brown as an American hero of near mythical proportions. Such an image is certainly not viewed as criminally deviant, nor does it suggest the status of criminal folk hero. But while a minority historical judgment has questioned his sanity or the radical end-justification logic he appeared to employ, few even in this camp would declare his actions truly terrorist. Civil War and military historian John Hubbell reflects this multidimensional view. Stating that while John Brown was, "in fact, a combination of humility and arrogance, submission and aggression, murder and martyrdom," his true motivation may not have been calculated terroristic cause and effect, but "an unresolved resentment of his father; his hatred of slaveholders may have been the unconscious resolution of his anger."

Thus, one can only question how and why this imagery has persisted throughout the decades. Is the terrorist label lacking due to the singular rationale of his crimes: the massive evil of slavery? Alternatively, are we correct in excluding Brown from the definition of terrorist because his actions simply fail to conform to contemporary elements that constitute such a criminal? For example, a similar definitional confusion currently exists regarding various violent attacks on abortion clinics and their personnel by those who, like Brown, rationalize their violence by moral or religious conviction. Some would define convicted murderer Paul Hill as a domestic terrorist for his premeditated attack on an abortion doctor and an escort during the summer of 1994. Yet others would fail to define his actions as terroristic due to Hill's justification of his act as a "lesser evil."

In order to define Brown precisely as a terrorist rather than as a martyr, the meaning of terrorism must be explored. As with many singular, emotion-producing labels of criminality, terrorism is easier to describe than define. The *Vice President's Task Force on Combating Terrorism* describes terrorism as a phenomenon involving "the unlawful use of threat of violence against persons or property to further political or social objectives." In a similar vein, the FBI's Terrorist Research and Analytical Center states that terroristic activity "is the unlawful use of force or violence against persons or property to intimidate or coerce a government, the civilian population, or any segment thereof, in furtherance of political or social objectives." Both definitions agree with views commonly provided by various governments. This traditional bureaucratic view stresses a triad in which both property and people are potential targets with the necessary presence of illegal actions and social or political motivations as the causative agent.

Additional attempts to conceptualize the terrorist often focus on the perpetrator's motive rather than legal definitions. To this economist Bill Anderson links the economic viewpoint, stressing that fundamental principles of economic theory are the real, often hidden, motives of such crimes. Anderson believes that after we "peel away the ideological skins and fig leaves that terrorists use to justify their violence, we come to the core reason for their actions: the terrorists' own desire for power and influence. In other words, the terrorists are seeking wealth transfers and/or power (all of which can be defined as economic or political rents) through violent means because they are not willing to pay the cost of participating in the political process."

Others prefer to explain away terrorism through an apologist approach, stressing the anger, hopelessness, and governmental violence brought against various victimized populations from which, inevitably, terrorists will be mobilized. Eqbal Ahmad, a research fellow at the Washington, D.C.–based Institute for Policy Studies, stresses this sympathetic theme when he links terrorism to government indifference to violence. He believes that individuals turn to terrorism to exercise "their need to be heard, the combination of anger and helplessness producing the impulse for retributive violence. The experience of violence by a stronger party has historically turned victims into terrorists." Thus, the apologist view firmly supports the recurring belief that terrorism is merely situational, constantly coming in and out of criminal focus according to prevailing political power or orientation. Sheikh Omar Abdel-Rahman clearly embraced the situational view when he claimed to be a victim rather than an alleged conspirator in the 1993 World Trade Center bombing. Angered over his conspiracy indictment and subsequent incarceration, he stated, "but what bothers me, and makes me feel bitter about the whole thing, is when a person who was called a freedom fighter then is now called, when the war is over, a terrorist."

A final view, particularly popular in fictional portrayals of terrorists, suggests individual psychopathology as the chief cause of terrorism. As detailed by political philosopher and professor of religion Moshe Amon, one form of terroristic crime may originate within the disturbed minds of some perpetrators, triggering myths and fantasies that can be categorized as messianic or apocalyptic. The messianic terrorist ideology streams from a conviction that one has special insight that produces an individual state of enlightenment. Terrorists are then convinced that "they are the only ones who see the real world, and the only ones who are not affected by its depravity. It is their mission, therefore, to liberate the blind people of this world from the rule of the unjust." Although this concept may be traced to early Hebrew origins, a more contemporary form is common among Latin American terrorists. Political scientist

John Pottenger concludes, "The existence of social injustice and [the] individual's commitment to human liberation, demand that a radical change can turn the Christian into a revolutionary vanguard demonstrating that God not only intervenes in human history but He does so on the right side of the oppressed."

Other psychological theorists believe that the most common type of terrorist has a psychopathic or sociopathic personality. The classic traits of the psychopath—impulsiveness, lack of guilt, inability to experience emotional depth, and manipulation—are perceived as ideally suited to the commission of terrorism. The ability to kill often large numbers of strangers without compunction or to manipulate others to unwittingly further criminal ends convinces many that the psychopathic personality is a requirement for terroristic action.

With such definitions of terrorism in mind, how are we to view John Brown? After almost a century and a half, the actions of Brown have been preserved with stark clarity, yet his personality and related psychological motivations can only be surmised. John Brown was fifty-nine years old when he was executed by the state of Virginia for treason, conspiring with blacks to produce insurrection, and murder in the first degree. His criminal activities of record include embezzlement and assault with a deadly weapon against an Ohio sheriff in 1842. In 1856 a warrant was issued by a proslavery Kansas district court charging Brown with "organizing against slavery." A month later he and eight other men kidnapped and murdered five Kansans, including a constable and his two sons. The killings were particularly brutal: the victims were hacked to death by repeated sword blows. In December 1858 the state of Missouri and the federal government offered a reward for Brown's capture because he was the chief suspect in yet another criminal homicide. Finally, Brown's criminal activities culminated in the seizure of the federal armory at Harpers Ferry on October 16, 1859. A company of U.S. Marines captured him the following day, and history records his execution less than fifty days after his attack against the armory.

The question of whether John Brown was indeed a terrorist must be based on a definitional standard that defies emotional or mythical distortion. The linkage of Brown's cause to the horrors of slavery circumvents the true nature of the man and of his crimes. According to Albert Parry, author of a best-selling work on the history of terror and revolutionary violence, terrorists and those who study them offer innumerable explanations of their violence; yet their motivations can be compacted into three main concepts:

1. Society is sick and cannot be cured by half measures of reform.
2. The state is in itself violent and can be countered and overcome only by violence.
3. The truth of the terrorist cause justifies any action that supports it. While some terrorists recognize no moral law, others have their own "higher" morality.

Comparing John Brown's actions to these criteria produces an inescapable match. On many occasions Brown expressed his solid belief that society, particularly a society that would embrace slavery, was sick beyond its own cure. Brown had clearly given up on public policy reforms or legal remedies regarding slavery when he drafted his own constitution for the benefit of his followers. The document attempts to define his justifications for the upcoming attack at Harpers Ferry and utterly rejects the legal and moral foundation of the United States: "Therefore, we citizens of the United States and the Oppressed People, who by a Recent Decision of the Supreme Court are declared to have no rights which the white man is bound to respect; together with all other people regarded by the laws thereof, do for the time being, ordain and establish for ourselves the following provisional constitution and ordinances, the better to protect our persons, property, lives, and liberties: and to govern our actions."

As to the terroristic belief that violent government can only be overcome by violence, Brown's convictions were preserved for posterity by a note he handed to a jailer while being led to the gallows: "I John Brown am now quite *certain* that the crimes of this *guilty land: will* never be purged *away;* but with Blood. I had *as I now think: vainly* flattered myself that without *very much* bloodshed: it might be done."

With similar conformity, Brown's beliefs and actions demonstrated his rigid "higher" morality, which served to justify numerous crimes, including multiple homicides. As described by historian Stephen Oates, "Brown knew the Missourians would come after him . . . yet he was not afraid of the consequences for God would keep and deliver him: God alone was his judge. Now that the work was done, he believed that he had been guided by a just and wrathful God."

Brown's deeds conform to contemporary definitions of terrorism, and his psychological predispositions are consistent with the terrorist model. As observed by David Hubbard, founder of the Aberrant Behavior Center and psychiatric consultant to the Federal Bureau of Prisons, the actions and personality of the terrorist are not "merely bizarre and willfully antisocial; but a reflection of deep-seated personal and cultural pathologies." Such behavioral pathology is commonly linked to the psychopathic personality or, less frequently, to some form of paranoia. Virtually unknown to mental health authorities during Brown's lifetime, the psychopathic personality is currently considered a relatively common criminal mental abnormality among violent offenders. Although psychopathic criminals account for a small percentage of overall lawbreakers, psychologist William McCord notes that they commit a disproportionate percentage of violent crime. While psychopaths may be encountered within any violent criminal typology, they appear to be particularly well represented in various crimes of serial violence, confidence fraud, and terrorism.

The concept of psychopathy focuses on the unsocialized criminal, who is devoid of conscience and consequently in repeated conflict with society; he or she fails to learn from prior experiences. As observed by Herbert Strean, professor of social work and psychotherapy researcher at Rutgers University, the psychopath is often arrogant, callous, and lacking in empathy and tends to offer plausible rationalizations for his or her reckless behavior. While John Brown demonstrated a guilt-free conscience on many occasions, his calculating leadership in the kidnapping and murder of five people in Kansas provided beyond question his capacity to free himself of normal emotion. On the night of May 26, 1856, Brown led a small party of followers to the various cabins of his political enemies, which included Constable James Doyle and his sons. During what would later be termed the Pottawatomie Massacre, the Brown party systematically dragged the five unarmed and terrified men from their homes and murdered them in a frenzy of brutal violence. "About a hundred yards down the road Salmon and Owen [Brown's sons] fell on the Doyles with broadswords. They put up a struggle, striking out, trying to shield themselves from the slashing blades as they staggered back down the road. But in a few moments the grisly work was done. Brown, who must have watched the executions in a kind of trance, now walked over and shot Doyle in the forehead with a revolver, to make certain work of it." When later questioned about his motives during the Kansas murders, Brown offered a classic messianic psychopathic rationalization. Without a trace of remorse, he stated that the victims all deserved to die as they "had committed murder in their hearts already, according to the Big Book . . . their killing had been decreed by Almighty God, ordained from eternity."

. . . John Brown does not stand alone in the annals of American-based terrorism. Yet he obviously remains a unique, paradoxical example of a terrorist whom history has often viewed through rose-colored lenses. As opposed to alarm or disgust, the deeds of John Brown have moved some to great literary inspiration, such as Stephen Vincent Benét's epic poem *John Brown's Body.* Ralph Waldo Emerson, writing shortly before Brown's execution, referred to Brown as "the Saint, whose fate yet hangs in suspense, but whose martyrdom, if it shall be perfected, will make the gallows glorious like the Cross." Other towering figures of the arts echo the purity of Brown while conveniently ignoring his murderous past. Henry David Thoreau wrote, "No man in America has ever stood up so persistently and effectively for the dignity of human nature, knowing himself for a man, and the equal of any and all governments. . . . He could not have been tried by a jury of his peers, because his peers did not exist." Other, more contemporary sources, including scores of textbooks, continue to echo such laudatory sentiments, informing generation after generation of young Americans that John Brown was a genuine hero. Typical of many such high school and middle school American history texts, one leading book praises Brown through Emerson's words as "a new saint," while another considers him "a martyr and hero, as he walked resolutely to the scaffold."

In a pragmatic sense, it is doubtful that the heroic legend of John Brown will ever include the terrorist truth of his crimes. As observed by guerrilla warfare essayist Walter Laqueur, "terrorism has long exercised a great fascination, especially at a safe distance . . . the fascination it exerts and the difficulty of interpreting it have the same roots: its unexpected, shocking and outrageous character." While many American terrorists exert a continuing fascination, none have occupied the unique position of John Brown. By contemporary definition, he was undoubtedly a terrorist to his core, demonstrating repeatedly the various axioms from which we shape this unique crime. Brown quite purposely waged war for political and social change while simultaneously committing the most heinous crimes. As political scientist Charles Hazelip would say when defining a terrorist, he had "crossed over the blurred line of demarcation between crime and war where political terrorism begins."

Yet John Brown's obsessive target, the focus of all his energy and murderous deeds, has by its nature absolved him from the cold label of *terrorist*. History and popular opinion have quite naturally found the greater criminality of slavery to far outweigh his illegal acts. The bold tactics at Harpers Ferry, coupled with his humanistic motives to free the Virginia slaves, compels us to forgive his disturbed personality and deadly past. The attack on a key government arsenal and armory, which in a contemporary context would horrify the nation, has been judged through the passage of time to be an inevitable, gallant first strike against the soon to be formed Southern Confederacy. When taken as a whole, and to the natural dismay of our justice system, Brown's actions quite convincingly demonstrate that if the weight of moral sentiment is on one's side, terroristic violence can be absorbed into a nation's historiography in a positive sense. [Christopher] Dobson and [Ronald] Payne conclude, "the main aim of terror is to make murderers into heroes." While many will continue to debate the magnitude of John Brown's terrorism, his heroic stature has been secured by the often paradoxical judgment of history.

JAMES N. GILBERT is a professor and former chair of the department of criminal justice at the University of Nebraska-Kearney, where he has taught since 1988. Specializing in criminal investigative theory, he is the author of *Criminal Investigation* (Pearson/Prentice Hall, 2009), now in its eighth edition, as well as numerous journal articles.

Scott John Hammond    **NO**

John Brown as Founder: America's Violent Confrontation with Its First Principles

John Brown moves at an angle through our history, a transfigured personage who is deemed a force of nature, an avenging angel wielding the scourge of God, a fearsome vessel of pure fanaticism that is seductive in the abstract as well as a terrifyingly demonic power in the flesh. Some would call him a tragic hero, flawed only in his insistence on purity in thought and action coupled with a mystical detachment from the political realities of his day; and some would see in him a prototerrorist, a criminal mind living on the lunatic fringe of history, condemned by rational people in both the North and South. Lincoln, in spite of his deep opposition to slavery, saw in Brown's raid the very archetype of lawless violence and was quick to distance both himself and his party from such obviously treasonous actions. For example, directing his remarks to Southern whites in a speech at the Cooper Union Institute on February 27, 1860, Lincoln declared: "You charge that we stir up insurrections among your slaves. We deny it; and what is your proof? Harper's [sic] Ferry! John Brown! John Brown is no Republican, and you have [yet] to implicate a single Republican in his Harper's [sic] Ferry enterprise." Conversely, Emerson praised Brown and remarked that Brown would elevate the gallows to a symbol of martyrdom on the same order and import as the Cross. It was, and perhaps still is, difficult for one to be objective or neutral about Osawatomie Brown: one was either with him or against him.

What we know of Brown's life fuels all these interpretations. As a lover of freedom steeled by a devotion to strict Calvinism, Brown appears to have been a practitioner of the Christian ethic framed by the imperative of universal love and compassion for others, especially those who suffer under the yoke of oppression and injustice. For in loving and caring for "the least" of his fellow human beings, he epitomized the purity of a love of human freedom that often comes from a sense of oneness with higher moral ends. Nonetheless, this is the same John Brown who, in the course of one night, assumed the visage of the Night Rider and personally directed and participated in the murder of five defenseless men. Since these men were supporters of slavery, and some of them had previously committed violence against Free State settlers, Brown's decision to kill them is perceived by some as part of his greater mission on behalf of even more defenseless slaves. Still, the manner in which Brown summarily executed these five resembles that of the vicious terrorist more than that of the righteous warrior, and the Pottawatomie Massacre chills the blood of even the most ardent foe of oppression.

These aspects of Brown's psyche reflect something about our own political soul—our "political psyche" writ large. If Brown embodies the essence of us all, then it might be conceded that Brown's more pathological qualities replicate a profound dissonance within our general political and social culture. We must consider the inevitable consequences inherent within a sociopolitical condition fractured by the collision between the ideals of democratic liberty and the appalling realities of slavery and racism. No American will impugn the principles of liberty and equality, for however they are construed or comprehended, the structuring principles of the American polity are derived from a noble vision and an aspiration for a free and dignified humanity. The presence of slavery in a country committed, at least in principle, to freedom is the worst possible incidence of ideational failure. Brown's fractured self is an embodiment of the tangled forces of light and darkness that grappled for the republic's soul; his character and actions demonstrate this, and in so doing, make him no different from the ruptured essence of our collective political self-consciousness. The Pottawatomie slaughter represents a symptom of the deeper malady, just as the abuse of any slave by an overseer represents the same type of symptomatic manifestation. In contrast to Brown's avenging violence in Kansas, the incident at Harpers Ferry was driven by a spirit imbued with the transfiguring fire of the idea of universal freedom, in the same manner as the Underground Railroad or the individual dissent of the most famous resident of Walden Pond. Both America and Brown reveal this self-negating duality.

That Brown could be so moved to action by the tragedy of his times further amplifies his character and conviction. Most citizens, absorbed in the daily process and considerations of private interest and obligation, ignore or suppress the maladies of the deeper social structure. The affairs of the state frequently demand too much concentration and emotional investment for the average citizen. Nevertheless, there will always be those among us who, like Brown, seriously regard the structuring principles of a political culture with unabashed sincerity and are thus impelled to hold our institutions and practices accountable to our own higher ideas and political ideals.

Brown judged society according to the laws of God, and he saw with a piercing clarity that neither the ruling political doctrine nor, more important, the commandments of Providence were being properly revered. Nothing could absolve us from the sin of slavery, and the distinctions between righteousness and evil were easily and sharply drawn. No ambiguity, no "gray in gray," no compromise or allowance would be tolerated; either one was with the warriors for freedom and divine righteousness or among the profane legions who served on behalf of sinful oppression. For Brown, unlike most of his fellow Americans, the only solution was an obvious one—brook no sympathy for or concession to the minions of evil, and unconditionally submit without hesitation or diffidence to the Higher Authority, never relenting until total emancipation was achieved or sublime retribution judiciously dispensed. This is what drove John Brown to act with such intensity of conviction, which magnified every hidden idiosyncrasy. Hence, Brown is at once liberator and fanatic, messiah and monster, the very incarnation of the conflicted American political soul.

This leads us to a more direct consideration of the notion of foundations and founding. The act of founding involves at least an abstract comprehension of those first principles that constitute a political soul and the resolve to forward those principles in an undiluted form. . . .

Upon examining those individuals who are noted for participating in an act of founding, we notice something unique that separates them from the ordinary politician, activist, or statesman. This is explained with considerable clarity by Machiavelli, who typically adds the ingredient of realpolitik to his observations of founding and reformative leadership. Given the fact that all founders and reformers will inevitably encounter resistance from those enemies who "profit from the old order," and assuming that a purely good leader will "bring about his own ruin among so many who are not good," Machiavelli notes that a lawgiver or prophet must go forth armed and prepared for struggle. Machiavelli's idea of a founder is consonant with the idea of virtue, or grandeur of soul—a character of extraordinary proportions, defined in terms of "ingenuity, skill, and excellence." Machiavelli seeks a type of transcending leadership, attaching a significant martial quality to his model founders. Even Moses, a religious founder, employs the might of God against Pharaoh in order to liberate the enslaved Israelites, something that those who follow the New Testament model of the suffering Christ would unequivocally reject.

Brown's actions are like those of a prophet-warrior. However, Machiavelli's armed prophet is also a conqueror; failure is associated with those who attempt to establish founding law without the enforcing power of arms. Brown does not seem to conform easily to the prophet-warrior model, for his arms were poor, his numbers few, and his plan thwarted by overextension and local hostility. Moses was at least able to extricate the Israelite slaves from their Egyptian oppressors. Moses conquered by overcoming the power of Egypt and then *founded* both a religion and a nation through the transmission of the Law of God. It is an understatement to say that Brown's achievement falls far short of this mark.

But if one considers the substance of Brown's commitment (the emancipation of the enslaved) and the method of Brown's action (confrontation with the sinful oppressor on behalf of the oppressed), Brown's character and actions do approximate the Machiavellian hero-founder. Furthermore, although he does not conquer in the physical or political sense, he does emerge triumphant. Brown was defeated but martyred, and in the end emancipation came for his people through the violence that he had prophesied. In a sobering moment of synchronicity, Lincoln's retrospective utterance in his second inaugural address, that "until every drop of blood drawn with the lash, shall be paid by another drawn with the sword," echoes Brown's last testimony. Two years earlier, Lincoln, at Gettysburg, had referred to a "new birth of freedom," and thus implicitly defined a new act of founding in the context and terms of the emancipation. From the blood and ashes of the war against slavery, the nation would be re-formed; Brown, who did not survive to witness the nation's second birth, nonetheless prophesied the act in his words. The nation was literally made anew but in a way that reaffirmed more completely the first principles of the republic. This represents an act of founding, and Brown's strike at Harpers Ferry was the prophetic prelude. Even though John Brown is distinct from Machiavelli's legendary types in a number of ways, he certainly shares in the role of founding/reforming visionary. Indeed, Lincoln, generally regarded as the heroic and tragic, even Christlike figure of the Civil War, resembles Brown in the end, only on a larger scale and from the comparatively more acceptable authority of his office. For Lincoln used violence to preserve the Union and purge the new nation of slavery. In his second inaugural address, he finally admits what he most likely knew from the beginning, that slavery was "somehow the cause of the war," and in so doing, for a brief moment toward the end of that war, the Great Emancipator shows himself akin to the Prophet of Osawatomie.

An alternative discussion of the founder-legislator is found in Rousseau's *Social Contract*. The Rousseauian founder is less applicable to the case of John Brown than the Machiavellian model. Rousseau's founder-legislator possesses a "superior intelligence" and is capable of "beholding all the passions of human beings without experiencing them." It is unlikely that Brown possessed a superior intelligence, and Brown's personality was far from the dispassionate character that Rousseau requires of his legislator. Furthermore, Rousseau's concept of the founder is identical to the concept of the first lawgiver and by no means resembles a prophet-warrior. Martial skill is not a requisite quality of Rousseau's founder, for Rousseau is always careful to mark an acute distinction between government based on consent and authority imposed by force. . . .

At another level, however, there is a similarity between Brown and Rousseau's founder. Rousseau's founder is an individual of superhuman qualities; indeed, Rousseau's description compares the creation of human first laws to the actions of gods. Rousseau's ideal founder is not afraid to act in a way that would challenge "human nature" itself. Brown seems to act against the natural order, but he does not intend to "change" human nature so much as to salvage it and even to save us from it. As a Calvinist, Brown undoubtedly believed that our nature is fixed by original sin; hence, he departed from Rousseau in yet another way. Brown fought against our sinful nature on behalf of redemption. Again, this seems to depart from Rousseau, but one must note that Rousseau's overall view of human nature was not much different from that of Calvin. Rousseau and Calvin both argued that humanity exists in a fallen condition, and although we cannot return to our original innocence, we can recover something of it through the affirmation of freedom and morality. For Calvin and John Brown, that higher state could be achieved through the Redeemer; for Rousseau, redemption is possible through the Social Contract. Both Rousseau and Brown sought a kind of recovery and affirmation of a better state of existence, and both insisted that in order to achieve such a goal, we must struggle mightily against our corrupted natures in order to reform and ennoble our humanity.

It should also be emphasized that the element of consent is vital to Rousseau. Brown's actions cannot admit of either direct or indirect consent of the governed for a number of reasons; most obvious of these is that Brown governed no one and possessed no legal or political authority, and that Brown was wholly dissociated from normal political channels. Even so, Brown acted in a way that relates indirectly to the notion of consensual governance. Brown sought neither the approval nor the consent of the populace, for the majority of the populace ignored, permitted, supported, or participated in the possession of human beings. More importantly, the law of God is not based on consent, but like Rousseau's general will, it is always right. Additionally, a minority of the population, both the enslaved victims and the various types of free dissenters and abolitionists, had been effectively deprived of their fundamental right to consent. The only rule that the slave knew was the rule of force, and the only rule that the abolitionist experienced was ultimately deemed immoral. The case of John Brown and his small group of followers and sympathizers exemplifies the latter, and it is compatible with Rousseau's theory of consent and resistance.

Even if Brown is not a founder-legislator in the strict Rousseauian sense, there are at least two arguments in the *Social Contract* that provide theoretical and moral support for Brown's extreme actions. First, Rousseau follows Locke in affirming that the notion of consent unequivocally requires unanimity. A political culture that either legitimizes or permits slavery violates this fundamental principle of universal consent. No one consents to be a slave; the enslaved population constitutes an excluded group that indicates a government based (partially) on force that is thus (wholly) illegitimate. Lincoln saw this as well and employed a similar argument in one of his many criticisms directed at the continued allowance of slavery. Even if one counters this argument by *incorrectly* objecting that Rousseau would not have included a slave population when considering the origins of the social contract, one would still have to take into account the abolitionists who, in acting against slavery from first principles, withdrew their consent to be governed by the current instrument. The unanimity that Rousseau demanded in theory never existed in practice under a regime that allowed slavery; thus, according to these standards, the Constitution, if it did indeed support or permit slavery (an issue that is in itself open to further analysis and argument within a different context) *was therefore not legitimate*. The founding act had occurred under an initial condition that was shaped by a great error.

This directs us back to our second point. Rousseau states without ambiguity that slavery is in every instance illegitimate and immoral. Freedom cannot be surrendered or usurped, for to "renounce liberty is to renounce being a man, to surrender the rights of humanity and even its duties." Thus, slavery can never be rendered legitimate or permitted by a government or any portion of its population. Rousseau makes this clear in the cases of both voluntary and involuntary submission. Slavery can be based neither on a voluntary arrangement nor on coercion or conquest. In the case of the former, one who agrees to be a slave is "out of one's mind," for it is madness to "renounce one's very humanity." Of course, American slavery was anything but voluntary, and for Rousseau, this form of slavery is equally inhumane. . . . As Rousseau powerfully states, "So, from whatever aspect we regard the question, the right of slavery is null and void, not only as being illegitimate, but also because it is absurd and meaningless. The words *slave* and *right* contradict each other, and are mutually exclusive. It will always be equally foolish for a man to say to a man or people: 'I make with you a convention wholly at your expense, and wholly to my advantage; I shall keep it as long as I like, and you will keep it as long as I like.'" Thus, not only is a social contract left unformed if it does not include the affirmation of *every* voice that is present within the polity, it is also morally incompatible given the presence of an enslaved group regardless of how the enslavement came about. In refusing to seek the consent of the majority, Brown chose to act on behalf of those who had been excluded from the founding act of consent and against a government that under Rousseau's definition can only be interpreted as illegitimate. Surely an analysis of Brown's actions from this perspective can better illuminate the questions that revolve around the accusation of his "lawlessness."

The notion of founding entails far more than establishment of institutions or governmental charters; it also, and above all, includes critical political and social reform in the pursuit of the higher principles of a given political culture. If we are to accept, along with such martyred luminaries as Lincoln and King, the proposition that the first principles of the American founding are to be understood as the guarantee of both individual liberty *and* the advance of political and legal equality, and if we add to this Rousseau's theoretical demolition of any claim to the alleged right to own human beings as property, then we can see in Brown's holy war against slavery an act that does indeed resonate with the spirit of the founding movement. . . .

Significantly, Brown made one major attempt to assume the mantle of legislator. The provisional constitution that was drafted and signed at the antislavery convention in Chatham, Ontario, was intended to provide the foundations for the new society that Brown envisioned establishing in the South after his successful liberation of the slaves and, as such, emulates the type of effort associated with a founder-legislator. In the Chatham document, Brown once again shares something in common with Lincoln in the latter's reaffirmation of the first principles established within the Declaration of Independence. Brown included in the Chatham document a statement that his provisional constitution was not meant to dissolve the federal constitution, but only to reaffirm the principles of the American Revolution through amendment and modification. The banner of the Spirit of '76 was to serve as the flag of the provisional government, thus echoing Lincoln's belief that the true founding of the nation began in the struggle for liberty and equality during the Revolution. In addition to the expression of higher political ideals, Brown also provided plans for framing a new government for the freed slaves and their allies, a proposed political system that, to many, was original and revolutionary. The Brown document departed dramatically from all previous constitutional examples because of such features as a supreme court that was to be elected by the widest possible popular vote; government officials who were "to serve without pay" and be removed and punished upon misconduct; extensive public reclamation of all property that was formerly acquired at the expense of the slaves; protection of female prisoners from violation; and plans for the "moral instruction" of the new citizens. Here again, Brown comes close to Rousseau's concept of the founder: a lawgiver who attempts to make human nature anew, one who is committed through law more than through force to the moral elevation of the human spirit. This is an example of Brown designing a more democratic government aimed toward human advancement and intended to restore the principles of the original American founding. . . . Brown's actions at Chatham are also similar to the steps taken at the convention of 1776, and once his supporters had signed the document, Brown felt prepared to enter the field of battle, knowing that his deeds were formally supported by written principles and political ideals as well as by his steadfast religious faith. At Chatham, Brown exchanged arms for pen and ink and, like Jefferson and Madison, attempted to establish a new order for humanity through law. . . .

In turning back to Harpers Ferry, we must also raise the following question: Why weren't more people of conscience moved to arms, as was John Brown? This can be partially explained by the close connection between abolition and nonviolent moral suasion, as in the case of William Lloyd Garrison and the Transcendentalists, but that connection notwithstanding, it is still remarkable that, after conceding the pacifism of most free opponents of slavery, we cannot remember another case that resembles or emulates the Harpers Ferry raid. This might be the best evidence on behalf of the case for Brown as founder, for his was an act consistent both with the tenets of scripture and with the political principles of the polity within which he lived. It was committed out of the purest motivations, it was directed to the achievement of the goal of purging the pathology responsible for the republic's social and cultural ills, and it anticipated the violent methods in which slavery was finally abolished. John Brown acted from high principles against evil, and while his methods were decidedly flawed, the moral necessity of his act of resistance remains evident. Although Brown's raid on Harpers Ferry was ultimately unsuccessful, he exemplifies the true spirit of just liberty; and while he contributed neither new law to support democracy nor any new concept to develop the idea of freedom, his deeds accelerated its progress. Thomas Jefferson proclaimed the egalitarian creed when he drafted the Declaration, but he was unable to renounce his own status as master or overcome his idiosyncratic ideas about racial difference. Abraham Lincoln sincerely and eloquently reaffirmed this creed on a higher and more authentically universal level at Gettysburg, but he was unable to act immediately and abolish the pernicious institution. John Brown, however, perhaps more than any founder since Thomas Paine, fully incorporated the creed into his actions and lived the idea of equality and racial friendship with unparalleled purity and ardor. John Brown compels us to think of him as a founder—one who, unlike Jefferson and Lincoln, appears to live and act on the fringes of society, but one who, on closer examination, springs from its very center.

Measuring the character and relevance of any historical figure is a task that lends itself to a certain degree of ambiguity. Figures such as Jefferson, Lincoln, and King have all been assessed differently by their champions and critics, and interpretations of their character and descriptions of their heroism as well as their lesser acts have all undergone continual redefinition. Yet they remain, for us, heroes all the same, for in spite of any inadequacies, they reflect the perpetual quest for the affirmation of higher political principle and remain among the great movers who helped shape the conscience and the development of the republic.

John Brown differs from these men because he shaped nothing tangible, at least nothing that we can point to today as the direct creation of his actions or product of his influence. However, he is similar to them because he represents the pursuit of high ideas consistent with action. In some aspects, John Brown is more relevant than they, for in his perpetually frustrated zeal for freedom and justice, he embodies the core of the American story; we see in the growth of the nation writ large the same constant buffeting between the idea of freedom and the reality of its interminable frustration that created a similar tension in the turbulent psyche of the Osawatomie Prophet. That tension was felt by the Sage of Monticello and was manifested in the visage of the Melancholy President, but it was *incarnate* in John Brown, and through that incarnation, the hope and dread of the American soul became flesh.

If some can embrace as a great hero the figure of Robert E. Lee, the defender of a commonwealth that included slavery as an accepted institution, then is it implausible to recognize heroism in the more astonishing figure of Brown? Lee never supported secession until the deed was committed, yet he chose to renounce his commission and past loyalties after years of distinction under arms only in order to side with his state. Other distinguished Southern warriors, such as David Farragut of Tennessee and Winfield Scott, Lee's fellow Virginian, went with the North, but Lee reluctantly followed the Old Dominion into the Confederacy. Is it fair to say that whereas Lee chose his homeland, Brown chose humanity? To his credit, Lee worried over the possibility of siding against his family and friends, thus exhibiting a tenderness for his communal roots and native land that is not as evident in Brown, so is it fair to argue that Lee chose to defend the hearth while Brown chose to fight for an abstraction? Whose abstraction is more meaningful: Lee's insistence on abiding with Virginia right or wrong or Brown's devotion to a people sealed in bondage? We must bear in mind that, in spite of his protestations, Lee owned slaves, and his wife owned even more than he did. Regardless of the answer to these questions, popular history has made its judgments, and Lee is known (by most) today as a gentleman warrior,

acting from duty and on principle, while Brown is considered (by many) as the guerrilla fanatic, blinded by undignified zeal and without honor. But we must ask which of the two acted on the higher principle, which violated the greater law, which one carries more blood on his hands, and who between them is a more genuinely American hero? If it is madness to conduct a private, unruly, and suicidal war against an enemy that one perceives as the very cause of sinful oppression, then what state of mind could cause a man of principle to lead thousands into death out of questionable loyalty to a political system that acknowledges oppression as a venerable institution? Who acted on the real spirit of liberty as expressed in the motto *Sic semper tyrannis?* Without intending to detract from the achievement of either man, it is still instructive to compare the actions and motivations of these past contemporaries, one widely deemed a hero, the other, quite often, a villain. At Harpers Ferry, these two men of different principles fatally met, and it is primarily on principle that their legacies stand before us today.

If we are to judge heroes on the principles that they attempt to advance, then we must develop a more comprehensive sense of the value and purity of those ideals that stir one to action. By any measure, John Brown represents the more startling manifestation of the murky dynamics that course within the continual process of the unfolding and founding of America's first principles; thus, he represents an individual of heroic, if still frightening, proportions who speaks powerfully to us today as we continue to confront our higher purposes as a political culture and democratic nation. Perhaps for this reason he is the most typical founder of all: the most consistently idealistic, the most existentially frustrated, the most American.

SCOTT JOHN HAMMOND is a professor of political science at James Madison University where he specializes in political philosophy. He is the author of *Political Theory: An Encyclopedia of Contemporary and Classic Terms* (Greenwood, 2008) and co-author of *Encyclopedia of Presidential Campaigns, Slogans, Issues, and Platforms* (Greenwood, 2008).

EXPLORING THE ISSUE

Was John Brown an Irrational Terrorist?

Critical Thinking and Reflection

1. Is it more appropriate to characterize John Brown as a domestic terrorist or a martyr? Explain.
2. What are the three main concepts that terrorists use to justify their actions? Did John Brown adhere to those concepts?
3. Is there a distinction to be drawn between Brown's antislavery activities in Kansas and his leadership of the raid on the federal arsenal at Harpers Ferry?
4. Is it legitimate to liken John Brown to Machiavelli's "prophet-warrior" and/or to Rousseau's "founder-legislator"?
5. Was Brown making "just war" on the institution of slavery?

Is There Common Ground?

Is John Brown representative of all abolitionists? While all of the abolitionists condemned the institution of slavery, few if any matched the behavior of John Brown. Some, like Garrison, used rhetorical or symbolic violence when speaking or writing of the immorality of the slave system in the United States. But burning copies of the Constitution of the United States was a far cry from executing proslavery settlers in Kansas or waging armed battle with local citizens and state troops in Virginia. But is such activity so different from American colonists waging war to free themselves from the bondage of an imperial power?

It is also important to remind ourselves that not all abolitionists agreed as to how best to attack the foundation of slavery in America. Some, like Garrison, took a moral suasionist approach that made no room for political action; others insisted that political involvement was essential in lobbying for the elimination of slavery. Most African American abolitionists, with the significant exception of Frederick Douglass who remained loyal to Garrison for a while longer, followed the political activists led by Theodore Dwight Weld and Arthur and Lewis Tappan. And as a group they tended to steer clear of John Brown. What does this suggest about the "radicalism" of abolitionists in general, whether black or white?

Create Central

www.mhhe.com/createcentral

Additional Resources

Henry Mayer, *All on Fire: William Lloyd Garrison and the Abolition of Slavery* (St. Martin's, 1998)

Richard S. Newman, *The Transformation of American Abolitionism: Fighting Slavery in the Early Republic* (University of North Carolina Press, 2002)

Merrill D. Peterson, *John Brown: The Legend Revisited* (University of Virginia Press, 2002)

David S. Reynolds, *John Brown, Abolitionist: The Man Who Killed Slavery, Sparked the Civil War, and Seeded Civil Rights* (Alfred A. Knopf, 2005)

John Stauffer, *The Black Hearts of Men: Radical Abolitionists and the Transformation of Race* (Harvard University Press, 2002)

Internet References . . .

Abolitionist Movement

www.history.com/topics/abolitionist-movement

John Brown-Harpers Ferry

www.nps.gov/hafe/historyculture/john-brown.htm

John Brown's Holy War

www.pbs.org/wgbh/amex/brown

The African-American Mosaic

www.loc.gov/exhibits/african/afam005.html

The Trial of John Brown

http://law2.umkc.edu/faculty/projects/ftrials/johnbrown/brownhome.html

Unit 4

UNIT

Conflict and Resolution

*T*he demand that the United States adhere to its principles of freedom and democracy and eradicate the evil of slavery finally erupted into violent conflict. Perhaps it was an inevitable step in the process of building a coherent nation from a number of distinct and diverse groups. The leaders, attitudes, and resources available to the North and the South were to determine the course of the war itself.

As part of the healing process that followed, most Americans concluded that the restoration of the Union superseded all local interests. Not all of the tensions generated by the war or by almost 300 years of political, economic, and social development had been resolved, but the framework had been established to secure a continuing commitment to the rights of citizenship in the American republic.

Selected, Edited, and with Issue Framing Material by:
Larry Madaras, *Howard Community College*
and
James M. SoRelle, *Baylor University*

ISSUE

Was the Civil War Fought Over Slavery?

YES: Charles B. Dew, from *Apostles of Disunion: Southern Secession Commissioners and the Causes of the Civil War* (University of Virginia Press, 2001)

NO: Gary W. Gallagher, from *The Union War* (Harvard University Press, 2012)

Learning Outcomes

After reading this issue, you will be able to:

- Describe the process used in the South to gain support for secession.
- Understand that white southerners were not of one mind when it came to the decision to leave the Union.
- Evaluate the major reason(s) why Union soldiers fought the Civil War.
- Evaluate Union soldiers' attitudes toward the South, secession, and slavery.
- Analyze the extent to which race and slavery were the keys to the sectional conflict leading to the American Civil War.

ISSUE SUMMARY

YES: Charles B. Dew uses the speeches and public letters of 41 white southerners who, as commissioners in 1860 and 1861, attempted to secure support for secession by appealing to their audiences' commitment to the preservation of slavery and the doctrine of white supremacy.

NO: According to Gary W. Gallagher, the letters of white northern soldiers during the Civil War reveal a limited concern about the institution of slavery and an often open hostility toward the use of African American troops that reinforces the conclusion that their main motivation was saving the Union.

I n April 1861, less than a month after his inauguration, President Abraham Lincoln attempted to send provisions to Fort Sumter in South Carolina, part of the newly formed Confederate States of America. Southern troops under the command of General P. G. T. Beauregard opened fire on the fort, forcing its surrender on April 1. The American Civil War had begun.

Numerous explanations have been offered for the cause of this "war between the states." Many contemporaries and some historians saw the conflict as the product of a conspiracy housed either in the North or South, depending upon one's regional perspective. For many in the northern states, the chief culprits were the planters and their political allies who were willing to defend southern institutions at all costs. South of the Mason-Dixon line, blame was laid at the feet of the fanatical abolitionists, like John Brown, and the free-soil architects of the Republican Party. Some viewed the secession and war as the consequence of a constitutional struggle between states' rights

advocates and defenders of the U.S. federal government, whereas others focused upon the economic rivalries or the cultural differences between North and South. Embedded in each of these interpretations, however, is the powerful influence of the institution of slavery.

In the 85 years between the start of the American Revolution and the coming of the Civil War, Americans made the necessary political compromises on the slavery issue in order not to split the nation apart. The Northwest Ordinance of 1787 forbade slavery from spreading into those designated territories under its control, and the new Constitution written in the same year held out the possibility that the Atlantic slave trade would be prohibited after 1808.

There was some hope in the early nineteenth century that slavery might die from natural causes. The Revolutionary generation was well aware of the contradiction between the values of an egalitarian society and the practices of a slaveholding aristocracy. Philosophically, slavery was viewed as a necessary evil, not a positive good.

The northern states were well on their way to abolishing slavery by 1800, and the erosion of the tobacco lands in Virginia and Maryland contributed to the lessening importance of a slave labor system.

Unfortunately, two factors—territorial expansion and the market economy—made slavery the key to the South's wealth in the 35 years before the Civil War. First, new slave states were created out of a population expanding into lands ceded to the United States as a result of the Treaty of Paris of 1783 and the Louisiana Purchase of 1803. Second, slaves were sold from the upper to the lower regions of the South because the invention of the cotton gin made it possible to harvest large quantities of cotton, ship it to the textile mills in New England and the British Isles, and turn it into cloth and finished clothing as part of the new, specialized market economy.

The slavery issue came to the forefront in 1820 when some northern congressmen proposed that slavery be banned from the states being carved out of the Louisiana Purchase. A heated debate ensued, but the Missouri Compromise drew a line that preserved the balance between free and slave states and that (with the exception of Missouri) prohibited slavery north of the 36° 30' latitude.

The annexation of Texas in 1845 and the acquisition of New Mexico, Utah, and California, as a result of the Mexican-American War (see Issue 12), reopened the slavery question. Attempts at compromises in 1850 and 1854 only accelerated the conflict. The Kansas-Nebraska Act of 1854, which repealed the Missouri Compromise, allowed citizens in the new territories to decide whether or not they wanted slavery on the basis of the doctrine of popular sovereignty. As the second party system of Whigs and Democrats fell apart, the Republican Party, whose members hoped to confine slavery to existing slave states, mounted a successful challenge against the Democrats and in 1860 elected Abraham Lincoln as president of the United States, a result that 11 slaveholding states in the South refused to accept. In *America in 1857: A Nation on the Brink* (Oxford University Press, 1990), Kenneth M. Stampp argues that conflict became inevitable after the election of James Buchanan (not Lincoln) to the presidency, the continuing firestorm in Kansas, and the Supreme Court's decision in *Dred Scott*. Eric Foner, who has written extensively on the influence of the free soil ideology and its impact on the coming of the Civil War in such works as *Free Soil, Free Labor, Free Men: The Ideology of the Republican Party Before the Civil War* (Oxford University Press, 1970), also points out that the argument for states' rights as an explanation for the cause of the war is largely a product of the post–Civil War era and, hence, more or less an afterthought on the part of southerners who hoped to distance themselves from the institution of slavery that dominated their region in the antebellum period.

A challenge to the belief that slavery was the sole cause of the war can be found in the works of Joel Silbey. In "The Civil War Synthesis in American Political History," *Civil War History* (June 1964); *The Partisan Imperative: The Dynamics of American Politics Before the Civil War* (Oxford University Press, 1985); and *Party Over Section: The Rough and Ready Presidential Election of 1848* (University Press of Kansas, 2009), Silbey argues that historians, by positioning slavery as the major issue that divided the United States, have distorted "the reality of American political life between 1844 and 1861." Silbey is one of the "new political historians" who have applied the techniques of modern-day political scientists in analyzing the election returns and voting patterns of Americans' nineteenth- and early twentieth-century predecessors. These historians use computers and regression analysis of voting patterns, favor a quantitative analysis of past behavior, and reject the traditional sources of quotations from partisan newspapers and major politicians because these sources provide anecdotal and often misleading portraits of our past. Silbey and other new political historians maintain that all politics are local. Therefore, the primary issues for voters and their politicians in the 1860 election were ethnic and cultural, and party loyalty was more important than sectional considerations.

Another approach is presented by Michael F. Holt in *The Political Crisis of the 1850s* (John Wiley & Sons, 1978). Holt also is interested in analyzing the struggles for power at the state and local levels by the major political parties, but he is critical of the ethnocultural school represented by Silbey. In Holt's view, Silbey's emphasis on voter analysis does not explain why the Whig Party disappeared, nor why the Republican Party became the majority party in the northern and western states in the 1850s. Holt also rejects the more traditional view that the Civil War resulted from the "intensifying sectional disagreements over slavery." Instead, he promotes a more complicated picture of the events leading to the Civil War. Between 1845 and 1860, he maintains, three important things happened: (1) the breakdown of the Whig Party; (2) the realignment of voters; and (3) "a shift from a nationally balanced party system where both major parties competed on fairly even terms in all parts of the nation to a sectionalized polarized one with Republicans dominant in the North and Democrats in the South."

More recently, Gary W. Gallagher has challenged several of the interpretations of modern scholars of the era of the Civil War. His book *The Confederate War* (Harvard University Press, 1997), for example, attacked historians of the Confederacy for attributing the loss of the Civil War to class divisions between planters and non-planters or religious guilt over slave ownership. Gallagher reverts back to older interpretations which maintain that the North had the larger military forces and an industrial base which the South could not match. He marveled that southerners fought for national pride and kept the war going for four years.

In the following essays, Charles B. Dew makes a very powerful argument challenging the neo-Confederate insistence that the decision to secede was driven by the U.S. federal government's abuse of states' rights. Whose attitudes would provide a better window into the thinking of white southerners on the eve of the Civil War than those individuals commissioned to travel throughout the region to drum up support for secession?

Gary W. Gallagher takes issue with a number of scholars who grew up in the midst of the 1960s civil rights era for overemphasizing the slavery issue as the primary cause that the war was fought. At the same time, Gallagher accuses modern scholars of downplaying nationalism as the primary reason for fighting the war. Based on his examination of the letters of 350 Union soldiers, their patriotic envelopes, and the contemporary regimental histories, Gallagher sees soldiers expressing their patriotic feelings about democracy and the freedom to express one's opinions, as well as the more basic goal of earning enough money to live a comfortable life.

YES

Charles B. Dew

Apostles of Disunion: Southern Secession Commissioners and the Causes of the Civil War

Slavery, States' Rights, and Secession Commissioners

"The Civil War was fought over what important issue?" So reads one of twenty questions on an exam administered by the Immigration and Naturalization Service to prospective American citizens. According to the INS, you are correct if you offer either one of the following answers: "Slavery or states rights."

It is reassuring to know that the INS has a flexible approach to one of the critical questions in American history, but one might ask how the single "issue" raised in the question can have an either/or answer in this instance—the only time such an option occurs on the test. Beyond that, some might want to know whether "slavery" or "states rights" is the more correct answer. But it is probably unfair to chide the test preparers at the INS for trying to fudge the issue. Their uncertainty reflects the deep division and profound ambivalence in contemporary American culture over the origins of the Civil War. One hundred and forty years after the beginning of that fratricidal conflict, neither the public nor the scholarly community has reached anything approaching a consensus as to what caused the bloodiest four years in this country's history. . . .

There is, however, a remarkably clear window into the secessionist mind that has been largely ignored by students of this era. If we want to know what role slavery may or may not have played in the coming of the Civil War, there is no better place to look than in the speeches and letters of the men who served their states as secession commissioners on the eve of the conflict.

As sectional tension mounted in late 1860 and early 1861, five states of the lower South—Mississippi, Alabama, South Carolina, Georgia, and Louisiana—appointed commissioners to other slave states and instructed them to spread the secessionist message across the entire region. These commissioners often explained in detail why their states were exiting the Union, and they did everything in their power to persuade laggard slave states to join the secessionist cause. From December 1860 to April 1861, they carried the *gospel of disunion* to the far corners of the South.

The overwhelming majority of the commissioners came from the four Deep South states of Mississippi, Alabama, South Carolina, and Georgia. In Mississippi and Alabama the commissioners were appointed by the governor and thus took the field first. In South Carolina, Georgia, and Louisiana, the secession conventions chose the commissioners.

The number of men sent on this vital mission varied from state to state. Mississippi and Alabama named commissioners to every one of the fourteen other slave states. South Carolina, however, only appointed commissioners to those states which had announced they were calling secession conventions, so only nine representatives eventually went out from the cradle of the secession movement—to Alabama, Mississippi, Georgia, Florida, Louisiana, Texas, Arkansas, Virginia, and North Carolina. Georgia dispatched commissioners to six of these same states—Alabama, Louisiana, Texas, Arkansas, North Carolina, and Virginia—and added the border slave states of Maryland, Delaware, Kentucky, and Missouri to the list. The Louisiana Convention appointed a single commissioner, to neighboring Texas, and he did not arrive in Austin until well after the Texas Convention had passed its ordinance of secession.

In all, some fifty-two men served as secession commissioners in the critical weeks just before the Civil War. These individuals were not, by and large, the famous names of antebellum Southern politics. They were often relatively obscure figures—judges, lawyers, doctors, newspaper editors, planters, and farmers—who had had modest political careers but who possessed a reputation for oratory. Sometimes they were better known—ex-governors or state attorney generals or members of Congress. Often they had been born in the states to which they were sent; place of birth was clearly an important factor in the choice of a number of commissioners.

The commissioners appeared in a host of different venues. They addressed state legislatures, they spoke before state conventions called to consider the question of secession, they took the platform before crowds in meeting halls and in the streets, and they wrote letters to governors whose legislatures were not in session. To a man, what they had to say was, and remains, exceedingly instructive and highly illuminating.

Despite their enormous value, the commissioners' speeches and letters have been almost completely overlooked by historians and, as a consequence, by the public at large. This scholarly neglect is difficult to understand. Contemporaries in both North and South paid close attention to the commissioners' movements and what they had to say. Many of their speeches were reprinted in full in newspapers and official state publications, and several appeared in pamphlet form and apparently gained wide circulation. Accounts of the secession crisis published during and just after the war also devoted considerable space to their activities. In the late nineteenth century when editors at the War Department were assembling a documentary record of the Civil War, they included extensive coverage of the commissioners in the volume dealing with the onset of the conflict—a clear indication that they considered these men to be key players in the sequence of events leading up to the war.

Dwight Lowell Dumond highlighted the importance of the commissioners in his 1931 study of the secession movement, a book that remains the most detailed scholarly treatment of this subject. He described the commissioners' words as extraordinarily important and revealing. "From the speeches and writings of the commissioners, as nowhere else, one may realize the depth of feeling and the lack of sympathy between the two sections of the country," Dumond wrote. "Vividly denunciatory of a party pledged to the destruction of Southern institutions, almost tragic in their prophetic tone, and pleading for a unity of allied interests, they constitute one of the most interesting series of documents in American history," he went on to say.

Yet Professor Dumond's book provides little detailed coverage of what these men actually said, and that pattern has persisted in the torrent of literature on the Civil War that has appeared in subsequent decades. As Jon L. Wakelyn notes in his recent *Southern Pamphlets on Secession,* "No adequate study of the Lower South delegates sent to the Upper South exists," and that same observation could be made about the commissioners who addressed their remarks to fellow Southerners in the states of the Deep South as well. Indeed, Professor Wakelyn does not include the full text of a single commissioner's speech in his otherwise superb collection of pamphlet literature, even though, in my opinion, several of the addresses published in pamphlet form are among the most powerful and revealing expressions of the secessionist persuasion put to paper on the eve of the war.

I have managed to locate the full texts or detailed synopses of forty-one of the commissioners' speeches and public letters. It is, as Professor Dumond suggested, a truly remarkable set of documents. What is most striking about them is their amazing openness and frankness. The commissioners' words convey an unmistakable impression of candor, of white Southerners talking to fellow Southerners with no need to hold back out of deference to outside sensibilities. These men infused their speeches and letters with emotion, with passion, and with a powerful "Let's cut to the chase" analysis that reveals, better than any other sources I know, what was really driving the Deep South states toward disunion.

The explanations the commissioners offered and the arguments the commissioners made, in short, provide us with extraordinary insight into the secession of the lower South in 1860–61. And by helping us to understand the "why" of secession, these apostles of disunion have gone a long way toward answering that all-important question, "The Civil War was fought over what important issue?" . . .

John Smith Preston spent the war years in uniform. After serving in a number of different staff positions in the army, he found a home in the Confederate Bureau of Conscription. He took over that agency in 1863, was promoted to the rank of brigadier general in 1864, and headed the Conscript Bureau until the South went down to defeat. Preston lived for a time in England after the war, but in 1868 he went back to South Carolina. His reputation as an orator still intact, Preston was invited to return to his native state in 1868 to address the Washington and Jefferson Societies of the University of Virginia. On June 30 of that year, Preston spoke in Charlottesville to the young Virginians.

Much of his address was an eloquent tribute to the Founding Fathers and their principal handiwork—the Revolution, the state constitutions, and the Constitution of the United States. Through their efforts "your fathers achieved that liberty which comes of a free government, founded on justice, order and peace," Preston said. In order to preserve the principles and the constitutional forms established by the Revolutionary generation, "you, the immediate offspring of the founders, went forth to that death grapple which has prevailed against you," he continued. It was the North, "the victors," who rejected "the principles," destroyed "the forms," and defeated "the promised destiny of America," Preston charged. "The Constitution you fought for"—the Confederate Constitution—"embodied every principle of the Constitution of the United States, and guaranteed the free Constitution of Virginia. It did not omit one essential for liberty and the public welfare," he claimed. The Confederacy was in ashes, however, and so was true constitutional liberty. "That liberty was lost, and now the loud hosanna is shouted over land and sea—'Liberty may be dead, but the Union is preserved. Glory, glory, glory to Massachusetts and her Hessian and Milesian mercenaries,'" Preston declaimed. Yet all was not lost. Even though "cruel, bloody, remorseless tyrants may rule at Fort Sumter and at Richmond . . . they cannot crush that immortal hope, which rises from the blood soaked earth of Virginia," Preston believed. "I see the sacred image of regenerate Virginia, and cry aloud, in the hearing of a God of Right, and in the hearing of all the nations of the earth—ALL HAIL OUR MOTHER."

Passionate, unregenerate, unapologetic, unreconstructed—all these and more apply to Preston's remarks on this occasion. But so do words like "conveniently forgetful," "strongly revisionist," and "purposely misleading." Nowhere to be found are references to many of the arguments and descriptions he had used over and over again before the Virginia Convention in February 1861—things like "the subject race . . . rising and murdering their masters" or "the conflict between slavery and non-slavery is a conflict for life and death," or his insistence that "the South cannot exist without African slavery," or his portrait of the "fermenting millions" of the North as "canting, fanatics, festering in the licentiousness of abolition and amalgamation." All this was swept aside as Preston sought to paint the Civil War as a mighty struggle over differing concepts of constitutional liberty. Like Jefferson Davis and Alexander H. Stephens in their postwar writings, Preston was trying to reframe the causes of the conflict in terms that would be much more favorable to the South.

Preston was not the only former secession commissioner to launch such an effort after the war. Jabez L. M. Curry, who had served as Alabama's commissioner to Maryland in December 1860, became a leading figure in the drive to improve primary and secondary education in the postwar South. As agent for both the Peabody and Slater Funds and as supervising director of the Southern Education Board, Curry worked tirelessly to establish public schools and teacher training for both races in the states of the former Confederacy. Curry also worked diligently to justify the Lost Cause of the Confederacy. In his *Civil History of the Government of the Confederate States, with Some Personal Reminiscences,* published in Richmond in 1901, Curry offered an analysis of the coming of the war that closely paralleled the argument used by John S. Preston in 1868. "The object in quitting the Union was not to destroy, but to save the principles of the Constitution," Curry wrote. "The Southern States from the beginning of the government had striven to keep it within the orbit prescribed by the Constitution and failed." The Curry of 1901 would hardly have recognized the Curry of 1860, who told the governor of Maryland that secession meant "deliverance from Abolition domination," and who predicted that under Republican rule the South's slave-based social system would "be assaulted, humbled, dwarfed, degraded, and finally crushed out."

In 1860 and 1861 Preston, Curry, and the other commissioners had seen a horrific future facing their region within the confines of Abraham Lincoln's Union. When they used words like "submission" and "degradation," when they referred to "final subjugation" and "annihilation," they were not talking about constitutional differences or political arguments. They were talking about the dawning of an abominable new world in the South, a world created by the Republican destruction of the institution of slavery.

The secession commissioners knew what this new and hateful world would look like. Over and over again they called up three stark images that, taken together, constituted the white South's worst nightmare.

The first threat was the looming specter of racial equality. The commissioners insisted almost to a man that Republican ascendancy in Washington placed white supremacy in the South in mortal peril. Mississippi commissioner William L. Harris made this point clearly and unambiguously in his speech to the Georgia legislature in December 1860. "Our fathers made this a government for the white man," Harris told the Georgians, "rejecting the negro, as an ignorant, inferior, barbarian race, incapable of self-government, and not, therefore, entitled to be associated with the white man upon terms of civil, political, or social equality." But the Republicans intended "to overturn and strike down this great feature of our Union . . . and to substitute in its stead their new theory of the universal equality of the black and white races." Alabama's commissioners to North Carolina, Isham W. Garrott and Robert H. Smith, predicted that the white children of their state would "be compelled to flee from the land of their birth, and from the slaves their parents have toiled to acquire as an inheritance for them, or to submit to the degradation of being reduced to an equality with them, and all its attendant horrors." South Carolina's John McQueen warned the Texas Convention that Lincoln and the Republicans were bent upon "the abolition of slavery upon this continent and the elevation of our own slaves to an equality with ourselves and our children." And so it went, as commissioner after commissioner—Leonidas Spratt of South Carolina, David Clopton and Arthur F. Hopkins of Alabama, Henry L. Benning of Georgia—hammered home this same point.

The impending imposition of racial equality informed the speeches of other commissioners as well. Thomas J. Wharton, Mississippi's attorney general and that state's commissioner to Tennessee, said in Nashville on January 8, 1861, that the Republican Party would, "at no distant day, inaugurate the reign of equality of all races and colors, and the universality of the elective franchise." Commissioner Samuel L. Hall of Georgia told the North Carolina legislature on February 13, 1861, that only a people "dead to all sense of virtue and dignity" would embrace the Republican doctrine of "the social and political equality of the black and white races." Another Georgia commissioner, Luther J. Glenn of Atlanta, made the same point to the Missouri legislature on March 2, 1861. The Republican platform, press, and principal spokesmen had made their "purposes, objects, and motives" crystal clear, Glenn insisted: "hostility to the South, the extinction of slavery, and the ultimate elevation of the negro to civil, political and social equality with the white man." These reasons and these reasons alone had prompted his state "to dissolve her connexion with the General Government," Glenn insisted.

The second element in the commissioners' prophecy was the prospect of a race war. Mississippi commissioner Alexander H. Handy raised this threat in his Baltimore speech in December 1860—Republican agents infiltrating the South "to excite the slave to cut the throat of his master." Alabamians Garrott and Smith told their Raleigh audience that Republican policies would force the South either to abandon slavery "or be doomed to a servile war." William Cooper, Alabama's commissioner to Missouri, delivered a similar message in Jefferson City. "Under the policy of the Republican party, the time would arrive when the scenes of San Domingo and Hayti, with all their attendant horrors, would be enacted in the slave-holding States," he told the Missourians. David Clopton of Alabama wrote the governor of Delaware that Republican ascendancy "endangers instead of insuring domestic tranquility by the possession of channels through which to circulate insurrectionary documents and disseminate insurrectionary sentiments among a hitherto contented servile population." Wharton of Mississippi told the Tennessee legislature that Southerners "will not, cannot surrender our institutions," and that Republican attempts to subvert slavery "will drench the country in blood, and extirpate one or other of the races." In their speeches to the Virginia Convention, Fulton Anderson, Henry L. Benning, and John S. Preston all forecast a Republican-inspired race war that would, as Benning put it, "break out everywhere like hidden fire from the earth."

The third prospect in the commissioners' doomsday vision was, in many ways, the most dire: racial amalgamation. Judge Harris of Mississippi sounded this note in Georgia in December 1860 when he spoke of Republican insistence on "equality in the rights of matrimony." Other commissioners repeated this warning in the weeks that followed. In Virginia, Henry Benning insisted that under Republican-led abolition "our women" would suffer "horrors . . . we cannot contemplate in imagination." There was not an adult present who could not imagine exactly what Benning was talking about. Leroy Pope Walker, Alabama's commissioner to Tennessee and subsequently the first Confederate secretary of war, predicted that in the absence of secession all would be lost—first, "our property," and "then our liberties," and finally the South's greatest treasure, "the sacred purity of our daughters."

No commissioner articulated the racial fears of the secessionists better, or more graphically, than Alabama's Stephen F. Hale. When he wrote of a South facing "amalgamation or extermination," when he referred to "all the horrors of a San Domingo servile insurrection," when he described every white Southerner "degraded to a position of equality with free negroes," when he foresaw the "sons and daughters" of the South "associating with free negroes upon terms of political and social equality," when he spoke of the Lincoln administration consigning the citizens of the South "to assassinations and her wives and daughters to pollution and violation to gratify the lust of half-civilized Africans," he was giving voice to the night terrors of the secessionist South. States' rights, historic political abuses, territorial questions, economic differences, constitutional arguments—all these and more paled into insignificance when placed alongside this vision of the South's future under Republican domination.

The choice was absolutely clear. The slave states could secede and establish their independence, or they could submit to "Black Republican" rule with its inevitable consequences: Armageddon or amalgamation. Whites forced to endure racial equality, race war, a staining of the blood—who could tolerate such things?

The commissioners sent out to spread the secessionist gospel in late 1860 and early 1861 clearly believed that the racial fate of their region was hanging in the balance in the wake of Lincoln's election. Only through disunion could the South be saved from the disastrous effects of Republican principles and Republican malevolence. Hesitation, submission—any course other than immediate secession—would place both slavery and white supremacy on the road to certain extinction. The commissioners were arguing that disunion, even if it meant risking war, was the only way to save the white race.

Did these men really believe these things? Did they honestly think that secession was necessary in order to stay the frenzied hand of the Republican abolitionist, preserve racial purity and racial supremacy, and save their women and children from rape and slaughter at the hands of "half-civilized Africans"? They made these statements, and used the appropriate code words, too many times in too many places with too much fervor and raw emotion to leave much room for doubt. They knew these things in the marrow of their bones, and they destroyed a political union because of what they believed and what they foresaw.

But, we might ask, could they not see the illogicality, indeed the absurdity, of their insistence that Lincoln's election meant that the white South faced the sure prospect of either massive miscegenation or a race war to the finish? They seem to have been totally untroubled by logical inconsistencies of this sort. Indeed, the capacity for compartmentalization among this generation of white Southerners appears to have been practically boundless. How else can we explain Judge William L. Harris's comments before the Mississippi State Agricultural Society in November 1858? "It has been said by an eminent statesman," Harris observed on this occasion, " 'that nothing can advance the mass of society in prosperity and happiness, nothing can uphold the substantial interest and steadily improve the general condition and character of the whole, but this one thing—compensating rewards for labor.' " It apparently never occurred to Harris that this observation might apply to the hundreds of thousands of slaves working in Mississippi in 1858 as well as to the white farmers and mechanics of his adopted state. His mind could not even comprehend the possibility that slaves, too, were human beings who, if given the opportunity, might well respond to "compensating rewards" for their labor.

In setting out to explain secession to their fellow Southerners, the commissioners have explained a very great deal to us as well. By illuminating so clearly the racial content of the secession persuasion, the commissioners would seem to have laid to rest, once and for all, any notion that slavery had nothing to do with the coming of the Civil War. To put it quite simply, slavery and race were absolutely critical elements in the coming of the war. Neo-Confederate groups may have "a problem" with this interpretation, as the leader of the Virginia Heritage Preservation Association put it. But these defenders of the Lost Cause need only read the speeches and letters of the secession commissioners to learn what was really driving the Deep South to the brink of war in 1860–61.

CHARLES B. DEW is the Ephraim Williams Professor of American History at Williams College. Two of his books, *Apostles of Disunion and Ironmaker to the Confederacy: Joseph R. Anderson* and the *Tredegar Iron Works* (Yale University Press, 1966), received the Fletcher Pratt Award presented by the Civil War Round Table of New York for the best nonfiction book on the American Civil War. He is also the author of *Bond of Iron: Master and Slave at Buffalo Forge* (W. W. Norton, 1994), which received the Elliott Rudwick Prize from the Organization of American Historians.

Gary W. Gallagher

The Union War

Introduction

The loyal American citizenry fought a war for Union that also killed slavery. In a conflict that stretched across four years and claimed more than 800,000 U.S. casualties, the nation experienced huge swings of civilian and military morale before crushing Confederate resistance. Union always remained the paramount goal, a fact clearly expressed by Abraham Lincoln in speeches and other statements designed to garner the widest popular support for the war effort. What Walt Whitman said of Lincoln and Union in the wake of the president's assassination applied equally to most loyal Americans. "Unionism, in its truest and amplest sense, form'd the hard-pan of his character," wrote the poet, who defined it as "a new virtue, unknown to other lands, and hardly yet really known here, but the foundation and tie of all, as the future will grandly develop." That hardpan of unionism held millions of Americans to the task of suppressing the slaveholders' rebellion, even as the human and material cost mushroomed. "By many has *this Union* been conserv'd and help'd," continued Whitman's tribute to Lincoln and Union, "but if one name, one man, must be pick'd out, he, most of all, is the Conservator of it, to the future. He was assassinated—but the Union is not assassinated—*ça ira!* One falls, and another falls. The soldier drops, sinks like a wave—but the ranks of the ocean eternally press on. Death does its work, obliterates a hundred, a thousand—President, general, captain, private—but the Nation is immortal."

Whitman celebrated a Union that carried great meaning for the mass of loyal citizens who joined him in equating it with "the Nation." It represented the cherished legacy of the founding generation, a democratic republic with a constitution that guaranteed political liberty and afforded individuals a chance to better themselves economically. From the perspective of loyal Americans, their republic stood as the only hope for democracy in a western world that had fallen more deeply into the stifling embrace of oligarchy since the failed European revolutions of the 1840s. Slaveholding aristocrats who established the Confederacy, believed untold unionists, posed a direct threat not only to the long-term success of the American republic but also to the broader future of democracy. Should armies of citizen-soldiers fail to restore the Union, forces of privilege on both sides of the Atlantic could pronounce ordinary people incapable of self-government and render

irrelevant the military sacrifices and political genius of the Revolutionary fathers. Secretary of State William Henry Seward encapsulated much of this thinking in one sentence pertaining to the Republicans' agenda: "Their great work is the preservation of the Union and in that, the saving of popular government for the world."

Issues related to the institution of slavery precipitated secession and the outbreak of fighting, but the loyal citizenry initially gave little thought to emancipation in their quest to save the Union. By the early summer of 1862, long before black men donned blue uniforms in large numbers, victorious Union armies stood poised to win the war with slavery largely intact. Setbacks on battlefields in Virginia dictated that the bloodletting would continue, however, and as months went by, casualties mounted, and a shortage of manpower loomed, emancipation and African American military service assumed increasing importance. Eventually, most loyal citizens, though profoundly prejudiced by twenty-first-century standards and largely indifferent toward enslaved black people, embraced emancipation as a tool to punish slaveholders, weaken the Confederacy, and protect the Union from future internal strife. A minority of the white populace invoked moral grounds to attack slavery, though their arguments carried less weight than those presenting emancipation as a military measure necessary to defeat the Rebels and restore the Union. African American freedom still seemed problematic in the bloody summer of 1864, when Union armies bogged down in Georgia and Virginia and antiemancipation Democrats looked hopefully toward the November elections. Only striking victories at Atlanta and in the Shenandoah Valley in September and October retrieved the situation, setting up Lincoln's reelection and guaranteeing that slavery's extinction would be a nonnegotiable condition for peace.

Union armies composed of citizen-soldiers occupied a central position in the grand drama. Their hard and costly service salvaged the Union and, more than any other factor, made possible emancipation. They functioned as the most powerful national symbol and unifying institution, bringing together men from all over the country regardless of political affiliation. In a conflict marked by deep divisions within the loyal states, they represented self-sacrifice reminiscent of the Continental soldiers who had followed George Washington. They confirmed notions of American exceptionalism based on a long-standing antipathy toward professional soldiers and large standing armies. Observers who watched 150,000 veterans parade down Pennsylvania Avenue in the Grand Review at the end of the war gloried in the fact that the men soon would be on their way home—citizens who had performed their civic duty with the expectation of returning to civilian pursuits as soon as the Rebels capitulated. The wartime generation viewed surviving veterans and the Union dead—300,000 of the latter reinterred in national cemeteries established soon after Appomattox—as honored reminders of a free society's reliance on citizen-soldiers.

This book seeks to recover what Union meant to the generation that fought the war. That meaning has been almost completely effaced from popular understanding of the conflict; indeed, "Union" as defined in a political sense in the nineteenth century has disappeared from our vocabulary. Students and adults interested in the Civil War are reluctant to believe that anyone would risk life or fortune for something as abstract as "the Union." A war to end slavery seems more compelling, something powerfully reinforced by films such as *Glory*—easily the best of Hollywood's treatments of the conflict—and, *Gettysburg*. Although Lincoln remains a towering figure in the popular imagination, few Americans associate him with the widely held idea of the Union, as he put it in his second annual message to Congress in December 1862, as "the last best, hope of earth." Even within the specialized world of Civil War enthusiasts who purchase prints and other contemporary artworks, the Union and its military idols take a decidedly secondary position behind such Lost Cause icons as Robert E. Lee and "Stonewall" Jackson. Apart from Col. Joshua Lawrence Chamberlain and his 20th Maine Infantry, the Army of the Potomac's famous Irish Brigade, and various commanders and episodes at the battle of Gettysburg, the Union cause scarcely exists in that art. Were it not for Michael Shaara's Pulitzer Prize–winning novel *The Killer Angels*, Ken Burns's documentary *The Civil War*, and the director Ron Maxwell's film version of Shaara's book, even Chamberlain would be largely unknown.

Much Civil War scholarship over the past four decades has diminished the centrality of Union. Slavery, emancipation, and the actions of black people, unfairly marginalized for decades in writings about the conflict, have inspired a huge and rewarding literature since the mid-1960s. No longer can any serious reader fail to appreciate the degree to which African Americans figured in the political, social, and military history of the war. This has been one of the most heartening developments in the field since the great successes of the civil rights movement in the 1950s and 1960s. But the focus on emancipation and race sometimes suggests the war had scant meaning apart from these issues—and especially that the Union victory had little or no value without emancipation.

Historical context is crucial on this point. Anyone remotely conversant with nineteenth-century U.S. history knows that democracy as practiced in 1860 denied women, free and enslaved African Americans, and other groups basic liberties and freedoms most white northerners

routinely attributed to their republic. Almost 99 percent of the residents in the free states were white (96.5 percent in the loyal states, which included slaveholding Missouri, Kentucky, Maryland, and Delaware), and their racial views offend our modern sensibilities. Yet a portrait of the nation that is dominated by racism, exclusion, and oppression obscures more than it reveals. Within the context of the mid-nineteenth-century western world, the United States offered the broadest political franchise and the most economic opportunity. Vast numbers of immigrants believed that however difficult the circumstances they might find, relocation in the United States promised a potentially brighter future. As one Irish-born Union soldier put it in early 1863, "this is my country as much as the man that was born on the soil and so it is with every man who comes to this country and becomes a citezen." If the Union lost the war, he added, "then the hopes of millions fall and. . . . the old cry will be sent forth from the aristocrats of europe that such is the common end of all republics." Without an appreciation of why the loyal citizenry went to great lengths to restore the Union, no accurate understanding of the era is possible.

The Union War focuses on one part of the population in the United States—citizens in the free states and four loyal slaveholding states who opposed secession and supported a war to restore the Union. This group encompassed Republicans as well as the portion of the Democratic Party that stridently opposed emancipation and other policies of the Lincoln administration but remained committed to a war against the rebellion. African American refugees who made their way to Union lines, soldiers in the United States Colored Troops (USCT), and antiwar Democrats or Copperheads receive some attention but remain peripheral to my main line of inquiry. White unionists in the Confederacy fall outside my purview. Many U.S. soldiers, it is important to keep in mind, acted from motives unrelated to unionist or any other ideology, including an indeterminate number of poor men who enlisted primarily for financial reasons. Similarly, some of their fellow citizens on the home front exhibited minimal interest in the war's large issues, hoping for the least possible disruption in the usual rhythms of their daily lives.

By exploiting evidence relating to the substantial majority of the U.S. population that supported a war for Union, this book examines three fundamental questions. What did the war for Union mean in mid-nineteenth-century America? How and why did emancipation come to be part of the war for Union? How did armies of citizen-soldiers figure in conceptions of the war, the process of emancipation, and the shaping of national sentiment? Consideration of these questions proceeds from knowledge that pro-Union support could be grudging, especially as emancipation became more prominent and the central government took unprecedented steps to raise money and find manpower. The Lincoln administration dealt with political fissures, war weariness, apathy, and fluctuating levels of outright hostility to the war. Yet loyal citizens remained steadfast enough to push through to victory, despite far more casualties than in any previous American war and the absence of a direct physical threat from Rebel armies to their homes, farms, businesses, towns, and cities. They did so because they believed to do otherwise would betray the generation who established the Union as well as future Americans who would reap its political and economic benefits.

Although concerned with ideas about nation, this is not a study of the formation of American nationalism. I do not believe a new nation was born amid military upheaval in 1861–1865—though the service of more than 2 million men surely strengthened bonds of nationhood across the free states and to a lesser degree in the Border States except for Kentucky, which so loathed emancipation that it aligned with the defeated Confederacy after Appomattox. Nation building had been in progress for a long time, and an expansionist, democratic republic built on the blueprint of the Constitution and convinced of American exceptionalism had used diplomacy and violence to overspread the continent by mid-century.

Continuity marked loyal citizens' opinions and attitudes between 1860 and the early postwar decades. They routinely deployed "United States," "the Union," "the country" and "the nation" as synonyms. A Republican broadside from the 1864 presidential election perfectly captured this phenomenon, referring to Union, nation, and country in just a few sentences: "CITIZENS OF MICHIGAN! To-day is to be decided whether this Nation *lives, or dies* at the *hands of traitors!* . . . Be sure and vote for the Union, GOVERNMENT, AND COUNTRY. If the Union and government is not maintained, the nation is disgraced before the CIVILIZED WORLD." The citizens who labored to save the Union subscribed to a vision of their nation built on free labor, economic opportunity, and a broad political franchise they considered unique in the world. They believed victory over the slaveholders confirmed the nation, made it stronger in the absence of slavery's pernicious influence, set the stage for the country's continuing growth and vitality, and kept a democratic beacon shining in a world dominated by aristocrats and monarchs. It is this belief that led them into battle and ultimately to victory over the Confederacy. . . .

Although some have placed emancipation at the heart of the presidential election of 1864, soldiers' comments left no doubt that saving the nation, to use General Rosecrans's language, easily trumped killing slavery as a motivation to vote for the Union ticket of Lincoln and Andrew Johnson. Most states permitted their soldiers to vote in the field—though Delaware, Illinois, Indiana, New Jersey, and Oregon did not. Democrats complained vociferously, and perhaps with some merit, that Republicans conspired to suppress the anti-Lincoln military vote. Only twelve states counted soldiers' ballots separately. Those that can be identified favored Lincoln by a margin of 119,754 to 34,291—78 percent compared to 55 percent among the electorate as a whole. For soldiers, votes for

Lincoln ensured that the war would be prosecuted vigorously until Rebels capitulated and the Union prevailed.

Three soldiers from New York, Maine, and Ohio recorded widely held opinions about the election. Edward King Wightman, a Democrat and noncommissioned officer in the 3rd New York Infantry, held "no very great respect" for Lincoln or McClellan and pronounced both parties' platforms "contemptible." He cast a ballot for Lincoln because the "main question seems to be whether we shall continue the war until the rebellion is subdued. "The integrity of the Union could "be restored only by force of arms and . . . such a course is necessary in order to vindicate the honor and establish the power of the Republic." Another noncommissioned officer, Abial Hall Edwards of the 29th Maine Infantry, believed the two parties in 1864 were "Unionists & Dis Unionists and I think as much of a war Democrat as I do of a Lincoln man." The Democratic platform called for a cessation of hostilities short of victory, which would "disgrace the memory of our fallin brothers[.]" Edwards craved peace but would vote for Lincoln, "remain here and if it need be lay down my life before we give up one iota of the victories we have gained to the Rebel hords." After Lincoln's victory, he explained to his future wife, "No Anna I do not desire the war to last 4 years longer. Neither do I want a peace that would disgrace us as a nation." John Marihugh of the 21st Ohio Infantry shared Edwards's sentiments. Deployed to Camp Butler near Springfield, Illinois, he summed up his ideas in one long sentence: "Wall a bout the election I think that Old Abe will be Electid with out mutch truble & if the *Cop[perhead]s* try too make truble down here we shall give them hell & that is whats the mater & I say three chears for Old Abe & the union."

Innumerable letters mirrored Marihugh's dislike of Copperheads and silence about emancipation as an issue in the election of 1864. Major Henry E. Richmond of the 4th New York Heavy Artillery touched on the nation, citizen-soldiers, and Copperheads in letters to his wife. He thought anyone who voted for McClellan would be "aiming a blow at & stabbing our National life to the heart." Pronouncing his military service "the noblest cause that a *loyal* citizen can do—the suppressing of the Rebellion against . . . our country & the best government that God ever vouchsafed to his children," Richmond insisted that "none but a copperhead or traitor" would support the Democrats or embrace peace short of Union victory. He considered any man who cast a ballot against Lincoln "no better than the enemy 100 yds in front, who fires his *bullets at us.*" A second lieutenant in the 76th Ohio Infantry used fewer, though equally inflammatory, words to make the same point. "The peace sneaks of the north should know by this time," wrote Lyman U. Humphrey from near Chattanooga, "that their damnable cause must go down to nothingness and their names be forever damned to eternal infamy." The soldiers "burn indignantly at the doings of the traitors behind us." Asa M. Weston, another Ohioan serving in Georgia, hoped Lincoln would be reelected but worried that men in Kentucky units "will vote for McClellan . . . so much the more willingly I suppose because he suits [Copperhead politician Clement L.] Vallandigham."

Early Union regimentals contain excellent material on emancipation and its consequences—though just more than a third of the sixty-four examined here ignore the end of slavery as a noteworthy outcome of the war. The ideas, arguments, and descriptive narratives published in the conflict's immediate aftermath conform closely to wartime soldiers' testimony about war aims, black military service, and the ways in which racial attitudes affected behavior and political opinions. These opinions regarding emancipation should not obscure the very widely held belief among Union soldiers that slavery had caused the war.

Taken as a group, these regimentals underscore the degree to which emancipation figured in most soldiers' minds primarily as a means to achieve and uphold Union. Four examples from Ohio, New York, and Illinois illustrate this point. Chaplain Thomas M. Stevenson of the 78th Ohio Infantry observed that "to suppress the rebellion without interfering with slavery, is an absurdity which would be only taking the effect and leaving the cause." A restored Union could be safe only with emancipation. No other course would "make a loyal people in the South . . . As well make a mocking-bird out of a moccasin snake, or make the substance of opposite affinities unite." Lincoln understood this, and his proclamation "was the key that turned all our efforts into success, and opened the doors of victory and complete success to our arms." The wartime regimental of the 23rd New York Infantry reprinted a letter about Lincoln's proclamation, which, asserted its author, "does not seem to offend any one in this part of the army." The letter took Benjamin Butler's pronouncement about runaway slaves literally: "It is pretty well settled in these military circles that negroes during the continuance of this war are as clearly contraband as cannon, 'hard tack,' quinine, saltpeter, or mercurial ointment."

Wales Wood, adjutant of the 95th Illinois Infantry, flatly denied that emancipation had been the principal goal of the war. "It was claimed by some people, and there are probably those who still adhere to the opinion," he wrote in the autumn of 1865, "that the war against secession was carried on by the Government from the beginning with the prominent idea on the part of the Administration of abolishing slavery . . . , and that the incipient plan of emancipating the slaves was fully illustrated and carried into practice by the Proclamation of President Lincoln." That interpretation misconstrued the president's intent to offer the proclamation "only as a *war measure* to hurt traitors and kill rebellion." Although emancipation hurt the Rebel military effort, Wood believed the "negro question at all times during the progress of the war, was an annoying subject to military commanders, in endeavoring to carry out the policy of the Government." Wood also mentioned General Frémont's plan to seize slaves of Rebel owners in Missouri as a policy designed to help fight the war for

Union, as did David Lathrop of the 59th Illinois Infantry. "General Fremont was far in advance of the nation's representatives, either in the field or cabinet," asserted Lathrop, "He realized that the only way to stop rebellion was to chastise rebels with the rod of justice."

Ovando J. Hollister of the 1st Colorado Volunteers detailed a lively discussion about emancipation among men in Company I of the 2nd U.S. Dragoons in September 1862. This group, who differed from the vast majority of Union men under arms because they were professional soldiers, "contained representatives of every shade of the idea, from the opposer of slavery on principle, to the tolerator of slavery on the ground of expediency, and the worshiper of slavery from long association and habit." Few Americans embraced fanatical devotion to any idea, mused Hollister, manifesting instead a very practical approach to life. Although motivation to fight the war against Rebels did not spring from a love of *"Liberty for all,"* true patriots "will rejoice that the destruction of chattel slavery in the United States, is an inseparable adjunct of the present upheaval of society." "Adjunct" was the crucial word for these men—though Hollister himself stood ardently against slavery on moral grounds—and set up the summary sentence. "We finally concluded," wrote Hollister with a swipe at slaveholders, "that because slavery is aggressive, if not because it is wrong, we muse necessarily war against it."

Chastising slaveholders through forced emancipation proved widely popular in the units covered by the regimentals. Lieutenant Bartholomew B. S. De Forest, quartermaster of the 81st New York Infantry, developed this theme. He hoped Rebel leaders would be punished severely in the aftermath of a war for "the preservation of our glorious Union." Black soldiers could help achieve that end, which would be complete only if slaveholders who "ruled with the iron hand of despotism" and "sought to perpetuate the institution of Slavery at the sacrifice of a Republican Government" had been utterly vanquished. Once Rebel armies had been dispersed and slavery abolished, "tyranny, that bitter foe of free institutions and humanity," would have been eradicated from American soil.

Regimental historians reached disparate conclusions about black military contributions. Very few perceived USCT regiments as decisive in any major battles, though several expressed admiration for black courage in smaller actions. Almost all welcomed the labor of African American soldiers because it freed white men from the kinds of noncombatant work they detested. A handful endorsed full citizenship for black soldiers based on their military service, though several drew a sharp line between the idea of equality within the wartime military sphere and in postwar society. Prejudice pervaded nearly all of the regimentals—often providing a jarring contrast to even the most appreciative accounts.

The chroniclers of the 117th and 115th New York Infantry acknowledged superior performances by USCT units at Petersburg and Olustee. Surgeon James A. Mowris of the 117th described the costly action outside Petersburg on June 15, 1864, where USCT men made their initial appearance on a big Virginia battlefield. The "brave fellows" had carried the outer line of Rebel works and then assaulted and captured a second line: "These black soldiers, were highly elated, even those who were severely wounded, greeted their white compatriots, with, 'Tell you boys, we made um get;' 'We druv em.'" The episode impressed white observers, noted Mowris with a touch of sarcasm: "Those who were politically the most conservative, suddenly experienced, an accession of respect for the chattel on this discovery of its 'equal' value in a possible emergency." Lieutenant James H. Clark of the 115th, a regiment that suffered heavy casualties at the battle of Olustee, described how one of the USCT regiments in that engagement "formed and maneuvered under fire, and suffered heavy losses." Although their colonel was killed, the black soldiers "preserved their line admirably and fought splendidly."

George W. Powers of the 38th Massachusetts Infantry typified those who found things to praise and criticize about black soldiers in combat. A veteran of operations in Louisiana and Virginia, he wrote in detail about two "native Louisiana regiments" in a skirmish on May 25, 1863, during the Port Hudson campaign. "A great deal of romance has been spoken and printed about this affair," Powers observed, "but, without wishing to detract in the least from the really valuable services rendered by the colored troops during the siege, especially in the engineer's department, it may be doubted if the exaggerated accounts of their bravery were of any real benefit to the 'colored boys in blue.'" Because it long had been fashionable "to decry the courage of the colored man, and deny him all the attributes of manhood, . . . when he proved himself something more than a beast of burden, public opinion went to the opposite extreme" and "asserted that this new freedman was the equal, if not the superior, of the Northern volunteer soldier." White soldiers even heard that General Banks said black soldiers "went where the white ones dared not go." Powers dismissed this as an improbable story that nonetheless "injured the general's popularity, and increased the prejudice already existing against the colored troops." On the night of May 26, Powers added in a short passage that twice damned African American comrades, a black regiment panicked and mistakenly fired a volley toward the 38th Massachusetts, but their aim was so bad "the bullets whistled harmlessly over head, and the panic soon subsided."

In his history of the 9th New Jersey Infantry, Hermann Everts ignored emancipation in the broader sense but inserted one comment critical of black soldiers. The 9th spent a good deal of time in proximity to USCT units, including in the trenches at Petersburg in the summer of 1864. Everts used a record of daily events in preparing the regimental, which included an entry for July 10, 1864, that suggested USCT soldiers lacked basic knowledge expected of veterans: "With the exception of the picket-firing, the night passed quietly. The picket-firing, so annoying, and so very unnecessary in most cases, was generally done by the negroes, as these troops need the sound of cannonballs around their heads and ears to keep their eyes open." Everts's observation accorded with other evidence from the first phase of the siege at Petersburg that suggested many white soldiers even doubted positive reports about the 54th Massachusetts in the assault at Fort Wagner—though some men changed their minds when they witnessed USCT troops overrun Rebel positions on June 15.

Black soldiers also emerged as less than exemplary in Col. W. W. H. Davis's narrative of the 104th Pennsylvania Infantry. Davis discussed the difficulty many white soldiers experienced with the idea of black enlistments, remarking that it took "some time to educate them up to this point." Deployed to South Carolina in early 1863, the 104th saw Col. Thomas Wentworth Higginson's 1st South Carolina Infantry (Union), the initial regiment of former slaves officially sanctioned by the War Department. "These African defenders of our national honor were lounging about camp and shore," recalled Davis with more than a hint of condescension, "clad in their blue dress coats and scarlet breeches. Our men gazed at them with strange interest, as it was the first time they had ever seen negroes equipped as soldiers. This sight carried me back to an earlier period in the history of the war, when arming the negroes to make soldiers of them dared not be talked about aloud." Davis also described how Brig. Gen. William Birney, son of the famous abolitionist James Gillespie Birney, detailed six men from the 104th to cook for a group of contraband laborers. This happened when two black regiments were posted near where the work was to be done and, insisted Davis, arose from Birney's wish "to degrade the white soldiers and insult the regiment . . . Is it then a cause of wonder that he was heartily despised by the white troops?"

The regimentals suggest that white soldiers reached no consensus about the postwar fate of USCT veterans and other freedpeople. Joseph Grecian, who wrote his history of the 83rd Indiana Infantry during the last part of the war, thought they should be educated "so as to be competent to take care and govern themselves. Meanwhile, they will be afforded means of accumulating a sufficient amount of wealth to take them to, and establish themselves in the Old World, from which they were brought, and thus they may become a 'polished shaft' in the hand of Providence to enlighten 'poor dark Africa.'" Lieutenant De Forest of the 81st New York printed a letter that affirmed USCT men "should be recognized as equal with the white soldier, when they are engaged in one common cause." Once a black soldier returned to civilian life, however, and "he lays off the blue jacket, he is a negro still, and should be treated as God designed he should be, as an inferior, with kindness and sympathy, but not as an equal, in a social point of view."

Henry T. Johns, a clerk in the 49th Massachusetts Infantry, presented deeply conflicting ideas about what the war would yield for African Americans. He presented his history in the form of letters to render the text "less didactic and stiff," signing his preface in early May 1864. Johns enthusiastically supported the Emancipation Proclamation and the enlistment of black soldiers, and in early 1863 predicted "Negro equality" but not "social equality" after the war. Talented black men would rise on their merits. Later in his text he envisioned a much bleaker future for freedpeople because they belonged to an inferior race. "Like the Indians," he prophesied, "they will disappear from before us"—perhaps returning to Africa. Yet at the end of the book he gave "all honor to our negro soldiers. They deserve citizenship. They will secure it." There would be much suffering in what he termed "the transition state," but a "nation is not born without pangs." . . .

GARY W. GALLAGHER is the John L. Nau III Professor of History of the American Civil War at the University of Virginia. He is the author of numerous scholarly studies of the Civil War, including *The Confederate War* (Harvard University Press, 1997), *Lee and His Generals in War and Memory* (Louisiana State University Press, 1998), and *Becoming Confederates: Paths to a New National Loyalty* (University of Georgia Press, 2013).

EXPLORING THE ISSUE

Was the Civil War Fought Over Slavery?

Critical Thinking and Reflection

1. What role did southern commissioners play in 1860 and 1861 in drumming up support for secession from the Union?
2. What arguments did southern commissioners make to justify secession?
3. Evaluate the continued support for the Union demonstrated by white southerners in several southern states right up to the time of secession.
4. Analyze the motivations of the Union soldiers for fighting the war.
5. Discuss the attitudes of northern soldiers toward the institution of slavery and the goal of preserving the Union.

Is There Common Ground?

Most historians of the Civil War era recognize the centrality of slavery in the sectional conflict that led ultimately to the secession of 11 southern states by 1861. The institution of slavery was so intricately wound into the fabric of southern society that even those who have insisted that the Civil War was a product of the propaganda of fanatics in either the North or South, blundering politicians, conflicting views of the Constitution of the United States, differences between the northern and southern economies, a conflict of cultures, or debates over majority rule and minority rights must realize how slavery imbedded itself into each of those factors. For those who insist that the debate was about states' rights, it is reasonably clear that the rights the southern states were seeking were the rights to keep the North and the federal government from meddling with the sanctity of the "peculiar institution." Similarly, scholars are hard-pressed to offer an economic explanation without recognizing that the most important economic institution in the South was slavery.

Charles B. Dew argues that the southern secessionist commissioners pushed the southern states into a Civil War in order to preserve the institution of slavery and the ideology of white supremacy. This interpretation is challenged in David Goldfield's recent book *America Aflame: How the Civil War Created a Nation* (Bloomsbury, 2011) which gives a more sympathetic portrait of the white slave owner who was proud of his ancestral heritage and felt himself losing political clout via attacks from abolitionists and northern evangelicals. At the same time, northerners were participating in slavery through their participation in the purchase of cotton goods for their factory.

Another comparison can be made regarding the motivations of the soldiers. Were they fighting to preserve the union and a democratic system that extended political and economic freedoms to its citizens? James McPherson's *For Cause and Comrade: Why Men Fought the Civil War* (Oxford, 1997) provides a variety of viewpoints on the grass-roots soldiers. Gary W. Gallagher finds sentiments toward African American soldiers that would be considered racist by modern standards. Most white soldiers believed that African Americans would make good support troops, serving as ditch diggers, supply officers, cooks, and laundrymen. Gallagher's critics say that the 350 soldiers' letters may not be a representative sample of attitudes. Is it possible that slavery and nationalism became fused together during the war? One may also argue that military necessity rather than human kindness was the main reason for Lincoln's Emancipation Proclamation in January 1863. Nevertheless, the president used all of his political leverage to attain the Thirteenth Amendment in March 1865, which freed the slaves and which passed the House of Representatives by only three votes. This is certainly the conclusion presented to viewers of Stephen Spielberg's recent movie *Lincoln*.

Create Central

www.mhhe.com/createcentral

Additional Resources

Edward L. Ayers, *What Caused the Civil War? Reflections on the South and Southern History* (W. W. Norton, 2005)

Steven A. Canning, *Crisis of Fear: Secession in South Carolina* (Simon & Schuster, 1970)

James Oakes, *Freedom National: The Destruction of Slavery in the United States, 1861–1865* (W. W. Norton, 2012)

Michael Perman, ed., *The Coming of the American Civil War*, 3rd ed. (D. C. Heath, 1993)

David Potter, *The Impending Crisis, 1848–1861* (Harper & Row, 1976)

Internet References . . .

History Detectives: Causes of the Civil War

www.pbs.org/opb/historydetectives/feature/causes
-of-the-civil-war

**The American Civil War Center: The
Causes of the Civil War**

www.tredegar.org/caused-civil-war.aspxhttp://

The Causes of the Civil War

www.historynet.com/causes-of-the-civil-war

The Civil War Home Page

www.civil-war.net/pages/troops_furnished_losses
.html

Selected, Edited, and with Issue Framing Material by:
Larry Madaras, *Howard Community College*
and
James M. SoRelle, *Baylor University*

ISSUE

Are Historians Wrong to Consider the War Between the States a "Total War"?

YES: Mark E. Neely, Jr., from "Was the Civil War a Total War?" *Civil War History* (vol. 50, December 2004)

NO: James M. McPherson, from "From Limited to Total War, Missouri and the Nation, 1861–1865," in *Gateway Heritage; Magazine of the Missouri Historical Society* 1992

Learning Outcomes

After reading this issue, you will be able to:

- Define "total war."
- Distinguish "total war," "unconditional surrender," and "modern war" from earlier types of warfare.
- List arguments for and against the Civil War as a total war and critically analyze the validity of these arguments.

ISSUE SUMMARY

YES: Professor Mark E. Neely, Jr., argues that the Civil War was not a total war because President Lincoln and the Union military leaders, such as General William T. Sherman, respected the distinction between soldiers and civilians, combatants and noncombatants. In addition, the North did not fully mobilize its resources nor engage in centralized planning and state intervention as was typical of twentieth-century wartime economies.

NO: Professor James M. McPherson argues that the Civil War was a total war. While conceding the distinction between combatants and noncombatants, he insists that the war accomplished the abolition of slavery and the extinction of a national state system—the Confederacy.

The confusion around the issue of whether the Civil War was a total war centers around the terms which historians use to describe the conflict. Are the terms "unconditional surrender" and "modern war" synonymous with total war? Was the policy of unconditional surrender that the Americans applied against Germany and Japan to end World War II also used by Lincoln against the Confederacy? Apparently Jefferson Davis thought so when Lincoln's negotiators at the Hampton Roads Peace Conference in early 1865 demanded "no cessation of hostilities short of an end of the war and the disbanding of all forces hostile to the government."

Yet even though Lincoln was determined to free the slaves, he stopped short of unconditional surrender when he drafted a bill after the Hampton Roads conference which would have compensated the former slave owners $400 per slave if they ended the war before April 1865. Professor Neely also points out that if Lincoln really believed in unconditional surrender, he could have demanded "the

exclusion of Confederate political leaders from future public office, disenfranchisement of Confederate soldiers, enfranchisement of freed blacks, legal protection for the Republican Party in former Confederate states, recognition of West Virginia's statehood, the partition of other Southern states, no reprisals against ex-slaves who served in Union armies, and so on."

Many historians consider the Civil War the most modern war because of the enormous number of casualties suffered—over 600,000 lives, 400,000 on the Union side and 200,000 on the Confederate. There is some question as to whether the weapons used, such as the development of the rifle musket, gave an advantage to the defense in repelling frontal assaults engaged by the infamous Pickett's charge at Gettysburg, which caused so many deaths. Professor Grady McWhiney and Perry D. Jamieson argue in *Attack and Die: Civil War Military Tactics and the Southern Heritage* (University of Alabama Press, 1982) that the "celtic heritage" caused Southerners to engage in these frontal attacks. But Professors Herman Hattaway and

Archer Jones in *How the North Won: A Military History of the Civil War* (University of Illinois Press, 1983) downplay the importance of specific battles and actions taken by individuals and believe that the North was victorious because the Union was more effective than the Confederacy in marshaling its resources.

Professor Mark Neely challenges the conventional wisdom of the time when he denies that the Civil War was a total war. According to Neely, not until after World War II when improved technology with its aerial bombing raids rendered the distinction between combatants and noncombatants meaningless that true "total war" was a reality. In his assessment of Sherman, Neely believes his rhetoric was more ferocious than his actions. Sherman did not make war against noncombatants. Whatever atrocities that were suffered in the war were mostly by soldiers against other soldiers on both sides. Whenever possible, Sherman tried to restrain his men from destroying the lives of civilians and their personal property. (South Carolina was the exception because it started the war.) If one seeks the earliest application of total war, Neely says it can be found in the speeches of President Jefferson Davis.

Neely also argues that the Lincoln administration did not mobilize its economy or its scientific community very well. There was no Manhattan Project that developed America's first atomic bomb. Nor were key industries mobilized under the rubric of state planning. Neely's argument on this point is partially substantiated by Stanley L. Engerman and J. Matthew Galman, "The Civil War Economy: A Modern View" in Steg Forster, et al., *The American Civil War and the German Wars of Unification, 1861–1871* (Cambridge University Press, 1997), who argue that it was the South and not the North that had to levy taxes, draft white Southerners, and engage in economic planning because its economic base was primarily agricultural.

Professor McPherson makes a strong case that the Civil War was a total war. Statistically, the war was devastating: 620,000 soldiers lost their lives, a number that equals almost all the number of soldiers killed in all the other American wars combined. One quarter of white men of military age lost their lives. Altogether, about 4 percent of southern people, black and white, were killed. Most were not killed in combat, but were victims of malnutrition and disease. It has been estimated that the war destroyed two-thirds of the region's wealth including the market value of slaves. In short, McPherson believes the Union war effort was "total" in its objectives because it destroyed the Confederate government and ended slavery.

McPherson argues familiarly that Lincoln shifted the objective of the war from restoring the Union with or without slavery intact to the destruction of both the Confederacy and slavery. His case for a shift from partial to total war is supported in his essay on "Union Generalship, Political Leadership and Total War" in the Forster collection cited above. Professor Edward Hagerman agrees with McPherson by saying that when Lincoln fired McClellan, he shifted his objective from a limited to a total war.

Did the North wage a total war against the South? In the YES selection, Professor Mark E. Neely, Jr., denies that the Civil War was a total war because the Union leaders respected the distinction between combatants and noncombatants and did not fully mobilize the country's economic resources. In the NO selection, Professor James M. McPherson says that Lincoln shifted the policy from limited to total war in the fall of 1862 and accomplished his objectives of abolishing slavery and destroying the Confederate government.

YES ↵

Mark E. Neely, Jr.

Was the Civil War a Total War?

... The idea of total war was first applied to the Civil War in an article about William T. Sherman published in the *Journal of Southern History* in 1948: John B. Walters's "General William T. Sherman and Total War."[1] After this initial use of the term, it was quickly adopted by T. Harry Williams, whose influential book *Lincoln and His Generals*, published in 1952, began with this memorable sentence: "The Civil War was the first of the modern total wars, and the American democracy was almost totally unready to fight it." Among the more popular Civil War writers, the idea also fared well. Bruce Catton, for example, wrote in a 1964 essay on "The Generalship of Ulysses S. Grant" that "He was fighting . . . a total war, and in a total war the enemy's economy is to be undermined in any way possible." Scholarly writers continued to use the term as well. In his masterful *Battle Cry of Freedom: The Civil War Era*, Princeton University's James M. McPherson writes, "By 1863, Lincoln's remarkable abilities gave him a wide edge over Davis as a war leader, while in Grant and Sherman the North acquired commanders with a concept of total war and the necessary determination to make it succeed." Professor McPherson's book forms part of the prestigious Oxford History of the United States. In another landmark volume, "*A People's Contest*": *The Union and the Civil War* (Harper & Row's New American Nation series), historian Phillip Shaw Paludan writes, "Grant's war making has come to stand for the American way of war. For one thing, that image is one of total war demanding unconditional surrender."[2]

Surely any idea about the military conduct of the Civil War that has been championed by Williams, Catton, McPherson, and Paludan, that is embodied in the Oxford History of the United States and in the New American Nation series, can fairly be called accepted wisdom on the subject. Most writers on the military history of the war, if forced to articulate a brief general description of the nature of that conflict, would now say, as McPherson has, that the Civil War began in 1861 with a purpose in the North "to suppress this insurrection and restore loyal Unionists to control of the southern states. The conflict was therefore a limited war . . . with the limited goal of restoring the status quo ante bellum, not an unlimited war to destroy an enemy nation and reshape its society." Gradually, or as McPherson puts it, "willy-nilly," the war became "a total war rather than a limited one." Eventually, "Union generals William Tecumseh Sherman and Philip Sheridan saw more clearly than anyone else the nature of

modern, total war, a war between peoples rather than simply between armies, a war in which the fighting left nothing untouched or unchanged." President Lincoln came to realize the nature of the military contest and "sanctioned this policy of 'being terrible' on the enemy." Finally, "when the Civil War became a total war, the invading army intentionally destroyed the economic capacity of the South to wage war." Northern victory resulted from this gradual realization and the subsequent application of new and harsh doctrines in the war's later phase. . . .

Northerner and Southerner alike have come to agree on the use of this term, total war, but what does it mean exactly? It was never used in the Civil War itself. Where does it come from?. . . .

Unfortunately, like many parts of everyday vocabulary, total war is a loose term with several meanings. Since World War II, it has come to mean, in part, a war requiring the full economic mobilization of a society. From the start, it meant the obverse of the idea as well: making war on the economic resources of the enemy rather than directly on its armed forces alone. Yet there was nothing really new about attacking an enemy's economic resources; that was the very essence of naval blockades and they long predated the Civil War. The crucial and terrible new aspect of the notion of total war was embodied in the following idea, part of a definition of the term cited in the *Oxford English Dictionary*: "Every citizen is in a sense a combatant and also the object of attack." Every systematic definition of the term embodies the concept of destroying the ages-old distinction between civilians and soldiers, whatever other ideas may be present. Another citation in the *OED*, for example, terms it "a war to which all resources and the whole population are committed; loosely, a war conducted without any scruple or limitations." *Webster's* . . . *Unabridged* dictionary describes total war as "warfare that uses all possible means of attack, military, scientific, and psychological, against both enemy troops and civilians." And James Turner Johnson, in his study of *Just War Tradition and the Restraint of War*, asserts that in total war "there must be disregard of restraints imposed by custom, law, and morality on the prosecution of the war. Especially, . . . total war bears hardest on noncombatants, whose traditional protection from harm according to the traditions of just and limited warfare appears to evaporate here."

Close application of this twentieth-century term (the product of the age of strategic bombing and blitzkrieg and powerful totalitarian governments capable of mobilizing science and psychology) to the Civil War seems fraught with difficulty. Surely no one believes, for example, that the Civil War was fought "without any scruple or limitations." From the ten thousand plus pages of documents in the eight full volumes of the *Official Records* dealing with prisoners of war, to the many copies of General Orders No. 100, a brief code of the laws of war distributed throughout the Union army in 1863, evidence abounds that this war knew careful limitation and conscientious scruple. Even World War II followed the rules bearing on prisoners of war. Any assessment of the Civil War's nearness to being a total war can be no more than that: an assertion that it *approached* total war in some ways. By no definition of the term can it be said to *be* a total war.

Occasionally, the term total war approximates the meaning of modernity. T. Harry Williams used the terms interchangeably, as in this passage from a later work in which he hedged a bit on calling the Civil War a total war: "Trite it may be to say that the Civil War was the first of the modern wars, but this is a truth that needs to be repeated. If the Civil War was not quite total, it missed totality by only a narrow margin."

Modernity is not a very useful concept in military history. Surely every war is thought to be modern by its participants—save possibly those fought by Japan in the strange era when firearms were consciously rejected. As a historian's term, modern when applied to warfare has a widely accepted meaning different from total. Modern warfare generally connotes wars fought after the French Revolution by large citizen armies equipped with the products of the Industrial Revolution and motivated more by ideology than the lash or strictly mercenary considerations. The Civil War certainly was a modern war in that sense, but it was not a total war in the sense that civilians were commonly thought of as legitimate military targets.

Perhaps no one who maintains the Civil War was a total war means it so literally. Historian Brian Bond provides a useful idea when he writes, "strictly speaking, total war is just as much a myth as total victory or total peace. What is true, however, is that the fragile barriers separating war from peace and soldiers from civilians—already eroded in the First World War—virtually disappeared between 1939 and 1945." Seeing how often that fragile barrier broke in the Civil War will tell how nearly it approached being a total war. All such matters of degree contain dangers for the historian trying to answer the question; the risk of sinking under a mass of piecemeal objections raised afterward by critics is very high. Even the most conservative of Civil War generals occasionally stepped over the boundaries of customarily accepted behavior in nineteenth-century warfare. General George B. McClellan, for example, did so in the Peninsula campaign, after only about a year's fighting. On May 4, 1862, he informed Secretary of War Edwin M. Stanton: "The rebels have been guilty of the most murderous & barbarous conduct in placing torpedoes [land mines] *within* the abandoned works, near wells & springs, near flag staffs, magazines, telegraph offices, in carpet bags, barrels of flour etc. Fortunately we have not

lost many men in this manner—some 4 or 5 killed & perhaps a dozen wounded. I shall make the prisoners remove them at their own peril." . . .

John B. Walters cited General Sherman's use of prisoners to clear mines as an example of his total war practices, but Sherman's reaction was in fact exactly like McClellan's. When Sherman saw a "handsome young officer" with all the flesh blown off one of his legs by a Confederate mine in Georgia in December 1864, he grew "very angry," because "this was not war, but murder." Sherman then retaliated by using Confederate prisoners to clear the mines. What at first may seem an incident suggesting the degeneration of warfare, in fact proves the belief of the protagonists in rules and codes of civilized behavior that have in the twentieth century long since vanished from the world's battlefields. The real point is that Union and Confederate authorities were in substantial agreement about the laws of war, and they usually tried to stay within them.

Leaving aside similar isolated instances caused by temporary rage, can a historian seeking to describe the war's direction toward or away from total war examine larger aspects of the war where the "fragile barriers" between soldiers and civilians may have broken down? Since the conscious application of a new doctrine in warfare forms part of the total war interpretation, can a historian focus on certain figures in high command who held such doctrines and applied them to the enemy in the Civil War? Throughout, can the historian keep an eye on the dictionary definition of total war to measure the proximity of the Civil War to it? Surely this can be done, and short of a study of the Civil War day by day, there can hardly be any other test. . . .

Sherman is the Civil War soldier most often quoted on the subject of total war. An article about him gave rise to this interpretation of the Civil War, and indeed it is now widely held that, as historian John E. Marszalek has expressed it, William T. Sherman was the "Inventor of Total Warfare." "We are not only fighting hostile armies, but a hostile people, and must make old and young, rich and poor, feel the hard hand of war, as well as their organized armies," Sherman told Gen. Hency W. Halleck on Christmas Eve 1864. As early as October 1862 he said, "We cannot change the hearts of these people of the South, but we can make war so terrible . . . [and] make them so sick of war that generations would pass away before they would again appeal to it."[3]

The gift of sounding like a twentieth-century man was peculiarly Sherman's. Nearly every other Civil War general sounds ancient by comparison, but many historians may have allowed themselves to be fooled by his style while ignoring the substance of his campaigns.

Historians, moreover, quote Sherman selectively. In fact, he said many things and when gathered together they do not add up to any coherent "total-war philosophy," as one historian describes it. Sherman was not a philosopher; he was a general and a garrulous one at that. "He talked incessantly and more rapidly than any man I ever saw," Maj. John Chipman Gray reported. "It would be easier to say what he did not talk about than what he did." Chauncey Depew said Sherman was "the readiest and most original talker in the United States." And what Sherman said during the war was often provoked by exasperating, momentary circumstance. Therefore, he occasionally uttered frightening statements. "To secure the safety of the navigation of the Mississippi River I would slay millions," Sherman told Gen. John A. Logan on December 21, 1863. "On that point I am not only insane, but mad . . . For every bullet shot at a steam-boat, I would shoot a thousand 30-pounder Parrotts into even helpless towns on Red, Oachita, Yazoo, or wherever a boat can float or soldier march." This statement was all the more striking, coming from a man widely reputed by newspaper critics to be insane. On another occasion, Sherman said, "To the petulant and persistent secessionists, why, death is mercy, and the quicker he or *she is* disposed of the better" (italics added).[4]

In other moods and in different circumstances, Sherman could sound as mild as Robert E. Lee. "War," the alleged inventor of total war wrote on April 19, 1863, "at best is barbarism, but to involve all—children, women, old and helpless—is more than can be justified." And he went on to caution against seizing so many stores that family necessities were endangered. Later, in the summer of 1863 when General Sherman sent a cavalry expedition toward Memphis from Mississippi, General Grant instructed him to "impress upon the men the importance of going through the State in an orderly manner, abstaining from taking anything not absolutely necessary for their subsistence while travelling. They should try to create as favorable an impression as possible upon the people." These may seem hopeless orders to give General Sherman, but his enthusiastic reply was this: "It will give me excessive pleasure to instruct the Cavalry as you direct, for the Policy you point out meets every wish of my heart."[5]

Scholars who pay less heed to the seductively modern sound of Sherman's harsher statements and look closely instead at what he actually did on his celebrated campaigns in Georgia and the Carolinas, find a nineteenth-century soldier at work—certainly not a man who made war on noncombatants. Joseph T. Glatthaar's study of Sherman's campaigns confirmed that, for the most part, Sherman's men did not physically abuse civilians who kept to themselves: atrocities were suffered mostly by soldiers on *both* sides; in Georgia and the Carolinas, Sherman's army recovered the bodies of at least 172 Union soldiers hanged, shot in the head at close range, with their throats slit, or "actually butchered." And only in South Carolina, the state blamed for starting the war, did Sherman fail to restrain his men in their destruction of private property. Before the idea of total war came to Civil War studies, shrewd students of the conflict had noted the essentially nineteenth-century nature of Sherman's campaigns. Gamaliel Bradford's *Union Portraits,* for example, written during World War I, observed: "Events . . . have

made the vandalism of Sherman seem like discipline and order. The injury done by him seldom directly affected anything but property. There was no systematic cruelty in the treatment of noncombatants, and to the eternal glory of American soldiers be it recorded that insult and abuse toward women were practically unknown during the Civil War."[6]

Though not a systematic military thinker, General Sherman did compose a letter addressing the problem of noncombatants in the Civil War, and it described his actual policies better than his frequently quoted statements of a more sensational nature. He sent the letter to Maj. R. M. Sawyer, whom Sherman left behind to manage Huntsville, Alabama, when he departed for Meridian, Mississippi, early in 1864. Sherman also sent a copy to his brother, Republican Senator John Sherman, with an eye to possible publication:

> In my former letters I have answered all your questions save one, and that relates to the treatment of inhabitants known or suspected to be hostile or "Secesh." This is in truth the most difficult business of our army as it advances and occupies the Southern country. It is almost impossible to lay down rules, and I invariably leave the whole subject to the local commanders, but am willing to give them the benefit of my acquired knowledge and experience. In Europe, whence we derive our principles of war, wars are between kings or rulers through hired armies, and not between peoples. These remain, as it were, neutral, and sell their produce to whatever army is in possession.
>
> Napoleon when at war with Prussia, Austria, and Russia bought forage and provisions of the inhabitants and consequently had an interest to protect the farms and factories which ministered to his wants. In like manner the allied Armies in France could buy of the French inhabitants whatever they needed, the produce of the soil or manufactures of the country. Therefore, the general rule was and is that war is confined to the armies engaged, and should not visit the houses of families or private interests. But in other examples a different rule obtained the sanction of historical authority. I will only instance one, where in the siege of William and Mary the English army occupied Ireland, then in a state of revolt. The inhabitants were actually driven into foreign lands, and were dispossessed of their property and a new population introduced.
>
>   . . . The question then arises, Should we treat as absolute enemies all in the South who differ from us in opinion or prejudice, kill or banish them, or should we give them time to think and gradually change their conduct so as to conform to the new order of things which is slowly and gradually creeping into their country?
>
>   When men take up arms to resist a rightful authority, we are compelled to use like force. . . . When the provisions, forage, horses, mules, wagons, etc., are used by our enemy, it is clearly

our duty and right to take them also, because otherwise they might be used against us. In like manner all houses left vacant by an inimical people are clearly our right, and as such are needed as storehouses, hospitals, and quarters. But the question arises as to dwellings used by women, children and non-combatants. So long as non-combatants remain in their houses and keep to their accustomed peaceful business, their opinions and prejudices can in no wise influence the war, and therefore should not be noticed; but if any one comes out into the public streets and creates disorder, he or she should be punished, restrained, or banished. . . . If the people, or any of them, keep up a correspondence with parties in hostility, they are spies, and can be punished according to law with death or minor punishment. These are well-established principles of war, and the people of the South having appealed to war, are barred from appealing for protection to our constitution, which they have practically and publicly defied. They have appealed to war, and must abide its rules and laws.

Excepting incidents of retaliation, Sherman by and large lived by these "principles of war."[7]

Leaving "the whole subject" to local commanders nevertheless permitted considerable latitude for pillage or destruction and was in itself an important principle. Moreover, Sherman, who was a critic of universal suffrage and loathed the free press, thought a volunteer army, the product of America's ultra-individualistic society, would inevitably loot and burn private property. His conservative social views thus led to a career-long fatalism about pillage.[8]

Sherman's purposes in the Georgia and Carolinas campaigns, usually pointed to as the epitome of total war in the Civil War, are obscured by two months of the general's letters to other generals describing his desire to cut loose from Atlanta and his long, thin line of supply to march to the sea. From mid-September to mid-November 1864, Sherman worried the idea, and his superiors, explaining it in several ways. At first he argued from his knowledge of the political disputes between Jefferson Davis and Georgia governor Joseph E. Brown that the march would sever the state from the Confederacy. "They may stand the fall of Richmond," Sherman told Grant on September 20, "but not of all Georgia." At the same time he belittled the effects of mere destruction: "the more I study the game the more I am convinced that it would be wrong for me to penetrate much farther into Georgia without an objective beyond. It would not be productive of much good. I can start east and make a circuit south and back, *doing vast damage to the State*, but resulting in no permanent good" (italics added).[9]

Less than three weeks later, Sherman gave a rather different explanation to Grant: "Until we can repopulate Georgia, it is useless to occupy it, but the utter destruction of its roads, houses, and people will cripple their military resources. By attempting to hold the roads we will lose 1,000 men monthly, and will gain no result. I can make the march, and make Georgia howl."

Ten days after that, he more or less combined his different arguments in a letter to General Halleck. "This movement is not purely military or strategic," he now said, "but it will illustrate the vulnerability of the South." Only when Sherman's armies arrived and "fences and corn and hogs and sheep" vanished would "the rich planters of the Oconee and Savannah" know "what war means." He spoke more tersely to his subordinates. "I want to prepare for my big raid," he explained on October 19 to a colonel in charge of supply, and with that Sherman arranged to send his impedimenta to the rear.

With plans more or less set, Sherman explained to Gen. George Thomas, who would be left to deal with Confederate Gen. John Bell Hood's army, "I propose to demonstrate the vulnerability of the South, and make its inhabitants feel that war and individual ruin are synonymous terms." Delays ensued and Sherman decided to remain in place until after election day. On the twelfth he cut his telegraph lines, and the confusing explanations of the campaign ceased pouring out of Georgia.

Sherman did not attempt the "utter destruction" of Georgia's "people." He did not really attack noncombatants directly or make any serious attempt to destroy "the economic capacity of the south to wage war," as one historian has described his purpose. After capturing Atlanta, for example, Sherman moved to capture Savannah and then attacked the symbolic capital of secession, South Carolina. He did not attack Augusta, Georgia, which he knew to contain "the only powder mills and factories remaining in the South." Though he did systematically destroy railroad lines, Sherman otherwise had little conception of eliminating essential industries. Indeed, there were few to eliminate, for the South, in comparison with the North, was a premodern, underdeveloped, agrarian region where determined men with rifles were the real problem—not the ability of the area's industries to manufacture high-technology weapons. Despite scorching a sixty-mile-wide swath through the Confederacy, Sherman was never going to starve this agrarian economy into submission, either. He had remarked in the past on how well fed and even shod the Confederate armies were despite their backward economy.

What Sherman was doing embodied traditional geopolitical objectives in a civil war: convincing the enemy's people and the world that the Confederate government and upper classes were too weak to maintain nationhood. He did this with a "big raid." "If we can march a well-appointed army right through his [Jefferson Davis's] territory," Sherman told Grant on November 6, 1864, "it is a demonstration to the world, foreign and domestic, that we have a power which Davis cannot resist." In *Battle Cry of Freedom* this statement is followed by ellipsis marks and the statement, "I can make the march, and make Georgia howl!" But that appears to be a misquotation. In fact,

Sherman went on to say something much less vivid and scorching:

> This may not be war, but rather statesmanship, nevertheless it is overwhelming to my mind that there are thousands of people abroad and in the South who will reason thus: If the North can march an army right through the south, it is proof positive that the North can prevail in this contest, leaving only open the question of its willingness to use that power.
>
> Now, Mr. Lincoln's election, which is assured, coupled with the conclusion just reached, makes a complete, logical whole.

And Mr. Lincoln himself endorsed the view. In his letter congratulating Sherman on his Christmas capture of Savannah, the president counted the campaign "a great success" not only in affording "the obvious and immediate military advantages" but also "in showing to the world that your army could be divided, putting the stronger part to an important new service, and yet leaving enough to vanquish the old opposing force of the whole—Hood's army." This, Lincoln said, "brings those who sat in darkness, to see a great light." Neither Sherman nor Lincoln put the emphasis on the role of sheer destructiveness or economic deprivation. . . .

In fact, no Northerner at any time in the nineteenth century embraced as his own the cold-blooded ideas now associated with total war. If one seeks the earliest application of the idea (rather than the actual term) to the Civil War, it lies perhaps in the following document, written in the midst of the Civil War itself:

> [T]hey [the U.S.] have repudiated the foolish conceit that the inhabitants of this confederacy are still citizens of the United States, for they are waging an indiscriminate war upon them all, with a savage ferocity unknown to modern civilization. In this war, rapine is the rule: private residences, in peaceful rural retreats, are bombarded and burnt: Grain crops in the field are consumed by the torch and when the torch is not convenient, careful labor is bestowed to render complete the destruction of every article of use or ornament remaining in private dwellings, after their inhabitants have fled from the outrages of a brutal soldiery.
>
> Mankind will shudder to hear of the tales of outrages committed on defenceless females by soldiers of the United States now invading our homes: yet these outrages are prompted by inflamed passions and madness of intoxication.

The source of the idea was, of course, Confederate, and it was a high Confederate source indeed: Jefferson Davis.

It may sound as though Davis was describing Sherman's march through Georgia or perhaps Sheridan in the Shenandoah Valley—most probably in a late speech,

in 1864 or 1865. In fact, President Davis made the statement in 1861, in his Message to Congress of July 20. Davis not only described total war three years before Sherman entered Georgia; he described total war before the First Battle of Bull Run had been fought. It was fought the day *after* Davis delivered his message to Congress.

The first application of the *idea* to the Civil War came, then, in Confederate propaganda. Though it may not be a sectional interpretation now, it was an entirely sectional idea in the beginning. Its origins give perhaps the best clue to the usefulness of the idea in describing the Civil War. Total war may describe certain isolated and uncharacteristic aspects of the Civil War but is at most a partial view.

The point is not merely semantic. The use of the idea of total war prevents historians from understanding the era properly. . . .

Likewise, the economic aspect of total war is misleading when used to describe characteristics of the Civil War reputedly more forward looking than naval blockades. The ideas of economic planning and control from World War II cannot be applied to the Civil War. Hardly anyone then thought in such macroeconomic terms. Abraham Lincoln did calculate the total daily cost of the war, but he did not do so to aid long-range economic planning for the Union war effort. Instead he used the figure to show how relatively inexpensive it would be for the U.S. government to purchase the freedom of all the slaves in the border states through compensated emancipation. At $400 a head, the $2 million daily war expenditure would buy every slave in Delaware at "less than one half-day's cost," and "less than eighty seven days cost of this war would, at the same price, pay for all in Delaware, Maryland, District of Columbia, Kentucky, and Missouri."

From the Confederate perspective, the economic insight seems ironically somewhat more appropriate. The blockade induced scarcities on which almost all Confederate civilian diarists commented—coffee, shoe leather, and needles were sorely missed. The Confederate government's attempts to supply scarce war necessities led some historians to call the resulting system "state socialism" or a "revolutionary experience." Yet these were the outcome less of deliberate Northern military strategy (the blockade aside) than of the circumstance that the South was agrarian and the North more industrialized.

For its part, the North did little to mobilize its resources—little, that is, that would resemble the centralized planning and state intervention typical of twentieth-century economies in war. There was no rationing, North or South, and the Yankees' society knew only the sacrifice of men, not of materials. As Phillip Paludan has shown, agriculture thrived, and other parts of Northern society suffered only modestly; college enrollments fell, except at the University of Michigan, but young men still continued to go to college in substantial numbers. Inflation and a graduated income tax did little to trouble the claims made by most Republicans of surprising prosperity in the midst of war. The Republican president stated in his annual message to the United States Congress in December 1864:

> It is of noteworthy interest that the steady expansion of population, improvement and governmental institutions over the new and unoccupied portions of our country have scarcely been checked, much less impeded or destroyed, by our great civil war, which at first glance would seem to have absorbed almost the entire energies of the nation.
>
> . . . It is not material to inquire *how* the increase has been produced, or to show that it would have been *greater* but for the war. . . . The important fact remains demonstrated, that we have *more* men *now* than we had when the war *began.* . . . This as to men. Material resources are now more complete and abundant than ever.
>
> The national resources, then, are unexhausted, and, as we believe, inexhaustible.

Democrats generally conceded prosperity by their silence and focused instead on race and civil liberties as campaign issues.

The essential aspect of any definition of total war asserts that it breaks down the distinction between soldiers and civilians, combatants and non-combatants, and this no one in the Civil War did systematically, including William T. Sherman. He and his fellow generals waged war the same way most Victorian gentlemen did, and other Victorian gentlemen in the world knew it. That is one reason why British, French, and Prussian observers failed to comment on any startling developments seen in the American war: there was little new to report. The conservative monarchies of the old world surely would have seized with delight on any evidence that warfare in the New World was degenerating to the level of starving and killing civilians. Their observers encountered no such spectacle. It required airplanes and tanks and heartless twentieth-century ideas born in the hopeless trenches of World War I to break down distinctions adhered to in practice by almost all Civil War generals. Their war did little to usher in the shock of the new in the twentieth century.

Notes

1. John B. Walters, "General William T. Sherman and Total War," *Journal of Southern History* 14 (November 1948): 447–80. See also John B. Walters, *Merchant of Terror: General Sherman and Total War* (Indianapolis, Ind.: Bobbs-Merrill, 1973). Phillip Paludan mistakes the origins of Walters's ideas as being a product of the Vietnam War era, ignoring the anti-Yankee roots of the idea apparent in the earlier article. See Philip Paludan, *"A People's Contest": The Union and the Civil War* (New York: Harper & Row, 1988), 456. Other books on Sherman embracing the total war thesis include: John G. Barrett, *Sherman's March through the Carolinas* (Chapel Hill: Univ. of North Carolina Press, 1956); Burke Davis, *Sherman's March* (New York: Random House, 1980); and James M. Reston Jr., *Sherman's March and Viet Nam* (New York: Macmillan, 1984).

2. T. Harry Williams, *Lincoln and His Generals* (New York: Alfred A. Knopf, 1952), 3; Bruce Catton, "The Generalship of Ulysses S. Grant," in *Grant, Lee, Lincoln and the Radicals: Essays on Civil War Leadership,* ed. Grady McWhiney (New York: Harper Colophon, 1966), 8; James M. McPherson, *Battle Cry of Freedom: The Civil War Era* (New York: Oxford Univ. Press, 1988), 857; Paludan, *"A People's Contest,"* 296.

3. OR 44:798; OR 17, 2:261.

4. McPherson, *Battle Cry of Freedom,* 809; John Chipman Gray and John Codman Ropes, *War Letters 1862–1865* (Boston: Houghton, Mifflin, 1927), 425, 427; Edmund Wilson, *Patriotic Gore: Studies in the Literature of the American Civil War* (New York: Oxford Univ. Press, 1962), 205; OR 31, 3:459; OR 32, 2:281.

5. OR 24, 2:209; John Y. Simon, ed., *The Papers of Ulysses S. Grant,* 16 vols. to date (Carbondale: Southern Illinois Univ. Press, 1967–), 9:155, 156n.

6. Joseph T. Glatthaar, *The March to the Sea and Beyond: Sherman's Troops in the Savannah and Carolinas Campaigns* (New York: New York Univ. Press, 1985), 72–73, 127–28; Gamaliel Bradford, *Union Portraits* (Boston: Houghton, Mifflin, 1916), 154n–155n, Paludan, though he says Sherman "helped announce the coming of total war," also states that "Sherman's idea of war was more description than doctrine." Paludan, *"A People's Contest."* 291, 302.

7. Rachel Sherman Thorndike, ed., *The Sherman Letters: Correspondence between General and Senator Sherman from 1837 to 1891* (New York: Charles Scribner's Sons, 1894), 228–30.

8. Ibid. 175–76,181–82,185; M. A. DeWolfe Howe, ed., *Home Letters of General Sherman* (New York: Charles Scribner's Sons, 1909), 209.

9. OR 39, 2:412.

MARK E. NEELY is currently the McCabe Greer Professor of Civil War History at Penn State University. A specialist on Abraham Lincoln and the American Civil War, he is the author of *The Fate of Liberty: Abraham Lincoln and Civil Liberties* (Oxford University Press, 1991), which won the Pulitzer and Bell I. Wiley prizes; *The Last Best Hope of Earth: Abraham Lincoln and the Promise of America* (Harvard University Press, 1993); *The Civil War and the Limits of Destruction* (Harvard University Press, 2007); and, most recently, *Lincoln and the Triumph of the Nation: Constitutional Conflict in the American Civil War* (University of North Carolina Press, 2011). From 1972 to 1992, he served as director of The Lincoln Museum in Ft. Wayne, Indiana.

James M. McPherson  **NO**

From Limited War to Total War, 1861–1865

A few years after the Civil War, Mark Twain described that great conflict as having "uprooted institutions that were centuries old, changed the politics of a people, transformed the social life of half the country, and wrought so profoundly upon the entire national character that the influence cannot be measured short of two or three generations." This profound transformation was achieved at enormous cost in lives and property. Fully one-quarter of the white men of military age in the Confederacy lost their lives. And that terrible toll does not include an unknown number of civilian deaths in the South. Altogether nearly 4 percent of the Southern people, black and white, civilians and soldiers, died as a consequence of the war. This percentage exceeded the human cost of any country in World War I and was outstripped only by the region between the Rhine and the Volga in World War II. The amount of property and resources destroyed in the Confederate States is almost incalculable. It has been estimated at two-thirds of all assessed wealth, including the market value of slaves.

This is the negative side of that radical transformation described by Mark Twain. The positive side included preservation of the United States as a unified nation, the liberation of four million slaves, and the abolition by constitutional amendment of the institution of bondage that had plagued the nation since the beginning, inhibited its progress, and made a mockery of the libertarian values on which it was founded. No other society in history freed so many slaves in so short a time—but also at such a cost in violence.

The Civil War mobilized human resources on a scale unmatched by any other event in American history except, perhaps, World War II. For actual combat duty the Civil War mustered a considerably larger proportion of American manpower than did World War II. And, in another comparison with that global conflict, the victorious power in the Civil War did all it could to devastate the enemy's economic resources as well as the morale of its home-front population, which was considered almost as important as enemy armies in the war effort. In World War II this was done by strategic bombing; in the Civil War it was done by cavalry and infantry penetrating deep into the Confederate heartland.

It is these factors—the devastation wrought by the war, the radical changes it accomplished, and the mobilization of the whole society to sustain the war effort that have caused many historians to label the Civil War a "total war." Recently, however, some analysts have questioned this terminology. They maintain that true total war—or in the words of Carl von Clausewitz, "absolute war"—makes no distinction between combatants and noncombatants, no discrimination between taking the lives of enemy soldiers and those of enemy civilians; it is war "without any scruple or limitations," war in which combatants give no quarter and take no prisoners.

Some wars have approached this totality—for example, World War II, in which Germany deliberately murdered millions of civilians in eastern Europe, Allied strategic bombing killed hundreds of thousands of German and Japanese civilians, and both sides sometimes refused to take prisoners and shot those who tried to surrender. In that sense of totality, the Civil War was not a total war. Although suffering and disease mortality were high among prisoners of war, and Confederates occasionally murdered captured black soldiers, there was no systematic effort to kill prisoners. And while soldiers on both sides in the Civil War pillaged and looted civilian property, and several Union commanders systematized this destruction into a policy, they did not deliberately kill civilians. Mark Neely, the chief critic of the notion of the Civil War as a total war, maintains that "the *essential* aspect of any definition of total war asserts that it breaks down the distinction between soldiers and civilians, combatants and noncombatants, and this no one in the Civil War did systematically."

Even William T. Sherman, widely regarded as the progenitor of total war, was more bark than bite according to Neely. Sherman wrote and spoke in a nervous, rapid-fire, sometimes offhand manner; he said extreme things about "slaying millions" and "repopulating Georgia" if necessary to win the war. But this was rhetorical exaggeration. One of Sherman's most widely quoted statements—"We are not only fighting hostile armies, but a hostile people, and must make old and young, rich and poor, feel the hard hand of war"—did not really erase the distinction between combatants and noncombatants, for Sherman did not mean it to justify killing civilians.

To note the difference between rhetoric and substance in the Civil War is to make a valid point. The rhetoric not only of Sherman but also of many other people on

McPherson, James M. Reprinted with permission from *Gateway Heritage Magazine*, Vol. 12, No. 4, Spring, 1992. Courtesy of the Missouri History Museum, St. Louis, MO.

both sides was far more ferocious than anything that actually happened. Northerners had no monopoly on such rhetoric. A Savannah newspaper proclaimed in 1863: "Let Yankee cities burn and their fields be laid waste," while a Richmond editor echoed: "It surely must be made plain at last that this is to be a war of extermination." A month after the firing on Fort Sumter, a Nashville woman prayed that "God may be with us to give us strength to conquer them, to exterminate them, to lay waste every Northern city, town and village, to destroy them utterly." Yankees used similar language. In the first month of the war a Milwaukee judge said that Northern armies should "restore New Orleans to its native marshes, then march across the country, burn Montgomery to ashes, and serve Charleston in the same way. . . . We must starve, drown, burn, shoot the traitors." In St. Louis the uneasy truce between Union and Confederate factions that had followed the riots and fighting in May 1861 broke down a month later when the Union commander Nathaniel Lyon rejected a compromise with pro-Confederate elements, which included the governor, with these words: "Rather than concede to the State of Missouri for one single instant the right to dictate to my Government in any matter . . . I would see you . . . and every man, woman, and child in the State, dead and buried."

These statements certainly sound like total war, war without limits or restraints. But of course none of the scenarios sketched out in these quotations literally came true—not even in Missouri, where reality came closer to rhetoric than anywhere else. Therefore, those who insist that the Civil War was not a total war appear to have won their case, at least semantically. Recognizing this, a few historians have sought different adjectives to describe the kind of conflict the Civil War became: One uses the phrase "destructive war"; another prefers "hard war."

But these phrases, though accurate, do not convey the true dimensions of devastation in the Civil War. All wars are hard and destructive in some degree; what made the Civil War distinctive in the American experience? It *was* that overwhelming involvement of the whole population, the shocking loss of life, the wholesale devastation and radical social and political transformations that it wrought. In the experience of Americans, especially Southerners, this approached totality; it *seemed* total. Thus the concept, and label, of total war remains a useful one. It is what the sociologist Max Weber called an "ideal type"—a theoretical model used to measure a reality that never fully conforms to the model, but that nevertheless remains a useful tool for analyzing the reality.

That is the sense in which this essay will analyze the evolution of the Civil War from a limited to a total war. Despite that fierce rhetoric of destruction quoted earlier, the official war aims of both sides in 1861 were quite limited. In his first message to the Confederate Congress after the firing on Fort Sumter by his troops had provoked war, Jefferson Davis declared that "we seek no conquest, no aggrandizement, no concession of any

kind from the States with which we were lately confederated; all we ask is to be let alone." As for the Union government, its initial conception of the war was one of a domestic insurrection, an uprising against national authority by certain lawless hotheads who had gained temporary sway over the otherwise law-abiding citizens of a few Southern states—or as Lincoln put it in his proclamation calling out seventy-five thousand state militia to put down the uprising, "combinations too powerful to be suppressed by the ordinary course of judicial proceedings." This was a strategy of limited war—indeed, so limited that it was scarcely seen as a war at all, but rather as a police action to quell a large riot. It was a strategy founded on an assumption of residual loyalty among the silent majority of Southerners. Once the national government demonstrated its firmness by regaining control of its forts and by blockading Southern ports, those presumed legions of Unionists would come to the fore and bring their states back into the Union. To cultivate this loyalty, and to temper firmness with restraint, Lincoln promised that the federalized ninety-day militia would avoid "any devastation, any destruction of, or interference with, property, or any disturbance of peaceful citizens."

None other than William Tecumseh Sherman echoed these sentiments in the summer of 1861. Commander of a brigade that fought at Bull Run, Sherman deplored the marauding tendencies of his poorly disciplined soldiers. "No curse could be greater than invasion by a volunteer army," he wrote. "No Goths or Vandals ever had less respect for the lives and properties of friends and foes, and henceforth we should never hope for any friends in Virginia. . . . My only hope now is that a common sense of decency may be infused into this soldiery to respect life and property."

The most important and vulnerable form of Southern property was slaves. The Lincoln administration went out of its way to reassure Southerners in 1861 that it had no designs on slavery. Congress followed suit, passing by an overwhelming majority in July 1861 a resolution affirming that Union war aims included no intention "of overthrowing or interfering with the rights or established institutions of the States"—in plain words, slavery—but intended only "to defend and maintain the supremacy of the Constitution and to preserve the Union with all the dignity, equality, and rights of the several States unimpaired."

There were, to be sure, murmurings in the North against this soft-war approach, this "kid-glove policy." Abolitionists and radical Republicans insisted that a rebellion sustained *by* slavery in defense *of* slavery could be crushed only by striking *against* slavery. As Frederick Douglass put it: "To fight against Slaveholders, without fighting against slavery, is but a half-hearted business, and paralyzes the hands engaged in it. . . . Fire must be met with water. War for the destruction of liberty must be met with war for the destruction of slavery." Several Union soldiers and their officers, some with no previous antislavery convictions, also began to grumble about protecting the property of traitors in arms against the United States.

The first practical manifestation of such sentiments came in Missouri. Thus began a pattern whereby events in that state set the pace for the transformation from a limited to a total war, radiating eastward and southward from Missouri. The commander of the Western Department of the Union army in the summer of 1861, with headquarters at St. Louis, was John C. Frémont, famed explorer of the West, first Republican presidential candidate (in 1856), and now ambitious for military glory. Handicapped by his own administrative incompetence, bedeviled by a Confederate invasion of southwest Missouri that defeated and killed Nathaniel Lyon at Wilson's Creek on August 10 and then marched northward to the Missouri River, and driven to distraction by Confederate guerrilla bands that sprang up almost everywhere, Frémont on August 30 took a bold step toward total war. He placed the whole state of Missouri under martial law, announced the death penalty for guerrillas captured behind Union lines, and confiscated the property and emancipated the slaves of Confederate activists.

Northern radicals applauded, but conservatives shuddered and border-state Unionists expressed outrage. Still pursuing a strategy of trying to cultivate Southern Unionists as the best way to restore the Union, Lincoln feared that the emancipation provision of Frémont's edict would

> alarm our Southern Union friends, and turn them against us—perhaps ruin our rather fair prospect for Kentucky. . . . To lose Kentucky is nearly the same as to lose the whole game. Kentucky gone, we can not hold Missouri, nor, as I think, Maryland. These all against us, and the job on our hands is too large for us. We would as well consent to separation at once, including the surrender of this capitol.

Lincoln thus revoked the confiscation and emancipation provisions of Frémont's decree. He also ordered the general to execute no guerrillas without specific presidential approval. Lincoln feared that such a policy would only provoke reprisals whereby guerrillas would shoot captured Union soldiers "man for man, indefinitely." His apprehensions were well founded. One guerrilla leader in southeast Missouri had already issued a counterproclamation declaring that for every man executed under Frémont's order, he would "HANG, DRAW, and QUARTER a minion of said Abraham Lincoln."

Lincoln probably had the Missouri situation in mind when he told Congress in his annual message of December 1861 that "in considering the policy to be adopted for suppressing the insurrection, I have been anxious and careful that the inevitable conflict for this purpose shall not degenerate into a violent and remorseless revolutionary

struggle." But that was already happening. The momentum of a war that had already mobilized nearly a million men on both sides was becoming remorseless even as Lincoln spoke, and it would soon become revolutionary.

Nowhere was this more true than in Missouri. There occurred the tragedy of a civil war within the Civil War, of neighbor against neighbor and sometimes literally brother against brother, of an armed conflict along the Kansas border that went back to 1854 and had never really stopped, of ugly, vicious, no-holds-barred bushwhacking that constituted pretty much a total war in fact as well as in theory. Bands of Confederate guerrillas led by the notorious William Clarke Quantrill, Bloody Bill Anderson, and other pathological killers, and containing such famous desperadoes as the James and Younger brothers, ambushed, murdered, and burned out Missouri Unionists and tied down thousands of Union troops by hit-and-run raids. Union militia and Kansas Jayhawkers retaliated in kind. In contrapuntal disharmony guerrillas and Jayhawkers plundered and pillaged their way across the state, taking no prisoners, killing in cold blood, terrorizing the civilian population, leaving large parts of Missouri a scorched earth.

In 1863 Quantrill's band rode into Kansas to the hated Yankee settlement of Lawrence and murdered almost every adult male they found there, more than 150 in all. A year later Bloody Bill Anderson's gang took twenty-four unarmed Union soldiers from a train, shot them in the head, then turned on a posse of pursuing militia and slaughtered 127 of them including the wounded and captured. In April 1864 the Missourian John S. Marmaduke, a Confederate general (and later governor of Missouri), led an attack on Union supply wagons at Poison Springs, Arkansas, killing in cold blood almost as many black soldiers as Nathan Bedford Forrest's troops did at almost the same time in the more famous Fort Pillow massacre in Tennessee.

Confederate guerrillas had no monopoly on atrocities and scorched-earth practices in Missouri. The Seventh Kansas Cavalry—"Jennison's Jayhawkers"—containing many abolitionists including a son of John Brown, seemed determined to exterminate rebellion and slaveholders in the most literal manner. The Union commander in western Missouri where guerrilla activity was most rife, Thomas Ewing, issued his notorious Order No. 11 after Quantrill's raid to Lawrence. Order No. 11 forcibly removed thousands of families from four Missouri counties along the Kansas border and burned their farms to deny the guerrillas the sanctuary they had enjoyed in this region. Interestingly, Ewing was William T. Sherman's brother-in-law. In fact, most of the Union commanders who subsequently became famous as practitioners of total war spent part of their early Civil War careers in Missouri—including Grant, Sherman, and Sheridan. This was more than coincidence. What they saw and experienced in that state helped to predispose them toward a conviction that, in Sherman's words, "we are not only fighting hostile armies, but a hostile people" and must make them "feel the hard hand of war."

That conviction took root and began to grow among the Northern people and their leaders in the summer of 1862. Before then, for several months in the winter and spring, Union forces had seemed on the verge of winning the war without resorting to such measures. The capture of Forts Henry and Donelson, the victories at Mill Springs in Kentucky, Pea Ridge in Arkansas, Shiloh in Tennessee, Roanoke Island and New Bern in North Carolina, the capture of Nashville, New Orleans, and Memphis, the expulsion of organized Confederate armies from Missouri, Kentucky, and West Virginia, the Union occupation of much of the lower Mississippi Valley and a large part of the state of Tennessee, and the advance of the splendidly equipped Army of the Potomac to within five miles of Richmond in May 1862 seemed to herald the Confederacy's doom. But then came counteroffensives by Stonewall Jackson and Robert E. Lee in Virginia and by Braxton Bragg and Kirby Smith in Tennessee, which took Confederate armies almost to the Ohio River and across the Potomac River by September 1862.

Those deceptively easy Union advances and victories in early 1862 had apparently confirmed the validity of a limited-war strategy. Grant's capture of Forts Henry and Donelson, for example, had convinced him that the Confederacy was a hollow shell about to collapse. But when the rebels regrouped and counterpunched so hard at Shiloh that they nearly whipped him, Grant changed his mind. He now "gave up all idea," he later wrote, "of saving the Union except by complete conquest." Complete conquest meant not merely the occupation of territory, but also the crippling or destruction of Confederate armies. For if these armies remained intact they could reconquer territory, as they did in the summer of 1862. Grant's new conception of the war also included the seizure or destruction of any property or other resources used to sustain the Confederate war effort. Before those Southern counteroffensives, Grant said that he had been careful "to protect the property of the citizens whose territory was invaded"; afterwards his policy became to "consume everything that could be used to support or supply armies."

"Everything" included slaves, whose labor was one of the principal resources used to support and supply Confederate armies. If the Confederacy "cannot be whipped in any other way than through a war against slavery," wrote Grant, "let it come to that." Union armies in the field as well as Republican leaders in Congress had been edging toward an emancipation policy ever since May 1861 when General Benjamin Butler had admitted three escaped slaves to his lines at Fort Monroe, labeled them contraband of war, and put them to work for wages to help support and supply *Union* forces. By the summer of 1862, tens of thousands of these contrabands had come within Union lines. Congress had forbidden army officers to return them. Legislation passed in July 1862 declared free all of those belonging to masters who supported the Confederacy. Frémont in Missouri turned out to have been not wrong, but a year ahead of his time.

By the summer of 1862 Lincoln too had come to the position enunciated a year earlier by Frederick Douglass:

"To fight against slaveholders, without fighting against slavery, is but a half-hearted business." Acting in his capacity as commander in chief with power to seize property used to wage war against the United States, Lincoln decided to issue a proclamation freeing all slaves in those states engaged in rebellion. Emancipation, he told his cabinet in July 1862, had become "a military necessity, absolutely essential to the preservation of the Union. . . . We must free the slaves or be ourselves subdued. The slaves [are] undeniably an element of strength to those who [have] their service, and we must decide whether that element should be with us or against us. . . . Decisive and extensive measures must be adopted. . . . We [want] the army to strike more vigorous blows. The Administration must set an example, and strike at the heart of the rebellion." After a wait of two months for a victory to give the proclamation credibility, Lincoln announced it on September 22, 1862, to go into effect on January 1, 1863.

With this action Lincoln embraced the idea of the Civil War as a revolutionary conflict. Things had changed a great deal since he had promised to avoid "any devastation, or destruction of, or interference with, property." The Emancipation Proclamation was just what the *Springfield Republican* pronounced it: "the greatest social and political revolution of the age." No less an authority on revolutions than Karl Marx exulted: *"Never* has such a gigantic transformation taken place so rapidly." General Henry W. Halleck, who had been called from his headquarters in St. Louis (where he was commander of the Western Department) to Washington to become general in chief, made clear the practical import of the Emancipation Proclamation in a dispatch to Grant at Memphis in January 1863. "The character of the war has very much changed within the last year," he wrote. "There is now no possible hope of reconciliation with the rebels. . . . We must conquer the rebels or be conquered by them. . . . Every slave withdrawn from the enemy is the equivalent of a white man put *hors de combat.*" One of Grant's field commanders explained that the new "policy is to be terrible on the enemy. I am using negroes all the time for my work as teamsters, and have 1,000 employed."

The program of "being terrible on the enemy" soon went beyond emancipating slaves and using them as teamsters. In early 1863 the Lincoln administration committed itself to a policy that had first emerged, like other total-war practices, in the trans-Mississippi theater. The First Kansas Colored Volunteers, composed mostly of contrabands from Missouri, were the earliest black soldiers to see combat, in 1862, and along with the Louisiana Native Guards the first to take shape as organized units. Arms in the hands of slaves constituted the South's ultimate revolutionary nightmare. After initial hesitation, Lincoln embraced this revolution as well. In March 1863 he wrote to Andrew Johnson, military governor of occupied Tennessee: "The bare sight of fifty thousand armed, and drilled black soldiers on the banks of the Mississippi, would end the rebellion at once. And who doubts that we can present that sight, if we but take hold in earnest?" By

August 1863 Lincoln could declare in a public letter that "the emancipation policy, and the use of colored troops, constitute the heaviest blow yet dealt to the rebellion."

Well before then the conflict had become remorseless as well as revolutionary, with Lincoln's approval. Two of the generals he brought to Washington from the West in the summer of 1862, John Pope and Henry W. Halleck, helped to define and enunciate the remorselessness. Both had spent the previous winter and spring in Missouri, where experience with guerrillas had shaped their hardwar approach. One of Pope's first actions upon becoming commander of the Army of Virginia was a series of orders authorizing his officers to seize Confederate property without compensation, to execute captured guerrillas who had fired on Union troops, and to expel from occupied territory any civilians who sheltered guerrillas or who refused to take an oath of allegiance to the United States. From Halleck's office as general in chief in August 1862 went orders to Grant, now commander of Union forces in western Tennessee and Mississippi. "Take up all active [rebel] sympathizers," wrote Halleck, "and either hold them as prisoners or put them beyond our lines. Handle that class without gloves, and take their property for public use. . . . It is time that they should begin to feel the presence of the war."

With or without such orders, Union soldiers in the South were erasing the distinction between military and civilian property belonging to the enemy. A soldier from St. Louis with his regiment in west Tennessee wrote home that "this thing of guarding rebels' property has about 'played out.'" "The iron gauntlet," wrote another officer in the Mississippi Valley, "must be used more than the silken glove to crush this serpent."

Inevitably, bitter protests against this harshness reached Lincoln from purported Southern Unionists. A few months earlier the president would have rebuked the harshness, as he had rebuked Frémont, for alienating potential Unionist friends in the South. But in July 1862 Lincoln rebuked the protesters instead. He asked one of them sarcastically if they expected him to fight the war "with elderstalk squirts, charged with rose water?" Did they think he would "surrender the government to save them from losing all"? Lincoln had lost faith in those professed Unionists:

> The paralysis—the dead palsy—of the government in this whole struggle is, that this class of men will do nothing for the government . . . except [demand] that the government shall not strike its open enemies, lest they be struck by accident! . . . This government cannot much longer play a game in which it stakes all, and its enemies stake nothing. Those enemies must understand that they cannot experiment for ten years trying to destroy the government, and if they fail still come back into the Union unhurt.

Using one of his favorite metaphors, Lincoln warned Southern whites that "broken eggs cannot be mended." The rebels had already cracked the egg of slavery by their own rash behavior; the sooner they gave up and ceased the insurrection, "the smaller will be the amount of [eggs] which will be past mending."

William Tecumseh Sherman eventually became the foremost military spokesman for remorseless war and the most effective general in carrying it out. Sherman too had spent part of the winter of 1861–1862 in Missouri where he stored up impressions of guerrilla ferocity. Nonetheless, even as late as July 1862, as commander of Union occupation forces around Memphis, he complained of some Northern troops who took several mules and horses from farmers. Such "petty thieving and pillaging," he wrote, "does us infinite harm." This scarcely sounds like the Sherman that Southerners love to hate. But his command problems in western Tennessee soon taught him what his brother-in-law Thomas Ewing was also learning about guerrillas and the civilian population that sheltered them across the river in Arkansas and Missouri. Nearly every white man, woman, and child in Sherman's district seemed to hate the Yankees and to abet the bushwhackers who fired into Union supply boats on the river, burned railroad bridges and ripped up the tracks, attacked Union picket outposts, ambushed Northern soldiers unless they moved in large groups, and generally raised hell behind Union lines. Some of the cavalry troopers who rode with Nathan Bedford Forrest and John Hunt Morgan on devastating raids behind Union lines also functioned in the manner of guerrillas, fading away to their homes and melting into the civilian population after a raid.

These operations convinced Sherman to take off the gloves. The distinction between enemy civilians and soldiers grew blurred. After fair warning, Sherman burned houses and sometimes whole villages in western Tennessee that he suspected of harboring snipers and guerrillas. The Union army, he now said, must act "on the proper rule that all in the South *are* enemies of all in the North. . . . The whole country is full of guerrilla bands. . . . The entire South, man, woman, and child, is against us, armed and determined." This conviction governed Sherman's subsequent operations which left smoldering ruins in his track from Vicksburg to Meridian, from Atlanta to the sea, and from the sea to Goldsboro, North Carolina.

When Mississippians protested, Sherman told them that they were lucky to get off so lightly: A commander

> may take your house, your fields, your everything, and turn you all out, helpless, to starve. It may be wrong, but that don't alter the case. In war you can't help yourselves, and the only possible remedy is to stop the war. . . . Our duty is not to build up; it is rather to destroy both the rebel army and whatever of wealth or property it has founded its boasted strength upon.

When Confederate General John Bell Hood charged him with barbarism for expelling the civilian population from Atlanta, Sherman gave Hood a tongue-lashing. Accusations of barbarity, he said, came with a fine irony from "you who, in the midst of peace and prosperity, have plunged a nation into war . . . who dared and badgered us to battle, insulted our flag . . . turned loose your privateers to plunder unarmed ships, expelled Union families by the thousands [and] burned their houses. . . . Talk thus to the marines, but not to me, who have seen these things." Sherman vowed to "make Georgia howl" in his march from Atlanta to Savannah, and afterwards expressed satisfaction with having done so. He estimated the damage to Confederate resources "at $100,000,000; at least $20,000,000 of which has inured to our advantage, and the remainder is simple waste and destruction." And this turned out to be mere child's play compared with what awaited South Carolina.

Sherman was convinced that not only the economic resources but also the will of Southern civilians sustained the Confederate war effort. His campaigns of devastation were intended to break that will as much as to destroy the resources. This is certainly a feature of modern total war; Sherman was a pioneer in the concept of psychological warfare as part of a total war against the whole enemy population. Sherman was well aware of the fear that his soldiers inspired among Southern whites. This terror "was a power," he wrote, "and I intended to utilize it . . . to humble their pride, to follow them to their inmost recesses, and to make them fear and dread us. . . . We cannot change the hearts and minds of those people of the South, but we can make war so terrible . . . [and] make them so sick of war that generations would pass away before they would again appeal to it."

This strategy seemed to work; Sherman's destruction not only deprived Confederate armies of desperately needed supplies; it also crippled morale both on the home front and in the army. Numerous soldiers deserted from Confederate armies in response to letters of despair from home in the wake of Sherman's juggernaut. One Southern soldier wrote after the march through Georgia: "I hev conckludud that the dam fulishness uv tryin to lick shurmin Had better be stoped, we have gettin nuthin but hell & lots uv it ever since we saw the dam yankys & I am tirde uv it . . . thair thicker than lise on a hen and a dam site ornraier." After the march through South Carolina, a civilian in that state wrote: "All is gloom, despondency, and inactivity. Our army is demoralized and the people panic stricken. To fight longer seems to be madness."

Philip Sheridan carried out a similar policy of scorched earth in the Shenandoah Valley. Interestingly, Sheridan too had spent most of the war's first year in Missouri. There as well as subsequently in Tennessee and Virginia he saw the ravages of Confederate guerrillas, and responded as Sherman did. If guerrilla operations and Union counterinsurgency activities in Virginia during 1864 were slightly less vicious than in Missouri, it was perhaps only because the proximity of Washington and Richmond and of large field armies imposed some restraint. Nevertheless, plenty of atrocities piled up in John Singleton Mosby's Confederacy just east of the Blue Ridge and in the Shenandoah Valley to the west. In retaliation, and

with a purpose similar to Sherman's to destroy the Valley's resources which helped supply Lee's army, Sheridan carried out a campaign of devastation that left nothing to sustain Confederate armies or even to enable the Valley's inhabitants to get through the winter. In little more than a week, wrote Sheridan in one of his reports, his army had "destroyed over 2,000 barns filled with wheat, hay, and farming implements; over seventy mills filled with flour and wheat; have driven in front of the army over 4,000 head of stock, and have killed and issued to the troops not less than 3,000 sheep." That was just the beginning, Sheridan promised. By the time he was through, "the Valley, from Winchester up to Staunton, ninety-two miles, will have little in it for man or beast."

Several years later, while serving as an American observer at German headquarters during the Franco-Prussian War, Sheridan lectured his hosts on the correct way to wage war. The "proper strategy," said Sheridan, consisted first of "inflicting as telling blows as possible on the enemy's army, and then in causing the inhabitants so much suffering that they must long for peace, and force the government to demand it. The people must be left nothing but their eyes to weep with over the war."

Abraham Lincoln is famed for his compassion; he issued many pardons and commuted many sentences of execution; the concluding passage of his second inaugural address, beginning "With malice toward none; with charity for all," is one of his most familiar utterances. Lincoln regretted the devastation and suffering caused by the army's scorched-earth policy in the South. Yet he had warned Southerners in 1862 that the longer they fought, the more eggs would be broken. He would have agreed with Sherman's words to a Southerner: "You brought all this on yourselves." In 1864, after the march to the sea, Lincoln officially conveyed to Sherman's army the "grateful acknowledgments" of the nation; to Sheridan he offered the "thanks of the nation, and my own personal admiration, for [your] operations in the Shenandoah Valley." And while the words in the second inaugural about malice toward none and charity for all promised a generous peace, the victory that must precede that peace could be achieved only by hard war—indeed, by total war. Consider *these* words from the second inaugural:

> Fondly do we hope—fervently do we pray—that this mighty scourge of war may speedily pass away. Yet if God wills that it continue, until all the wealth piled by the bond-man's two hundred and fifty years of unrequited toil shall be sunk, and until every drop of blood drawn with the lash, shall be paid by another drawn with the sword, as was said three thousand years ago, so still it must be said "the judgments of the Lord, are true and righteous altogether."

The kind of conflict the Civil War had become merits the label of total war. To be sure, Union soldiers did not set out to kill Southern civilians. Sherman's bummers destroyed property; Allied bombers in World War II destroyed hundreds of thousands of lives as well. But the strategic purpose of both was the same: to eliminate the resources and break the will of the people to sustain war. White people in large parts of the Confederacy were indeed left with "nothing but their eyes to weep with." This was not pretty; it was not glorious; it did not conform to the image of war held by most Americans in 1861 of flags waving, bands playing, and people cheering on a spring afternoon. But as Sherman himself put it, in a speech to young men of a new generation fifteen years after the Civil War, the notion that war is glorious was nothing but moonshine. "When . . . you come down to the practical realities, boys," said Sherman, "war is all hell."

JAMES M. MCPHERSON is the George Henry Davis '86 Professor Emeritus of United States History at Princeton University. The author of 17 books, his major works include *The Struggle for Equality: Abolitionists and the Negro in the Civil War and Reconstruction* (Princeton University Press, 1964); *The Negro's Civil War: How American Negroes Felt and Acted During the War for the Union* (Pantheon Books, 1965); *Ordeal by Fire: The Civil War and Reconstruction* (3rd ed., McGraw-Hill, 2001); and *Battle Cry for Freedom: The Civil War Era* (Oxford University Press, 1988), for which he won the Pulitzer Prize.

EXPLORING THE ISSUE

Are Historians Wrong to Consider the War Between the States a "Total War"?

Critical Thinking and Reflection

1. (a) Define total war.
   (b) Given your definition, compare the arguments of Professors Neely and McPherson for their respective positions.
   (c) For example, do you agree with McPherson that the distinction between combatants and noncombatants refers to the twentieth-century world wars and that it is possible to have a total war without such a distinction? Critically evaluate the arguments of both authors.
2. Critically evaluate the different arguments of Neely and McPherson about the rhetoric and actions of General William T. Sherman. Did Sherman wage a total war? How similar and how different were Sherman's actions compared to those of the Allied Commanders in World War II?
3. Professor Neely argues that neither Lincoln, Grant, nor Sherman had a total war philosophy. Critically analyze what he means by this. How does Professor McPherson counter this argument?
4. Professor Neely argues elsewhere that President Lincoln's surrender terms—end hostilities, abolish the Confederacy, and emancipate the slaves—were lenient surrender terms. McPherson disagrees. Critically discuss.
5. Was it politically possible for Lincoln to have been tougher when Lee surrendered and have demanded the following?

   - Exclude all Confederate political leaders from public office.
   - Disenfranchise all Confederate soldiers.
   - Give free blacks the right to vote.
   - Give legal protection to the Republic party in former Confederate states.
   - Recognize the statehood of West Virginia.
   - Partition the Southern states.
   - Protect the ex-slaves who fought in the Union from reprisals.

   Critically discuss.

Is There Common Ground?

The "total war" issue raises a side question. Was the North's victory inevitable because of its superior leadership, nationalist ideology, and its overwhelming numbers in terms of population and natural resources? Most historians argue yes, but Professor James M. McPherson disagrees with the conventional wisdom. In a Gettysburg symposium, edited by Gabor S. Boritt, on *Why the Confederacy Lost* (Oxford University Press, 1992), McPherson dismisses all the external and internal explanations for the South's defeat listed above. In his critique, McPherson applies the theory of *reversibility*. Briefly stated, the hindsight provided by knowing the outcome of the war allows the writer to attribute causes that explain the northern victory. But what if the South had won the Civil War? Could the same external explanations that are attributed to the Union victory also be used to explain a Confederate win? Would Jefferson Davis's leadership emerge as superior to Abraham Lincoln's? Would the great military leaders be Robert E. Lee, Thomas "Stonewall" Jackson, and Braxton Bragg instead of Grant, Sherman, and Sheridan? Would one Confederate soldier be considered equal to four Union soldiers? Would a triumvirate of yeoman farmers, slaveholding planters, and small industrialists have proven the superiority of agrarian values over industrial ones?

In addition to the theory of reversibility, McPherson advances the theory of *contingency* as an explanation for the Union victory. During the war, four turning points that altered the course of the war could have gone either way. First, during the summer of 1862 the southern victories prolonged the war. Second, at the Battle of Antietam in the fall of 1862, the southern advance into the North stalled. Third, the battle of Gettysburg in July 1863 turned the tide of war in favor of the Union. Fourth, the Atlanta and western campaigns in the fall of 1864 enabled Lincoln to win the presidential election and eventually led the northern forces to defeat the Confederacy and abolish slavery. These arguments merit serious consideration by students and scholars seeking to characterize the nature of the American Civil War.

Create Central

www.mhhe.com/createcentral

Additional Resources

Edward Ayers, *Valley of the Shadow: Two Communities in the American Civil War* (W. W. Norton, 2000)

Stig Forster and Jorg Nagler, eds., *On the Road to Total War: The American Civil War and the German Wars of Unification, 1861–1871* (Cambridge University Press, 1997)

James M. McPherson, *Battle Cry of Freedom: The Civil War Era* (Oxford University Press, 1998)

James M. McPherson and William J. Cooper, Jr., eds., *Writing the Civil War: The Quest to Understand* (University of South Carolina Press, 1998)

Robert Toplin, ed., *Ken Burns' The Civil War: The Historians Respond* (Oxford University Press, 1996)

Internet References . . .

AmericanCivilWar.com

http://americancivilwar.com/index.html

Images of Battle—The American Civil War

www.lib.unc.edu/mss/exhibits/civilwar/index.html

The Valley of the Shadow Project

http://valley.vcdh.virginia.edu/

Selected, Edited, and with Issue Framing Material by:
Larry Madaras, *Howard Community College*
and
James M. SoRelle, *Baylor University*

ISSUE

Was Abraham Lincoln America's Greatest President?

YES: Phillip Shaw Paludan, from *The Presidency of Abraham Lincoln* (University Press of Kansas, 1994)

NO: Melvin E. Bradford, from *Remembering Who We Are: Observations of a Southern Conservative* (University of Georgia Press, 1985)

Learning Outcomes

After reading this issue, you will be able to:

- Evaluate the criteria historians use to assess presidential performance.
- Analyze Lincoln's leadership from the perspective of the concept of the "imperial presidency."
- Identify and assess Lincoln's policies as a wartime president.
- Summarize the major points of criticism of Lincoln's presidency.

ISSUE SUMMARY

YES: Phillip Shaw Paludan contends that Abraham Lincoln's greatness exceeds that of all other American presidents because Lincoln, in the face of unparalleled challenges associated with the Civil War, succeeded in preserving the Union and freeing the slaves.

NO: Melvin E. Bradford characterizes Lincoln as a cynical politician whose abuse of authority as president and commander-in-chief during the Civil War marked a serious departure from the republican goals of the Founding Fathers and established the prototype for the "imperial presidency" of the twentieth century.

The American Civil War (1861–1865) produced what Arthur Schlesinger, Jr. has called "our greatest national trauma." To be sure, the War Between the States was a searing event that etched itself on the collective memory of the American people and inspired an interest that has made it the most thoroughly studied episode in American history. During the last century and a quarter, scholars have identified a variety of factors (including slavery, economic sectionalism, cultural distinctions between North and South, the doctrine of states' rights, and the irresponsibility of abolitionists and proslavery advocates) that contributed to sectional tensions and that ultimately led to war. Although often presented as "sole causes," these factors are complicated, interconnected, and controversial. Consequently, historians must consider as many of them as possible in their evaluations of the war, even if they choose to spotlight one or another as the main explanation (see Issue 14).

Most historians, however, agree that the war would not have occurred had 11 southern states not seceded from the Union to form the Confederate States of America following Abraham Lincoln's election to the presidency

in 1860. Why was Lincoln viewed as a threat to the South? A southerner by birth, Lincoln's career in national politics (as a congressman representing his adopted state of Illinois) apparently had been short-circuited by his unpopular opposition to the Mexican War. His attempt to emerge from political obscurity a decade later failed when he was defeated by Stephen Douglas in a bid for a Senate seat from Illinois. This campaign, however, gained for Lincoln a reputation as a powerful orator, and in 1860 Republican Party managers passed over some of their more well-known leaders, such as William Henry Seward, and nominated the moderate Mr. Lincoln for the presidency. His victory was guaranteed by factionalism within Democratic ranks, but the election results revealed that the new president received only 39 percent of the popular vote. This fact, however, provided little solace for Southerners, who mistook the new president's opposition to the extension of slavery into the territories as evidence that he supported the abolitionist wing of the Republican Party. Despite assurances during the campaign that he would not tamper with slavery where it already existed, Lincoln could not prevent the splintering of the Union.

Given such an inauspicious beginning, few observers at the time could have predicted that future generations would view Lincoln as our nation's greatest president. What factors have contributed to this assessment? The answer would appear to lie in his role as commander-in-chief during the Civil War. Is this reputation deserved?

Lincoln's assassination at the hands of John Wilkes Booth shortly following the end of the Civil War pretty much guaranteed for the fallen leader a martyrdom that had the potential to cloud balanced appraisals of his leadership. Biographer Stephen B. Oates, in *Abraham Lincoln: The Man Behind the Myths* (Harper & Row, 1984), accurately reminds us that Lincoln, at the time of his assassination, was perhaps the most hated president in history. But since Arthur Schlesinger, Jr. first polled experts on the subject in 1948, historians consistently have rated Lincoln the nation's best chief executive. George Washington, Thomas Jefferson, Theodore and Franklin Roosevelt, and Woodrow Wilson have done well in presidential polls conducted by Gary Maranell (1970), Steve Neal (1982), and Robert K. Murray (1983), but none so well as Abraham Lincoln. Another president, Harry Truman, himself ranked Lincoln in the category of "great" chief executives. Truman wrote of Lincoln: "He was a strong executive who saved the government, saved the United States. He was a President who understood people, and, when it came time to make decisions, he was willing to take the responsibility and make those decisions, no matter how difficult they were. He knew how to treat people and how to make a decision stick, and that's why his is regarded as such a great Administration."

Some of the most insightful writing on various aspects of Lincoln's life appeared almost 50 years ago but still offer incisive interpretations of many aspects of Lincoln's political career and philosophy. See, for example, David Donald, *Lincoln Reconsidered: Essays on the Civil War Era* (Knopf, 1956) and Richard Current, *The Lincoln Nobody Knows* (McGraw-Hill, 1958). Lincoln's responsibility for the precipitating event of the war is explored in Richard N. Current, *Lincoln and the First Shot* (Lippincott, 1963). Doris Kearns Goodwin, *Team of Rivals: The Political Genius of Abraham Lincoln* (Simon & Schuster, 2005) is a beautifully written more recent appraisal of Lincoln's approach to leadership. Goodwin, in particular, notes that in the selection of cabinet members, Lincoln chose individuals representing many different factions but who overcame their contentiousness to handle competently the burdens of wartime governing.

The best studies of Lincoln's attitudes toward race and slavery are by the generally sympathetic Benjamin Quarles, *Lincoln and the Negro* (Oxford University Press, 1962), and by LaWanda Cox, *Lincoln and Black Freedom: A Study in Presidential Leadership* (University of South Carolina Press, 1981). Lerone Bennett, *Forced Into Glory: Abraham Lincoln's White Dream* (Johnson Publishing, 2000) characterizes Lincoln as a white supremacist and argues that African American slaves themselves were far more effective agents of emancipation than was the "Great Emancipator."

The selections that follow assess Lincoln's presidency from dramatically different perspectives. Phillip Shaw Paludan sees unparalleled greatness in the leadership of the United States' 16th chief executive. Lincoln's greatness, Paludan concludes, derived from his ability to mobilize public opinion in the North behind his goal of saving the Union and freeing the slaves. Significantly, Paludan does not separate these accomplishments. Rather, he argues that they were inextricably connected; one could not be realized without the other.

Melvin Bradford offers a sharp critique of the conclusions reached by Paludan. By pursuing an anti-southern strategy, Bradford argues, President Lincoln perverted the republican goals advanced by the Founding Fathers and destroyed the Democratic majority that was essential to the preservation of the Union. Furthermore, Bradford asserts, Lincoln abused his executive authority by cynically expanding the scope of presidential powers to an unhealthy extent. Finally, Bradford charges that Lincoln was uncommitted to the cause of black Americans.

YES ↙

Phillip Shaw Paludan

The Presidency of Abraham Lincoln

The oath is a simple one, made all the more austere because there is no coronation, no anointing by priest or predecessor. The office has passed from one person to another months before, first by popular election and then by a ritualistic casting of votes by presidential electors, whose names are forgotten if anyone knew them in the first place. The only requirement on the day the president takes office is an oath or affirmation: "I do solemnly swear that I will faithfully execute the Office of President of the United States, and will to the best of my ability, preserve, protect and defend the Constitution of the United States."

Each president in the history of the nation has tried to protect and defend the Constitution—some with more dedication than others. Each responded to the challenges and the opportunity that his time gave him. No president had larger challenges than Abraham Lincoln, and the testimony to his greatness rests in his keeping of that oath, which led him to be responsible for two enormous accomplishments that are part of folk legend as well as fact. He saved the Union and he freed the slaves.

He preserved the unity of the nation both in size and in structure. There were still thirty-six states at the end of his presidency; there might have been twenty-five. The population of the nation when he died was 30 million; it might have been 20 million. The constitutional instrument for changing governments was still in 1865 what it had been in 1861—win a free election and gain the majority of the electoral votes. Another option might have existed—secede from the country and make war if necessary after losing the election. A divided nation might have been more easily divided again—perhaps when angry westerners felt exploited by eastern capitalists, perhaps when urban minorities felt oppressed by powerful majorities. And there were lasting international consequences from Lincoln's achievement: Foreign oppressors of the twentieth century were not allowed to run free, disregarding the two or perhaps three or four countries that might have existed between Canada and Mexico.

Because of Lincoln, 4 million black Americans gained options beyond a life of slavery for themselves and their children. Men, women, and children were no longer bought and sold, denied their humanity—because of Lincoln, but certainly not because of Lincoln alone. Perhaps 2 million Union soldiers fought to achieve these goals. Women behind the lines and near the battlefields did jobs that men would not or could not do. Workers on farms and in factories supplied the huge army and the society that sustained it. Managers and entrepreneurs organized the resources that helped gain the victory. But Lincoln's was the voice that inspired and explained and guided soldiers and civilians to continue the fight.

Black soldiers, too, preserved the Union and freed slaves. And these black soldiers were in the army because Lincoln wanted them there, accepted the demands of black and white abolitionists and growing numbers of soldiers and sailors that they be there. Hundreds of thousands, perhaps millions, of slaves, given the chance, walked away from slavery and thus "stole" from their masters the labor needed to sustain the Confederacy and the ability of those masters to enslave them. No one would ever again sell their children, their husbands, their wives; no one would rape and murder and mutilate them, control their work and much of their leisure.

Lincoln kept his oath by leading the nation, guiding it, insisting that it keep on with the task of saving the Union and freeing the slaves.

Too often historians and the general populace (which cares very much, and may define itself in vital ways by what Lincoln did and means) have divided his two great achievements. They have made saving the Union, at least for the first half of his presidency, a different task from freeing the slaves. They have noted that Lincoln explained to Horace Greeley that he could not answer Greeley's "Prayer of Twenty Million" and simply free the slaves. His prime goal, he told Greeley, was to save the Union, and he would free none, some, or all the slaves to save that Union. But before Lincoln wrote those words he had already decided that to save the Union he would have to free the slaves.

. . . Freeing the slaves and saving the Union were linked as one goal, not two optional goals. The Union that Lincoln wanted to save was not a union where slavery was safe. He wanted to outlaw slavery in the territories and thus begin a process that would end it in the states. Slave states understood this; that is why they seceded and why the Union needed saving.

Freeing the slaves, more precisely ending slavery, was the indispensable means to saving the Union. In an immediate practical sense, those 180,000 black soldiers were an essential part of the Union army in the last two years of the war. They made up almost 12 percent of the total Union land forces by 1865, adding not only to Union numbers but subtracting from the Confederate labor force. Moreover, those black soldiers liberated even where they did not march. Their example was noted throughout the South so that slaves far from Union occupation knew that blacks could be soldiers, not just property, and they began to march toward freedom.

Ending slavery also meant saving the Union in a larger sense. Slavery had endangered the Union, hurting black people but also hurting white people, and not only by allowing them to be brutes, as Jefferson had lamented. Slavery had divided the nation, threatening the processes of government by making debate over the most crucial issue of the age intolerable in the South and, for decades, dangerous in the Congress of the United States. To protect slavery the Confederate States of America would challenge the peaceful, lawful, orderly means of changing governments in the United States, even by resorting to war. Lincoln led the successful effort to stop them and thus simultaneously saved the Union and freed the slaves.

Why does it matter that Lincoln linked saving the Union and the emancipation of the nation from slavery? First, it is necessary to get the historical record straight. It matters also because in understanding our history Americans gain access to the kind of faith that Lincoln held that our means, our legal processes, our political-constitutional system work to achieve our best ideals. Too many people, among them the first black justice of the United States Supreme Court, Thurgood Marshall, have doubted that respect for the law and the Constitution can lead to greater equality. "The system" too often has been the villain, "institutional racism" the disease that obstructs the struggle for equality. The underlying premise of this book is that the political-constitutional system, conceived of and operated at its best, inescapably leads to equality. Lincoln operated on that premise and through his presidency tried to achieve that goal.

But how did he do that? One of his accomplishments, the one that took most of his time, was fighting and winning a war. He chose the generals, gathered the armies, set the overall strategy; he restrained the dissenters and the opponents of the war; he helped to gather the resources that would maintain the Union economy and that would enable the Union military to remain strong and unrelenting. He kept himself and his party in office, the only party that was dedicated to saving the Union and ending slavery. And he kept an eye on foreign affairs, seeing to it that Great Britain remained willing to negotiate and to watch the conflict rather than joining or trying to stop it. . . .

I am particularly interested in what Lincoln said, for the most important power of a president, as Richard Neustadt has argued, is the power to persuade. Thus it is vital for a president to inform and to inspire, to warn and to empower the polity, to bring out the "better angels of our nature"—better in the sense of allowing the nation to achieve its best aspirations. "Events have controlled me," Lincoln said, but what he did most effectively was to define those events and to shape the public opinion that, he noted, was "everything in this country." In the 1840s a Whig newspaper came close to the mark I am admiring in assessing Lincoln:

> Put the case that the same multitude were addressed by two orators, and on the same question and occasion; that the first of these orators considered in his mind that the people he addressed were to be controlled by several passions . . . the orator may be fairly said to have no faith in the people; he rather believes that they are creatures of passion, and subject to none but base and selfish impulses. But now a second orator arises, a Chatham, a Webster, a Pericles, a Clay; his generous spirit expands itself through the vast auditory, and he believes that he is addressing a company of high spirited men, citizens. . . . When he says "fellow citizens," they believe him, and at once, from a tumultuous herd they are converted into men . . . their thoughts and feeling rise to an heroical heights, beyond that of common men or common times. The second orator "had faith in the people"; he addressed the better part of each man's nature, supposing it to be in him—and it *was* in him.

At their best American presidents recognize that their duty as the chief opinion maker is to shape a public understanding that opens options and tells the truth about what the people can be and what their problems are. Appealing to the fears we have, manipulating them to win office or pass a law or achieve another goal, does not so much *reflect* who we are as it in fact *creates* who we are. It affirms us as legitimately fearful—afraid of something that our leaders confirm to be frightening—and as being citizens whose fears properly define us.

Appealing to better angels is more complicated—it requires calling on history for original aspirations—reminding Americans for example that the basic ideal of the nation is that "all men are created equal." Equally vital, such an appeal also requires reminding Americans that they have in fact established institutions that work to that end—not only reminding them of their aspirations but also reassuring them that their history, their lived experience, reveals legitimate paths to achieving those goals. History thus acts to recall the nation's best dreams, but it also restores faith that the means to approach the dream live, abide in the institutions as well as in the values that shape the nation.

I believe that a history of the presidency of Abraham Lincoln can show how Lincoln managed to shape a public understanding, how at times he failed, but how he usually succeeded. Thus he set a standard that makes it legitimate that we, when the better angels of our nature prevail, define ourselves in important ways by who Lincoln was, by what he did, and by what he said.

The Lincoln presidency did not end through the operation of the political-constitutional system. There was no joyous ritual, no abiding process that had gone on for generations. It was the first assassination of a president in history. A single bullet erased the decision by the people of the Union that Abraham Lincoln should be their president. It was stunning, an awful repudiation of the system that helped define them as a people, that they had been fighting for over the last four years, that had cost them such blood and treasure.

Yet the process endured. Reacting to the murder of the president newspapers throughout the country spoke of the need to "let law and order resume their sway," as the *San Francisco Chronicle* noted. "The law must reign supreme," the *Philadelphia Evening Bulletin* declared, "or in this great crisis chaos will overwhelm us, and our own maddening feeling bring upon us national wreck and ruin which traitor arms have failed to accomplish." More specifically there was admiration and recognition for a system that could overcome even assassination. "When Andrew Johnson was sworn in as President," the Reverend Joseph Thompson told a New York audience, "the Statue of Liberty that surmounts the dome of the Capitol and was put there by Lincoln, looked down on the city and on the nation and said 'Our Government is unchanged—it has merely passed from the hands of one man into those of another.'"

The words reflected part of a larger legacy. The Union was saved, and thus the political-constitutional process endured—the nation would change governments, settle controversies, and debate alternatives at the polls, in legislative halls, and in courtrooms, not on bloody battlefields. It would be a nation whose size and diversity gave it wealth and opportunities for its citizens and huge potential influence in the world. Future autocrats would have reason to fear that influence, just as future immigrants would be drawn to it. Its power would not always be used well. Native Americans who "obstructed" national mission, foreign governments deemed "un-American" had reason to fear and to protest against invasions of their rights and the destruction of their people. But within the nation itself, because of what it stood for and fought for and preserved, there remained a conscience that could be appealed to in the name of the ideals it symbolized and had demonstrated in its greatest war. Saving the Union had meant killing slavery.

Slavery was dead. Its power to divide the Union, to erode and destroy constitutional and political debate was over. No longer was the highest court in the land able to rule that under the Constitution black people had no rights that white people had to respect and that no political party legally could say otherwise. No longer could men, women, and children be bought and sold: treated as things without ties to each other, without the capacity to fulfill their own dreams. The Thirteenth Amendment, ending slavery throughout the nation and moving through the states toward ratification, ensured that. And in the vain of that amendment came protection for civil rights and suffrage. Blacks were promised that they would enter the political arena and the constitutional system—this time as participants, not as objects.

This more perfect Union was achieved chiefly through an extraordinary outreach of national authority. Certainly Lincoln extended presidential power beyond any limits seen before his time—the war demanded that; Congress agreed, the Supreme Court acquiesced, and the people sustained his power. If one compares Lincoln's use of power with executive actions before 1861, popular and even scholarly use of a word such as "dictatorship" makes limited sense. Lincoln had produced, as Edwin S. Corwin observes, "a complete transformation in the President's role as Commander in Chief." Yet war was about the expansion of power, and Congress also stepped forward, expanding national power, extending its authority. Even state governments reached further than precedent admitted, increasing expenditures, strengthening their police powers over health, morals, and safety, and establishing new regulatory agencies to shape the economy.

After the war public pressures demanded a return to peacetime boundaries. Executive authority in most areas, once the fight between Johnson and Congress was settled, rapidly contracted. A few outbursts of presidential influence showed that the White House was still occupied. Grant fought senators bitterly over the Santo Domingo Treaty and presided over an effective Treaty of Washington, which resolved claims against the British for building rebel raiders. Hayes sent federal troops to settle labor protests and worked for civil service reforms. Garfield, Arthur, and Harrison also kept busy; Cleveland's vetoes showed signs of vigor. Generally, however, the presidency declined in power. With the exception of Grant a series of one-term presidents did little to inspire demands that they stay in office. For the rest of the century no president came within miles of Lincoln's power or even close to Polk or Jackson, for that matter. By 1886 Woodrow Wilson was able to write that national government in the United States was "congressional government." M. Ostrogorsky, telling foreign audiences about America, described a lawmaking environment in which "after the [civil] war the eclipse of the executive was complete and definitive"; Lord Bryce told British and American audiences in 1894 that "the domestic authority of the President is in time of peace small." These late-nineteenth-century images may have inspired Theodore Lowi to assert in 1992 that "by 1875 you would not know there had been a war or a Lincoln."

But Lord Bryce had added a caveat about the president's domestic authority: In time of war, "especially in a civil war, it expands with portentous speed." Clearly it had been thus with Lincoln. Despite calls to retreat from the vast domains of Civil War there is a sense in which Lincoln's legacy of power in the presidency survived the retreat. Certainly presidential authority, like the national authority with which it was connected, diminished when the war was over. But national power was still available after Appomattox and for the fundamental purpose that had called it forth originally: to destroy slavery and its vestiges. The fight between Congress and Lincoln's successor has obscured the fact that congressional Republicans were acting in the same cause for which Lincoln had acted. They were not recapturing power lost to the president; they were claiming power that they had shared increasingly with Lincoln.

Before Lincoln died many of the more radical Republicans had been attacking him for moving too slowly toward emancipation and then for yielding too much to military necessity and Southern loyalists. After early statements of satisfaction with Johnson they quickly came to their senses as Johnson proved not only to be slower than Lincoln to march to their goals but also to be a bitter racist obstructionist. Thus they fought against Johnson and for goals that Lincoln had espoused and had used his power to try to achieve: civil rights, education, suffrage for the freedmen. The army, which had been the major instrument of Lincoln's expanding egalitarianism and which looked to its commander in chief for direction, shifted its allegiance to Congress. Soldiers such as Grant, whom Lincoln had charged with leading the army to save the Union, did not think it incongruous to support Congress in its battle to preserve the gains of war. And when legislators moved to weaken executive power over the army with the Tenure of Office and the Command of the Army acts, they were trying to save Lincoln's legacy by weakening Johnson.

Although President Grant retreated on other issues, he tried to protect former slaves from white Southerners' efforts to restore as much of the prewar South as they could. Grant sent troops into Louisiana, Mississippi, North Carolina, and South Carolina to effect the Force Acts and to destroy the Ku Klux Klan. A vocal element in the Republican party continued to push for federal intervention in the South in the form of national civil rights and suffrage-enforcement laws well into the 1890s. Despite retreating from the broadest definitions of federal power when it interpreted the Civil War amendments, the Supreme Court struck down laws that kept blacks off juries, and that denied Chinese Americans equal chances to work, and it upheld federal power to protect blacks from political violence. The Justice Department prosecuted thousands of election officers under this power. Local juries usually acquitted their white neighbors, but the national prohibition remained. Because of the Lincoln presidency the constitutional system carried promises of equality, and the processes to bring those promises to life endured. One hundred years after Lincoln had been awakened by the Kansas Nebraska Act to the dangers of slavery to the constitutional system, blacks and whites would see the United States Supreme Court strike down inequality in that system (that case would, interestingly enough, also involve Kansas).

Not every element, even in that reformed constitutional system, promised equal justice. The Union that Lincoln and his forces had saved remained a Union of states. Lincoln's respect for those states, demonstrated in his commitment to reconstruct them rather than to allow Congress to govern territories and in his insistence that only a constitutional amendment, ratified by states, would secure slavery's death, strengthened later arguments that states should control the fate of their citizens, old and new. Lincoln's abiding insistence that the Constitution guided his actions meant that black equality could be hindered or denied by constitutional claims of states' rights and local self-government. Brutal racism could find shelter in such legal arguments.

Yet the triumph and the irony of his administration resided in Lincoln's commitment to the Constitution; without that there would have been no promises to keep to 4 million black Americans. Because so many Americans cherished the Union that the Constitution forged, they made war on slave masters and their friends, on a government that Alexander Stephens claimed rested "on the great truth that the negro is not the equal of the white man; that slavery . . . is his natural and normal condition."

Without the president's devotion to and mastery of the political-constitutional institutions of his time, in all probability the Union would have lacked the capacity to focus its will and its resources on defeating that Confederacy. Without Lincoln's unmatched ability to integrate egalitarian ends and constitutional means he could not have enlisted the range of supporters and soldiers necessary for victory. His great accomplishment was to energize and mobilize the nation by affirming its better angels, by showing the nation at its best: engaged in the imperative, life-preserving conversation between structure and purpose, ideal and institution, means and ends.

PHILLIP SHAW PALUDAN (1938–2007) was a professor of history at the University of Kansas for over 30 years before accepting the distinguished chair in Lincoln studies at the University of Illinois, Springfield. In addition to his study of Lincoln's presidency, which won the Lincoln Prize, he is the author of *Victims: A True Story of the Civil War* (University of Tennessee Press, 1981) and *A People's Contest: The Union and Civil War, 1861–1865* (Harper & Row, 1988).

Melvin E. Bradford  **NO**

Remembering Who We Are: Observations of a Southern Conservative

The Lincoln Legacy: A Long View

With the time and manner of his death Abraham Lincoln, as leader of a Puritan people who had just won a great victory over "the forces of evil," was placed beyond the reach of ordinary historical inquiry and assessment. Through Booth's bullet he became the one who had "died to make men free," who had perished that his country's "new birth" might occur: a "second founder" who, in Ford's theater, had been transformed into an American version of the "dying god." Our common life, according to this construction, owes its continuation to the shedding of the sacred blood. Now after over a century of devotion to the myth of the "political messiah," it is still impossible for most Americans to see through and beyond the magical events of April 1865. However, Lincoln's daily purchase upon the ongoing business of the nation requires that we devise a way of setting aside the martyrdom to look behind it at Lincoln's place in the total context of American history and discover in him a major source of our present confusion, our distance from the republicanism of the Fathers, the models of political conduct which we profess most to admire. . . .

Of course, nothing that we can identify as part of Lincoln's legacy belongs to him alone. In some respects the Emancipator was carried along with the tides. Yet a measure of his importance is that he was at the heart of the major political events of his era. Therefore what signifies in a final evaluation of this melancholy man is that many of these changes in the country would never have come to pass had Lincoln not pushed them forward. Or at least not come so quickly, or with such dreadful violence. I will emphasize only the events that he most certainly shaped according to his relentless will, alterations in the character of our country for which he was clearly responsible. For related developments touched by Lincoln's wand, I can have only a passing word. The major charges advanced here, if proved, are sufficient to impeach the most famous and respected of public men. More would only overdo.

The first and most obvious item in my bill of particulars for indictment concerns Lincoln's dishonesty and obfuscation with respect to the nation's future obligations to the Negro, slave and free. It was of course an essential ingredient of Lincoln's position that he make a success at being anti-Southern or antislavery without at the same time appearing to be significantly impious about the beginnings of the Republic (which was neither anti-Southern nor antislavery)—or significantly pro-Negro. He was the first Northern politician of any rank to combine these attitudes into a viable platform persona, the first to make his moral position on slavery in the South into a part of his national politics. It was a posture that enabled him to unite elements of the Northern electorate not ordinarily willing to cooperate in any political undertaking. And thus enabled him to destroy the old Democratic majority—a coalition necessary to preserving the union of the states. Then came the explosion. But this calculated posturing has had more durable consequences than secession and the Federal confiscation of property in slaves. . . .

In the nation as a whole what moves toward fruition is a train of events set in motion by the duplicitous rhetoric concerning the Negro that helped make Abraham Lincoln into our first "sectional" president. Central to this appeal is a claim to a kind of moral superiority that costs absolutely nothing in the way of conduct. Lincoln, in insisting that the Negro was included in the promise of the Declaration of Independence and that the Declaration bound his countrymen to fulfill a pledge hidden in that document, seemed clearly to point toward a radical transformation of American society. Carried within his rejection of Negro slavery as a continuing feature of the American regime, his assertion that the equality clause of the Declaration of Independence was "the father of all moral principle among us," were certain muted corollaries. By promising that the peculiar institution would be made to disappear if candidates for national office adopted the proper "moral attitude" on that subject, Lincoln recited as a litany the general terms of his regard for universal human rights. But at the same time he added certain modifications to this high doctrine: modifications required by those of his countrymen to whom he hoped to appeal, by the rigid racism of the Northern electorate, and by "what his own feelings would admit." The most important of these reservations was that none of his doctrine should apply significantly to the Negro in the North. Or, after freedom, to what he could expect in the South. It was a very broad, very general, and very abstract principle to which he made reference. By it he could divide the sheep from the goats, the wheat from the chaff, the patriot from the conspirator. But for the Negro it provided nothing more than a technical freedom, best to be enjoyed far away. Or the valuable opportunity to "root, hog, or die." For the sake of such vapid distinctions he urged his countrymen to wade through seas of blood.

To be sure, this position does not push the "feelings" of that moralist who was our sixteenth president too far from what was comfortable for him. And it goes without saying that a commitment to "natural rights" which will not challenge the Black Codes of Illinois, which promises something like them for the freedman in the South, or else offers him as alternative the proverbial "one-way-ticket to nowhere" is a commitment of empty words. It is only an accident of political history that the final Reconstruction settlement provided a bit more for the former slave—principally, the chance to vote Republican; and even that "right" didn't last, once a better deal was made available to his erstwhile protectors. But the point is that Lincoln's commitment was precisely of the sort that the North was ready to make—while passing legislation to restrict the flow of Negroes into its own territories, elaborating its own system of segregation by race, and exploiting black labor through its representatives in a conquered South. Lincoln's double talk left his part of the country with a durable heritage of pious self-congratulation. . . .

The second heading in this "case against Lincoln" involves no complicated pleading. Neither will it confuse any reader who examines his record with care. For it has to do with Lincoln's political economy, his management of the commercial and business life of the part of the Republic under his authority. This material is obvious, even though it is not always connected with the presidency of Abraham Lincoln. Nevertheless, it must be developed at this point. For it leads directly into the more serious charges upon which this argument depends. It is customary to deplore the Gilded Age, the era of the Great Barbecue. It is true that many of the corruptions of the Republican Era came to a head after Lincoln lay at rest in Springfield. But it is a matter of fact that they began either under his direction or with his sponsorship. Military necessity, the "War for the Union," provided an excuse, an umbrella of sanction, under which the essential nature of the changes being made in the relation of government to commerce could be concealed. Of his total policy the Northern historian Robert Sharkey has written, "Human ingenuity would have had difficulty in contriving a more perfect engine for class and sectional exploration, creditors finally obtaining the upper hand as opposed to debtors, and the developed East holding the whip over the underdeveloped West and South." Until the South left the Union, until a High Whig sat in the White House, none of this return to the "energetic government" of Hamilton's design was possible. Indeed, even in the heyday of the Federalists it had never been so simple a matter to translate power into wealth. Now Lincoln could try again the internal improvements of the early days in Illinois. The difference was that this time the funding would not be restrained by political reversal or a failure of credit. For if anything fell short,

Mr. Salmon P. Chase, "the foreman" of his "green printing office," could be instructed "to give his paper mill another turn." And the inflationary policy of rewarding the friends of the government sustained. The euphemism of our time calls this "income redistribution." But it was theft in 1864, and is theft today.

A great increase in the tariff and the formation of a national banking network were, of course, the cornerstones of this great alteration in the posture of the Federal government toward the sponsorship of business. From the beginning of the Republican Party Lincoln warned his associates not to talk about their views on these subjects. Their alliance, he knew, was a negative thing: a league against the Slave Power and its Northern friends. But in private he made it clear that the hidden agenda of the Republicans would have its turn, once the stick was in their hand. In this he promised well. Between 1861 and 1865, the tariff rose from 18.84 percent to 47.56 percent. And it stayed above 40 percent in all but two years of the period concluded with the election of Woodrow Wilson. Writes the Virginia historian Ludwell H. Johnson, it would "facilitate a massive transfer of wealth, satisfying the dreariest predictions of John C. Calhoun." The new Republican system of banking (for which we should note Lincoln was directly accountable) was part of the same large design of "refounding." The National Banking Acts of 1863 and 1864, with the earlier Legal Tender Act, flooded the country with $480 million of fiat money that was soon depreciated by about two-thirds in relation to specie. Then all notes but the greenback dollar were taxed out of existence, excepting only United States Treasury bonds that all banks were required to purchase if they were to have a share in the war boom. The support for these special bonds was thus the debt itself—Hamilton's old standby. Specie disappeared. Moreover, the bank laws controlled the money supply, credit, and the balance of power. New banks and credit for farms, small businesses, or small town operations were discouraged. And the Federalist model, after four score and seven years, finally achieved.

As chief executive, Lincoln naturally supported heavy taxes. Plus a scheme of tax graduation. The war was a legitimate explanation for these measures. Lincoln's participation in huge subsidies or bounties for railroads and in other legislation granting economic favors is not so readily linked to "saving the Union." All of his life Lincoln was a friend of the big corporations. He had no moral problem in signing a bill which gifted the Union Pacific Railway with a huge strip of land running across the West and an almost unsecured loan of $16,000 to $48,000 per mile of track. The final result of this bill was the Credit Mobilier scandal. With other laws favoring land speculation it helped to negate the seemingly noble promise of the Homestead Act of 1862—under which less than 19 percent of the open lands settled between 1860 and 1900 went to legitimate homesteaders. The Northern policy of importing immigrants with the promise of this land, only to force them into the ranks of General Grant's meatgrinder or into near slavery in the cities of the East, requires little comment. Nor need we belabor the rotten army contracts given to politically faithful crooks. Nor the massive thefts by law performed during the war in the South. More significant is Lincoln's openly disgraceful policy of allowing special cronies and favorites of his friends to trade in Southern cotton—even with "the enemy" across the line—and his calculated use of the patronage and the pork barrel. Between 1860 and 1880, the Republicans spent almost $10 million breathing life into state and local Republican organizations. Lincoln pointed them down that road. There can be no doubt of his responsibility for the depressing spectacle of greed and peculation concerning which so many loyal Northern men of the day spoke with sorrow, disappointment, and outrage. . . .

A large part of the complaint against Lincoln as a political precedent for later declensions from the example of the Fathers has to do with his expansion of the powers of the presidency and his alteration of the basis for the Federal Union. With reference to his role in changing the office of chief magistrate from what it had been under his predecessors, it is important to remember that he defined himself through the war powers that belonged to his post. In this way Lincoln could profess allegiance to the Whig ideal of the modest, self-effacing leader, the antitype of Andrew Jackson, and, in his capacity as Commander-in-Chief, do whatever he wished. That is, if he could do it in the name of preserving the Union. As Clinton Rossiter has stated, Lincoln believed there were "no limits" to his powers if he exercised them in that "holy cause." Gottfried Dietze compares Lincoln in this role to the Committee of Public Safety as it operated in the French Revolution. Except for the absence of mass executions, the results were similar. War is of course the occasion for concentration of power and the limitation of liberties within any nation. But an internal war, a war between states in a union of states, is not like a war to repel invasion or to acquire territory. For it is an extension into violence of a domestic political difference. And it is thus subject to extraordinary abuses of authority—confusions or conflations of purpose which convert the effort to win the war into an effort to effect even larger, essentially political changes in the structure of government. War, in these terms, is not only an engine for preserving the Union; it is also an instrument for transforming its nature. But without overdeveloping this structure of theory, let us shore it up with specific instances of presidential misconduct by Lincoln: abuses that mark him as our first imperial president. Lincoln began his tenure as a dictator when between April 12 and July 4 of 1861, without interference from Congress, he summoned militia, spent millions, suspended law, authorized recruiting, decreed a blockade, defied the Supreme Court, and pledged the nation's credit. In the following months and years he created units of government not known to the Constitution and officers to rule over them in "conquered" sections of the South, seized property throughout both sections, arrested upwards of twenty thousand

of his political enemies and confined them without trial in a Northern "Gulag," closed over three hundred newspapers critical of his policy, imported an army of foreign mercenaries (of perhaps five hundred thousand men), interrupted the assembly of duly elected legislatures and employed the Federal hosts to secure his own reelection—in a contest where about thirty-eight thousand votes, if shifted, might have produced an armistice and a negotiated peace under a President McClellan. To the same end he created a state in West Virginia, arguing of this blatant violation of the explicit provisions of the Constitution that it was "expedient." But the worst of this bold and ruthless dealing (and I have given but a very selective list of Lincoln's "high crimes") has to do with his role as military leader per se: as the commander and selector of Northern generals, chief commissary of the Federal forces, and head of government in dealing with the leaders of an opposing power. In this role the image of Lincoln grows to be very dark—indeed, almost sinister.

The worst that we may say of Lincoln is that he led the North in war so as to put the domestic political priorities of his political machine ahead of the lives and the well-being of his soldiers in the field. The appointment of the venal Simon Cameron of Pennsylvania as his secretary of war, and of lesser hacks and rascals to direct the victualing of Federal armies, was part of this malfeasance. By breaking up their bodies, the locust hoard of contractors even found a profit in the Union dead. And better money still in the living. They made of Lincoln (who winked at their activities) an accessory to lost horses, rotten meat, and worthless guns. But all such mendacity was nothing in comparison to the price in blood paid for Lincoln's attempts to give the nation a genuine Republican hero. He had a problem with this project throughout the entire course of the war. That is, until Grant and Sherman "converted" to radicalism. Prior to their emergence all of Lincoln's "loyal" generals disapproved of either his politics or of his character. These, as with McClellan, he could use and discharge at will. Or demote to minor tasks. One thinks immediately of George G. Meade—who defeated Lee at Gettysburg, and yet made the mistake of defining himself as the defender of a separate Northern nation from whose soil he would drive a foreign Southern "invader." Or of Fitz John Porter, William B. Franklin, and Don Carlos Buell—all scapegoats thrown by Lincoln to the radical wolves. In place of these heterodox professionals, Lincoln assigned such champions of the "new freedom" as Nathaniel P. ("Commissary") Banks, Benjamin F. ("Beast") Butler, John C. Fremont, and John A. McClernand. Speaking in summary despair of these appointments (and adding to my list, Franz Sigel and Lew Wallace), General Henry Halleck, Lincoln's chief-of-staff, declared that they were "little better than murder." Yet in the East, with the Army of the Potomac, Lincoln made promotions even more difficult to defend, placing not special projects, divisions, and brigades but entire commands under the authority of such "right thinking" incompetents as John Pope (son of an old crony in Illinois) and "Fighting Joe" Hooker. Or with that "tame" Democrat and late favorite of the radicals, Ambrose E. Burnside. Thousands of Northern boys lost their lives in order that the Republican Party might experience rejuvenation, to serve its partisan goals. And those were "party supremacy within a Northern dominated Union." A Democratic "man-on-horseback" could not serve those ends, however faithful to "the Constitution as it is, and the Union as it was" (the motto of the Democrats) they might be. For neither of these commitments promised a Republican hegemony. To provide for his faction both security and continuity in office, Lincoln sounded out his commanders in correspondence (much of which still survives), suborned their military integrity, and employed their focus in purely political operation. Writes Johnson:

> Although extreme measures were most common in the border states, they were often used elsewhere too. By extreme measures is meant the arrest of anti-Republican candidates and voters, driving anti-Republican voters from the polls or forcing them to vote the Republican ticket, preventing opposition parties from holding meetings, removing names from ballots, and so forth. These methods were employed in national, state and local elections. Not only did the army interfere by force, it was used to supply votes. Soldiers whose states did not allow absentee voting were sent home by order of the President to swell the Republican totals. When voting in the field was used, Democratic commissioners carrying ballots to soldiers from their state were . . . unceremoniously thrown into prison, while Republican agents were offered every assistance. Votes of Democratic soldiers were sometimes discarded as defective, replaced by Republican ballots, or simply not counted.

All Lincoln asked of the ordinary Billy Yank was that he be prepared to give himself up to no real purpose—at least until Father Abraham found a general with the proper moral and political credentials to lead him on to Richmond. How this part of Lincoln's career can be reconciled to the myth of the "suffering savior" I cannot imagine.

We might dwell for some time on what injury Lincoln did to the dignity of his office through the methods he employed in prosecuting the war. It was no small thing to disavow the ancient Christian code of "limited war," as did his minions, acting in his name. However, it is enough in this connection to remember his policy of denying medicines to the South, even for the sake of Northern prisoners held behind the lines. We can imagine what a modern "war crimes" tribunal would do with that decision. There may have been practicality in such inhumane decisions. *Practicality* indeed! As Charles Francis Adams, Lincoln's ambassador to the Court of St. James and the scion of the most notable family in the North,

wrote in his diary of his leader, the "President and his chief advisers are not without the spirit of the serpent mixed in with their wisdom." And he knew whereof he spoke. For practical politics, the necessities of the campaign of 1864, had led Lincoln and Seward to a decision far more serious than unethical practices against prisoners and civilians in the South. I speak of the rejection by the Lincoln administration of peace feelers authorized by the Confederate government in Richmond: feelers that met Lincoln's announced terms for an end to the Federal invasion of the South. The emissary in this negotiation was sponsored by Charles Francis Adams. He was a Tennessean living in France, one Thomas Yeatman. After arriving in the United States, he was swiftly deported by direct order of the government before he could properly explore the possibility of an armistice on the conditions of reunion and an end to slavery. Lincoln sought these goals, but only on his terms. And in his own time. He wanted total victory. And he needed a still-resisting, impenitent Confederacy to justify his re-election. We can only speculate as to why President Davis allowed the Yeatman mission. We know that he expected little of such peace feelers. (There were many in the last stages of the conflict.) He knew his enemy too well to expect anything but subjection, however benign the rhetoric used to disguise its rigor. Adams's peace plan was perhaps impossible, even if his superiors in Washington had behaved in good faith. The point is that none of the peace moves of 1864 was given any chance of success. Over one hundred thousand Americans may have died because of the Rail-Splitter's rejection of an inexpedient peace. Yet we have still not touched upon the most serious of Lincoln's violations of the Presidential responsibility. I speak, finally, of his role in bringing on the War Between the States.

There is, we should recall, a great body of scholarly argument concerning Lincoln's intentions in 1860 and early 1861. A respectable portion of this work comes to the conclusion that the first Republican president expected a "tug," a "crisis," to follow his election. And then, once secession had occurred, also expected to put it down swiftly with a combination of persuasion, force, and Southern loyalty to the Union. The last of these, it is agreed, he completely overestimated. In a similar fashion he exaggerated the force of Southern "realism," the region's capacity to act in its own pecuniary interest. The authority on Lincoln's political economy has remarked that the Illinois lawyer-politician and old line Whig always made the mistake of explaining in simple economic terms the South's hostile reaction to anti-slavery proposals. To that blunder he added the related mistake of attempting to end the "rebellion" with the same sort of simplistic appeals to the prospect of riches. Or with fear of a servile insurrection brought on by his greatest "war measure," the emancipation of slaves behind Southern lines, beyond his control. A full-scale Southern revolution, a revolution of all classes of men against the way he and some of his supporters thought, was beyond his imagination. There was no "policy" in such extravagant behavior, no human nature as he perceived it. Therefore, on the basis of my understanding of his overall career, I am compelled to agree with Charles W. Ramsdell concerning Lincoln and his war. Though he was no sadist and no warmonger, and though he got for his pains much more of a conflict than he had in mind, Lincoln hoped for an "insurrection" of some sort—an "uprising" he could use.

The "rational" transformation of our form of government which he had first predicted in the "Springfield Lyceum Speech" required some kind of passionate disorder to justify the enforcement of a new Federalism. And needed also for the voting representatives of the South to be out of their seats in the Congress. It is out of keeping with his total performance as a public man and in contradiction of his campaigning after 1854 not to believe that Lincoln hoped for a Southern attack on Fort Sumter. As he told his old friend Senator Orville H. Browning of Illinois: "The plan succeeded. They attacked Sumter—it fell, and thus did more service than it otherwise could." And to others he wrote or spoke to the same effect. If the Confederacy's offer of money for Federal property were made known in the North and business relations of the sections remained unaffected, if the Mississippi remained open to Northern shipping, there would be no support for "restoring" the Union on a basis of force. Americans were in the habit of thinking of the unity of the nation as a reflex of their agreement in the Constitution, of law as limit on government and on the authority of temporary majorities, and of revisions in law as the product of the ordinary course of push and pull within a pluralistic society, not as a response to the extralegal authority of some admirable abstraction like equality. In other words, they thought of the country as being defined by the way in which we conducted our political business, not by where we were trying to go in a body. Though once a disciple of Henry Clay, Lincoln changed the basis of our common bond away from the doctrine of his mentor, away from the patterns of compromise and dialectic of interests and values under a limited, Federal sovereignty with which we as a people began our adventure with the Great Compromise of 1787–1788. The nature of the Union left to us by

Lincoln is thus always at stake in every major election, in every refinement in our civil theology; the Constitution is still to be defined by the latest wave of big ideas, the most recent mass emotion. Writes Dietze:

> Concentrations of power in the national and executive branches of government, brought about by Lincoln in the name of the people, were processes that conceivably complemented each other to the detriment of free government. Lincoln's administration thus opened the way for the development of an omnipotent national executive who as a spokesman for the people might consider himself entitled to do whatever he felt was good for the Nation, irrespective of the interests and rights of states, Congress, the judiciary, and the individual. . . .

But in my opinion the capstone of this case against Lincoln . . . is what he has done to the language of American political discourse that makes it so difficult for us to reverse the ill effects of trends he set in motion with his executive fiat. When I say that Lincoln was our first Puritan president, I am chiefly referring to a distinction of style, to his habit of wrapping up his policy in the idiom of Holy Scripture, concealing within the Trojan horse of his gasconade and moral superiority an agenda that would never have been approved if presented in any other form. It is this rhetoric in particular, a rhetoric confirmed in its authority by his martyrdom, that is enshrined in the iconography of the Lincoln myth preserved against examination by monuments such as the Lincoln Memorial, where his oversized likeness is elevated above us like that of a deified Roman emperor. . . .

MELVIN E. BRADFORD (1934–1993) was a professor of literature at the University of Dallas from 1967 until his death. His publications include *Against the Barbarians and Other Reflections on Familiar Themes* (University of Missouri Press, 1992) and *Original Intentions: On the Making and Ratification of the United States Constitution* (University of Georgia Press, 1993).

EXPLORING THE ISSUE

Was Abraham Lincoln America's Greatest President?

Critical Thinking and Reflection

1. What were the major issues Abraham Lincoln faced as president of the United States, and how effective was he in addressing these matters?
2. What were Lincoln's major goals in the Civil War?
3. How did Lincoln respond to his opponents during the war?
4. Based on your understanding of his leadership during the Civil War, was Abraham Lincoln an effective commander-in-chief?
5. What approach did President Lincoln take with respect to the institution of slavery?

Is There Common Ground?

Historians consistently rank Abraham Lincoln in the highest echelon of American presidents even when they do not place him in the top spot. Over the years, Lincoln has had competition from George Washington, mainly for being the first president and providing a sterling role model for those who followed, and Franklin D. Roosevelt, for his leadership during the Great Depression and most of World War II. Nevertheless, Lincoln more often than not ends up on the top of the heap. Melvin Bradford's assessment, therefore, is extreme in its departure from tradition. At the same time, however, most Lincoln scholars, without embracing many of Bradford's specific conclusions, would agree that during the Civil War, Lincoln plumbed the well of executive powers and found it almost limitless. Lincoln himself told Senator Chandler in 1864, "I conceive that I may in this emergency do things on military grounds which cannot be done constitutionally even by Congress." To this end, he suspended the writ of habeas corpus, suppressed hostile newspapers, declared a blockade of southern ports before war was declared, raised a national army without an enabling act, and prepared for the reconstruction of the Union without seeking anyone's advice on how best to proceed. Clearly, however, most historians view these steps as necessary in prosecuting the war against the recalcitrant Southerners who formed the Confederacy.

Create Central

www.mhhe.com/createcentral

Additional Resources

Gabor S. Boritt, ed., *The Historian's Lincoln: Pseudohistory, Psychohistory, and History* (University of Illinois Press, 1988)

David Donald, *Lincoln* (Simon & Schuster, 1996)

Allen C. Guelzo, *Lincoln's Emancipation Proclamation: The End of Slavery in America* (Simon & Schuster, 2004)

Mark E. Neely, Jr., *The Fate of Liberty: Abraham Lincoln and Civil Liberties* (Oxford University Press, 1991)

Stephen B. Oates, *With Malice Toward None: The Life of Abraham Lincoln* (Harper & Row, 1977)

Internet References . . .

Abraham Lincoln Historical Digitization Project

lincoln.lib.niu.edu/

Abraham Lincoln Institute

www.abrahamlincoln.org/

Abraham Lincoln Online

www.abrahamlincolnonline.org/

American President—Abraham Lincoln (1809–1865)

millercenter.org/president/lincoln

Two Hundred Years of Abraham Lincoln

www.smithsonianmag.com/history-archaeology/life-of-lincoln.html

Selected, Edited, and with Issue Framing Material by:
Larry Madaras, *Howard Community College*
and
James M. SoRelle, *Baylor University*

ISSUE

Did Reconstruction Fail as a Result of Racism?

YES: LeeAnna Keith, from *The Colfax Massacre: The Untold Story of Black Power, White Terror, and the Death of Reconstruction* (Oxford University Press, 2008)

NO: Heather Cox Richardson, from *The Death of Reconstruction: Race, Labor, and Politics in the Post–Civil War North, 1865–1901* (Harvard University Press, 2001)

Learning Outcomes
After reading this issue, you will be able to:
• Explain several factors that prevented the Reconstruction process from being more successful.
• Analyze the political, economic, and social implications of the era of Reconstruction.
• Evaluate the role played by race in the reaction to the Reconstruction governments in the South following the Civil War.
• Define free labor ideology and explain its influence on Reconstruction.

ISSUE SUMMARY

YES: LeeAnna Keith characterizes the assault on the Grant Parish courthouse in Colfax, Louisiana on Easter Sunday in 1873 as a product of white racism and unwillingness by local whites to tolerate African American political power during the era of Reconstruction.

NO: Heather Cox Richardson argues that the failure of Radical Reconstruction was primarily a consequence of a national commitment to a free labor ideology that opposed an expanding central government that legislated rights to African Americans that other citizens had acquired through hard work.

Given the complex issues of the post–Civil War years, it is not surprising that the era of Reconstruction (1865–1877) is shrouded in controversy. For the better part of a century following the war, historians typically characterized Reconstruction as a total failure that had proved detrimental to all Americans—Northerners and Southerners, whites and blacks. According to this traditional interpretation, a vengeful Congress, dominated by radical Republicans, imposed military rule upon the southern states. Carpetbaggers from the North, along with traitorous white scalawags and their black accomplices in the South, established coalition governments that rewrote state constitutions, raised taxes, looted state treasuries, and disenfranchised former Confederates while extending the ballot to the freedmen. This era finally ended in 1877 when courageous southern white Democrats successfully "redeemed" their region from "Negro rule" by toppling the Republican state governments.

This portrait of Reconstruction dominated the historical profession until the 1960s. One reason for this is that white historians (both Northerners and Southerners) who wrote about this period operated from two basic assumptions: (1) the South was capable of solving its own problems without federal government interference; and (2) the former slaves were intellectually inferior to whites and incapable of running a government (much less one in which some whites would be their subordinates). African American historians, such as W. E. B. Du Bois, wrote several essays and books that challenged this negative portrayal of Reconstruction, but their works seldom were taken seriously in the academic world and rarely were read by the general public. Still, these black historians foreshadowed the acceptance of revisionist interpretations of Reconstruction, which coincided with the successes of the civil rights movement (or "Second Reconstruction") in the 1960s.

Without ignoring obvious problems and limitations connected with this period, revisionist historians identified a number of accomplishments of the Republican state governments in the South and their supporters in Washington,

D. C. For example, revisionists argued that the state constitutions that were written during Reconstruction were the most democratic documents that the South had seen up to that time. Also, although taxes increased in the southern states, the revenues generated by these levies financed the rebuilding and expansion of the South's railroad network, the creation of a number of social service institutions, and the establishment of a public school system that benefited African Americans as well as whites. At the federal level, Reconstruction achieved the ratification of the Fourteenth and Fifteenth Amendments, which extended significant privileges of citizenship (including the right to vote) to African Americans, both North and South. Revisionists also placed the charges of corruption leveled by traditionalists against the Republican regimes in the South in a more appropriate context by insisting that political corruption was a *national* malady. Although the leaders of the Republican state governments in the South engaged in a number of corrupt activities, they were no more guilty than several federal officeholders in the Grant administration, or the members of New York City's notorious Tweed Ring (a Democratic urban political machine), or even the southern white Democrats (the Redeemers) who replaced the radical Republicans in positions of power in the former Confederate states. Finally, revisionist historians sharply attacked the notion that African Americans dominated the reconstructed governments of the South.

There can be little doubt that racism played some role in the failure of the Radical Republicans to realize their most ambitious goals for integrating African Americans into the mainstream of American society in the years following the Civil War. After all, white supremacy was a powerful doctrine. At the same time, we should not so cavalierly dismiss some of the more positive conclusions reached by that first generation of revisionist historians who built upon W. E. B. Du Bois's characterization of Reconstruction as a "splendid failure." For example, Kenneth Stampp's *The Era of Reconstruction, 1865–1877* (Alfred A. Knopf, 1965) ends with the following statement: "The Fourteenth and Fifteenth Amendments, which could have been adopted only under the conditions of radical reconstruction, make the blunders of that era, tragic though they were, dwindle into insignificance. For if it was worth a few years of civil war to save the Union, it was worth a few years of radical reconstruction to give the American Negro the ultimate promise of equal civil and political rights." Eric Foner, too, recognizes something of a silver lining in the nation's post–Civil War reconstruction process. In *Reconstruction: America's Unfinished Revolution, 1863–1877* (Harper & Row, 1988), Foner claims that Reconstruction, while perhaps not all that radical, offered African Americans at least a temporary vision of a free society. Similarly, in *Nothing But Freedom: Emancipation and Its Legacy* (Louisiana State University Press, 1984), Foner advances his interpretation by comparing the treatment of ex-slaves in the United States with that of newly emancipated slaves in Haiti and the British West Indies. Only in the United States, he contends, were the freedmen given voting and economic rights. Although these rights had been stripped away from the majority of black Southerners by 1900, Reconstruction had, nevertheless, created a legacy of freedom that inspired succeeding generations of African Americans.

On the other hand, C. Vann Woodward, in "Reconstruction: A Counterfactual Playback," an essay in his thought-provoking *The Future of the Past* (Oxford University Press, 1988), challenges Foner's conclusions by insisting that former slaves were as poorly treated in the United States as they were in other countries. He also maintains that the confiscation of former plantations and the redistribution of land to the former slaves would have failed in the same way that the Homestead Act of 1862 failed to generate equal distribution of government lands to poor white settlers.

Thomas Holt's *Black Over White: Negro Political Leadership in South Carolina During Reconstruction* (University of Illinois Press, 1977) is representative of state and local studies that employ modern social science methodology to yield new perspectives. While critical of white Republican leaders, Holt (who is African American) also blames the failure of Reconstruction in South Carolina on freeborn mulatto politicians, whose background distanced them economically, socially, and culturally from the masses of freedmen. Consequently, these political leaders failed to develop a clear and unifying ideology to challenge white South Carolinians who wanted to restore white supremacy.

In the essays that follow, LeeAnna Keith and Heather Cox Richardson present thought-provoking analyses of the influence racism played in the failure of Reconstruction. In the first selection, Keith describes the events surrounding the military assault by white Louisianans on the Grant Parish courthouse located in the town of Colfax. Rumors had circulated for some time that such an attack would take place, and African American militiamen, who had been empowered by the Republican leaders in Louisiana, were prepared to protect the building that had become the symbol to whites of "Negro rule" in their region. The resulting massacre (most of the casualties occurred as a result of wholesale executions after a surrender had occurred) of over 150 blacks by Southerners seeking to uphold the doctrine of white supremacy represented the deadliest incident of racial violence in United States history and paved the way for the end of Radical Reconstruction in Louisiana.

Heather Cox Richardson offers a post–revisionist interpretation of the failure of Reconstruction and contends that the key barrier to postwar assistance for African Americans was the nation's commitment to a free labor ideology. Believing that social equality derived from economic success, most Americans opposed legislation, such as the Civil Rights Act of 1875, which appeared to provide special interest legislation solely for the benefit of the former slaves.

YES ↵

LeeAnna Keith

The Colfax Massacre: The Untold Story of Black Power, White Terror, and the Death of Reconstruction

The Battle of Colfax Courthouse

The Republican faction in control of the courthouse was prepared for trouble, but Jesse McKinney was not. McKinney tried to stay out of trouble—a goal that required a black man to steer clear of politics in general and to keep away from the town of Colfax in particular, after the seizure of the courthouse initiated its militarization. In the two weeks before his death, McKinney had observed the passage of armed men of both races from his home near the ferry crossing on Bayou Darrow. He stuck close to his wife and six young children. The family was watching on April 5, 1873 when the white men shot him in the head. They heard him scream—"like a pig," as a black neighbor remembered it—and they heard some of the white men asking if McKinney was killed. "Yes," came the answer, "he is dead as hell."

Republican commentators in Louisiana would later deplore the killing of a man at work, as they said, "peaceably building a fence around his property." In fact, in the charged environment of post–Civil War Louisiana, where black ownership seemed to threaten the social and economic order, the act of building a fence approximated a kind of defiance. McKinney had money. Like his father and brother, he acknowledged almost $500 in personal property in the 1870 census. Late in the season, his corn crib and pantries were fully stocked.

The white men who killed him were far from home. They needed food for their horses and water and provisions for their growing ranks. After they shot McKinney, they dismounted and "danced like mad" for two hours, then settled in to feed their horses out of his supply.

Jesse McKinney did not die instantly, but lingered for six or eight hours. Assisted by another woman, Eliza Smith, his wife Laurinda loaded him and the children into a wagon while the whites in the yard mocked them, hooting lecherously and calling them "bad names." Laurinda McKinney drove to her stepfather's house and laid her husband's body on the floor. At sundown, when he died, his wife found her way to Mirabeau Plantation to ask for a coffin and a safe place to sleep. All of her neighbors had fled. The body remained unburied, attracting so many turkey vultures by the end of the week that the roof of the house was covered with birds.

The raiding party at McKinney's farm brought together an unlikely handful of area whites. Among participants later identified by the widow and other eyewitnesses, representatives from distant parishes made up the party that pulled the trigger. Denis Lemoine, a rollicking Creole from 60 miles away in Avoyelles Parish, joined his cousins from the extensive Natchitoches clan of Lemoines. On April 5, Lemoine was riding with Bill Irwin, a poor farmer from the Rapides section of Grant Parish. Their unlikely company suggested the reach and strategy of the white supremacist organizations that planned the attack on the Colfax courthouse. In fact, the Knights of the White Camellia and a group calling itself the "Old Time Ku Klux Klan" played a major organizational role. Acting as scouts, Lemoine, Irwin, and their associates secured a site to feed and water the horses of a growing contingent of armed men. They would visit the abandoned McKinney house on patrol and make liaisons there until supplies ran out.

Like many who would join their ranks in the area around Colfax, Irwin and Lemoine were Confederate veterans. Apart from the killing of civilians and other excesses, white preparations betrayed a jaunty military spirit. Where former officers such as George Stafford and David Paul took the lead, volunteers formed "companies" and even designated ranks. Rapides Parishes offered three such units, under Captains Stafford, Paul, and Joseph W. Texada, all prominent planters and former slaveholders. Contingents from Catahoula, Concordia, and Winn Parishes traveled long distances under similar leadership. Others, such as Denis Lemoine, arrived as individuals or in small groups. Local residents offered directions and hospitality, putting up out-of-towners and providing meals as possible. Veterans figured prominently in the mix, but a significant number of young men joined in, including many, such as Stafford, who had lost older brothers and other relatives in the Civil War.

The talk around their campfires was of genocide. Many expressed the strong conviction that the seizure of the Colfax courthouse was the first step in a war of conquest to eradicate the white race.

> The Negroes at Colfax shouted daily across the
> river to our people that they intended killing

every white man and boy, keeping only the young women to raise from them a new breed [explained the organizer of an elite Rapides Parish contingent]. On their part if ever successful, you may safely expect that neither age, nor sex, nor helpless infancy will be spared.

"[T]he open threats of the negroes were to kill the white men and violate the white women," remembered one participant. Another account suggested the participation of militant organizations in fanning the rumor.

We were all startled and terrified at the news by a Courier who had just gotten in from our Parish Site, that the Negroes under the leadership of a few unprincipled white men had captured the Court House & driven all white inhabitants out of the Town, and were raiding stealing & driving the cattle out of the surrounding country. The Negro men making their brags that they would clean out the white men & then take their women folks for wifes.

Another fragment of the rhetoric of such claims referred in Klan-style idiom to the way the "Tytanic Black Hand was sweeping over the Red River Valley in 1873," and to the urgent response of white manhood in the state. . . .

As Easter Sunday approached, the military character of the confrontation became increasingly pronounced. Blacks in Colfax drilled in formation and worked to stockpile ammunition, including homemade "blue whistlers" for bullets. With the assistance of the remaining Union veterans in the crowd . . . the men prepared three makeshift cannons using stovepipe and gunpowder and constructed shallow breastworks on two sides of the courthouse. . . .

Fortified by their faith in their rights as citizens, blacks in Colfax girded for the fight.

Whites made their own preparations, taking advantage of their control of the countryside surrounding Colfax to steal horses and mules from undefended black households. Creating army-style squadrons under the leadership of selected men, the whites assembled a version of a cavalry outfit. The white paramilitary patrolled constantly, assessing the strength of black defenses and scouting for the arrival of new recruits. . . . By Easter Sunday, according to their own estimate, the white line consisted of 140 men and teenage boys. . . .

Despite the intensity of the buildup on both sides, Easter Sunday started slowly in Colfax. A handful of lost stalwarts departed the radical camp in the morning. A prominent African American from Rock Island came to town to implore the men to surrender the fight. No formal observance of the holiday could be discerned. A bustle of activity, in contrast, occupied the white force as it prepared to move in concert from its network of campsites around the town. Riding to a designated spot on Bayou Darrow, the white captains paused to review the plan of attack. Captain Dave Paul read the muster roll and made a final address to the men.

"I close my eyes [and] his face and form comes before my mind just as he was that morning," wrote a participant, 50 years afterward. "Boys," said Paul, "there are one hundred and sixty-five of us to go into Colfax this morning; God knows how many will come out of it alive."

Upon the signal, the men swam their horses across the Bayou Darrow, crossing onto the Calhoun estate and initiating the hostile phase of their maneuvers. They rode in one company to the main road to Colfax and paused in battle formation where they could be seen from the courthouse and Smithfield Quarters. Christopher Columbus Nash—the former lieutenant—yielded military authority to Captains Paul, Stafford, and Wiggins but assumed formal responsibility for the fight as the Fusion ticket sheriff of the parish. . . . As such, Nash rode forward, accompanied by two men, to issue a final order for the blacks to disperse.

Bearing a white flag, Nash approached the Smithfield Quarters and asked for John Miles, a man later celebrated as a favorite of the white community. Miles would make the journey to the courthouse on Nash's behalf, walking out along the open road between the main positions of the armed rivals. Nash withdrew with his seconds to a point forward of the white line and observed as a black man exited the courthouse and mounted a dappled gray horse.

Benjamin L. Allen—known locally as Levy, Levin, or Lev—identified himself as the commander of the courthouse defense. Allen was one of two Buffalo Soldiers to remain in the radical camp. . . . Like the storekeeper, Peter Borland, who also chose to stay, Allen had long years of military experience, including the defense of stationary targets, such as garrisons and telegraph and railroad installations, against mounted Apaches on the Texas frontier. Though he never stood for office or played a visible role in Republican Party affairs, his commitment to preserving the possibility for black advancement in the parish was second to none. Allen had traveled the countryside during the buildup to the conflict, recruiting new men by appealing to the pride of their race. Even if he had no arms, he insisted, all black men should lend their hands to the defense. As for weapons, he said, "they could have his when he was killed."

The interview between Allen and Nash was dignified and brief, despite the breach of protocol that placed the black military commander, not the sheriff, as the counterpart of the would-be white officeholder. In fact, Sheriff Dan Shaw, the last of the white men in the courthouse defense, had headed for Mirabeau Plantation just as Nash and the others rode into view. Lev Allen himself had given Sheriff Shaw the go-ahead. "Old man," said Allen, "go away and save yourself, if you can." . . .

Having stated their cases, the two sides agreed to proceed with hostilities. Allen rode back to the courthouse redoubt, where he "received the approbation of the whole posse, the men all believing that the proposal of their assailants was a ruse to entrap them into disarming, that they might be incapable of resisting in case of a massacre."

Nash had agreed to give Allen 30 minutes to remove the women and children from the line of fire. Most headed for Mirabeau Plantation on the open road. Stragglers, a group that included the elderly and mothers of small children, became reluctant to enter the line of fire as the deadline approached. Scaling the riverbank, six to eight feet to a narrow shore, a contingent waited out the battle from just below the action.

A flanking maneuver brought one of the three white squadrons face to face with the noncombatants at the Red River shoreline, as a picked group of 30 men sought a new angle on the courthouse, some 75 yards from the riverbank. The encounter must have marked the interlude before the fighting with considerable tension down below, as the white men warned the gathering not to betray their location. No injuries or killings were reported, however, and the white squadron retained the element of surprise until the critical moment.

Up in the town, a kind of comic indolence set in as the warning period extended to about two hours. The improbability of the coming confrontation taxed the comprehension of men on both sides, the majority of whom knew one another by long acquaintance or at least reputation. In fact, the interlude of silence was repeatedly broken by shouted threats against specific individuals and their families, with most of the taunting emanating from the white side. Some of the white irregulars went into the Smithfield cabins, even helping themselves to hot lunches abandoned in haste. Another group played cards.

Black defenders showed defiance and disbelief (except for Baptiste Elzie, one of three local brothers in the fight, who had fallen asleep in the trench). A sniper on the courthouse roof took potshots in the vicinity of the card game, causing the whites to reform their ranks around 2 P.M. As the white line moved forward, firing a few shots, one man jumped to the top of the courthouse earthworks in a dramatic show of begging and pleading, "bowing his head and throwing up his hands several times, adding some expression, the precise words not being understood," as a white eyewitness remembered it. By some gesture, the black supplicant made clear that he was mocking them. Then the firing began in earnest.

The white offensive proceeded in three parts. Wheeling the cannon into action, a crew of artillerymen led by a northern-born white Union veteran fired on the courthouse, using a supply of iron slugs cut from two-by-two-inch bars in lieu of cannonballs. To protect the artillery charge, a squadron of men dismounted, approaching on foot in infantry formation. A mounted component, essentially disengaged from the action, maintained the rear.

Cannon fire penetrated the line of defenders in the courthouse earthworks, claiming the first fatality of the fight. According to the account of Baptiste Elzie, who described it years afterward, a slug cut across the abdomen of Adam Kimball, who was standing. His bowels torn open, Kimball ran inside the courthouse, where his intestines fell out. . . .

Some of the black defenders broke for the road, where they were shot. Others, such as Zach White, made their way to the river, where White swam a mile and a half to safety wearing clothes and carrying his shot pouch and powder horn. A white contingent led by Captain J.P.G. Hooe of Alexandria—who carried a sawed-off shotgun—awaited black militiamen who fled to the nearby black community of Cuny's Point. Those who ran for the woods—including Captain Lev Allen, who fled on horseback—fared best, capitalizing on the whites' uncertainty about black defenses that could not be seen. Allen freed his horse and found a hiding place with a view of the courthouse where he would remain until the fighting was done. Another handful of survivors spent the night up to their chins in a pond.

The largest contingent—an estimated 65 men—retreated into the courthouse, where accommodations for a siege had been prepared. Only one of the 25th Infantry veterans, the storekeeper Peter Borland, remained with the defense, which also included the local Union soldiers [Cuffy] Gaines, [Alabama] Mitchell, and [Edmund] Dancer. Shots from inside the courthouse felled the Yankee artilleryman, who survived, and fatally wounded a local man, Stephen Parish, also in the cannon crew. The black militia's jury-rigged artillery malfunctioned, but the brick walls and shuttered windows of the courthouse held firm against the last blasts of shrapnel. For the space of an hour, desultory gunshots (and the sound of shots fired in pursuit nearby) marked the standoff phase of the fight.

In their cleanup operations around town, the Fusionists and Klansmen had taken prisoner a handful of men in the warehouse and one hiding under a building nearby. From these, the captains chose a man named Pinkney Chambers and handed him a pole they had affixed to a saddle blanket doused in coal oil. "[Here's] a chance to save your life," they said; "we are going to light this and you must take it and put it on the roof." With "ten [double barrel] shotguns trained on him from his back, and I suppose 50 guns in front of him [in the courthouse]," as a white man remembered it, Chambers put the torch on the cypress shingles to start a lively fire.

The men inside the courthouse observed as Pinkney Chambers set the roof on fire, but did not shoot him. Instead, they tried to knock the burning cypress shingles from the roof from the building's rough upper story. The cause was hopeless, and many of the men inside began to despair.

> I warned our people not to go into the courthouse [a black participant told a reporter one month after the event]. I knowed it would be the end of 'em. But when the cannon went off we were all skeered, and huddled into the building like a herd of sheep. Then the burning roof began to fall on us, and every one was praying and shrieking and singing and calling on God to have mercy. The flesh of those furtherest from the door began to roast. I could smell it. . . . The hair bunt off our heads, our clothes burn[ed] and our skin roast[ed].

Among those fighting the fire on the second storey, a local man named Shack (or Jack or Jacques) White strayed too close to an open window. With the invaders deliberately shooting at the fire, providing cover as it grew, White took a bullet to the neck.

By this time, the white line had mostly dismounted and drawn close to the burning building. They were close enough for Shack White to recognize a friend among the men nearby. "Save me, Bill Irwin," he called from the window. Irwin replied that he owed him one, perhaps assuring him of the services of the surgeon and doctor in the company of whites. White tore the sleeve from his white shirt (some accounts say a large sheet of paper), put it out the window, and shouted, "We surrender!" Too late to save his life, he brought the courthouse siege to an unexpected halt.

Was he heard downstairs above the crackling of the fire on the roof? Could they know below about the improvised flag of truce? What they saw, within the incalculable space of time between two incidents, was the approach of armed white men to the door. The first, Sidney Harris, carrying a gun, opened the door. At his rear walked a man dressed in a sword and wearing the red rosette of his secret order, James West Hadnot.

Fast as thought, Harris was dead and Hadnot lay mortally wounded in the gut. . . .

The horror that gripped the body of whites at the courthouse—a group that included "Old Man" Hadnot's three young adult sons—turned the momentum of the fighting as if on a switch. By this time, a handful of black men had emerged from the courthouse and begun to stack their arms. They were overwhelmed by a blast of gunfire from the white side. With men pressing out of the burning building amid continuing fire, bodies fell in a stack by the door, including several who were slightly injured or not hurt. Using pistols and Bowie knives, the whites killed several in close combat. The door slammed. Those afraid to surrender hid under the floorboards. The cinders crackled overhead, as white men sorted out the living from the dead at the doorway and just beyond.

"Get up, old man, you're not dead," said a man. Benjamin Brimm was 56 years old, the father of four girls, a former slave. He was directed to the base of a pecan tree some distance from the courthouse and made to wait with other prisoners. Fifteen minutes later, he was told to go inside the burning courthouse to retrieve the last of the holdouts before it collapsed.

"They was under the floor in the little back room," he later testified. "[Y]'all had better come," he called. They agreed, all but one. "I might just as well to be burned up as to be shot," said the man, who burned to death some time in the next hour. The others, including Alabama Mitchell, emerged safely and were taken prisoner. A few dozen—28 or 48, in typical accounts—waited under the pecan tree to learn the final resolution of the fight.

After sunset it began to rain. The wounded blacks were moved to the porch of the nearby boardinghouse, while the remainder of the prisoners made do under the shelter of the tree. Black women, emboldened by the lack of gunfire, left their hiding places and moved within sight of the battlefield, staying well away from both the prisoners and the dead.

The armed force of whites was breaking up, with hungry men eager to make camp and others preparing for a long journey home. . . . The semblance of military discipline abated, as the remaining white chiefs discussed the fate of the last living black men in the town.

Nash wanted to set them free. "[N]ow boys," he asked Benjamin Brimm and the others, "if I take you all and send you home to your cotton, will you go to work?"

"I answered quick," remembered Brimm, "[as] I knowed Mr. Nash and he knowed me." Brimm promised he would.

A white man objected: "[B]y God, Nash . . . if you send these God Dam Negroes home you won't live to see two weeks." Having killed 50 or more in the courthouse fight and cleanup operations, many in the crowd may have feared reprisals, legal and personal, after the prisoners returned home. . . . Liquor whetted the appetite for violence in the group. One man said that he had ridden 60 miles to kill niggers, and was not yet prepared to stop. Overriding Nash's objections, the remainder of the white force decided to execute the prisoners. "Unless these niggers are killed," a Grant Parish man, Thomas Hickman, told Nash, "we will kill you." . . .

The white men told the remaining prisoners to line up and prepare to be marched to the sugarhouse, where they would spend the night and be set free in the morning. Luke Hadnot, whose dying father had recently departed on a boat to Alexandria, called out the names of five men. The five stepped forward; Hadnot lined them up in close ranks, and killed all five with two gunshots. Others likewise identified their victims of choice. Clement Penn, for example, selected and killed Etienne Elzie while Elzie's wife, Annie, stood by only a few feet away. "I was looking directly at Penn when he shot my husband," Annie Elzie later testified. "I heard him beg for his life." . . .

Chaos reigned in Colfax on Monday, when the excesses of the previous hours saw light of day. Scores of white men, including many who had not participated in the fight, came to town to witness the outcome of the struggle. The distribution of the bodies told much of the story. In the shallow breastworks around the courthouse, the bodies of the earliest victims could be seen. A significant number of corpses fanned out from the courthouse door, with piles on either side of the door in mute witness to the gunfire that greeted those trying to escape the fire. The ruins of the courthouse contained the smoldering remains of the man who feared to exit, and a few others were found killed beneath the warehouse and other buildings in the town.

Something special—still secret—could be found in the vicinity of the old pecan tree, which later became the object of special pride among area whites. According to some accounts, thirteen prisoners were hanged from its branches, and may have remained visible to visitors on April 14. By the time authorities arrived on Tuesday, however, the only bodies near the tree were the victims of gun violence. Most revealed gunshots to the head. One man's skull had been crushed. He had died with his hands still clasped in the act of begging for his life.

Whites in Colfax Monday attempted to count the number of dead, a task complicated by the pursuit of some black participants by men on horseback. At least three of the identifiable victims on April 13 had been killed outside the town, one more than ten miles downriver in Cotile, Louisiana. The removal and burial of some of the bodies on Monday further disrupted the count. Among those who attended to the numbers, the final tally varied on a wide range, with the most conservative reckoning the number of victims at 71. Whites may have indulged in exaggeration, but the most morbidly diligent white veteran historian of the massacre accepted the high number presented in Oscar Watson's reminiscences, "An Incident of My Boyhood Days":

> Next morning myself & 8 or 10 others went back to look and count the dead[.A]fter making the rounds of the town 165 dead was reported within the entrenchment [and] no one will ever know how many met their fate further out[,] as some 25 or 30 men scoured the Country for 4 or 5 miles [and] no report ever reached us of how many they killed in this raid.

The black men had brought it on themselves, he reasoned.

> [I]t was a sorry blunder the negroes made in [firing] on our men after surrender, for only their leaders would have been dealt with[.B]ut after their treachery the order went let none escape. The order was carried out.

Whether 70 or 165 or many more, the accepted number of victims was larger than any other incident of racial violence in American history (the only comparable number of casualties, the victims of the New York City Draft Riot of 1863, included large numbers of unfortunate whites). In surveying the damage, white men in Colfax were taking the measure of their terrible success.

White men also took liberties with the bodies of dead men and the possessions of those displaced by the violence. They mutilated the bodies, most often by shooting the corpses. In one awful case, mischief-makers used gunpowder or some other means to blow up the corpse of a local man known as Big Frank. One widow reported finding her husband's corpse with the pockets ripped open and wallet missing. Blacks in the area later complained about the theft of horses, mules, wagons, furniture, and money. "[Y]ea, even the clothes and shoes of the murdered men were taken and carried off," according to victims, "and this practice was being pursued for days after the massacre." W. R. Rutland, still aggrieved by his own loss of property in the burglary of his Colfax home, was seen riding a stolen horse around town.

Whites in Colfax sought to publicize their victory on Monday while most of the bodies remained unburied, encouraging blacks they encountered to go view the dead. "Go to town, if you want to see a mess of dead beeves," said a man to a woman whose husband was killed in the fight. Others used bad language, forced strangers to bury bodies or cook food, and taunted the widows with references to sexual favors.

Dorcas Pittman, the mother of one of the victims, arrived in Colfax on Monday to learn the fate of her son Lank, who had perished in the fight.

> When I went to Colfax the day after the fight I found my dead son's body; dogs were eating him; I took the remains home and buried them; I felt so bad that I didn't know what I did.

Whites permitted the removal of Lank Pittman's body because of the extreme circumstances, and may have allowed other burials as well. On the whole, however, they were satisfied to leave the bodies where they fell.

Their pride in display revealed the symbolic significance of the white raid on the town. Conceived as a lesson to those who advanced the black cause in politics, the rout of the courthouse defense served notice of white determination. The white men of Louisiana would unite to defeat their enemies within, killing and dying for white supremacy and home rule.

LeeAnna Keith earned her PhD at the University of Connecticut and currently teaches history at Collegiate School, a boy's day school in New York City, which is the oldest independent school in the United States.

Heather Cox Richardson    **NO**

The Death of Reconstruction: Race, Labor, and Politics in the Post–Civil War North, 1865–1901

Civil Rights and the Growth of the National Government, 1870–1883

Northern Republican disillusionment with African-American attitudes toward social issues compounded the Northern association of Southern freedmen with labor radicals who advocated confiscation of wealth. Taking place during and immediately after the South Carolina tax crisis, the civil rights debates of the 1870s seemed to confirm that African-Americans were turning increasingly to legislation to afford them the privileges for which other Americans had worked individually. Civil rights agitation did more than simply flesh out an existing sketch of disaffected black workers, however; it suggested that advocates of African-American rights were actively working to expand the national government to cater to those who rejected the free labor ideal.

"Civil rights," in the immediate aftermath of the war, meant something different than it gradually came to mean over the next several years. *Harper's Weekly* distinguished between "natural rights" to life, liberty, and "the fruits of . . . honest labor," and "civil rights," which were critical to a freedperson's ability to function as a free worker. Civil rights, it explained, were "such rights as to sue, to give evidence, to inherit, buy, lease, sell, convey, and hold property, and others. Few intelligent persons in this country would now deny or forbid equality of natural and civil rights," it asserted in 1867. The 1866 Civil Rights Act, written by the man who had drafted the Thirteenth Amendment, Illinois senator Lyman Trumbull, was intended to secure to African-Americans "full and equal benefit of all laws and proceedings for the security of person and property as is enjoyed by white citizens." It guaranteed only that the legal playing field would be level for all citizens; state legislatures could not enact legislation endangering a black person's right to his life or his land. By 1867, hoping to woo conservative Republican voters into the Democratic camp and to undercut the justification for black suffrage, even moderate Democrats claimed to be willing to back civil rights for African-Americans "with every

token of sincerity . . . from a free and spontaneous sense of justice."

"Social" equality was a different thing—it was a result of a person's economic success rather than a condition for it. It was something to be earned by whites and blacks alike. Directly related to economic standing, a man's social standing rose as he prospered. A good social position also required that a person possess other attributes that the community valued. A place in upwardly mobile American society required religious observance and apparently moral behavior, as well as the habits of thrift and economy dictated by a plan for economic success. This gradual social elevation became a mirror of gradual economic elevation through hard work as a traditional free laborer.

Immediately after the Civil War, as Democrats insisted that black freedom would usher in social mixing between races and intermarriage, almost all Northern Republicans emphatically denied that emancipation was intended to have any effect on social issues and reiterated that African-Americans must rise in society only through the same hard effort that had brought other Americans to prominence. In 1867, a correspondent to the radical *Cincinnati Daily Gazette* from Louisiana painted a complimentary portrait of Louisiana African-Americans, then concluded that they had neither the expectation nor the desire for "social equality, that favorite bugbear." They would ridicule any attempt to break down social distinctions by legislation, knowing that the government could give them only political equality, the writer claimed, quoting his informants as saying, "Our own brains, our own conduct, is what we must depend upon for our future elevation; each one of us striving for himself and laboring to improve his mental and moral condition." Adding credence to the correspondent's representations, the Georgia Freedmen's Convention of 1866 resolved, "We do not in any respect desire social equality beyond the transactions of the ordinary business of life, inasmuch as we deem our own race, equal to all our wants of purely social enjoyment."

As the Republicans enacted legislation promoting the interests of African-Americans, however, racist Democrats insisted they were forcing social interaction to promote African-Americans artificially, at the expense of whites. When the Civil Rights Act of 1866 took effect, Democrats charged that the Republican concept of black equality before the law meant Republicans believed that blacks and whites were entirely equal. The *New York World* predicted interracial marriages; the *Columbus (Ohio) Crisis* insisted that a black orator in Richmond had told his black audience to "vote for the man who will bring you into his parlor, who will eat dinner with you, and who, if you want her, will let you marry his daughter." In 1868, *De Bow's Review* argued that negro suffrage meant that African-Americans would "next meet us at the marriage altar and in the burial vault," where they would "order the white ancestors' bones to be disinterred and removed elsewhere, and their own transferred into these hitherto held sacred white family sepulchers."

In response to Democratic attacks, in 1868 the *New York Times* reiterated that Republicans planned only for African-Americans to share the rights and opportunities of typical free laborers. It maintained that "reconstruction did not fly in the face of nature by attempting to impose social . . . equality," it simply established political and legal equality. These rights would eventually "obliterate" social prejudices as white men sought black votes. The next year the *Times* approvingly reported that abolitionist agitator Wendell Phillips had said that "the social equality of the black race will have to be worked out by their own exertion." Frederick Douglass put out the best idea, it continued later, namely: "Let the negro alone."

❦

Republican insistence that social equality would work itself out as freedpeople worked their way up to prosperity could not provide an answer for the overwhelming discrimination African-Americans faced. While many black and white Southerners accepted the established patterns of segregation, those practices meant that African-Americans' public life was inferior to that of their white counterparts. Black people could not sit on juries in most of the South, they could not be certain of transportation on railroads or accommodation at inns, their schools were poor copies of white schools. In addition to creating a climate of constant harassment for African-Americans, discrimination, especially discrimination in schooling, seemed to hamper their ability to rise economically. The Fourteenth and Fifteenth Amendments had made all Americans equal before the law, but they could not guarantee equal access to transportation, accommodations, or schools, and while many ex-slaves accepted conditions as an improvement on the past and dismissed civil rights bills as impractical, those African-Americans who had worked hard to become members of the "better classes" deeply resented their exclusion from public facilities. "Education amounts to nothing, good behavior counts for nothing, even money cannot buy for a colored man or woman decent treatment and the comforts that white people claim and can obtain,"

complained Mississippi Sheriff John M. Brown. Prominent African-Americans called for legislation to counter the constant discrimination they faced.

African-American proponents of a new civil rights law to enforce nondiscrimination in public services had a champion in the former abolitionist Senator Charles Sumner of Massachusetts. An exceedingly prominent man, the tall, aloof Sumner was the nation's leading champion of African-American rights after the war and had advocated a civil rights measure supplementary to the Civil Rights Act of 1866 since May 1870, when he introduced to the Senate a bill (S. 916) making the federal government responsible for the enforcement of equal rights in public transportation, hotels, theaters, schools, churches, public cemeteries, and juries.

But Sumner's sponsorship of a civil rights bill immediately made more moderate congressmen wary of it; his enthusiasm for black rights frequently made him advocate measures that seemed to remove African-Americans from the free labor system and make them favored wards of a government that was expanding to serve them. Only two months after the ratification of the fifteenth Amendment had reassured moderate Republicans and Democrats alike that they had done everything possible to make all men equal in America, Sumner told the Senate that black men were not actually equal enough, but that his new bill would do the trick. When it passes, he said, "I [will] know nothing further to be done in the way of legislation for the security of equal rights in this Republic." . . .

❦

By 1874, most Republicans were ready to cut the freedpeople's ties to the government in order to force African-Americans to fall back on their own resources and to protect the government from the machinations of demagogues pushing special-interest legislation. When Mississippi Republicans asked President Grant in January 1874 to use the administration to shore up their state organization, the *Philadelphia Inquirer* enthusiastically reported his refusal. Grant "remove[d] his segar from his mouth and enunciate[d] a great truth with startling emphasis," according to a writer for the newspaper. The president said it was "time for the Republican party to unload." The party could not continue to carry the "dead weight" of intrastate quarrels. Grant was sick and tired of it, he told listeners. "This nursing of monstrosities has nearly exhausted the life of the party. I am done with them, and they will have to take care of themselves." The *Philadelphia Inquirer* agreed that the federal government had to cease to support the Southern Republican organizations of freedpeople and their demagogic leaders. The *New York Daily Tribune* approved Grant's similar hands-off policy in Texas, thrilled that "there [was] no longer any cause to apprehend that another State Government will be overturned by Federal bayonets."

Benjamin Butler's role as the House manager of the civil rights bill only hurt its chances, for he embodied the connection between freedpeople and a government in thrall to special interests. The symbol of the "corruption" of American government, Butler was popularly credited with strong-arming the House into recognizing the Louisiana representatives backed by the Kellogg government, which was generally believed to be an illegal creation of Louisiana's largely black Republican party, supported not by the people of the state but by federal officers. Honest men wanted to destroy "the principle which Mr. Butler and his followers represent," wrote the *New York Daily Tribune* and others. "The force in our politics of which he is the recognized exponent, and of which thousands of our politicians of less prominence are the creatures." "But-lerism" meant gaining power by promising an uneducated public patronage or legislation in their favor, and all but the stalwart Republicans and Democratic machine politicians hoped for the downfall of both Butler and what he represented.

Despite the fact that it was prosperous African-Americans who advocated the bill, it appeared to opponents that the civil rights bill was an extraordinary piece of unconstitutional legislation by which demagogues hoped to hold on to power in the South, and thus in the nation, by catering to the whims of disaffected African-Americans who were unwilling to work. The proposed law seemed to offer nothing to the nation but a trampled constitution, lazy freedpeople, and a growing government corrupted into a vehicle for catering to the undeserving.

The civil rights bill would probably never have passed the Senate had it not been for the sudden death of Charles Sumner on March 11, 1874. Before he died, Sumner charged fellow Massachusetts senator George F. Hoar to "take care of the civil-rights bill,—my bill, the civil-rights bill, don't let it fail." Even Republican enemies of the bill eulogized the "great man"; the *Chicago Tribune* reflected that "there is no man, friend or enemy, who does not pause to pay respect to the memory of Charles Sumner." African-Americans across the country mourned Sumner's death and called for the passage of his "last and grandest work," and on April 14, 1874, from the Committee on the Judiciary Senator Frederick T. Frelinghuysen reported Sumner's civil rights bill protecting African-Americans from discrimination in public facilities, schools, and juries. The committee's amendments placed firmly in the national legal apparatus responsibility for overseeing violations of the proposed law. In caucus on May 8, some Republican senators objected to "certain features" of the bill but expressed a desire to act "harmoniously" on the measure. In the next caucus, the Republicans decided to support the bill without amendments.

After an all-night session of the Senate, a handful of African-American men in the galleries applauded as the Senate passed the bill on May 23, 1874, by a vote of twenty-nine to sixteen. Rumors circulated that the president had "some doubts about signing it" if it should pass the House,

and many Republicans indicated they would not mind the loss of the bill. "Respect for the dead is incumbent on us all," snarled the *New York Times*, "—but legislation should be based on a careful and wise regard for the welfare of the living, not upon 'mandates,' real or fictitious, of the dead." Referring to the apparent African-American control of Southern governments, the *Times* asked whether the freedman "stands in need of protection from the white man, or the white man stands in need of protection from him." The House Judiciary Committee could not agree on its own civil rights measure and decided to replace its bill with the Senate's. The House then tabled the bill for the rest of the session, despite the continued urging of "leading colored men" that Benjamin Butler get it taken up and passed. . . .

The civil rights bill was rescued from oblivion only by Democratic wins in the 1874 elections. Republican congressmen's desire to consolidate Reconstruction before the Democrats arrived barely outweighed party members' fears that the measure was an attempt of corrupt politicians to harness the black vote by offering African-Americans extraordinary benefits that would undermine their willingness to work. When the lame-duck Congress reconvened in December 1874, House Republican leader Benjamin Butler tried to pass a bill protecting freedmen at the polls and an army appropriations bill to shore up stalwart Republicans in the South. Democrats filibustered. Butler was unable to get a suspension of the rules to maneuver around them as fifteen Republicans joined the opposition, worried that Butler's attempt to suspend the rules was simply a means "to get through a lot of jobbing measures under cover of Civil Rights and protection of the South." With his reputation as a special-interest broker, Butler had a terrible time getting the civil rights bill off the Speaker's table. Finally Republicans agreed to let Butler take it to the floor in late January.

The galleries were full as the House discussed the bill in early February. After omitting provisions for integrated schools, churches, and cemeteries, the House passed the bill on February 5 by a vote of 162 to 100. While African-Americans in favor of a civil rights bill were horrified at the sacrifice of the school clause, all but the most radical Republicans approved the omission. "The bill . . . is worthy [of] the support of every congressman who wishes to deal equitably with the citizens of the United States, white and black," wrote even the *Boston Evening Transcript*. "This measure simply provides for the education of the blacks, and does not force their children into association with white scholars," at the same time demanding that the schools be equal. "The Republicans can stand upon such a platform as that," the *Transcript* chided unwilling party members. "The great desire and solicitude of the people are to support 'civil rights' and so execute in good faith the constitutional pledges of the nation." After initial reluctance, the Senate passed the school amendment by a vote of 38 to 62, and despite Democratic plans to talk the bill to death, the Senate repassed the civil rights bill without further amendment on February 27, 1875, with Democrats in the opposition. Grant signed the civil rights bill into law on March 1, 1875.

While some radical papers like the *Boston Evening Transcript* defended the bill—wondering "[i]f the blacks and whites cannot shave and drink together . . . how can they remain tolerably peaceful in the same community?"—its passage drew fire from conservative and moderate Northern Republicans who still read into the measure a larger political story of the corruption of a growing government by those determined to advance through government support rather than through productive labor. The *New York Times* noted that Nothern African-Americans were "quiet, inoffensive people who live for and to themselves, and have no desire to intrude where they are not welcome." In the South, however, it continued, "there are many colored men and women who delight in 'scenes' and cheap notoriety." It was these people, the "negro politician, . . . the ignorant field hand, who, by his very brutality has forced his way into, and disgraces, public positions of honor and trust—men . . . who have no feeling and no sensibility," who would "take every opportunity of inflicting petty annoyances upon their former masters." The author concluded that the law would not be enforceable, and that "it is a great mistake to seek to impose new social customs on a people by act of Congress." Noticing the immediate efforts of Southerners to circumvent the law by giving up public licenses and legislating against public disturbances, the *San Francisco Daily Alta California* agreed that the act was likely to produce more trouble than equality, and reiterated that social equality must be earned rather than enforced by law.

The true way for African-Americans to achieve equality, Republicans argued, was to work. The *New York Times* approvingly quoted an African-American minister in the South who reiterated the idea that laborers must rise socially only as they acquired wealth and standing. The *Times* recorded his warning that "character, education, and wealth will determine their position, and all the laws in the world cannot give them a high position if they are not worthy of it." Even a correspondent for the staunchly Republican *Cincinnati Daily Gazette* reflected that "Sambo . . . can go to the hotels, ride in first-class cars, and enjoy a box in the theater. To what good is all this? . . . He needs now, to be let alone, and let work out his own destiny, aided only as his wants make him an object of charity. . . .

⋅⟨◎⟩⋅

In 1883, the U.S. Supreme Court considered five civil rights cases, one each from Tennessee, New York, Kansas, Missouri, and California. On October 15, 1883, the court decided that the Civil Rights Act of 1875 was unconstitutional because federal authority could overrule only state institutional discrimination, not private actions; Justice John Marshall Harlan of Kentucky cast the only dissenting vote. With the decision, Northern Republicans stated that they had never liked the law, because it removed African-Americans from the tenets of a free labor society, using the government to give them benefits for which others had to work. The *New York Times* declared that African-Americans "should be treated on their merits as individuals precisely as other citizens are treated in like circumstances" and admitted that there was, indeed, "a good deal of unjust prejudice against" them. But the *Times* remained skeptical that legislation could resolve the problem. Even newspapers like the *Hartford Courant*, which supported the law, said it did so only because it proved that Americans were sincere in their quest for equal rights. Three days later that newspaper mused that the law had been necessary only for "the reorganization of a disordered society," and that freedpeople no longer needed its protection. The *Philadelphia Daily Evening Bulletin* agreed that public sentiment had changed so dramatically that the law was now unnecessary. Even the radical African-American *Cleveland Gazette*, which mourned the court's decision, agreed that the law was a dead letter anyway. The *New York Times* welcomed the decision, going so far as to charge the law with keeping "alive a prejudice against the negroes . . . which without it would have gradually died out."

Instead of supporting the Civil Rights Act, Republicans reiterated the idea that right-thinking African-Americans wanted to succeed on their own. The *New York Times* applauded the public address of the Louisville, Kentucky, National Convention of Colored Men that concentrated largely on the needs of Southern agricultural labor and referred not at all to civil rights. That the convention had pointedly rejected chairman Frederick Douglass's draft address, which had included support for civil rights legislation, made the *Times* conclude that most attendees were "opposed to the extreme views uttered by Mr. Douglass," and that the great African-American leader should retire, since his "role as a leader of his race is about played out."

Despite the *Times*'s conclusion, African-Americans across the country protested the decision both as individuals and in mass meetings, reflecting, "It is a mercy that Charles Sumner is not alive to mourn for his cherished Civil Rights bill." At a mass meeting in Washington, D.C., Frederick Douglass admonished that the decision "had inflicted a heavy calamity on the 7,000,000 of colored people of this country, and had left them naked and defenceless against the action of a malignant, vulgar and pitiless prejudice." When the African Methodist Episcopal (AME) Church Conference of Western States, in session in Denver, discussed the decision, delegates made "incendiary" speeches and "[a] Bishop declared that if the negroes' rights were thus trampled upon a revolution would be the result." . . .

Republicans and Democrats agreed that the only way for African-Americans to garner more rights was to work to deserve them, as all others did in America's free labor system. The *Philadelphia Daily Evening Bulletin* repeated this view:

[F]urther advancement depends chiefly upon themselves, on their earnest pursuit of education, on their progress in morality and religion, on their thoughtful exercise of their duties as citizens, on their persistent practice of industry, on their self-reliance, and on their determination to exalt themselves, not as proscribed or despised Africans, but as American men clothed with the privileges of citizenship in the one great republic of the earth. They have it in their power to secure for themselves, by their own conduct, more really important "rights" than can be given to them by any formal legislation of Congress.

The Democratic *Hartford Weekly Times* agreed, and asserted that true black leaders, "not men like Fred. Douglass, who are 'professional' colored men, and who have been agitating something and been paid for it all of their lives," approved of the decision. "They say there is no such thing as social equality among white men, and that the colored man cannot get it by law, but by the way he conducts himself."

Republican and Democratic newspapers highlighted those African-Americans who cheerfully told their neighbors "to acquire knowledge and wealth as the surest way of obtaining our rights." From Baltimore came the news that "Mr. John F. Cook, a colored man of character, who deservedly enjoys the respect of this entire community, who has held and administered with marked ability for years the responsible office of Collector of Taxes for the District of Columbia," told a reporter that he had no fears of white reprisals after the decision, expecting whites to accord to African-Americans "what legislation could never accomplish." "These are golden words, and if all men of his race were like Mr. Cook there would never be any trouble on this subject," concluded the Republican *Philadelphia Daily Evening Bulletin*.

Even many Northern Democrats painted their own picture of an egalitarian free labor society that had no need of a civil rights law. First they restated the idea that Republican efforts for African-Americans had simply been a ploy to control the government by marshalling the black vote. Trying to make new ties to African-American voters, the Democratic *San Francisco Examiner* emphasized that Republicans had only wanted to use the black vote to create a Republican empire and that the reversal showed that Republicanism no longer offered advantages to black citizens. A reporter noted that members of the black community had said that "it was about time to shake off the Republican yoke and act in politics as American citizens, not as chattels of a party who cared but for their votes."

While the rhetoric of the *San Francisco Examiner* repeated long-standing Democratic arguments, it also reinforced the idea that some hardworking African-Americans had indeed prospered in America, and that these upwardly mobile blacks were fully accepted even in Democratic circles. In San Francisco, the paper noted, "there are . . . many intelligent and educated men and women of African descent." Using the Republican pattern of according prosperous African-Americans names, descriptions, and their own words, it interviewed the Reverend Alexander Walters, whom it described respectfully as an educated and well-traveled young man, and happily printed both his assertion that in cities across the nation and "in the West . . . race prejudice has died out," and his prediction that the court's decision would drive black voters from the Republican party. Similarly, it quoted P. A. Bell, "the veteran editor of the *Elevator*, the organ of the colored people," as saying that in California—a Democratic state—"we people are treated just as well as if there were fifty Civil Rights bills."

With the overturning of the 1875 Civil Rights Act, mainstream Republicans and Democrats, black and white, agreed that there must be no extraordinary legislation on behalf of African-Americans, who had to work their way up in society like everyone else. Stalwart Republicans who advocated additional protection for black citizens were seen as either political demagogues who wanted the black vote to maintain their power or misguided reformers duped by stories of white atrocities against freedpeople. Northern black citizens who advocated civil rights legislation, like Frederick Douglass, were either scheming politicians who, like their white counterparts, needed the votes of uneducated African-Americans, or they were disaffected workers who believed in class struggle and wanted to control the government in order to destroy capital.

Southern blacks seemed to be the worst of all these types. They appeared to want to increase the government's power solely in order to be given what others had earned, and to do so, they were corrupting government by keeping scheming Republican politicos in office.

HEATHER COX RICHARDSON is professor of history at Boston College. Her other books include *The Greatest Nation of the Earth: Republican Economic Policies during the Civil War* (Harvard University Press, 1997) and *West from Appomattox: The Reconstruction of America after the Civil War* (Yale University Press, 2007).

EXPLORING THE ISSUE

Did Reconstruction Fail as a Result of Racism?

Critical Thinking and Reflection

1. What were the key factors that contributed to the Colfax massacre?
2. In what ways does an economic interpretation play a significant role in the essays by both Keith and Richardson?
3. In what ways does a racial interpretation play a significant role in the essays by both Keith and Richardson?

Is There Common Ground?

The question posed in this issue assumes that Reconstruction policy ended in failure. Certainly, many of the goals formulated by the Radical Republicans in Congress remained unfulfilled by the time the Compromise of 1877 removed federal troops from the South. If the goal of Reconstruction was to bring the former Confederate states back into the Union, however, that task was accomplished despite the fact that relations between the North and South remained uneasy. If the goal was to rebuild the South economically, positive steps were taken in that direction, as well. And coinciding with the end of Reconstruction were the efforts by some white Southerners to demonstrate their willingness at reconciliation with the hated Yankees by attracting industrial and manufacturing interests to the "New" South as a means of diversifying the region's economy. In addition, state constitutions were democratized, and public education was made available on a large scale for the first time.

For those few forward-thinking Radicals who envisioned a multiracial society in the South that extended full rights of citizenship to African Americans, many of whom had lived their entire lives in slavery until the end of the Civil War, failure was likely foreordained given the strength of the doctrine of white supremacy, not only in the South but also nationally. Absent a firm economic foundation that could guarantee self-sufficiency, sustained

access to the ballot box, and a broad-based commitment to equality of the races, African Americans in the South possessed little protection from poverty, political powerlessness, and the privilege of whiteness. Quiet, small victories would have to be crafted from within segregated black communities while African Americans held out hope for future enforcement of the Fourteenth and Fifteenth Amendments.

Create Central

www.mhhe.com/createcentral

Additional Resources

W. E. B. Du Bois, *Black Reconstruction in America: An Essay Toward a History of the Part Which Black Folk Played in the Attempt to Reconstruct Democracy in America, 1860–1880* (Harcourt, Brace, 1935)

Richard N. Current, *Those Terrible Carpetbaggers: A Reinterpretation* (Oxford University Press, 1988)

Carol Faulkner, *Women's Radical Reconstruction: The Freedmen's Aid Movement* (2004)

Leon F. Litwack, *Been in the Storm So Long: The Aftermath of Slavery* (Alfred A. Knopf, 1980)

Forrest G. Wood, *The Era of Reconstruction, 1863–1877* (Harlan Davidson, 1975)

Internet References . . .

America's Reconstruction: People and Politics After the Civil War

www.digitalhistory.uh.edu/exhibits/reconstruction/

Freedmen's Bureau Online

www.freedmensbureau.com/

Reconstruction

www.gilderlehrman.org/history-by-era/civil-war-and
-reconstruction-1861-1877/reconstruction